THE JEWISH MIND

THE
JEWISH
MIND

Raphael Patai

CHARLES SCRIBNER'S SONS · NEW YORK

Copyright © 1977 Raphael Patai

Library of Congress Cataloging in Publication Data

Patai, Raphael.
  The Jewish mind.

  Includes bibliographical references and index.
    1. Jews—Civilization.   2. Jews—Civilization—
Foreign influences.   3. Civilization—Jewish influences.
4. Judaism—Relations.   5. Jews—Psychology.   I. Title.
DS112.P29   909'.04'924   76-58040

ISBN 0-684-14878-1 (cloth)
ISBN 0-684-16321-7 (paper)

1 3 5 7 9 11 13 15 17 19 V/C 20 18 16 14 12 10 8 6 4 2
3 5 7 9 11 13 15 17 19 F/P 20 18 16 14 12 10 8 6 4

PRINTED IN THE UNITED STATES OF AMERICA

CONTENTS

PREFACE   xiii

PART I. PRELIMINARIES

1. Some Introductory Questions and Answers   3

   1. *What Is Meant by Group Mind?*   3
   2. *Why Should the Jewish Mind Differ from the Gentile
      Mind?*   4
   3. *What Are the Causes of Jewish Diversity?*   6
   4. *Why Is There Intra-Community Variance?*   6
   5. *Which Were the Major External Influences upon the
      Jewish Mind?*   6
   6. *What Is the Essence of Jewishness?*   8
   7. *Are There Constants in the Jewish Mind?*   12
   8. *Is There Such a Thing as Global Jewish Influence?*   12

2. Who Is a Jew?   15

3. Ethnohistory and Inner History   28

PART II. SIX GREAT HISTORIC ENCOUNTERS

4. Israel and Canaan   42

   1. *The Language*   42
   2. *Ethnic Antagonism*   44
   3. *The Religious Influence*   46
   4. *The Lasting Effects*   50
   5. *Israelite Iconography*   53

5. Jews and Hellenes   57

   1. *The Reappearance of Aramaic*   57
   2. *The Hellenistic Sweep*   59

   3. *Jewish Separatism*   61
   4. *The Lure of "Greek Wisdom"*   62
   5. *Greek and Latin in the Talmud*   63
   6. *The Archeological Evidence*   64
   7. *The Problem of Jewish Iconography*   67
   8. *The Cherubim and the Menora*   74
   9. *Formal Borrowing*   75
 10. *The Apocrypha*   77
 11. *Tannaitic Literature*   80
 12. *The Bible in Greek*   81
 13. *Historiography and Fictionalized History*   83
 14. *Philosophy*   85
 15. *Apologetics*   89
 16. *Why No Science?*   92
 17. *Conclusion*   94

6. **Hebrew Arabesque**   96

   1. *The* Dhimmis   96
   2. *Arabization and the Use of Romance*   99
   3. *The Eastern Prelude*   104
   4. *The Move to the West*   107
   5. *Hebrew Linguistics*   109
   6. *Poetry and Swagger*   113
   7. *The Breakthrough into Science*   122
   8. *Philosophy: Faith and Arrogance*   126
   9. *Kabbala and Hinduism*   134

7. **The Renaissance Jew**   152

   1. *The Jews of Italy*   152
   2. *The Sephardim in Italy*   153
   3. *The Pre-Renaissance South*   155
   4. *The Dawn of the Renaissance*   156
   5. *The New Culture*   158
   6. *Medicine and Magic*   159
   7. *The World of the Arts*   161
   8. *Crime, Gambling, and Sports*   163
   9. *Sexual License*   164
 10. *The Position of Women*   165
 11. *Literacy and Education*   166
 12. *Learning and Literature*   167

13. *Religious Laxity*   171
14. *Between Jews and Christians*   173
15. *Cultural Synthesis*   175

8. Jewish Dionysians: The Hasidim   180

    1. *Hasidism as Seen by Its Historians*   181
    2. *The Gentile Religious Environment*   182
    3. *The Jews of East Europe in the Eighteenth Century*   188
    4. *The BeShT—Peasant Prophet*   191
    5. *Dionysian Features in Hasidism*   196
    6. *Other Gentile Influences and Parallels*   206
    7. *The Jewishness of Hasidism*   217

9. Enlightenment: Triumph and Tragedy   222

    1. *Introductory*   222
    2. *The Forerunners*   224
    3. *Dutch Interlude*   229
    4. *The (Helping) Hands of Esau*   234
    5. *The Voice of Jacob*   241
    6. *Women and the Salons*   246
    7. *Outer Opposition: Anti-Semitism*   250
    8. *Inner Opposition: Orthodoxy*   253
    9. *The Problem of Nationalism*   258
   10. *Jews of the East and the West*   265
   11. *In Summary*   271

10. The Trend of Millennia   275

PART III. JOURNEY INTO THE JEWISH MIND

11. Jewish Intelligence   287

    1. *What Is Intelligence?*   287
    2. *What Is the I.Q.?*   289
    3. *The Findings*   292
    4. *What Goes into the I.Q.?*   294
    5. *What Is the Meaning of Group Differences in the I.Q.?*   296
    6. *Brain Damage: Nutritional and Sociogenic*   298
    7. *The Jewish Home Environment*   302
    8. *Hereditary Factors*   304
    9. *Intra-Jewish Differences*   306

12. Giftedness and Genius   315

    1. Medieval Scholarship   316
    2. Post-Enlightenment Upsurge and Reaction   318
    3. The Terman Study   321
    4. Early Views of Jewish Preeminence   324
    5. Fritz Lenz and Rabbi Dreyfuss   327
    6. Marginality and Eminence   331
    7. A Factor Analysis of Jewish Excellence   335
    8. The Jewish Nobel Prize Record   339

13. Special Talents   343

    1. Three Basic Questions   343
    2. The "Semites"; or, The Desert and Monotheism   347
    3. Views of Jewish Talents   352
    4. Painting and Sculpture   355
    5. Architecture   360
    6. Music   362
    7. Literature   367

14. Personality and Character   372

    1. The Problem of the "Jewish Personality"   372
    2. Historical and Modern Views   375
    3. Two Special Cases: Sephardim and Italian Jews   380
    4. Variance   384
    5. Profile of the American Jew   388
    6. Intensity, Sensitivity, and Impatience   391
    7. Galut-Jew, Sabra, and Kibbutznik   394
    8. Religiosity and Identity   397

15. Health: Physical and Mental   408

    1. Physical Health   408
    2. Mental Health   413
    3. "On the Fence"   428

16. Three Problem Areas: Alcoholism, Overeating,
     and Drug Addiction   433

    1. Alcoholism   433
    2. Overeating and Obesity   447
    3. Drug Addiction   453

17. Jewish Self-Hate   456

    1. Parasitism   456
    2. Collective Guilt and Collective Excellence   460
    3. Sephardi Pride and Prejudice   463
    4. A Miscellany of Critics   465
    5. The French Infection   471
    6. Between East and West in Israel   477
    7. The New Left   479

18. The World of Values   481

    1. The Family   483
    2. An Excursus on Sex   497
    3. Education   509
    4. Charity   524

19. Conclusion   534

    NOTES   541

    INDEX   593

PREFACE

----◆◆◆◆----

This book is the direct outgrowth of a chapter on the Jewish mind which forms part of the book *The Myth of the Jewish Race* written jointly by my daughter, Dr. Jennifer Patai Wing, and myself, published in 1975. Its origins, however, go much farther back than that. They stem from my lifelong interest in the culture of the Jews and of the Middle East which has been the motivating and unifying factor in the two dozen volumes and hundreds of articles I have written. It was inevitable that this preoccupation should sooner or later converge on the two themes of the Arab mind and the Jewish mind. My book *The Arab Mind* was published in 1973. Its counterpart, *The Jewish Mind,* is presented herewith.

Once again I am indebted to many individuals and institutions without whose help this book could not have been written. Among them my special thanks are due to my daughter Jennifer for her comments on chapter 11, "Jewish Intelligence"; to Professor Victor Sanua for his comments on chapter 15, "Health: Physical and Mental"; to Professor Meir M. Bravmann for elucidations of Semitic linguistic problems; and to my wife, Frances, for reviewing and discussing the material contained in this book, and for her patience with a husband immersed in his work to the point of neglecting many other aspects of life.

Also to Miss Annette Bruhwiler, director of the library of Fairleigh Dickinson University at Rutherford, N.J., and her staff; Dr. Leonard S. Gold, chief of the Jewish Division, New York Public Library, and his staff; Mr. Francis Paar of the Oriental Division, New York Public Library; Mrs. Sylvia Landress, director of the Zionist Archives and Library, New York, and her staff; the staffs of the libraries of the New York Academy of Medicine and of the Hebrew Union College—Jewish Institute of Religion, New York; Mlle. Madeleine Neige, chief of the Service Hébraïque of the Bibliothèque Nationale of Paris; and the staffs of the libraries of the Hebrew University of Jerusalem, the Tel Aviv University, and Yale University.

R. P.

Forest Hills, N.Y.
September 1976

THE JEWISH MIND

I

PRELIMINARIES

1

Some Introductory Questions and Answers

This book is an attempt to consider the Jewish mind as a product of Jewish culture, and Jewish culture as a product of the Jewish mind. Jewish religion—unquestionably the most important element in Jewish culture—is likewise considered as a product of the Jewish mind. We shall see how this collective mind reacted to the incessant flow of outside cultural influences to which the Jews were exposed throughout their history. And the reverse influences, those exerted by Jews on the Gentile world, will be treated, albeit briefly, as manifestations of the extraordinary force of the Jewish mind which has made itself felt around the globe for two thousand years. As a foil to the constant two-way exchange between the Jews and the Gentiles, the persisting differences between the Jewish and the Gentile mind are pointed up. The inquiry also stresses the internal variations evinced by the Jewish mind between one local Jewish group and another, and between different sectors of the same community.

In dealing with such complex subjects, a number of points must be understood before any meaningful inquiry can be undertaken. These clarifications, presented summarily, follow next; some of them will be taken up again in greater detail later in the book.

1. What Is Meant by Group Mind?

To begin with, we must touch upon the problem of what is meant by "mind" when applied, not to an individual, but to a human group. As I have discussed this question at some length in two recent books,[1] I may perhaps be permitted to give my understanding of it here in the briefest possible form.

3

Social psychologists and anthropologists have found that the plurality in any given population share certain motives, traits, beliefs, and values. In a large aggregate, such as a nation, the sum total of these shared mental traits is referred to as "national character," or "basic personality," or (since the plurality is the statistical mode) "modal personality." In other words, when a social scientist speaks of, say, the "Polish national character" and states that the "Polish mind" is characterized by traits A, B, and C, he does not mean that every Pole exhibits them, but merely that these traits are found more frequently among the Poles than, say, traits D or E. It is with this qualification in mind that we shall discuss "Jewish" intelligence, "Jewish" talents, "Jewish" character traits, etc., as well as the differences between the "Jewish mind" and the "Gentile mind."

2. Why Should the Jewish Mind Differ from the Gentile Mind?

Were we to set the peoples of the world in a series ranging from those who had the least exposure to outside influences to those who had the most, the Jews would undoubtedly rank highest in the variety, intensity, and duration of such exposure. More than that, the difference in this respect between the Jews and the Gentiles is not merely quantitative but also qualitative. This, in effect, places the Jewish people in a category *sui generis*. Thus history has supplied a profound justification for the taxonomical dichotomy of mankind into Jews and Gentiles which has been a fundamental feature of the Jewish world view ever since antiquity, when the Bible put the prophetic words about Israel into the mouth of the pagan seer Balaam: "Lo, it is a people that shall dwell alone, and shall not be reckoned among the nations." [2]

The qualitative differences between the Jews and other peoples so far as the role of foreign contacts in their history is concerned become apparent as soon as one considers a few basic historical facts. Many nations had to endure foreign occupation or domination, which meant intensive contact with intrusive foreigners. Such contacts, in turn, resulted in cultural influences absorbed by the native nationals from the outsiders. But these experiences were nothing more than temporary interludes which, while they may have caused upheavals in the nation's life, did not result in basic changes. Foreign occupation aside, all countries, unless geography effectively isolates them from their neighbors, constantly absorb cultural influences from across their borders. But again, these influences bring about only minor and gradual modifications, while the national character preserves its continuity. The identity of the national population aggregate, entrenched within a territory of its own, speaking its own language and adhering to its own variety of religion, ruled or governed autocephalously, and informed by its own cultural traditions, endures.

Jewish history in two thousand years of Diaspora presents a strong contrast to this picture. Throughout this long period, the typical mode of Jewish existence was dispersal in many countries—communities, in many cases no more than splinter groups, wedged in among various majorities, fulfilling special limited roles in disparate social and economic structures; isolated from, and yet in daily contact with, the Gentiles; and existing on sufferance in circumstances ranging from the fairly tolerable to the extremely painful and perilous. Under these conditions, constant exposure to powerful radiation from the host culture was the rule. The influences of material culture were ubiquitous; that is to say, whether or not a Jewish community considered the culture of its Gentile neighbors attractive, circumstances forced it to adopt their styles of housing, furniture, clothing, food (with certain exceptions contingent on the laws of *kashrut*), and to confine itself to the particular niches in the occupational structure assigned to it by the powers that be. As for the intellectual components of the Gentile culture, they were adopted, or emulated, by the Jews only when they found them attractive, as for instance in medieval Arab Spain and Renaissance Italy.

As far as character traits were concerned, one of two psychological mechanisms could determine the Jewish reaction. If a Gentile trait was found attractive, it was first behaviorally imitated (despite the general Biblical-Talmudic prohibition of "walking in the ways of the Gentiles"), and then internalized; if not, its opposite was emphasized in both Jewish behavior and ethos. An example of the former is the adoption by the Jews of the Spanish pride which continued to haunt the Sephardim for four hundred years after their expulsion from Spain; [3] and an example of the latter is the East European Jewish insistence on sobriety, which received added emphasis as a reaction to the endemic drunkenness of the Polish and Russian peasants. [4]

The entirely unique circumstances in which the Jews have lived for the last two thousand years have left their traces on their specific psychological development, both as communities and as individuals. For the Gentiles, the contact with, and influences from, other cultures, while they existed, were of minor significance in relation to the developments brought about by internal forces. Thus the Gentile mind, by and large, is the product of endogenous processes. The Jewish mind, on the other hand, has for two thousand years been exposed to two equally powerful forces—the Jewish tradition and the Gentile influence. And it is itself a product of the tension between the two; by contrast to the Gentile mind, it is, to a much greater extent, exogenous. For this reason it is evidently not possible to discuss the Jewish mind without constant reference to the Gentile environment whose impact so greatly contributed to its formation.

3. What Are the Causes of Jewish Diversity?

The remarks so far contain the gist of an answer to the next question, which touches on the causes of the diversity that characterizes the Jews in their global Diaspora. Since all Jews ultimately derive—if not genetically, then certainly culturally, religiously, and tradition-wise—from one common source, their Biblical-Israelite ancestry, obviously there can be only two factors which could have produced these differences. The first is a variance in the development among the Jews themselves within various countries; and the second, the exposure to, and absorption of, disparate Gentile influences. In fact, all over the Diaspora both processes went hand in hand, although the relative shares varied greatly from time to time and from country to country. This subject is of such importance to understanding the bases and meaning of Jewish diversity, and the workings of the Jewish mind, that a separate chapter will have to be devoted to it.[5]

4. Why Is There Intra-Community Variance?

A related question is that of the variance within Jewish groups located in one and the same country or even city. Here again, the two factors just mentioned will be found responsible for much of this variance. Both the internal developments and the rate and quality of external influences absorbed may be found to be disparate within two parts of the same local Jewish community, depending on such variables as religious observance, class status, occupational structure, and so on. To these is added a third factor—that of the Jewish migrations, which have brought together in one place groups of different origins and hence dissimilar historical antecedents. These origin groups, in general, have tended to preserve certain features which characterized them in the places they left behind. This is the basis of the "*Landsmannschaften*" well known especially in America, and of the ethnic communities comprised in the Jewish population of Israel.

5. Which Were the Major External Influences upon the Jewish Mind?

Of the many encounters experienced by the Jews in the course of their long history, six are outstanding in salience and lasting in the influence they exerted on the development of the Jewish mind. The dimensions of their effect were varied, but they had one feature in common: each in its turn brought about a departure into new realms of cultural activity and the adoption of a new language or its utilization as a medium for a new mode of expression.

The first was the encounter with the Canaanites, from the days of the first patriarchs down to the Babylonian Exile (c. seventeenth century to 586 B.C.E.). In its earliest phase, the Children of Israel switched from their ancestral Aramaic to the "language of Canaan," which they soon developed into their unique national and religious tongue, Biblical Hebrew. Equally decisive and lasting was the religious influence, which, in that early and formative period of their religious conceptualization and practice, penetrated them from the Canaanite environment. This first encounter was seminal in influencing the course of Jewish history in the Biblical period, and, through the Bible, the development of Judaism in all its subsequent phases.

The second great encounter was with Hellenism (late fourth century B.C.E. to second century C.E.), which resulted in the superimposition of Greek on the Aramaic colloquial dominant among the Jews since the fifth century B.C.E. This prompted them to add to their own Biblical-rabbinic tradition important elements of Hellenistic culture, and to produce a special Hellenistic-Jewish variety of literary, intellectual, religious, and artistic activity.

The third followed the Arab conquest of Southwest Asia and North Africa in the seventh century. This encounter made Arabic the language of the majority of the Jews and induced the Jewish mind to tackle, for the first time, great intellectual tasks of a secular nature. Moreover, it enabled Spanish Jewry to occupy an important position in the vanguard of the great Arab cultural flowering and in the transmission of Greek philosophy and science to the West.

The fourth, localized in its geographic extent but no less important from the standpoint of Jewish cultural history, was the encounter with Renaissance Italy. From the fourteenth century on, Italian-speaking Jewry was swept along by the effervescence of the Renaissance while retaining its Jewishness. This demonstrated that it was feasible for the Jewish mind to be equally at home in a secular culture and in its own traditional Judaism and thus pointed the way in which Jews could cope with the great cultural developments that were to take place north of the Alps in the eighteenth century.

The fifth encounter was that between East European Jews and the Christian sectarian movements in the Ukraine and Poland, which influenced the development of Hasidism in the eighteenth century. With Hasidism the Yiddish language became a vehicle of a great and vital religious development in Judaism, which represented a revolutionary departure from the Talmudic-halakhic trend dominant in Judaism ever since antiquity.

The sixth and last of this series of great historic encounters was the voluntary self-subordination of the Jews in the eighteenth century to modern Western culture. The resulting Jewish Enlightenment brought about the adoption by the Jews of the national language of each country which, in the nineteenth century, emancipated them. It broke down the age-old social and cultural barriers which everywhere had separated Jew from Gentile and enabled the Jews to become not merely participants, but in many cases leaders and pioneers, in the culture of the modern West. From the standpoint of Jewish survival, this encounter was more crucial, more transfigurative, and potentially fraught with more dangers than any of the preceding five. Its final outcome is still veiled in the future.

Part Two of this book will be devoted to a closer look at each of these six great historic encounters between the Jews and the world, which have immeasurably contributed to the formation of the Jewish mind and whose residual effects are still inescapably at work in the depths of the modern Jewish psyche.

6. What Is the Essence of Jewishness?

If, as I have just indicated, the Jewish mind has absorbed so many disparate influences from the Gentile environments, the question must inevitably arise as to what, if any, are the essential features which have informed it throughout history. In looking for an answer to this question we can get some help from the sages of the Talmud, who themselves could look back upon more than a thousand years of Jewish history. They had definite views on the mental traits which, they felt, were most characteristically Jewish. Thus a Talmudic passage puts these words in the mouth of King David: "There are three traits in this nation: they are compassionate, modest, and charitable. . . . Only he who has these three traits is worthy of being admitted into it." [6] Since the Bible does not record any such statement by King David, it is clear that it presents the Talmudic view on what were the outstanding characteristics of the Jews.

Other Talmudic passages cast similar ideas into different forms and speak of three basic "things" on which the existence of "the world" (read: the Jewish people) depends. The High Priest Shim'on the Just (who lived in the third or second century B.C.E.) used to say: "The world stands on three things: on the Tora, and on the [Temple] Service, and on Charity." When using the expression "the world" he did not, of course, mean the world at large, which bore no relationship to the Tora and to the Temple service, but the Jewish world. One must therefore interpret this saying as meaning that the existence of Jewry depended on the study of the Law, the performance of the Temple ritual, and the practice of charity. Against this view, which assigns a pivotal place to ritual as one would expect of a sage who was also a priest, Rabban Shim'on ben Gamliel (in the first half of the second century C.E.) stated that the three things on which the world (that is, again, Jewry) stood were justice, truth, and peace [7]—three moral features which were "Jewish" only inasmuch as they were made into fundamentals of Jewish existence.

More famous than these pronouncements is the formulation of the great first-century B.C.E. sage Hillel. When a Gentile came to him saying, "You may make me a proselyte provided you can teach me the whole Tora while I stand on one foot," he answered: "Do not unto others what is hateful to you. This is the whole Tora, the rest is commentary. Go and study." [8] That is, Hillel saw the essence of Judaism in being considerate of others; a Gentile who accepted this was admitted by him into the community of Israel. However (I mention this here only in passing), once admitted, he was expected to engage in the major preoccupation of Israel: studying the Law.

The common denominator in these distillations of the essence of Jewishness, except for the earliest one which was partly ritualistic, is that they all insist on moral qualities only, nothing else. One can therefore conclude that in Talmudic times the crucial distinction the sages perceived between the "nations of the world" (that is, mainly Greeks and Romans) and the Jews was neither in the ritual, nor in the credal, but in the moral realm. They considered the Jews the moral people *par excellence*. A Gentile could join the Jewish community by accepting the Jewish morality.

Hillel's formulation of the essence of the Tora is, of course, but a recasting into negative form of what in the Bible itself appears as a positive commandment: "Thou shalt love thy neighbor as thyself." [9] It is remarkable, and characteristic of the direction the development of Judaism took in Talmudic times, that it was this commandment which was considered "the whole Tora," rather than the complementary one which imposes the duty of *amor dei*: "Thou shalt love the Lord thy God with all thy heart and with all thy soul and with all thy might." [10] This second "Thou shalt love" is, incidentally, part of the *Sh'ma'* prayer whose daily recitation has been a religious duty for Jews for at least two thousand years. The two commandments of love are, therefore, unquestionably traditional essentials of Judaism. That they were so considered is amply attested by the rich religious literature which the Jews have produced throughout their history.

Only in modern times did the emphasis in isolating the essential features of Jewishness shift from the love aspect to the feeling of belongingness. The core of Jewishness was now conceived as a "national consciousness," an innermost commitment to Jewish identity, which was also considered the key to the secret of Jewish survival. One of the many who expressed this thought was Bernard Lazare (1865–1903), the outstanding French-Jewish author and defender of Dreyfus. He wrote that the Jews survived "because they preserved, tenaciously and forcefully (*vivace et vivante*), their national consciousness." [11] One of the contemporary writers who expressed the same idea is David Hadler (Ferdynand Zweig): "The core of Judaism is the belief in Israel and the will to Judaism which is the source of its miraculous survival." [12]

This psychologistic view of Jewish endurance was enriched by Christian historians and theologians with a mystical note. Erich von Kahler, a foremost German philosopher of history, emphasized that there was a bond which unified Israel and which was not simply the bond of flesh and blood, nor that of an ethico-historical community, but a supra-historical, sacred bond of promise and yearning. [13] The same idea was expressed by the Catholic philosopher Jacques Maritain in saying that Jewish thought is aware that "Israel is a *corpus mysticum,* a mystical body." [14] While none of these thinkers speaks of the core of Jewishness as such, it is clear that for them the Jewish awareness of the existence of a unifying sacred bond which makes Israel into a mystical body is the essential feature of Jewishness.

The reason that these and other such modern views about the essence of Jewishness are unsatisfactory is that they are applicable to the Jews only in certain times and certain conditions. Jewish "national" consciousness certainly could not exist in times prior to the emergence of nationalism in the Western world, and even thereafter it remained foreign to Jews who lived in the Muslim orbit. As for "sacred bond" and "mystical body," such concepts smack more of Christianity than of the down-to-earth Jewish view of the relationship between man and man and man and God.

In my own search for the core of Jewishness, I was led by two basic considerations. I felt that any trait, in order to be pronounced as essential, must meet two criteria: it must be an irreducible minimum; and it must have informed the Jewish mind at all times and in all places. It seems to me that two beliefs and two duties meet these requirements. They are the belief in the one God; the belief in the special relationship between God and Israel; the duty toward God; and the duty toward one's fellow man. The two duties, as we have just seen, were given early concrete formulation in two Biblical commandments. The two beliefs were not formulated at that time, at least not in pithy, general, and explicit statements similar to those referring to the two duties of love just mentioned. But while remaining unexpressed, both were taken for granted and are implicit in Biblical pronouncements based on them. Not until late in the First Temple period do we find in the Bible the imperative: "Believe in the Lord your God," [15] reported to have been uttered by Jehoshaphat, king of Judah, in an exhortation to his army before a decisive battle. All of the Ten Commandments, except the first, are cast in the form of "Thou shalt" or "Thou shalt not." The first, instead of saying, "Thou shalt believe in Me," merely says, "I am the Lord thy God who brought thee out of the land of Egypt, out of the house of bondage." [16] Nahmanides, the great medieval Bible commentator, aware of the formal deviation represented by the First Commandment when compared to the other nine, explains: "This commandment is a positive precept. It means: 'I am the Lord,' which teaches and commands Israel to know and to believe in the Lord. . . ."

Similarly, a belief in the special relationship between God and Israel is not demanded explicitly in the Bible, but it is the underlying axiom of much that is said about Israel's duties toward God. The Bible often refers to the election of Israel by God—an election, to be sure, not to a privileged position but to serving God. In a great passage in Deuteronomy the doctrine is explained in detail: God chose Israel, the smallest of all peoples, because He loved Israel; hence, Israel is a holy people unto the Lord, and must love God and keep His commandments.[17] In other Biblical passages, too, the two ideas—Israel's chosenness and its duty to serve God and observe the Law— are causally interconnected: "Unto Me the Children of Israel are servants; they are My servants whom I brought forth out of the Land of Egypt."[18] The same idea is poetically expressed in the Book of Isaiah: "Thou, Israel, My servant, Jacob whom I have chosen . . . I said to thee, 'Thou art My servant . . .'"[19] And, reciprocally, Israel chose God to serve Him: "Ye have chosen you the Lord to serve Him. . . ."[20]

In Talmudic times, Israel's chosenness was felt to be a status God had literally forced upon it. As a Midrash puts it: When God revealed the Law on Mount Sinai, He lifted up the mountain, held it over the heads of the people, and said to them: "If you accept the Tora, it is well; if not, here will be your burial."[21]

In the Middle Ages, in vastly different circumstances, Maimonides felt that a formulation of Jewish credos was required, and when he undertook to do so, in his famous Thirteen Principles of the Faith, he included explicitly the belief in the one God, and implicitly the belief in the special relationship between God and Israel. Throughout Israel's history, its chosenness has always remained an obligation, a duty, a yoke to be carried, never a privilege to be frivolously enjoyed. But it has also become the religious, mythical, mystical, and emotional ground of Israel's enduring existence in the world.

From Biblical times down to the present the essence of Jewishness has comprised the same four basic features, the same two behavioral and two credal demands. Any person, whether or not born to Jewish parents, who accepted them and submitted to them was a Jew and belonged to the Jewish community, which therefore can be described as the aggregate of all those individuals who subscribe to these four tenets.

Because of the irreducible nature of these four elements, whatever the Jews absorbed from their Gentile environments was never, until the Enlightenment, allowed to encroach upon them. They remained the Jewish elixir of life, the source of Israel's *élan vital*, the leitmotif of Jewish existence, always clearly recognizable even though played in many different keys, to changing rhythms, and on a variety of instruments. Whenever in this book I refer to "the core" or "the essence" of Jewishness, or to "the Jewish content," these four elements are what I have in mind.

7. Are There Constants in the Jewish Mind?

The inner core of Jewishness, comprised of the two duties and two beliefs just discussed, constitutes a constant in the Jewish mind which has been informed by them throughout Jewish history. Despite their incessant exposure to outside influences, the Jews remained in this sense fundamentally true to themselves, at least until the Enlightenment. Whatever components of foreign religious thought and practice they adopted—from the Canaanites, the Zoroastrian Iranians, the polytheistic or philosophical Greeks, the Muslim Arabs and Persians, or the Christian Europeans—their traditional Jewish religion continued its own evolutionary course through the ages; and while it may have been tinged, it was never transformed by these external influences. In making their adjustments to the social forms and norms, to the cultural orientations and occupational structures of their Gentile neighbors in their ever-widening dispersion (both in the lands of the Muslim East and the Christian West), they always retained their integral cohesion and consistency, remaining the carriers of a complete, self-contained, and all-encompassing Jewish religious culture. Whatever the degree of autonomy granted to it, the Jewish community continued to function as the framework for what all Jews knew to be their traditional way of life. Even if Gentile values succeeded in penetrating the psychological barriers of the separate and self-contained Jewish existence, they could never amount to more than manageable modifications in the traditional Jewish value system, whose basics remained untouched, unaltered, undiluted.

8. Is There Such a Thing as Global Jewish Influence?

This is a crucial question to which many distorted answers have been given. The answers, in most cases affirmative, range from the most rabidly anti-Semitic to those which amount to unrestrained ethno-religious self-aggrandizement.

On the one hand, there are those who believe, with the czarist fabrication known as *The Protocols of the Elders of Zion* (recently resuscitated by the Arab enemies of Israel), that the Jews form a global cabal—a sinister, secret, and incredibly powerful conspiracy which somehow can and does work its will upon mankind all over the world. Among those who followed the paranoid path of this argument were otherwise intelligent men who had a blind spot only when it came to the Jews. The nineteenth-century examples are too well known to mention; in the present century, such beliefs supplied fuel to the Nazi genocide, to Horacio Calderon's *Argentina Judia*, published in 1975 and ranting about a "Jewish synarchy" which dominates the world, and—*mutatis mutandis*—to such fantasy-filled but not quite harmless books as Roger Peyrefitte's *Les Juifs*.

On the other hand, there is also a Jewish over-estimation of the global significance of the Jews. This goes back to Talmudic times, when some sages were convinced that the whole world existed only for the sake of Israel and that, conversely, the existence of the whole world depended on Israel's fulfilling the role, the religious function, allotted to it by God.[22] A late, faint echo of this view could be found in the teachings of Reform Judaism in their "classical" form, which date from the nineteenth century, and which maintained that while Judaism was nothing but a religion, it had a global mission: to spread the faith of pure ethical monotheism all over the world.

A more restrained but no less strongly pro-Jewish view is the one embraced by a number of modern historians who have presented, eloquently and in considerable detail, the Jewish contribution to civilization. Essentially, these books consist of systematic enumerations and evaluations of the work of outstanding Jewish writers, poets, artists, musicians, scholars, scientists, industrialists, economists, legal experts, statesmen, and the like, especially in modern times.[23] They show, among other things, that in all the occupations mentioned the Jews have achieved, since the Emancipation, a considerable over-representation, and that their influence has been disproportionately large. But the influence of the Jewish mind transcends the sum total of these individual achievements. There are views and conceptions of man, of life and fate, of human quiddity and destiny, of what in certain Oriental philosophies is called "suchness," which have spread over almost the entire globe, prefiguring (or perhaps serving as the basis for) a Chardin-like "noosphere."[24] Not only have the Jews contributed most significantly to this global network of views and their underlying *Weltanschauung*; they have done so to an extent not duplicated, or even approximated, by any other people. As Ernest van den Haag observed,

> . . . Jews are human, we all are, but Jews are in a sense more human than any one else: they have witnessed and taken part in more of the human career, they have recorded more of it, shaped more of it, originated and developed more of it, above all, suffered more of it, than any other people. No other nation has witnessed so much, argued and bargained so much, and yet clung to its own inner core as much as Jews have. . . .
>
> The lives of all of us in the West (as well as in Russia) and even of vast areas in the rest of the world have been strongly influenced, if not altogether shaped, by a view of human fate which is essentially Jewish in cast and origin. Jewish

influence continues, not only through our common religious heritage, which clearly bears the mark of its Jewish origin, but also through the constant addition of new, nonreligious ideas produced by Jewish scientists and scholars.[25]

This Jewish ability to create ideas and values destined to influence the majority of mankind testifies to the extraordinary capacity for transference of precisely the greatest products of the Jewish mind, their universal human appeal, their propensity of becoming the property of all or most of mankind. Through the two great world religions of Christianity, initiated by the Jew Jesus and established by his Jewish disciples, and Islam, developed by the Arab Muḥammad under the impact of Jewish teachings, Jewish thoughts have radiated out in ever-widening circles around the globe and changed man and his world. After achieving religious insights which have conquered a major part of mankind, the Jews were, for two thousand years, prevented by Gentile oppression and their own reaction to it from bringing forth new globally influential ideas. But even so, they produced a Maimonides in the twelfth century, considered one of the two greatest minds of the Middle Ages, and a Spinoza in the seventeenth, regarded as the greatest modern philosopher. And no sooner were they emancipated in the nineteenth century than they returned most energetically to the age-old Jewish specialization of changing the conceptual framework of humankind. The teachings of Marx, who was called a latter-day Jewish prophet, spread with phenomenal speed, especially outside the modern Western world, until today Marxism can claim about as many adherents as Christianity and Islam together. Psychoanalysis, created by the Viennese Jewish physician Sigmund Freud, and its several offshoots have been widely accepted in the modern world and form both a therapy and a basic approach to man and his works. Albert Einstein, a German Jew, not only influenced more than any other modern scientist the development of both the warlike and the peaceful utilization of atomic power, but also opened up a new understanding of the world of energy and matter, and thus of the entire physical universe. So (to put it perhaps somewhat hyperbolically) the twentieth-century views of the socioeconomic dynamics, of the inner forces of the human psyche, and of the physical universe all contain major Jewish-produced components. Without naming the many dozen Jewish geniuses who appear as stars of secondary magnitude only in relation to such luminaries of the human race as Moses, Isaiah, Jesus, Maimonides, Spinoza, Marx, Freud, and Einstein, one can generalize and assert that, apart from some isolated areas of the globe which are shrinking daily, all mankind today is affected in one way or another by the products of the Jewish mind. And, one may add, no other human group can boast of an even remotely comparable record.

2

Who Is a Jew?

Before embarking on our voyage into the Jewish mind we must, first of all, make sure we know whose mind precisely we are setting out to investigate. That is, we must come to a clear understanding of who is a Jew.

The very fact that this question can arise indicates to what extent the *Halakha*, the traditional Jewish religious law, has lost its hold over the Jewish mind. Prior to the Jewish Enlightenment, when all Jews (with a very few exceptions) observed and obeyed the *Halakha*, its definition of a Jew was accepted as axiomatic. Halakhically, a Jew is an individual who was either born to a Jewish mother, or converted to Judaism. Since the Enlightenment, and the profound changes it wrought in Jewish life—including, in the first place, a disregard of the *Halakha* as the sole basis of Jewish existence—the halakhic definition of a Jew has become unsatisfactory. The halakhic consensus gave way to a multiplicity of opinions as to Jewish identity, each emphasizing a different aspect of Jewishness. Today, the most frequent answers to the question, Who is a Jew? are:

> A Jew is a member of the Jewish race.
> A Jew is an adherent of (or believer in) Jewish religion.
> A Jew is a member of the Jewish people.
> A Jew is a person born of Jewish parents.[1]

The first three of these answers can be reformulated into statements about the nature of that aggregate of individuals which is referred to as "the Jews." The first says that the Jews are a *race*; the second, that they are a *religion*; and the third that they are a *people*. The fourth is about as helpful as answering the question, What is a sheep? by saying, A sheep is an animal born of a ram and a ewe.

Let us have a critical look at each of the first three answers.

The view that the Jews are a race, and that therefore a Jew is a member of the Jewish race, has recently been subjected to intensive examination. A

15

detailed analysis of the historical, demographic, and anthropological data, as well as the available anthropometric, serological, and other genetic evidence (including the complex phenomena of Jewish morbidity), led to the conclusion that the Jews are definitely not a race in the genetic sense of the term, which defines a race as "a population which differs from others in the incidence of certain genes." [2] All the multi-faceted evidence that could be marshaled pointed unmistakably to the conclusion that genetically the Jews show great variations among themselves, that the genetic differences between Jews in one country and Jews in another can be as great as those between the Gentile populations of the same two countries, and that the genetic characteristics of every Jewish group manifest remarkable resemblances to those of the non-Jewish peoples among whom the Jews have lived in the lands of the Diaspora. The striking Jewish physical diversity becomes most apparent when one compares one Jewish group of the Diaspora with another native to a remote country, such as the Polish Jews with the Yemenite Jews. As for the similarity between any given Jewish group and the Gentile population, this is most pronounced in those countries in which the Jews have resided for many generations—one can refer to any Central or East European country and to any Middle Eastern land for contrasting examples. In making these observations one must, of course, keep in mind that whether we are speaking of diversities among the Jews themselves or of Jewish-Gentile similarities, the reference is always to statistical averages.

The second answer, that a Jew is an adherent of the Jewish religion, is of course true in a general way, inasmuch as most Jews adhere to Judaism in one form or another. But the exceptions are too numerous to be overlooked. There are many individuals who will answer "Yes" to the question "Are you a Jew?" and who not only belong to no Jewish congregation or organization, but observe nothing of Jewish religion. Even if an individual born to Jewish parents takes the step of formally converting to another religion, he does not thereby automatically cease being Jewish. After his baptism he becomes a "Jew converted to Christianity," never simply a Christian. In those cases where conversion was forced upon the Jews, as happened in Catholic Spain in the late Middle Ages, they become not "Christians" but "New Christians," with social barriers persisting between them and the "Old" Christians for several generations. Similarly, the forced conversion of Jews to Islam in seventeenth- and eighteenth-century Persia resulted in separate "New Muslim" communities. On the other hand, there have occasionally been Gentiles who converted to Judaism, that is, have been formally admitted into the community of Israel, and yet they did not become "Jews" but merely *gerim*, proselytes. Hence the religious definition of a Jew is not coterminous with historical fact.

The concept of the Jew as one of the Jewish people suffers from the same shortcoming. While many Jews agree on their peoplehood—in fact, the

expression "People of Israel" is an age-old Jewish term of Biblical origin—
there are many others who vehemently deny that Jewishness has any connotation whatsoever beyond the purely religious one. Prior to the Zionist
movement and the reestablishment of the State of Israel in which the Jews
form a people like any other people in the world, the concept of Jewish
peoplehood had become repugnant to most Jews in Central and Western
Europe, although in East Europe many non-religious and anti-religious Jews
were attracted to the doctrine of "Galut Nationalism" propounded by Zhitlovsky and Dubnow. Both of these views will be discussed in the chapter on
the Jewish Enlightenment and are here mentioned only to show that the definition of the Jews as a people would exclude all those Jews who define their
own Jewishness in purely religious terms.

·The fourth answer, as already hinted, is also inadequate. Although most
persons born of Jewish parents are Jews, biological parenthood in itself does
not confer Jewishness on a child. If such a child is placed at birth with Christian or Muslim foster parents, certainly no traces of Jewishness will remain
or develop in it. On the other hand, if a Gentile child is placed at birth into a
Jewish home where it receives a Jewish upbringing, it will become a Jew
whatever its biological parentage. And, if biological parentage were the de-
termining factor, what about the child of a mixed Jewish-Gentile couple?
Evidently here again the decisive factor is not genetic descent but the cultural transmission that takes place within the family.

Jewish traditional law (the *Halakha*) considers the child of a Jewish mother
and a Gentile father a Jew, but the child of a Gentile mother and a Jewish father a non-Jew. While this rule happens to reflect the closer relationship that
exists between mother and child than between child and father, it is based
on the harsh realities of Jewish history in which Gentile males not infrequently fathered children on willing or unwilling Jewish women, who
thereupon were faced with the necessity of bringing them up, which, of
course, meant bringing them up as Jews. Hence, according to Jewish law
codes—the last of which, the *Shulḥan 'Arukh*, is still followed by Orthodox
Jews today—such children are considered Jews.[3]

In modern times most Jewish men or women who have children with a
Gentile partner do not know or care about halakhic rulings as to the Jewishness of their offspring. Irrespective of the sex of the Jewish parent, they
make their own individual choice as to the religion in which they wish to
bring up their child, or they may elect not to instill into it any religious ideas
at all. Depending on these decisions, as well as on other influences to which
the child becomes exposed, it may develop the feeling that it is a Jew, a
Christian, or neither; it may have any of these feelings to varying degrees of
intensity; it may know nothing, or a little, or much of the religious or ethnic
antecedents of one or both of its parents; and so on. What the child comes to
feel about its group identity, and to know about the group with which it

identifies itself, will depend on its environmental conditioning; it has nothing to do with its biological parentage.

The same holds good, of course, in the case of children who are the off-spring not of a mixed couple, but of Jewish parents. Such children, in the great majority of cases, grow up as Jews, but not because of their genetic antecedents. They become Jews if the parents, being Jews, wish to transmit to them the cultural heritage of Judaism, and succeed in doing so.

One of the most tenacious popular beliefs transmitted in this way from generation to generation of Jews is that of Abrahamic descent. While in fact they were (and are) in many cases not the genetic descendants of the Biblical Hebrew patriarchs, the Jews have throughout their history maintained the tradition that they were the children of Abraham. This popular Jewish belief has become a psychological fact which was more important, because it was more effective in holding the Jews together, than the purest "blood line" could have been. The image of "Abraham our father" has been focal in Jewish consciousness throughout history, beginning with Biblical times. The stories of Genesis—that great mythical charter of Jewish existence for all ages—tell about the divine covenant with Abraham, through which he received the promise of becoming the father of a "multitude of nations." [4] In the Book of Deuteronomy, the statement: "A wandering Aramean was my father," refers to Abraham as the father of the Children of Israel.[5] And in a later age, Deutero-Isaiah admonishes the people:

> Look unto the rock whence you were hewn
> And to the vault of the pit whence you were carved
> Look unto Abraham your father
> And unto Sarah who bore you;
> For he was but one and I called him,
> And blessed him and made him many.[6]

The grand myth of the one who was childless until, by the grace of the Lord, he became many, so that his seed multiplied "as the stars of heaven and as the sand which is upon the seashore," [7] has from earliest times been the Magna Charta of Jewish existence. So important was this belief in the descent of all Jews from "our father Abraham" that to this day a proselyte is given the name "N. son of Abraham," to signify that by converting to Judaism he has become an adoptive son of the father of all Jews.

This mystical affiliation of all Jews to Abraham was complemented by an even more fictitious one to "Rachel our mother." Every Jew who had the slightest familiarity with the Bible knew that Rachel was the mother of but two of the twelve sons of Jacob from whom the twelve Biblical tribes of Israel descended. Those who had a more thorough acquaintance with Biblical history were aware that the three Rachel-tribes—Ephraim, Manasseh, and

Benjamin—were relatively insignificant compared to the major tribe of
Judah, and that, moreover, the Assyrian conquest in 721 B.C.E. of the Kingdom of Israel resulted in the virtual disappearance of most of the descen-
dants of Rachel. This happened some three generations prior to the days of
Jeremiah. Nevertheless, by his time the myth of Rachel, the tragic mother of
the nation who laments and weeps for her children, was firmly established.[8]
Throughout the long exile, Rachel remained the symbol of the mother of
Israel, the closest Judaism ever got to a counterpart of the Christian *mater
dolorosa*, and in the Kabbalistic imagination of the Middle Ages the image of
Rachel became mystically identified with the Matronit, the loving and long-
suffering spouse of God the King and mother of the People of Israel.[9]

Mysticism and Kabbala aside, the descent of all Jews from Abraham remained a basic concept in normative Judaism throughout the ages until the
Enlightenment began to nibble away at it. Throughout the centuries the
Jews considered themselves one large family, going back ultimately to Abraham "the rock" whence all of them were hewn. They had no conception of
the extent to which "foreign blood" was infused into the Jewish aggregate in
every generation. It was clearly a case of "where ignorance is bliss"; but even
had they known it, they would have managed to ignore it just as they were
able to ignore the Biblical evidence contradicting Rachel's motherhood of all
Jews. I am perhaps belaboring the point, but what I am aiming at is not to
show the erroneousness of the pre-Enlightenment Jewish belief in the Abrahamic descent of the Jews, but to emphasize that Jewish affiliation, far from
being a matter of genetics, is part of the traditional Jewish belief system.
Which leads us to a preliminary answer of our own to the question of who is
a Jew: A Jew is a person who believes, or feels, that he, together with all
other Jews, is a descendant of Abraham—a descendant, that is, symbolically,
mystically, and emotionally.

This generalization is subject to two qualifications. One is that since the
Enlightenment, an increasing number of Jews have known at least as much
of Jewish history as made them aware that not all Jews were the descendants
of Abraham, that conversions to Judaism have occurred at all times, and that
non-Jewish "blood" has entered the Jewish aggregate in numerous other
ways as well. This new understanding meant that no Jew could be certain he
was actually a descendant of Abraham, even if descent was reckoned only in
the patriline, that is, through father, father's father, and so on, back to the
beginnings of Biblical history. In actuality, of course, such genealogical tracing back of one's descent could not be carried out, because most Jews do not
know even who their great-grandfather was. This holds good even for the
Kohens and Levis, although among them the tradition of Aaronic and Levite
descent, respectively, has been preserved. The second qualification is that
even prior to the Enlightenment some Jews in all periods knew about the
accretion of foreigners to the Jewish body politic. The most conspicuous ex-

ample of such knowledge is presented by the Talmudic discussions as to who, and after how many generations following the conversion of his ancestor, can be admitted to connubium with Jews and accorded other Jewish privileges.[10]

Despite these and some other possible qualifications, the overwhelming majority of Jews at all times considered themselves the progeny of Abraham. From this self-attribution to Abrahamic descent, several weighty consequences followed. First of all, the Bible records that beginning with Abraham, a series of mutual pledges and undertakings were exchanged between God on the one hand, and Abraham and his descendants on the other. Among the divine pledges was the promise of giving the Land of Canaan to the seed of Abraham, of making it a great nation, and of elevating it to the position of God's chosen, holy people. The progeny of Abraham on its part undertook to serve only God and to observe His laws. The most solemn of these pledges was given by the Children of Israel (as they were called by that time) at Mount Sinai when they said, "All that the Lord hath spoken will we do, and obey."[11] A millennium and a half later, the sages of the Talmud considered this pledge as having bound not only the generation which pronounced it but all its descendants for all time to come. Every Jew, they held, because he was the offspring of those who had stood at the foot of Mount Sinai, was *eo ipso* sworn and subject to obeying the Law of God. Thus the Abrahamic descent and the pledge of obedience given to God became in Jewish consciousness like two sides of a coin: each and every Jew existed only because God gave Abraham the promise of numerous progeny; and each and every Jew was pledged personally[12] to fulfill God's commandments.

All this, of course, meant that the question, Who is a Jew? could never arise as long as these twin beliefs were living realities. A Jew was a child of Abraham upon whom, ever since the Sinaitic Revelation, lay the "yoke of the Law." If, as occasionally happened in every generation, a Jew felt that the burden was too heavy and threw it off, this made him a bad Jew, a sinful Jew, but "even though he sinned he was a Jew." His defection did not eradicate his Jewishness because nothing could.[13] This was what he himself felt, and this was what others felt about him.

To believe oneself a descendant of Abraham had another important consequence. It brought Biblical history closer. The greater and lesser characters about whom the Bible speaks, its heroes and villains, its saints and sinners, the entire people—all were one's ancestors; one was directly, genetically involved in everything that happened to them. What they did, and also what was done to them, was of great moment, of inevitable effect, in one's own life. The Exile—to mention only one example, and the most painful at that—was caused by the sins of the fathers; and the sons, dozens of generations later, had still to suffer it. Thus Biblical history had a direct relevance to one's own life; it was, so to speak, one's family history, which one would want to know as a matter of course, just as one would want to know what had happened to one's grandfather in his early days before he had become the old man one remembered from one's own youth.

All this changed radically for those Jews who, after the Enlightenment, became acquainted and enchanted with Western culture and consequently allowed a distance to develop between them and their Jewish antecedents. As a result of these changes, a new type of Jew appeared in ever-increasing numbers. True, also in the pre-Enlightenment past individual Jews occasionally turned from the Jewish to the Gentile culture. Cases are known from Talmudic times when Hellenism was the seductive force, from medieval times when Muslim Arab culture proved irresistible to some Jews, and from Renaissance Italy, to name only three typical examples. But all these examples were few and far between, while the overwhelming majority remained securely wrapped in the Jewish fold. What was new after the Enlightenment was the large number of Jews whom the Jewish heritage was no longer able to hold, who became indifferent, and often even hostile, to their Jewish past, and who considered Jewish tradition and Jewish culture something inferior to the secular, enlightened culture of Western Europe. In many cases this led to formal apostasy, to conversion to Catholicism or Protestantism; in others, it led to intermarriage and therewith to the grafting of the next generation on foreign family trees. Most frequently it meant simply removing oneself, informally and without any declaration of intent, from the Jewish community—an act, however, which in effect had the same consequence of severing social and emotional ties with the Abrahamic family.

It was in this circumstance that the question, Who is a Jew? arose. It was soon to assume considerable importance for the secessionists themselves as well as for the community they abandoned. Was it really possible that one's Jewishness could be reduced to a matter of credal choice? That a person could simply state that he no longer subscribed to the tenets of the Jewish faith, and therewith cease to be a Jew? In the pre-Enlightenment past, in those rare cases when a Jew took this option, the community could react by placing a ban on him—excommunicating him, which, to be sure, did not transform the culprit into a non-Jew but cut him off effectively from all contact with the Jewish community. In the post-Enlightenment period, such direct action was no longer possible because the laws of the country did not allow it and because the number of those who turned their backs on Judaism was too great. The problem had to be faced in a different way, and part of facing it was to seek ways and means to prevent either formal or informal apostasy, and to establish a stance toward the phenomenon as such and toward individuals caught up in it. In this connection, the question, Who is a Jew? had to be tackled. Was the apostate a sinful Jew, as the old Talmudic position had it, or did he actually cease to be a Jew? And what about a person who stopped short of officially embracing another religion but ceased to be Jewish to all intents and purposes? When did a Gentile become Jewish? What if he observed Jewish ritual but did not undergo a conversion ceremony? Or, if he did formally convert but failed to observe any part of the Jewish religion? And what of the children of such people or of the children of mixed couples? In which cases are they Jewish and in which are they not, and at what age is their Jewishness decided?

These problems, as one notes, were the outcome of the greatly increased interaction between Jews and Gentiles which followed in the wake of the Jewish Enlightenment and the Emancipation. As the legal and civil barriers between Jews and Gentiles crumbled, the lure of the Gentile world became greater, and the old Jewish self-assurance faded away in the consciousness of many Jews. Once this situation arose and marginal or alienated Jews of various types emerged, the question of what constituted Jewishness assumed practical significance as well in the life of Jewish congregations. The laws of some European countries (e.g., Germany, Hungary) in the post-Emancipation era gave Jewish communities the right to tax all Jews residing in the locality. This "congregational tax" was the main financial basis of all the institutions maintained by the community, such as synagogues, schools, hospitals, orphans' asylums, old people's homes, and the like. In this connection it was necessary to have a clear definition of who was a Jew over whom the community had taxing powers, and who was not. The state law, in accord with the *Halakha*, defined as a Jew every person born of Jewish parents or legally converted to Judaism. Only a Jew who personally appeared before the congregational authorities to give formal notice of his decision to secede could thereafter be accepted into one of the Christian churches. There was, however, the option of renouncing one's Jewish affiliation and therewith removing oneself from the taxing jurisdiction of the Jewish community, without embracing another religion, and becoming instead "confessionless." [14] Underlying all these regulations was the legal assumption that a person born to Jewish parents was a Jew and that his Jewish birth imposed on him certain duties toward the Jewish community. Only by formally seceding from Judaism could he sever his ties with his ancestral faith and, simultaneously, with the Jewish community.

All that, however, is a thing of the past. At present, the most important legal context in which the question of who is a Jew must be answered is the Law of Return enacted by the Knesset (parliament) of the State of Israel on July 5, 1950. The main provision of this law states, "Every Jew has the right to come to this country as an immigrant." The term "Jew" in the law is vague; it is not clear whether it is used in a strictly religious or an ethnic sense. In a famous 1963 case, in which a Catholic monk of Jewish parentage claimed the status of a Jew immigrating under the Law of Return, the Israeli Supreme Court, interpreting the term in accordance with its popular meaning, found against the claimant. Subsequently the monk, Brother Daniel, originally Oswald Rufeisen, nevertheless acquired Israeli citizenship by naturalization, a procedure that is available to all non-Jews who wish to settle in Israel.[15]

This case, and several others which have arisen since the independence of Israel, kept the issue of who is a Jew alive and made it a *cause célèbre* between the Orthodox Israeli Chief Rabbinate and other rabbinical bodies, especially those of American Jewry. The halakhic definition of a Jew as a person who either was born to a Jewish mother or has converted to Judaism was adopted by the Knesset in 1970, but this legislative act could not settle the question of what precisely constitutes conversion to Judaism. The Israeli Rabbinate insisted that conversion had to conform to strict halakhic rules and that therefore it could be performed only by an Orthodox rabbi. American Conservative and Reform rabbinical organizations argued for the equal validity of conversions performed under their auspices. The common feature in both positions was the requirement that a formal conversion take place which could be effected only by a rabbi. As against this official position, it is interesting to note that a significant proportion of Israeli students in an attitude study (11 percent of the religious students surveyed and 34 percent of the non-religious) considered a person a Jew solely on the basis of his feeling of belongingness to the Jewish people.[16]

The discussion so far should have made it clear that, whatever the Law of Return or halakhic law says, to be Jewish is primarily a matter of feeling, of emotional commitment. To feel Jewish can, of course, be the result of one or more of several factors. Some Jews feel Jewish because they believe that they are of the seed of Abraham; others, because they adhere to the Jewish religion. Still others feel themselves Jews because they consider themselves members of the Jewish people, or because they feel a close identification with the State of Israel, or because they were traumatically shaken by the Nazi holocaust, or because they resent the latent (or not so latent) anti-Semitism they encounter in their professional and/or social life, or because the Jewish past lives in their consciousness, or for one of several other possible reasons. The common denominator in all these cases of feeling Jewish is their cognitive nature: they all derive from *knowing* something about the Jews, and from feelings produced by that knowledge. Thus, in the ultimate analysis, to be Jewish is a state of mind.

While this is undoubtedly true, it does not yet give the complete answer to who is a Jew. To consider or feel oneself Jewish is certainly a necessary condition of Jewishness, but is it a sufficient condition? In some cases, admittedly unusual, a person may feel himself Jewish and yet others may not consider him to be a Jew. This can happen especially when a Gentile converts to Judaism: in the eyes of the Gentiles he becomes a renegade; in the eyes of the Jews, a proselyte. Neither side will consider him a Jew, unless convinced

of his total identification with Judaism. Hence we must add a second necessary condition to the first one: a person must be considered a Jew by others
as well in order to be a Jew. The two necessary conditions together amount
to a sufficient one. Thus we reach the conclusion that *a Jew is a person who
considers himself a Jew and is so considered by others*. Which, of course,
does not change the fact that to be Jewish is a state of mind, except that now
we have recognized that the state, or position, of more than one mind is involved: that of the individual whose Jewishness is being adjudged, and that
of his social environment. If we run down the list of all the marginal
categories of Jewishness, we will find that the two criteria when taken
together constitute as clear a dividing line between Jew and non-Jew as can
be had.

Persons belonging to these marginal categories, I must stress, constitute
only a small fraction of the total aggregate of individuals generally subsumed
under the term "Jews." In the great majority of cases, whether a person is or
is not Jewish is not in doubt. Practically all the Jews who live today in the
world are children of Jewish parents and grandparents, and most children of
Jewish parents have some consciousness of being Jewish. In all these cases,
that is, Jewish descent (as far as the immediate ancestry is concerned) and
Jewish consciousness coincide. A problem arises in the case of converts both
from and to Judaism, and of the children of mixed marriages. Were Heine,
Marx, Disraeli, and the others like them, who were born to Jewish parents
and subsequently converted to Christianity, Jewish or not? Did Marilyn
Monroe, Elizabeth Taylor, Sammy Davis, Jr., to name only three who have
received much publicity, and all the others who were born Christians and at
a certain stage of their lives converted to Judaism thereby become Jewish or
not? And what about the children of mixed Jewish-Christian couples? Are
they Jews or Christians, or neither, and what determines which they are?

Borderline cases are notoriously resistant to taxonomy. Nevertheless, the
criteria of Jewishness in all the marginal categories mentioned must be
sought in the realm of consciousness: offspring of mixed marriages as well as
converts to and from Judaism are Jews if they retain or acquire a Jewish consciousness, if they feel Jewish, if they consider themselves in some sense as
belonging to the Jewish community. And, since inevitably there is interaction between what we feel and what the society that surrounds us feels about
us, whether others consider an individual Jewish or not bears importantly on
his own Jewish identification. In most cases, however, the individual's feelings in the matter are reflected in those of his society, and vice versa, so that
both point in the same direction. It is precisely because this is the case in
general that it was so devastating for the descendants of Jews, who had considered themselves Christian Germans and had been so considered by their
environment, to be stigmatized as "non-Aryans" by the Nuremberg Laws of
1935.

As for proselytes, if we take a category encountered in the United States more frequently than others, a Gentile woman who falls in love with a Jew and undergoes the ritual of conversion because without it he would not marry her does not through this formal act itself become a Jew. Despite the ritual of admitting her as a proselyte, neither she, her husband, nor their friends will consider her Jewish, nor will she feel Jewish. A contrasting example is that of the Polish count Valentine Potocki, who converted because he had come to believe in the tenets of Judaism, joined the Jewish community, and died a martyr's death at the stake in 1749. He unquestionably was a Jew; the strictly Orthodox Jews among whom he lived and together with whom he devoted his life to Talmudic study considered him Jewish, as Jewish as themselves. Similarly, the Marranos who fled Portugal and returned to Judaism after their forebears had been Christians for four or five generations became thereby wholly and fully Jewish, not because of the act of conversion itself but because of their wholehearted commitment to Judaism and to the Jewish community.

An example of a Gentile who became a Jew without formally converting to Judaism is Aimé Pallière (1875–1949). Born into a devout French Catholic family, Pallière was attracted to Judaism and without full conversion lived the life of an ardent and ascetic Jew, recognizing only Orthodox Judaism as authentic; he acted as a spiritual guide to the Paris Liberal synagogue and wrote several deeply Jewish books.[17] Quite a number of proselytes in recent centuries became famous because of personal achievements which, by their very nature, leave no doubt as to their sincerity in embracing Judaism.[18]

The same criterion is applicable to those who take the formal step of leaving the fold. Heine, who converted to Christianity because he felt he needed the baptismal certificate as an entrance ticket to European culture, but continued to the end of his life devoted to Jewry and Judaism, remained a Jew. So did Disraeli, whose Jewish feelings and proud Jewish self-awareness never diminished. By the same token, Proust, the son of a Christian father and a Jewish mother, born and brought up a Christian, proved himself a Jew in making the hero of his great autobiographical novel, Swann, a Jew, and endowing him with the traits which he considered most precious in man.[19]

As these examples show, the perceptual-cognitional definition of those who are Jews applies even to the marginal cases of individuals whom mixed parentage places in an ambiguous position or who have taken the formal step of moving away from, or into, the Jewish community. In all of them the decisive criterion is not the formality of introduction in infancy into Christianity, or Judaism, nor of conversion in later life from one religion to the other, but the consciousness of belonging.

This consciousness of belonging as the ultimate criterion of Jewishness applies also to those individuals who were born to Jewish parents and never took the formal step of converting to another religion. Such persons are commonly referred to as Jews, and they are the ones to whom Jewish census takers or demographers refer when they say that, for example, the number of Jews in the United States in the early 1970's was 5,800,000. If it were possible to question them, or the 14,150,000 Jews estimated to have lived in that period in the world,[20] about their Jewishness, one would find that an unknown but certainly not negligible percentage could not be considered Jews because no traces of "feeling of belongingness to the Jewish people" are left in them. More easily ascertainable is the fact that they observe none of the precepts of Judaism and know only those details about Jews, Jewry, and Israel that they could not help absorbing from papers and news broadcasts. They have become, so to speak, neutralized Jews. Left to their own devices, these non-Jewish children of Jewish parents (or grandparents, because their parents may already have reached this stage) would put the seal on their own removal from Jewishness by totally merging into the Gentile majority of their environment.

If the Jews (including Israel) drew no more global attention than, say, the Danes or the Dutch; if they were exposed to no more attacks, threats, denunciations, and accusations than, say, the Guatemalans or the Paraguayans; if their position in the world were similar to that of many a people left in peace by others; then there can be no doubt but that most of these neutralized Jews, these Jewishly indifferent descendants of Jewish forebears, would never experience anything like the faintest stirrings of Jewish consciousness.

However, history so far has not allowed this to happen. With inexorable regularity it has thrust the Jews, often not without help from themselves, into the forefront of international attention. During and since World War II, events have taken place in which the Jews were passively or actively involved and which touched the conscience of the civilized world. Three-quarters of European Jewry were exterminated by the Nazis. Four times since the foundation of Israel the Arabs have tried to throw its Jewish population into the sea. In Russia, where the Jews were the favorite victims for hundreds of years, they are still singled out for the worst treatment of all minorities. With the exception of the Western democracies, Jew baiting is something of a national pastime in many a country. Most recently, a large majority in the United Nations equated Zionism (for which read Judaism) with racism. And throughout all this, Jews in the free world have continued to make the most significant contributions to all fields of science for the betterment of the human condition. Yes, history makes it impossible for the world to be oblivious of the Jews. Their very existence forces people to take a stand: to be either for or against them.

If this is the reaction of the world at large to Jewish existence, one need not be surprised that many of the un-Jewish offspring of Jews, too, feel compelled to react to what Jews do or what is done to them. Faced with such events, their neutral stance turns out to be a spurious one. In some, it becomes transformed into a veritable hatred of everything Jews as a group do and stand for; without being aware of it, because they are ignorant of Jewish history, they follow the two-hundred-year-old path trodden by Jewish Jew-haters ever since the Enlightenment (see Chapter 17 on "Jewish Self-Hate"). Others, when willy-nilly made aware of a Jewish triumph or a Jewish tragedy, feel a twitch of Jewish pride or a twinge of Jewish conscience; to their own greatest surprise, they are forced to recognize that somewhere in the depths of their psyche, under the ashes of their Jewish indifference, there smoldered all the time a latent, residual Jewishness. As long as these feelings last—and they may rapidly dissipate in the event that things about the Jews become "normal"—they bear witness to a rudimentary Jewish be-longingness.

Such intermittent Jewishness, however, is rare and in the overall tax-onomical division between Jews and Gentiles can safely be overlooked. For the overwhelming majority of Jews, the distinction between Jew and Gentile is never in doubt: a Jew is a Jew because he considers himself a Jew. Com-pared to this one overriding factor of self-identification, the question of why he considers himself a Jew is of minor significance. Whether he does so because he believes himself to be one by race, by religion, by ethnicity, by nationality, or simply because his parents are or were Jewish makes little dif-ference. What matters is the feeling of belongingness, which usually trans-lates itself into efforts to pass the same feeling on to one's children. Herein lies the secret of Jewish survival.

3

Ethnohistory and Inner History*

In the mind of every people the image it has of its own history is a most weighty constituent. More than that, to a great extent national character is influenced by the knowledge people have of their own past. The achievements remembered of past centuries, the virtues extolled in retrospect in former generations, the attitudes and traits believed to have characterized the forefathers—this is of the stuff that forms and informs the modal personality in every country. Since the invocation of the past is a propensity and a practice common to all nations, the use of history has everywhere been institutionalized: national holidays commemorate and celebrate great historical events, novels and plays dramatize them and their protagonists, schools teach about them and present the deeds of famous men as examples to be followed. In this way, history shapes the present and points to the future.

General education, through which most of these influences are channeled today, while it is one of the proudest achievements of the Western world is also a relatively new development. But the effect of the national or ethnic past on the present did not start with the introduction of compulsory schooling for all. Long before this and before the inception of a critical study of history—whose simplified findings in a saccharine solution are fed to schoolchildren—there was the folk memory of the past, which played the same role of shaping the minds of the people by holding up to them the images of their historical or mythical ancestors. Even today, after history has become entrenched in the school curricula for several generations and history texts are available by the thousands, the millennial role of folk memory has not yet been completely eliminated: witness the story of little George Washington and the cherry tree in this country, or of the foundation of Rome by Romulus and Remus in Italy, or the miraculous giving of the Law on Mount Sinai in Jewish tradition. The sum total of such incidents, events, or processes, remembered by the people and considered by them historical, has been termed "ethnohistory." Ethnohistory is that part of folklore which comprises the traditional historical knowledge of the people, transmitted from genera-

tion to generation. In the ethnohistory of each people, the deeds of its own
ancestors play the central role. Whether or not what the ethnohistory of a
nation tells about the past is historically true is of minor importance compared to the function it has in molding and shaping the national character.

Among the Jews, ethnohistory was almost entirely confined to religious
history as presented in the Bible. This meant, first of all, that Jewish ethnohistory, in contrast to that of all other peoples, had a sacred character. It was
a religious duty to accept every event related in the Bible as a true historical
fact, above and beyond critical questioning. Moreover, because it was sacred
history—in which the will of God manifested itself, and even the knowledge
of which was revealed from on high—it had a much more powerful formative
impact on the Jewish mind than other ethnohistories had on the minds of
other peoples. And thirdly, because the Bible, this sacred sourcebook of
Jewish ethnohistory, contains an account of the history of the Jewish people
combined with a presentation of Jewish religious doctrine and practice, Judaism in post-Biblical times became the unique combination of religion and
ethnicity which set it apart from the Gentile world.

The Jews have often been characterized as a people strongly dominated by
a sense of history. As a closer look shows, this is true only inasmuch as Jewish religion is inseparably intertwined with certain periods and events in
Jewish history, among which the central place is held by the Exodus.[1] It is
not at all true if it is meant to refer to a strong Jewish *interest* in Jewish history. In fact, the exact opposite is the case: the Jews have had less interest in
their own history (with the exception of the Biblical period, of which more
later) than many another people has had in its past. This general assertion
can easily be documented. Only a knowledge of Biblical history was both inevitable and religiously necessary. Inevitable, because the recitation of the
Five Books of Moses, portions of the Prophets, the Psalms, and other Biblical books were part of the religious ritual, so that a knowledge of whatever
historical accounts they contained was acquired almost automatically. Religiously necessary, because many religious injunctions are embedded in historical narratives and could be neither understood nor observed without a
knowledge of their historical context. As a result of this organic interrelationship between Jewish religion and Biblical history, there has always been
a significant positive correlation between a Jew's knowledge of Biblical history and his religious observance. Both together constituted the ground of
his self-identification as a Jew and of his identification with the Biblical
Children of Israel.

Compared to his familiarity with Biblical history, the Jew's knowledge of
post-Biblical Jewish history was minimal. Biblical history ends with the age
of Ezra and Nehemia (c. 450 B.C.E.), and with it ends Jewish historical
knowledge and interest. Characteristically, as against hundreds of sages

whose religious discussions have been preserved in the two Talmuds, and as against dozens of apocryphal books, Midrashim, and Hellenistic Jewish literary products, the works of only one Jewish historian, Josephus Flavius, have survived from antiquity; and even they escaped oblivion only because of Christian interest in them. From Josephus to the *Shevet Y'huda* of the Ibn Vergas, for about a millennium and a half, during which the Jews had a phenomenal output of religious and secular literature, they produced not a single historian.

This absence of Jewish historiography expressed not just a lack of interest in history but a denial of all value to its study. Typical in this respect was the view of the great Maimonides, who held that to occupy oneself with history was "a useless waste of time." [2] If the greatest mind of medieval Jewry had this attitude toward history, one can easily imagine what thick cloud of historical ignorance must have cast its shadow over the minds of the less learned. The fact is that almost complete ignorance of post-Biblical Jewish history and lack of interest in it remained characteristic of the Jews until the Enlightenment. Even Moses Mendelssohn and the period of Jewish Enlightenment "had little use for historical thought," and it was not until two generations later that enlightened Jews felt "the need of presenting their story in terms of history"—a position which found its classical expression in the works of Zunz, Jost, Geiger, and Graetz. [3] As for Orthodox Jews of the traditional persuasion, among them both ignorance of, and lack of interest in, post-Biblical history have continued down to this day. Thus, equally in past and present, historical awareness in the most history-bound element among the Jews has focused on the Biblical age, Biblical events, and Biblical heroes.

As for the post-Biblical ages, the little that was known about them was derived from the occasional references contained in religious literature; or rather, in that part of it which became the basis of the standard halakhic curriculum. This consisted, in the main, of the Babylonian Talmud (completed c. 500 C.E.) and its medieval commentaries, and the four great religio-legal codes of Yitzhaq Alfasi (1013–1103), Maimonides (1135–1204), Jacob ben Asher (c. 1270–c. 1343), and Joseph Caro (1488–1575). These codes, being legal compendiums, could not be expected to contain any historical material. The Talmud, a major part of which is non-halakhic, does yield considerable historical information for the scholar who studies it as a historical source. Traditional Jews, however, never studied it for the sake of learning about Jewish history, but for the halakhic rules which it contains and which form the basis of the decisions by the authors of the medieval codes. In fact in the yeshivot, the Talmudic academies, which to this day are centers of traditional Jewish studies as they have been pursued for many centuries, all non-halakhic material contained in the Talmud is treated with much condescension as mere *"agad'te,"* non-serious exercise of fancy, which can as well be skipped or glossed over. Consequently, whatever historical information is contained in the Talmud was in general overlooked. This explains why even the halakhically most learned Jew knew pitifully little of post-Biblical Jewish history.

There is actually nothing surprising in this lack of historical interest among the Jews. Until the Enlightenment, ignorance of their own history and at best a lukewarm interest in it were characteristic of all the peoples among whom the Jews lived. In general, people were satisfied with their ethnohistory, that is, popular historical traditions, which are always disjointed and fragmentary and in most cases at variance with critically ascertainable historical fact. The same held good for the Jews; the circumstance that they were "the people of the book," that almost all of them were literate, and that so many of them devoted much of their lives to the study of the *Halakha* should not make us expect otherwise. On the contrary, precisely because all their intellectual interest was focused on, and satisfied by, halakhic study, little mental energy was left over for other intellectual pursuits.

Nevertheless, there was a marked difference between Gentile and Jewish ethnohistory. The Gentiles, generally illiterate until the Enlightenment, shaped their ethnohistory on a folkloristic basis: it contained fabled exploits of folk heroes, great deeds of kings, local legends, and the like. In brief, their ethnohistory told them what it knew and remembered about the great events of their past, whether real or imaginary, and was transmitted orally. Jewish ethnohistory, on the other hand, had a written basis. It was grounded in the historical books of the Bible and in the scattered historical references contained in that part of the post-Biblical literature which the Jews studied as halakhic sources, or which, like the story of Hanukka, became part of a religious ritual.

I referred earlier to the Jewish self-identification with the Biblical people of Israel; this statement, however, requires careful qualification. Being religiously observant but historically ignorant—a description that fits almost all of them until the Enlightenment—the Jews identified themselves not with the Biblical Israelites as a whole but only with their pious, God-fearing, and God-loving leaders: with Abraham, Isaac and Jacob, Moses and Aaron, David, the prophets, Ezra and Nehemia, as well as with those of the people who obeyed the divine injunctions conveyed to them by these saintly men. The existence of such a pious contingent of Biblical Israelites was imaginatively assumed and emotionally taken for granted, although a critical scrutiny of the Biblical sources (never, of course, undertaken by religious Jews) would have yielded little factual basis for it. Jewish ethnohistory instilled into the Jews an identification with a prototypal Jewish piety which was modeled after medieval Jewish religiosity and projected back into Biblical times. They certainly did not identify with those Israelites who were the target of bitter reproaches by the Biblical historians, prophets, and leaders for their incessant backsliding, idolatry, and moral transgression. They viewed those sin-

ners with abhorrence, and with resentment as well since it was to their transgressions that Jewish ethnohistory (or, if you wish, the Jewish religious view
of their condition) attributed the misery of the Galut.

The fact that Biblical historiography became the one major formative influence dominating the ethnohistory, or historical awareness, of the Jews down
to the age of Enlightenment was crucial in the development of the Jewish
view of the interrelationship between Jews and Gentiles and of Jewish versus
Gentile values. By the end of the Biblical period itself the Bible had become
the charter of Jewish life, which not only regulated religious belief and
conduct but also imparted to all future generations its own specific view of
history and of Israel's relationship to God. The Biblical historians, prophets,
and poets were all convinced and devoted Yahwists, who looked upon history as the stage on which the consequences of the people's and their leaders'
religio-moral conduct were acted out. Therein alone lay for them the essence
of history, and they never tired of reiterating their uncompromising religious
judgment of kings, leaders, and the people as a whole. This viewpoint inevitably impressed itself as the only possible one upon the post-Biblical Jewish
understanding of Biblical history.

Moses in this perspective is the lawgiver rather than the liberator; David,
"the sweet singer of Israel," the psalmist, rather than the warrior-king who
conquered Israel's enemies; Solomon, the builder of the Temple, the wise
ruler, and the author of the Song, the Proverbs, and Ecclesiastes, rather
than the Oriental despot, talented administrator, and cunning diplomat who
cemented Israel's alliances with its neighbors. In the Books of Kings and
Chronicles, the only angle from which the rulers of Israel and Judah are
judged is whether they served God or idols; compared to this one main issue
their political, military, and other exploits are treated as secondary matter.
The end of the divided monarchy is the great age of the prophets who
preached lofty religious ideas, not the period of decline of Israelite and
Judaite power that ended in the destruction first of Israel and then of Judah
and Jerusalem. Of the early Second Commonwealth, Ezra and Nehemia are
known and remembered not as political leaders of their people but as the
pious reestablishers of pure religious observance.

The same viewpoint dominated whatever Jewish ethnohistory was able to
retain from post-Biblical ages. The three centuries following the close of
Biblical history are an almost total blank as far as Jewish ethnohistory is concerned; then follows the Maccabean uprising, again remembered not for the
military victory it achieved over a powerful foreign oppressor but for the
cleansing of the Temple of Jerusalem desecrated by the pagans, the miracle
of the oil, and the reestablishment of the Temple ritual. The period of the
Tannaim—the sages whose teachings and rulings are contained in the
Mishna—began about a century before the fall of Jerusalem; but Jewish
ethnohistory remained almost oblivious of Roman repression and persecu-

tion, and of the loss of the last vestiges of Jewish sovereignty which took place in that period, remembering it only as the age of the great and saintly sages who laid the foundations for the Talmudic elaboration of the Law. Of the Jewish revolt which led to the Jewish-Roman war Jewish ethnohistory knows practically nothing. The defeat of the Jews by the Romans which ended the war in the year 70 was mourned not as the loss of Jewish national independence it signified, but as a religious catastrophe, the destruction of the Second Temple of Jerusalem. The memory of this spiritual tragedy was coupled with, and to some extent counterbalanced by, that of the simultaneous founding of the Talmudic academy in Yavne by Rabban Yoḥanan ben Zakkai, which ensured the uninterrupted continuation of the study and development of the Law, henceforward the only basis of Jewish religious existence.

The subsequent four centuries are remembered only as the age of the Talmud, in which Jewish life is imagined to have revolved around the religio-legal discussions which took place in the great academies of Sura, Pumbeditha, and Nehardea in Babylonia, and in schools of lesser importance in Palestine. With the end of the Talmudic period (c. 500 C.E.), Jewish ethnohistory becomes even vaguer; generations are merged or telescoped or pass unnoticed because they left behind no religio-legal monuments of sufficient magnitude to impress themselves upon folk memory. Remembrance revives only sporadically, as when it can recall an outstanding religious authority who produced a code which subsequently became incorporated into the halakhic curriculum; even in this case, the knowledge retained is not of the life of the code's author but only a vague notion of the time in which he lived in relation to others. This alone is the essential, since each subsequent code supersedes its predecessor and a knowledge of their chronological order is therefore mandatory.

Jewish ethnohistory, then, evinces a pattern which curiously reverses the one usually characterizing folk memory. In most cases a people remembers little of what took place long ago, and more and more of successive ages as they approach the present. This is inevitable in ethnohistories whose medium of transmission is oral tradition. But in the book-based ethnohistory of the Jews, it was not the distance in time but the character of and the regard for its written sources that determined the extent of popular retention. The oldest Jewish sourcebook, the Bible—being considered the most sacred, and in addition containing much historical information—was incorporated into Jewish memory and consciousness in a most detailed manner. Thereafter, every successive Jewish religious sourcebook was considered less sacred and also happened to contain less and less historical material; the nearer the period to the present, the less information about it survives in Jewish folk memory. Thus pre-Enlightenment Jews in the eighteenth century knew incomparably more about what happened to their remote forebears in Biblical

Palestine in the days of David and Solomon than about events that had transpired in their own city a hundred years before their own time.

A much more crucial difference between Gentile and Jewish ethnohistory is that the former emphasizes external history, while the latter concentrates on inner history. The distinction between external and inner history requires a word of explanation.

External history consists of that chain of events in which the leaders of the people—whether tribal, feudal, military, or political—are the main protagonists. Wars, conquests, revolutions, famines, pestilences, and other such major upheavals are the typical links in this chain; its typical mode is action—group action led from above, or group reaction provoked by social, economic, or political conditions, or the individual action of a great popular hero. Inner history, on the other hand, takes place primarily on the mental plane: its landmarks are new ideas, new insights, new attitudes, new values, whose birth may or may not be followed by action. It is what is termed in German *Geistesgeschichte*—the history of what went on in the human mind and of its consequences for human life. Religious movements are the prime examples of what inner history is about; the transformations of human life they brought about dwarf the effects of the greatest military conquests.

Gentile ethnohistory dwells, in general, on external rather than inner history. Its typical heroes are not great men of the spirit whose works, thoughts, and teachings folk memory can neither grasp nor retain, but kings and queens, heroic men and beautiful women, whose images fascinated the folk and whose acts impressed themselves on its memory. Jewish ethnohistory constitutes an exception from this general rule for reasons that require looking into.

Measured by all external criteria, the Jews in the Diaspora were never masters of their history. For two thousand years they were not actors but were acted upon in the continuing drama of their encounter with the Gentile world. They settled in every country at the pleasure of its Gentile rulers. They lived in areas or quarters assigned to them by the Gentiles. They engaged in occupations permitted to them by the Gentiles and had to resign themselves to discrimination, oppression, and contemptuous treatment. They were the victims of attacks, atrocities, pogroms, and massacres, forced on pain of death to convert to the religion of the ruling majority. They experienced the trauma of expulsion from nearly every country in which they had been allowed to dwell. And, recently, they were singled out as the main target of the only systematic genocide ever conceived and executed by human inhumanity.

Jewish passivity and defensiveness were typical of Jewish-Gentile relations all over the world. There were, to be sure, variations: in some places at some times the Jewish condition within Gentile society was neither hard nor harsh. Historical scrutiny can even unearth totally exceptional cases—places from which the Jews have never been exiled, or where their position in certain periods was a favored one. Yet these exceptions cannot alter the validity of the observation that the basic theme of Jewish history was one of endurance of, or adaptation to, the will of massive Gentile majorities.

All this only touches upon the external aspect of Jewish life and does not tell the whole story of the Jewish past. In fact, it relates only to that part of Jewish history which, in the eyes of the Jews themselves, was of lesser importance, and much of which remained unknown to them or was soon forgotten. Far more important for the Jews was the internal aspect of their life, which consisted primarily of three interrelated elements in those areas of existence in which they themselves could determine how to act, feel, and think: their conduct and attitudes toward fellow Jews, their devotion in fulfilling God's will, and their concentration on studying and perfecting the Law. Not that the Jews had not been conscious of their sufferings or did not bemoan the bitterness of their Exile. Of course, they could not help being painfully aware of having been cast in the role of victims by the inscrutable will of God; of course they never ceased, they could not cease, praying and hoping for deliverance and for what in modern terminology would be called national self-determination. But the fact that they were mere pawns in ruthless games played by kings and dukes, by city potentates and church prelates, never diminished their feelings about themselves, their self-valuation, their conviction that they ranked highest in the only true global hierarchy, in which man's standing depended on nothing else but his fulfillment of the will of God. No amount of persecution could make them doubt in the slightest that they were the chosen people of God, make them forget that only they of all mankind had bent their necks into the "yoke of the commandments," or shake their conviction that their own morality towered mountain high above that of the rest of mankind, and that intellectually as well they were princes, albeit forced to wear paupers' disguise. It was this consciousness of their inner worth that enabled the Jews to endure, in the double sense of continuing to exist and withstanding all adversity. The fact that this, too, exacted its price in the form of cultural and intellectual isolation from the Gentile world in most places and at most periods never crossed their minds—never, that is, until the onset of the Jewish Enlightenment in the late eighteenth century.

Thus external history, for the Jews, consisted of all those events, processes, and conditions which were imposed upon them by the Gentile majority in whose midst they lived; while their inner history comprised in the main the autonomous area of their preoccupation with religious life, practice, belief, and study. Of the two, the external history was the chronicle of powerless, passive endurance, the history of all the factors whose sum total made up the Galut, the Exile. The inner history was the record of Israel's enduring chosenness, its continuous search for the will of God, and its ceaseless reassertion of the special relationship between it and its Father in Heaven.

It was a psychological necessity that in popular retrospect (which ethnohistory basically is) the inner history should appear as the main thing, the overriding aspect of Jewish existence, and that the political and socio-economic circumstances and the mundane, material aspects of life determined by them should be considered nothing more than incidental, insubstantial, and ephemeral. The temporal was looked upon as temporary, while the spiritual was seen as the eternal ground of Jewish life. This explains how it could come about that the external history was retained in Jewish folk memory only in the vaguest, haziest terms, occasionally referred to in lamentations about unusually cruel *g'zerot* or persecutions, but in general allowed to sink into oblivion. Memories of the inner history, on the other hand, although they too were few and poor compared to what the average Jew knew of Biblical times, were cherished as the authentic manifestation of the essential in Jewish life, as a sequence of great intellectual achievements recorded in an increasingly voluminous religious literature and absorbed by the Jewish mind. To illustrate this by a single poignant example, until the Enlightenment all Jews, even the least learned, knew of Rashi (1040–1105), the greatest of all Biblical and Talmudic commentators, even if they had only a vague idea of the period in which he lived. But very few indeed were those who knew that during Rashi's lifetime the Jewish communities of the Rhine, to the east of the French city of Troyes in which Rashi lived, were attacked and massacred (in 1096) with unprecedented cruelty by bands of Crusaders. Of this and the many other waves of persecution that swept over Jewish communities in most places, Jewish ethnohistory preserved nothing more than a generalized awareness that life in the Galut was cruel, the feeling rather than the knowledge that the Jewish condition in the Diaspora was to be victimized by the Gentiles, and that the proper Jewish reaction to suffering was to turn even more fervently to God, to obey His will even more scrupulously, and to devote oneself to the study of the *Halakha* even more diligently. In this manner the pattern of turning from the external to the inner history came to be confirmed anew again and again.

The distinction between the external history which is best overlooked and forgotten, and the inner history which is of the essence and must therefore be remembered as clearly as possible, is as old as the Bible. In Biblical historiography, too, the emphasis is always on the inner rather than the external history of Israel. It is evident that the anonymous historians, whose work is preserved in the historical books of the Bible, had little interest in the wars, the victories and defeats, the political ups and downs, the alliances and diplomatic relationships, the economic and social life of the people, and in all the other aspects of external history, except as these events had a bearing upon the inner history of Israel. More than that, in accordance with their strictly religio-centric and Yahwistic point of view, even in presenting the inner history of Israel, they did not write *Kulturgeschichte* (cultural history) or *Geistesgeschichte* (intellectual history) in general, but concentrated on *Religionsgeschichte* (history of religion). All the historical events they presented were for them nothing but illustrative material which made manifest the fateful consequences of the people's and its leaders' behavior in the innermost sanctum of inner history—their self-subordination to the will of God. Herein, according to the Biblical historians and prophets, lay the deeper meaning of history; in fact, the only meaning. The external events that befell the people of Israel were but the consequences of what they themselves had wrought in relation to the will of God. Obedience led to national prosperity; disobedience to national peril. Inner history, that is, was of the essence; external history was merely its palpable manifestation.

This Biblical view of history indelibly impressed itself upon the Jewish mind for all times. It made Jewish ethnohistory neglect the external and emphasize the inner aspects of the Jewish past. It even made Jews perceive their contemporary condition in its light, enabling them to endure with relative equanimity the trials and tribulations of the Galut, all of which were, after all, things external, and to find solace in living an essentially Jewish life, obeying the divine commandments to love God and one's neighbor, and faithfully fulfilling one's duties toward God and man. From Biblical times to the Enlightenment, this traditional concentration on inner history, which hinged on the retention of and adherence to the essence of Jewishness, remained the Jewish position in all historic encounters between the Jews and the Gentile world.

We are now ready to have a closer look at the six most important of these great historic meetings, each of which contributed in its own way to the formation of the Jewish mind.

II

SIX GREAT HISTORIC ENCOUNTERS

For no other people have encounters with outside forces played so important a role as for the Jews. Beginning with the earliest, semi-mythical phase of their history, the Jews were exposed to the most varied foreign influences impinging upon all areas of their life. This process began when Hebrew nationhood was but a divine promise made to the Biblical patriarchs and has continued down to the present, for almost four millennia. It encompassed such areas as language (discussed elsewhere in this book), religion, social life, cultural orientation, occupational structure, and values and in all of them wrought changes ranging from ephemeral to radical. Yet despite these metamorphoses, throughout their history from the Biblical period to the age of their Enlightenment, the Jews remained fundamentally true to themselves, their destiny, their God. Whether they spoke (and wrote) in Hebrew, Aramaic, Greek, Arabic, Persian, or any of the languages they acquired in Europe, their speech was primarily a Jewish medium of communication, and what they produced in writing was, in the main, Jewish literature.

In the following pages we shall take a closer look at six great historic encounters between the Jews and the world which have immeasurably contributed to the formation of the Jewish mind and whose residual effects are still inescapably at work in the depths of the modern Jewish psyche.

4

Israel and Canaan

The first encounter, that between the Children of Israel and the people of Canaan, had two lasting outcomes. One was their acquisition of the Hebrew language; the second was the incorporation of certain Canaanite elements into the religion of the pre-exilic Israelites and Judaites.

1. The Language

The account given in Genesis of the lives of the Hebrew patriarchs contains clear indications to the effect that the Hebrew language was acquired by them from their Canaanite neighbors. While the historicity of the patriarchal family is still doubtful, and some scholars assume that the adventures told about its epic figures mask the movements of a sizable clan, there is no reason to doubt the tradition which attributes an Aramaean origin to the Children of Israel. According to Genesis, Abraham and his wife Sarah, who was also his half sister, came to Canaan from Haran in Upper Mesopotamia, which, in the seventeenth century B.C.E. (the probable period of this event), was an Aramaic language area. Those members of Abraham's family who remained behind in Mesopotamia are consistently termed Aramaeans.[1] Many centuries later, when the Book of Deuteronomy was written, Abraham himself, or the entire patriarchal family, was referred to in a ritual invocation as "a wandering Aramaean."[2] In this case, the mother tongue of Abraham and Sarah, as well as of their son Isaac, would have been Aramaic, although after their arrival in Canaan they undoubtedly learned Canaanitic as well in order to be able to communicate with their new neighbors. Isaac's wife, Rebekah, was the daughter of Bethuel the Aramaean, a nephew of Abraham. She grew up in Paddan-aram in Aram-naharaim (that is, Mesopotamia) and was brought to Canaan by Abraham's faithful servant Eliezer of Damascus.[3] There can be little doubt, therefore, that the mother tongue of Jacob, the favorite son of Rebekah, was also Aramaic, although Canaanitic must have been his second language. The two wives of Jacob, Rachel and Leah, for whom he served for fourteen years in Haran, or Paddan-aram, were the daughters of Laban the Aramaean, brother of Rebekah.[4] So they were Aramaic-speaking girls, as were the two concubines who were the "handmaids," that is, slave girls, of Jacob's wives. This means that the mother tongue of the twelve sons of Jacob whom these four women bore to him—all of them except the youngest, Benjamin, in Mesopotamia—was Aramaic; but they, too, must have learned Canaanitic from contact with their neighbors after the family's return to Canaan.

It can further be assumed that this early bilingualism, which characterized the patriarchal family for three generations, ceased with the children of Jacob's twelve sons, all of whom (with the exception of Joseph, who while still a boy was sold by his brothers into slavery and taken to Egypt) must have married Canaanite girls. These Canaanite women, of course, brought up their children with Canaanitic as their mother tongue. By the time Jacob went down to Egypt with his large family,[5] Canaanitic was firmly entrenched as the sole language of all of Jacob's grandchildren. Once adopted, this language became the national language of the clan which soon took the name of "Children of Israel." But even centuries after its adoption, it was still known among the Israelites as "the language of Canaan," [6] next to its more common designation of *Y'hudit* or *"Judaic."* [7] Only as late as in Mishnaic days was the term *"(Lashon) 'Ivrit,"* i.e., "Hebrew (language)," to appear for the first time.

It is unnecessary to dwell here on the extent to which the Children of Israel made this originally Canaanite language their own, developed it so as to be able to express in it lofty theological concepts and ethical thoughts, created in it great literary and religious masterpieces collectively known as the Bible, elevated it to a position of sanctity, and cherished it throughout their long history in the far-flung communities of their Diaspora. The pagan Canaanitish origin of Hebrew became forgotten soon after the end of the Biblical period. In Talmudic times, the Hebrew language was viewed with rather ethnocentric romanticism as the original language of mankind. Hebrew, the sages taught, was the language God used when He created the world, the language spoken by Adam, Eve, and the Serpent, and shared by all men until they split up into many tongues at the Tower of Babel.[8]

Such Agadistic fantasies apart, we have, in the passages of Genesis referred to above, historical echoes of the acquisition within two or three generations of a new language. This is followed by its adaptation to the cultural needs of the Hebrew community, and by its transformation, in the process, from a foreign into an authentically Israelite cultural property and a medium of Hebrew and Jewish literary creativity. This remarkable process of language acquisition by the Jewish people was subsequently repeated with Aramaic, Greek, Arabic, Ladino, and Yiddish (and to a more limited extent also with other languages). Each of those processes can be considered an example of the Jewish intellectual faculty to make a virtue out of necessity, to acquire a vernacular from the Gentile environment, and to "Judaize" it intellectually, spiritually, and emotionally. These linguistic absorptions and incorporations succeeded to such an extent that, in the case of the major historical Jewish languages, in the first place Hebrew, Aramaic (cf. the Talmud), Ladino, and Yiddish, not a trace of their foreign origin remained in the Jewish consciousness. On the contrary, each of them became surrounded by an aura of sanctity, or at least was hallowed as a venerable Jewish cultural treasure and a basic feature of Jewish tradition, religious expression, and folk life.

2. Ethnic Antagonism

No evidence is contained in the Biblical sources as to any resistance the patriarchs may have put up against the acquisition by their children of "the language of Canaan." Canaanite mores, however, were an entirely different matter. Objection to them must have been a factor in Abraham's apprehension lest his son Isaac marry a Canaanite girl. "I will make thee swear," Abraham said to his faithful steward, the Damascan Eliezer, "by the Lord, the God of heaven and the God of the earth, that thou shalt not take a wife for my son of the daughters of the Canaanites among whom I dwell," [9] and forthwith dispatched him to Mesopotamia, to his kindred, to take a wife for Isaac. When Isaac's son Esau took two Hittite girls to wife (the Hittites were one of the ethnic groups in Canaan), "they were a bitterness of spirit unto Isaac and Rebekah." [10] Therefore Isaac, at Rebekah's initiative, instructed Jacob to go to the house of his mother's brother in Paddan-aram and find himself a wife there. When "Esau saw that the daughters of Canaan pleased not Isaac his father," he went to Ishmael, Isaac's half brother, and took the daughter of Ishmael to wife, in addition to the Hittite wives he had married earlier. [11]

After the return of Jacob from Mesopotamia twenty years later, we no longer find such overt evidence of antagonism to marriages with Canaanite girls. From the story of Jacob's encounter with Esau upon his arrival in Canaan, it appears that none of the eleven sons who were born to him in Mesopotamia was yet married. [12] Hence they all married in Canaan, and the only inference possible is that their wives were Canaanite women. The only two sons of Jacob to whose marriages in Canaan reference is made in Genesis are Simeon—one of whose sons, Shaul, is stated to have been born to him by a Canaanite woman—and Judah, who married a daughter of the Canaanite Shua. Years later, Judah took a Canaanite girl by the name of Tamar as wife for his firstborn son Er. [13] Joseph, of course, grew up in Egypt and married an Egyptian woman. [14] While all this is recorded without any reprobation, one suspects that the marriage of their sons and grandsons to Canaanite women must have been regarded by Jacob and his wives (who were his first cousins) with as much disapproval as such outgroup marriages were by his own parents and grandfather. Whatever the express or unspoken wishes of Jacob and his wives, their sons evidently disregarded them and married Canaanite women. However, when it came to giving a sister of theirs, Dinah, in marriage to a Canaanite prince, they opposed this bitterly, although by allowing Dinah to marry her seducer they would have enabled her to regain her destroyed honor. On the other hand, the story which tells of the bloody revenge taken by the sons of Jacob on the entire city of Shechem also contains an indication that they themselves were not averse to "taking captive" the Shechemite women,[15] which could mean only one thing—that the attractive ones among them were destined to serve as concubines or even wives.

Precisely why Isaac and Rebekah were so strongly opposed to "the daughters of Canaan" as actual or prospective daughters-in-law is a moot question. The religious difference, which comes first to mind, cannot be the answer, because Rebekah's brother Laban, to whom they sent Jacob to find himself a wife, was as much an idolater as were the Canaanites. Laban's daughter Rachel, the beloved wife of Jacob, was a devoted follower of her father's idolatrous religion, as we know from the incident of her theft of Laban's household gods, the *Teraphim*,[16] recorded in Genesis without any trace of disapproval. Once the religious issue is excluded, the only possible remaining reason for the first two patriarchs' objection to their sons' marriages with Canaanite women must be sought in what today would be described as "ethnic" differences: that is, they were repelled by the Canaanite girls' behavior and manners, mentality and values.

Jacob himself, as well as his wives, may have been no more accustomed to Canaanite ethnicity than his father and grandfather had been before him. Nevertheless, Jacob and his wives did not follow the example of Isaac and Rebekah and of Abraham: they did not instruct their sons to take wives from the family in the old country. With the sons marrying local girls, the ethnic assimilation of the patriarchal family to Canaanite culture began, and their adoption of "the language of Canaan" was completed.

By the time Jacob and his sons went down to Egypt their entourage consisted of some 150 "souls," counting the females as well as the traditional 70 males. This was no longer an extended family; it was a lineage, large enough to return to the traditional preference of their forefathers for close in-family endogamy. Whatever the precise duration of the Israelites' sojourn in Egypt, and whatever the historical process—as against the traditional story—of their exodus from "the house of bondage," their wanderings in the desert, and their penetration into the Land of Canaan, endogamy must have been observed by them throughout this period. Outgroup marriages in this period did occur but seem to have been very rare. Moses married a non-Israelite, and so did an unnamed Hebrew woman. Attached to the Israelites who left Egypt was a contingent of non-Israelites referred to as 'erev rav, or "mixed multitude," and, of course, intermarriages with them occurred.[17] Nevertheless, on the whole the Israelites of the time were a homogeneous ethnic group, whose endogamous preference enabled them to retain "the language of Canaan" (Hebrew) with only the slightest traces of Egyptian linguistic influence.

3. The Religious Influence

The acquisition by the Abrahamic family of the language of Canaan lies too far back in the dawn of Israelite history to have left behind more than a few quasi-mythical traces in Biblical references. We know of no struggle put up by the Aramaic-speaking patriarchs against the adoption of Canaanite-Hebrew by their children or grandchildren. By contrast, a few centuries later but still in the early period of Biblical history, the penetration of another Canaanitish cultural element provoked bitter opposition on the part of Hebrew religious purists who, while few in number, had the distinction of producing the only literary documents which survived from the Biblical period—the Bible itself. I refer, of course, to the impact of the Canaanite religion on the Israelites, which began soon after their conquest of the Promised Land and lasted until their exile to Mesopotamia some seven centuries later.

The clash between these two peoples—closely related racially, speaking almost the same language, and competing for control of the narrow strip of fertile land between the Mediterranean and the desert—was inevitable. In historical perspective, more important than the issue of political and military supremacy was the question of religious differences. As one can gather from the Biblical references, the lure of the Canaanite polytheistic and sensuous cults was too much for the Israelites. "They served the Baals and the Asherahs," and the Astartes, and other Canaanite deities, and had it not been for the zealous and tireless struggle of a few utterly devoted Yahwists in each generation against these pagan "abominations," the old, tribal, Mosaic Yahwist monolatry would have been submerged in Canaanite polytheism. Thus the monotheism of the Hebrew prophets would have never developed to serve as the foundation for Talmudic Judaism, and beyond it as a "light unto the nations." This momentous development requires more detailed consideration.

Whatever the precise historical circumstances of the settlement of the Israelite tribes in Canaan, it brought about a major complex of socio-cultural transformations which involved the giving up of the nomadic pastoral way of life for a settled, agricultural existence. This led, in turn, to the development of commerce, artisanship, trades, territorial organization, and at least partial urbanization. The magnitude of this transformation and its attendant problems can be well appreciated from our present-day perspective, for the same process has been repeated on and off throughout the history of the Middle East and in fact is still continuing more rapidly today than ever in the past as a result of the undreamed-of riches pouring into the area from an oil-hungry world.[18]

As far as the Biblical Israelites were concerned, their sedentarization in the "Land of Promise" meant—in addition to their transformation from nomads (or, as Albright has argued, donkey-caravaneers)[19] to settled people—"Canaanization." They conquered and subjected many of the petty Canaanite kingdoms, which in most cases consisted of nothing more than a central town, occasionally fortified, with a few square miles of surrounding countryside dotted with several villages—the latter in Biblical language termed the "daughters" of the town which held the position of "mother" to them. But, as often happens when a warlike people conquers weaker but more civilized foes, the conquerors in turn were, if not conquered, at least profoundly influenced by the culture of those they defeated. This process (which the genius of Ibn Khaldūn some twenty-six centuries later recognized as a historical law) meant first of all in the case of the Israelite tribes that they acquired agricultural methods from the Canaanites, including the techniques of making and using agricultural implements, of building structures for the storage of the crops and as shelters for the farm animals, and of making vessels for carrying and keeping farm produce of various kinds. It also meant that they adopted the Canaanite way of building houses, villages, towns, and fortifications; the Canaanite methods of owning and leasing land, of selling and buying property, of keeping slaves and concubines, of litigation and adjudication, and of communal, social, and ultimately national leadership centered on the sacred person of the king. In brief, during the transitional period known in Biblical history as the Age of the Judges, in the course of which the Israelites solidified their hold over a major portion of the Land of Canaan on both banks of the Jordan, they acquired practically the entire gamut of Canaanite civilization. It is an eloquent testimony to the openness of Israelite society and its readiness to adopt the ways of its neighbors that the entire Biblical literature contains not a single critical word of this all-encompassing process of the Canaanization of Israelite life. Not a word, that is, with the exception of the torrent of scathing denunciations directed at Canaanite religious influence.

Unfortunately, we know much too little about the religion of the Children of Israel in the pre-Conquest period.[20] Direct contemporary evidence is altogether lacking, because like all nomadic peoples everywhere, they left behind neither buildings nor monuments, neither inscriptions nor other written documents. As to the Biblical account, however old the oral tradition on which it is based, in its extant form it bears the marks of editorial work done in much later periods and in the spirit of uncompromising Yahwism. Despite these limitations, there can be no reasonable doubt that pre-Conquest Israelite religion had as its credal basis the belief in one God, named Yahweh, who was considered the sole God of Israel but whose power and dominion extended only over Israel. Other peoples had their own gods, although the Israelites' victories over their enemies confirmed them in the belief that Yahweh was stronger than those other deities. This was a kind of monolatry, inclining toward an ethnic monotheism, which is reflected even in such a late source as the Book of Chronicles which puts into Solomon's mouth the words, "Great is our God above all gods." [21] The relationship between Yahweh and Israel was believed to have been based on a covenant which made Israel into a sacral community obliging it to worship only Yahweh, in return for which Yahweh undertook to stand by his people in war and peace.[22] The aniconic character of Yahwism, too, had its origins in the pre-Canaanite period, although the figural representation of subordinate household gods, the so-called *Teraphim*, which had been a very old feature in Israelite religion, persisted and was tolerated until at least the eighth century B.C.E. Next to the *Teraphim*, whose main function seems to have been connected with female fertility,[23] many other types of cult images were also in use; but the visual representation of Yahweh himself had become anathema at a very early age, and even verbal reference to his image became restricted to the most daring *Merkava* ("Chariot") vision of Ezekiel.[24]

Certainly pre-Conquest was the belief in demons, often appearing in the form of animals found in the desert, the sea, and lonely places, and including snakes, satyrs, Liliths (night hags), Azazel, and several other such frightening creatures, although the names of some of them, such as Leviathan, reflect Canaanite influences.

When we come to pre-Conquest Israelite ritual, we are on even more uncertain ground. However, it would seem that the Children of Israel did have a Tent-Sanctuary, which they carried along with them in their wanderings, which was attended by special functionaries, and which contained a sacrificial altar. First and foremost, however, the Mosaic "Tent of Meeting" was the repository of the "Ark of Yahweh," the most sacred cult object of the Israelites, in which or on which God was believed to dwell. They had some sort of Sabbath observance, although it is doubtful whether a regularly recurring day of rest is either necessary or possible for pastoral-nomads or even semi-sedentary peoples such as the Israelites had been prior to their conquest of Canaan. The day on which the new moon appeared seems to have been an occasion for celebration. The night of the full moon nearest to the spring equinox was the time for the Passover ritual—the pastoral practice of slaughtering and eating a lamb, which served several purposes: to ensure the fertility of the flocks by sacrificing a lamb, to establish, or renew, the bond between the worshippers and their God by eating a common meal, and to protect their homes and flocks from evil influences by smearing blood on the doorposts. Some rituals performed on the Day of Atonement, such as the purification of the Ark and the offering of the Scapegoat to the demon Azazel, are certainly pre-Canaanitish. Finally, there can be no doubt that the rite of circumcision, which had been practiced by many peoples in the area, was adopted by the Children of Israel a long time prior to their conquest of Canaan. These, in the main, were the salient features of pre-Canaanitish Hebrew religion; I have purposely abstained from touching upon the question of its origins. It was the religion of a male-dominated pastoral nomadic or semi-nomadic tribal society centered on a jealous male god, of a society in which women played a very small role, relegated as they were to a subordinate position even in its myths, which validated and explained the existing natural and social order and gave meaning to the rituals.

In the course of adopting the Canaanite agriculture, technology, arts and crafts, social system, and political organization, the Israelites could not avoid coming under the influence of Canaanite religion, which permeated all aspects of Canaanite culture. Agriculture can illustrate the point. Canaanite agricultural practices, as those of other peoples, comprised not only rational techniques based on the experiences of many generations of farmers, but also religious rituals which were considered just as indispensable for obtaining good crops as any of the successive technical steps of cultivation. The two aspects, the technological and the religious, were so closely intertwined that their separation was entirely unthinkable. For the Israelite newcomers to the mysteries of cultivation, it would have been totally impossible even to imagine that Canaanite agricultural practice consisted of two disparate categories of procedures, and that they could have adopted the one without the other. Hence they had no choice but to take over from the Canaanites not only the methods of their agricultural technology, but also their ways of ensuring the benevolent assistance of their gods on whose good graces the success of the crops depended. In this way the Canaanite early summer feast of Pentecost was adopted as the feast of offering up the first fruits of the field to God; the Canaanite ritual of mourning the death of Tammuz (identified by the Phoenicians with *Adon*, Greek Adonis, meaning Lord) was adopted and observed in midsummer, chiefly by women [25] bewailing the death of nature brought about by the pitiless rays of the hot summer sun; the Canaanite celebration of the vintage in the early fall was adopted and became the Feast of Tabernacles, the most joyous and abandoned feast of the year, which also served the magical purpose of causing the autumn rains to come.[26] These and several other Canaanite observances connected with agriculture became integral parts of the Israelite calendar of annual feasts. Before long their foreign origin was forgotten and all distinction between them and the older, pre-Conquest, feasts disappeared. Nor did any of the Hebrew prophets, who from the eighth century B.C.E. on took a dim view of all ritual, whether feast or fast, sacrifice or assembly, ever include in their generalized denunciations of these ceremonials any reference to their Canaanite origin. The thrust of their objection was that the Israelites, while observing what by general consensus was considered the traditional Israelite ritual, neglected the moral commandments which the prophets considered the chief religious duty.

In addition to the rituals which had become incorporated into Israelite observance, however, there were rites which, to the mind of devoted Yahwists, were objectionable to Yahweh and therefore execrated by the prophets. Foremost among these was what was generically referred to as "the worship of other gods." For the Israelite people at large, the worship of Canaanite gods was an inevitable outcome of having adopted Canaanite agricultural practices and other cultural features. If you cultivated the land as the Canaanites did, you had to observe the rituals without which no crops would succeed; and you also had to worship those gods who were in control of the rains, the growth of the vegetation, the fertility of the domesticated animals, and ultimately the human generative process. In the Canaanite and Phoenician pantheons there were numerous gods with specialized powers and domains, and it was inevitably felt that one was well advised to pay due homage to them by observing their rites—including sexual rituals and the sacrifice of the firstborn. All this was, of course, abhorred and decried by the faithful Yahwists, in whose eyes worshipping other gods became the most heinous sin.[27] This was the crucial issue in the clash between Yahweh and the gods of Canaan—or, if one prefers, in the struggle between Israelite ethical monotheism and Canaanite sensuous polytheism.

4. The Lasting Effects

This contest had two ultimate outcomes. On the one hand, Canaanite polytheism, and all it stood for, became first absorbed into and then gradually eliminated from the religion of the Israelite folk. Its last vestige—the worship of the goddess Anath or the "Queen of Heaven"—seems to have disappeared from the main concentrations of the Judean exiles in Babylonia and Egypt soon after their arrival in those countries following the destruction of Jerusalem in 586 B.C.E.[28] Never again thereafter were the Jews as a group (as contrasted to individuals) tempted by polytheism, or for that matter by any other religion. This immunization of the Jews against other gods was one of the two historic outcomes of the encounter of their ancestors with Canaanite paganism.

The second was the incorporation into Jewish worship of Canaanite rituals and other religious elements. As the genius of Maimonides recognized a long time ago, the entire Israelite sacrificial ritual was adopted from the pagans (i.e., the Canaanites): they offered sacrifices to their gods, and the Israelites offered the same sacrifices to their one and only God. Any other way of weaning the Israelites from idolatry, Maimonides says, would have been psychologically impossible.[29]

In Biblical times, these sacrifices were the central feature of all ritual: on weekdays, on Sabbaths, and on feast days, of which several, as we have seen, were in themselves adaptations from the Canaanite environment. After the demise of the Second Temple of Jerusalem, sacrifices have become obsolete in Judaism, although a recital of the Biblical sacrificial orders still forms part of Jewish holyday prayers. But the holydays themselves are still very much alive, still form essential ingredients of Jewish religion, and are still celebrated with fervor and feeling by observant Jews who, of course, have no idea of their indebtedness for them (or part of them) to the pagan Canaanites.

Another debt Judaism owes the Canaanites is connected with Biblical poetry, in particular, with its theocentric imagery. Even Jews who have totally abandoned all religious observance know, if they are educated at all, that the Bible is one of the greatest masterpieces of world literature. Among both Jewish and Christian students, "The Bible as Literature" is one of the more popular courses in many universities and colleges. What escapes many is the extent to which Biblical poetry reflects its Canaanite and Phoenician background. Many phrases, expressions, poetic forms, and above all ideas which contribute to the greatness of Biblical poetry have their origin in Canaanite and Phoenician antecedents. Much has been written on this subject, particularly since the discovery in the 1920's of the rich fifteenth- to fourteenth-century B.C.E. literature at Ugarit (modern Ras Shamra, near the northeastern corner of the Mediterranean), which is recorded in a language that closely resembles Biblical Hebrew but antedating by one or two centuries even the earliest written formulations of any part of the Bible. The most important Ugaritic texts are mythological, and they document very fully the Canaanite fertility cult which so influenced the Israelites, and against which the Hebrew prophets inveighed. These texts prove that the Hebrews were indeed well acquainted with the mythology of Canaan and used it in their literary works; or at least, to put it as cautiously as possible, that much of the imagery of Hebrew prophecy and poetry on the one hand, and of Canaanite mythological literature on the other, goes back to a common, very ancient tradition. The Biblical prophets and poets used epithets, phrases, and even descriptions which occur in Ugaritic poetry in connection with the gods of Canaan and applied them with little or no change to Yahweh, thereby making them part of the religious thought and vocabulary of Judaism and Christianity to this very day. Just one or two examples will suffice to illustrate the point.

The Song of Moses, dating from the thirteenth century B.C.E., contains this praise of God:

> *Who is like unto Thee among the gods, O Yahweh?*
> *Who is like unto Thee, feared in holiness?* [30]

Compare with this the following Ugaritic distich from the fifteenth century B.C.E.:

> *Who is like unto thee, O Baal?*
> *Who is like unto thee among the gods?* [31]

Again, in one of the Psalms we read:

> *Behold, Thine enemies, O Yahweh*
> *Behold, Thine enemies shall perish*
> *All the workers of iniquity shall be scattered.* [32]

which is an almost literal reproduction of the Ugaritic:

> *Behold, thine enemies, O Baal,*
> *Behold, thine enemies shalt thou crush,*
> *Behold, thou shalt crush thy foes!* [33]

In these two examples both the formal and the ideational similarities are striking. No less remarkable is the recurrence of a divine epithet in Ugaritic myth and in the Psalms. In Ugaritic, Baal is termed "Rider of Clouds," [34] and the same term (translated "Rider of the Skies") appears as an epithet of Yahweh in the Psalms. The ancient Canaanite myth about the god who kills the dragon also figures in the Bible. In the Psalms we read: "Thou didst crush the heads of Leviathan . . ." and in Isaiah: "In that day Yahweh with His sore and great and strong sword will punish Leviathan the winding serpent and Leviathan the crooked serpent, and He will slay the dragon [tannin] that is in the sea." [35] The same myth is referred to in the Ugaritic texts:

> *When thou dost smite Lotan the primordial serpent*
> *When thou dost destroy the winding serpent*
> *Shalyat of the seven heads . . .*

And again:

> *Have I not muzzled the dragon,*
> *Nor crushed the crooked serpent*
> *Mighty monster of the seven heads?* [36]

The great seven-headed dragon reappears in Revelation,[37] the only apocalypse in the New Testament, composed in the late first century C.E. by a Jew who was well versed in the Scriptures.

In the course of time, these old mythological allusions eventually paled into mere poetical imagery. Prophetic universal ethical monotheism became victorious and was to remain the core of Jewish religion, as well as the core of the Jewish psyche, for all times to come. In reviewing the subsequent great historic encounters between Jews and the Gentile world, a discussion of the retention of this psycho-religious core will serve as our leitmotif. Meanwhile, these remarks should suffice to show that despite the fundamental antagonism between Yahwism and Canaanitish polytheism, the latter nevertheless made lasting contributions to Judaism. Long after the Canaanite gods and goddesses were expunged from the post-Biblical religion of the Jews, which became solidly and unshakably grounded in the belief in and worship of the one and only wholly transcendental Deity, this masculine, all-powerful, and awe-inspiring God acquired a feminine aspect which, in the form of the divine "Presence" (Hebrew *Shekhina*), developed into something like a mediator, or rather mediatrix, between God and man. The Talmudic Shekhina, whose late Kabbalistic successor, the Matronit, was to become God's mystical spouse, can in no way be directly derived from an old Canaanite goddess prototype, such as "the Queen of Heaven" who was still worshipped in Judah shortly before, and by the Judean exiles in Egypt long after, the fall of Jerusalem. Yet the historical experience of the adoration of a goddess must have left its mark, in the psychological subsoil from which grew, perhaps under the stimulus of Greek goddess cults, the concept and image of the Shekhina.[38]

5. Israelite Iconography

Another equally important contribution to Judaism by the Canaanite (and general Near Eastern) religious environment can be seen in the belief in angels, a belief which was subsequently to be taken over in toto by the two daughter-religions of Judaism, Christianity and Islam. Winged human-looking figures appear frequently in ancient Near Eastern monuments, in which they usually depict deities. These winged gods can be either male or female, although in Canaanite religion they are most frequently female. Thus, a fifteenth–fourteenth-century B.C.E. cylinder seal from Ras Shamra-Ugarit shows the goddess Anath as a seated woman with wings. Female divinities with wings, standing and facing palm trees, appear on ivory plaques found in the palace of Hazael, king of Damascus (late ninth century B.C.E.), and in Arslan Tash, North Syria. Much older than these is the winged, naked figure of Lilith, with bird's claws instead of feet, standing on the back of a lion

shown on a Sumerian terra-cotta relief (c. 2000 B.C.E.). The oldest extant
Israelite counterpart of these female winged deities is shown on an ivory
plaque found in King Ahab's palace in Samaria and dating from circa 870
B.C.E.[39]

The common Biblical designation of these winged deities, unless they can
be identified as Anath, Lilith, etc., is *k'ruvim* (i.e., Cherubim, sing. *k'ruv*),
derived from the Akkadian *karibu*, meaning "intercessor." In ancient Mesopotamia, especially Assyria, the *karibu* were winged bulls or lions with
human heads whose statues often guarded the entrances to temples and palaces. The religious concept behind these huge and impressive sculptures was
that the *karibu* were secondary gods, called *lamassu* or *shedu*, whose function was to intercede with the chief gods for the benefit of man. Also in Syria
and Palestine, numerous animal Cherubim were found—composite figures
with a lion's body, a human head, and outstretched wings. In addition, totally human-looking Cherubim are often shown on ivory plaques, with their
wings the only indication of their divine nature.[40]

There is general agreement among archeologists and historians of religion
that the Cherubim who figure frequently in the Bible entered the religion of
the ancient Hebrews from their polytheistic pagan environment. In addition
to their name, their form (or forms) and functions point unmistakably to
Mesopotamian, Syrian, Canaanite, and perhaps even Egyptian influence.
Like the Assyrian gate-keeping *karibu*, the Biblical Cherubim were the
guardians of the Garden of Eden and of the Ark of the Covenant and the
Sanctuary.[41] As for the Cherubim shown on the ivory tablets from Ahab's
palace, they must have had the same decorative purpose as the one served
by the Cherubim on the ivory tablets found in other royal palaces, in Damascus or in Arslan Tash.

Whatever the original concept of the Cherubim, when the Israelites
adopted it from their neighbors they soon modified it so as to fit into their
monotheistic religion. Israelite monotheism could not tolerate other gods
next to Yahweh; hence the Cherubim which in Assyria, Syria, and Canaan
were gods or goddesses had to be reduced, within the context of the Israelite
religion, to creatures that, while superhuman, were definitely subordinated
to Yahweh and, moreover, were created by Yahweh just like all the other living beings. Such creatures, however, are none other than *angels*. Thus the
angels who were to play such an important role in later Judaism (as well as in
Christianity and Islam) were derived by the Biblical Israelites from the ancient Near Eastern prototype of the Cherubim.

Let us mention only in passing that relatively early in Biblical times the
Cherubim were given the main function of serving as Yahweh's bearers or
throne. The phrase, "The Lord of Hosts who is enthroned on the Cherubim," occurs many times in the Bible.[42] In Ezekiel's vision, Yahweh appears
seated upon the Cherubim.[43] By the time the Book of Enoch was written

(the last two centuries B.C.E.), the Cherubim had been incorporated among the angelic orders as high-ranking angels.[44]

The Cherubim serve as the best refutation of the view that Biblical Yahwism was totally aniconic. It was emphatically not aniconic in its heterodox form: in the Israelite sanctuaries of Dan and Bethel, there stood golden images of bulls which were worshipped (as their predecessor was in the wilderness) as symbols of Yahweh, or, perhaps, regarded as the pedestal on which he stood.[45] Legitimate, recognized (or orthodox) Yahwist worship became centered on the Temple of Jerusalem, which was suffused with Cherubim images. They figured as the main decorative motif on the walls and doors of the Temple, on the panels of the bases, on the curtains, and on the veil which separated the Holy Place from the Holy of Holies.[46] And, most importantly, two huge golden statues of Cherubim stood above the Ark of the Covenant in the Holy of Holies: they were 10 cubits (15 feet) high, and their wing span measured the same; their inner wings touched each other, while their outer wings reached the opposite walls of the holy chamber.[47] Copies of these statues were placed in the Second Temple, although at a certain date their configuration was altered and they were given the form of a winged man and a winged woman in sexual embrace, to symbolize, according to the Talmudic rabbis, the love of God and Israel.[48]

At the time of the Israelite-Canaanite encounter, the religion of Israel was still in its formative stage and relatively open to foreign influences. The northern Israelite heterodox Yahwism admitted the sculptural representation of God in the bull image which went back to a primitive ancient Near Eastern practice of depicting the chief divinity as a storm-god standing on a young bull. This practice was doubtless shared by the pre-Mosaic Hebrews with the pagans among whom they lived, and its restoration by Jeroboam at Dan and Bethel, although it must have been politically motivated (to bolster his political independence from Jerusalem by making his kingdom also religiously independent of the Jerusalem Temple), was simply a return to early Hebrew tradition.[49]

No such paganizing iconic tendency was evinced at Jerusalem. True, a statue of Asherah was introduced into the Temple by Solomon's son Rehoboam, or his widow Maacah, in the late tenth century B.C.E.; and thereafter, with some interruptions, this goddess was worshipped in the Jerusalem Temple next to Yahweh until its destruction in 586 B.C.E.[50] But no visual representation of Yahweh himself is known to have ever been placed in the Jerusalem Temple. Thus, as far as Yahweh was concerned, his worship in the Jerusalem Temple was aniconic indeed. But his mounts, the Cherubim, were shown in statuary in the oversized golden figures, in relief on the walls, and in embroidery on the curtains. Wherever one's eyes fell, they lighted on Cherubim images. The statues of the Cherubim were features of great importance in the Second Temple as well, at a time when the Cherubim were considered angels. Their presence in the Holy of Holies habituated the Jews to the idea that their religion, although strictly aniconic where God Himself was concerned, countenanced the visual, two- or three-dimensional representation of lesser superhuman beings, such as angels who were subordinated to the one and only God. This view would have a crucial role in opening the doors of synagogues to the profusion of Greco-Roman pagan symbols which surrounded them everywhere in the Hellenistic age.

5

Jews and Hellenes

When dealing with a period which lies as far back in history as that of Hellenism (from 300 B.C.E. to c. 100 C.E.) one does not, of course, expect to find statistical data. Yet the question of the number, and even more of the proportion, of Jews in the Hellenized world is an important one if we are to view the relationship between Jews and Hellenes, and between Judaism and Hellenism, in the proper perspective. Hence, in the absence of hard data, we shall have to look at least at the estimates, which are available from the first century C.E. At that time, according to Philo and Josephus, there were 1 million Jews in Egypt within a total population of 7.5 million, or 13.5 percent of the total. In the same century there were about 4.5 million Jews in the entire Roman empire, including Egypt and Palestine, in a total population of 54 million, or about 8.4 percent.[1] Equally significant is the fact that, in addition to their main concentrations in Alexandria and Palestine, the Jews of the Hellenistic age were dispersed all over the Greco-Roman world, but very few of them lived outside it. Thus the one major Gentile culture to which all of them were exposed was the Hellenistic.

1. The Reappearance of Aramaic

Some two centuries before the end of the Biblical period, that is, from the seventh century B.C.E., the Aramaic language (which had been the ancestral tongue of the first patriarchs of Israel) gained international currency in the Near East. Even before the First Exile (586 B.C.E.), the leadership of Judah knew it, since it was most useful as the international language of diplomacy. Following the Exile, Aramaic gradually replaced Hebrew in popular usage as well, with the result that major portions of the late Biblical books were written in it, or, more precisely, in its Western variety which was current in Palestine from the fourth century B.C.E.[2]

The Biblical era of Judaism ended with the work of Ezra and Nehemia who, about the middle of the fifth century B.C.E., were leaders of the Jewish community in Judah. While Nehemia had secular powers—he was appointed governor of Judah by Artaxerxes (probably the first, surnamed Longimanus, r. 465–424 B.C.E.)—Ezra, of priestly descent and the first to be termed *sofer* or "scribe," led the people of Jerusalem and Judah in religious matters. What precisely the work of Ezra was in his "scribal" capacity remains rather vague from the Biblical account, although it is assumed by some Biblical scholars that it must have concerned the compilation, in conjunction with a whole school of writers in Babylonia, of the book of "the Law of God" which he brought to Jerusalem and which is generally identified with the so-called Priestly Code (P) in the Pentateuch. In any case, a passage in the Book of Nehemiah informs us that Ezra and his colleagues and the Levites read and explained to the people the Law of God.[3] Among the scribes who succeeded Ezra were the teachers of Wisdom and the authors of the Jewish Wisdom literature.

The main activity of the Scribes (*sof'rim*), however, consisted of interpreting the Bible and occasionally emending the sacred text; this, of course, meant that they were experts in the ways in which the Law had to be understood and observed. Some of the spiritual heirs of these early Scribes became members of the Sanhedrin, the highest religio-legal and administrative body in the Jewish theocratic state, which came into being after the successful Maccabean uprising (168 B.C.E.). Others joined the religio-political party of the Pharisees, who subsequently developed the Oral Law, the basis of the Mishna and the Talmud. It was the work of the Scribes, Pharisees, and sages (rabbis) which laid the foundations of Jewish life from Talmudic times on.

By Talmudic times (which began perhaps in the second, but certainly in the first century B.C.E.), various Aramaic dialects were the dominant colloquials among the Jews of Palestine and Babylonia, which necessitated the translation of the Hebrew Bible, no longer understood by the average synagogue-goer, into Aramaic. Thus the so-called *Targums* (Aramaic Bible translations) came into being. From the perspective of the Talmudic sages, the reading of the Bible in the synagogues in both Hebrew and Aramaic was so old that they attributed the introduction of this rite to Ezra.[4] The sages and scholars, of course, retained full mastery of Hebrew; and the fact that the Hebrew of the Mishna (c. A.D. 200) differs somewhat from Biblical Hebrew indicates that the language was still sufficiently alive to evolve and change. Most of the texts of the Palestinian or Jerusalem Talmud (compiled c. 425) and of the much larger and authoritative Babylonian Talmud (c. 500) are written in western and eastern Aramaic respectively. Both Talmuds are structured around the Mishna, but their bulk is made up of the *G'mara* (lit. "completion"), which is several times larger than the Mishna and is, in essence, an amplification of the Mishna, giving further clarification, expansion, and codification of the rabbinic Law. Apart from this legal material, which is called *Halakha* (lit. "Walking"), each of the two Talmuds contains also much *Aggada* (lit. "Telling"), exposition or interpretation of Scripture aiming at edification, and homilies, as well as many other types of non-legal matter.

2. The Hellenistic Sweep

Hellenism made its impact on Palestinian Jewry when this religio-legal work was at its very inception. In the late fourth century B.C.E., when Alexander the Great conquered the East, the Jews had only the Bible and some of its oral interpretation developed by the Scribes as the basis of their religious, cultural, and communal life. Yet this was sufficient to create a barrier against the spread of Greek religion among them both in Palestine and in their rapidly expanding Diaspora in the Near East and North Africa.

Greek religion, which permeated Greek art, literature, architecture, gymnasium education, and even philosophy, had no difficulty in becoming accepted by all the peoples that had come under the rule of Alexander and his successors. Whatever problems religious differences presented were solved by the simple but ingenious method of identifying the local gods with Greek gods, and by working out a religious synthesis on this basis. This procedure was appropriate to all Gentiles since they were all polytheistic. Only the Jews proved intractable: no common ground could be found between their monotheistic religion and Greek polytheism.

While the religious chasm between Judaism and Hellenism proved unbridgeable, other aspects of Greek civilization did penetrate Jewish life and wrought a considerable transformation in it. As in other countries conquered by Alexander, Greek cities sprang up in Palestine and all around it. From them Greek cultural influences spread into the Jewish population. By Mishnaic times (that is, c. 100 B.C.E. to 200 C.E.), Jewish material culture in the urban centers of Palestine, as well as in the neighboring Diasporas, had become largely Hellenistic. The Greek language vied with Aramaic and gradually replaced it in wide circles. Side by side with the sages and rabbis who taught in Hebrew and Aramaic and produced the materials that were to go into the Mishna and later the Talmud, there were Jewish authors, philosophers, historians, and dramatists who wrote in Greek. In Alexandria, which harbored the greatest concentration of Jews at the time, Greek had totally replaced Hebrew and Aramaic. This necessitated a Greek translation of the Bible, several versions of which, known by the generic name of *Septuagint*, are extant. Scions of the well-to-do Jewish urban classes both in Egypt and in Palestine enrolled in *gymnasia*—the Greek educational institutions in which athletics played a central role. So as not to differ in any way from their Greek

classmates when participating naked in the games, these Jewish youths subjected themselves to the painful operation known as *epispasm* which made
them appear uncircumcised.[5]

As early as the Maccabean period (in the second century B.C.E.), the *gymnasion* was considered by both tradition-bound Jews and their Hellenizing
brothers the "acme of Hellenism." Just before the uprising, Jason, the High
Priest of the Jerusalem Temple (174–171 B.C.E.), who was a fervent Hellenizer (he himself had changed his name from the Hebrew Joshua to the Greek
Jason) and who had managed to be appointed High Priest in place of his
brother Onias by promising a tribute of 440 talents to Antiochus, promised to
pay the king another 150 talents for permission to build a *gymnasion* and an
ephebeion in Jerusalem. These were the two educational institutions of a typical Greek city that were to signify the transformation of the ancient city of
David into a Greek *polis*, to be called Antioch. The *gymnasion* was built on
the Temple hill itself, directly under the fortress of Jerusalem; the youth of
the Jewish bourgeoisie, including young priests, flocked to it wearing the *pe-
tasos*, the broad-brimmed hat of the god Hermes, patron of the *epheboi*. The
gymnasion and the *ephebeion*, attendance at which was the monopoly of the
sons of the wealthy, served as the educational institutions for those young
men who aspired to the honor of being admitted to the citizen corporation.[6]

It was therefore with good cause that the strongly Jewish-conscious author
of the second Book of the Maccabees, written sometime between 125 B.C.E.
and the fall of Jerusalem in 70 C.E., decried these Jasonian Hellenistic reforms in the sternest terms:

> And to such a height did the passion for Greek fashions rise, and the influx of
> foreign customs, thanks to the surpassing impiety of that godless Jason—no
> high-priest he!—that the priests were no longer interested in the services of
> the altar, but despising the sanctuary, and neglecting the sacrifices, they hur-
> ried to take part in the unlawful displays held in the palaestra after the quoit-
> throwing had been announced—thus setting at naught what their fathers hon-
> ored and esteeming the glories of the Greeks above all else.[7]

These events were symptomatic of conditions in Jewish Palestine on the
eve of the Maccabean uprising. The restoration which followed the Has-
monean victory checked, but was unable to stem, the progress of Hellenization among the Jews. A little more than thirty years after the victory of Mat-
tathias and his sons, Yohanan (John), a grandson of his, became the secular
and religious leader of the Jewish state. His surname was Greek, Hyrcanos,
testifying to his Hellenizing tendencies; and from this time until the end of
the Jewish state in 70 C.E., all the kings and high priests in Jerusalem had
Greek names. Herod (r. 37–4 B.C.E.), who succeeded the last Maccabean
king and became the founder of the last royal house in Jewish Palestine, was
a convinced Hellenizer. His great passion was building: cities with Roman

imperial names, theaters and amphitheaters, other public buildings in and out of Palestine, and a resplendent new replacement for the old Temple of Jerusalem. These buildings, with the exception of the last, all served Hellenistic purposes and pastimes. In his Jerusalem amphitheater Herod had spectacular combats staged between gladiators and wild beasts. Every four years he organized splendid games in honor of Caesar, including chariot races, wrestling, and other athletic performances, to which competitors, musicians, and other contestants were attracted from many countries to vie for the costly prizes. These events, which brought together immense crowds, could be interpreted as nothing else but enthusiastic demonstrations in honor of Hellenism. In view of such manifestations, the rabbis had no choice but to take a stand on the religious and cultural problem presented by Hellenization; the surprising thing is that their stand was not more negative than appears from the contemporary sources.

3. Jewish Separatism

The basic law of Jewish history—that centrifugal forces were constantly tearing away some individuals or even classes from the Jewish body politic, while centripetal forces kept the others together—now obtained. It would be entirely futile to speculate on the relative strength of the two forces at any given period. During the Hellenistic age—judging from the persistence of the Greek language and culture among the Jews for centuries—most of those who were Hellenized remained Jews; and, incidentally, their numbers were greatly augmented by proselytes in all parts of the Roman empire.[8]

The Jews of Babylonia on the eastern borders of the Roman empire also lived in a Hellenized environment under the Seleucids and Arsacids from 321 B.C.E. to 227 C.E., that is, for more than half a millennium.[9] The cultural assimilation to Hellenism could be observed among the rabbis as well as the simple people. It manifested itself in their language and their appreciation of "Greek Wisdom," and even in their admittance of statues into their homes and synagogues. Rabban Gamliel, Rabbi Y'huda, and no doubt other sages as well, set up in their houses statues made by Gentiles, and in the Shaf weyathiv synagogue in Nehardea, Babylonia, there was a bust.[10]

Apart from the sharp boundary line which the rabbis, and most Jews, drew between cultural assimilation to Hellenism (which was considered permissible) and religious assimilation (which was not only prohibited but unthinkable), there was another important factor which enabled the Jews to survive in a Hellenistic environment. This was their settlement pattern in closed urban groups, often quite large. Their communal organization bound all Jews of one locality into a single body, centered on the synagogue and adhering to the basic tenets of Judaism. While Hellenistic forms could and did penetrate deeply into Jewish life and even into the very synagogue, the compact Jewish society which they formed favored a way of life that was separate and different from that of the Gentiles. This is unequivocally attested by numerous Roman authors, who—by no means friendly to the Jews—describe them as a people apart. As late as the third century C.E., the Greek rhetorician Philostratus who lived in Rome wrote of the Jews: "These people mingle with others neither for common meals nor in prosperity, prayer, or sacrifice; they are farther away from us than are Susa, Bactria, or India . . ." [11]

These words were written after more than half a millennium of Jewish Hellenization. Many other classical authors held it against the Jews that they kept themselves apart and aloof from the Romans. There is no reason to doubt their testimony, which is borne out by Jewish sources as well.

4. The Lure of "Greek Wisdom"

Hellenism was the first in the series of historic encounters between the Jews and Gentile cultures whose study was approved, albeit usually only grudgingly, by the Jewish intellectual and spiritual leaders, the rabbis. In earlier encounters—with Egyptians, Canaanites, Babylonians—however strong the popular attraction of their cultures, the prophets, Scribes, and teachers of God's Law always and uncompromisingly rejected them lock, stock, and barrel. There was, of course, one fundamental difference between these earlier cultures on the one hand, and Hellenism and the subsequently encountered Arab-Spanish, Italian, and enlightened European cultures on the other. Those ancient Near Eastern cultures were religious cultures through and through. They were totally permeated by religion, so that practically any of their component cultural elements which proved attractive to the Jews or were in fact adapted by them meant the potential or actual penetration of an idolatrous polytheistic feature into the still frail structure of Hebrew-Jewish ethical monotheism. Therefore, rejection and exclusion could be the only answer.

This was not true of Hellenism, nor of the three subsequent cultures to be dealt with later. Although Hellenism comprised a strong religious component and had a pronounced polytheistic coloring, it embraced numerous features which, at least on the surface of it, had little or nothing to do with religion, or in which the religious element could be disregarded without preventing one from enjoying them in their other aspects. The ability—and preparedness—of the rabbis to discern between the acceptable and the non-acceptable aspects in Hellenism was paralleled by the distinction they made between the right teachings and the wrong behavior of single individuals. The latter is epitomized in the Talmudic references to the second-century

sage Rabbi Meir, a pupil and friend of the apostate Rabbi Elisha ben Abuya:
"Rabbi Meir found a pomegranate, ate its inside and threw away its shell." [12]
In a similar manner, the Talmudic sages in general saw nothing wrong in
studying Greek and reading Homer, enjoying "the charm of his style and
plots"; but they certainly perceived "Homer's mythology as mere fairy tales
and as a good occasion of making fun of idol worship." [13] More important,
the Greek philosophers themselves, long before Hellenism reached Palestine, had dethroned the gods of Olympus and made short shrift of Greek
mythology. Thus the "Greek Wisdom" (as the Talmudic sources refer to
Greek philosophy) which attracted the Palestinian and Egyptian Jewish in-
telligentsia was from a liberal Jewish religious viewpoint relatively innocu-
ous. In this manner it was possible for the Talmudic sages, despite their unquestioning adherence to the religious tenets of Judaism as axiomatic, to
study "Greek Wisdom" and to allow its teaching to students, except young
children. [14] As a result of this attitude, it was, in fact, studied by many: according to a semi-anecdotal reference in the Talmud, one-half of all the
young men in the house of Patriarch Rabban Gamliel studied "Greek Wisdom"; the books of Homer were known in certain Jewish circles; and occasional Homeric phrases and mythical references (e.g., to sirens and centaurs) found their way into the Talmudic text. [15]

5. Greek and Latin in the Talmud

"Greek Wisdom" and Homer apart, Talmudic literature bears most eloquent testimony to the ubiquitous influence of Hellenistic culture and languages. The Greek and Latin vocabulary contained in the Hebrew and Aramaic religious sources (most of which date from about 100 B.C.E. to 500 C.E.)
has been estimated at 3,000 words. A full listing of the categories represented by these borrowed "culture words" would be much too lengthy and
tedious, but a few can serve as examples. Some designate political concepts
or refer to public life and office, commerce, religion, music, folklore, the
arts, literature, writing, and the calendar; others pertain to cosmography, geography, minerals, plants, and animals. The realm of medicine is well represented by terms designating ailments, medicaments, and physicians. The
world of material culture is covered by terms for architectural features, furniture, clothing, food, ornaments, jewelry, coins, weights, weapons, tools, vessels, and raw materials. To these must be added the large number of proper
names. All in all, we have in these loan words a mirror of cultural influences
that pervaded all realms of life, even that of religion. [16]

In order to illustrate the highly pervasive nature of Hellenistic influence
on the Hebrew and Aramaic of the rabbis—as shown in the Tannaitic and
Amoraic works they left behind in the Mishna, Tosefta, the Talmuds, the

Midrash, and the Targums—we could confine ourselves to the one area in which such influence would be least expected: that of Jewish Law. Traditional rabbinic Law, the *Halakha*, is the focus of attention in much of Talmudic and Midrashic literature; it was the domain proper of rabbinic thought, and the theory behind it was that every interpretation of the Law, every discernment of even the most minute nuance in its meaning, is implicit in the Biblical text itself or is based on a tradition going back to Moses at Mount Sinai. One would therefore expect that in the realm of the *Halakha*, the concepts with which they operated would be Hebraic or at least Aramaic, and that the terminology used to express them would be taken from the religio-legal vocabulary of those two traditional Jewish languages. Remarkably, this is not the case.

The fact is that Greek terms abound in the Mishnaic, Talmudic, and Midrashic passages which deal with this most Jewish of all cultural realms. The very court of law was denoted not only by the Hebrew term *bet din* (lit. "house of judgment"), but also by the Greek term *synédrion*, which received the Aramicized form *sanhedrin*. Its presidium was *parhedrin*, from the Greek *próedroi*. The term for the prosecutor was *qategor*, from the Greek *katégoros*; for the defense attorney *sanegor*, from the Greek *synégoros*, or *praqlit*, from the Greek *parákletos*. An object pledged as a security was *ipotiki*, from the Greek *hypothéké*; a will, *diatiqi*, from the Greek *diathéké*; a guardian, *epitropos* (usually pronounced *apotropos*), from the Greek *epítropos*. Even such a specifically Jewish legal innovation as the one introduced by Hillel (consisting of a deposition at the court to the effect that the law of limitation by the entrance of the Sabbatical year shall not apply to the loan to be transacted) was given a Greek name: *prozbol*, from the Greek *prosbolé*. This brief list could easily be multiplied and similar lists of Greek (and Latin) loan words assembled for every subject mentioned above.

6. The Archeological Evidence

The lexicographic evidence is supplemented and, in fact, topped by the archeological evidence of pictorial, sculptural, and architectural remains. These show that Hellenistic influence was ubiquitous in the visual appurtenances of Jewish worship. Remains of synagogues, which by the time the Second Temple of Jerusalem was destroyed by the Romans (70 C.E.) were an ancient and well-established institution in both Israel and the Diaspora, have been unearthed in recent decades in various parts of Israel and other countries and give us a fair idea of what synagogue architecture and decorations were like in the Hellenistic period. In brief, both were dominated by Greek styles. Erwin H. Goodenough's magnum opus, *Jewish Symbols in the Greco-Roman Period*, which consists of thirteen quarto volumes with thousands of illustrations, presents a clear picture of the extent of this influence. From it we learn that not only was the general architectural design of the synagogues Hellenistic, but the carvings, paintings, and mosaics which decorated them showed numerous pagan motifs.

Several of Goodenough's volumes are devoted to the synagogue at Dura Europos, on the right bank of the Upper Euphrates, which was built in 245 C.E. and partially destroyed in 256. Fortunately, enough of its walls remained standing protected by covering sand to preserve what is the richest Hellenistic pictorial material found to date in any Jewish structure.[17] The symbols taken from the Jewish cult which appear as decorations of synagogues (as well as Jewish tombs) consist of the Menora (the seven-branched candelabrum), the Tora-shrine (in which the Scrolls of the Law were, and still are, kept in the synagogues), the Lulabh and the Ethrog (the unopened palm branch and the citron fruit, used in the ritual of Tabernacles), the Shofar (the ram's horn, blown as the most revered ritual, primarily on the two days of the New Year festival), and the Incense-Shovel which was used in synagogues in those days. There are also representations of fish (including dolphins and sea-monsters), depictions of bread, and symbols pertaining to wine, all of which appear frequently in the synagogues but their provenance is not clear. These motifs were ubiquitous in the Greco-Roman world; yet their appearance among synagogal decorations could simply mean that those foodstuffs, which had figured ever since Biblical times in the Jewish ritual, were developed into decorative motifs under Hellenistic influence. Similar caution is needed in evaluating the significance of pictures of the bull, the lion and other felines, the tree, the crown, rosettes, wheels, and round objects. While the idea of using these images as synagogal and funereal decorative motifs may have entered the Jewish world from the Greco-Roman, and while the style in which they are presented shows the influence of Hellenistic art, the symbols themselves may refer back to traditional Biblical imagery.

With the image of Victory, a female figure carrying a crown or wreath, we enter definitely into the realm of Greco-Roman pagan influence. Among other decorative figures appearing in the synagogues, such as that of Dura Europos and several in Palestine (including those at Bet Alpha, Hamat of Tiberias, Capernaum, Chorazin, and many more), are the figures interpreted by Goodenough as depicting Helios driving his quadriga through the Zodiac, Orpheus, Ares, the Cavalier God, Cupid, Psyche, Aphrodite, her Persian counterpart Anahita, the Mystic Temple, Dionysiac felines, masks, birds symbolizing love, sheep, the hare, the scallop shell, the cornucopia, the centaur, the cudgel of Heracles, psychopomps (superhuman carriers of the human soul to the Other World) including the eagle, the griffin, Pegasus, the ladder and the ship, and astronomical symbols, including the Zodiac, the four seasons, the sun and the moon, and other heavenly bodies.[18] This list,

rich in itself, is augmented by similar symbols found in Jewish burial
chambers and on sarcophagi, and by a different type of evidence presented
by the large number of Jewish amulets and charms relying on the magic supposedly present in the Jewish divine names (such as Lord God, The Name,
Adonai, Lord of Hosts) in conjunction with the names of pagan divinities
(such as the Greek Helios, Eros, Hecate, Heracles, Aphrodite, Zeus, or the
Egyptian Ammon, Ptah, Thoth). In many cases these charms and amulets
display indisputably Jewish emblems such as the Menora, or Jewish words
and names, which make their Jewish provenance certain. [19] While one may
question the pagan meaning or derivation of several of these pictorial representations or verbal references (as indeed I have done elsewhere in connection with the picture of a naked woman shown on a mural in the Dura
Europos synagogue, whom Goodenough identified as Anahita while I interpreted it as depicting the Shekhina), [20] there can be no doubt that Goodenough is correct in his general conclusion that on the popular level there
was "a widespread invasion of Judaism by Hellenism." [21]

The pictorial and magical material is supplemented by the evidence of
inscriptions which point to a widespread popular use of Greek as the colloquial language of the people at large. According to the funerary inscriptions
and others found in Jerusalem, until the end of the second century C.E.,
"Aramaic prevailed over Greek in a proportion of roughly two to three." In
the Galilee, Greek predominated. The great majority of the inscriptions in
the Bet Shearim catacombs (near Haifa), and in the Hamat synagogue, are
Greek. It seems therefore correct to conclude, as Goodenough did, that
"Jews, even in Palestine, and certainly through the Diaspora in general,
seem as Hellenized in language as they were in architectural ornament and
funerary symbols." [22]

This archeological evidence indicates that Hellenistic influences spread to
the simple people, and in particular to the rural Jewish population of the
country. Certain aspects of Hellenism, we know, attracted the urban masses;
witness the *circenses* performed in amphitheaters. Others, such as the participation in *gymnasion* education, were confined to the urban upper classes.
However, Greek seems to have replaced Aramaic in the country to a considerable extent. Interestingly, such a development was desired by some sages,
as we can gauge from a saying of Rabbi Y'huda the Prince (c. 135–c. 220
C.E.), who had such a contempt for Aramaic that he referred to it by the
cacophonistic pun "*Sursi*" (for *Suri*, Syrian), meaning something like "emasculated speech." He is quoted as having exclaimed, "What has *Sursi* to do
in the Land of Israel? Speak either the Holy Tongue [i.e., Hebrew] or
Greek!" [23]

In addition to the Greek language there were two lessons which (as Louis
Finkelstein has pointed out) the Jewish plebeians learned from the Greeks:
the strength inherent in organizing themselves into identifiable groups, and

the value of formulated doctrines. The first resulted in the emergence of the plebeian *Hasidim*, or pietists, with formal membership, rules for admission and expulsion, probationary periods, recognized beliefs, duly chosen leaders, and methods for reaching decisions. The spiritual offspring of the Hasidim were the Pharisaic and Essenic orders. The second lesson, the systematization of plebeian belief, resulted in a body of doctrine, subsequently taken over by the Pharisees. The very concept of doctrinal formulation was "so definitely foreign to the Judaite mind, which always liked the concrete and shunned the abstract, that we cannot be wrong in imputing the tendency to the influence of the example set by the Athenian philosophical schools." [24] Among the tenets thus formulated were the belief in the resurrection of the dead, in the existence of angels, in Divine Providence as relating to the individual, and in the validity of the Oral Law. [25]

7. *The Problem of Jewish Iconography*

The fundamental question to be weighed in view of such rich evidence of Greek influences on the Hellenized Jews is this: Did these influences go beyond the modalities of expression and become factors modifying the content, the core, of Jewish belief? We have seen that the material culture of the Jews was Hellenized; that they adopted Greek as a colloquial; that Grecian symbols were admitted into the synagogue and the cemetery; that pagan magic names were used together with Jewish ones on amulets and charms; that sages of the Mishna (and subsequently of the Talmud) showed interest in, and had an appreciation of, "Greek Wisdom" and in their halakhic work borrowed a profusion of Greek terms; and finally that the simple people emulated the Greek example in civic organization and doctrinal formulation. What, then, of their Jewishness did remain?

The question is difficult to answer for a number of reasons. Minute deviations from an established belief system may be elusive. The Jews of the period, as of other times, comprised elements greatly varying in their tenets and in adherence to religious tradition; and, in addition, the various Diasporas differed considerably in their positions toward Hellenism. To touch first, briefly, on the last point, the Alexandrian Jews were more Hellenized than the Palestinian, while the latter were more Hellenized than the Babylonian. And, of course, it is well known that in Palestine the position on Hellenism was a major dividing line between the Sadducees, Pharisees, and Essenes.

The first point, however, is the most difficult to come to grips with. How can one gauge deviation from the belief in the one and only God? If we find in a synagogue a mural depicting a Greek divinity, say, Winged Victory or Helios with his quadriga, does this mean that the people who frequented that synagogue (and presumably entrusted the muralist with the task of decorating its walls) believed in a goddess named Nike and a divine chariot-eer of the sun named Helios, that is, were not monotheists in the traditional Jewish sense? Or does it mean something entirely different, something that in no way impinged on their monotheistic Jewish faith?

Although Goodenough has devoted much attention to the subject, one looks in vain for a clear answer to this question in his thirteen volumes. In summarizing his results, he states that "Jews throughout the Roman empire were worshipping Yahweh with a quite conscious awareness of their kinship to pagan cosmic worship"; that they had a "recognition of God through cos-mic order such as we properly associate with Greek thinking, and that a Jew could believe, as Philo did, that this was the true meaning of Torah and Jew-ish cult." And he goes on to say:

> Outside the circles of rabbinic teaching there seem to have been a great number of Jews everywhere who had been influenced by paganism, to the point not only that, like Philo, they expressed their religious aspirations in the language of Greek mystery and metaphysics, but also that they found the sym-bolic vocabulary of later Greco-Roman art equally suitable to their thinking. I have seen no evidence that the Jews were worshipping other gods than Yah-weh; hence in that sense no trace of syncretism has appeared. But there is a great deal of evidence that they ascribed to Yahweh Helios' rulership as chariot-eer of the universe, such saving power as that of Heracles and Ares, such gracious mercy as that offered by Aphrodite and the Nymphs. Yahweh made available to men such spiritual triumph as was represented to pagans in Nike, the goddess Victory, and her crown. Yahweh seems to have had the ferocity and glory of the lion, the bull, and the eagle, and to have been the spurting Stream of Life. At the same time he still kept his People together in the ancient Covenant, so that the delivery from corruption and sin he offered in this life and the heavenly glory at his throne in the next were oriented in the same Torah and in the same proof texts as those on which Talmudic rabbis were bas-ing their own Judaism.[26]

In these passages (and several others), Goodenough makes two points. One, that the Hellenized Jews remained monotheists who worshipped only Yahweh; and two, that they were nevertheless sufficiently influenced by Greek paganism to find the Greek deities meaningful, and to admit that divine reality was expressed in, and manifested through, the Greek gods. The second point is given more emphasis in Goodenough's treatment of indi-vidual instances: he says, for example, that in a painting in the Dura Europos synagogue the naked woman who is depicted holding the infant Moses "is unmistakably Aphrodite." [27] I cannot go along with this view for several rea-sons, which lead me to different conclusions as to what the pictures of pagan divine figures and other symbols found in the synagogues of the Hellenized Jews meant to them.

First, we must remember that the ubiquitous Cherubim figures in both the First and the Second Temples of Jerusalem (as we saw in the last chapter) had long habituated the Jews to the idea and the practice of including in their places of worship visual representations of superhuman beings lesser than God and subordinated to Him. While the presence of Cherubim in the Temple did not mean that the Jews worshipped them, it certainly meant that they recognized (or, if you will, believed in) the existence of such beings, and that they attributed certain functions to them, such as serving as the throne or vehicle of God, carrying out God's will and command, acting as messengers and intermediaries between God and the world. The importance of the Cherubim, bridging as they do the times of the First and the Second Jerusalem Temple, is such that we shall have to return to them below.

Next, we must be aware that Jewish theology, as it had developed on a traditional basis by Hellenistic times, comprised the concept of divine hypostases, that is, superhuman or angelic intermediaries between God and the world. The most important of these were Wisdom, the Word, and the Shekhina, each of which began its existence as an attribute of God and gradually assumed a more and more independent character. The Shekhina or "Presence," in particular, became an entirely separate and distinct entity, to the extent of being barely subordinated to God. At the same time the belief in angels also developed—heavenly beings who had been created by God for the express purpose of serving as His messengers, and who, when not on their way carrying out a divine command, surrounded God in adoration and sang His praise.

Third, the Jews in the Hellenistic period lived in an environment in which the visual representation of gods and divine powers and functions was ubiquitous. Being strongly influenced by Hellenistic culture in many fields, the Jews wished to adopt the style of Greek temples for their own religious structures and the methods used by the Greeks to represent their deities for embellishing the synagogues. Considering that pictorial and sculptural representation of the Cherubim was part of old Jewish religious tradition, there could be no objection in principle to such depiction of other divine hypostases or powers.

Fourth, the Hellenistic environment was one of religious syncretism, of which the identification of the gods of different religions was an integral part. Greek Zeus was identified with the Roman Jupiter and the Egyptian Ammon; Greek Aphrodite with the Roman Venus and the Persian Anahita; the Greek Dionysus was identified with the Roman Bacchus and the Egyptian Osiris—the examples are too numerous to list. In their totality these identifications across religious boundaries amounted to a consistent system of divine equations. As we shall see, as early as circa 200 B.C.E. Hellenistic Jewish thinkers adopted this method, equating the one and only Jewish God with the Greek chief deity Zeus who, they maintained, was originally the only god recognized by the Greeks. On this basis the Hellenized Jews saw no problem in reinterpreting the visual images of certain Greek deities as referring to those hypostases, divine messengers or powers, which formed part of their own monotheistic religious system.

All these considerations explain, I believe, not only how the Jews could admit what appear to be pagan divine figures and symbols into their synagogues, but also how they understood those figures and symbols. There can be no doubt that in the process of placing these pagan features on the walls and floors of the synagogues, they gave them meanings compatible with Jewish theology and religious doctrine. This is why, to revert to the most salient example, the naked woman holding the infant Moses on the striking Dura mural is not, because she cannot be in the Jewish context, Aphrodite or Anahita, although the form and style in which she is painted certainly are copied from the pictures of these goddesses as found in pagan structures. Rather, she is a representation (unquestionably quite a daring one) of the Shekhina, the most important Jewish hypostasis of the period, whom the Midrash closely associates with Moses. And this is why, in general, out of the plethora of Greek gods only those were borrowed for synagogal use who could be similarly reinterpreted as representing traditional Jewish concepts of divine messengers or intermediaries between God and the world.

To what extent this is indeed the case becomes clear if we consider, for a moment, all those Greek deities whose images were *not* utilized by Hellenistic Jews. Not one of the chief Greek gods, the members of the Olympian family, were so used: Zeus, the king of the Olympus, could not be shown because his image in a synagogue would have been interpreted as a depiction of Yahweh himself which, of course, was anathema. The other Olympians were likewise excluded for two reasons: first, because they had no counterparts in Jewish theology among the divine hypostases, messengers, or angels with whom, so as to make them acceptable, they could have been identified. This is why the Hellenistic synagogues contain no pictures modeled after those of Zeus' sister and wife Hera, or their children, Ares,[28] Hephaestus, and Hebe, or Zeus' brothers Hades and Poseidon, his other sisters Hestia and Demeter, or his children by other women, Hermes, Apollo, Artemis, Dionysus, or Athena. Secondly, these most important Greek deities were unacceptable to Jews precisely because they were siblings or children of Zeus, and thus it would have been difficult, if not impossible, to reinterpret their pictures as showing divine beings created by, and subordinated to, God.

As against these major Greek deities of whom no trace can be found in the Hellenistic Jewish art, there are several Greek mythical figures of lesser rank whose routine pagan representation has its echo in the contemporary Jewish art. Of these, the most frequently shown is a human face or figure with four horses which closely resembles the pagan pictures of Helios. Helios, in

Greek myth, was the son of the Titan Hyperion and the Titaness Eury-
phaessa or Theia, whose task was to drive his four-horse chariot daily across
the sky. In Greek and Hellenistic art he is often shown driving his quadriga,
which was generally understood to symbolize the passage of the sun from
east to west. This image struck a familiar chord in the minds of Hellenized
Jews. God riding a divine chariot was an old Hebrew mythical motif which
appeared in the Bible in numerous variants: God rides upon Cherubim,
upon clouds, upon the wings of the wind; His very throne is a chariot carried
by four winged "living creatures" and wheels within wheels; His messengers
take the shape of four horse-drawn chariots that go out to the four winds. [29]
On this Biblical basis, Philo considered God the divine charioteer who controlled the universe. [30] In the Midrashic elaboration of this idea, God's
chariot is drawn by Cherubim, glory and magnificence are in it, and it is
decorated by the figure of a steer. Occasionally even an angel of God rides in
a chariot of fire drawn by four steeds of fire. [31]

There can be no doubt that the divine chariot was an integral part of the
Jewish concept of the power of God, so integral, indeed, that it simply had to
be shown in graphic illustration once the idea became implanted in the
Hellenized Jewish mind that religious ideas can be expressed visually. But
how? The lack of an indigenous Jewish tradition for the visual presentation of
historical and conceptual traditions was the great hurdle that the Hellenistic
Jewish artists had to overcome with almost every subject to which they
turned. This is why Jewish art of the period so often is confined to showing
simple objects whose prototypes were either extant or known: the Menora,
the Shofar, the Lulabh, the Ethrog, etc. In the case of God's chariot, as in
that of the Temple, the strumming David, the Shekhina (see below), the way
out of the difficulty was for the artist to copy the nearest Greek equivalent—of which there was an abundance in every Hellenistic town. Thus the
quadriga of Helios had to stand in for the fiery four-horse or four-creature
chariot of God. Of course—and one cannot emphasize this too often—by
producing a picture inspired by or even copied from a Greek original showing Helios, the Jewish artist did not intend to express anything like belief in
the existence of a god separate from Yahweh, nor did the congregation which
frequented the synagogue take it in this way. What the picture of a deity
with the quadriga meant to all of them was: Yahweh is in control of the
world. And since even the prophet Ezekiel (whose vision of the dry bones
forms the subject of another Dura mural) goes so far as to state explicitly, albeit guardedly, that upon the divine chariot-throne he saw "a likeness as the
appearance of a man" which was none other than "the appearance of the likeness of the glory of Yahweh," [32] the Hellenized Jews, inured as they were to
pictorial representation of the Greek deities, could consider it permissible to
depict in this context (though not in any other) a human face as the "appearance of the likeness" of God, or of an angel of God.

Another such image closely resembling a pagan prototype is that of the man with a lyre at Dura. The Greek paradigm is, of course, Orpheus. Orpheus, the son of King Oeagrus and the Muse Calliope, was the most famous poet and musician of Greek mythology; he was a mortal and was killed by the Maenads. The picture of a man with a lyre at Dura is interpreted by Goodenough as being that of Orpheus, although in fact it appears more likely that it depicts David, the greatest poet and musician known to Biblical tradition. If the artist styled his David in a similar way to the pictures of Orpheus in Greek art, he could have done so for either or both of two reasons: because he had no Jewish artistic tradition to show David the musician, and thus had to use a Greek prototype; or because he wanted to indicate that David was a greater poet and musician than Orpheus. A third Greek hero, who while not himself shown at Dura lent his weapon, the cudgel, to Moses, is Heracles. He was the son of human parents, King Amphitryon and his wife Alcmene, but was reputed to have been begotten on her by Zeus. The greatest hero of Greek myth, Heracles performed twelve famous labors and other great feats, but in the end death overtook him. In the Dura mural, Moses is not shown holding a staff, as described in the Bible, but a cudgel, the weapon of Heracles. By this transposition the artist seems to have intended to express the idea that Moses was as great a hero as, perhaps greater than, the Greek Heracles.

About the provenance of Aphrodite, the Greek Goddess of Desire, there are variant myths: she was born of the foam of the sea, or of the genitals of Uranus, or was begotten by Zeus. She was identified with the Canaanite Astarte, the Mesopotamian Ishtar, the Roman Venus, and the Persian Anahita. Goodenough suggested that it is she who appears at Dura in the scene showing the infancy of Moses. However, for the artist to want to say, and for the congregation to read, that Moses was rescued from the Nile by the pagan love-goddess would be as absurd as it would be blasphemous. Hence, despite the formal similarity between the naked woman holding the infant Moses and the pagan depictions of Aphrodite and Anahita, the Dura painting cannot refer to that goddess. Rather (as mentioned above) it must be an illustration of the Midrash according to which the Shekhina was with Moses at that perilous moment, as she was with him later throughout his long and heroic life.

The last of the human figures appearing in Dura and identified by Goodenough with a Greek deity is that of Nike, the Winged Victory. The figure is shown in triplicate, holding a crown and riding the three visible roof corners of the Jerusalem Temple, which itself is depicted twice. She is also shown at the two top sides of the open gate of the wall of Egypt. The incorporation of the figure of Winged Victory at Dura and elsewhere was facilitated by her resemblance to the Cherubim and to the winged Seraphim and "living creatures" spoken of by Isaiah and Ezekiel. However, the fact that

Nike appears over the gate of Egypt as well as over the roof of the Jerusalem Temple seems to indicate that her figure had lost all religious meaning and become reduced to a mere architectural decorative feature, such as the Greek columns on the picture of the Jerusalem Temple. The Mesopotamian artist who lived and worked at Dura in the middle of the third century C.E. had no tradition as to how the Temple of Jerusalem, destroyed almost two hundred years earlier, looked. Therefore, he took as the model for his mural representation of the Temple the Greek temples, of which there were several at Dura, or representations of such temples familiar to him. His Temple of Jerusalem is a Greek temple, complete with Corinthian columns, gabled pediment—and Nike figures at the corners of the roof. The whole representation of the Temple is so strongly stereotyped and so closely resembles reliefs of Greek temples which contain *all* these features that one feels Kraeling is right in terming the Victories at Dura "a cliché." [33]

How closely the artist observed the limits placed by Jewish tradition on the representation of God Himself in pictorial terms can be seen in several panels in the upper part of which large hands are visible. These, evidently, are the "hand of God" and the "arm of God," often mentioned in the Bible as the anthropomorphic expression of God's manifest power.[34] Occasionally these hands are cut off, halfway between the wrist and the elbow, by the upper frame of the picture. In other cases the hand is cut off at the same spot even though it is well below the frame, as if the artist intended to say, "Thus far and not farther am I allowed to depict God's presence." No other evidence could more eloquently testify to a strict adherence to Jewish aniconic tradition.

The environmental influence is strongly felt in the clothes worn by the Biblical figures depicted at Dura. They are in contemporary Roman or Persian garb: some of the men are dressed in Roman togas, others in Persian tunics and trousers; the women wear sleeved tunics and long skirts, with long head-kerchiefs over their heads; the soldiers are protected by a mail-coat and carry oval shields. When the widow whose son Elijah resuscitated is shown in mourning, she is naked from the waist up, although such denudation was certainly not a Jewish mourning ritual. Much greater artists than the Dura muralist manifested the same nonchalance when presenting Biblical scenes. Like them, the Dura artist used the forms and styles he could see around him to depict scenes which, he knew, had taken place a thousand years earlier but about whose costumes he knew nothing.

In conclusion one might summarize the evidence of the Dura synagogue (which can be taken as typical of Hellenistic intrusion into Jewish houses of worship in general) as follows: The Hellenistic influence is evident in the presence of murals showing human figures, and in the style of these murals. However, all the major murals depict Biblical scenes, sometimes in the version of their Midrashic interpretation. Moses is shown many times, David three times; several pictures show scenes from the life of Elijah; two show the Temple, represented as a Greek-style edifice. One picture shows the Ark of the Covenant in the Philistine temple of Dagon with the pagan statues broken into pieces. Another shows the Ark in battle. One picture cycle is devoted to the vision of Ezekiel; one to the triumph of Mordecai. These central panels are surrounded and interspersed by smaller decorative elements showing ritual objects or objects that figure in Biblical symbolism: the seven-branched Menora, the Lulabh and the Ethrog, the Scroll of the Law, the Ark of the Covenant, the altar of Elijah with the bull on it. They also show animals which play a role in Biblical literature: horses, oxen, sheep, lions, tigers, leopards, or panthers, as well as birds such as the dove and the eagle. They show trees, stalks of grain, and wines, and fruits such as grapes, apples, pomegranates. A sea-monster, with a goat's head, a horse's neck and forelegs, a snake's body, and a fishtail, closely resembles the dragons shown on the base of the seven-branched Menora on the triumphal arch of Titus in Rome. These dragons seem to represent (again following a Greek prototype) the Biblical Leviathan or Dragon in the Sea.

These comments are still a long way from touching on all the pictorial material contained at Dura, let alone in Jewish art all over the Greco-Roman world. Among the details omitted there are certainly some that indicate the penetration of Greek religious ideas. Nonetheless, the conclusion is clear. By and large, Hellenistic Jewish art was unquestionably Jewish: it expressed Jewish religious ideas, although it often had no choice but to use patently Greek forms and images. It copied Greek artistic style and even modeled itself after the manner in which Greek artists depicted their gods, goddesses, and religious symbols. But while adopting these forms, styles, and models, Hellenistic Jewish art conveyed Jewish ideas about the one and only Jewish God, His messengers and works—ideas that were anchored in the Bible or its Midrashic amplification.

8. The Cherubim and the Menora

It has been indicated that religious iconography was an integral part of Biblical Jewish religion long before the encounter between Jews and Hellenes. The Biblical descriptions of the decorations and vessels of the Desert Tabernacle and the Solomonic Temple of Jerusalem show that, whatever the historical realities behind these literary accounts, Jewish religion had comprised an orthodox iconography. The Cherubim, those winged human figures depicted graphically all over the Temple and sculpturally in its Holy of Holies, are undoubtedly the most striking example. The original meaning of the Cherubim in the sanctuary can no longer be retrieved with certainty, but by Hellenistic times they were interpreted as symbols. According to Philo, they symbolized God's two "chief powers," goodness and sovereignty, and several other paired divine attributes. According to Pinhas ben Yair, a second-century C.E. Palestinian sage, the Cherubim stood for God's two "holy names." And according to Rab Qetina, a third–fourth-century Babylonian teacher, and other rabbis, the Cherubim were erotic-symbolic statuary: the two winged figures, one male and one female, were "intertwined with one another" in the manner of a couple in marital embrace; and when they were shown to the crowds of pilgrims, who were allowed to catch a glimpse of them from the Temple court, they were told, "Behold, your love before God is like the love of male and female!" [35]

The Cherubim as a symbol in Jewish iconography did not survive the destruction of the Temple of Jerusalem in 70 C.E., although they did continue to be referred to in Jewish literary sources. Even the number of Jewish ritual objects which survived in graphic form was small. They comprise five cult objects which were used in the Temple: the Lulabh, the Ethrog, the Shofar, the Incense-Shovel, and the Menora (of which below), which continue to be depicted upon Jewish graves and in synagogues. One more important ritual object which did not figure in the Temple must be added: the Tora-shrine or facade. All these are essentially not symbols in the sense of representing an idea in a graphic, shorthand version, or as Goodenough, following Ovid, put it, "a form which means more than we actually see." [36] They are simply graphic representations of cult objects used in Jewish religious ritual; this is what they mean, and nothing more.

With the Menora, the seven-branched candelabrum, the situation is different. On the surface, of course, this too is merely a depiction of a cult object, but a cult object which had a cosmic-symbolic meaning: it represented the lights in the firmament, or the seven planets, or heaven, or (since there were ten seven-branched candlesticks in the Temple) the seventy nations. [37] The Menora became in Hellenistic times, and remained throughout Jewish history, the most frequently employed Jewish emblem. [38] Nevertheless, it is questionable whether the Menora, so often depicted on Jewish tombs and in synagogues, meant anything "symbolic" to the Jews or was merely used as an identification mark, as were the other cult objects, as if to say: This is a synagogue in which we worship God by using our ancient Biblical cult objects, the Menora, the Shofar, the Lulabh, the Ethrog. In a similar manner, the depiction of the same objects on tombs could have meant: Here rests a Jew, who in his life worshipped God by using these Jewish cult objects.

9. Formal Borrowing

This was the Jewish baseline upon which Hellenism made its impact. Greek religion, as it appeared to the Jews, was of course sheer idolatry with which Judaism could have no truck. But closer acquaintance with Greek religion taught the Jews that it attributed to its gods features not unlike those ascribed to God by Jewish religion. Moreover, Greek religion had developed a rich graphic vocabulary in which it expressed its ideas about the gods. These graphic symbols were attractive for the Jews, as were many other features of Hellenistic culture—its architecture, its language, its poetry, its historiography, its philosophy. Hellenistic Jewish authors learned to talk about the remarkable history of the Jews, and about the unique religion of Judaism, in the Greek language, in the style of Greek historians and philosophers, and with the utilization of Greek philosophical approaches. Similarly, Jewish artists and those responsible for building and decorating synagogues borrowed the Hellenistic mode of visually expressing ideas and concepts about God. As to the ideas and concepts themselves about the nature of the attributes of the godhead—of those they had a rich supply in their own traditions, whether written or oral. But they borrowed from the Hellenistic world the modes of expressing in graphic symbols those ideas which the Greeks had about their gods and which coincided with, or corresponded to, the Jewish traditional concepts about their one and only invisible deity. Given the Hellenistic influence on the visible and tangible environment in which the Jews lived, and given the extreme paucity of indigenous Jewish graphic traditions, when they wished to express pictorially certain features which their traditions attributed to God, they had no other way of doing so than by using Greek symbols and images.

A few examples of how this worked in practice have been given. Others can easily be found. The Bible describes God as the creator of two great luminaries and the stars: hence the pictures of the sun, the moon, and the Zodiac in Hellenistic synagogues. Dragons as a part of Jewish thinking (under very old Babylonian influence) antedate Homer and Hesiod. Yet when the unknown Hellenistic Jewish artist wished to depict them on the base of the famous Menora (a plastic representation of which can still be seen on the triumphal Arch of Titus in Rome), he had no choice but to show them in a form familiar to him from Hellenistic art.

What underlies all this, and indeed the entire gamut of Hellenistic Jewish art, is the desire to express in visual form traditional Jewish religious ideas about God. The implantation of this desire in the Jewish mind was due to Hellenistic influence—this must be admitted without reservation. But this is all. The presence of two- or three-dimensional portraits, such as those referred to, certainly cannot mean that the Hellenized Jews believed in any of the Greek deities, nor that they identified God with them. A picture modeled after that of a Greek god or goddess on the walls of a synagogue was read by those who prayed in it as a statement about certain aspects of God. Figures of dragons served as a reminder of God's victory over Leviathan and other sea-monsters, and the like. All these and many more were adaptations of pagan forms which, in the synagogal context, were filled with Jewish contents.

An analogy to the process can be found in modern Jewish life. When the Jews embraced religious reform, the European and American Reform congregations introduced the use of the organ in their synagogues, now called "temples." The example they followed was that of the Christian churches, and their motivation in doing so was the feeling that organ music will be a suitable and attractive enrichment of the synagogue services. To this extent the organ in synagogues unquestionably represents Christian influences. But it would be utterly mistaken to conclude from the introduction of the organ into Jewish houses of worship that the Jews have succumbed to Christian religious influence beyond the purely formal one of adopting a musical instrument. Again, numerous synagogues in Europe and America were built in the nineteenth century in a pseudo-Moorish style. The formal influence is unmistakably there, but it has nothing to do with any influence of Islam upon Judaism.

Similarly, the utilization of Hellenistic graphic symbols by the Jews, including the decoration of their synagogues with paintings modeled after those of Greek deities, while it undoubtedly testifies to a strong *formal* influence, in no way proves, or even implies, that Hellenistic influences penetrated the Jewish belief system, the core and content of Jewish religion.

10. The Apocrypha

This conclusion is confirmed by the contemporary literary evidence left behind by the Hellenistic Jewish authors. The Jewish Hellenistic literature, which by any standard is the most important manifestation of the Hellenistic impact on the Jews, was written in Greek, the third language adopted by them, first as a colloquial and soon thereafter as a literary language. The first such linguistic acculturation, as we have seen, was to Hebrew, which the patriarchal clan adopted from the Canaanites and in which the Israelites a few generations later began to produce, first orally and then in writing, that unique literature which is known as the Bible. It happened the second time toward the end of the Biblical period when Aramaic replaced Hebrew as the colloquial of the Jews, and when they began to write in that language parts of the late Biblical books and, subsequently, the bulk of their rabbinic literature. And it happened for the third time when Greek became the dominant Jewish tongue.

Not that the Jews had not written in Hebrew and Aramaic during the Hellenistic period. On the contrary, this was the time when several new categories of Jewish literature came into being in both Hebrew and Aramaic. Culture, as every student of anthropology knows, is cumulative; and what happened in the literary field in Judah from the third century B.C.E. can be taken as a striking illustration of this general thesis. First of all, Jewish poets, moralists, and other authors continued to write, in Hebrew, works which followed older, Biblical prototypes. They wrote religious poems, such as Psalms, several of which were included in the Biblical Book of Psalms (the Psalter was completed not much before 100 B.C.E.), while others were put together in an extra-canonical collection known as the Psalms of Solomon (probably written by a Pharisee between 70 and 40 B.C.E.). They continued to write moralistic "Wisdom" literature, of which the most outstanding Hebrew examples are the Wisdom of Yeshuʻa ben Sira (Jesus ben Sirach, also known as Ecclesiasticus), written by a Palestinian Jew about 180 B.C.E., and the *Pirqe Avot* or Sayings of the Fathers, which was subsequently included in the Mishna (described later). Sometime between 100 B.C.E. and 50 C.E., probably in Alexandria, lived the unknown Jewish author of the Wisdom of Solomon, written in Greek.

Another popular genre, represented by quite a number of Jewish books, was that of the apocalyptic literature. "Apocalypse" is the Greek term (meaning literally "Disclosure") used to designate quasi-prophetic writings which purport to reveal what is hidden. The Hellenistic age saw a proliferation of apocalyptic literature produced mostly by Jews in Palestine, primarily in Hebrew or Aramaic, but occasionally in Greek as well. This literature comprises numerous elaborations of a single, basic Biblical theme: the Day of Yahweh on which, as the prophets taught, God would punish Israel's enemies, establish His people as a world power, and sit in judgment over Jews as well as Gentiles.[39] The apocalyptic authors, of whom Zechariah can be considered the earliest, utilized the symbolism and myths of Babylonia to illustrate in frightening detail how God's judgment of the wicked and deliverance of the just would come to pass. The symbols they used were as a rule animals—sheep, bulls, birds—or often composite creatures whose various parts represent certain qualities, or mythological beings such as Beliar. The purpose of the apocalypses is to hold out future hope to a people beset by troubles and misery. In order to make their message effective, they resort to the device of attributing their books to old and famous figures who are represented as foretelling what is to happen in the future, both in times that had preceded the actual writing of the book (which establishes the fictitious author as creditable) and in times that still lie ahead.

Among the ancient worthies to whom the unknown authors of the apocalypses attribute their books are Enoch, who is especially suited to the role of an apocalyptic author because the Bible says of him enigmatically: "And Enoch walked with God and he was not; for God took him";[40] also the twelve sons of Jacob, Moses, Solomon, Isaiah, Baruch, and Ezra. All in all, this literature is as distinctly Jewish and hence as unique as the Biblical literature which preceded and the Talmudic which followed it. Most of it is subsumed under the term *pseudepigrapha*, that is, "spurious writings," so named because of the false attribution of authorship, and is excluded from the Biblical Canon. But one of them, in fact the one which is considered the parent and prototype of all apocalypses, was admitted. The Book of Daniel, which appeared in the Maccabean period (it is usually dated 164 B.C.E), is the latest book contained in the Bible and is written partly in Hebrew and partly in Aramaic.

During the same period the Jews of Palestine produced other literary works as well which were not found worthy of admission into the Biblical Canon. These books are called *apocrypha*, meaning books that are "hidden away." The apocrypha contain a large variety of writings. They include, first of all, genuine historical books such as the First Maccabees (of unknown authorship), which tells the story of the heroic exploits of Judah Maccabi and his family. It was written in Hebrew circa 100 B.C.E. and is an important historical source. Many apocrypha contain legends or moralizing stories, such as the books of Tobit and Judith. Related to this type of apocryphal literature are those books which, written in Greek before the beginning of the common era, contain paraphrases, amplifications, and additions to the latest books which were admitted to the Biblical Canon. Among them is the free and much augmented Greek version of the Book of Ezra, known as the First Book of Esdras (or, in the Vulgate, as the Third Esdras); the additions to Esther; several additions to Daniel, probably going back to Hebrew originals and consisting of the Prayer of Azariah, the Song of the Three Young Men (who were thrown into the fiery furnace), the Story of Bel and the Dragon (in which Daniel unmasks the chicanery of the priests of Bel), and the Story of Susanna (whom Daniel saves from the accusations of the lecherous Elders). The last three, as well as the books of Judith and Tobit, are novelistic in character, but they all drive home a definite moral lesson.

A third category of apocrypha consists of prophetic books, attributed, in a pseudepigraphic manner, to prophets or pious men of old. Among these is the Prayer of Manasseh, which pretends to be the full text of the supplication offered up by the distressed King Manasseh according to the Bible; [41] the Book of Baruch, attributed to the scribe of Jeremiah; and the Letter of Jeremiah, ostensibly written by the prophet to the Babylonian exiles warning them against idolatry. The didactic apocrypha, written in the manner of the Biblical Book of Proverbs and containing words of wisdom and warning, have already been referred to. All the apocrypha, whether written in Hebrew, Aramaic, or Greek, are firmly Jewish in spirit and content.

The question of why such worthy and pious books as the Wisdom of Yeshu'a ben Sira and the First Maccabees were excluded from the Canon, while others, which were neither older nor loftier in spirit—such as Daniel, Esther, Ecclesiastes, and the Song of Songs—were included is difficult to answer. But we know that it was in the academy of Yabne (founded by Yohanan

ben Zakkai in 70 C.E.) that the canonization of the Biblical books took place
about 90 C.E., and that thereafter all the books current among the Jews
which were not admitted into the Canon were considered unworthy of study
or preservation. If they nevertheless survived—in many cases in translation
only—this was primarily due to the early Christian Church, which intermin-
gled them with the canonical books of the "Old Testament" and recognized
them as parts of a more complete Biblical Canon.

11. Tannaitic Literature

In the latter part of the Hellenistic period the Tannaim lived and taught in
Palestine—those rabbinical scholars who devoted their entire intellect to
studying and interpreting the Biblical law. In contrast to the pseudepigraphic and apocryphal literatures, which remained outside the mainstream
of Jewish developments, Tannaitic literature is the major connecting link between Biblical Hebrew religion and rabbinic Judaism. The magnum opus of
the Tannaites, the Mishna, compiled in Hebrew by Rabbi Y'huda the Prince
about 200 C.E., is second only to the Bible itself in its importance for
normative Judaism; in fact, the acceptance of the Mishna (and of the subsequent Talmudic literature based on it) as the authoritative formulation of
the Law which in the Bible itself is often obscure, laconic, and fragmentary is
the dividing line between Jews and such semi-Jewish sects as that of the Samaritans and the Karaites. The Mishna, in turn, forms the basis of the much
more voluminous Talmuds: the Talmud of Jerusalem (compiled c. 425 C.E.),
and the even larger and more authoritative Babylonian Talmud (compiled c.
500 C.E.). Both Talmuds contain further refinements and elaborations of the
traditional law as codified in the Mishna—this part is called *Halakha* or "The
Walking"—as well as stories, anecdotes, homilies, moral teachings, and
other non-legal material which is called *Aggada* or "Telling." Parts of both
Talmuds are in Hebrew; much of them is in Aramaic. The Babylonian Talmud, incidentally, with its commentaries written from the eleventh century
on, formed practically the sole subject of unending study among the
Ashkenazi Jews until the Enlightenment.

It is in the Talmud that much of the Tannaitic teachings is preserved. A
special Aramaic technical term in the Talmudic text introduces every quote
from a Tannaitic source, known as *Baraita* (Aramaic for "External"). The Talmudic Baraitas contain those Tannaitic traditions which, for various reasons,
were not incorporated into the Mishna. The relationship, therefore, between
Baraita and Mishna is like that between the apocrypha and the Bible, except
that Tannaitic halakhic traditions were considered as having authority (unless
they clashed with the Mishna) even if found only in a Baraita. There are also
Aggadic Baraitas, that is, such as contain homiletic elucidations and legen-

dary amplifications of Biblical passages supplied by Tannaites. In addition to these brief and scattered passages, Tannaitic literature comprises a sizable collection of Baraitas called the *Tosefta* (or "Addition"), which treats traditional halakhic subjects in a more complete form than the Mishna. Finally, there are extant several volumes of Tannaitic *Midrashim* (literally "Explanations"), written in the form of comments, often of considerable length, to Biblical passages, of either a legal nature (these are known as halakhic Midrashim) or comprising moralizing, edifying, or legendary writings (known as Aggadic or Haggadic Midrashim). The language of the Midrash literature which comprises several dozen books is either Hebrew or Aramaic, and the period which they represent extends from the Tannaitic era to the tenth or eleventh century C.E. In many cases it is impossible to pinpoint the time in which they were written: constituent materials may be centuries older than the date of their final compilation.

12. *The Bible in Greek*

The types of Jewish literature discussed so far aimed primarily at a Jewish readership. Not so the Hellenistic Jewish literature, which, written in Greek, addressed itself to the Gentiles as well as to the Hellenized Jewish reader. Its aim was to acquaint the Greek-speaking world with the greatness of the history of Israel, to make it aware of the folly of paganism, and to convince it that the anti-Jewish attacks, which multiplied with the spread of the Jewish Diaspora in the Hellenistic world, were utterly baseless. At the same time, the Hellenistic Jewish writers endeavored to impress their assimilated fellow Jews with the great past of which they were heirs, to strengthen them in their Jewish consciousness, and to demonstrate to them the lasting value of Jewish religion.

In the earlier part of this chapter we discussed the Jewish adoption of Hellenistic forms of education and entertainment, the attraction "Greek Wisdom" held for the educated Jews (including the rabbis), the frequent use of Greek cultural terminology, and the widespread knowledge of Greek among all layers of Jewish society. We saw that, despite these ubiquitous adoptions of Hellenistic cultural forms, the Jews nevertheless managed to preserve their Jewishness. However, the clinching argument that they phenomenally succeeded in doing so is supplied by the Hellenistic Jewish literature, to a rapid survey of which we now turn.

The first thing to be said of this literature is that it rivals in richness the rabbinic literature of Talmud and Midrash which was produced in subsequent centuries. The second is that in its variety, although not always in its quality, it equals that of the Greek literature produced by the Gentiles. It comprises translations of the Bible, reworkings of and supplements to Scripture, historical books, epics, dramas, philosophy, apologetics, and various forms of Jewish propaganda, some of it under a pagan mask. The list of the known Hellenistic Jewish authors contains dozens of names. The number of their known works runs into hundreds. Evidently, they must have written many more works of which all traces were lost.

So convinced were the Hellenizing Jews of the supreme historical, religious, moral, and legal value of their divine book, the Bible, that the first literary work they undertook in Greek was its translation into that language. In fact, they embarked on this great venture at a time when the Bible as a whole was not yet canonized, that is, long before the Tannaim of Yavne had decided which of the many books that circulated among the Jews of Palestine and were considered sacred should be admitted to that most sacred and exclusive anthology known as the Bible. We have no precise historical information as to the circumstances in which this work of translation was undertaken. However, there can be no doubt that, apart from their understandable desire to present their Holy Book to the Gentile world, an important motivation was concern about the increasing ignorance, among the Hellenized Jews, of Aramaic, and still more of literary Hebrew. To counteract this estrangement from the fountainhead of Judaism and to enable Greek-speaking Jews to reacquaint themselves with their own Scripture—these were the main aims of the early bilingual Jewish scholars who undertook the formidable task of translating the Bible into Greek.

As to the time of the first translation, and the way in which it was carried out, there is a legendary account in the Greek *Letter of Aristeas to Philocrates*, the apologetic intent of which will be discussed later in this chapter. According to the unknown Alexandrian Jewish author of this *Letter*, which purports to have been written by a Greek high official at the court of Ptolemy II Philadelphus (285–247 B.C.E.), but in reality was composed about 130 B.C.E., it was Demetrius of Phalerum who took the initiative by suggesting that the Law of the Jews should have a place in the great Alexandrian Library. Thereupon the king dispatched an embassy to the High Priest at Jerusalem, and in due course six scholarly elders from each of the twelve tribes of the Jews arrived in Alexandria and undertook the work of translation. In the brief span of seventy-two days, the seventy-two elders completed the translation of the Pentateuch, which, after they reconciled the differences "by mutual comparisons," was submitted to Demetrius. This, in itself legendary, account of the origin of the Septuagint (as the translation became known) was further embellished by Philo of Alexandria (c. 20 B.C.E.–c. 45 C.E.), who maintained that the translators worked independently of one another and yet, by divine inspiration, arrived at the identical phraseology.

Whatever the circumstances of its preparation, the Septuagint remained for several centuries the only Greek translation of the Bible (subsequently the other Biblical books were also translated). It is written in the *koinē dialektos*, or common Hellenistic Greek, although it is tinged with many Hebraisms in its syntax. It follows the original as closely as possible, but includes most of the apocryphal books (excluded from the Hebrew Bible), without making any distinction between canonical and non-canonical books.

The influence of the Septuagint on the development of a Jewish literature in the Greek language was immeasurable. For one thing, it enabled the Hellenized Jews to become acquainted with the Bible, and even to study it thoroughly, without having to learn Hebrew; for another, it showed them the way to present Jewish ideas and concepts to a Greek-speaking public, whether Jewish or Gentile; and thirdly, it could be referred to as the authoritative source, in Greek, whenever proof texts were required in arguing a point of Jewish religion, law, or history. Without the Septuagint one cannot imagine the development of a Hellenistic Jewish literature in Greek.

Because the early Christian Church appropriated the Septuagint, the Jews repudiated its authority and thus the need arose for a new Jewish Bible translation into Greek. In the course of the second century C.E. no less than three such translations were produced, all of them, it seems, by proselytes to Judaism. Their names, in contrast to those of the earlier linguists who worked on the Septuagint, are known: they were Aquila, Theodotion, and Symmachus. These translations were based on the Masoretic Hebrew text of the Bible, which had not yet existed at the time the Septuagint came into being. However, only fragments of them survive.

13. Historiography and Fictionalized History

The Hellenized Jewish authors—like writers of other peoples who came under the influence of Hellenism—felt that only a nation possessed of an old and venerable history could hold up its head in the civilized world, and they set about to present the history of the Jews, in Greek, in the style of the Greek historians, emulating their approach, viewpoint, and even manner. Yet the purpose of all Hellenistic Jewish historiography remained totally Jewish. It is permeated throughout by a deep desire to show the readers, whether Jewish or Gentile, the greatness of the Jewish people (as manifested in its Biblical and later history), the truth of its monotheistic religion, and the superiority of its ethics.

The majority of the Jewish historians lived in Alexandria. Regrettably, the works of most of them are lost and known to us only from scattered references and occasional quotations found in later historical books. Several Hellenistic Jewish historians who lived in the second and early first centuries B.C.E. were referred to and excerpted by Alexander Polyhistor (c. 80–40 B.C.E.) in his book *Peri Ioudaion*, or *About the Jews*. However, this book itself is lost, and its contents are known to us only from the extant *Praeparatio*

Evangelica of Eusebius, bishop of Caesarea (260/65–339 C.E.), which incorporates considerable parts of it. These third-hand quotes of quotes not only inform us of the names of Eupolemus, Artapanus, Kleodemus, Demetrius, Theodotus, Aristeas, Ezekiel, but also give us an idea of their styles and approaches. Thus we know that their way of writing ranged from the dry annalistic style of Demetrius to the unbridled fantasies of Eupolemus and Artapanus, who embellished their histories with much legendary material. In addition to those named, there was a Jewish historian by the name of Jason of Cyrene who lived in the second century B.C.E. and devoted five volumes to the history of the Hasmoneans. Nothing of his work survived; it is known only from its brief summary in the Second Book of the Maccabees. The Third Maccabees, whose author was an unknown Alexandrian Jew, is a religious historical novel which tells about the victories of the Jews over their enemies through divine intervention during the reign of Ptolemy IV Philopator (222–204 B.C.E.). Yet another Hellenistic Jewish historian is known by name: he was Justus of Tiberias, who lived in the second half of the first century C.E. and wrote a history of the Jewish kings from Moses to Agrippa II, and a history of the Jewish war. However, nothing of these books survived.

On the other hand, the voluminous writings of Justus' contemporary, Josephus Flavius (c. 38–early second C.E.), survived in toto. Josephus, originally Joseph ben Matityahu, was of priestly descent and a scion of the Maccabean royal house. He received a thorough education and mastered the three Jewish languages of his era, Hebrew, Aramaic, and Greek. At the age of twenty-six he was sent to Rome on a diplomatic mission. Two years later, when the Jewish revolt against the Romans started, he was one of those entrusted with organizing the defense of the Galilee. The fort of Yotapata, of which he was in charge, was the last in Galilee to fall to Vespasian. Joseph was captured, but claiming prophetic ability, saluted the general as Caesar, won his favor, and upon the election of Vespasian as emperor was given his freedom and took his patron's family name, Flavius. When the son of Vespasian, Titus, took over the siege of Jerusalem, Josephus accompanied him, observed the death throes of the city from close quarters, and after its fall (70 C.E.) retired to the estate in Judea given to him to write his first work, the seven-book history of *The Jewish War*. He first wrote it in Aramaic (which is lost), then switched to Greek, completed it before the death of Vespasian (79 C.E.), and presented the book to him. In 93 C.E. his second, greatest work, the twenty-book *Antiquities of the Jews*, was published. It covers the history of the Jews from the earliest Biblical times to the outbreak of the revolt in 66 C.E. While the first book—written, it seems, at the behest of Vespasian—is an apology for both the Romans and the Jews, the second is a wholeheartedly Jewish book and serves one purpose only: to inspire the Greek readers with respect for the Jews whose history went back to oldest times, who produced a long line of great men outstanding in war and in peace, and who had the finest record of laws and institutions.[42] In his later years, Josephus wrote two smaller works: *Against Apion* and his own *Life*. Apion, a grammarian of Alexandria in the first half of the first century C.E., wrote an attack against the Jews; Josephus in his *Against Apion* repudiates him and defends the Jews against others of their enemies and calumniators. His autobiography, published after the death of Agrippa II (that is, in the early second century C.E.), was written in response to Justus of Tiberias who accused Josephus of having instigated the Jewish revolt against the Romans.

The works of Josephus as historical sources are invaluable. But beyond their purely documentary value, they are great historiography, written with a dramatic force, an artist's eye for detail, an unsparing precision, and a consistency in the organization of the material which equal the best of Greek historical writing.

Almost nothing has survived of the work of the Hellenistic Jewish poets who wrote numerous epic and dramatic works. A certain Philo (not to be confused with the philosopher Philo of Alexandria who lived later) living in the second century B.C.E. wrote an epic poem *About Jerusalem*, of which only small fragments survive. Theodotus, who was his contemporary and may have been a Hellenized Samaritan, wrote a history of the city of Shechem in epic form, of which a piece is preserved in Eusebius' *Praeparatio Evangelica*. The Hellenistic Jewish tragedian Ezekiel, also of the second century B.C.E., wrote several Jewish tragedies, but excerpts from only one survive. It was titled *The Exodus* and dealt with the liberation of the Israelites from Egypt. These few fragments from the work of three poets afford a tantalizingly brief glimpse of what may have been a rich field of literary activity.

14. Philosophy

The earliest, and entirely incidental, testimony to the interest Jews took in Greek philosophy pertains to a meeting between Aristotle and an educated Jew in Asia Minor which took place between the years 348 and 345 B.C.E.[43] Hence we know that there were individual Jews familiar with Greek philosophy even before the Hellenization of the East began, and that at least one of them had personal contact with one of the greatest Greek philosophers. After the conquests of Alexander (who, incidentally, was a pupil of Aristotle), the Hellenizing Jews acquired Greek culture, as we have seen, on varying levels. For some it meant athletic games and gymnasium education; for others, the absorption of Greek terminology; for the great majority, the acquisition of Greek as their colloquial; and for the most learned, acquaintance with the ideas and methods of the great Greek philosophers. We have also seen that Greek philosophy, which they termed "Greek Wisdom," was tolerated by many rabbis and even considered a desirable accomplishment by some. While we know of several Palestinian rabbis who studied or encouraged the study of "Greek Wisdom," not one is known to have entered the ranks of those select few who, in addition to studying it, also wrote Greek philosophy. This ultimate Hellenizing accomplishment was, however, achieved by several Alexandrian Jewish intellectuals.

For a Jew to write Greek philosophy was a most complex task. Apart from the language problem which had to be overcome, it required a painstaking process of familiarizing oneself with the teachings of the major Greek philosophers and philosophical schools; and it meant the use of terminology, expressions, and concepts developed within the context of Greek thought ultimately reaching back to (even though quite considerably removed from) ancient Greek polytheism and mythology. Finally, since all Hellenistic Jewish philosophers were, as we shall see, totally committed to Judaism, it involved the attempt to make understandable, within the Greek confines, tenets of belief anchored deep in quite a different, monotheistic, moral, and aniconic tradition; in other words, to recast Jewish ideas in Greek garb. Because of this fundamental incongruity between the two traditions the Hellenistic Jewish philosophers had to bridge, they put the emphasis not on logic and physics, but on ethics; and their main purpose was the practical and traditionally Jewish one of educating man to true morality and piety. The proportion of Jewish to Greek ideas varies greatly in the writings of the Hellenistic Jewish philosophers: in some, the Greek element is stronger, in others weaker. But, as Schürer stated,

> even those who are most strongly permeated by Greek ideas, nevertheless stood essentially on a Jewish ground. For they not only emphasize the oneness and transcendence of God, and the rule of divine providence, which punishes those who are evil and rewards those who are good, but also uphold unswervingly that the Mosaic revelation contains the most complete cognition of things divine and human, so that Judaism is therefore the way to true wisdom and true virtue.[44]

While their method of presentation and argumentation was Greek throughout—drawing eclectically upon the teachings of Plato, Aristotle, the Stoics, and the Pythagoreans—in literary form some of the Hellenistic Jewish philosophers hark back to Biblical and rabbinic prototypes. Thus the apocryphal book known as the Wisdom of Solomon follows in style the Biblical Book of Proverbs but contains philosophical exhortations to true faith and genuine zeal for God and His laws, as well as arguments on the truth of Judaism and the folly of idolatry. It is, in fact, a Hellenistic Jewish counterpart to the more traditional Hebrew Wisdom of Yeshu'a ben Sira. Divine wisdom, says the unknown author, is the most exalted of all goods, the source of all truth, virtue, and bliss. This basic idea is described in terms reminiscent of the Stoic doctrine of the world soul and of God as the immanent world reason which permeates the whole universe. The psychology of the author, on the other hand, is Platonic-dualistic: the human soul is preexistent; if the soul is good, it enters a pure body. The body is but an "earthly hut" for the soul which, after a short sojourn in the body, must be returned like a loan, leaving the body to decompose into dust.[45]

One early Alexandrian Jewish philosopher was Aristobulus, who lived in the middle of the second century B.C.E. His opus, which is lost, was a free reproduction of the contents of the Pentateuch. From quotations contained in the works of the Church Fathers, we know that Aristobulus was a trained philosopher, familiar with Pythagoras, Socrates, Plato, and the Peripatetics. But at the same time he was a convinced Jew, who held that the Greek philosophers had derived their teachings from Moses, and that even Greek poets, such as Homer and Hesiod, had drawn certain things from the Pentateuch which had been translated into Greek long before the Septuagint. This claim, that Moses was the father of Greek philosophy and culture, would be reiterated by later Hellenistic Jewish philosophers, among them Philo of Alexandria.

Either shortly before or shortly after the beginning of the Common Era lived yet another, anonymous, Jewish philosopher in Alexandria, whose work, known as Fourth Maccabees, is a long sermon on the supremacy of pious reason over the passions. This, of course, is a basic Stoic doctrine which the author uses for the purpose of presenting his predominantly Jewish idea that the persecutions and death suffered by the Maccabean martyrs "were a ransom for our nation's sins."[46] Of all the Hellenistic Jewish philosophers known to us, this author is closest to Pharisaic Judaism: what he praises in the Maccabean martyrs is precisely their strict adherence to ritual law. On the other hand, his belief in immortality differs from that of the Pharisees and is identical with that of the other Jewish Hellenists: the belief in an eternal and blissful survival of the pious souls in heaven.

I have left to the last the greatest Hellenistic Jewish philosopher of all, Philo of Alexandria (c. 20 B.C.E–c. 45 C.E.), also known as Philo Judaeus, in whose work Hellenistic Jewish creativity reached its pinnacle. Although several of his writings are lost, what survives of them is most impressive in its volume, variety, and quality. His writings, which comprise twelve volumes in the Loeb Classical Library edition, fall into three main categories:

1. Brief explanations to the Pentateuch in the form of catechistic questions and answers, intended for wide circles.
2. A great, allegorical commentary to selected passages of Genesis.
3. A systematic presentation of Mosaic legislation.

The second of these three groups of works centers on one basic idea: The history of the men who figure in Genesis is essentially a great psychological

and ethical treatise. The individual persons who appear in this first book of
the Bible, both the good ones and the evil ones, stand for the various psychological conditions which occur in man. Philo's purpose is to analyze these
conditions in their relationships to one another and to the deity, and to draw
moral lessons from them. In accordance with this approach, his theology is
allegorical and moralistic. To take but one example, he interprets the two
golden Cherubim which stood in the Holy of Holies of the Jerusalem Temple
as symbolizing two groups of divine powers (or virtues or attributes). One
Cherub stood for God (*Elohim*), the Father, Husband, Begetter, Creator,
who is Reason, Goodness, Peaceable, Gentle, and Beneficent. The other
symbolized the Lord (*Yahweh*), the Mother, Wife, Bearer, Nurturer, who is
Wisdom, Sovereignty, Legislative, Chastising, and Correcting.[47]

Philo was not only a master of Greek style but much more at home in
Greek literature than Jewish. He knew Homer, Euripides, and the other
great Greek poets and dramatists and was suffused with a knowledge of the
Greek philosophers. His familiarity with Hebrew, on the other hand, was
limited: he read the Bible only in its Greek translation, the Septuagint, and
knew little of the rabbinic *Halakha*, although he was well acquainted with
the Aggadic methods of Scripture interpretation. Nevertheless, his favorite
method of allegorical interpretation of the Bible owes more to the Greek use
of this approach in reinterpreting myths than to its Jewish use in the *Aggada*.
His metaphysics, too, with its *hypostases* (or mediators between God and the
world) and its uncreated primal matter, places him in the Greek rather than
the Jewish world of thought. On the other hand, one must not lose sight of
the fact that the central *hypostasis* of the Philonian system, the divine *Logos*
("Reason"), which he conceived as a quality of God and yet distinct from
God, has not only Greek philosophical antecedents (e.g., in Aristotle and the
Stoics), but also Biblical paradigms. Such concepts as the "Wisdom" and the
"Word" of God, which figure prominently in the Biblical Book of Proverbs
and in the apocryphal Wisdom of Yeshu'a ben Sira (which the author's grandson translated into Greek), must have been familiar to Philo and influential
in the development of his *Logos* and other *hypostases*. Where he was totally
Jewish was in his acceptance of the Tora of Moses as the highest, indeed the
only, authority—the complete revelation of Divine Wisdom. In agreement
with the Talmudic rabbis, he was convinced that everything in the Tora is
the word of God, and that therefore it contains not a single word without definite meaning. Consequently, all true wisdom is contained in that divine
book, and all the Greek philosophers—Plato, Pythagoras, Zeno, and the
rest—derived their wisdom from Moses, the one great teacher of mankind.[48]

When it comes to the core of his Jewish belief, Philo is as uncompromising
as any orthodox Pharisee teacher: God is one, eternal, unchanging, simple,
free, self-sufficient, devoid of all human failings, and towering high above all
human virtues. In Him is united all perfection; He fills and encompasses ev-

erything. And yet, He is also *apoios*, without any quality whatsoever, that is to say, can in no way be defined—an apparent logical contradiction which would have been a stumbling block to a native Greek philosopher but could pass unnoticed by a Jewish thinker, inured to inconsistency by the innumerable contradictory statements about God contained in the Bible.

True Jewish content is reflected also in Philo's anthropology, although the mode of its expression is Hellenistic-philosophical. He considered the human body the source of all evil: sensuality in itself is evil, therefore man is born sinful. Yet God created man by breathing His spirit into him; [49] thus the human soul is derived from the Divine Source, and man has the capacity of attaining to a conception of the nature of divinity through the spirit of prophecy or through mystical meditation. [50]

Philo envisaged and fulfilled two missions. He demonstrated to his Jewish readers that Greek philosophy was valuable because it taught what God had revealed to Moses and what is contained in the Bible. And he showed to the Greek readers that all those insights and understandings which were reached by the Greek philosophers had been achieved before them by Moses. Thus it was Moses who was the first and greatest philosopher, as well as the best lawgiver. [51]

Our present task does not permit us to enter into a discussion of the significance of Philo as a philosopher and of the influence he exerted on rabbinical Judaism, on Neo-Platonism, and on the development of Christian dogma. [52] But we cannot take leave of him without pointing out that this master of Greek philosophy and allegorical interpretation was a strictly traditional Jew (today we would call him Orthodox), who believed that the observance of the Mosaic Law, including the ritual laws of circumcision, the Sabbath rest, and the dietary laws, was obligatory; and who reproached those who regarded those laws as mere *symbola* and did not observe them literally. He also believed that the Jews were God's chosen people, and that the Messianic promise of a blissful age on earth would come true and would be enjoyed by the Jews as well as those Gentiles who convert to the faith in the only true God. [53]

In sum, Philo was a virtuoso of the delicate art of pouring the old wine of Jewish theocentrism into the glittering amphorae of Greek philosophy. A whole millennium had to elapse before the Jewish mind was again to achieve a similarly remarkable feat by decanting the same old precious draft into the new jars made available by the medieval Arab philosophers.

15. Apologetics

To the Greeks and the Romans, all Oriental peoples seemed outlandish or exotic with their strange appearance, peculiar garb, foreign speech, uncouth manners, and, above all, their religions—perceived either as mysterious or as superstitious. Yet all could somehow be accounted for within the Greco-Roman polytheistic frame of reference, by the simple but ingenious method of identifying their gods and goddesses with the homegrown deities of the Greco-Roman pantheons. All, that is, except the Jews. In contrast to the rest of the world, which, like the Greeks and Romans, was polytheistic, the Jews believed in one god only; as against all other peoples, who worshipped their gods in statues and other visible representations, the Jews maintained that their god could not and must not be depicted in a graphic or plastic medium. And not only was their religion aniconic, which in itself was a reproach to, and a denial of, the proper accepted ways of worship; they also displayed an annoying tendency to keep themselves apart from the Gentiles, they refused to work on one particular day of the week, and they had many other disagreeable laws of their own which they insisted on observing even in the most cultured Hellenistic environment.

Because they were felt to be an anomaly in the civilized world, the populace was always ready to attack them. The educated people, for their part, had contempt for the peculiar Jewish rites and considered them atheists, seeing that they worshipped no visible god and denied the existence of the Greco-Roman deities. These sentiments underlie the numerous anti-Jewish remarks or passages found in the works of many Greek and Roman authors. Some felt so strongly about them that they devoted special treatises to attacking and denigrating the Jews.

To counter these feelings and anti-Semitic writings, numerous Hellenistic Jewish authors produced apologetic works, or wrote about Jewish history and religion with an apologetic purpose in mind. Philo wrote a book, regrettably lost, entitled *Apology for the Jews*; Josephus, in his *Against Apion*, marshals cogent arguments against Apion and all others who defamed the Jews.

Apart from these specifically and avowedly apologetic tracts, however, all the other works of Philo and of Josephus, the two dominant figures of Hellenistic Jewish literature, are permeated by a strong pro-Jewish spirit, as are all the writings of their predecessors.

The apologetic orientation of the Jewish Hellenists produced a peculiar type of literature which, too, pursued the aim of propagandizing for Judaism, but did so under the mask of pagan authorship. The precise purpose of these writings varied greatly, and so did the literary form in which they were cast. The most remarkable are undoubtedly the Sibylline Oracles. The Sibyls were half-mythological and half-historical figures in Greek religion, who uttered oracular prophecies in a state of *manía*, that is, divinely inspired ecstasy. Several collections of these Sibylline Oracles existed in various parts of the Greco-Roman world, and as late as 363 C.E. the emperor Julian ("the Apostate") consulted them. They were regarded very highly by the religiously and mystically inclined, and it was this circumstance that motivated some Jewish authors to use this literary form for their own propagandistic purposes. Beginning in the second century B.C.E., they composed and circulated "Sibylline Oracles" written, like their pagan prototypes, in Greek hexameters. These contained prophecies, put into the mouth of the old Sibyl, about the past and future fate of the world (presenting for the early ages much Greek mythological material), threatening the pagan peoples with punishment for their idolatry and immorality, warning them to repent before it was too late, and upholding the faithfulness of the Jewish people to God's law and their freedom from unnatural vices. (With the emergence of Christianity, Christian authors in their turn produced additional "Sibylline Oracles," in order to impress their new faith upon the Greco-Roman world.)

A few other Hellenistic Jewish apologetic works under the mask of pagan authorship can be mentioned. There was an apocalyptic-eschatological treatise attributed to Hystaspes, the legendary father of King Darius; there was a book *About the Jews*, whose unknown author attributed it to the late fourth-century B.C.E. Hecataeus of Abdera, a pro-Egyptian political and philosophical propagandist; and there was the famous *Letter* of the pagan Aristeas to Philocrates, already referred to; which tells about the translation of the Bible into Greek. More important, however, than the legend of the seventy-two translators is the purposive intent of the *Letter of Aristeas*. This presents Judaism as identical in the main with Greek philosophy, but characteristically tries to bridge the gap between the Greek and Jewish religions by arguing that originally all peoples had one God, like the Jews, but called him by different names. Among the Greeks he was known as Zeus; therefore, Zeus is identical with the Jewish God. Having thus established a common ground between the two religions on purely Jewish terms, Aristeas has no qualms in suggesting that the Jews must acquire a Greek education and abandon the barbarous features of their character, while continuing to cleave with all their hearts to the Law of Moses which contains lofty philosophical elements. This will enable the two peoples, Greeks and Jews, to draw closer together in everyday life.[54] While Aristeas is willing to make every formal concession to Hellenism, he draws the line when it comes to monotheism and the Jewish Law, the ultimate essence of Judaism. In general, Aristeas reads like a panegyric on Jewish Law, Jewish wisdom, and Jewish religion. Incidentally this *Letter* is one of the few writings of this type extant in toto.

Another work that survived is the "Warning Poem," which calls in 230 hexameters for morality and belief in one God, in an entirely Biblical manner. Its unknown author was a Hellenistic Jew, who attributed his poem to the sixth-century B.C.E. moralistic poet Phocylides of Miletus. Yet another anonymous Jewish Hellenist wrote a collection of proverbs which are strongly reminiscent of the Biblical Book of Proverbs and the apocryphal Wisdom of Yeshu'a ben Sira, and which he attributed to the Attic comedian Menander who had become famous as the author of proverbs.

In conclusion, we should also mention the numerous interpolations of pro-Jewish passages into the works of the most famous Greek poets. This was evidently done by Hellenistic Jews who were trying to demonstrate that the best Greek minds were favorably inclined toward the Jews, Jewish Law, and Jewish wisdom. These attempts date from the third century B.C.E. and consist of verses attributed to Homer, Hesiod, Linus, Aeschylus, Sophocles, Euripides, the comedian Philemon, Menander, Diphilus, and even Orpheus himself.

The result of these manifold Jewish efforts to present Judaism in a form acceptable to Greeks and Romans was that conversion to Judaism became a widespread phenomenon in the Hellenistic world, and that by the early first century C.E. there were many Jews, as well as full or half proselytes, in all parts of the Roman empire. The large number of Jews was due chiefly to proselytism, which, in turn, would not have come about had not the Jews influenced the pagan world with their rich crop of Hellenistic literature.

16. Why No Science?

So far this chapter has described what the Jews adopted from Hellenism and the many fields of Greek culture in which they actively participated. To complete the picture, a few words at least must be said about those areas of Greek civilization from which the Hellenized Jews were conspicuously absent. There were two such areas: that of the sciences and that of language studies.

The scientific breakthrough accomplished by the Greeks is often referred to as the Greek "miracle." Although George Sarton has emphasized that it "was prepared by millennia of work in Egypt, Mesopotamia and possibly in other regions," [55] the Greek systematic approach to scientific problems remains miraculous in its uniqueness. The development of Greek science reached its zenith in the Hellenistic age, just as the preceding two centuries, circa 500–300 B.C.E., were the great classical age of Greek philosophy, literature, and art. While Athens continued in the Hellenistic age "to exercise its special authority in philosophy . . . in philology and the mathematical sciences Alexandria reigned without serious challenge." [56] Most of the great Hellenistic Greek scientists lived and worked in Alexandria which, with its Museum and Library, became the intellectual capital of the world in the third century B.C.E. This was the place and the time of Euclid, Archimedes, Diophantus of Alexandria, Aristarchus of Samos, the engineers Philo and Ctesibius, Eratosthenes, and Apollonius of Perga, who (together with a few of their colleagues elsewhere within the realm of eastern Hellenism) constituted a unique galaxy of great mathematicians, geometricians, geographers, physicists, astronomers, and engineering scientists. Nor was this outburst of scientific productivity confined to the third and second centuries B.C.E. in which all the men just named lived. It continued for at least three centuries thereafter; witness Hero of Alexandria, the great first-century C.E. mathematician, physicist, geometrician, and engineer, and Claudius Ptolemy (c. 100–178 C.E.), the famous astronomer, mathematician, and geographer.[57]

Given this scholarly environment—to which must be added the influence of the Alexandrian Library, the biggest and greatest in the ancient world—it is puzzling indeed that the Hellenized Jews, whose great center was in the same city, took no part at all in this remarkable Greek scientific activity.

The only science, or rather pseudo-science, in which the Jews took sufficient interest to claim Biblical origin for it was astrology: some Hellenistic Jewish authors maintained that Enoch was its inventor, and that Abraham taught it to the Egyptian king Pharethothes.[58] Apart from this single exception, the entire rich literary output of the Jewish Hellenizers contains not a single contribution, as far as we know, to mathematics, geometry, geography, astronomy, physics, mechanics—the subjects which stood in the center of the scientific attention of their pagan Hellenized contemporaries.

No less astounding is the fact that the Jewish Hellenists did not even write medical studies, although the practice of medicine was well established among them, and quite a few Hellenistic cities in Asia (e.g., Ephesus and Venosa) had Jewish "chief physicians" in their employ.[59] Nor did they take any interest in grammar, whether Hebrew, Aramaic, or Greek, although Alexandria was a great center of Greek grammarians, linguists, philologists, and lexicographers, from Zenodotus (who flourished c. 325 B.C.E.) through Callimachus (c. 310–c. 240 B.C.E.) and Aristophanes of Byzantium (c. 257–c. 180 B.C.E.), to Apollonius of Alexandria (second century C.E.), all four of whom, incidentally, were associated with the great Alexandrian Library.

It is tempting to speculate on the possible reasons for this total absence of Jews from the domain of the sciences and linguistics at a time when they participated so intensely in literature, historiography, and philosophy. It would seem that the Hellenistic Jewish intellectuals were attracted only to those fields of Greek cultural activity in which their works could be used for demonstrating, upholding, and arguing Jewish excellence. They tried their hand at the epic and the drama, because in these fields they could, as they actually did, write about great Jewish historical figures in epic and dramatic form; they wrote books of history because they could, and did, give inspiring accounts of the Jewish past; and they produced volumes of philosophy which they used as vehicles for convincing the Hellenistic world of the unique values of Jewish monotheism, morality, and law. By the same token, they were not attracted to the sciences and linguistics, because any contribution they could have made to them, while it might have advanced the discipline in question, would not have served the Jewish cause, the one overriding purpose to which they were committed. We shall be in a better position to appreciate the remarkable quality of this self-enforced intellectual ethnocentrism after we become acquainted with the great change that transpired in the so-called Spanish Golden Age. In it the greatest Jewish minds divided their attention between subjects of Jewish interest (where they continued the tradition of their Talmudic and Hellenistic forebears) and secular subjects in many a scientific field, striking out into what for the Jews had been *terrae incognitae*.

17. Conclusion

This rapid survey of the main *oeuvres* of Hellenistic Judaism leads to one important conclusion about the relative predominance of the Jewish and the Greek elements in the minds of those who produced them. In form, style, and character, all of these works were Greek; the architectural styles the Hellenized Jews employed were Greek; the decorations with which they embellished buildings and objects were Greek; the language in which they expressed their ideas was Greek; the literary categories—history, epic, drama, philosophy, apologetics, propagandistic writings, etc.—to which they resorted were Greek. In all formal aspects of their cultural output the Hellenized Jews were as Greek as the best Greek-born and Greek-descended representatives of Greek culture.

But when we shift our attention from the *how* to the *what*, from the form to the content, the husk to the core, we find something entirely different. Surprisingly, in each of the manifold artistic, literary, poetic, and philosophical works left behind by the Hellenized Jews, the core, content, and intent are exclusively Jewish. They used Greek architectural styles to build Jewish places of worship; they employed Greek decorative motifs, figures, and images to embellish their Jewish religious structures—synagogues, cemeteries, catacombs, monuments; and they acquired a mastery of writing Greek-style history, epic, drama, and philosophy for the one purpose of conveying in them Jewish ideas, of presenting in them the greatness of Jewish history, the truth of Jewish religion, the value of Jewish Law and morality. The Jewishness of the Jewish Hellenists comes through in all their works like a leitmotif that was not allowed to be absent from anything they produced. As far as we know, there is not a single work left behind by the Jewish Hellenists which was not filled by a Jewish content, not motivated by a Jewish conviction, not intended to be "good for the Jews." Therefore—in marked contrast to the works which the Jews were to produce subsequently in the Spanish Golden Age and later—the totality of the Hellenistic Jewish opus was fundamentally Jewish and was not only, as Tcherikover put it, "a hymn in praise of the one, unique and supreme God," [60] but also a panegyric on Jewish religious and moral supremacy.

A specific form in which the Hellenized Jews presented their views about
Jewish superiority was the argument that Jewish culture was older than
Greek; in fact that it was the oldest, and that the best of Greek knowledge
was derived from Jewish sources. The Jewish historians and apologists were
able to make such a good case for this ethnocentric idea that it became accepted by some of the keenest Greek minds. Thus Alexander Polyhistor in
the first century B.C.E. reiterates this idea, which crops up after him repeatedly in the works of respectable scholars throughout the ages, including
French and English savants in the sixteenth to eighteenth centuries.[61]

In his synopsis of the Hellenistic Jewish literature, Emil Schürer, the outstanding Protestant theologian and historian of the Jews in the Hellenistic
period, came to the conclusion that

> although the Jews, like other Near Eastern peoples, became Greek, at the
> same time they demonstrated that Judaism was something different from the
> pagan religions. Its inner *power of resistance* was infinitely greater than that of
> the latter. While the other Oriental religions dissolved in the general religious
> intermingling of the times, Judaism, as far as its core was concerned, endured
> unbroken. It held fast, strictly and unshakably, to the oneness of God and his
> aniconic worship; as well as to the belief that God's ways with mankind lead to
> a goal of bliss. In this unwavering adherence to the Jewish core as against the
> pressure of Hellenism it proved its superior religious strength.[62]

6

Hebrew Arabesque

The Talmud, that huge masterpiece produced by the joint effort of hundreds of sages through hundreds of years, bridges the time gap that separates the Hellenistic and the Muslim-Arab periods in Jewish history. The work of the Tannaim, the early teachers whose legal opinions and decisions are contained mainly in the Mishna, began in the first century B.C.E. and continued until about 200 C.E. The Amoraim, who supplied the bulk of the Talmudic text built around the Mishna, lived from circa 200 to circa 500 C.E. They were followed by the Saboraim, the principals and scholars of the Babylonian Talmudic academies, who for another two centuries were engaged in editorial work on the Talmud.[1] Thus the completion, or final codification, of the Talmud, which was to remain the mainstay of Jewish religion until the Enlightenment, took place about half a century after Babylonia (i.e., Iraq) had become Islamized and Arabized. In resisting submergence in the Hellenistic world, the Jews had only the Bible to lean upon; in maintaining their identity in the face of the new challenge by the young and dynamic religious culture of Islam, which in addition was as strictly monotheistic as Judaism, they could base themselves on the broad expanses of Talmudic law and lore. Secure in their rabbinic Judaism, the Jews under Islam had no qualms about following the Arabs, or marching abreast with them, into each and every cultural venture, including the sciences which had remained a closed territory for the Hellenized Jews.

1. *The* Dhimmis

In contrast to the Israelite-Canaanite encounter, which was localized in and on the borders of the Land of Israel, and to the Jewish-Hellenistic encounter, which took place mainly in Egypt (Alexandria) and Palestine, the encounter of the Jews with the Muslim Arabs had as its stage the far-flung domains which, by the early eighth century, had been conquered by the

Arabs. The Arab conquest, it has often been remarked, was the most phenomenal in speed and extent to have occurred in the history of man. When
Muḥammad died, in 632, he was the recognized leader only of the towns and
tribes of the Arabian peninsula. Eighty years later, the Umayyad caliphs
were in control of the entire Middle East (except Anatolia), from the Indus
River and Transoxania in the east to the Mediterranean in the west, as well
as of the whole of North Africa from the Red Sea to the Atlantic, and were in
the process of conquering Spain. The Arab empire stretched to the incredible distance of some 4,500 miles from east to west. In contrast to Alexander's
empire, which fell apart at his death, the Arab empire remained united
under the Umayyads and the Abbasids until 945, although in the latter part
of this period the caliphs' control over the outlying parts was more nominal
than effective. Another difference between Alexander's Hellenistic empire
and the Arab empire was that, in the former, both the Greek religion and
the Greek language, imposed upon the conquered countries, disappeared
sooner or later; after the Arab conquests, on the other hand, Islam remained
the dominant religion in all areas ever to come under Arab rule (with the exception of Spain), and Arabic remained the dominant tongue from the Tigris
and the Persian Gulf in the east to the Atlantic coast of North Africa in the
west.

In all parts of this huge territory Jews had lived for many centuries prior to
its conquest by the Arabs, in some places since early antiquity. A rapid rundown of their major concentrations with settlement dates shows that from
Palestine, where they had lived since the thirteenth century B.C.E., they
spread to Babylonia (Iraq) in the eighth, to Persia in the sixth, to Syria and
Egypt in the third, and to Arabia in the second. In North Africa and Spain
they settled in the first century C.E. Everywhere they established communities of their own, and constituted a people, or a religio-ethnic group, which
differed emphatically from the majority population and was a group *sui generis* in relation to other ethnic groups.

The Arab policy toward the conquered populations was clear-cut. If they
were idolaters, they were forced to convert to Islam under the pain of death;
if they were monotheists, they were reduced to the status of *dhimmis*, subject peoples, and allowed to retain and continue in their religious customs,
with certain restrictions, in exchange for a special head tax, *jizya*. In this way
the Jews, the Christians, and the Zoroastrians were enabled to retain internal autonomy, to follow their own traditions, and to constitute separate
religio-ethnic communities within the *Dār ul-Islām*, or House of Islam.

The restrictions placed upon the *dhimmis* were more in the nature of an-
noyances and indignities than serious disabilities. Their general intent was to
keep the *dhimmis* in a lower status compared to the Muslims. Thus, while
the *dhimmis* were welcomed and, indeed, often pressured to convert to
Islam, no Muslim was allowed to embrace a *dhimmi* religion. A Muslim man

could marry a *dhimmi* woman, but a *dhimmi* man was not allowed to marry a
Muslim woman. A *dhimmi* could not own Muslim slaves. If a *dhimmi* was
murdered, the blood-wit payable to his kin was half (or two-thirds) that due
for a Muslim. *Dhimmis* had to wear a distinguishing article of dress, such as a
special belt; they were forbidden to wear fine clothes or to own or ride noble
steeds, and they had to cut their forelocks. They were not allowed to construct or even reconstruct places of worship and were subject to many more
such restrictions. It must, however, be mentioned that these restrictions
were often disregarded by the Muslim authorities. Nevertheless, under pressure by a generally contemptuous Muslim majority, the *dhimmis* in every
country conquered by the Arabs gradually lost in numerical strength. Within
a few centuries, the Zoroastrians were reduced to an insignificant minority
on the eastern peripheries of the Muslim world. Christians remained as sizable communities only in Egypt (the Copts) and in Lebanon (Maronites, Orthodox, and others). Only the Jews maintained themselves more tenaciously;
while their numbers were relatively small everywhere, they remained ubiquitous in all parts of the Arab world until the establishment of Israel in 1948.

In the classical centuries of Islam only one persecution of the *dhimmis* has
been recorded: it was perpetrated by the Fāṭimid caliph al-Ḥākim
(985–1021), who was a visionary, cruel and unbalanced. His excesses were
directed mostly against Christians. As for the Jews, one can say that their
position in the House of Islam was, on the whole, much better than in Christian Europe. Even though in the later Middle Ages the Arab attitude toward
them hardened, they never experienced large-scale persecutions or expulsions, let alone massacres like those carried out by the Crusaders and others
in Western and Central Europe, by Cossacks in Eastern Europe, and by the
Nazis in the countries under their control.

Despite their *dhimmi* status, and the Qur'ānic sanction of keeping them
low and separate, the Jews assimilated to Arab culture and attained positions
of influence in royal courts, in scientific, scholarly, and literary circles, in internal and international commerce. This led to a social and cultural assimilation to the Arab majority which, however, was largely checked by the Jews'
stubborn adherence to their ancestral faith and countered by an intense
pride in their own religio-national tradition.

In Spain, the country we are concentrating on in this chapter, the Almohad invasion of 1136 made the Jews experience what was probably the worst
that has ever happened to them under Arab rule. But when life in Arab-
dominated Andalusia became nearly impossible for them for several decades,
they found a friendly reception in the north, in the expanding Christian
domains of Castile and Aragon. Then the tide turned, and Jews fleeing from
Christian persecution again found refuge in the Muslim realm, in Spain and
overseas.

Quite a specific aspect of Jewish life in Spain was the great love the Jews had for the country as such. Their poets never tired of singing of the beauty of the land. The same Y'huda haLevi who poured his longing for Zion into a magnificent ode in many other poems extolled the beauties of Spain. Others mourned in somber dirges the sorrows of living in exile, but sang jubilantly of the pleasures of the fields, mountains, gardens, and rivers of Spain. For many of them, "exile" meant leaving Arab Spain and living in the Christian north. We shall have occasion to get acquainted with this feature when speaking of the Spanish Hebrew poetry. Even at the very end, when Jews and Marranos had to flee from Spain and the claws of the Inquisition, they still carried in their hearts the love of Spain, as expressed in a Spanish poem Luis de Carvajal wrote when he was forced to embark for Mexico (where, incidentally, the Inquisition caught up with him):

> *Adios Espagna, tierra bonita*
> *Tierra de la consolation . . .*

A word must be said here about a particularly tragic feature in the life of the Spanish Jews. For centuries, while they lived in both the Muslim south and the Christian north, these two inimical powers were intermittently engaged in fighting each other. The Jews participated in these wars on both sides; on occasion, brother faced brother across the battle lines. The fact that these wars appear to us as minor skirmishes did not diminish the pain and tragedy for those involved. Not until World War I, and then of course on a vastly larger scale, would Jewish combatants again find themselves in such a situation.

2. Arabization and the Use of Romance

One of the most reliable measures of the cultural rapprochement of the Jews to the Gentile population in any country is language. Where the rapprochement was strong, the language of the country rapidly became the mother tongue of the Jews; where such a relationship did not develop, the Jews, while learning the local language sufficiently to be able to communicate with the Gentiles, retained their old language. An example of the latter case is the retention of Yiddish for centuries by the Jews in East Europe. The former development could be observed in the Arab world. Take, for instance, the Jews of Babylonia (Iraq). For centuries prior to the Arab conquest (633–642), they spoke Aramaic, in which language they produced their magnum opus, the Talmud. In pre-Islamic times, al-Ḥira, to the southeast of present-day Najaf in southwestern Iraq, was the capital of the small Arab Lakhmid state and attracted Arab poets, but that was a strictly local phenomenon. After the Arab conquest, the linguistic Arabization of the country (except for its northern, Kurdish-inhabited part) proceeded apace; and under the Umayyads (661–750), although their capital was Damascus, Iraq became the most important Arab intellectual and literary center. The rapid Arabization of the Aramaic-speaking Jews of Iraq may have been aided by the settling in Kufa, the capital of 'Alī, of Jews who were expelled from Arabia (about 641). In any case, already in the early eighth century, a Jewish physician, Masarjuwayh of Basra, was translating medical writings from Greek and Syriac into Arabic and also writing original Arabic medical works. [2]

Masarjuwayh's work can be considered the beginning of Jewish literary activity in Arabic. In all the other countries conquered by the Arabs, the Jews rapidly adopted Arabic as their colloquial, producing in it a literature which is so vast that it is impossible to survey it within the confines of one chapter, just as it is impossible to review the other, non-literary, cultural results of the Arab-Jewish encounter in all the far-flung domains of the Arab world. This is why we have to concentrate on one country in which the cultural contacts between the two peoples were most intense and most fruitful, and on the few centuries in which the Jewish cultural flowering reached its full bloom. I am, of course, referring to the famous Golden Age of Spain.

As the conquest of Iraq in the East, so that of Spain in the West (711) was followed by a rapid Arabization of the country, although in the rural areas Romance dialects survived. As for the Jews, Arabic became, within a short time, not only their everyday colloquial but the language in which they wrote their scholarly works: philosophical treatises, mathematical and other scientific studies, books of Hebrew grammar, and even many of their halakhic studies. The only holdout against this pervasive Arabization was, as we shall see, poetry.

With the devastation wrought in the twelfth century by the invasion of the North African Almohads into Spain, the Jewish center of gravity gradually shifted northward. The Christian Spanish rulers, who at the same time were engaged in their own energetic campaign to carry the *reconquista* as far south as possible, welcomed the Jews who fled from the Almohad persecution. Thus Spanish gradually (in fact, very gradually) replaced Arabic as the Jewish colloquial in the expanding Christian-held areas of Spain, until a time was reached when the rabbis could term Spanish "our language." [3] Now the foundations were laid for Ladino, which was to be retained as their mother tongue by the Sephardi Jews down to the twentieth century.

The major difference between the history of the Jews in Muslim Spain and in Christian Spain was that while in the former Jewish life was interrupted periodically by persecutions, in the latter the persecution of Jews was interrupted from time to time by peaceful periods. Perhaps this is one of the reasons why Spanish was so slow in being adopted by the Jews as their colloquial, and why it never became the medium for Jewish scientific work. Even centuries after the transfer of political control to the Christian rulers, the

Jews in many parts of Spain remained predominantly Arabic-speaking, and it is known that, for example, in Toledo, which was reconquered by the Christian Spaniards from the Arabs in 1085, the Jews still spoke and wrote a colloquial Arabic as late as the fourteenth century. However, a decline of Arabic as the vehicle for Jewish scholarly work did set in, and from circa 1200 halakhic works were no longer written in Arabic but in Hebrew.

Hebrew seems also to have been the language of instruction in the yeshivot. As for their colloquial, only from about 1400 did the Jews adopt the local languages: Catalan in the northeast, Portuguese in the southwest, and Castilian Spanish in all the rest of the peninsula, with the exception of the small strip of land along the southern Mediterranean coastline which until 1492 remained the Moorish kingdom of Granada, and in which, of course, the Jews continued to speak Arabic. Jewish scholars acquired a sufficient knowledge of the Romance colloquials, as well as of Latin, to be able to maintain contact with kings and authorities, and to conduct religious disputations in these languages. They even translated into them important Hebrew religious works. Thus, in the twelfth century, at the behest of Archbishop Raimundo (d. 1152), they translated Arabic scientific and philosophical works into Castilian; and in the thirteenth, at the initiative of Alfonso X of Castile (r. 1252–84), who wanted to make the Castilian colloquial into a language of culture and literature, they cooperated with Christian scholars in translating the Bible into Castilian, as well as translating Arabic scientific writings (including astronomical tables). The thirteenth century was also the epoch in which the Jews began to translate Arabic, Latin, and Spanish works into Hebrew.[4]

As for original works by Jews in Spanish, they were conspicuous by their almost total absence. The little they did write consisted of polemical works, which, if they dared to write them at all, had to be written in Spanish in order to reach the Christian derogators of Judaism for whom they were intended. Also, they were written in a late period, within a century of the expulsion of the Jews from Spain. Thus the philosopher Ḥasdai Crescas (1340–1410), who wrote his major work, the *Or Adonai* (*Light of the Lord*), in Hebrew, composed in 1398 a *tratado* (tractate) in Spanish entitled *Refutation of the Cardinal Principles of the Christians* (extant only in the Hebrew translation of Joseph ibn Shem Tov). In it Crescas presents the reasons which held the Jews fast to their ancestral faith. Another Spanish work of similar intent was written by the pupil of Crescas, Joseph Albo (c. 1380–c. 1444), known for his major philosophical treatise written in Hebrew and entitled *'Iqqarim* (*Principals*), detailing the fundamentals of Judaism. Albo was one of the Jewish participants in the great and protracted religious debate held at Tortosa in 1413–14, and it is possible that his polemical treatise had some connection with his role in this disputation. Apart from these translations and polemics, Jews wrote little in Spanish—nothing more than a few rather insignificant poems (written in the eleventh century). No new discovery has supplied a reason to change Steinschneider's judgment made a century ago to the effect that there was no Jewish literature in Spanish prior to the 1492 expulsion.[5]

In this connection a word must be said of Jewish literature in Ladino. Ladino is the language which originated among the Jews in Christian Spain prior to the expulsion (1492), beginning, it seems, with the thirteenth century, when the earliest translations into it were produced. Only after the expulsion did Ladino reach its full development, containing a medieval Castilian base element and numerous Hebrew endings (suffixes), as well as a Hebrew vocabulary of "culture words." Like Yiddish, Judeo-Arabic, and Judeo-Persian, Ladino is written in Hebrew script. In the sixteenth century, the Bible was translated into Ladino, as were Hebrew exegetical and ethical works, moral handbooks, and prayer books. Soon original works in Ladino began to appear, and about the same time also a certain amount of Jewish literature in Spanish began to be produced by Sephardi communities in the West, mainly in Amsterdam.[6]

There is some similarity between the attitude of the Iberian Jews to Spanish and that of their ancestors of more than a thousand years earlier to Latin. In those earlier days the Jews eagerly adopted Greek, the language of the dominant culture of Hellenism, both as their colloquial and as their medium of literary expression. Some two centuries later, after Rome had extended its dominion over the entire Hellenized world, Latin became the colloquial of the Jews in many parts of the Roman empire. Yet they did not switch to Latin for whatever literary work they engaged in. At a time when Latin literature just had its golden age behind it, when it could boast of Cicero, Lucretius, Varro, Virgil, Horace, Ovid, and many others, the Jewish authors continued to write in Greek. In fact it was in this age, the first century C.E., that they produced their most important works in Greek. And in quite a similar way, while Spanish replaced Arabic as the Jewish colloquial in Spain, the Jews in Christian Spain continued to write in Arabic; with the exception of translations from Arabic into Spanish, they did not use Spanish as a vehicle of literary expression until after their expulsion from Spain in 1492.

But to return to Muslim Spain, there the Arabization of the Jews was total. Of course, they also knew Hebrew, and the instruction of children in the Holy Tongue was a prime concern of all communities, even the smallest ones. Education was extended, occasionally at least, to girls as well as boys, and among the teachers some women were found. However, for three centuries, from the tenth to the twelfth, Arabic was not only the Jewish colloquial but also the primary vehicle for Jewish literary and scholarly activities. It was the language in which the earliest systems of Jewish philosophy were formulated, in which ethical, theological, and halakhic works were written, as were Talmudic commentaries, codes of law, and rabbinic responsa. And, needless to say, Arabic was the medium of the Jewish contributions to the sciences, such as mathematics, astronomy, medicine. When the Jewish centers in Muslim Spain were destroyed under the Almohads, the knowledge of Arabic remained preserved in northern Spain, under Christian rule. An important school of Jewish translators arose, who rendered Arabic works into Hebrew and Spanish, as well as into Latin; the latter, though it never again became a Jewish language as it was in antiquity, was mastered by members of the Jewish élite for practical as well as scholarly reasons. Thus they embarked on the great historic task—subsequently carried on by Italian Jews—of making Greek and Arabic science accessible to Christian Europe.[7]

It has repeatedly been discussed why, as against all their other varied literary products in Arabic, the Jews in Spain wrote their poetry in Hebrew.[8] There can be no doubt that rather than force the straitjacket of rigid Arabic meters on the Hebrew language, it would have been simpler and easier for the Jewish poets to write in Arabic. Arabic, after all, was their mother tongue and everyday colloquial; and they were unquestionably more fluent in it than in Hebrew, which they studied in school as a sacred but second language, and in which only the most thoroughly educated could acquire a sufficient mastery to produce poetry. If they nevertheless chose Hebrew as the sole medium for their poems (with a few insignificant exceptions), there must have been weighty reasons for doing so. Three of these seem to have been most decisive.

First, a tradition of Hebrew poetry had existed among the Jews from times which antedated the Muslim-Arab impact. True, those old Hebrew poets were mere *paytanim*, whose liturgical poems, the *piyyutim*, were written in a forced and artificial Hebrew and fell short in every respect of the accomplished Hebrew poetry of Muslim Spain. But they nevertheless constituted a connecting link between the great Biblical poetry of the Psalms and the prophets on the one hand, and the period in which, following the Arab example, the Jewish poets in Spain began to give poetical expression to their thoughts and feelings.

The second reason seems more important, and curiously, it again had to do with Arab influence. The Arabs' intense love of, and great pride in, their language has often been commented upon.[9] The Qur'ān, believed by orthodox Muslims to this day to be the word of God dictated to Muḥammad by the angel Gabriel, is written in an Arabic style which they consider inimitable in its miraculous perfection. Although medieval Arabic poetry owes much to pre-Islamic Arabian poets, it leans heavily on the poetic language of the Qur'ān. Thus, to write poetry in Arabic meant, in a way, to pay homage to the linguistic glories of the Qur'ān. The same was not the case with prose, whether scholarly or philosophical, since in prose the language played a secondary role in relation to the thoughts or subjects discussed.

The Jews on their part were, of course, convinced that no other book could be compared in any way to the Bible. Seeing that the Arabs produced poetry in the language of their holy book, the Jews felt the desire to write their poems in the language of their own Holy Writ. Thus, while adopting Arabic prosody in toto, and while devoting a major part of their poetry to themes standard with the Arab poets, they wrote in Hebrew and, in fact, endeavored to utilize Biblical language and phraseology to the fullest.

The third factor is connected with, and derived from, the second. One of the important features of Arab poetry was the utilization of the so-called *musive* (or mosaic or emblematic) style. This consisted of frequently weaving Qur'ānic expressions, phrases, and even sentences into their poems, thereby enriching them with the peculiar allure of associations from that most sacred book. (The Arabs did not invent the musive style; it was used by the Greeks who, in the same way, wove Homeric expressions and phrases into their writings.)

The musive style had enormous appeal for the Hebrew poets, who were as saturated with the Bible, Biblical expressions, and quotable quotes as were their Arab colleagues with the Qur'ān. The Bible was available in Arabic translation, but that was for the ignorant. A poet, equally proud of his poetic ability and his learning, would not stoop to quoting it in Arabic; but quotes from the Bible in its original language could only be woven into poems written in the same language. The writings of the Spanish Hebrew poets are replete with Biblical names, symbols, images, metaphors, expressions, phrases, proverbs, and other references. It is no exaggeration to say that only a person well versed in the Bible could fully appreciate the great Hebrew poems of the Middle Ages.[10] (A few examples of the musive style will be given in the course of the discussion of Spanish Hebrew poetry.)

3. The Eastern Prelude

From the historical perspective afforded by the Jewish Golden Age in Spain, the intellectual, literary, and scholarly work done in Arab-dominated Iraq and other Eastern countries was nothing more than a prelude. Apart from the time element and the geographical distance between the two centers, the two periods are distinct also from a purely cultural point of view. In the East, although the burgeoning young Arab culture gave the Jews the required impetus to strike out into new fields from "the four cubits of the *Halakha*" to which they had devoted all their attention for half a millennium, the new territories they began to explore remained limited. They consisted, in the main, of codes of law, Midrashim, Talmudic dictionaries, analytical works on the Talmud, legal treatises; as well as liturgical poetry, the so-called *piyyut*, whose best-known practitioner was Eleazar Kallir (sixth or seventh century), a Babylonian; the beginnings of the vocalization and accentuation of the Biblical text; and the translation of the Bible into Arabic, the writing of commentaries on the Bible (in Arabic), and the compilation of Biblical vocabularies and religious philosophy (in Arabic). As we can see, whatever the nature of the scholarly fields into which the Iraqi Jews entered, they all had one thing in common: they were predominantly centered on Jewish religion, and primarily on the Bible. They were also characterized by the use of Arabic as the medium, with the exception of such works as liturgical poetry which was intended for synagogal use (written in Hebrew) and most of the responsa (written in Aramaic).

No other savant illustrates the scope and the limitations of Jewish literary and scholarly activity in the Arab East more clearly than Sa'adya Gaon, who was born in Dilaz, Upper Egypt, 882; became Gaon of Sura in 928; and died at Sura, 942. The genius of Sa'adya made him an outstanding contributor to every field he chose to enter, and his versatility was astounding.

The works of Sa'adya are so numerous that their listing alone would be too lengthy. But they can be subsumed under six headings, covering six areas, in each of which he not only proved himself an outstanding master but was an original innovator: exegesis, Hebrew linguistics, halakhic writings, liturgical works, philosophy of religion, and polemics. Sa'adya wrote almost all his works (except for his poems and some responsa) in Arabic, and the areas of research to which he devoted himself were also precisely those whose Muslim-Arab counterpart flourished in early Abbasid Iraq. Since his interest focused exclusively on Jewish religious subjects, he did not branch out into fields beyond the religious realm, where the Iraqi Muslim scholar-scientists who preceded him or were his contemporaries excelled. The same limitation was characteristic of the other Iraqi Jewish scholars, who also fell far short of Sa'adya in point of versatility.

The Muslim-Arab intellectual and scholarly activity under the Umayyads and their successors, the early Abbasids, in addition to areas centered on religion, comprised scientific fields which had no ostensible connection with Islam—mathematics, geometry, geography, astronomy, chemistry, physics, natural history, medicine, pharmacology (to mention only the major subjects), as well as the two pseudo-sciences of alchemy and astrology.

Of all these fields, the Jews entered only those which they could connect with their own religio-centric world view. This is what Sa'adya did, and the same limitation characterizes every other Jewish scholar of the Arab East with the exception of three or four whose chief interest was astrology or medicine, both old Jewish specializations. One of them was Mashallah (c. 770–820), whose original name was probably Manasseh, and who was one of the earliest astronomers and astrologers in Islam. He wrote numerous books, all in Arabic, but only one of them is extant in the original: a treatise on the prices of wares. Another book of his, on astronomy, became popular in the Middle Ages in Latin translation under the title *De scientia motus orbis*. The second was Sahl Rabbān al-Ṭabarī (i.e., Sahl, the rabbi of Tabaristan), who flourished in the early ninth century and was an astronomer and physician. He was the first translator into Arabic of Ptolemy's great astronomical encyclopedia, the *Almagest* (c. 800). His son 'Alī al-Ṭabarī converted to Islam in 835 and wrote a book dealing chiefly with medicine, but also with philosophy, meteorology, zoology, embryology, psychology, and astronomy, based on Greek and Hindu sources. He also wrote a defense of Islam and was the teacher of al-Rāzī. The third (or the fourth, if we count 'Alī al-Ṭabarī) was Abū 'Uthmān Sahl ibn Bishr ibn Ḥabīb ibn Hānī (or Hāyā), who flourished in Khurasan (northeast Persia) in 820–30 and wrote many treatises in Arabic on astrology, as well as a book on algebra. These few Jewish scientists in the Arab East are certainly a poor crop in relation to the great abundance of scientific investigators produced by the Muslims.[11]

This, then, was the Arab-inspired Jewish cultural baseline from which the Iberian Jews started out on their phenomenal intellectual journey in the tenth century. To be sure, aside from its poverty in the sciences, the baseline was quite impressive. In addition to halakhic studies, which were a direct continuation of the great Talmudic work of their immediate Babylonian predecessors, and to religious philosophy and polemics, which had been absent from the Jewish horizon since Hellenistic days, the cultural production of the Iraqi Jews comprised several entirely new fields—Biblical exegesis, Hebrew linguistics, and liturgical poetry. However, whether the areas of intellectual activity in which they engaged were a thousand years old or entirely new, the Iraqi Jewish scholars had one thing in common with both the Talmudists and the Hellenists: their interests were totally absorbed by the various, and expanding, areas of Jewish religious studies. With a few insignificant exceptions, everything they investigated, everything they wrote, was directly connected with a better understanding or a defense of their Jewish faith. For twenty-two centuries (c. 1300 B.C.E.–c. 900 C.E.), while the center of Jewish life was in the East—in Palestine, Egypt, and Babylonia-Iraq—all the intellectual efforts of the Jewish mind were thus devoted to religion. This dominant preoccupation seems to have immunized the Jews against all desire to follow the Gentiles into those fields of secular endeavor in which the latter excelled, whether in Hellenistic Alexandria or Muslim-Arab Iraq. The change which came about in this respect in the Jewish "Golden Age" in Iberia was as dramatic as it was seminal in implanting into the Jewish mind a totally new and, we may add right here, emphatically positive attitude toward science. It also fostered the practice of using one's intellectual powers for scholarly and scientific investigations which (despite all pious avowals to the contrary) had only the most tenuous connection with religion.

4. The Move to the West

In the transplantation of the Jewish intellectual center from the Arab East to the Arab West, Ḥasdai ibn Shaprut (c. 915–970) played a key role. Ḥasdai was minister and personal physician to the caliph ʿAbd al-Raḥmān III (r. 912–61), whose capital was in Cordova. Without the official title of vizier, Ḥasdai was in effect the caliph's minister of foreign affairs, who secured great diplomatic triumphs for the king in his dealings with the Christian rulers of Germany, northern Spain, and Byzantium. Although he himself was a scholar of no mean achievement, his fame in Jewish history rests primarily on two things: the diplomatic contact he established with the Jewish king of Khazaria, of which more need not be said in the present context; and his highly successful efforts in ushering in the Jewish Golden Age in the Iberian peninsula.

Prior to Ḥasdai, the Andalusian Jews, like the Jewish communities in all other parts of the world, were dependent intellectually and religiously on the great Talmudic academies of Sura and Pumbeditha in Babylonia. If a serious religious problem arose which the local rabbis were not equipped to resolve, they would send a question to the Gaon of either of those two central seats of Jewish learning, and in due course a learned answer would arrive. This relationship between the Babylonian schools and the Jewish world of the period gave rise to the rich responsa literature, which is an invaluable source for the cultural and social life of medieval Jewry. Now Ḥasdai brought from Babylonia to Andalusia a number of outstanding Jewish scholars, thereby securing religious and intellectual independence for Spanish Jewry from the Babylonian center and launching it on the great period of efflorescence known as the Golden Age. He appointed Moses ibn Ḥanokh (d. c. 965) rabbi of Cordova and principal of the Talmudic School. He brought to his court and supported two men who pioneered the study of the Hebrew language, M'naḥem Yaʿaqov ibn Saruq (c. 910–c. 970), and Dunash ibn Labrat (c. 920–c. 990), the latter a pupil of the famous Saʿadya Gaon. Because of disagreements over fine points in the science of Hebrew grammar, these two scholars were to become bitter enemies—a fact which had significant repercussions to be discussed later.

Following the example of the Arab princes and viziers who were great patrons of Arabic literature and scholarship, Ḥasdai made his house a gathering place for Hebrew writers and scholars—it was perhaps the first Jewish "salon" of intellectuals known in history—where writers would read aloud their poems and other works and hold literary debates. Among the Arabs a gathering held in the house of a prince or vizier was called *majlis*, the generic Arabic term for any kind of "sitting together," and correspondingly its

Jewish counterpart was called *moshav*, a literal Hebrew translation from the Arabic. Ḥasdai's protégés, for their part, followed the example of their Muslim colleagues in devoting themselves to two main pursuits: writing poetry (in Hebrew), and studying Hebrew grammar and writing up (in Arabic) the results of their linguistic investigations.[12]

From the tenth century on, the Jews of the Spanish Golden Age achieved marvels of intellectual productivity in every field in which Arab culture, with the incomparably greater manpower at its disposal, excelled. Religious studies, linguistics, philosophy, poetry, medicine, the sciences—all were cultivated, with remarkable success, by both Arabs and Jews. There was only one field into which the Jews did not follow the Arabs: historiography. Not only was history a neglected stepchild among the Spanish Jews, but according to Maimonides, the greatest intellect of medieval Jewry, to occupy oneself with history (and with music) was "a useless waste of time."[13] Judging from the almost total absence of any interest in history, as evidenced by the extreme paucity of studies which had even a remote affinity to historiography, the view of Maimonides must have been shared by all the Jewish scholars in medieval Spain.

This remarkable disinclination to historical studies becomes the more puzzling if one considers that historiography was a favorite subject of the Hellenized Jewish *literati* (cf. pages 83–85), and that the Arab environment in Spain and elsewhere contained at least as many stimulating examples of historical writing as did the Hellenistic. In fact, Muslim historiography was a rich and variegated scholarly field, which flourished wherever Arabic literature thrived, and which produced, from the ninth century on, fine annalistic works, serial biographies, local histories, etc., before it culminated in the unique figure of Ibn Khaldūn (d. 1406), the great Arab philosopher of history.[14]

And yet, the Spanish Jews (or the Jews in the Arab world in general) wrote next to nothing in history. The qualification "next to" is inserted because there were two Jewish scholars in Spain who lived three and a half centuries apart, each of whom did write a book which can qualify as historiography by stretching the concept to some extent. The earlier was Abraham ibn Daud (c. 1110–1180), an Andalusian astronomer, philosopher, and physician, whose book *Sublime Faith* (written in Arabic) anticipated in many respects and certainly influenced Maimonides' *Guide of the Perplexed*. Provoked by the Karaite heresy, Ibn Daud wrote a polemical work in 1161 to prove that rabbinical Judaism was justified by a claim of unbroken tradition from Moses down to his own time. This book, entitled *Sepher haQabbala* (*Book of Tradition*), although written in the rhetorical manner of the Arab traditionalists, nevertheless contains valuable information about the Gaonim and the Jews in Spain. The next quasi-historical work was written after the Spanish expulsion. It was by Abraham Zacuto (1450–after 1510), a professor of astronomy at Salamanca and Saragossa until the 1492 expulsion, after which he served

as court astronomer in Portugal but had to flee from there too, first to Tunis
and then to Turkey. While in Tunis he wrote his *Sepher Yuhasin* (*Book of
Genealogies*) in 1504, wishing, like Ibn Daud before him, to give an account
of the Oral Law as transmitted through the ages.

From the sixteenth century on, when Jews no longer lived on the Iberian
peninsula, their historiography is somewhat more abundant, but that is a development which does not concern us in the present context. We might,
however, mention in passing that these sixteenth-century and later works
were mostly chronicles of the persecutions of the Jews. They are best exemplified by the *Shevet Y'huda* ("Rod of Judah"), to which brief reference
was made above in Chapter 3. This is an account of sixty-four persecutions of
the Jews, of many disputations, and of Jewish customs. It was written in
Turkey by Solomon ibn Verga (flourished fifteenth to sixteenth centuries)
and completed by his son Joseph in Adrianople. Jewish historiography in the
full sense of the term began only after the Enlightenment, with Isaac Marcus
Jost, who wrote his history of the Jews in 1820–28, and his history of Judaism
in 1857–59; and with Heinrich Graetz, who wrote his great Jewish history in
1853–70.

It is tempting to speculate about the possible reasons for this abstention
from historiography by Spanish Jewish scholars who in all other fields of intellectual endeavor gave such a splendid account of themselves. The explanation offered for the absence of Jewish scientific writings in the Hellenistic
age—that the Jewish intellectuals were interested only in fields in which
their work could redound to the greater glory of Jews and Judaism—does not
hold good in the present case, first, because historiography is a most excellent vehicle for singing the praise of the people whose history is being
told; and second, because the Spanish Jews most eagerly threw themselves
into all kinds of scientific fields—mathematics, astronomy, geometry, etc.—
which had nothing to do with Judaism or with their devotion to it. Could the
fact that the Jews of Spain lived on both sides of the advancing and retreating
borderline between the Muslim and the Christian worlds have something to
do with it? And if so, how precisely? Or was it that the Jews, more than their
Arab neighbors, were absorbed in the issues and affairs, in the exigencies
and uncertainties, of their everyday life, and that therefore they devoted
themselves to what they considered to be pragmatic disciplines—whether
religious, philosophical, linguistic, or scientific—that is, knowledge which
had a bearing on their existence and its problems as history they felt had
not? I am sorry to have to admit that the answer eludes me.

5. Hebrew Linguistics

The central place that the Arabic language occupies in Arab culture and
Arab consciousness has often been commented upon.[15] It is a phenomenon

which has no counterpart in other cultures. In most countries conquered by
the Arabs, they imposed their language upon the native populations and instilled into them an attitude of reverence toward it. This veneration of Arabic
spread even into countries which were not Arabized but only converted to
Islam; in them, as in Arabic-speaking countries, studying the Qur'ān in the
original Arabic became a religious duty, and the prayers, based largely on
Qur'ānic passages, could be recited only in Arabic. The traditional prohibition of translating the Qur'ān into other languages has been observed by the
Muslims for centuries.

Compared to this veneration of and attachment to Arabic in the Muslim
world, the Jewish position on Hebrew was always a much more flexible one.
While the Jews considered Hebrew their Holy Tongue and referred to it as
the *l'shon haqodesh* (lit. "language of holiness"), they never clung to it with
anything comparable to the fervent, almost sensual, attachment the Arabs
had for Arabic. Well before the end of the Biblical period they substituted
Aramaic for Hebrew as their colloquial, incorporated several Aramaic parts
into the Bible, spoke and wrote in both Greek and Aramaic during the
Hellenistic and Talmudic periods, and switched readily to Arabic soon after
the Arab conquest of the countries in which most of them lived. Because of
these changes in their vernacular, they translated the Bible into Aramaic,
Greek, and Arabic (and later into many other languages as well). Moreover,
despite the general emphasis on prayers in Hebrew, Aramaic texts did enter
the Jewish prayer book, and the Mishna states that among the religious functions which can be performed "in any language" are the recitation of the
Sh'ma' (the most important Jewish prayer), all other prayers, and the after-
meal grace. This rule was followed in practice; thus we hear that in Hellenized Caesarea there were Jews in the fourth century who read the Sh'ma' in
Greek. Similarly, the "bedtime Sh'ma'" used to be recited in Ladino in
various Sephardi communities down to recent times.[16]

In their new Arab environment the Jews absorbed more than the Arabic
language itself. They assimilated the Arab attitude to Arabic and, after centuries of neglect or indifference, came to relate to their own Hebrew with
the same infatuation which the Arabs had for their language. The love of Arabic, together with the centrality of the "noble Qur'ān" in Muslim life, gave
the impetus to the Arabs to develop several sciences which focused on the
linguistic aspects of the Qur'ān and of the Arabic tongue in general. Within a
generation after the death of Muḥammad, hundreds of Arab scholars were
engaged in compiling Arabic dictionaries, investigating Arabic grammar and
writing books about it, and studying the Qur'ān from many different view-
points. As a result of this dedicated concentration, soon after the establishment of Islam the Qur'ān became the most thoroughly studied book in the
medieval world and Arabic the most thoroughly analyzed language. This is

the background against which one must view the sudden emergence of Jewish scholarly interest in Hebrew linguistics in the Arab environment.

The Jews could have developed Hebrew language studies a thousand years earlier, in the Hellenistic world in which the linguistic study of Greek played an important role. That they did not can be attributed to several areas in which the attitudes and culture of the Greek-speaking Hellenized Jews differed from those of the Arabic-speaking Jews. First of all, the Greek language was totally different from Hebrew, so that the methods developed for the study of Greek did not seem applicable to Hebrew. Secondly, Greek was the language of an all-pervasive pagan mythology; to treat the Hebrew language as the Greek scholars treated the texts of Homer, Hesiod, and other Greek authors must have appeared, to say the least, improper in the eyes of the Jews. Thirdly, Hebrew, while sacred, was a foreign tongue for the Hellenistic Jewish authors and became increasingly so after the Greek translation of the Bible, the Septuagint, was at their disposal. Even Philo, unquestionably the greatest of them, was far from knowing Hebrew thoroughly. Thus they had neither the incentive nor the ability to subject Hebrew to the linguistic scrutiny which the Greek scholars brought to bear upon their language.

In the Arab environment the situation was entirely different. In the first place, Arabic and Hebrew are two closely related languages—this much was clear to anybody who had a smattering of both. The similarities in the vocabulary and grammatical structure of the two languages are readily apparent. The methods developed by the Arabs for a grammatical and lexicographic study of their language did therefore seem almost automatically applicable to Hebrew. Second, although the Jews did not accept Muḥammad as a prophet and the Qur'ān as the revealed word of God, they recognized in the Qur'ān a spirit kindred to their own and found in it many passages and stories taken from the Bible. Hence, they felt that there could be no objection to applying to the Bible and the Hebrew language a linguistic science developed on the basis of the Qur'ān. Third, between the Hellenistic and the Arab periods intervened the development of the Hebrew *Masora*—the science of vocalizing the unvoweled Hebrew text of the Bible, and thereby fixing uniform rules for its pronunciation. This inevitably brought about an interest in the grammatical rules that underlay the readings. And lastly, in contrast to the Hellenized Jews, among the Jews in the Arab age Hebrew was a living tongue in which they produced a body of poetry and prose literature. These works required linguistic innovations which could be accomplished only on the basis of a knowledge of the grammatical rules of Hebrew. Thus, the creation of a science of the Hebrew language became an inevitable part of the Hebrew culture which developed in the Muslim-Arab environment.

After some hesitant beginnings in the Arab East, Hebrew linguistic studies matured suddenly in the West. An early forerunner was the North African philologist Y'huda ibn Quraysh (born at Tahort, Algeria; flourished in the ninth century). He wrote a dictionary and a book on the commandments which did not survive. But his claim to fame rests solidly on a short treatise in Arabic in the form of a letter addressed to the Moroccan Jewish community of Fez, which is the earliest contribution to comparative Semitic linguistics. In it Ibn Quraysh compares Biblical Hebrew with Aramaic, Mishnaic Hebrew, and Arabic and recognizes the affinity of these languages, their derivation from one source, and the fact that they are all subject to the same linguistic laws.

In the tenth century, M'nahem ibn Saruq and Dunash ibn Labrat, both of whom were mentioned earlier (page 107), advanced Hebrew linguistics considerably. The final breakthrough was accomplished by Y'huda ben David Hayyuj, who was born about 950 in Fez and went at an early age to Cordova. There he became a pupil of Ibn Saruq and resided until his death in the early eleventh century. Thoroughly familiar with Arabic grammatical literature, Hayyuj applied to the Hebrew language the theories developed by Arab linguists and established the basic grammatical law according to which all Hebrew verbal stems consist of three consonantal root letters. Characteristically, his works were all written in Arabic, although it was thanks to their Hebrew translation that they became the lasting foundation of Hebrew grammar to this day.

While Hayyuj is thus the father of modern Hebrew grammar, it fell to another Cordovan Jewish scholar, who lived a generation later, to complete what he had begun. Abu 'l-Walid Merwan (Yona) ibn Jannah (b. at Cordova, between 985 and 990; d. at Saragossa before 1050) was by profession a physician, but all his works dealt with the Hebrew language, except for one medical book on simple remedies which is no longer extant. He wrote everything in Arabic, in which he had a graceful style; he knew also Latin, quoting the Vulgate. Although he criticized Hayyuj and corrected his mistakes, Ibn Jannah considered him his master and speaks of him with great respect. It was in the spirit of the time and place that Ibn Jannah should get involved in debates with Jewish, Muslim, and Christian scholars, the most memorable of which was his acrimonious dispute in Saragossa with the most illustrious pupil of Hayyuj, Samuel haLevi ibn Nagrela, better known as Samuel haNagid (993–1056). This was the great Granadan statesman, scholar, and poet who played a role in Andalusian Jewish culture similar to that of Hasdai ibn Shaprut a century earlier. A native of Cordova, Samuel studied rabbinics and was tutored in Hebrew philology by Hayyuj, and in Arabic, Latin, and Berber by non-Jewish masters. Starting out as a small businessman and letter writer, he became the secretary of the vizier of King Habus of Granada, then rose to the position of vizier himself, which he retained under the king's son and successor, Badis. As such he headed the army of Granada from 1038 to

1056 and led it to many victories. He also functioned as the authorized head, or Nagid, of the Granadan Jewish community and was a generous patron of Jewish scholars and poets, among them Solomon ibn Gabirol. Samuel was admired by both Arabs and Jews. The Arab poet Muntafil extolled him in verse, and the Hebrew poet Moses ibn Ezra said of him (in Arabic): "In Samuel's time the kingdom of science was raised from its lowliness, and the star of knowledge once more shone forth. God gave him a great mind which reached to the spheres and touched the heavens so that he might love Knowledge and those that pursued her, and that he might glorify Religion and her followers." [17]

As well as an astute statesman and a true Maecenas, Samuel was a scholar and a poet of no mean accomplishments. He wrote responsa, Talmudic decisions, an *Introduction to the Talmud* (in Hebrew) which was translated into Latin, and several poetical works. His poetry (in Hebrew), collected in his *Diwan*, includes devotional poems, aphorisms and maxims, and philosophical meditations, as well as war poems which are unique in Hebrew poetry. One of his poems was a veritable linguistic *tour de force*: addressed to King Ḥabus, it was written in seven languages. HaNagid, whose work in Hebrew grammar was only a small part of his many interests, had such reverence for his teacher Hayyuj that he organized a campaign against Ibn Jannaḥ for the latter's strictures on Hayyuj's writings, wrote a pamphlet against him, and caused others to publish treatises attacking him. All this, it should be noted, was done in Arabic. In his own grammatical works (which are lost) Samuel haNagid refrained from going beyond what his revered master Hayyuj laid down.

All these jealousies and partisanships, which began with the fight between Ibn Saruq and Ibn Labrat and their respective followers, resulted within one century (c. 950–1050) in the production of a solid Hebrew grammatical science that left very little for later generations to improve. Without the example of Arabic grammarians to follow and emulate, such a development could not have been accomplished.

6. Poetry and Swagger

However, it is not Hebrew grammar but Hebrew poetry for which the Spanish Golden Age receives most accolades from those who know Hebrew well enough to understand the exceptionally difficult style fancied by the Spanish Hebrew poetic school. We shall presently return to this issue, but first let us use a few figures to convey something of the phenomenal abundance of the poetic output in Hebrew in the medieval Arab environment. Israel Davidson, in his great *Thesaurus of Medieval Hebrew Poetry*, lists about 37,000 poems by close to 3,000 poets! And this excludes the so-called occasional poems. Perhaps even more impressive is the fact that at the peak of the Spanish Golden Age in the eleventh to twelfth century, the names of about fifty Hebrew poets are known, all of whom were contemporaries and who included such great masters as Samuel haNagid, Solomon ibn Gabirol, Moses ibn Ezra, Abraham ibn Ezra, and Y'huda haLevi. This unparalleled outflow of poetry has been well studied and general introductions to it are readily available. Translations into English, on the other hand, are few and poor—none of them comes even close to the beauty and strength of the original.[18]

Medieval Hebrew poetry reached its zenith only after it had adapted the syllabic meters developed by Arab poets several centuries earlier. This is the more remarkable since the Arabic meter is basically unsuited for the Hebrew language, as felt and expressed by Y'huda haLevi in his *Kuzari*.[19] The Arabic meter is based on the principle of selecting a fixed sequence of alternating short and long vowels for a line, and then repeating the same sequence in all the lines contained in the poem. In Arabic, which has short and long vowels, this works fine, lending a characteristic rhythm to the poem. In Hebrew, the difference in length between the short and the long vowels had long been lost; in adapting the Arabic meter, the Hebrew poets therefore established a system in which all full vowels were considered equivalent to the Arabic long vowels, while the Arabic short vowels were represented by the the the Hebrew *sh'va na'* (sh'va mobile), and *ḥataf* semi-vowels. In this system the first two lines of Y'huda haLevi's famous ode to Zion look as follows:

> Tzīyōn hălō tīsh'ălī līsh'lōm ăsīrāyīkh
> Dorshe sh'lomekh w'hem yeter adarayikh
> (*Zion, will you inquire about the peace of your captives*
> *Who send peace unto you, and they are the remnant of your flocks*)[20]

A simpler example is supplied by the liturgical hymn *Adon 'Olam*:

> Ădōn 'ōlām ăshēr mālākh
> B'terem kol y'tzir nivra
> (*Lord of the world who ruled*
> *Before all creatures were created*)

The man responsible for introducing this Arabic meter into Hebrew poetry was the linguist and poet Dunash ibn Labrat, whom we have already met. After some initial objection, the system was adopted by all Hebrew poets, and many centuries had to pass before Hebrew poetry liberated itself from its artificial shackles.

Equally important was the thematic influence exerted by Arabic on Hebrew poetry. Of the fewer than a dozen themes which dominate the rich poetic crop of the Spanish Hebrew Golden Age, all but one are in imitation of contemporary and earlier Arabic poetry. Love songs (often erotic and occasionally addressed to a beautiful youth), songs of friendship, wine songs, songs celebrating the beauty of nature, religious songs which speak of the love of God, poems describing personal misery and desolation, poems of invective, poems of self-praise, paeans for patrons—all these have their prototypes in the work of Arabic poets whom nearly all their Jewish colleagues sought to imitate.[21] The one theme which was original with the Hebrew poets was derived from their consciousness of the Galut, the Exile. The Spanish Hebrew poets often sing about Jewish suffering under Gentile rule, and about their longing for the Holy Land, Zion, and Jerusalem. These "Zionist" songs have, of course, no counterpart in Arabic poetry.

The most typically Arab of all the other themes are those of self-aggrandizement and self-praise, and of invective and denigration directed against opponents—two themes which, in many cases, are combined in a single poem. These sentiments also happen to be the most un-Jewish: they fly in the face of long-established Jewish religious traditions of modesty (one of the greatest praises the Bible has to tell about Moses is that "the man Moses was very humble"), and of consideration for the sensitivity of others (the Talmud says, "He who shames his fellow man is as if he had spilled his blood").[22] Hence, the frequent self-glorification and verbal abuse of opponents found in the verses of the Spanish Hebrew poets must be taken as even clearer evidence of the intensity of Arab environmental and literary influence than the presence of other Arab-derived poetic themes. In adopting the Arabic meter, rhythm, rhyme, stanza structure, and all the other themes enumerated above, the Hebrew poets were, at the utmost, guilty of superimposing foreign forms on their Hebrew verse; in so doing they did not violate any entrenched Jewish value. But this is precisely what they did when they echoed the spirit of pride and conceit with which Arabic poetry had been suffused ever since the famous *hijā* (poetic diatribe) of pre-Islamic times.[23] The influence of the environment must have been powerful indeed for them to do so. A few examples will show the form taken by this Arab-inspired poetic self-aggrandizement *cum* invective directed against others in the writings of the Hebrew poets of the Spanish-Arab Golden Age. We shall confine ourselves to the poems of those who are generally considered the greatest of the fifty near-contemporaries, for the greater a poet, the less one would expect him to be impelled either to self-praise or to diatribe. If these men succumbed to such temptations, one can assume that to sing in this vein was simply *de rigueur* in that day and age.

We have met Samuel haNagid—statesman, military leader, and Hebrew poet of considerable merit. His influence and power at the court and his many successes on the battlefield, one would think, should have rendered him immune to the poetic pettiness of his colleagues. But not so. These are some of the things Samuel haNagid has to say about himself in relation to others:

> Myriads listen to me like to their father,
> Hope for the words of my mouth like for rain,
> And admire, like a vision, my brain . . .

In another poem, Samuel haNagid compares himself to King David, the greatest warrior and the greatest poet of Biblical Israel:

> I work miracles in song; it'll be
> On the lips like the sweet song of David.
> It's cut from words like unto pearls
> and mined like pure gold from rocks.
> . . . .
> When its sound rises, people rejoice
> . . . .
> It lights the paths of those who walk by night
> And brings joy to all the suff'ring souls . . .

In this vein the poem, like other poems of haNagid, goes on and on. One more example:

> In my presence the wise are silent
> And the enlightened, as if beset by guilt
> Keep quiet and muzzle their mouths. [24]

Solomon ibn Gabirol (1021–53), the younger contemporary and protégé of Samuel haNagid, is considered one of the three greatest Hebrew poets of the Spanish Golden Age. He was, in addition, a philosopher of stature whose *Fons Vitae*, written in Arabic, became extremely popular in its Latin translation and was long believed to be the work of a Christian thinker. Many of his poems are suffused with a mystical-erotic note and touch upon themes that were to be taken up two centuries later by the Kabbala. A few lines will indicate their tenor. In one of his poems the Community of Israel addresses her lover, God, who, she feels, has abandoned her:

> The gate which has been closed–arise and open it,
> And send to me the hart that took to flight.
> Return to me today and lie betwixt my breasts
> Upon me there do leave your fragrant spoor. [25]

Yet this unquestionably great poet and profound thinker was also infected by the kind of two-edged malaise of conceit and contempt one would only expect to find in a small mind. In his early youth he wrote:

I am the prince, and song is slave to me,
I am the harp of all poets and minstrels.
My song—a royal crown to kings
A coronet to deck the heads of nobles.
Although I am but sixteen years of age
My wisdom is like that of one who's eighty. [26]

Ibn Gabirol's opinion of other poets is expressed in a long poem which begins: "How can I sing when every fool sings tasteless songs?" and goes on for dozens of lines to decry the folly and ignorance of the poets of his generation, and to praise to high heavens his own wisdom and greatness as a poet. His friends, Ibn Gabirol says, tell him: "You are the brilliant star that shines over our generation, and lovelier than the richest necklace of pearls are your measured words and divine song . . ." which accolade is answered by the poet: "I am the man who is young in years only, rich in knowledge alone, like the wisest elders. My body wanders in the depths, but my spirit rises higher than the clouds . . . I cannot look on calmly and see how petty and vain minds pass for pillars of wisdom, and clumsy versifiers wish to shame me with their songs. I am repelled by the shameful tribe! They wish to compare themselves with me, but how can they, the blind, appreciate my true worth? I am the master of song, the guardian of the well of wisdom. . . . From melodies, words, and sounds, I create, as if through magic, divine songs. . . ." etc. etc. And yet this man who was so full of conceit was so unaware of his shortcomings that he could write in his *Choice of Pearls*: "Wise is a man as long as he seeks wisdom; but as soon as he thinks he has already attained the goal, he becomes foolish." [27]

When his fellow townsmen in Saragossa remonstrated with Ibn Gabirol and asked him to moderate his attacks upon them, his answer was: "Shall I seal my lips because dumb dogs bark?" [28] Accustomed as they were to poetic diatribe, the abuse pouring from the pen of Ibn Gabirol became too much for his community to bear. Sensing that some of its members planned to avenge themselves on him, the twenty-four-year-old poet fled to Granada. There he obtained the support of Samuel haNagid and in exchange for his patronage celebrated him in a large number of poems of praise.

For Moses ibn Ezra (1055–after 1135), the second of the three greatest Spanish Hebrew poets, self-aggrandizement and the denigration of others are almost as important as they were for Ibn Gabirol. In his youth Ibn Ezra wrote dazzling secular poems, all suffused with an enormous joy of life, about women, love, wine, nature. In his mature years he composed more than three hundred religious and penitential poems, many of which found their way into the Jewish prayer book. Self-conceit and the derogation of others, as can be expected, are more apparent in his secular than his religious poems. In his long poem entitled *Tarshish (Beryl)*, he devotes a chapter to celebrating the power and greatness of poets in general and his own creativity in particular. The poet, he says (evidently speaking of himself), can raise unknown men to the summit of honor and greatness; with his power he can crown kings but also break the might of rulers and princes. Like his Arab colleagues, Ibn Ezra resorts to what we would feel is jarring exaggeration in glorifying his own poems. He compares them to "God's script and tablets," which one should carry on one's heart; his poetry, he asserts, "is the Mistress of Song compared to whom all others are maidservants." [29] His fame, he felt, would last forever: "My golden songs will not be forgotten as long as night follows day. They are created out of words, refined by poetic fire, and irradiated with God's spirit. At their birth the ink was the darkness of the night, the pen the golden rays of the sun, and the paper the ocean." [30]

Ibn Ezra was as proud of his wisdom and his ability to fathom the depths of philosophy as of his poetic powers. In one of his poems he relates how he immersed himself in philosophical mysteries, how he comprehended the nature of God and His power and "understood that the Lord dwelt in him."

The reverse of the garish coin of conceit is contempt for others. Of this, too, Ibn Ezra had a full measure:

> In spite of those who hate and envy me
> At all times high will rise my eminence.
> They aimed their arrows at my heart
> But the hands of God deflected them . . .
> . . . .
> What has the grass of roofs with the cedars of God?
> And how can little foxes run after the lion? [31]

In a poem sent to his young friend Y'huda haLevi, Ibn Ezra complains that he must dwell

> Among wolves who live in darkness
> Who never heard the name of man.
> Better to meet a bear of whelps bereft
> Or face a pride of hungry lions
> Than to meet them . . . [32]

It was because of his unhappy and frustrated love for his niece, whose hand was denied to him, that Ibn Ezra left his beloved Granada to live the life of a wanderer in Castile, in Christian Spain. Life away from Granada appeared to him a bitter "exile," as he repeatedly states in his poems. The people in Castile filled him with contempt, and he called them "wild asses." "When I hear their barbarous talk," he says, "I sit full of shame, and my lips remain sealed." However, even those whom he left behind in Granada are accused by him of "vile deeds" and his brothers, who prevented him from marrying the daughter of one of them, of having committed "an evil deed

the like of which has never been done since the world exists." [33] Again, as in
the case of Ibn Gabirol, one wonders how the man who was so full of the
greatness of his poetry and wisdom could write (in his Arabic book on rhetoric and poetry) that, although the public shows regrettable indifference to
scholars, this did not affect him personally because he possessed a virtue
which permitted him to renounce any pretension to public recognition—the
virtue of contentment and moderation! [34]

The man whom critical consensus considers the greatest of all medieval
Hebrew poets, Y'huda haLevi (1075–1141), was born in Toledo, in Christian
Castile, and was sent south by his father to study in Muslim Spain, the major
cultural center of the period. He became a physician, and, like Solomon ibn
Gabirol and Moses ibn Ezra, he wrote not only poetry but also philosophy.
His famous theological-philosophical book, *The Kuzari*, in which he set out
to prove the superiority of Judaism over Greek philosophy, Karaism, and
other religions, was written, like most medieval Jewish philosophy, in Arabic. (Interestingly, there is a passage in it in which Y'huda haLevi discusses
the excellence of Hebrew over all other languages.) In his early poetry.
Y'huda haLevi, too, wrote of nature, of wine and love (some of his love songs
are highly erotic), as well as of friendship (another favorite theme of the Arab
poets); in his mature years, religious and "Zionist" poems predominate.

The twin subjects of self-praise and contempt for others are evident in the
writings of Y'huda haLevi also. In one of his poems (which can be taken as an
indication that he was a physician to the Castilian court) he says, "I am a man
friendly to all; hateful to me are only the flattering grandees." [35]

Having tasted the culture of Arab Spain Y'huda haLevi felt unhappy in
Christian Castile, which appeared to him backward, and settled in Cordova
(which was to remain in Arab hands until its conquest in 1236 by Ferdinand
III of Castile). But even there he felt immensely superior to all the people
who kept him company.

> How could I be afraid of any man
> When my soul's whelps can make a lion tremble?
> Shall I be troubled by poverty and want
> When pearls I dig from Wisdom's mount?
>
> . . . .
> How should I want a friend to entertain me
> When e'en the wisest of his words
> But make my harp and violin fall silent . . . [36]

His view of the many poets who were his contemporaries was, to put it
mildly, dim. When his friends asked him why he had kept silent for such a
long time, he replied: "The fount of poetry is corrupted and defiled, it
awakens in me only disgust and indignation. The lion can no longer walk in
his path when little foxes scrabble around in it." [37] And his philosophical

Kuzari refers contemptuously to the mechanical versifiers of his day, "who apply themselves to prosody and practice scanning metres. There we can hear braying and a babel of words in an art which offers no difficulties to those naturally gifted." [38]

In our discussion of the influence of Arabic on Hebrew the musive style was mentioned. It remains to show, with a few examples, how this most characteristic poetic device worked. When Y'huda haLevi was informed that his friend Moses ibn Ezra had left Granada and gone to Christian Spain, he wrote a poem in which he expressed his sorrow over his friend's departure and concluded:

> *You who are pure of speech, what do you among stammerers?*
> *What has the dew of Hermon with the Gilboa?* [39]

The last line will only impress the reader if he instantly associates with it Ps. 133:3, in which "the dew of Hermon" is mentioned as a simile for something most precious, and with 2 Sam. 1:21, where David, in his lament over Saul and Jonathan, curses the mountains of Gilboa on which they died: "Ye mountains of Gilboa, let there be no dew nor rain upon you . . ." Those who knew these Biblical passages recognized the allusion to them and found the line immensely evocative; to those who did not, it meant nothing.

Moses ibn Ezra's poems contain many examples of a frivolous and erotic use of Biblical allusions in the musive style. In his *Tarshish*, he says:

> *O gazelle, be gentle to the sojourner*
> *And do not slay the voyager*
> *With breasts like arrows*
> *In whose mouth honey flows.* [40]

In the Hebrew original, both the second and fourth line end with the word *hēlekh*. This word occurs only twice in the entire Bible: once in the sense of "voyager" (2 Sam. 12:4), and once in the expression *hēlekh d'vash*, meaning "a flow of honey" (1 Sam. 14:26). Only a Biblical scholar would know this and could understand the meaning of Ibn Ezra's lines. Incidentally, this use of the same word in two different Biblical meanings, the so-called dilogistic musive technique, forms a special subvariety of the musive style to which the Spanish Hebrew poets resorted very frequently, and which would not have been possible in Arabic.

Occasionally a poet showed his mastery of the nuances of Biblical Hebrew, and of his poetic inventiveness, by using a word not in two but three meanings from the Bible. The complexity of this procedure is such that it must be given in the Hebrew original as well as in translation. Y'huda haLevi says in one of his love poems:

> *Leḥi k'ritzpat esh b'ritzpat shesh*
> *Nirqam s'vivav mor k'riqmat shesh*
> *Yosef b'libi esh b'qorvo li*
> *Ki yaḥ'mol pa'am v'yivgod shesh*

Which can be translated:

> *Her cheeks like glowing fire upon a floor of marble,*
> *Around them perfumed locks like woven silk.*
> *They near and cause a fire in my heart,*
> *If once she pities, six times she betrays.*[41]

It must be explained that in line 1, *ritzpa* in the sense of "glowing" is taken from Isa. 6:6, and that *ritzpat shesh*, in the sense of "marble floor," occurs in Esth. 1:6. In line 2, *riqmat shesh*, literally "woven byssus," is taken from Ezek. 16:13; while in line 4, *shesh* is the common word for "six" in Biblical and later Hebrew.

In conclusion, let us look at two rather contrasting verses which show the range of Arab-influenced erotica in Hebrew poetry. The first is a straightforward love poem written by the early Spanish Hebrew poet Yitzḥaq ibn Khalfūn (c. 970–?), one of the protégés of Samuel haNagid, to his beloved, a young man of great charm whom he addresses, as was usual in this type of poetry, as *tz'vi*, or "hart."

> *The sickness of my heart and all its woes*
> *And pain and anguish, suffering and cries*
> *Come from your lovely eyes, o fairest hart,*
> *Which can inflict a deep yet bloodless wound*
> *And rob the sleep of those you have enslaved*
> *While undisturbed you sleep on on your couch.*
> *O hart, your eyes and neck resemble those*
> *Of a young deer, but you don't wear its antlers.*
> *When sweet to me you fill my heart with greatest joy*
> *When wroth, you hurl it into depths of misery.*
> *Alas, my heart cannot shake off this sickness*
> *And none can see the pain caused by your eyes.*[42]

The second sample is from the pen of the great Y'huda haLevi, whose religious poetry was accorded the highest honor that can be paid by a people as religio-centric as the Jews were until the Enlightnment—three hundred of his poems were adopted into Jewish liturgy. Yet the same Y'huda haLevi had no peer in secular Hebrew verse, combining as he did an unexcelled mastery of form with an unflinching explicitness of expression. He could easily duplicate the structure, rhythm, and rhyme scheme of any of the Arabic song hits of the day. At the same time—under the transparent guise of symbolism—he could outdo them in licentiousness and eroticism. Shalom Spiegel has called attention to the truly amazing formal duplication by haLevi of a *muwashshah* (a poem with a refrain or master rhyme) by the popular Sevillian poet al-Abyad.[43] To appreciate haLevi's virtuosity, one must juxtapose the two poems in the originals. The Arabic of al-Abyad is on the left and the Hebrew of Y'huda haLevi on the right:

barrid ghalīl	*raqiq blil*
ṣabb al-'alīl	*nofet klil*
lā yastaḥīl	*yofi w'lul-*
fīhi an ahdi	*ot s'fat maddi*
walā yazāl	*hatter w'gal*
fī kulli ḥāl	*shad qam k'gal*
yarju 'l-wiṣāl	*kish'de sh'gal*
wahwa fī 'ṣ-ṣaddi	*ḥen w'as daddi* [44]

The lines of al-Abyad are part of a simple love poem, and not particularly erotic at that. In literal translation they say, addressing the sweet lips of the beloved, "Cool the thirst / refresh the sufferer / who will not change / his faithful constancy / and will not cease / in all circumstance / to hope for a union / though she shun him." Y'huda haLevi's poem expresses much more sophisticated and erotic thoughts. It is written to Moses ibn Ezra who, Y'huda haLevi says, is thus addressed by Wisdom personified as a woman: To you a fullness of beauty, the pleasure of God, is prepared, with the kisses of my mouth whose taste is like the taste of (and here follow the quoted lines) "a cake mixed with / honey, a wreath of / beauty. Open the loops edging / my garment, and uncover / a bosom rising like a wave / like the bosom of a concubine / fair, and press my breast."

So much for the Arab influence on Spanish Hebrew poetry.

7. The Breakthrough into Science

On the eve of their encounter with the Arabs, the Jews had been for more than two thousand years a highly literate, cultured, and intellectually active people. During the same two millennia, however, their entire creativeness was focused on religion, as witnessed by all the writings they left behind, in Hebrew, in Aramaic, and in Greek. It was not until they were exposed to the influence of the young and dynamic Arab culture that the Jews, stimulated by it, entered into the fields of science which had formerly been totally ignored by them. As a consequence, for the first time in their history, the Jewish mind no longer concentrated on Jewish religion, Jewish history, Jewish philosophy, Jewish Law, and other things Jewish, but struck out into sciences in which the interest held by the subject matter and the treatment it demanded had little or nothing to do with the religion or ethnic background of the investigator. Thus, again for the first time in their history, the Jews not only made important *Jewish* contributions to the intellectual and spiritual life of mankind, as they had done, for example, when they gave prophetic universal ethical monotheism to the world; they also became members of the international community of scholarship and science which had been founded by the Greeks of Hellenistic Alexandria.

Two sets of figures can illustrate the magnitude of the change in Jewish intellectual preoccupation in response to the Arab challenge. Although astronomy was used by Talmudic scholars as an auxiliary science aiding religious observances, until Judeo-Arab times no Jew turned to the study of astronomy or wrote a single astronomical treatise. Yet in the Arab orbit suddenly a large number of Jewish astronomers appear, and from circa 800 to 1500 the names (and in many cases the works) of some hundred are known.

Astronomy was considered by Arab scientists one of the seven disciplines which were comprised in mathematics, the other six being arithmetic, algebra, geometry, astrology, optics, and music. Each of these found its devotees among the Jews in the Arab world. Moritz Steinschneider, the great Jewish bibliographer, described the work of some two hundred Jewish mathematicians (plus more than fifty anonymous Jewish mathematical works), the great majority of whom lived in Spain in the tenth to fifteenth centuries and wrote in Arabic.[45] These numbers speak for themselves.

As a matter of historical interest, it should be mentioned that mathematics was regarded by the Arabs, and hence by the Jews as well, as a science introductory to philosophy. Therefore the move from philosophy, which was cultivated by the Jews in the Hellenistic age, to the mathematical sciences into which they entered in the Arab age was not as great as one would be inclined to imagine today. The contribution of Jews to the mathematical sciences, as far as originality is concerned, was not a major one. Nevertheless, while they did little to advance theory, they had a considerable share in making mathematical and astronomical knowledge available for practical use. An important chapter in applied science was that of the astronomical tables, an indispensable navigational aid, in whose compilation and improvement the Jews played a leading part. Another Jewish specialization was map making, which was concentrated in the hands of Jews on the island of Majorca. Most important, however, was the role of the Jews as translators and thereby transmitters of Greek and Arab science to Christian Europe. They translated mathematical, astrological, astronomical, geometrical, and other works from Arabic into Spanish, Latin, and Hebrew, from Hebrew into Latin, and from Greek and Latin into Hebrew.[46]

These generalized statements can be illustrated by a brief account of the work of one Spanish-Jewish scientist and philosopher, Abraham bar Hiyya (d. c. 1136), frequently called Savasorda, which is a corruption of the Arabic official title *sāhib al-shorṭa* (originally "captain of the guard," but denoting a judicial and civil functionary). Bar Hiyya lived in Barcelona but spent some time in Provence (at the time under the rule of the count of Barcelona), where he was rather unhappy because of the low state of mathematical knowledge among the Jews. His significance in the history of science is due partly to his original works, all written in Hebrew; partly to his translations from Arabic; and partly to his function, shortly before his death, as an interpreter of Arabic for another important translator, Plato of Tivoli, the oldest known translator from that language.[47]

An encyclopedic work by Bar Hiyya, of which only small fragments have been preserved, was *Foundations of Understanding and Tower of Faith*. This book treated arithmetic, geometry, optics, astronomy, and music. Probably intended to be part of it is Abraham's extant treatise on *Mensuration and Calculation*, whose original purpose was to help French Jews in the measurement of their fields. This is the first Hebrew work to show that the area of the circle equals $r^2\pi$, and the first known work (after an Egyptian papyrus of the eighteenth century B.C.E.) to give the formula of a truncated pyramid. In 1145, Plato of Tivoli translated it into Latin under the title *Liber Embadorum* (or *Book of Areas*), thus introducing Arab trigonometry to the West.

An astronomical work by Bar Hiyya consists of two parts. *Form of the Earth and Figure of the Celestial Spheres* is a geography containing a brief review of lands according to the seven climes; and *Calculation of the Courses of the Stars*, which was annotated by another outstanding Spanish-Jewish poet, philosopher, and scientist, Abraham ibn Ezra (1092/93–1167), himself the author of several mathematical, astronomical, and astrological works in Hebrew. Next, Bar Hiyya compiled astronomical tables known also as *Tables of al-Battani*, because he followed in them the Arab astronomer of that name. His *Book of Intercalation* (written in 1122) is the oldest Hebrew work treating problems of the calendar.

In addition to these works in science, Bar Hiyya wrote an important book of moral philosophy entitled *Meditation of the Sad Soul*, which follows Neo-Platonic and Aristotelian arguments, and in which the author reveals himself as a staunch believer in the superiority of Israel in relation to other peoples. He devoted a separate work, *Scroll of the Revealer*, to calculating, on Scriptural basis, the year of the advent of the Messiah. The year he arrived at was 5118 of the Jewish calendar, or 1358 C.E., to be followed in 1448 by resurrection.

Bar Hiyya's translations include numerous Arabic scientific books which he interpreted to Plato of Tivoli and the latter then put into Latin. These translations played an important role in the transmission of Arab scientific knowledge to Europe.

In the thirteenth century, at the behest of Alfonso X (r. 1252–84) of Castile, Isaac ibn Sid, the cantor of the Toledo Jewish community, undertook (with the help of others) the compilation of the so-called Alfonsine Tables—a revision of the Ptolemaic planetary tables, which gave the exact hours for the rising of the planets and fixed stars. The original language of these Tables is unknown, but they survived in Latin, from which version they were translated into Hebrew by Moses ben Abraham of Nîmes in 1460. These Tables, revised by Abraham Zacuto (c. 1450–after 1510), were used by Columbus and enabled him to reach the New World.

The history of science in the Spanish Arab orbit is replete with colorful Jewish figures who would require more space than we can devote to this subject in the present context.[48] Instead, we must fall back again on numbers. The numerical dimensions of the Jewish participation in the scientific life of Spain can be roughly estimated on the basis of two separate sets of figures made available by Sarton and Baron respectively. Sarton found that in 1150–1200, there were in Spain fifteen Muslim, eight Jewish, and three Christian scientists whose work he considered important enough to be included in his general history of science; in 1200–1250, eight Muslim, seven Jewish, and six Christian scientists; and in 1250–1300, seven Muslim, twenty Jewish, and eleven Christian scientists.[49] This gives for the entire 150-year period from 1150 to 1300 a total of eighty-five scientists, of whom thirty-five were Jewish, thirty Muslim, and twenty Christian, or about 41 percent Jewish, as against 35.3 percent Muslim and 23.5 percent Christian scientists. According to Sarton's figures, therefore, the Jews were the scientifically most productive religious group in Spain, with two out of every five scientists Jewish.

The true significance of this finding becomes clear if we relate it to the total number of Jews in Spain in the period in question. In the absence of statistics, estimates will have to do. Regrettably, these vary greatly. According to Yitzhaq Fritz Baer, the eminent historian of the Jews in Spain, at the end of the thirteenth century there were about 40,000 Jews in the three Christian kingdoms of Castile, Aragon, and Navarre, which at the time comprised all of Spain except for the small Muslim kingdom of Granada on the Mediterranean coast in the south of the peninsula. Salo W. Baron, on the other hand, estimates that their number in 1300 in the same area was 150,000, in a total population of 5,500,000.[50] Using this higher estimate, which we modify only to the extent of including in it the Muslim-held Granadan corner of the peninsula, we find that the Jews constituted 2.7 percent of the total population of Spain. Combining Baron's estimates with Sarton's figures, we reach the conclusion that the number of scientists among the Spanish Jews was about twenty-five times higher than among the Spanish non-Jews. Never again were the Jews to attain such a disproportionate predominance in the sciences compared to their Gentile contemporaries.[51]

8. Philosophy: Faith and Arrogance

The world of medieval Jewish philosophy has been explored many times. Its development, main ideas, and relationship to Jewish religion have been analyzed, its sources and influence on subsequent Western philosophy clearly demonstrated. Thanks to these numerous and excellent studies we know that, after a deep sleep of nine centuries following Philo of Alexandria, Jewish philosophy awakened to new life under the impact of Arab philosophy, which in turn was a result of the Hellenization of Islam. Alexander Altmann put it categorically: "Medieval Jewish philosophy is an offspring of the Arabian culture." [52] It was the intellectual climate of Islamic thought which largely inspired the rationalistic bent of Jewish philosophy. In its initial phase, medieval Jewish thought was modeled on the Arabic *Kalām* (lit. "speech," but meaning dogmatic theology), although the latter, in turn, owed a certain debt to Jewish thought. Sa'adya Gaon (882–942), the earliest Jewish philosopher in the Arab orbit and the outstanding representative of the Jewish *Kalām*, was dependent on its Mu'tazilite school.

Sa'adya sounds the theme that was to become a leitmotif in medieval Jewish philosophy: there is no conflict between Reason and Revelation, that is, between philosophical speculation and the teachings of Judaism as revealed in the Bible. He shares with all *Mutakallimūn* (followers or exponents of the *Kalām*, Kalāmists) "the view that God's existence is proved by establishing the fact of creation and thus necessitating a creator." [53] While the "Kalām remained the guiding star" of the Eastern (Babylonian) as well as North African Jewish philosophers until the early eleventh century, from about 900 a second phase of Jewish philosophy began, which was influenced by the Islamic tradition of Neo-Platonism and by the attempts of three great Arab philosophers, al-Kindī (late ninth century), al-Fārābī (c. 870–950), and Avicenna (Ibn Sina, 980–1037), to combine it with Aristotelianism.

The first Jewish Neo-Platonist was Isaac ben Solomon Israeli (d. 950), a court physician at Kairuwan, Tunisia, who was reputed to have known all the seven medieval sciences. The most outstanding was Solomon ibn Gabirol (c. 1021–53), of whose poetry we heard above. His *Fons Vitae* (*Fountain of Life*), written, like almost all medieval Jewish philosophy, in Arabic, was preserved only in a Latin translation with the corrupted author's name of Avicebron or Avicembrol—for this reason, and because of the complete absence of any reference to traditional Jewish sources, it was considered by the Scholastics to have been the work of a Christian. This book "exercised a profound influence on the Schoolmen of the thirteenth and fourteenth centuries, notably on Albertus Magnus and Duns Scotus," and also "influenced the Jewish Neoplatonists and the Jewish mystics of Gerona," who were the immediate forerunners of the Spanish Kabbala. The most popular of all medieval Jewish thinkers was yet another Kalāmist-Neo-Platonist, Baḥya ibn Paquda (d. c. 1100), whose book *The Duties of the Heart*, which shows also the influence of Muslim mysticism, became the standard work of Jewish moral philosophy.[54]

With the gradual elimination of Muslim rule from Spain, Hebrew replaced Arabic as the language of the Jewish philosophers. But whether they wrote in Arabic or in Hebrew, the major influence on their thought came from the Muslim philosophers. The greatest of these, Averroës (Ibn Rushd, 1126–98), dominated the last phase of medieval Jewish philosophy with his radical Aristotelianism. His influence is felt even in the Florentine Jewish philosopher of Portuguese birth, Judah Abravanel or Leone Ebreo (c. 1460–c. 1521), who wrote in Italian his *Dialoghi d'Amore*, which became the most successful philosophic work of the Italian Renaissance and was translated several times into French and Spanish and once into Latin and Hebrew. He was the son of the last great Spanish Jewish thinker, Don Isaac Abravanel (1437–1509), and symbolizes in his life and work the transmission of Spanish Jewish culture into Renaissance Italy. However, he was not the last Jewish Averroist of importance. That role was held by Elijah Delmedigo (1460–93), who, at the request of Pico della Mirandola, translated Averroës' writings from Hebrew into Latin.[55]

A younger contemporary of Averroës was Moses ben Maimon, better known as Maimonides (1135–1204). Maimonides is not only considered the greatest Jewish philosopher, but also one of the two greatest creative minds of the medieval world in general, the other being Averroës.[56] In addition to being a philosopher, Maimonides was also an outstanding practicing physician and medical author, a great halakhist and codifier of the Jewish Law, a commentator on the Mishna and the Talmud, and an authoritative source of advice on moral conduct and of spiritual comfort to the many who turned to him in person and in writing. Incidentally, he was also the head of the Jewish community at Fostat, Egypt, a great center of Jewish life in his time, and physician to the royal court. Except for his great code, the *Mishne Tora (Second Tora)*, also known as *Yad haḤazaqa (Strong Hand)*, which he wrote in Hebrew, almost all his other writings, too numerous to list, were written in Arabic.

The present context allows us only to dwell on Maimonides' *Guide of the Perplexed*, which he completed in Arabic in 1190 (before becoming acquainted with the work of Averroës), and which for centuries exercised a profound influence on Jewish and Christian philosophy and, to a lesser extent, on Muslim thought as well. Before doing so, however, some general remarks are in order on the nature of medieval Jewish philosophy, of which Maimonides was generally recognized as the greatest exponent.

The central problem which preoccupied most of the medieval Jewish philosophers was how to reconcile Reason and Faith, or philosophy and religion. All were firm believers in the absolute truth of Scripture—this was a cardinal doctrine from which nothing could make them deviate. On the other hand, they also believed that philosophy, or to be more precise, the teaching of certain Greek philosophers which reached them in a Muslim Arab garb, also was true. Since two truths cannot contradict each other, the teachings of the Bible and of the philosophers, even though cast in different idioms, must contain the same truth. The great task, then, to which one Jewish philosopher after another devoted much of his life's work was to show, by using the reasoning faculty, that these two apparently different truths were fundamentally identical. To achieve this great aim, two ways suggested themselves. One was traditionally Jewish in the sense that the Talmudic rabbis—as well as the Hellenistic Jewish philosophers—had resorted to it, although the Muslim Arab philosophers also used it with great skill. It consisted of the method of allegorical interpretation. Maimonides not only constantly uses allegorical interpretation of Biblical passages in his *Guide* but elevates it to the position of a central exegetic principle. Thus at the very beginning of the *Guide* he states categorically that in the Bible, "we are told about those profound matters of natural science—which divine wisdom has deemed necessary to convey to us—in parables and riddles and in very obscure words." [57] Moreover, he applied the same method to the Midrash: in his Commentary to the Mishna, he says, he "promised to explain all the difficult passages in the Midrashim where the external sense manifestly contradicts the truth and departs from the intelligible. They are all parables." [58] In fact, he goes so far as to maintain that, in the Biblical account of Creation, "the external sense of the texts leads either to a grave corruption of the imagination and to giving vent to evil opinions with regard to the deity, or to an absolute denial of the deity and to disbelief in the foundation of the Law." Instead, one must examine the Scriptural texts "with what is truly the intellect, after one has acquired perfection in the demonstrative sciences and knowledge of the secrets of the prophets." [59]

The second method was not so much an attempt at reconciling differences between the philosophical and the Biblical views as an effort to show that logical reasoning proves the Biblical teaching right and the philosophers' views which contradict it wrong. The classical example of this procedure is Maimonides' position of the problem of *creatio ex nihilo*, or "creation out of nothing." Maimonides devotes a major part of the second of the three books of his *Guide of the Perplexed* to an elucidation of this issue, since, as he says, the theory that God created the universe out of nothing is "undoubtedly a basis of the Law of Moses our Master, peace be upon him. And it is second to the basis that is the belief in the unity [of God]." On the other hand, Aristotle and his followers maintain that "the first matter" of the universe "is not subject in its essence to generation and passing away, but that various forms succeed each other in it." With his inexorable logical progression, Maimonides next describes the methods used by the Aristotelians to prove their theory; then he indicates the inadequacy of the proofs put forward by the *Mutakallimūn*, the Muslim Arab philosophers of the *Kalām*, for the *creatio ex nihilo*; and then he proceeds to show that both theories, that of the eternity of the universe and that of *creatio ex nihilo*, are admissible. Next, by philosophical reasoning, he indicates that the latter is more acceptable and, in addition, has on its side the authority of "prophecy which explains things to which it is not in the power of speculation to accede." In the sequel Maimonides states that, had his reasoning led him to accept the Aristotelian view on the eternity of the universe, he would not have found it difficult to present a suitable interpretation of those Biblical passages which, in their literal form, speak of Creation.[60] Nevertheless, one cannot escape the impression that it was rather the traditional Jewish doctrine of *creatio ex nihilo* which determined Maimonides' position on the issue and set in motion his reasoning faculty in the direction of finding logical proofs for it. In any case, since the issue was for him a fundamental Jewish principle, next in importance to that of God's unity, he adheres to it even though this means parting with Aristotle, whom he regarded as "the chief of philosophers" and his great master in logical reasoning. No better example could be found to illustrate the point that despite their adoption of Arabic literary and poetic forms, Greco-Arab science and philosophy, and many other aspects of Arab culture, when it came to fundamentals the Jews in the Muslim world remained impenetrably Jewish.

Having given some indication of the method used by Maimonides in his *Guide*, it remains to sum up briefly its contents. It opens with a discussion of Biblical expressions apt to be theological pitfalls because of their anthropomorphism, then proceeds to discuss the nature of God, and especially the vexing problem of the divine attributes. Next follows the presentation of proofs that, despite Aristotle, the world was created by God (as stated in the Bible). After an analysis of the nature of prophecy, Divine Providence is discussed, and the purpose of the Law in general as well as that of individual laws, whereby their educational intent is stressed. Two of the last three chapters outline the higher religion of the "perfect man," which consists of true knowledge of God and is identical with the "Love of God." Throughout the book Maimonides stresses that he could not disclose everything, which creates the impression that he possessed much additional esoteric knowledge not divulged in the *Guide*.[61]

This briefest and barest summary of Maimonides' philosophical position indicates that he was an out-and-out rationalist, although his rationalism is obscured somewhat by his acceptance of the tenets of his age, for example, that the constellations are intelligent living beings. Another characteristic was his unrelenting intellectual élitism, which reminds one of the inordinate pride the Spanish Hebrew poet-philosophers took in their own wisdom, and which, we might add, he shared with many other Jewish philosophers who were not poets. Maimonides, of course, was much too controlled a thinker to let slip from his pen any remark about his own superior intellect. But he repeatedly goes on record to the effect that intelligence is the supreme human value, and his elevation of the intellect to the position of *summum bonum* is matched by his contempt for the ignorant and foolish masses. These attitudes are apparent in almost all of his writings and color even his cosmogony and cosmology. Thus in the preface to his Commentary on the Mishna, on which he began to work at the age of twenty-three while wandering about in Spain, Maimonides states that the purpose of all creation was to serve the intellectually and morally superior. The Active Intellect in the Maimonidean cosmogony, which closely follows Aristotle, is the tenth and last or lowest of the concentric spheres comprising the universe, each of which is endowed with a soul and moved by an intelligence, in accordance with the dictum of the Psalms (19:2), "The heavens declare the glory of God." Parting with Aristotle, who taught that the spheres coexisted with the Primal Cause, Maimonides holds that they were created by God and are identical with the angels of Jewish tradition. The tenth sphere, the Active Intellect, he maintains, is the one under whose influence stands the sublunar world, and through which knowledge is bestowed on the human mind.[62]

Maimonides' theology is likewise intellectually based. God is "the Intellect" (*al-'aql*), the Primal Cause, whose direct emanation is the First Intelligence—the agent of motion for the first and uppermost all-encompassing sphere. God's intellect is so much superior to that of man that man's mind can in no way grasp or imagine it. In fact, no comparison whatsoever is possible between human knowledge and God's knowledge, the latter being absolutely incomprehensible to human intelligence.[63]

An intellecto-centric cosmology and theology requires an anthropology which is likewise intellectually centered. If God is intellect, then the knowledge of God, as far as it is possible for man to attain it, is man's greatest good. It surpasses the pious life and the knowledge of the Law—these are merely prerequisites to the highest human achievement, "the philosophic grasp of the physical and metaphysical truths that culminate in a purified conception of the nature of God." Maimonides argues that the ultimate aim of the creation of this world is man; the ultimate aim of man is happiness; and happiness consists, not of activities which man has in common with the animals, but in the exercise of his intellect, which leads to the cognition of truth. The highest cognition is that of God and His unity; hence the greatest good is the knowledge of God through philosophy.[64]

Traces of élitism are clearly discernible also in Maimonides' psychology, as can be illustrated by his explanation of the function of animal sacrifices. He starts out with the observation that just as in the structure and development of animals and men gradual transition is the rule, so psychologically it is impossible for man to go suddenly from one extreme to the other: "Man, according to his nature, is not capable of abandoning suddenly all to which he was accustomed." Now in the days of Moses the general mode of worship among all men, shared by the Israelites, consisted in sacrificing animals and the like. Hence God's wisdom "did not require that He give us a Law prescribing the rejection, abandonment, and abolition of all these kinds of worship. For one could not then conceive the acceptance of such a Law, considering the nature of man which always likes that to which it is accustomed." Instead, God "suffered the above-mentioned kinds of worship to remain, but transferred them from created or imaginary and unreal things to His own name, may He be exalted, commanding us to practice them with regard to Him . . ." and "He forbade the performance of any of these actions with a view to someone else." This was the "Divine ruse" which "effected that the memory of idolatry was effaced and that the grandest and true foundation of our belief—namely the existence and oneness of the deity— was firmly established; while at the same time the souls had no feeling of repugnance and were not repelled because of the abolition of modes of worship to which they were accustomed and than which no other mode of worship was known at that time." Only the prophets, whom Maimonides considered intellectual giants, recognized that the sacrifices "are not the object of a purpose sought for its own sake and that God can dispense with them"; this is why Samuel, Isaiah, Jeremiah, and others denied that God commanded Israel to offer up sacrifices to Him and demanded instead, in God's name, that the people obey His voice.[65]

The intellectual élitism of Maimonides permeates his sociology as well. Over against the intellectual man, who has attained or at least approached human perfection by exercising his intellect, stand the great masses of mankind comprised of fools and ignoramuses with whom Maimonides wants to have nothing to do. According to one of his letters addressed to his beloved pupil Joseph ben Y'huda, Maimonides was inaccessible to the ordinary people even in his medical practice and confined himself to treating princes, judges, and grandees.[66] His *Guide* was written for the same Joseph ben Y'huda, and in its Introduction addressed to him Maimonides states that he composed the *Guide* "for you and for those like you, however few they are." In the text of the *Guide*, the intelligent and the ignorant are contrasted. The latter are referred to as "rash fools" and "vulgar ones." At the very beginning of the *Guide*, he says that, in teaching the truth, he prefers to please "a single virtuous [i.e., intelligent] man" and does not mind "displeasing ten thousand fools." Moreover, he purposely wrote the *Guide* in such a way that only the intelligent could understand it: "It is not the purpose of this Treatise to make its totality understandable to the vulgar or to beginners in speculation." [67]

His contempt for the ignorant and the common people comes through in unexpected places. In his medical treatise *On the Regulation of Health*, which Maimonides composed for the sultan al-Afḍal Nūr al-Dīn 'Alī (r. 1198–1200), he writes, "Generally speaking, most of what the common people think to be happiness is in reality misfortune, and what is thought by them to be misfortune is happiness." Similarly, in a letter written to his son, Maimonides goes on record with a wholesale condemnation of the Jews of North Africa on account of their ignorance. [68]

Even Divine Providence, Maimonides teaches, has a direct relationship with human intellectual attainment. The truth taught by the prophets is that Providence is "watching over human individuals according to the measure of their perfection and excellence," that is, intellectual development; and philosophical research leads to the same conclusion. This being the case, he says: "As for the ignorant and disobedient . . . they have been relegated to the rank of the individuals of all the other species of animals: 'He is like the beasts that speak not' (Ps. 49:13 and 21). For this reason it is a light thing to kill them and has even been enjoined because of its utility."

His contempt for the ignorant masses is complemented by his dim view of the value of his Jewish predecessors' work in philosophy. He states that the writings of the Gaonim and the Karaites contain nothing more than "a scanty bit of agreement regarding the notion of the unity of God"; even the little they wrote about it "was taken over by them from the *Mutakallimūn* of Islam" and "is very scanty indeed if compared to what Islam has compiled on the subject." [69]

Maimonides does not hesitate to criticize even the sages of the Talmud—whom all Jews in the Middle Ages considered authoritative beyond challenge and infallible as the heirs to the *Halakha* which went back to "Moses on Mount Sinai," in other words, was ultimately divine in its origin. He, too, accepts the authority of the Talmud and closely follows the Talmudic *Halakha* in his Code. But he draws the line when it comes to matters in which his own conclusions, based on his philosophical grasp or medical knowledge, contradict Talmudic statements. The most important of the cases in which he allows his own judgment to supersede that of the Talmudic rabbis is his condemnation of their belief in witchcraft, and his castigation of them because of this belief. After recapitulating the Talmudic laws concerning sorcery, astrology, incantation, necromancy, etc. (e.g., "The witch must be punished by stoning to death"), without any comment, at the end of the chapter dealing with this subject he bursts out:

These things are all things of lie and falsehood, with which the idolaters of old misled the nations of the countries so that they should follow them. And it is unseemly that Jews, who are intelligent and wise, should be drawn to such nonsense, or should believe that they are effective, for it is written, "For there is no enchantment in Jacob, nor divination in Israel" (Num. 23:23), and it is written, "For these nations, that thou art to dispossess, hearken unto sooth-sayers and unto diviners, but as for thee, the Lord thy God hath not suffered thee to do so" (Deut. 18:14). Whosoever believes in these things and the like of them, and thinks in his heart that the Tora has forbidden them, is a fool and an ignoramus, and belongs to the category of women and children whose minds are not fully developed. But those who have wisdom and understanding will know, with clear proofs, that all these things which the Tora forbade are not things of wisdom but nothingness and vanity to which are drawn those who lack knowledge and who have abandoned all the ways of truth for their sake. . . .[70]

As to his evaluation of his own intellect, without ever deigning to utter a single word of self-praise, the writings of Maimonides betray the fact that he was full of self-importance. His *Guide* is dotted with phrases and sentences such as: "A most extraordinary speculation has occurred to me just now through which doubts may be dispelled and divine secrets revealed." Or: "This book then will be a key permitting one to enter places the gates to which were locked," "I hold," "I assert," "I am of the opinion," "Hear now the intent of our reply," "Know this," "If, however, an individual of insuf-ficient capacity should not wish to reach the rank to which we desire him to ascend . . ." "We open a gate and draw your attention . . ." Even when he tries to be modest, he does it in such an exaggerated fashion that one cannot help feeling it is insincere: "I shall not . . . refrain from saying what I in my inadequacy have apprehended and understood."

As Zinberg put it, an "arrogant scorn and contempt for the 'foolish, igno-rant multitude' is very clearly discernible in Maimonides' work generally and in his *Guide for the Perplexed* particularly." [71]

I have dwelt at some length on the intellectual élitism of Maimonides because he was the greatest of medieval Jewish philosophers. To show that this was indeed a trait shared by Jewish philosophers in general, let us refer to three of them very briefly. Isaac Albalag (thirteenth century), the transla-tor into Hebrew and commentator of al-Ghazālī, of whose Kabbalistic teach-ings we shall hear below, constantly speaks of the "masses" who "lack every-thing, that is, intellect," and, like Maimonides, avers that "the purpose of philosophy is not to teach the masses or to make them succeed, but to cause success to those who are accomplished, a success which depends on a true knowledge of all existing things." Both Albalag and his colleague and con-temporary Levi ben Abraham (c. 1245–c. 1315) express the idea that the par-ables and overt language of the Bible are for the fools, while its inner mean-ing is understood only by the wise. An older contemporary of these two,

Moses of Marseilles, also speaks of this "double meaning" of the Tora, which says something entirely different to the foolish masses and to the wise few.[72]

In fine, whether poets or philosophers, the Jewish intellectuals of the Arab orbit amply exhibited the human failing of having succumbed to the arrogance, boastfulness, and contempt for the "foolish masses," or the common people, that were characteristic features of their Arab environment.

9. Kabbala and Hinduism

As the Golden Age of Jewish poetry, philosophy, science, and *Halakha* was drawing to a close in Spain, the Jewish community of the peninsula produced a new intellecutal phenomenon, that of Kabbalism or Jewish mysticism. Jewish mysticism shares with other Jewish religious and cultural phenomena the feature of having Talmudic and even Biblical antecedents. The Psalmist's exclamation, "O taste ye and see that God is good" (Ps. 34:9), has reverberated in the teachings of many mystics, including those of Thomas Aquinas (1225–74), who defined mysticism as *cognitio dei experimentalis*, or "the experiential knowledge of God." [73] The mystical visions of Isaiah and Ezekiel describing the divine throne-chariot occupied by God and surrounded by seraphim are too well known to require more than a passing reference. Based on them, in Talmudic times an entire science of mystical speculation developed which at the time was termed *Ma'ase Merkava* (lit. "Work of the Chariot") but which in scholarly literature is usually referred to as Merkava mysticism.

But these and other such groping and hesitant excursions in antiquity into what was regarded as the highly dangerous terrain of mystical speculation were but a preamble or prefiguration of the fullness of the Kabbala as it sprang into bloom in thirteenth-century Spain. Again, the mystical teachings of the German "Hasidim of Ashkenaz" (c. 1150–c. 1250; not to be confused with East European Hasidism, which was founded in the eighteenth century by Israel Ba'al Shem Tov) appear as mere preludes, important only because they exerted a certain influence on the development of the Spanish Kabbala.

The earliest important figure in the galaxy of Spanish Kabbalists was Moses ben Naḥman (1194–c. 1270), often referred to as Nahmanides. True to the tradition of the great Jewish intellectuals who preceded him, Nahmanides was a versatile scholar, a halakhist, a Biblical exegete, and a physician; but he added to these traditional Jewish accomplishments one more— he was also a Kabbalist, who exerted considerable influence on his younger contemporary, the author of the Zohar (see below). Of the approximately fifty works by Nahmanides which have been preserved, most deal with *Halakha*. However, they contain numerous Kabbalistic references, as do his liturgical poems. His only work dealing exclusively with the Kabbala is his commentary on the first chapter of *Sepher Y'tzira* (or *Book of Creation*), the famous obscure treatise on cosmology which was probably written between the third and sixth centuries in Palestine or Babylonia. Despite the paucity of his Kabbalistic writings, Nahmanides came to be known in his later years as a leading Kabbalist, and the deep respect he enjoyed as the foremost rabbinical authority of his age contributed greatly to establishing the Kabbala as a legitimate branch of Jewish religious study.

The other important Jewish scholar of the age who fulfilled a similar role in legitimizing the Kabbala was the Provençal halakhist and critic of Maimonides, Abraham ben David of Posquières (c. 1125–98). The fact that he and Nahmanides joined the ranks of the Kabbalists was "a guarantee to most of their contemporaries that, despite their novelty, kabbalistic ideas did not stray from the accepted faith and the rabbinic tradition. Their undisputed conservative character protected the Kabbalists from accusations of deviation from strict monotheism or even of heresy." [74] Had Hasidism, in the eighteenth century, been similarly embraced by the leading rabbinical authorities of that age, the acrimonious conflict between it and its opponents could have been prevented. The role of Nahmanides and Abraham ben David in legitimizing the Kabbala has a remarkable parallel in what happened in Muslim mysticism in the eleventh century, when respected Arab theologians, and above all al-Ghazālī (1058–1111), secured Sufism its place within Muslim orthodoxy. [75]

One of the most colorful figures of this colorful age was Abraham Abulafia (1240–after 1291), who was a restless mystic, a world traveler in search of the legendary mysteries of the Orient, and a seer of visions, some of which, as he himself acknowledged, were inspired by demons. Abulafia nurtured Messianic ambitions in whose pursuance he went to Rome to present himself before the pope, from which venture he barely escaped with his life. He was a prolific author of prophetic, inspired, and apocalyptic, or else theoretical and doctrinal writings. His prophetic and quasi-Messianic activities in Sicily provoked the wrath of Solomon ben Adret (c. 1235–c. 1310), the recognized leader of Spanish Jewry for forty years. [76]

Solomon ben Adret himself, a disciple of Nahmanides, was an outstanding halakhist who wrote about 11,000 responsa and decisions and, while he was opposed to mystical excesses and Messianic pretensions, was nevertheless a Kabbalist. But he was also a conservative traditionalist, who, although himself well versed in the scientific literature of his day, headed the movement aimed at preventing the spread of these subjects among the masses. In 1305 he proclaimed a ban against the study of physics and metaphysics until the age of twenty-five, but placed no restriction on the study of astronomy, medicine, and the works of Maimonides. Like his teacher Nahmanides, Adret acquired great knowledge in the Kabbala, and mystical comments abound in his works.

All the men mentioned so far were completely overshadowed by Moses ben Shem Tov de Leon (c. 1240–1305), who lived until 1290 in the small Castilian town of Guadalajara northeast of Madrid, then, after some years of wandering, spent the last ten years of his life in Avila. From 1286 to after 1293 he wrote a considerable number of Hebrew books on the commandments and other traditional religious subjects which, like the works of other authors of the period, are full of mystical allusions. Between about 1280 and 1286 de Leon produced his magnum opus, the *Sepher haZohar* (*Book of Splendor*), which subsequently acquired the position of the holiest book of the Kabbalists. De Leon wrote the Zohar mostly in Aramaic (some of it is Hebrew); and, in order to make sure that it would be accepted as an authoritative work, he attributed its authorship to the second-century Talmudic teacher and miracle worker Rabbi Shim'on ben Yoḥai. De Leon was influenced by the prophetic Kabbalism of Joseph Gikatila, a pupil of Abraham Abulafia, although the influence was reciprocal, and the later writings of Gikatila are, in turn, influenced by the Zohar. While through the Zohar and under its influence Aramaic became the dominant language of the Kabbala, there was at least one Kabbalist, Joseph ibn Waqar of Toledo (flourished c. 1340), who wrote in Arabic.[77]

It is difficult to present the essence of the Zohar within the compass of a brief statement.[78] It is a very long work—comprising about 850,000 words (or 1,700 pages in the most popular Vilna edition)—much of it written in the form of a Kabbalistic Midrash, or mystical commentary, to sections of the Pentateuch, Song of Songs, Ruth, and Lamentations, and is actually a collection of several books or sections. Nowhere does it put forth a coherent or systematic doctrine, but instead repeats in a rather haphazard manner all over its great bulk a number of ideas about the deity, the forces of evil, cosmology, man, and so on.[79] Moreover, although the Zohar comprises the central and most influential formulation of early Kabbalistic thinking (as distinct from that of the great sixteenth-century Safed Kabbalists), it builds to a very great extent on its predecessors and, in turn, had an immense influence on the subsequent development of the Kabbala. Hence, while one must keep in mind that there is no such thing as a single uniform Kabbalistic system but only many different Kabbalas, it is nevertheless more expedient to summarize the main teachings of "the Kabbala" despite the abstraction and schematization that this involves, rather than those of the Zohar alone. While doing so, I shall repeatedly digress to present the analogies between the Kabbala and the one ancient Oriental religion which it resembles more than any other, namely, Hinduism, or rather, certain Hindu schools. For the absence of a uniform system which we pointed out in the Kabbala is even more characteristic of Hinduism, whose dimensions of time, space, and number of devotees are incomparably greater than those of the Kabbala. While Hinduism is unquestionably an enormously complex subject, and "the endless diversity of

Indian religious life" [80] is most intimidating for the nonspecialist, one can nevertheless point to a number of generally prevalent concepts which show a remarkable similarity to Kabbalistic ideas.

Let us begin with the one detail to which Scholem has called attention. He observed that Abraham Abulafia's teachings represent "but a Judaized version of that ancient spiritual technique which has found its classical expression in the practices of the Indian mystics who follow the system known as *Yoga*." He cites, as one instance out of many, the important part played in Abulafia's system by the technique of breathing, which in the Indian *Yoga* is commonly regarded as the most important instrument of mental discipline:

> Again Abulafia lays down certain rules of body posture, certain corresponding combinations of consonants and vowels, and certain forms of recitation, and in particular some passages of his book *The Light of the Intellect* give the impression of a Judaized treatise on *Yoga*. The similarity even extends to some aspects of the doctrine of ecstatic vision, as preceded and brought about by these practices. [81]

Turning now to Kabbalistic doctrine, the first thing to tackle is, of course, its theology (or theosophy) which occupies the central place in the entire Kabbala. Compared to that of the Kabbala, the theologies of the Bible, the Talmud, and Philo are simplicity itself. In the Kabbala, God is not a static but a dynamic concept. He is presented as having gone through stages which today we would call evolutionary. These stages are also thought of as aspects of the deity. In one of His aspects, God is the absolute essence who lies beyond speculation or even ecstatic comprehension. This unknowable aspect of the Divine is expressed in the Hebrew term *En Sof*, that is, "Infinite"; but, and here we run into our first major difficulty, it is also referred to as *Ayin*, "Nothing"—because, as the rather lame explanation has it, no created being can intellectually comprehend it. According to some Kabbalists, this Nothing is the region of pure absolute Being; according to others, it is infinitely more real than all other reality. Again others refer to God in this state as dwelling "in the depths of nothingness." It is from this primal and mystical Nothingness that all the subsequent stages of God's gradual unfolding emanate, in the course of which the Nothing becomes the divine *ego*, the Hebrew word for which, *ani*, as was pointed out by some Kabbalists, has the same consonants as the word for Nothing—AYiN-ANiY [82]—and is thus anagrammatically identical with it.

This Kabbalistic primal Nothing has its counterpart (or prototype?) in Hinduism. According to one of the basic Brāhmanic texts, the Śatapatha Brāhmana, "The non-existent, verily, was here in the beginning. What was this non-existent? Life energy." In the Shiva symbolism, the primal nothing is deprived even of life energy. The god Shiva "denotes the Absolute in that state in which nothing comes to pass. Nishkala Shiva, i.e., Shiva 'without parts' is the unchanging, sterile Absolute, devoid of every urge of energy towards procreation and cosmogonic transmutation. This is the Absolute as sublime lifelessness, primary and ultimate inertia, the supreme void; here nothing whatsoever throbs or stirs." Even the Hebrew play of words between *ani* and *ayin* has its Hindu analogue: the name Shiva, without the vowel element that converts the *a* into *i*, is Shava, corpse. Only by adding that element, which of course stands for Shiva's consort, the goddess Shakti (the supreme representative of movement and life) does the lifeless Nothing, Shava, become the god Shiva, full of life essence and energy.[83]

In Kabbalistic theogony-cosmogony the divine Primal Will is either separate from, or identical with, the *En Sof*. In any case, their joint manifestation is the first *Sephira* or Emanation, named *Keter* ("Crown") which is still identical with the mystical Nothingness, the incomprehensible absolute, and from which issues the first sexually differentiated and contraposited pair: the Supernal Father, Wisdom, and the Supernal Mother, Intelligence, identified as the second and third *Sephira* respectively. We shall soon return to this supreme divine couple but mention here in passing that in a similar way Indian mystical theogony speaks of Shiva and his consort of many names as "the primeval twofold personalization of the Absolute," and as "the first and primal unfolding of the neuter Brahman into the opposites of the male and the female principles."[84] The remaining seven Kabbalistic *Sephirot* are termed in most systems: (4) Mercy (or Greatness); (5) Power (or Judgment); (6) Compassion (or Beauty); (7) Eternity; (8) Majesty; (9) Foundation (or Righteous One); and (10) Kingdom (or Diadem). This theory of the ten *Sephirot*, which ultimately goes back to the *Sepher Y'tzira*, became the backbone of Spanish Kabbalistic teaching. The *Sephirot* are intermediary states between the first Emanator and all things that exist apart from God and thus represent the roots of all existence in the Creator. The term *Sephira*, it should be noted, has nothing to do with the Greek *sfaira* ("Spheres") but is related to the Hebrew *sappir* ("sapphire"), which in Ezekiel's great chariot vision symbolizes the radiance of God (Ezek. 1:26).

The ten *Sephirot* are replete with mystical symbolism. They are frequently taken to be symbolic of the body of *Adam Qadmon*, the "Primordial Man." The first three represent the head; the fourth and fifth, the arms; the sixth, the torso; the seventh and eighth, the legs; the ninth, the male sexual organ; while the tenth refers either to the all-embracing totality of the image or to the female companion of the male, since both together are needed to constitute a perfect man.

Other symbolisms read into the *Sephirot* are the names of God, the four elements, the four winds, the four metals (gold, silver, copper, lead), the sun and moon, the seven days of Creation, the mythical cosmic tree, and so on.

Essentially the *Sephirot*, as developed in the Zohar, are "various phases in the manifestation of the Divinity which proceed from and succeed each other." They are the "ten fundamental categories" which "embrace the archetypes of all being." The world of the *Sephirot* "is a world of divine being, but it overflows without interruption or new beginning into the secret and visible worlds of Creation, all of which in their structure recapitulate and reflect the intradivine structure." As the Italian Kabbalist Menahem Recanati (flourished c. 1300) put it: "All created beings, earthly man and all other creatures in this world, exist according to the archetype [*dugma*] of the ten Sephirot." [85] A favorite Kabbalistic method of showing the ten *Sephirot* in a visual form is that of concentric circles, which duplicate the ten concentric spheres that comprise the universe according to medieval philosophy.[86]

This entire system of *Sephirot* has its analogue in Hindu Shivaism. We have heard above of Nishkala Shiva, the sterile, absolute void. Another aspect of Shiva is Parama Shiva, "Ultimate Reality," or "Supreme Experience," from whom emanated ten *Tattvas* (Principles, basic categories, or essences) which make up the metaphysical and physical universe. To put it differently, Shiva, "the Lord Creator, Maintainer and Destroyer of the World . . . out of his own boundless essence evolved the perishable universe and its creatures." [87] Shiva himself is above and beyond all the *Tattvas*, unaffected by time, space, and relation, but alone making possible the existence of the universe. Like the *Sephirot* in the Kabbala, so in the *Tattva* system of Shivaism, the *Tattvas* emerge from each other gradually, each successive *Tattva* pervading and permeating all the *Tattvas* which are its immediate or indirect products, and each successive *Tattva* containing the presence of all the preceding ones, in the manner of "concentric circles" (as in the Kabbala). The gradual descent from the divine to the mundane—which is expressed in the Kabbala in the progression from the first *Sephira*, *Keter*, the Supreme Crown of God, to the tenth, Kingdom, the most earthbound one (see below)—is paralleled in the Shivaic *Tattvas* in the descent from the first *Tattva*, the ever-existing inseparable realities of Shiva and his consort, Shakti, to the tenth, the physical orders or states, namely, ethereality, aeriality, formativity, liquidity, and solidity.[88]

Of the ten *Sephirot*, four stand in a special relationship to one another. They are: the second, Wisdom, referred to as the Supernal Father; the third, Intelligence, called the Supernal Mother; their son, the sixth *Sephira*, Compassion (or Beauty), termed in this context God the King; and finally their daughter, the tenth *Sephira*, Kingdom, called Shekhina, Matronit, or Community of Israel. These four emanations or aspects of the deity are represented, according to the Kabbala, in the letters of the name YHWH (Yahweh). Elsewhere I have shown that this Kabbalistic tetrad is but the Jewish variant of a well-attested tetradic myth cycle whose older versions are found in several ancient religions, including those of Egypt, Sumer, the Hittites, the Canaanites, Japan, and India, with the last-named evincing the greatest similarity to it.[89] In the Zohar, the relationship between the Father and the Mother (as we shall refer to this divine couple for the sake of brevity) is described in highly erotic terms such as one could expect to find only in an atmosphere permeated by the erotic poetry popularized under Arab influence by the Spanish Hebrew poets in the preceding three centuries. To give just one example:

> When the seed of the Righteous One [i.e., the Supernal Father] is about to be ejaculated, he does not have to seek the Female [i.e., the Supernal Mother], for she abides with him and is always in readiness for Him. His seed flows not save when the Female is ready, and when they both as one desire each other; and they unite in a single embrace, and never separate.[90]

The Zohar has much to say about the constancy of the love between the Father and the Mother. They are locked in an eternal marital embrace, like any other ancient divine couple of world parents: "They never separate and never leave each other. They are together in complete union." [91] Passages such as this, with many variations, abound in the Zohar and in the subsequent Kabbalistic literature. It is more than doubtful whether, when reading or hearing them, the average Kabbalist was able to keep it fixed in his mind that he was being told of nothing more than the mystical interrelationship between two of the ten phases of the manifestation of the deity.[92] I would rather guess that the appeal of these passages was the same as that of Y'huda haLevi's poem, in which he speaks of uncovering and pressing the swelling breasts of the enticing concubine, Wisdom.

The Zohar supplies numerous details about how the Father first brought forth the Mother, and how they assumed their permanent position of marital embrace. At long last the Mother became pregnant and brought forth the Son and the Daughter—in an androgynous form: "They emerged together, joined together back to back." But the Son managed to separate himself from the Daughter and soon thereafter their own love life began.[93]

A similar myth is told about Shiva: in his manifestation as Ardha-nārīshvara, he was half male and half female, symbolizing the union of Puruṣa ("the True and Real") and Prakṛiti ("the Covering," or "the undifferentiated primordial material"), which is the central idea in Hindu nature worship. Shiva, fused with the goddess Shakti into one body, presents the oneness of opposites which constitutes the essence of the divine and of reality.[94]

As for the relationship between the older and the younger divine couple, we read in the Zohar of the exceeding love the Father had for his Daughter, the Shekhina-Matronit: He called her not only Daughter, but also Sister, and even Mother, and constantly kissed and fondled her.[95] While the Zohar stops short of ascribing to the Father the desire to seduce his Daughter, the erotic attraction he felt issuing from the Daughter is unmistakable. One is

reminded of the Hindu myth about "the primeval father of creatures, Pra-
jāpati, who desired to commit incest with his daughter, the lovely maiden
Dawn," but was stopped by Shiva with his mighty bow.[96]

We are now ready to have a closer look at the relationship between the
Son, or God the King, and the Daughter, or the Shekhina-Matronit. The
sexuality of the King (as we shall henceforth refer to him) is emphasized by
attributing to him one physical organ in particular—a divine phallus or
lingam, represented by the ninth *Sephira*, *Y'sod*, or Foundation. It is
through this organ that all the eight higher *Sephirot* are combined in the
image of the King. Inevitably, all the powers contained in the entire Se-
phirotic structure flow into the Shekhina through this Foundation. The happiness and pleasure the King and the Matronit found in each other is described in what is perhaps the most beautiful passage in Kabbalistic
literature:

> The Matronit, surrounded by her maidens, repaired to her couch set up in the
> Temple, there to await the coming of the Groom. The curtains round about
> were decorated with myriads of precious stones and pearls. At midnight, the
> tinkling of bells he wore around his ankles announced the coming of the King.
> As he approached, he was accompanied by a host of divine youths, and the
> maidens of the Matronit welcomed him and them by beating their wings with
> joy. After singing a song of praise to the King, the Matronit's maidens with-
> drew, and so did the youths who accompanied him. Alone, the King and the
> Matronit embraced and kissed, and then he led her to the couch. He placed his
> left arm under her head, his right arm embraced her, and he let her enjoy his
> strength. The pleasure of the King and the Matronit in each other was inde-
> scribable. They lay in tight embrace, she impressing her image into his body
> like a seal that leaves its imprint upon a page of writing, he playing betwixt her
> breasts and vowing in his great love that he would never forsake her.[97]

How anybody, reading this poetically and sensuously described scene, could
keep in mind that what he is reading is not a love scene at all but a mystical-
symbolic description of the interrelationship between two *Sephirot*, emanations of God's essence, is totally beyond me. I am rather inclined to believe
that passages such as this, which abound in the Zohar, struck the untutored
or semi-tutored reader by what they overtly said and not by their hidden esoteric meaning. This apparent eroticism, among other factors, must have
been responsible for the popularity attained by the Zohar and by the Kabbala
in general.

The marital happiness of the King and the Matronit is paralleled by that of
Shiva and his goddess in India. In Hindu mythology Shiva, in one of his
most important aspects, is the generative principle, the gigantic linga(m) or
phallus, the great lord of procreation. His home is in the Himalayas, where
he lives in perfect marital happiness with his wife, Shakti (i.e., "Power"),

who is the daughter of Himalaya, whence her name Parvati ("Daughter of the Mountain"). She is also the Great Mother, the female aspect of the Great God, and is symbolized by the *yoni*, the female symbol of creative energy. Like the King and the Matronit, Shiva and Shakti are united in a sacred marriage, and their delight in each other is made manifest in many Indian works of art. A splendid example of these, described in detail by Zimmer, shows the god and goddess regarding each other with intense emotion. Gazing with a deep and everlasting rapture, she sits on his left thigh with her right arm around his shoulder, while his left arm holds her by the waist and presses her left breast gently upward. With the numerous retinue surrounding the divine couple, this could be a visual representation of the scene we just quoted from Kabbalistic literature. As in the written presentation of the Kabbala, so in Hindu visual representation, "though the outward symbolization in images is strikingly erotic, the connotations of all the forms are almost exclusively allegorical." [98]

The joyous and intense love relationship between the King and the Matronit was disrupted from time to time by the sins of Israel, and, most catastrophically, by the destruction of their divine bedchamber, the Temple of Jerusalem, and the subsequent exile of the Shekhina in her aspect as the Community of Israel. The separation of the King from the Matronit robbed him of his power: "The King without the Matronit is not a king, is not great, and is not praised." [99] The same idea is found in Hinduism: "If Shiva is united with Shakti, he is able to exert his powers as lord; if not, the god is not able to stir." [100] As to the exile of the Shekhina, remarkably even this seemingly most Jewish concept—because it is a reflection of the historical tragedy of the Jewish people—has its counterpart in Hindu mythology. In it we hear of a demon-tyrant, Maya by name (not to be confused with Māyā), who, leading his hosts, conquers the entire created cosmos, as a result of which the great gods, "the brilliant denizens of Mount Meru [are] driven from their paradise into the bitter void of exile." [101] As a consequence of the sins of Israel and of the Exile, the Shekhina is being defiled by Samael: he glues himself to her body "with the adhesive force of resin," and "other gods" are able to take possession of her; she becomes tied to them, and the children of those other gods, the Gentiles, are able to suck from her just as the Children of Israel had done while the Temple still stood. [102] In an analogous manner, in Hindu mythology, the union between Shiva and Shakti is interrupted by a period of separation, and the goddess is subject to the satanic claim of the titan tyrant Jalandhara. Shakti is "ever desired, won, and lost again in the endlessly revolving strife for world dominion between the demon-giants and the gods." [103] In the Kabbala, the Shekhina-Matronit has the same role and fate: God, other gods, forces of impurity, and the pious of Israel, all want to possess her—and succeed. [104]

There is yet another striking analogy between Shivaism and Kabbalism. In contrast to Western ways of thinking, which consider energy, activity, and aggressiveness as male characteristics, while the female sex is associated with softness, passivity, and placidity, in both Shivaism and Kabbalism these archetypes are reversed. In Hindu mythology, Shiva, the male god, "is the personification of the passive aspect which we know as Eternity," while his consort Shakti, the goddess, is that of "the activating energy [*sakti*], the dynamism of Time." His name means "Beneficent," while the name Shakti means "Universal Power." [105] In Judaism, this identification of the male deity with passivity and the female divinity with activity and power is found in its initial form as early as the writings of Philo. In Philo's theology, *Elohim*, God (symbolized by one of the two Cherubim in the Jerusalem Temple), was the father, who was goodness, was peaceable, gentle, and beneficent; while *Yahweh* (the Lord), symbolized by the other Cherub, was the mother, characterized by sovereignty, and was legislative, chastising, and correcting. [106] That is to say, of the two, the male aspect of the deity was the more passive and the female the more active. In the Kabbala, these role allocations are more pronounced. According to the Zohar, the King entrusts all his warlike activities to the Shekhina (or Matronit). She commands myriads of supernatural soldiers, armed with terrible weapons, who wreak bloody vengeance on the forces of the idolatrous nations, the sinners, the enemies of Israel. "In fact, the King completely renounced all direct control of his forces" and entrusted to the Matronit "all his weapons, spears, scimitars, bows, arrows, swords, catapults, as well as his fortifications, wood, stones, and subordinated all his war-lords to her." When the King wishes to take revenge on the idolatrous nations, the Shekhina herself becomes filled with blood and metes out bloody punishment to the sinners. [107] This aspect of the Shekhina-Matronit is completely analogous to the role of the primeval Shakti, the One Force, as the "unconquerable, sublime warrior-maid," to whom the gods willingly abdicated "their various masculine attitudes—royal, valiant, and heroic," and into whose hands they delivered their various weapons, utensils, ornaments, and emblems containing their particular energies and traits. Shiva handed her his trident; Kala, the God of Time, presented her with sword and shield; her own father, the mountain-god Himalaya, gave her the lion that she was to ride. Representations in relief and mythic descriptions show the goddess as a brilliant Amazon, provided with the weapons of all the gods, defeating the giant buffalo-demon. [108]

The one trait of the Shekhina-Matronit least consonant with traditional Jewish ideas of the divinity is her monstrous aspect, more horrifying even than her characterization as the warrior-queen. For in using even the most lethal weapons entrusted to her by the King, the Shekhina-Matronit only fights evil in its manifold manifestation; and, however gory the incidents of the combat, the destruction of evil is a good. In the monstrous Shekhina we cannot escape the impression that we are faced with a goddess who is a source of unspeakable suffering meted out indiscriminately to the good and the evil; moreover, the fantastically enormous size attributed to her characterizes her as a universal menace, as the embodiment and concretization of anguish and death which are the inescapable fate of all men. The Shekhina, referred to in this context by the name "Moon" (one of her many names), is described as a demonic, cosmic woman monster who swallows a thousand rivers at one draught, whose nails reach out in a thousand and seventy directions while her hands in twenty-four thousand. A thousand shields cling to her hair. Nothing can escape her. It is in this aspect that the Shekhina is the bringer of death. "From betwixt her legs," as the Zohar puts it with a clearly discernible intention to shock, issues forth a youth, who is none other than the angel Metatron, who stretches from one end of the world to the other, wields sixty clubs of fire, and commands hosts of *ḥayyot,* angelic beasts.[109]

The manifestation of Shakti corresponding to this monstrous Shekhina is Kali, one of the many names and aspects of Shakti. Kali is depicted as black, which emphasizes her frightening character. The Zohar, too, says, "At times the Shekhina tastes the other, bitter side, and then her face is dark." [110] In the Tantra texts, Kali is described as "standing on a boat that floats upon an ocean of blood . . . the life blood of the world of children that she is bringing forth, sustaining, and eating back. . . ." [111]

In both Hinduism and the Kabbala, the forces of evil are referred to as "the other side." The Hindu deities have, in addition to their "benevolent aspect," also their terrifying destructive phase. This "other side" of Mother Shakti is the Black Kali; while her son, the beloved and immensely popular Ganesha, also known as "Lord of the Hosts" (just as the son of the Shekhina, Metatron, is commander of great hosts of angelic beasts), has his "other side" in the monster Kīrttimukha, terrifying, devouring, and exhibiting carnivorous teeth.[112] While the monstrous Shekhina, described above, is not referred to in the Kabbala as "the other side," she clearly represents it, and is related to the Shekhina in exile, that is, in separation from her husband the King and in submission to and entanglement with "the other side"—the *sitra aḥra,* or the forces of evil. According to the Zohar, the ten holy *Sephirot* have their counterparts in ten unholy or impure ones, that is, an ordered hierarchy of the potencies of evil, produced by "left emanations." Thus the ultimate source of evil is God: His "right hand" is the quality of love and mercy; His "left hand" is that of stern judgment. The latter can, and did, break away from God altogether and was transformed into the radically evil, the dark world of Satan.[113]

A favorite Kabbalistic image for the forces of evil is *q'lippot* ("husks"). The husks imprison the holy sparks of the soul and need to be removed from them.[114] Similarly Shivaism teaches that the husk *(Mala)* is coexistent with the grain, and that only with Arul Shakti (i.e., the Grace of God) can Mala be removed from the soul which is the grain, so as to enable it to free itself from the painful and fateful chain of rebirth. Mala is impurity, which attaches itself to the soul and binds it to the world of empirical existence and selfishness. Its removal is one of the functions of Shiva's cosmic dance.[115]

The eroticization of the Divine, which we have discussed above, is complemented in the Kabbala by a divinization of human sexuality. The latter is the outcome of a concept which, although spiritualized in the Zohar, is a direct derivative of the age-old human belief in sympathetic magic. If you want the forces of nature to do something that redounds to your benefit (this belief holds), you have to show them what you want of them, then they will follow suit. If you want rain to fall, you pour water on the earth; if you want the male and female powers of nature to have union—necessary for the fertility of the land, animals, and men—you must perform a ritual copulation. Beliefs and practices of this type existed in ancient Judaism in Biblical and Talmudic times.[116] On these antecedents the Kabbala built its theory that, in order to ensure blessings for the world, one must cause the King and the Matronit to have union. Each and every religious commandment was performed by the Kabbalists with this one purpose in mind and on their lips; "This is done for the sake of the reunion of God and His Shekhina." [117] However, beyond these generalities, in performing the act of sexual union— the one act which could most directly and immediately bring about a magical-sympathetical response from on high in the form of a sexual union between the King and the Matronit—the Kabbalists were supposed to be fully conscious of the sacral significance of the act. They were not simply indulging their carnal lust; they were not even merely performing the religious commandment of procreation but were causing the King and the Matronit to couple and thereby ensuring the flow of blessing from above to Israel and the world.[118]

These concepts fitted the fundamental Kabbalistic doctrine according to which "the impulse from below calls forth that from above," [119] that is to say, the impulse which originates from a human deed is magically reflected in the upper region of the *Sephirot*; thus the devotee, through his acts, exercises control over the deity. Let us mention only in passing that the same concept is found in Hinduism, where it is expressed in the words of Shiva himself who says that "he is the slave of his devotees." [120]

The comparison between Kabbalistic and Hindu mysticism should be brought to a close with a brief reference to an important doctrine in anthroposophy: that of metempsychosis, the transmigration of souls. This doctrine, of course, formed part of Pythagorean, Orphic, Platonic, Neo-Platonic, and Gnostic teachings, and it could have reached the Kabbala from any of these sources via Arab (e.g., *Mu'tazila*) mediation. The Muslim authors who deal with it attribute it to the Indians rather than to Greek philosophical schools. It is a fact that in no Western system did reincarnation play as important a role as in India where, from the time of the Upanishads (eighth–fourth century B.C.E.) it forms a pervasive feature in practically every religious doctrine including Buddhism. The precise form taken by the belief in metempsychosis varies from sect to sect; but in general, it assumes that upon death a person's soul (or the substance of his soul) is being reborn in a life-form which is determined by the person's thoughts, words, and deeds. To put it in the simplest possible terms, if a person is good throughout his lifetime, the new individual in whose body his soul will be reborn will have a happy and joyful life; while an evil or sinful person's soul is reborn to a life of pain and suffering and can sink so low as to be reborn in the body of a dog. This doctrine solves at one stroke the difficult problem of how a good person can suffer and an evil one enjoy a pleasurable life—each is enjoying, or suffering, the consequences of his acts in a previous reincarnation. If a man can reach a state of enlightenment, he can brake this wheel of Karma, so that after his death his soul enters Nirvana, which in a classic definition is neither existence nor non-existence.

The Kabbalistic belief in metempsychosis, termed *gilgul* (a translation of the Arabic *tanāsukh*), is first encountered in the twelfth-century book *Bahir*, written or edited in Provence and manifesting, according to Scholem, Gnostic and possibly also Catharist influence.[121] Soon it appears as a fully developed doctrine with variants and details, in writings of Isaac the Blind (c. 1160–1235), Nahmanides, and, of course, in the Zohar. In its full form the doctrine of *gilgul* closely resembles the one familiar to us from India; for example, *gilgul* is used to explain the problem of the suffering of the righteous and the prospering of the wicked referred to above. Similar to the Indian view is the Kabbalistic position that the process of *gilgul* itself—irrespective of the quality of the new life-form the soul has to enter—is a painful experience. After 1400, the belief in the transmigration of souls into animals or plants as a punishment became common among the Kabbalists—again a belief familiar to us from India. A typical example from the Zohar reads:

> How many and how wondrous are the cycles of the soul. . . . Truly all souls must undergo transmigration; but men do not perceive the ways of the Holy One, how the revolving scale is set up and men are judged every day at all times. . . . They perceive not the many transmigrations and the many mysterious works which the Holy One accomplishes with many naked souls. . . .[122]

Does this random harvest of similarities add up to a proof that the Kabbalistic ideas discussed are derived from Hinduism? No. But the cumulative evidence of detail after detail makes it appear likely that the Hindu concepts were known to some Kabbalists in thirteenth-century Spain, just as certain *Yoga* practices were, and that they influenced them in the formulation of the doctrines referred to.

The main channel through which the ideas and practices of Hindu mysticism could reach the Spanish Kabbalists were, of course, the Arabs. The Arabs' conquest of India began in 711, in the very year in which they penetrated Spain. From the tenth century, Muslim rule expanded in northwest India and conversions of Hindus to Islam became numerous. Beyond proselytism, the two religions, Hinduism and Islam, strongly influenced each other. Although the origin of Sufism antedated this period, many mystic practices—meditation, concentration, control of breath, and so on—were borrowed by Indian Islam from the Hindu Yogis and the Buddhists. The religious teachings of the Upanishads were found to have an affinity with the pantheistic thought of Muslim mystics, resulting in a rapprochement on the theoretical level. On the popular level, the Hindu faith in magic, sorcery, miracles, grave-worship, apotropaic practices, and the like could not be resisted by Muslims. Also, after their conversion to Islam, many Hindus continued in their customs and traditions. Inevitably, these influences could not remain isolated in Indian Islam but spread all over the Caliphate. To mention only two instances, the great Muslim mystic al-Ḥallāj (857–922) undertook a long tour in India and after his return to Baghdad won many followers to his teachings. And al-Bīrūnī, one of the greatest scholars of medieval Islam, wrote a *Description of India* in 1030 which deals mostly with the beliefs of the Brāhman community.[123]

In addition to Arab mediation, the Jews of Spain could have learned about Hindu ideas and practices directly. The Jews in medieval times, and in the first place the Spanish Jews, were great international merchants and travelers whose commercial ventures took them, by land and sea, as far as India and China. The activities and routes of these Jewish merchant travelers, known as *al-Rhādaniyya* or Radanites, are described as early as the middle of the ninth century by Ibn Khurradādhbih.[124] Others, such as Benjamin of Tudela in 1167–73, and the Kabbalist Abraham Abulafia a century later, traveled to the East not because of commercial interests but driven by a curiosity to find what we today would call "exotic" Jewish communities. Given the great fascination religion had for the Jews of the period, it cannot be imagined that at least some of these travelers did not bring back reports of Hindu mysticism. In fact, occasionally at least, direct references of Hindu doctrines or practices are found in Kabbalistic writings. Thus the anonymous author of the Hebrew *Book of Life*, written about 1200, mentions that "magicians in India and the Arab countries still make animals of men" by giving them a magic potion to drink.[125] Isaac Albalag, the thirteenth-century Spanish Kabbalist who translated into Hebrew and annotated al-Ghazālī's well-known *Tendencies of the Philosophers*, writes in detail about the Hindu doctrine of the repeated destruction and recreation of the world:

> According to the sages of India this is how the world is being renewed: the astronomers among them found that the place of the apogee of the sun, which

today is on the northern side, moves with a slow movement until, at the end of 70,000 years, the apogee of the sun will be in the place which today is its perigee, in the south. And as the sun moves away from the north side, that side becomes dark and humid, and the element of water increases in it, while the south side which is opposite it, becomes warm and dry, until, at the end of 70,000 years, the waters which today are in the south side will gather in the north, and the waters will be in the north, and the dry land will become visible in the south, which today is the place of the waters called seas. And this region will become a new world, and in this manner the world always becomes renewed after the destruction of the [preceding], at the end of 70,000 years. . . .[126]

While the precise Hindu source of Albalag's cosmic cycles of 70,000 years has not yet been traced,[127] the general doctrine of successive creations and destructions of the world is a widely prevalent Hindu idea, as is the teaching that at the beginning of each *yuga* ("world age") the sun, moon, and planets stand in the initial point of the ecliptic and return to the same point at the end of the age, which evidently is identical with the doctrine referred to by Albalag. However, the Hindu cosmogonical myths speak of world-ages generally much longer than Albalag's 70,000 years: they assign a duration of from 12,000 to hundreds of millions of years to a *yuga*. It is possible that Albalag, confusing time with distance, took the number 70,000 from the 70,000 *yojanas* (1 *yojana* = c. 2 miles) which, according to Hindu cosmogony, is the distance to which the nether worlds extend below the surface of the earth. As for the destruction of the world by water at the end of every cycle, which Albalag reports as a tenet of the Indian sages, this indeed is the way in which Hindu mythology envisages the end of each cycle.[128]

Beyond such direct mentions of Hindu sources, several Kabbalistic doctrines, as we have seen, bear a remarkable resemblance to Hindu features. The androgyneity of the deity; the splitting of the traditionally one and only God into ten mystical emanations, several of whom are spoken of in terms of male and female divine personages; the eroticization of the relationships between these complementary *Sephirot* of the godhead; the discernment of the realm and the forces of evil as the "husk," the "other side," or the "left side" of the Divine; the concept and details of metempsychosis or transmigration of souls; the divinization of human sexuality—this and much more is so vividly reminiscent of Hindu mythology, theosophy, and anthropology that one simply must rule out the possibility of mere coincidence. However, this is an enormously complex subject whose full investigation will have to await the attention of a scholar who is equally at home in the Kabbala and in Hinduism.

Pending the outcome of such a major study, we must face up to another question. Do these Kabbalistic concepts—irrespective of their origin—

represent a substantial deviation from the traditional essence of Judaism grounded in Biblical-prophetic and Talmudic doctrines? As in the case of Hellenistic Judaism (cf. above, pages 94–95), our answer to this question is again a definite no. There can be no doubt that the Kabbalists erected a new superstructure on the old foundations. But nowhere did they even as much as shake those foundations, let alone damage them. This was precluded, among other things, by the very method they employed in supporting novel ideas with constant reference to Biblical passages—even if in a daringly reinterpreted form. The same conclusion is the only one possible if we consider that the emergence of the Kabbala did not lead to a religious struggle in any way comparable to that provoked by Hellenism some fifteen centuries before it, or to that which was to follow the rise of Hasidism in the eighteenth century. Judaism was able to take the Kabbala in its stride because the Kabbala managed to "Judaize" Sufi ideas, *Yoga* practices, and, possibly, Tantric, Shivaic, and other Hindu teachings and concepts. Although the Kabbalists speak without surcease of divine potencies, of hypostases, of stages in an intra-divine life process, of interrelations and even tensions between the various aspects of the deity, their basic axiom is the unity of God, a unity which, while living and dynamic, is nonetheless so solidly knit that its very incomprehensibility assures its totally unique character. The statement contained in the *Credo* of the greatest rationalistic Jewish philosopher, Maimonides, "I believe with a full faith that the Creator, blessed be His name, is One and there is no oneness like Him," [129] was unquestioningly and wholeheartedly subscribed to by all Kabbalists, although the forms and forces they discerned within that Oneness would have shocked Maimonides.

In conclusion, we should briefly mention the influences that "emanated" from the Kabbala. Its influence on Muslim and Christian mysticism was considerable, but that subject does not belong in this book. [130] Among the Jews, its influence lasted until the Enlightenment combated and eliminated it except for small groups of the faithful who have preserved it in its Hasidic transfiguration. Until at least 1800 the Kabbala, although never systematized or catechized, was widely considered the true Jewish theology, and its teachings left their mark on all aspects of Jewish life: the ritual as laid down in the *Halakha*, the *Aggada*, and, above all, the three interrelated areas of prayer, custom, and ethics. To dwell for a moment on the one issue which seems to me the most crucial: as a result of the permeation of Jewish folk life with Kabbalistic ideas, the belief became widespread that the behavior and actions of human beings on earth here below bring about mystically, but also automatically and quasi-magically, corresponding events in the realm of the Divine above. It has therefore become an accepted tenet of Jewish religious faith and practice that man must behave in such a manner that his conduct and every individual act should bring about results that are beneficial to both the godhead and Israel. Foremost among these aims was to redeem the Shekhina from the impurity of her exile and to cause her to be reunited with her husband, the King.

While these and the many other mystical teachings contained in the Kabbala brought about a greater religious inwardness, they also led to a magicization and demonization of life. With the passage of time and the growth of religious ignorance among the Jewish masses in seventeenth- to eighteenth-century East Europe, this magic element became a dominant characteristic of traditional Jewish life. Those developments were, of course, accompanied by the emergence of a great quantity of writings, mostly small booklets, purporting to serve practical-magical purposes, which were directed at every Jewish home and which even today have not yet entirely ceased being produced or reissued. In fine, whether or not one looks with sympathy upon the changes brought about by the Kabbala in Jewish life, one has to agree with the judgment of Scholem to the effect that the Kabbala has been "one of the most powerful forces ever to affect the inner development of Judaism." [131]

In 1492, Ferdinand of Aragon and Isabella of Castile defeated the Moorish king of Granada and thus brought the *reconquista* to an end. For more than a decade before this event the position of the Jews in Christian Spain had gone from bad to worse. Those of them who under the threat of persecution and expulsion had converted to Christianity had to face a new danger: the Inquisition, which employed torture to extract the admission by the "New Christians"—or Marranos ("Pigs") as they were called by the populace—that they adhered in secret to their old Jewish faith. The punishment was death. Those who were found guilty were burned alive in a public spectacle called *auto-da-fé* or Act of Faith; those who admitted their guilt, professed repentance, and recognized the Church as the sole source of salvation were first strangled and then burned. Thousands of Marranos thus ended their lives in flames. Not satisfied with this, three months after their victory over Granada the "Catholic kings" issued their decree ordering the expulsion of all Jews from Spain within four months. On August 2, 1492, the very day on which the last ships sailed from Palos with Jewish exiles aboard, Columbus set out on his epoch-making voyage of discovery, supplied with navigational charts which had been prepared by Jews, and with several Marranos in his crew. As the *Santa Maria*, *Pinta*, and *Niña* passed the ships which carried the refugees, Columbus noted this fact in his diary. It has been estimated that about 200,000 Jews left Spain in 1492; some 50,000, unable to tear themselves away from their beloved Spain, embraced Christianity and remained.

The tragic end of Jewish life in Spain did not, however, mean the end of Spanish Jewry. Carrying with them their Sephardi heritage, the Ladino language, an inordinate pride in their Spanish extraction, their intellect, and their manners, and convinced of their superiority in relation to all other Jews, they rapidly managed to become the dominant element in almost every Jewish community in whose midst they settled: in Morocco, Algeria, Tunisia, Egypt, Palestine, and Greece (at the time under Turkish rule); and somewhat later in southern France, Holland, and England. For two centuries after the expulsion, the momentum of the Sephardi cultural excellence continued, and all the important developments in Jewish history were initiated by Jews who had been born in Spain or by their descendants. Among these can be mentioned such diverse feats as the final codification of the *Halakha*—by Joseph Caro; the completion and popularization of the Kabbala—by the mystics of the Safed circle; the most widespread pseudo-Messianic movement—by Shabbatai Zevi in Turkey; the most significant advance in philosophy since Maimonides—by Baruch Spinoza in Holland; the fight for and achievement of the readmission of Jews to England—by Manasseh ben Israel; and the settlement of the first Jews in the New World, in Brazil, Peru, Chile, and Mexico, and later in the West Indies and in New Netherlands (which was to become the United States)—by Marranos from Spain and Portugal and by Sephardi Jews from Holland.

To what extent the Sephardi heritage is still a living reality in Jewish life in the last quarter of the twentieth century is a moot question. But even if their Hebrew cultural arabesque should be felt no longer relevant for us, the Jews of Spain had their age of splendor and made their inestimable contribution to moving Jewish history ahead toward the Renaissance, Hasidism, Enlightenment, Emancipation (the seminal role of the Sephardim in the struggle for Emancipation will be touched on in Chapter 9), and modern times by absorbing what the Arabs of Spain had to offer and yet holding their own in that great cultural encounter.

7

The Renaissance Jew[1]

To begin with, a word must be said about the number of the Jews in Italy whose encounter with the forces of the Renaissance constitutes the subject of this chapter. While precise information is not available, estimates made by the most competent historians and demographers show that this figure was subject to phenomenal fluctuations. Baron estimated that the total number of Jews in Italy in 1300 was 50,000; and in 1490, 120,000.[2] The figure in 1600 was estimated by Roberto Bachi at 21,000, and in circa 1638, by Simone Luzzatto, at 25,000. For 1700, estimates give 26,500; and for 1800, 31,400. As for the total population of Italy, it too was small: in 1600, it was 10,804,000; in 1700, 10,071,000; and in 1800, 17,860,000.[3] The number of Jews, therefore, was quite insignificant both in absolute figures and in relation to the total population of Italy.

Similarly, the individual Jewish communities were small in size. In sixteenth-century Rome, 1,500 to 3,500 Jews lived in a total population of 55,000 to 97,000; in Venice, there were about 400 to 1,700 in a city of 100,000 to 150,000.[4] It was this small Jewish community which, under the impact of the Renaissance and moved by its own intellectual energy, struck out into dozens of new fields of cultural activity.

1. The Jews of Italy

Italian Jewry is the oldest in Europe among the still existing Jewish communities. Jews first settled in Rome in the second century B.C. and soon thereafter were found in many parts of the peninsula. Originally they were Greek-speaking, but by the close of the imperial period they had become Latinized, with the exception of those who lived in the southern tip where Greek was retained down to the twelfth century. In Sicily, which was under Moorish rule from the late ninth to the eleventh century, the Jews spoke Arabic until the fourteenth, that is, for more than two hundred years after the

Christian reconquest of the island. Elsewhere, as soon as Italian established itself among the Gentiles, the Jews too adopted the language—the use of Judeo-Italian for synagogal purposes is attested from about 1200. From those days to the present, the bulk of Italian Jewry remained Italian-speaking.

In the Middle Ages the ranks of the Italian Jewish community were augmented by refugees from East and West who sought and found a haven in Italy. In the thirteenth century came the first Moroccan Jewish contingent and, still before the end of the century, the first wave of refugees from German lands. This immigration from across the Alps reached its peak in about 1400. The first Spanish exiles arrived in the fourteenth century, with this influx peaking after the 1492 expulsion. Before the end of the fifteenth century the influx of refugees from the island of Rhodes, where Jews had lived since pre-Christian times even before they settled in Rome, began.

The attitude of the established Italian Jewish community to the newcomers was, on the whole, friendly and helpful. Many spared no effort in aiding the refugees. Some, however, feared that their own position could be adversely affected by the influx of foreign Jews; these put up stiff opposition and even went so far in violating basic Jewish ethics as to petition the Italian authorities to exclude the refugees. A notorious early case of such unbrotherly behavior was that of certain Roman Jews who submitted such a request, accompanied by a gift of 1,000 ducats, to Pope Alexander VI. The pope, however, refused to comply and demanded instead another 2,000 ducats to permit the petitioners themselves to remain.

At the end of the fifteenth century the Jews were expelled from Sicily, at the time under Spanish rule, and at the same time the first exile of Marranos from Venice occurred. Local expulsions had been ordered before from various parts of Italy—especially from domains controlled by foreigners (e.g., the French or the Spaniards)—and continued to occur later. But whenever the Jews were expelled from one place, they were admitted in another, and before long they usually were invited or allowed to settle again in the city which had ousted them. Despite these local occurrences, the fact remains that throughout their long history in Italy, there was never a countrywide general expulsion of the Jews from the peninsula, who were thus spared the fate that sooner or later overtook their co-religionists in all other parts of Europe. Equally important is the fact that Italy remained the only country of the continent in which the Jews never experienced a general persecution.

2. The Sephardim in Italy

As mentioned in Chapter 6, wherever Sephardi exiles settled they established themselves as a dominant element above the preexisting local Jewish communities, retaining their separate identity and their language, Ladino.

This happened not only in North Africa, in Greece, and in other parts of the Ottoman Empire, but also in the Netherlands and England. Only in Italy was the course of events different. For a relatively short time, it is true, the Sephardim maintained their separate identity here too, as did the German Jews (hence the term *tre nazioni* or three nations, applied to the Jews of Italy in the sixteenth century, the third being that of the Italian Jews); but after the end of the Renaissance this threefold division disappeared and all the Jews, whatever their provenance, became Italianized. As far as the Sephardim were concerned, this meant that in Italy, alone of all the countries in which they settled, they were unable to maintain for long their superior posture. The memory of the glory that was the Spanish Jewish Golden Age faded in the face of the attraction of Italian Jewish culture, and their Sephardi ethnocentrism gave way to a larger and more comprehensive Italian Jewish ethnicity.

There was, of course, much in Italian Jewish culture to appeal to the Sephardi Jews. In other countries the Sephardim found, at best, Jewish excellence in traditional religious studies. But the narrow confines of "the four cubits of the *Halakha*" had long ceased to be the only, or even the main, concern for the Sephardim. Given their background, experiences, and achievements, they could not but feel superior to those who knew little of Hebrew poetry and grammar or of Jewish philosophy, let alone such non-Jewish subjects as sciences, the arts, and secular literature. The fact that the Jewish religious leaders in the countries which admitted the Sephardi exiles considered these accomplishments *un-*Jewish, and that the appearance, behavior, manner, and customs of the "native" Jews were not only strange but uncouth and unrefined—or so they appeared in the eyes of the Sephardim—added to the latter's feeling of superiority and to their disdain of the Ashkenazim or Oriental Jews.

Not so in Italy. Here the time of the arrival of most of the Sephardim coincided with the high Renaissance and the intensive Jewish participation in it. From the thirteenth century, the Italian Jews had absorbed considerable cultural influences through contact with individual Spanish Jews who settled in Italy; but thereafter they creatively expanded what the Sephardi Jews had begun centuries earlier. True, the Sephardi exiles of 1492 were heirs to the glorious heritage of the Jewish Golden Age in Spain; but by the time of their arrival in Italy, that age was a thing of the past. If the Sephardim took a hard look at themselves, they had to recognize that they were nothing but epigones of epigones. Woefully few, indeed, were the poets, linguists, philosophers, scientists, and other intellectuals of any significance, nor could they point to such in the two or three generations that preceded them. In Italy, on the other hand, they found all these, and many more, creative activities flourishing among the Jews as among the Gentiles. Thus they had to recognize that *grandezza*, or pride in being Sephardim instead of Italian

Jews, would have been utterly inappropriate and misplaced in view of the actual situation.

Another factor was added to all this. In retrospect, from the perspective of the Renaissance, the cultural accomplishments of the Spanish Golden Age must have appeared limited, or at least incomplete. The Jewish talents in Spain, we recall, manifested themselves in those fields in which the Muslims excelled: they were grammarians, translators, poets, philosophers, mystics, students and codifiers of the religious Law, commentators of Scripture, astrologists and astronomers, mathematicians, geometers, and, of course, physicians. When writing books whose subjects fell within the traditionally approved Jewish religious studies they used Hebrew; for their other works, they used Arabic. It in no way diminishes the greatness of the Spanish Golden Age to point out that the participation of the Italian Jews in the Renaissance extended to all these fields and more. But it was precisely this "more"—this complement of additional realms of scholarly, literary, artistic, and even technological activity—which could not but impress itself upon the Sephardi Jews, long sensitized to secular intellectual interests, to the extent of rendering it impossible for them to resist assimilation into Italian Jewry. A glance at the accomplishments of the Renaissance Jew will substantiate the point.

3. The Pre-Renaissance South

First, however, a pre-Renaissance phase of the Jewish cultural efflorescence must be described, whose locale was southern Italy and Sicily, important way-stations in the transmission of Jewish and secular culture from the East to the West. Here Hebrew poetry and Midrashic compositions were produced as early as the eighth century—antedating the inception of the Jewish Golden Age in Muslim Spain. Here in the tenth century lived and worked the well-known Jewish physician, astronomer, mystic, and commentator Shabbatai Donnolo (913–82), one of the first Italian scientists of the Middle Ages. Other Jewish physicians, scholars, and poets of lesser fame both preceded and followed him. This profusion of Jewish creativity in southern Italy in the pre-Renaissance Middle Ages is the background against which one must view and understand the paraphrase of a verse from Isaiah (2:3) by a twelfth-century scholar: "Out of Bari comes forth the Law, and the word of the Lord from Otranto." Most of the Jews were agriculturists, merchants, and craftsmen (including cheese makers, soap manufacturers, dyers, weavers, potters, silk manufacturers, and the like), but among them were also Talmudic scholars, of whom one of the earliest and best known was Nathan ben Yehiel of the famous Anau family, who completed his most important work, the 'Arukh, in 1101. Talmudic academies flourished not only in

Bari, Otranto, and Palermo in the south, but also in Rome, Verona, and other Italian cities in the north. Some of the masters of these schools had studied in the great and ancient Talmudic academies of Babylonia, which at the time were on the verge of collapse.

The same role was fulfilled by southern Italian Jewish scholars in passing on the heritage of classical antiquity and the great contemporary Muslim Arab culture to pre-Renaissance Europe. They participated (or so it was rumored) in the development of the oldest, and for long the most famous, medical school in Christian Europe at Salerno, where Jewish scholarship, too, flourished. It is said that at the University of Naples, established in 1224, lectures were at one time given in Hebrew. To enable Jewish scholars to translate Arabic works directly into Latin, rather than into Hebrew as was their wont, Charles of Anjou, who employed several Jewish translators, had at least one, Moses of Palermo, tutored in Latin. The number of books rendered from Arabic, Greek, or Hebrew into Latin by Jewish translators amounted to several dozen and included philosophical and medical works, as well as collections of folk stories (e.g., the famous *Kalila waDimna*). The share of Jews in the great early medieval revival of learning, often referred to as the "Latin" Renaissance, was considerable. The extent of the external assimilation of the south Italian Jews to their Christian environment in clothing and appearance—always indicative of social and cultural rapprochement—can be gauged from two edicts issued in 1222 by Frederick II of Hohenstaufen, king of Sicily with Apulia: he ordered all Jews to wear a badge of bluish color in the shape of the Greek τ (tau) and to grow beards. Without such distinguishing marks, the Jews evidently could not be told from the Christians.

The flowering of south Italian Jewry came to an end in the late thirteenth century, when the Jews were given the choice between death and conversion to Christianity. Many managed to flee; thousands accepted baptism, although they retained their separate identity for generations. Everywhere, synagogues were converted into churches, and a glorious chapter in early Italian Jewish history came to a tragic end. However, the fall of southern Italian Jewry was closely followed by the rise of the Renaissance Jews in central and northern Italy.

4. The Dawn of the Renaissance

From the fourteenth century on, the Jewish communities in Upper Italy rapidly gained in importance. The process was one familiar from other places. The Jews established themselves in an increasing number of localities by supplying needed services: they served the cities as loan bankers under carefully regulated conditions (the so-called *condotta*, or "conduct"), or as merchants in furs, skins, paper, cloth, old clothes, precious stones, and the like; or as peddlers, tailors, pawnbrokers, goldsmiths, silversmiths, printers, booksellers, musicians, and even dancing masters. And, of course, there were everywhere practitioners of that most famous of Jewish specializations, medicine. Thus Jewish communities sprang up in many places from Rome to the north, and the fourteenth century—a time of trouble and suffering for the Jews in Germany, France, and even Spain—proved a period of general well-being for Italian Jewry, disrupted only rarely by cases of anti-Jewish attacks and other setbacks.

Again, as it happened elsewhere, the establishment of an economic basis and relative tranquillity proved to be the soil in which the seeds of intellectual activity could strike root and blossom forth. The time lag between the foundation of a Jewish community and the first signs of intellectual achievement was, as in other places, from two to three generations as a rule.

The Roman Jewish community numbered but two hundred families in the late twelfth century when the famous Spanish Jewish traveler Benjamin of Tudela passed through Italy. After some hesitant beginnings going back to the eleventh century, it produced its first major figure in the late thirteenth century, in the person of Immanuel haRomi ("of Rome"), also known as Manuel da Gubbio (c. 1261–after 1328). The son of a wealthy Jewish family, Immanuel studied Bible and Talmud, as well as mathematics, astronomy, medicine and philosophy; and in addition to Italian and Hebrew he knew also Latin and Arabic. He wrote Biblical commentaries, a work on the symbolism of the Hebrew alphabet, and other "Jewish" studies. But first and foremost he was a poet. Although only a few of his Italian poems survive, some of his contemporary fellow poets considered him second to none but Dante. It used to be assumed that Immanuel and Dante were acquaintances or even friends, though this has been shown by Umberto Cassuto and Cecil Roth to lack a historical basis. However, it is a fact that the influence of Dante's *Divina Commedia* is strongly felt in Immanuel's Italian and Hebrew verses, and especially in his Hebrew poem *HaTofet w'ha'Eden*, or *Hell and Paradise*, which forms the concluding part of his collection, the *Maḥbarot 'Immanuel (Immanuel's Compositions)*. Other Italian Hebrew poets, such as Moses Rieti and Abraham Yaghel Gallichi, also imitated Dante. In his Hebrew poetry, Immanuel followed the strict metric rules introduced into Hebrew verse by the great Jewish poets of Spain (who, in turn, took it from the Arabic poetry of their day); but he combined this with typical Italian poetic forms such as the sonnet. More important than these formal influences were Immanuel's thematic borrowings from contemporary Italian literature, and the spirit and mood of Italian poetry which pervades his poems. They are elegant, witty, flippant, frivolous, and often erotic, for which reason their reading was banned by some of the contemporary rabbis. Nevertheless, Immanuel became the founder and prototype of a distinguished line of Jewish authors who throughout the ages made important contributions to Italian literature.

Since we can but touch on the highlights of the Jewish participation in the Italian Renaissance, I will mention only in passing that numerous other Jewish poets, scholars, commentators, Kabbalists, and philosophers, whose work often included Italian as well as Hebrew writings, lived all over Italy in the fourteenth and fifteenth centuries.

5. The New Culture

Compared to medieval man, Renaissance man was possessed by a phenomenally wide range of intellectual interests and curiosity. He was interested in the history of the human race, in the geography of the entire known world, in geometry and technology, in anatomy, physiology, and medicine, in philosophy and politics, and, of course, in literature, poetry, music, the dance, the theater, painting, sculpture, and all the minor arts. This preoccupation with man, his world and his work, led to an intensive cultivation of all these fields and to an unparalleled cultural breakthrough. As for the Jews, this was an entirely new world the like of which they had never before known. Until the Renaissance, as Cecil Roth put it, "the Jew, with a high standard of civilization which embraced the Arab version of ancient Hellenic science and philosophy, and with cosmopolitan elements such as no other section of the population enjoyed, was culturally in advance of Europe as a whole in many respects." [5] With the cultural explosion of the Renaissance, those Jews who became acquainted with it suddenly felt that they had been culturally outstripped—the first time that such an awareness dawned upon them in Christian Europe. This recognition was followed by an intense movement of acculturation, which led to a complete absorption by the Jews of the interests, endeavors, ambitions, and orientations—including the extraordinary intellectual curiosity, the artistic activities, the philosophical inquiry, and the literary productivity—which characterized their Gentile compatriots. The resulting similarities between the Christian and the Jewish life-forms and thought-forms were so many that to enumerate them would mean to present a catalogue of practically everything the adherents of both religions did—all the activities they engaged in, as well as a list of almost all the patterns of thinking and feeling which were predominant in their minds.

The Jewish participation in the Italian Renaissance can be seen both from the general Italian viewpoint and from the specifically Jewish one. As far as the first is concerned, the share of the Jews in the great outpouring of Renaissance creativity was minor. There were a few Jewish translators; some Jews belonged to the circle of Pico della Mirandola, who had a leading part in the revival of Hebrew as the third humanistic language next to Greek and

Latin; and the work of at least one Jew, the *Dialoghi d'Amore* of Judah Abravanel (Leone Ebreo, d. 1535), was one of the most popular and influential philosophical treatises of the time. But their participation in the plastic arts—never until the Enlightenment a strong domain of Jewish talent—was negligible. In music and the theater they were more strongly felt, but even here their absence would not have made much difference. All in all, one cannot say that the Jews made a significant contribution to the Italian Renaissance.

For our purposes the second aspect is the important one. Whether or not the Jewish participation resulted in something significant within the total picture of Renaissance culture, from the Jewish aspect the very fact of the participation had great importance and far-reaching consequences. For the first time in their long history, the Jews acquired for themselves the totality of an alien culture. This had not happened either in the Hellenistic world of antiquity or in the Muslim Middle Ages. At the height of the Renaissance nothing but religion separated Jews from Christians, and since the attitude to religion was rather lukewarm among many in both camps, even the religious difference did not really amount to much.

This situation required major readjustments on the part of the Jews. The alien culture, which they soon came to feel was their culture as well, threatened to submerge their Judaism completely. We know that this did not come to pass. What were the manifestations of this Jewish-Christian cultural rapprochement, and what were the factors which nevertheless enabled the Jews to save the preserve their own separate, ethnic identity? The rest of this chapter will discuss these questions in detail.

6. Medicine and Magic

Although interest in medicine was not something the Jews had to acquire from their Renaissance environment, the importance of the healing art as a Jewish specialization was such that it warrants discussion in the first place.

As in the Muslim world, so in Renaissance Italy Jewish doctors played a prominent role in all aspects of medicine—including its teaching at universities, its practice, and its discussion in scholarly and popular books. Most of the Jews who received appointments at Italian universities taught medicine. Understandably, medicine was also the most favored curriculum pursued by Jewish students enrolled in the universities. Thus in Padua alone, between 1517 and 1619, no less than eighty Jews graduated in "philosophy and medicine." In medical practice Jews predominated. There was scarcely a pope or a ruling prince in Italy whose personal physician was other than Jewish. Jewish physicians served also as medical officers in the armies of various Italian states or functioned as official city physicians (e.g., in Sicilian towns). Others specialized in dentistry. The ranks of Jewish medical men were augmented by Jewish women physicians. As early as in 1376, Virdimura, the wife of the physician Pasquale of Catania, was licensed to practice medicine throughout Sicily. There were numerous Jewish medical dynasties whose members practiced healing for generation after generation. The fame of the Italian Jewish doctors spread far and wide, and many of them were invited to practice at the Sublime Porte in Constantinople. One spent some time in England attending to the ailing King Henry IV; another was called in 1490 to Russia to treat the heir apparent of the Grand Duke of Muscovy and upon failing to cure him was summarily executed. A bull issued in 1581 by Pope Gregory XIII, which prohibited Jewish physicians from treating Christians and Christians from summoning Jewish doctors, put an end to the golden age of Jewish medicine in Italy. Nevertheless, the great University of Padua remained the center of study for aspirant Jewish physicians from all over Europe until the middle of the eighteenth century.

The Jewish contribution to medical literature was significant. Jews helped Vesalius in his great anatomical work at Padua. The first work ever written in otology (diseases of the ear) was composed by Abraham Portaleone at the request of Duke Gugliermo Gonzaga of Mantua. Portaleone also wrote a study on the medicinal use of gold. The ex-Marrano Amatus Lusitanus compiled a history of his outstanding cases in his *Centuriae curationum*, which became a classic in its day. A Sardinian physician known as Hayim of Cyprus wrote a work on the medicinal plants of the island. Most of the Jewish doctors wrote their medical works neither in Latin nor in Hebrew but in Italian, which was of course the language most commonly understood by their intended readership, whether Gentile or Jewish. Many of these books are decidedly popular: they include manuals of prescriptions and remedies and, in keeping with the prevalent medical beliefs of the times, bristle with superstitious folk cures—one of them prescribes the wearing of a salted wolf's eye against eye disease.

Superstitions constituted the one medieval heritage which Renaissance man had the greatest difficulty in shedding. The blatant discrepancy between the humanistic scholarly orientation and the persistent belief in magic, sorcery, and witchcraft was as much a characteristic of the Christian as of the Jewish mind. As far as the Jews were concerned, they did not have to borrow this type of belief from their Gentile contemporaries. The venerable pages of their own Talmud abound in descriptions of, or allusions to, the realm of magic, demons, and other infernal manifestations. A Jewish true believer, therefore, had to accept these as part of the things existing between heaven and earth. But the Renaissance burgeoning of superstition reinforced this ancient Jewish tendency and opened up new avenues for it. Thus not only did both Christians and Jews believe in the existence and power of demons, spirits, ghosts, satyrs; in the magic efficacy of amulets, talismans, jewels, and precious stones (some of which were used as medicaments); in vows and oaths; and in palmistry and physiognomy as means to learn the future. They also engaged side by side in the two great quests which Renaissance man inherited from the Middle Ages: the search for the elixir of life, and for a method of transforming cheap metals into gold by means of the elusive "philosopher's stone." Thus alchemy became a most attractive preoccupation for a certain type of people in both camps. Moreover sorcery—that Damoclean sword which hung over Renaissance man's head and which was believed in by the Jews as well—was considered by the Christians a nefarious practice in which the Jews were both especially adept and frequently engaged. To mention one example, in 1600 a seventy-seven-year-old Jewess, Judith Franchetti, and an alleged pupil of hers, Jacob Fano, were burned alive in the public square of Mantua on a charge of sorcery.

While in traditional Judaism superstitious beliefs often fitted neatly into a niche of the total religious world view, the Renaissance belief in the power of the stars tended to undermine the religious attitude among both Jews and Christians. On the one hand, the belief that man's fate and luck were influenced by the stars made them face losses, whether at the gambling table or in other walks of life, with a resigned acceptance of the inevitable. On the other, this belief in the power of the heavenly constellations, equally firm among Jews and Christians, made for a fatalism which was antithetical to both religions. As for the Jews, they felt that if everything depended on the force of the stars, then repentance—one of the most fundamental demands of Jewish religion—was of no use, and even corruption could be condoned. Needless to say, under these conditions astrology was a very popular science.

7. The World of the Arts

In the representational and decorative arts, the great Italian masters were eagerly imitated by the Jews. There were Jewish painters (two were members of the painters' guild at Perugia), engravers, goldsmiths (one in the service of Cesare Borgia), metalworkers, majolica workers, and art purveyors. Such a development would not have been possible had not rich Jews, and in the first place loan bankers, emulated the Italian nobility and princes of the Church in playing the role of patrons of the arts.

Music making, dancing, and the theater, in which the Jews contributed more to Renaissance culture than in any other field, were a part of Jewish everyday life. All Jewish boys and girls received instruction in music and dance. Noble ladies took dancing lessons from Jewish women, and male Jewish dancing masters taught the art to Christian clients. Mixed dancing of men and women together was accepted. These activities led to intercourse between Christians and Jews which was vehemently opposed by both civic and

Church authorities. The frequently repeated orders to close down Jewish schools of music and dancing in places like Venice indicate that these rescripts were only temporarily obeyed, and that the Gentile clients who knocked on the doors soon enabled them to reopen. There were numerous Jewish composers; the names of an even larger number of Jewish performers are known, among them violinists, flutists, and both male and female singers, the most outstanding of whom played to princely and ducal audiences. In Venice in the 1620's and 1630's, there was a Jewish musical society, patterned after the "academies," or cultural associations, that proliferated throughout Italy and was directed by Leon da Modena, the famous rabbi and author. Another Jewish musical center was in Mantua, where the House of Gonzaga employed Jewish musicians. In disregard of explicit Talmudic injunction, Italian Jews considered it permissible to listen to women singing. This intense interest in music led to the emergence of a considerable literature, written by Jewish authors, on music and dancing and including studies on the history of music and musical instruments.

Equally important were the role of Jews in the Italian theater and the role of the theater in Jewish life. Jewish dramatists wrote plays in Italian, which were well received by a mixed Jewish-Christian public. Some wrote Italian dialect comedies; others authored Purim dramas in Italian, combining the traditional Jewish story of Queen Esther with contemporary treatment. The most famous was the playwright Leon Sommi, who wrote pastorals and comedies studded with mythological figures. There was even a Jewish theatrical producer who also wrote a book on stage management. From the early sixteenth century there were Jewish theaters in Mantua, Venice, and other Italian cities, and Jewish actors performed in the ducal court of Mantua, where the court theater was served also by Jewish choreographers and engineers as technical advisers. Some of the *istrioni Ebrei* achieved great fame among Jews and Christians alike.

The Renaissance technology, of which Leonardo da Vinci is the great paragon, also attracted Jews. They participated in developing machines, constructing bridges, diverting rivers, improving silk manufacture; they invented an invisible ink and new methods of polishing mirrors and cut glass; they designed weapons and advised Italian rulers on problems of warfare, security, fortifications, and the like. Others wrote technical monographs in Italian on such subjects as the refraction of light.

Such close involvement with civic and military affairs could not but create among the Jews sincere patriotic feelings for the city or republic in which they lived (such as Florence, Rome, Siena, Venice, Verona, etc.). We know of many Jews who made intense efforts to be allowed to bear arms, and of others who were involved in political affairs and served various Italian states in a diplomatic capacity. This interest, too, is reflected in the writings in which they discuss political issues. Remarkable among these is the plan of

Abraham Portaleone (d. 1612), the eminent physician and scion of a famous Mantuan family of physicians, for establishing a society based on several different classes.

8. Crime, Gambling, and Sports

With all his thirst for knowledge, his intellectual curiosity, and his interest in the arts and sciences, Renaissance man was intent on what today would be termed ego satisfaction. This expressed itself in many ways: in a blatant disregard of the law, whether secular or religious; in an unwillingness or inability to control one's passions; in violence and vengefulness; in criminal acts; in addiction to games of chance; and in an overindulgence in sex and especially in illicit sexual adventures. All these phenomena could be observed among the Jews as well as among the Gentiles.

The Jewish crime pattern—which even in such a highly assimilated Jewish community as that of the present-day United States differs markedly from that of the non-Jewish population—conformed in Renaissance Italy closely to the Gentile Italian prototype. There were Jewish bandits and gangsters who terrorized people; there were Jewish informers, looters, robbers, murderers; some even "worked" as hired killers. To resort to murder was not beyond the horizon of the educated, whether Jew or Christian. At least two cases of the murder of Jewish physicians by other Jewish physicians are known. Others, who did not go to such lengths, were known to have been aggressive and violent, with cases attested among Jewish bankers and humanists. It was in the spirit of the times to give vent to one's passions, and this led to strife and feuds, often lasting decades, and to trickery and vengefulness of which elaborate examples are extant. The same atmosphere also of course fostered great courage and the Renaissance determination to achieve one's goal at any cost.

As for the games of hazard, dice and cards were the main attractions. The passion of card playing is known to have engulfed even rabbis, some of whom were reduced to the verge of ruin as a result. As early as 1418, the Jewish conference held at Forli issued a decree against the vice—to no avail, as can be seen from the frequent reiteration of the prohibition down to the late eighteenth century. Gambling knew no religious barriers, and Jewish gamblers could play even against ducal partners. On one such occasion, in 1479, an unfortunate Jew lost 3,000 ducats at one sitting to the duke of Ferrara. Experiences such as this motivated Jewish gamblers to make vows of abstention from the game, as we know from a note on the flyleaf of a prayer book also from Ferrara. Rabbi Judah ben David, known as Bonjudes ben Davin (or Bondavin), who was the rabbi of all Sardinia as well as a physician, was an expert dice player; on one occasion in 1408, he had some difficulty in excusing himself from playing with the king at the royal invitation. About two centuries later, Leon da Modena (1571–1648), one of the greatest figures of Italian Jewry, famous rabbi, orator, and poet, was a lifelong gambling addict. At the age of thirteen, he wrote a dialogue against gambling which was published in no less than ten editions as well as in Latin, French, German, and Yiddish translations; but despite his awareness of its dangers, he could not resist a passion for all games of chance which contributed greatly to his many other troubles and misfortunes. At the age of sixty he was still not rid of his addiction and got involved in a struggle with the Venice community which he served as rabbi and which issued a decree of excommunication against all persons guilty of playing cards.[6] The epidemic of card playing, incidentally, enabled Jewish artisans to engage in the lucrative business of manufacturing (i.e., hand-painting) and selling playing cards.

The Jews indulged in all the favorite sports and pastimes of the Renaissance. In addition to the pursuit of amorous adventures and gambling, they took part in fencing and ball playing. Of the outdoor sports, the Jews practiced hiking, hunting, horse racing, and the "ball game," i.e., rackets or tennis. The last became such a passion with many Jews that they would not refrain from it on the Sabbath, and the rabbis felt constrained to permit it on the Jewish holyday of rest.[7] This game was a spectators' sport as well, and the onlookers would place bets on the player.

9. Sexual License

In the sexual area, things were made complicated and dangerous for Jews due to the civil laws. All over Italy these made Jewish-Gentile sex relations a criminal offense, punishable, as far as the Jewish culprit was concerned, by a great variety of penalties ranging from fines through imprisonment, expulsion, flogging, and galley slavery to death at the stake.[8] The Christian partner of such illicit affairs got away with a relatively light punishment or none at all. The fact that in these circumstances young Christian men, especially of the noble class, regarded Jewish women as fair game is understandable, considering the highly eroticized Renaissance ambience. Many a Jewish girl and woman fell victim to such amorous approaches, which were facilitated by the frequent social contact that existed between Jewish and Gentile families. Some Jewish women, it is known, had to pay with their lives for such dalliance. Thus in 1628 the Jewish mistress of the son of the duke of Parma was burned.[9] Others, especially well-educated ones, entered the time-honored profession of prostitution, became sought-after courtesans, and mingled with high Christian society. As in Spain so in Italy, landlords accepted prostitutes as tenants in their houses; when some people complained to the civil authorities, they were rebuffed and told that it was entirely proper to have houses of prostitution so as to prevent men from the sin of carnal intercourse with married women.[10]

The Jewish men were just as adventurous as the Christian men, despite the much greater danger even a single encounter with a Christian woman represented for them. Numerous cases are known in which Jews were caught in immoral acts with Christian women, including nuns—for the latter sin the entire Jewish community was punished by exile. These Jewish-Christian intrigues occasionally had a truly Boccaccio-like flavor. In Reggio, in 1536, a Christian couple developed an ingenious get-rich-quick scheme. Their plan was for the wife, who had been courted by a rich Jew, to consent to receiving him in her home, and then let them be "surprised" by her husband. To make things more effective, the husband brought along the *podestà* and his two assistants, and the four burst in upon the frightened Jew, from whom they extorted 400 *scudi* in hush money. It so happened that, at the end, the *podestà* was publicly punished for the conspiracy.[11] One can get some idea of the frequency of sexual offenses from the fact that in fifteenth-century Florence, which had a Jewish population of not more than a hundred families, of the eighty-eight cases against Jews tried before the civic magistrates, thirty-four were for moral misdemeanors, while seventeen were for gambling. Since we can assume that only a small percentage of the transgressions committed came to the notice of the civil authorities, the actual incidence of fornication and gambling among the Jews must have been quite considerable. Historical evidence shows that the frequently repeated prohibitions, issued with great regularity every few years by both secular and Jewish authorities, could stem the tide of immorality neither in the area of sex nor in that of games of chance.[12]

Slave ownership, a widespread practice in the Renaissance, contributed its share to what by Jewish tradition was considered gross immorality. The female slaves (most of the slaves of both sexes were Negroes) were often used as concubines by their masters, a practice which was well known among the Jewish communities in the Muslim world and which received added impetus in Italy from its prevalence among the Gentiles.

10. The Position of Women

The position of the Jewish woman was an exact replica of that of her Christian sister. Not only did Jewish women, in general, have Italian names (in contrast to the Jewish men, most of whom had Biblical names which, of course, were used by Christian men as well), but they enjoyed an education like that of the Christian women and, again like them, participated in business, in public life, in politics, and in literature (they wrote in Italian). Indeed, some of them attained prominent positions. There were Jewish

women physicians and beauticians advising and serving the women of
princely houses, selling them unguents and beauty preparations. There were
even female ritual slaughterers, authorized by the rabbinate. They shared
the same ideal of female beauty, which was discussed in a vast literature
produced by Gentile authors and, following in their footsteps, by Jewish
writers also. Ardent love letters, in the best Renaissance style, were exchanged between the Jewish affianced, as well as between men and women
connected only by emotional ties. The Jewish women, like the Christian,
loved luxurious clothes and expensive jewelry (which they refused to give up
despite repeated rabbinical anti-luxury decrees) and took great pride in
beautifully appointed homes. The Jewish families adopted the Christian custom of sitting together in a group and being entertained by reading and
storytelling.

11. Literacy and Education

One of the important differences between Jews and Gentiles throughout
the Diaspora has been the much higher rate of literacy among Jews. Baron
remarked in this connection that the Jews in the Middle Ages were as literate as the Christian clergy. This difference between Jewish and Gentile literacy persisted in Renaissance Italy as well, although here the Gentile literacy
rate was relatively high. Among the educated people, and especially the
wealthy, the Renaissance produced a great interest in books and old manuscripts. This spread rapidly to the Jews, who took to collecting first manuscripts, and later printed books, and to establishing libraries. In Cremona,
the Inquisition destroyed at one time 12,000 books which were in the possession of the eighty Jewish families in the city. This astounding figure indicates
the extent of Renaissance Jewish bibliophilism; for some Jews, it became a
veritable passion. In any case, the Jewish interest in books enabled hundreds
of Jewish scribes to make a living from copying manuscripts. In the last
quarter of the fifteenth century, when Hebrew printed books made their appearance, a lively Jewish book trade developed, and the number of Jewish
libraries increased considerably. The available information shows the extraordinarily wide range of subjects covered by the books amassed by Jewish
bibliophiles: they included, of course, all the traditional and not-so-tradi-
tional Jewish subjects, as well as philosophy, astronomy, geography, history,
and non-Jewish *belles lettres* in Italian, or in Yiddish translation.

Before the end of the fifteenth century, Hebrew printing presses were established in several Italian cities—in many cases, interestingly enough, by
Jewish physicians. This led to a further increase in Jewish literacy, already
high all over Italy, and in Jewish-owned libraries. Some of the Jewish presses

also printed books in Italian and Latin, and many of the incunabula and later books produced by them are of exquisite craftsmanship.

Literacy is, of course, a function of education, and the emphasis on education has been a Jewish characteristic everywhere. In Renaissance Italy the nature of Jewish education was strongly influenced by the Gentile environment.

The Renaissance emphasis on knowledge and learning inspired the Jews to efforts at raising the educational level of their own young. They either had their children, both boys and girls, tutored privately or sent them to Jewish schools in which they were instructed in Jewish and secular subjects—including Italian grammar, fencing, music, and dancing. Thus, in addition to a Jewish education, the Jewish child studied the subjects which comprised the curriculum in well-to-do Italian circles. The close social relations between Jews and Christians were indicated by the fact that Christian tutors were employed in Jewish families to teach secular subjects, while Jewish tutors fulfilled the same service in Christian homes. In addition, the Renaissance interest in the Hebrew Bible and even in rabbinic literature opened up a new avenue of tutorial activity for learned Jews, who taught these subjects privately to individual Christian humanists.

While Jews had access to Italian universities both as students and as teachers, some felt that those institutions of higher learning were deficient from a Jewish point of view since they did not provide an education in Jewish subjects. To remedy this situation, they made plans to organize Jewish academies or universities in which both Tora and philosophy, that is, Jewish and secular subjects, would be taught. Such an institution was planned in 1466 in Sicily but did not materialize. Another was mooted in Ferrara in 1556 and reached the stage of receiving a letter patent from the duke. A third one was actually established in Mantua in 1564 and functioned for at least ten years, with a curriculum comprising, in additon to Jewish subjects, Latin and Italian composition, logic, mathematics, oratory, astronomy, and, of course, medicine.

12. Learning and Literature

As we saw in the preceding chapter, under the impact of the Muslim Arab environment the Jewish scholars struck out into new fields of Jewish intellectual creativity. They began to study Hebrew grammar, wrote poetry, explored religious philosophy (including mysticism), and occupied themselves with the codification of the *Halakha*—all this in addition to the secular studies in which they were already engaged. This expansion of the intellectual horizon, embracing all secular subjects as well as those which can be loosely termed "Jewish studies," was carried forward in Renaissance Italy to an unprecedented extent. Perhaps the most remarkable phenomenon in the life of Renaissance Jews was the rapid spread of the Renaissance zest for learning from the Christians to their ranks. Learning was, of course, nothing new for the Jews; but it had meant, as it was to mean again after the Renaissance had run its course, devoting oneself to the study of the Tora, that is, the Law, the *Halakha*. During the Renaissance, learning in an entirely different sense—that of acquiring a familiarity with all branches of knowledge, of exploring the unknown in the most varied fields—became as much an obsession with the Jews as it was with the Gentiles. Just as the Italian princes, the high clergy, and the aristocrats of wealth supported artists and scholars, so did the wealthy Jews. In return, Jewish authors dedicated their works to their patrons in a way that closely copied their Christian colleagues' usage. Excellence in a field of learning was the key to the courts of kings and princes, in which Jewish and Christian scholars mingled and exchanged ideas. To facilitate this, the rabbis gave permission to Jewish savants to wear the *cappa*, the distinguished and distinctive garb of the Christian scholars.

The literary activities of the Jews in Renaissance Italy, which have been touched on occasionally and in passing in connection with other subjects, constitute the richest and most variegated chapter in their life and work. Because of their traditional preoccupation with literature, the Jews in every period of contact with the Gentile world evinced a greater readiness to absorb non-Jewish cultural influences in the literary than in any other field. Thus the most important formal influences of the ancient Canaanite culture, of Hellenism, of the Muslim Arab civilization are discernible in the literary works of the Jews who were exposed to them. The same holds good for the Renaissance as well.

The Renaissance Jews, of course, had the advantage of being heirs to the broad and rich literary tradition that had developed among the Jews in the Muslim Arab lands. Thus they began with the knowledge that Jewish literary works do not have to be confined to traditional religious subjects but can extend over many other fields as well. Yet, from the very beginning they went far beyond the Mediterranean and Arab Jewish literary heritage. Earlier, I mentioned Immanuel haRomi, the late thirteenth- and early fourteenth-century grand master of Hebrew letters, who played an important role in introducing the Italian sonnet form into Hebrew poetry. Subsequently, Renaissance Jewish poets borrowed other forms as well from Italian prosody and wrote Hebrew terzinas (*"terza rime"*), sestinas, canzonas, canzonettas, and madrigals, while simultaneously retaining the Arabic meters used by their Spanish Hebrew predecessors.

More important than the formal influence was that of the contents and tone of Italian poetry and prose on Hebrew authors. Jewish poets wrote hymns, elegies, love poems, and, above all, occasional verses in an endless outpouring. Birth, marriage, death, events in the life of the community—everything was an event to be greeted by poetic efforts. Obscene language, or at least a flippant tone, was common in both Italian Renaissance poetry and prose, with sexuality and sexual pleasure forming the theme of countless short stories. This literature was eagerly read by the Jews (almost all of whom knew Italian) and was emulated by Jewish writers, a situation which only sporadically provoked protests from conservative rabbis. For those new-comers from across the Alps who had not mastered Italian, the most popular Italian romances were translated into Yiddish, while some tried their hand at original secular literary pieces in that language. For the Italian-speaking majority of the Jews in Italy, translations were produced in the reverse direction. Thus the Jews created a literature in Italian as well as in Judeo-Italian dialects, into which they translated the Bible, liturgical works, sermons, and, as already mentioned, the prayer book.

A blurring of the boundaries in the literary world is indicated by the fact that while the Italian Jews read much non-Jewish literature, including the works of the great Italian poets, Jewish authors wrote poetry and prose for the non-Jewish public. On the other hand, Hebrew was still sufficiently alive among the Jews to prompt writers to translate Italian novels and other genres of literature into that language. In fact, the interest in Hebrew linguistics was considerable, the study of Hebrew grammar was very popular, and consequently the Renaissance Jews knew Hebrew better than the Askhenazim. Some even undertook an investigation of the Samaritan alphabet.

However, *belles lettres* were only one of many literary fields to which Renaissance Jews devoted their attention. They wrote numerous historical works—by no means confined to the Jewish past—whose scope and depth paralleled those of Italian Renaissance historiography. To mention only one of the many historians of the period, Joseph ben Joshua haKohen (1496–c. 1575), who spent much of his life as a physician in Genoa, wrote two important historical works in Hebrew. One is a *Chronicle of the Kings of France and Turkey*, an account of the conflict between Christianity and Islam; the other is his *Vale of Tears*, a Jewish martyrology, containing a history of the persecutions of Jews down to the year 1575. His lesser works, also in Hebrew, include a history of the conquest of Mexico, and others of both Jewish and non-Jewish content. [13]

The great Renaissance preoccupation with the ancient world was reechoed among the Jews in a keen interest in both Jewish and non-Jewish antiquities and archeology. The literary expression of this interest was a series of books on subjects the like of which could not have been imagined by Jews living in other environments, including the Spanish Golden Age. One of those who embarked on such formerly untrodden or even unknown paths of research was Abraham Portaleone, already mentioned, who, in addition to his medical works, wrote an important treatise on Biblical and Talmudic antiquities. He was preceded by Azariah de Rossi (1513–78), whose study of Hebrew literature, archeology, and history in the light of Greek sources applied to the subject the critical principles developed in the Renaissance. Another work of Rossi's, his magnum opus entitled *M'or 'Enayim* or *Light of the Eyes*, contains criticism of Talmudic beliefs and stories, and consequently provoked sharp opposition among conservative rabbis. In the very year it was printed (1575), no less an authority than Joseph Caro, the celebrated author of the *Shulḥan 'Arukh*, was about to issue a decree ordering the Jewish communities to burn the book when he died. Others wrote studies on general and Jewish history, and on Biblical chronology and archeology, including lengthy descriptions of the Jerusalem Temple.

In addition to the literary pursuit of archeological studies, many Jews became collectors of antique objects of art—bronze figures, vessels, medals, coins, and so on. Another consequence of this preoccupation with the ancient world among both Christians and Jews was a fascination with Greek and Roman mythology, with ancient religions, and with the ancient way of life in general. All this was of course facilitated because it was so easy for Italians to learn Latin and to read the classical authors in that language. Many Italian Jews mastered Latin to the extent of being able to translate Arabic works of science and philosophy into it, or to write original prose and poetry or use it in making speeches. The knowledge of Greek was less widespread, but an appreciation of it was not lacking, and some Jews considered Greek the most beautiful language in the world. Even those who did not know Latin and Greek were familiar with classical literature from the Italian translations, and frequently quoted from Latin and Greek authors in their own books.

Incidentally, scholarship, and the ability to translate sought-after Arabic books into Latin, could secure for Jews employment by rulers and princes. Occasionally, Christian patrons of the sciences granted stipends to Jewish scholars without any stipulated service in exchange.

Next to history and archeology, geography and cosmography were favorite Renaissance subjects. Abraham Farissol (or Farrisol) wrote numerous Bible commentaries and a polemical work against Christianity and Islam. But he was also the author of a pioneering cosmography and geography entitled *Iggeret Orḥot 'Olam*, or *Epistle of the Paths of the World*, which was first published in the Hebrew original in Ferrara in 1524 and reissued in a Latin translation in Oxford in 1691. Farissol himself translated Aristotle's *Logic* into Hebrew, among other writings. Others wrote on the geography of the Holy Land. Abraham Farissol's contemporary and relative was Judah Farissol, who wrote a description of the astronomical sphere with diagrams in 1499, under the title *Iggeret S'fira* (*Epistle of the Sphere*).

Other subjects to which Jewish authors devoted their writings can be mentioned only briefly. Solomon Jedidiah Norsa produced for the first time a scientific text of the Hebrew Bible. The famous Judah Messer Leon wrote a Hebrew book on rhetoric, in which he quotes profusely standard Jewish authorities as well as such classical writers as Cicero and Quintilian. The financial problems and moral issues which arose in connection with Jewish loan banking could not fail to be treated in scholarly work; a treatise written in 1559 by the banking magnate Vitale, or Yehiel Nissim da Pisa, discusses the mechanism of financial transactions and their permissibility under Biblical law. Abraham Portaleone also wrote a treatise entitled *Shilte haGibborim* or *The Heroes' Shields*, which contains, among other things, a comprehensive plan of how to conduct a war, including detailed instructions on how to carry out surprise attacks, how to make gunpowder, and other military matters. (We might add that Jews served alongside their Gentile compatriots in the armies of the cities and republics of Italy.)

Even when they wrote on subjects well established within Jewish tradition, the Renaissance Jews introduced an original note. The writing of Biblical commentaries had been a standard practice among the great Spanish rabbis, and of course Rashi, the greatest of all Bible commentators, had already been at work in the eleventh century in France. Yet when Yohanan Alamanno put pen to paper to write a Hebrew commentary to the Song of Songs—which he did at the suggestion of his Gentile friend Pico della Mirandola—he produced something entirely new and unheard-of in this venerable field. His commentary was in the tradition of contemporary Tuscan philosophical thought; moreover, he prefaced it by a pen portrait of Lorenzo the Magnificent and his circle, and a penetrating analysis of the Florentine character.

13. Religious Laxity

Social contact inevitably brought about a weakening of Jewish religious observance, much of which had as its explicit or implicit purpose the erection of a barrier between Jew and Gentile in an attempt to prevent assimilation. Some of the laxity in religious observance was due to the Jewish desire to adopt the customs and forms of the Christians and so diminish the visible differences between them. Thus the traditional Jewish religious rule of wearing a head covering was frequently disregarded, as was the rule imposed by the Italian authorities of wearing the "Jewish badge" as a clear distinguishing mark. Frequent commensality with Christians led to the disregard of the old Jewish ban on wine made by Gentiles. In fact, wine drinking was very common on both sides, and joint meals, which were frequent in Jewish and Christian homes, could not be imagined without the cup. In Jewish homes the laws of *kashrut* seem to have been observed in general, although the dishes favored were the same as those in Christian homes; but it is more than doubtful whether such dietary laws were observed by Jews when visiting the homes of Christian friends for convivial feasting. On these occasions social dancing was also indulged in—again, a violation of the traditional Jewish rules of sexual modesty.

Equally serious was the deviation from the generally respectful attitude toward religious values demanded by Jewish tradition. Enchantment with secular knowledge led many a thoughtful individual among both Christians and Jews to take a critical view of the traditional doctrines of their religion. In general, a rather nonchalant position developed toward religious observance, institutions, and doctrines. Even such a basic Jewish doctrine as that of the immortality of the soul was apparently undermined by a rampant religious skepticism.

The synagogue, that last stronghold of Jewish religious observance and conservatism, was also penetrated by Gentile Renaissance influences—a phenomenon that was to be repeated after the Jewish Enlightenment with much more dire consequences. The synagogue buildings imitated the Italian Renaissance architectural style. Their walls were decorated with murals showing birds and flowers; the sacred vessels used in it were made occasionally by Gentile silversmiths, including the famed Benvenuto Cellini, or more often by Jewish craftsmen who carefully imitated the Italian style. The very copies of the Bible and the tomes of halakhic literature showed the Italian influence. They were frequently and beautifully illustrated with Italian-style pictures, showing animals, human figures, Cherubim, and non-Jewish motifs. Next to the eye, the Italian influence was perceived through the ear: cantors and choirs sang the Hebrew prayers to the melodies of Italian folk tunes. Even the sermons preached by the rabbis in the synagogues were not only given in Italian but were in many respects imitations of Italian religious oratory. Instead of the traditional discourses displaying rabbinical scholarship and based on Bible, Talmud, and Midrash, they were ethical, moral, and hortatory, not dissimilar to those of the friars who exhorted the multitudes to repentance during Lent. The very structure of these sermons was greatly influenced by contemporary Italian homiletics and was built on frequent references to classical authors such as Aristotle and Cicero. Some rabbis, such as Judah del Bene, were so thoroughly imbued with the Renaissance spirit that they could not help (or did not mind) introducing pagan allusions into their sermons. Several rabbis gained great fame as outstanding orators, made speeches in Latin as well as in Italian, spoke on secular subjects, and were listened to with rapture by Christians who would come to their synagogues to enjoy an extraordinary oratorical feat. Another sign of the Italianization of religious life was the translation of the prayer book into Judeo-Italian, for the benefit of the womenfolk.

Religious celebrations outside the synagogue also manifested strong

Italian influences. In emulation of the Italian carnival, the Feast of Purim became an occasion for Jewish revelry, complete with elaborately produced theatrical plays, with masks worn by young and old alike, and much carrying on in the streets. (The American reader will have no difficulty in recognizing the same process which made Hanukka in the United States a Jewish counterpart of the highly commercialized and secularized Christmas.) [14]

Elaborate, luxurious, and ostentatious celebrations of family occasions, with gatherings in *piazzas* and festive processions in the streets, were a typical expression of the Renaissance love of pomp and circumstance, and the Jews could not but vie with the Christians in this area as well. Weddings and circumcisions were occasions for sumptuous masquerades, the bridegroom was accompanied by numerous torch bearers as he went or rode to visit his bride, flowers and sweets were thrown down on the bridal party, and so on. Things came to such a pass that almost every Jewish community felt it advisable to issue repeatedly sumptuary laws forbidding such excesses and setting a limit on the number of guests the celebrant family was allowed to invite, on cavalcades, on richly caparisoned horses, on large gatherings in the streets, on what dresses and jewelry the women might wear, on the amount they were permitted to spend on wigs, muffs, fans, flowers, and even on the preparation of an illuminated *ketubba* or marriage contract. One of the first such lists of restrictions was issued by the Jewish Vigilance Committee which met at Forli in the Romagna in 1418; and as late as 1748 in Ferrara, and 1766 in Ancona, the Jewish leadership felt it necessary to repeat essentially the same sumptuary laws.

Oddly enough, the greatest ostentation was reserved, not for these joyous occasions, but for funerals. Even in poverty-stricken Sicily, incredibly lavish funerals were the order of the day. The grandiose funeral of Rabbi Judah Minz of Padua in 1509 was a garish testimony to the extent to which Renaissance Jews had succumbed to the Italian love of ostentatious pomposity.

14. Between Jews and Christians

The very nature and composition of Jewish society was a mirror image in miniature of the Christian. The Italian ruling nobility had its Jewish counterpart in the rich loan bankers and merchant princes: both groups prided themselves on being patrons of the arts and of literature. To the Christian Church leaders corresponded the rabbis: in the clergy of both faiths there were many in whose minds worldly preoccupations and interests predominated. As we have seen, all the arts and crafts, the branches of literature, science and philosophy, in which the Christians excelled attracted Jews as well. In two, translation and medicine, the Christians were definitely outdis-

tanced; and in another three—music, dance, and the theater—the Jews gave
a remarkable account of themselves.

However, because the Jews in every Italian city were a small group living
in the midst of a large Christian majority, the distance between the Jewish
élite and lower classes could never be as great as it was between the top and
bottom layers of the Christian society. This meant that the interests and accomplishments of the Jewish élite had a greater influence on the rest of the
Jewish community than was the case among the Gentiles. The old famous
Jewish trait of literacy, not confined, as it was among the Christians, to the
élite, was an important factor in reducing the distance between the Jewish
upper and lower classes and in making the literary achievements of the
former available to the latter. Adherence to the other old Jewish value, that
of charity, which made it a moral and religious duty to help the needy, had
the result of practically eliminating the most dire forms of poverty which
claimed so many victims among the Christians. The Jewish concern for the
poor was so strong that occasionally Jews would leave bequests to the *Monti
di Pietà*, the civic charitable lending institutions, although the activities of
these "Funds of Piety" represented a dangerous competition to Jewish loan
banking.

Needless to say, in those fields of everyday life which were not circumscribed by their religious law, the Jews emulated the Gentiles with a
limitless abandon. The houses of those who could afford it were in the best
style prescribed by contemporary taste. Well-to-do Jews, like the Christian
patricians, had villas in the country to which they would repair for the hot
summer months and from which they would go out hunting—a most un-
Jewish pastime in traditional terms—or hiking. They furnished their houses
like the Christians and kept pet animals and birds. The Jewish home, like
the Christian, manifested the artistic taste of its owner in that its walls were
hung with pictures. These were often portraits of the head and other
members of the family. The Jews, like the Gentiles, were patrons of the fine
arts, becoming thus the first Jewish community long before the Enlightenment to take an interest in painting and sculpture.

Not the least purpose of having one's portrait painted was to perpetuate
one's name and memory. For the same reason Jews, like Gentiles, had their
likeness struck on medallions. Both groups were obsessed with the idea of
leaving behind their image in a tangible or visible form, which was the more
important for them since they had lost their belief in an afterlife. Many Jews,
on a somewhat higher plane, emphasized in the books they wrote that their
works would serve the preservation of their memory.

Social contacts between Jews and Gentiles were intensive, despite the
"tolerated" status of the former and the "Jewish badge" which was mandatory all over Italy. A few Jews obtained exemption from the odious duty;
many more, risking severe punishment, disregarded the law, dressed like

the Christians, and vied with them in elegance and luxurious attire. Motivated by a powerful desire to become part of the effervescent and scintillating Renaissance life, they spared no effort not only to dress like the Christians, but also to behave like the Christians, to speak like the Christians, and to acquire a mental equipment which would enable them to match the best of the Christians in brilliant conversation. Jews and Christians frequently visited each other's homes, celebrating family feasts in each other's company. Jewish and Christian children played together, and the genuine closeness between Jews and Christians, brought about by a similarity in family life patterns, could not be disrupted even by repeatedly issued bans on such social contact. In fact, anticipating by four or five centuries what in modern American parlance has become known as "interfaith in action" and in liberal Christian circles is termed "ecumenism," the Renaissance Jews and Christians, motivated by mutual esteem, frequently engaged in friendly debate for the purpose of understanding each other's faiths. All this resulted in a close relationship between Jews and Gentiles and in a participation by Jews in the intellectual and social life of Gentile society to an extent not duplicated anywhere until the Emancipation.

Some Jews, to be sure, went to ridiculous or pathetic lengths in their eagerness to achieve the great purpose of social acceptance. They provided themselves with elaborate heraldic coats-of-arms, acquired the title *cavaliere*, of which they were immensely proud, or, as a poor substitute, sought the degrees of *Rabbi* or *Haver*. They fought for the right to bear arms—an important status symbol in Renaissance society. The Renaissance Jew, like the Renaissance Gentile, was an individualist whose major goal in life was to stand out from among other men and to be admired for extraordinary deeds or attainments. In pursuing this goal both Christians and Jews spared no effort, often performing even bizarre and discreditable acts. Another great aim, again shared by Jews and Gentiles, was to attain the unattainable: ultimate bliss. This concept, as well as such ideals as "true human success" and "perfection," are often mentioned in popular Jewish guides to human happiness. Some of these books include descriptions of "the perfect man" complete with concrete examples: King Solomon and Lorenzo the Magnificent. The references to great figures of the Jewish past are, typically, couched in resounding Renaissance phraseology. Thus a Talmudic sage is described as "*divino*," divine—a strange epithet indeed for a Jewish religious scholar.

15. Cultural Synthesis

What emerges from this depiction of the mind of the Renaissance Jew as mirrored in his life, letters, and works is that the convergences between his cultural interests and those of his Christian contemporaries were so numerous as to appear almost overwhelming. There were striking similarities between Jews and Christians in attitudes and aspirations, manners and mores, intellectual endeavors and orientation, as well as in everyday life and activity. These similarities—it would not be amiss to term them identities—were so comprehensive and all-embracing that the question must inevitably arise whether in the deepest ground of the Renaissance Jewish psyche that innermost core of Jewish consciousness, of Jewish commitment and identification, still persisted. In the earlier great historical encounters, this had unmistakably marked off Jew against Gentile. In the case of the Renaissance Jew, it must be admitted, the traces or manifestations of such a Jewish core and content are more difficult to discern than they were in the Spanish-Arab, Hellenistic, or Canaanite epochs. Nonetheless, they were there, ready to disclose themselves to the searching eye.

In the first place, this residual but still essential Jewishness becomes manifest in the endeavor to aggrandize and glorify the cultural achievements of the Jewish past in typically Renaissance terms. That is to say, those forms of intellectual activity which were highly valued in the Renaissance were shown by Renaissance Jews, whenever possible, to be of Jewish origin or invention. Thus, since music was a major preoccupation in Renaissance Italy, the Italian Jews, who of course participated wholeheartedly and enthusiastically in Italian musical life, also went out of their way to emphasize that music was actually a "Jewish" invention. Does not the Bible state (in Gen. 4:21) that Juval was the originator of this noble art? Since the dialogue had become a favorite Italian literary form, the Jews not only adopted it but tried to prove that this, too, was an ancient Jewish invention, pointing as proof to the Biblical Book of Job which is undeniably written in the form of a series of dialogues. And Judah Messer Leon, who was known in secular records as "Leo the Jew, Doctor of Arts and Medicine, and Knight, as well as Doctor of the Hebrew Law," wrote a book entitled *Nofet Tzufim* (or *Honeycomb*, 1478), in order to raise the prestige of the Jew by demonstrating to the Gentile world that Jews were not hostile to secular culture. In this way all kinds of Renaissance activities were claimed to have been originated by Jews, or at least to be in conformity with ancient Jewish doctrine and practice.

Efforts to conform to the traditional *Halakha* in the midst of all these varied Renaissance activities are also indicative of the persistence of Jewish commitment and identification. For example, those who were addicted to the fashionable sport of rackets felt that they had to make sure that, if they played it on the Sabbath, they did not violate the precepts of the Jewish day of rest. A similar desire to comply with Jewish Law while conducting Renaissance activities motivated the banking magnate Vitale or Yehiel Nissim da Pisa in writing the treatise in which he discusses the permissibility of financial transactions under Biblical law. At the other end of the range of Renaissance preoccupations, those Jews who were interested in philosophy made efforts to show that there was no prohibition of philosophical speculation in the Bible. Again, they used Jewish occasions such as circumcisions, weddings, funerals, or Purim celebrations to indulge in a genuinely Renaissance-style display of luxury, thus exhibiting their pride in their Jewishness for all to see.

In general, the Renaissance Jew, however great his fascination with Renaissance culture, neither tried to hide his Jewish affiliation nor become indifferent to, or uninterested in, traditional Jewish culture. Just the contrary: he was determined to "harmonize the religious and cultural values of Judaism with Renaissance values and its life style." [15] And he succeeded, to a degree which is quite astounding if we contrast this with what happened in nineteenth-century Germany in the wake of the Jewish Enlightenment. The German Jewish Enlighteners' (*Maskilim*) total self-subordination to, and infatuation with, modern European culture led them to abandon Jewish culture, Jewish tradition, and often even Jewish religion. The Renaissance Jews, on the other hand, were so firmly anchored in their Jewishness that however greatly they were smitten by Renaissance culture, this merely spurred them to ingenious intellectual attempts to prove that the ancient Hebrews had a decisive role in that tide of human culture which crested in their Renaissance environment. All these efforts must be interpreted and can be understood only as manifestations of a vital Jewish psyche in the midst of the Renaissance turmoil and ferment.

In numerous instances, the cultural interest which was awakened in the Jews by their Renaissance environment was either totally or at least partially chaneled by them into Jewish fields. That is to say, while they became acculturated to the Renaissance, they also adopted Renaissance culture to Jewish use or enriched their Jewish culture with Renaissance features. To give a rapid rundown of the clearest examples, they did this in the arts by using Renaissance styles and motifs to illustrate and illuminate Jewish books, such as the Bible and the prayer book, and Jewish documents, such as the *ketubba* or marriage contract. In music, they took Italian melodies to enrich their Jewish prayers both in the synagogue and at home. They acquired the Renaissance theatrical techniques and utilized them for the dramatic presentation of the most emphatically Jewish consciousness-raising story: that of Queen Esther. They learned the latest critical historiographic methods and applied them to studies of Jewish history. The Renaissance interest in archeology took the form of investigating the antiquities of the Jews. In other sciences, even when writing on secular subjects which could not be given a Jewish angle, they frequently composed their treatises in Hebrew, making thereby a contribution if not to Jewish literature at least to Hebrew letters and the Hebrew language. Likewise, when they wrote poetry, secular in content and flippantly Italian in form, they often wrote in Hebrew, and the same poets also wrote Jewish religious poems in Hebrew. When adding their voices to the Renaissance quest for the ultimate in bliss and perfection, they presented great Jewish historical figures, such as King Solomon, as the ideal image of the perfect man. In all this, and much more along the same lines, the Renaissance Jew accomplished the seemingly impossible: he produced a synthesis of two widely different, if not antagonistic, cultures.

A second, perhaps even more telling manifestation of the enduring Jewish consciousness and identity among the Renaissance Jews can be seen in their fidelity to their religion and community. This, again, becomes especially impressive if one compares it with the rapid path to total assimilation and conversion to Christianity that was followed by the children and grand-children of those German Jews who in the late eighteenth century either ini-tiated the Jewish Enlightenment or became its first followers. It is a well-known fact that, for instance, not a single grandchild of Moses Mendelssohn remained Jewish, and that in the early nineteenth century there was a verita-ble epidemic of conversions among the Enlighteners or Assimilants, although they were the first generation of Jews to receive an upbringing which was not entirely traditionally Jewish. As against this, the descendants of even the most fervent Jewish adherents of and participants in the Italian Renaissance remained within the fold down to modern times. This, of course, does not mean that the phenomenon of conversion to Christianity was unknown in Renaissance times. But, in general, when conversions did take place, they were in response to extreme duress. Given the choice between death or con-version, or between expulsion and conversion (as occasionally happened in various places in Italy), there were always some who chose conversion. From the seventeenth century on, in the wake of the Catholic reaction, forced bap-tisms of Jews (including children) became frequent in all parts of Italy, often involving outrageous procedures. Yet only in rare instances did the Renais-sance skepticism about religious values, even if combined with considerable pressure on the part of the Church, result in voluntary conversion to Chris-tianity by individual Jews, sometimes members of ancient families and per-sons of learning. Self-interest, too, played a part in these conversions, and even motivated some of the *neofiti* (or New Christians) to engage in vicious anti-Jewish activities.

These cases notwithstanding, the fact remains that while for the German Jewish Enlightener Judaism as such became an oppressive ballast which he discarded at the earliest opportunity, the Italian Renaissance Jew considered his Jewish heritage a treasure whose true value became enhanced for him when he could look at it through Renaissance eyes. In contrast to the *Has-kala*, whose Teutonic grip often uprooted the Jewish psyche from its ancient moorings, the Italian Renaissance, with all its Latin exuberance, never pene-trated the deepest reserves of the *Ebreo* soul. It thus appears that despite his near-total absorption of all the characteristics of the Italian Renaissance man, including an uncanny mimesis of his personality traits, the Renaissance Jew nevertheless remained essentially Jewish in the one ultimate issue—his Jew-ishness, which formed the ground of his being.

A third eloquent testimony to the abiding Jewish identification and com-mitment of the Renaissance Jews is supplied by the reception they accorded to David Reubeni, the mysterious Oriental adventurer who arrived in Italy in 1524. Reubeni claimed that he was a prince of the House of Reuben and that his brother Joseph was the king of a powerful and independent country located somewhere east of Egypt and inhabited by a warlike Jewish people of the Reubenite tribe. He had been sent by his royal brother, he maintained, in order to form an alliance between his forces and the Christian powers of Europe for the purpose of launching a joint attack against the Turks, who had gained control of the Holy Land and were menacing Christendom. The plan found immediate and fervently positive response among the Jews of Italy. Immersed though they were in the tide of Renaissance culture, they reacted with a boundless enthusiasm to the strange, stocky, and swarthy Jewish "prince" and his scheme. The extent to which this reaction to Reubeni was the result of Jewish rather than Italian sentiments becomes evident if one compares it with the lukewarm interest he evoked in the pope, Clement VII, the cardinals, and other Christian potentates, although for them Turkey represented a menace while for the Jews it was a friendly power and a haven of refuge. One would expect the Jews to have felt some hesitancy toward a project aimed at reducing or eliminating Turkish dominance over the eastern Mediterranean. But the news that there existed a faraway powerful Jewish kingdom, a Jewish nation of warriors who had been fighting the "terrible Turk" and were planning to deal him a mortal blow, struck a chord in the psyche of the Italian Jews which drowned out all notes of caution and pru-dence. The hearts of the richest and most acculturated Renaissance Jews swelled with pride as they listened to the strange, guttural Hebrew speech of the presumed Arabian Jewish prince, and they surrounded him with the same adulation he received from the simplest common folk. "All the wealth and cultures of Italian Jewry lay at his feet. He was lavishly supplied with money. He never appeared in the streets without an escort of ten young Jews and a crowd of inquisitive Christians. . . . He made an almost royal progress through Bologna, Mantua, and Ferrara, giving it to be understood that the hour was near for the regathering of the Diaspora under the auspices of his non-existent brother." [16] The story of the suspicions Reubeni soon was to arouse among the Christian kings who deigned to grant him audiences, and of his arrest and death in a dungeon in Llerena, Spain, does not belong in this context. What is important for our attempt to understand the mind of the Renaissance Jew is the light the Reubeni episode throws on its enduring and basic Jewishness. This continued undiminished, despite all the Renais-sance trappings and an almost complete formal assimilation to the Renais-sance way of life and thought.

8

———◆◆◆◆———

Jewish Dionysians: The Hasidim

Hasidism represents one of the most significant and most original phenomena not only in the history of Judaism, but also in the history of the development of religions in general. . . . It did not aim at an improvement of the tenets of the faith or at a reform of religious practices; what it endeavored was something greater and deeper: the perfection of the *soul*. By means of exerting a powerful psychological influence Hasidism succeeded in creating a type of *believer* who valued the ardor of feeling higher than the observance of rites, piety and religious fervor higher than speculation and Tora-study.[1]

Although I agree with this characterization of Hasidism given by the great Jewish historian Simon Dubnow, my own readings about Hasidism have convinced me that from the point of view of general Jewish cultural typology, what Hasidism effected was to introduce a strongly Dionysian element into traditional Jewish culture, which had earlier been characterized by an overwhelmingly Apollonian configuration.

It was Nietzsche who named and described those two diametrically opposed Greek ways of arriving at the values of existence. But it was Ruth Benedict who, by utilizing the contrasting Nietzschean concepts of the Apollonian and the Dionysian for a general cultural typology, popularized them to the extent of making them bywords in cultural studies. The Apollonian " 'knows but one law, measure in the Hellenic sense!' He keeps the middle of the road, stays within the known map, does not meddle with disruptive psychological states. . . . The known map, the middle of the road, to any Apollonian is embodied in the common tradition of his people. To stay always within it is to commit himself to precedent, to tradition."[2] The Dionysian, by contrast, pursues the values of existence through

"the annihilation of the ordinary bounds and limits of existence"; he seeks to attain in his most valued moments escape from the boundaries imposed upon him by his five senses, to break through into another order of experience. The desire of the Dionysian, in personal experience or in ritual, is to press through it towards a certain psychological state, to achieve excess. The closest analogy to the emotions he sees is drunkenness, and he values the illuminations of frenzy. With Blake, he believes "the path of excess leads to the palace of wisdom." . . . In their religious ceremonies the final thing [the Dionysians] strove for was ecstasy." [3]

It is so apparent that the general trend of Jewish life and culture for the last two thousand years was Apollonian that this does not require detailed argument, although it will be touched upon briefly later in this chapter. The Dionysian nature of Hasidism, on the other hand, must be demonstrated in detail, which is the task of the present chapter, together with a tracing of its extraneous (i.e., Gentile) sources. It will also be shown that despite the strong influence of the foreign environment on Hasidism, this last great religious movement in Judaism was an essentially *Jewish* development, and that in this respect it did not differ from the other great Jewish religious and cultural efflorescences that preceded it.

1. Hasidism as Seen by Its Historians

The history of Hasidism has often been told from its beginnings as a response to the physical and spiritual oppression of the Jewish masses in eighteenth-century Eastern Europe, through its triumphant development into the religious expression of the major part of the Jewish people in Poland and neighboring lands, to its decline in the nineteenth century which turned it into Tzaddiqism, a sorry caricature of its former self. Outstanding Jewish historians have analyzed Hasidism, painted pen portraits of its major figures, presented in detail its doctrines, and followed step by step its struggles with its bitter opponents, the Mitnagdim.[4] As a result of this painstaking work there is perhaps no other phase in Jewish history, except the most recent one, of which so much is known. We can therefore confine ourselves to the briefest presentation of the teachings of Hasidism and its significance for Judaism before tackling the question of what kind of encounter it represented with the Gentile environment in which it arose.

Hasidism, then, can be described as the Jewish religious and social movement founded in Podolia and Volhynia by Israel Ba'al Shem Tov (1699?–1760), usually referred to by the acrostic BeShT. It taught that what God wanted of man was not asceticism and the mortification of the flesh, as represented by Lurianic Kabbala, nor concentration on halakhic study as demanded by Polish Talmudism, but devotion, or "cleaving" (*d'vekut*) to Him. God, the BeShT taught, must be served with joy. One must surrender oneself to Him with enthusiasm (*hitlahavut*) so that one can give up the consciousness of separate existence and be joined to the eternal being of God. Since, however, most men cannot achieve this high state of spiritual union with God, they need the intermediacy of the Tzaddiq (the "saintly" or "pious one"), who is a manifestation of God and a connecting link between the Creator and Creation. This, in barest outline, is the basic doctrine of Hasidism. Its immediate psychological effect was an enormous uplift for the downtrodden masses of East European Jews, for whom the new teaching opened up a road to self-assurance, to belief in their own worth, to ecstatic experience, and to an existence in which joyous trust in God and His Tzaddiq scattered the black clouds of misery which had for so long enveloped them.

Were one to judge from the major works dealing with Hasidism, one would have to conclude that this movement was based solely on Jewish antecedents (notably on the Kabbala), was a response to the internal Jewish condition, and that its values, concepts, beliefs, and rituals were all specific Jewish developments. This indeed is how Hasidism has been treated and presented by the foremost Jewish historians—Horodezky and Dubnow, to mention only two—and by the authoritative analyst of Jewish mysticism, Gershon G. Scholem.[5]

As far as I am aware, the first student of Hasidism who commented on the non-Jewish influences it absorbed was S. J. Hurwitz, a bitter opponent of the movement, whose purpose in writing a booklet about it was to attack it and to heap ridicule on Hasidic leaders and followers alike.[6] Some twenty years later, Torsten Ysander called attention to similarities between Hasidism on the one hand, and Russian Orthodoxy and the Russian dissenting sects on the other. He did this in a massive book which, however, was summarily and I think too harshly dismissed by Scholem as having "failed completely."[7] Finally, a few years ago Yaffa Eliach published a brief but useful study about the influence of Russian dissenting sects on the BeShT.[8]

2. The Gentile Religious Environment

In the eighteenth century the Kingdom of Poland comprised a huge area stretching from the Baltic in the north to the Black Sea in the south, and from Central Europe in the west to the Dvina and Dnieper rivers in the east. Its major population elements belonged to either of two churches: the Poles and Lithuanians in the northwest were Catholics, while the White Russians and the Ukrainians in the southeast were Orthodox. In addition, the territory in question contained a large minority of religious dissenters. Hence, in trying to sketch briefly the environmental matrix in which Hasidism arose—which is necessary for an understanding of what we shall have to say about it—we must deal separately with these three greatly disparate Christian religio-cultural configurations.

RUSSIAN SECTARIANISM

Long before the emergence of Hasidism, the Russian culture had absorbed a goodly portion of Jewish influences.[9] The beginnings of this influence are lost in the mists of antiquity, but from the eleventh century on the Hebrew Biblical elements in Russian thought are unmistakable. Subsequently, Jewish religious attitudes, literary works, and musical traditions left their mark in Russia. The Russian Old Believers expected the end of the world in 1666—the Messianic year of the followers of Shabbatai Zevi. There was a striking similarity between the Shabbataians and the Old Believers in their apocalypticism, fascination with occult numerical computations, ecstatic sense of elation, and semi-masochistic acceptance of suffering. The Old Believers made common cause with the Jews and other minorities in order to survive under conditions of persecution. The sectarians and the Jews interacted, and the Jews played a definite role in the Russian religious ferment of the late seventeenth century, although its extent has never been systematically investigated. Some, like the Molokans (or "Milk-Drinkers") who arose in the early eighteenth century in the Tambov region, incorporated certain Jewish practices into their worship. All Russian sectarians shared the belief that man was capable of establishing direct links (if not actual identity) with God outside the established churches. The way they tried to achieve this was by vigorous group action: wrestling, drinking, flagellation, and even self-castration. The sectarian movements found the greatest response in the depressed agrarian regions of southern and western Russia.[10]

Jewish mysticism influenced Russian religious philosophy in a more roundabout way, through the intermediacy of Jacob Böhme (1575–1624). As Scholem has pointed out, this highly influential mystic shows a close affinity to Kabbalism and may have deliberately assimilated elements of Kabbalistic thought to the extent that the connection between his ideas and those of the theosophic Kabbala was quite evident to his followers.[11] Böhme's influence on seventeenth- and eighteenth-century Christian mystics in Germany, Holland, and England has long been known; but, as Billington shows, he was also "the most important single influence on the formation of a Russian philosophical tradition."[12] Böhme's ideas about God as an infinitely transcendent and at the same time omnipresent force; about man's intellectual pursuits, sexual longings, and social impulses as expressions of the "homesickness" for the lost unity between man and God; about God's own longing for Sophia, "the auspicious eternal virgin of Divine Wisdom" and the principle of "eternal femininity"; about man's return to God as the attainment of perfect androgyny, that is, a union of male and female characteristics—all of these contain ringing echoes of Kabbalistic thought, and all made a deep impression on Russian thinkers.

The seventeenth and eighteenth centuries were a time of intense religious ferment and hysteria in Russia. The great Schism of 1666–67 created bitter enmity between the opposing factions and a will among the Nonconformists to die for their faith: between 1672 and 1691, more than 20,000 of them committed suicide by self-immolation in thirty-seven communal conflagrations,[13] offering themselves as holocausts in an extreme Dionysian annihilation of the bounds of existence. In the following two centuries numerous dissenting sects sprang up, calling themselves by such fetching names as Shore-dwellers, Wanderers, Saviorites, Runners, Prayerless, Khlysty (or "Flagellants"), Dukhobors (or "Spirit Wrestlers"), Molokans (or "Milk-Drinkers"), Skoptsy (or "Castrated"), and the like. All told, their numbers ran into hundreds and their adherents into millions.[14]

The titles assumed by the leaders of the sects varied. Some were satisfied to be styled "prophet" or "prophetess"; others were termed "Czar"; quite a number were called "Christ" and claimed, and were believed, to be the reincarnations of Jesus Christ. A woman leader of the Khlysty was called "Mother of God." Many would be seized by fits, fall to the ground in convulsions, and then recount their visions, prophesy, and foretell the future. The old Russian idea of the Lord dwelling in man's soul and speaking through man's mouth was reaffirmed with new vigor. Miracles, such as the descent of a chariot of fire, were reported to have occurred.[15]

This was also the time in which the famous Ukrainian mystic Gregory Skovoroda (1722–94) wandered throughout Russia with the Hebrew Bible in his knapsack, preaching and expounding his ideas in writing. Skovoroda's teachings evince a remarkable formal similarity to the Kabbalistic and Hasidic doctrine. The concept of the divine spark, which is central to the Kabbalistic-Hasidic doctrine of the relationship between God and the world, plays an important role in Skovoroda's thought. Christ's voice, he taught, resounded ceaselessly from every heart in which the divine spark had not been extinguished by carnal passion. In our craving to satisfy our carnal desires, which are but seeds of evil sown into our hearts by Satan, we became subordinated to the flesh and thereby extinguished the divine flame. By mortifying the flesh, the spirit can be freed from bodily servitude and ascend toward its supreme nature, its eternity. These ideas were very similar to those of the Ukrainian Dukhobors, who regarded the body as the temporary prison of the spirit and taught that the aim of the sojourn of the spirit in the body is to restore God's image in man, thereby breaking the material bonds.[16]

Another Kabbalistic-Hasidic idea, that of the "husk"—the profane or evil physical aspect of existence, which surrounds and hides the kernel that is the spirit—also has its parallel in Skovoroda's teachings. "Compared to faith," he explained, "the [ritual] ceremonies are as husks to the grain, or complements to true kindness." Similarly, the official confession of the Ekaterinoslav Dukhobors, written in 1791, stresses that the ritual observances, and even the

Scriptures themselves, were only signs and "symbolic images," and that it was "hypocrisy" to obey them without possessing the inner inspiration.[17]

By the early nineteenth century, mystical sectarianism had reached Russian aristocratic circles. One of these movements centered on Catherine Tatarinova, who was first influenced by Conrad Selivanov, the founder of the Skoptsy, and then, feeling that she herself was a prophetess, organized meetings in her own home. These meetings—in which princes, princesses, and high army officers participated—developed into ecstatic exercises in which the participants were "so carried away that they forgot themselves, played, sang, broke out into jumping, whirling, and clapping their hands." [18]

At this point figures would be helpful to give an idea of the extent of sectarianism in Russia in the eighteenth century. Regrettably but not at all unusually, statistics are non-existent. However, we do know that in 1738 the estimated number of Orthodox Christians in all Russia was 16 million, and a century later, in 1840, 44 million. During the reign of Alexander II (1855–81), an attempt was made to determine the number of Schismatics. An imperial commission was appointed which found in 1859 that they numbered about 9,300,000. But this was a gross underestimate, because, as one member of the commission stated, in the province of Yaroslav the Orthodox formed only one-fourth of the population. Thus the proportion of Schismatics to Orthodox must have been much higher than the ratio of 1:5 given by the commission.[19] The same proportion, or an even higher one, must have existed in the eighteenth century before the numbers of the Schismatics were reduced by systematic government persecution. In addition, the high visibility of the Schismatics and sectarians, their concentration in villages, and their ecstatic and defiant behavior would seem to be among the factors which explain why they were in a position to make an impression on the Jews who lived among them or in their immediate vicinity.

RUSSIAN ORTHODOXY

Russian Orthodoxy itself contained numerous elements which bore a marked resemblance to Hasidic practice and doctrine. In the Orthodox Church there was a strong mystical trend. The followers of this trend held that the true believer was filled with the Divine, and that therefore, in a sense, one could speak of the divinization of man. They believed that the deepest essence of religion and the most complete union with God could be achieved in joy and in religious-ecstatic rapture. The mystical Russian soul was filled with a desire for infinity and oneness with God. The mystics held that the purpose of human existence was to become part of the universal Divine and to become dissolved in it. They also maintained that love was the greatest value in life, love that filled the heart and embraced all—men, animals, birds, demons, and the totality of creation.[20] As we shall see later, these Russian mystical doctrines are paralleled by the teachings of Hasidic mysticism.

Another parallel, and quite a striking one, is that between the Tzaddiq in Hasidism and the Starets in the Russian Orthodox Church. The rise of the Tzaddiq and the Starets took place simultaneously. The Starets (pl. Startsy) was a holy man, usually a monk, who commanded wide popular respect for his gift of spiritual guidance in the Russian Church of the eighteenth and nineteenth centuries. The influence of the Startsy was not related to that of the priesthood; they were mostly simple people who relied on direct guidance from the Holy Spirit and were not connected with the official Church hierarchy. While the first Starets was a fifteenth-century Russian saint and mystic named Nil Sorski, who preached mental asceticism, the Startsy did not become important figures in Russian religious life until the eighteenth century, when they extended their activities from the monasteries to the lay public at large. They became pastors and counselors to the people, who began to make pilgrimages to them and considered them spiritual leaders, father confessors, and saints inspired by God.[21] In the first half of the nineteenth century, at the very time when Tzaddiqism reached its height among the Hasidim, many famous Startsy were active among the Russians paralleling in a number of respects the position, function, and activities of the Tzaddiqim. The religiously devout would choose themselves a Starets and would then become completely subordinated to him. The believer became totally dependent on his Starets; he abdicated his own will entirely and gave himself up to the Starets, who thus acquired great power and influence. However, his influence was not derived from his office or his scholarship, but stemmed from his personality alone. He managed to break through all religious formalism to draw upon the living source of the spirit. His attitude to life was positive and optimistic. He was believed to possess the divine power of judgment, wisdom, humility, gentleness, and devotion. And his influence extended even over the monasteries: the monks confessed to him every day their sins, their thoughts, their desires.[22]

POLISH FOLK RELIGION

In contrast to the fermentation which characterized religious life in White Russia and the Ukraine, Poland and Lithuania experienced no major religious upheaval in the seventeenth and eighteenth centuries. Here Catholicism was the acknowledged, indeed the only, dominant religion. But, as Thomas and Znaniecki have shown, beneath the Catholic veneer the Polish peasant retained old animistic concepts, beliefs, and practices; and it is in these, rather than in their official Catholic counterparts, that one must look for features which may have influenced Hasidism.

One of the most important characteristics of this old Polish folk religion was the intense interest in and the concern about nature. The Polish peasant tended to animate and personalize all natural objects—trees, rocks, pits, meadows, and fields—to endow them with an individuality and call them by personal names. He would speak to the animals, especially the horses and cattle, and believed that each species had its own rulers, could act and react intelligently, had knowledge of things unknown to man, and that its members had a strong feeling of solidarity for one another. It was a sin to kill an animal unless its meat was needed as food or as a medicament (the meat of a snake boiled in oil was believed to be a most effective remedy). The earth itself was considered a living being, with feelings and a will of its own. Fire was treated with great deference. The simplest act of using nature's gifts assumed a religious character and was accompanied by religious rites, thanksgivings, blessings, or expiatory acts. Even the meanest natural beings glorified God by their life as man did.

Beyond and within the visible nature, the world was full of spirits, vampires, demons, devils. God, of course, reigned supreme; but His attitude toward man depended on the magical relation which man by his acts established between God and himself. If a man committed a sin, it could bring calamities not only upon him but also on his family, community, farm stock, and even the natural environment.

From the seventeenth century on, there was an increasing cult of patron saints. Every parish, corporation, fraternity, city, and province had its own patron saint. Moreover, every individual had a guardian angel. For added protection, much use was made of amulets and talismans, often consecrated by the priest, to ward off the evil eye and other nefarious forces. A curse, once pronounced, had terrible power. Particularly powerful was the curse of a father or a mother—it simply had to be fulfilled by God.

The Polish peasant felt that he lacked any control over the world, but believed that those who were his intellectual superiors had almost unlimited power. He also showed a particular kind of credulity toward the effect which could be expected from any incident.

The parish was considered something like a large family, headed by the priest. The church was often a magnificent structure, contrasting sharply with the poverty of the peasants' own houses. The meetings for service in the church unified the group—in almost every parish there were religious associations and fraternities whose aim was a particular kind of worship. These cultivated religious songs and music, some had also humanitarian and practical ends—the care of the sick and the poor, help to widows and orphans, funeral and dowry insurance. Under the leadership of the priest, groups were formed for the purpose of making pilgrimages to miraculous places, in the country or abroad (Rome, Lourdes, or even Jerusalem). The priest was the trusted adviser; they went to him to ask for advice, to listen to his remonstrances. He was obeyed more readily than any secular power.

The important thing in prayer was not the form, the letter, but the meaning and the religious feeling which accompanied it; this was what influenced
God or the saint. It was generally believed that confidence in God and the
love of God would compel Him to grant men what they needed. Yet withal,
the Polish peasant never dared to imagine any religious attitude other than
the teachings of the Church. In this respect, at least, he was very different
from the Russian peasant with his strong inclination to schismatic sectarianism.[23]

Before leaving this subject it must be emphasized that, despite its dominant position, Catholicism did not hold universal sway in Poland. For one
thing, it never succeeded in completely eliminating or superseding the
pagan Polish folk beliefs and practices which continued to flourish under a
Catholic veneer. For another, Poland became a place of refuge for Russian
sectarian dissenters who crossed its borders from western Russia in order to
escape persecution. Thus a sizable Raskol community was established in
Vetka, Poland, in the early part of the eighteenth century.[24]

3. The Jews of East Europe in the Eighteenth Century

Having sketched the religious mentality of the Gentiles in the lands where
Hasidism originated and spread, we must next inquire into the extent of the
contact that existed between the Jews and the Christians. Was this contact
sufficiently close to give the Jews the opportunity to be influenced by the
popular-religious ideas and practices of Christianity?

Before answering this question, a general statistical feature must be
pointed out. In the eighteenth century, four-fifths of the Jewish people as a
whole lived in Europe. Of the European Jews, numbering more than 2
million, fewer than one-tenth lived in Western Europe (England, Holland,
France, and Italy); fewer than one-fourth in Central Europe (Germany, Bohemia, Moravia, Austria, and Hungary); and some two-thirds, or more than a
million and a quarter, in the backward, feudal, agrarian countries of Eastern
Europe.[25] Hence, whatever developments took place in the life of East European Jewry affected the great majority of the Jewish people. And the one
development which did take place, and which first shook Jewish life to its
foundations and then reshaped it thoroughly and entirely, was the rise and
spread of Hasidism.

The partitions of Poland resulted first in a reduction of the territory of the
kingdom (1772, 1793), and then in its total elimination (1795). After Napoleon's defeat in 1815 most of the Polish area was brought under Russian control, and the lands with the densest Jewish population, from the Baltic to the
Black Sea, came to constitute the so-called Jewish Pale of Settlement. The
Jews of this region differed from other Jewries in the high proportion of their

rural distribution. Almost one-third of them lived in villages, and a major part of the others in small towns which were much more village-like than urban in their character. Almost all the Jews who lived in villages, and many of those who lived in the towns, were leaseholders, innkeepers, and liquor sellers, constituting the connecting link between the manorial lords and peasants and burghers. The other urban Jews were either traders, active in the exchange of agricultural and urban products, or itinerant traders or peddlers, or were engaged in artisanship, working mainly as tailors, furriers, and cap-makers. In the White Russian small towns, about one-tenth of the Jews were carters or porters. In addition, even the smallest Jewish community had its musicians: a fiddler, a bass viol player, and a cymbalist. The only academic profession open to Jews, apart from the rabbinate and teaching, was medicine—as in other countries, almost all the kings, princes, and magnates had their Jewish physicians.

The cultural environment was no less backward than the economic. Except for members of the *szlachta* (the Polish nobility) and the priesthood, illiteracy was general, as was belief in spirits, devils, witchcraft, and the evil eye. The latter was shared by the *szlachta* as well and led to numerous witch trials and burnings at the stake. The Catholic Church incited the nobility and the populace to unbridled fanaticism and persecution of non-Catholics, including the Greek Orthodox in the Ukraine and White Russia, and, of course, the Jews. Because of their wide dispersion all over the country, the Jews of Poland had closer contact with the peasants than in other lands. In the Ukraine, for instance, in 1765 Jews lived in no less than 99 percent of all villages. In the villages and small towns, agriculture and animal husbandry were widely practiced by the Jews as auxiliary sources of income, and in some places (e.g., Kolomyja in eastern Galicia), Jews mowed hay in the meadows side by side with their Christian neighbors.[26]

Close contact with the Gentiles, however, did not necessarily mean friendly relations; quite the contrary. This was a time of cruel oppression of the peasantry—a fate the Jews had to share. In addition, the Jews had to bear a much greater tax burden and were even more ruthlessly brutalized. They were forced to enter into public disputations with the Frankists (e.g., in 1757 in Podolsk, and in 1759 in Lwow) and to listen to Catholic sermons (having to pay the priests for preaching to them). Their holy books were burned in marketplaces and ritual murder charges were leveled against them in a bloody wave that swept all provinces and led to the torture and execution of many. For the slightest reason, or no reason at all, Jews would be apprehended by nobles, whipped, imprisoned, tortured, or forcibly converted. The peasantry, for its part, hated the Jews, in whom they saw exploiters and the nobles' lackeys, and attacked them, most bloodily in the 1768 Haidamak uprising which claimed tens of thousands of Jewish lives and left an even greater number in utter destitution. The Jews were assaulted

also by Jesuit students who rioted in many places in Poland and were victimized by the Bor Confederacy Rebellion which lasted four years.[27]

To cap all this, the Jewish masses had to suffer from their own leaders as
well. The Kehillot, the Jewish communal organizations, were headed by a
hereditary oligarchy which exploited the people with the support of government dignitaries and city owners. They imposed exorbitant taxes on almost
everything a Jew owned, used, and consumed (including food). The situation
resulted in frequent bitter struggles and even rebellions by the Jewish artisans and other poor Jews against their own Kehilla leadership, which in
many cases enjoyed the subservient support of the rabbis. Little wonder that
in these conditions the number of destitute and homeless Jews grew to sizable proportions, and that many Jews turned to theft and robbery. There
were gangs composed of Jews, gypsies, dispossessed burghers and peasants,
and even impoverished members of the *szlachta*, as well as all-Jewish groups
of bandits—a phenomenon quite unusual in Jewish history. Nor is it surprising that in these circumstances Jews too fell victim to the main vice of East
European peasantry and townsmen—alcohol. The consumption of alcohol
among the common people was extremely high. What was worse, it was
made a duty for the peasants; in most parts of Poland the peasant was forced
to purchase a fixed quota of liquor at the nobleman's tavern (which was
usually leased to a Jew), and he was frequently remunerated not with cash
but with manorial credit slips redeemable in kind by the liquor lessee.[28]

I have said nothing so far of the spiritual degradation to which the Jewish
masses were exposed in addition to their poverty, insecurity, and brutaliza-
tion. By the middle of the eighteenth century, Jewish religious and intellectual life in Eastern Europe could look back upon more than two centuries of
Talmudism. This meant, as it did in other places but more intensively so,
exclusive concentration on Talmudic study by all those who could afford it.
The ideal way of life was to marry the daughter of a rich Jew in order to be
relieved of the necessity of earning a living, and to devote all one's time to
studying the Talmud. Those who managed to achieve great proficiency in
Talmudic knowledge and were either forced by economic circumstances or
prompted by their own ambition would seek rabbinical positions in one of
the many Polish Jewish Kehillot. The overwhelming majority of the Jews
had, of course, to eke out a living as best they could with the sweat of their
brow, which meant that they were condemned to remain ignorant. The age-
old Jewish veneration of scholarship—which here meant Talmudic scholarship more exclusively than in most other places and other times—brought
about a sharper division between the Polish Jewish scholars and ignorant
masses than elsewhere, perhaps because the general poverty reduced the
number of the scholars in relation to the ignorant to smaller proportions than
obtained in more prosperous Diasporas. Whatever the reason, the masses of
East European Jews, persecuted and hounded by the Gentiles, exploited

economically by both the Gentiles and the Jewish leadership, were reduced by Talmudism to the status of religious pariahs. A more wounded human animal has rarely lived on earth. This was the creature whose misery Hasidism tried to heal.

4. The BeShT—Peasant Prophet

Any analysis of the external influences on Hasidism must begin with the life and teachings of its founder, the BeShT. Right here, however, we run into considerable difficulties since unfortunately very little about the life of the BeShT can be historically established. He himself did not put his teachings in writing, although some letters purportedly written by him are extant. Twenty years after his death his disciples began to collect and print the master's sermons, teachings, and sayings, but it took several more decades before his life story became the subject of a book, the *Shivhe haBeShT* (or *Praises of the BeShT*), compiled by Dov Ber ben Samuel of Linits, son-in-law of Alexander Shohat, who was for many years the BeShT's scribe.[29] The *Praises* is not a biography but a collection of legends about the BeShT, whose historical kernel is most elusive.[30] However, one consideration allows us to isolate what is historically trustworthy from the profusion of evidently legendary material. The legends, as one would expect, are frankly adulatory. They show the BeShT as a man of superior intelligence, a miracle worker, possessed of great piety, a veritable saint. Interspersed among the legends, however, are bits and pieces of information which are quite incongruous with the general tone of admiration characterizing the *Praises*. Some of these details can, from a traditional Jewish point of view, in no way be considered as redounding to the BeShT's credit. Since such details could certainly not have been invented by admiring disciples, they must be assumed to be based on what the BeShT actually said and did. That they were included in the *Praises* despite their unflattering nature can be explained as attesting to the boundless, totally uncritical veneration which surrounded the BeShT, and to which even the most unseemly acts of the master appeared pregnant with mysterious significance.

On this basis, then, it can be considered a fact that from his early youth the BeShT had a great love for nature, the forests, the animals, and the peasants to whose songs he liked to listen. It was his custom to take long walks in the forests and meadows. One of the stories about him has him wandering "in a great desert." He loved solitude in his youth as well as in his later life, when he built himself a "house of seclusion" in the forest where he stayed all week long, going back to his home and joining his wife only for the Sabbath, on which he wore white garments in the manner of the Russian sectarians.[31] There can be little doubt that he was attracted to the ways of the peasants, their songs, their dances, their folk beliefs, their gaiety, to the extent of attributing to them the ability of relating in a childlike, immediate manner to the Divine Father of all. He was so fond of the peasants' and shepherds' singing that he saw elements of sublimity in it. According to his grandson, Rabbi Ephraim of Sudilkov (c. 1737–c. 1803), he would say, "In all the songs sung by the Gentiles there is a breath of the fear and love of God, of those feelings which, as they spread from On High to earth below, reach down to the Lowest Levels." [32] Many Hasidic rabbis, following the example of the BeShT, would later adopt the songs of Gentile folk and impute a sacred and secret meaning to their simple lyrics.

The *Praises* have much to say about a mysterious and otherwise entirely unknown Rabbi Adam who bequeathed to the BeShT an untraceable book which became the seminal influence on his thinking and teaching. In fact I suspect that it was rather the environment which played this role in his formative years. One particular feature which the BeShT must have acquired during his childhood in the Carpathians was his inordinate fondness of horses—a decidedly un-Jewish trait. His *Praises* describe how he liked to wander about in the marketplaces and how he would "play with the horses, stroking them in the manner of one familiar with animals." He learned to ride well, and later in life he himself owned "good horses." On one occasion, when he arrived at the house of an adherent, he wanted to know whether his host had good horses. He went to see them, liked one in particular, and asked his host to give it to him as a present. When the host refused, he became most upset. On another occasion he unashamedly admitted that he "coveted" a man's horse. [33]

He was equally fond of, and knowledgeable about, wine. On his journeys he would often drop in at a tavern. When his fiery prayers exhausted him, he would ask for "a very good wine" to recover his strength. Once he amazed everybody by drinking a large amount of very strong Walachian wine without any visible effect. He often drank brandy as well, and his opponents in later years accused him of habitual drunkenness. [34]

He also had quite an eye for female beauty, as can be concluded from his parables in which beautiful women often figure. One of these parables begins, "If a man suddenly beholds a comely woman, he may well wonder whence came she by such comeliness. . . ." Another tells of a king's son, who "espied a virgin and lusted for her charms." [35] (There will be more said of his attitude toward sex later.)

He was passionately fond of his long-stemmed pipe or *lolkeh*, which he smoked almost incessantly. He smoked on weekdays before the morning prayer, before he had anything to eat; he took it along with him to the synagogue; he smoked it while traveling and lit it first thing after the *Havdala* ceremony at the end of the Sabbath, when he would lie down to enjoy it. [36]

In this connection it must be mentioned that the *Praises* contain several references to a recurrent behavior pattern of the BeShT which can best be explained as symptoms of epilepsy. While engaged in prayer or preaching a sermon, he would be seized by a violent trembling. His face would burn like a torch. "His eyes were bulging and fixed straight ahead like someone dying." These trembling fits would last a long time. On one occasion, during the Yom Kippur afternooon prayer, "he made terrible gestures and bent backwards until his head came close to his knees and everyone feared that he would fall down. . . . His eyes bulged and he sounded like a slaughtered bull. He kept this up for about two hours. Suddenly he stirred and straightened up" and concluded the prayers in a great hurry.[37] He also would often lie (or be found lying) on the floor or the ground, with arms and legs outstretched, and have visions or cry bitterly, tearing at his hair. At least once he lost the power of speech.[38] After these seizures he would tell people that he had "moved from one world to another without any hindrance" and had "entered the palace of the Messiah," or had visions of thousands of souls coming to him.[39] All the manifestations described—the violent trembling, the bulging of the eyes with a fixed glare, "terrible gestures," bending over backwards, stertorous breathing ("sounded like a slaughtered bull"), falling to the ground, and visions during the seizure remembered afterward—have often been described in medical literature as epileptic symptoms.[40] At the same time one must not overlook the marked resemblance between these seizures of the BeShT and those of Russian sectarian prophets and prophetesses discussed earlier.

As we have seen, the BeShT was an inveterate pipe smoker. Eliach suggested that he smoked something other than tobacco.[41] In the eighteenth century opium was available in Volhynia and Podolia, which neighbored on Turkish-controlled lands. From 1672 to 1699 Podolia and parts of Polish Ukraine belonged to Turkey, and the town of Okop or Okopy in which the BeShT was born was located near the old Polish-Turkish border.[42] The BeShT himself visited Istanbul,[43] where he could have easily got acquainted with the pleasures of opium smoking. In one incident recounted in the *Praises* we hear that two Gentile soldiers who snatched the BeShT's pipe while he was smoking it were found an hour later fast asleep,[44] possibly because they were unused to opium smoking. Many of the seizures of the BeShT are reported to have occured on holydays (such as the Day of Atonement) on which smoking was forbidden; being thus deprived of the narcotic to which he was habituated, the BeShT could have suffered withdrawal symptoms. It is a well-known fact that opium (and other drug) withdrawal produces seizures of an epileptic character.[45] This explanation is offered merely as a tentative suggestion pending the full investigation the subject requires.

While temper is a matter of individual proclivity, the amount of control a person exercises over his temper is largely determined by the values inculcated into him by his environment. Jewish tradition has always favored mild, modest, peaceable, and temperate behavior. Temper tantrums and outbursts of anger were considered unbefitting a Jew, and most unworthy of a rabbi or scholar. Numerous Talmudic sayings, well known to all educated Jews, decried temper and upheld meekness as the ideal behavior. If the BeShT did not follow these directives, it must have been due to the influence of the peasants with whom he associated and who were uncouth, unmannered, and would make no attempt to control their temper. For, as it transpires from the *Praises*, the BeShT was prone to violent temper tantrums. He would rudely accost those who aroused his anger, calling them "fool," "idiot," or worse. On one occasion he shouted at a barren woman, "See to it that you give birth to a son! If not, I will break your bones with this stick!" On another, he administered a thorough beating to a man who was feigning death. For relatively minor transgressions he would prophesy death to people and destruction by fire to entire cities—predictions which, according to the *Praises*, invariably came true.[46]

His peasant-like behavior extended also to his relationship with his wife. The *Praises* mentions that "in the way of the peasants his wife sat next to him at the table," and that he slept in one bed with his wife.[47] The first detail was merely a minor deviation from the Jewish custom; but the second was in flagrant disregard of the traditional Jewish rules of sexual modesty and ritual purity, which required that man and wife sleep in separate beds, since for about two weeks in every month a woman is ritually impure and must not be touched by her husband. To make things worse, although the context is not quite clear on this point, it seems that the BeShT lay down next to his wife in the presence of a houseguest who slept in the same room.

The rusticity of the BeShT is palpable on every page of the *Praises*. He liked to crack jokes, used profane language, and comes through as a thoroughly earthy character. At the same time he must have been possessed of a powerful charisma, which is the psychological explanation of his successes as a dispenser of amulets and magic remedies, as a healer of the blind and the paralyzed, as an exorcist and a reviver of the presumedly dead, as well as of the fear with which he inspired even Gentile peasants and robbers.[48] The belief in demons and spirits had good credentials in Talmudic lore, but it also received a powerful impetus from the folklore of the Gentile environment. The preoccupation of the BeShT with this realm must therefore be explained by a convergence of both factors.

Related to his belief in evil spirits was the BeShT's preoccupation with the dangers and impurities of sex. In his imagination he frequently dwelt on the pollution caused to men by nocturnal (and daytime) accidental emissions, which, according to old Jewish folk belief, were caused by the dangerous and malicious queen of the night, Lilith.[49] The subject of illicit sexual intercourse also held an irresistible fascination for him, and the *Praises* tell of many occasions on which he miraculously (or, as we would say, intuitively) felt that a person was guilty of it, or that a bed had been the scene of fornication or adultery.[50]

Intense preoccupation with sex has prompted many a sectarian to a pathological resolve to abstain from it altogether. According to one tradition included in the *Praises*, the BeShT stated that for fourteen years he had refrained from intercourse with his wife, and that his son Hershele was conceived by her "through the word." [51] Another story about him reports that a girl conceived from the BeShT's prayer. These statements bear an uncanny resemblence to the Khlysty doctrine, which preached sexual abstention and taught that if God wanted a virgin to conceive He would impregnate her with His Holy Spirit.[52]

Enough has been said about the BeShT to show that his behavior as well as his relationship to nature and the supernatural was deeply influenced by his Gentile environment. It remains to add that in his appearance, too, he cultivated a resemblance to the Gentile holy men, many of whom were active in his days among the Raskol ("dissenting") peasantry of Ruthenia, Podolia, Volhynia, and the Ukraine. The leaders of some sects, and often the members as well, wore long white shirts or caftans, and the wearing of white by the BeShT was considered one of the misdemeanors for which some of the Jews of Ostraha pronounced a ban against him.[53] The peasants could easily mistake him for one of their own holy men (who were called "Christs" in the Khlysty sect) and react to his appearance among them with trembling fear. Some of the stories about the BeShT tell how, when he stepped out of a house, the hostile peasants who had assembled in the front of it began to tremble and fell to the ground, remaining there until he went back into the house.[54] In fact, the first people who recognized his holiness and ability to perform miracles, and who were awed by him, were none other than Gentile highwaymen.[55]

A fondness for horses, wine, strong drink, beautiful women, and powerful smoke, an uncontrolled temper, sexual immodesty, the use of profane language, love of singing and dancing, a preoccupation with nocturnal demonic dangers, proneness to epileptic fits, and a charismatic presence strong enough to fell groups of trembling peasants—all these are not merely accretions from the Gentile environment; they are also Dionysian features, which ill fitted into the Apollonian structure of traditional Judaism. Yet it was precisely this foreign Dionysian intrusion which gave Hasidism its specific character in the lifetime of the BeShT, and even more so after his death, when the movement he initiated conquered for itself the majority of East European Jewry.

5. Dionysian Features in Hasidism

Hasidism broke the shackles of a millennial Diaspora Apollonianism to infuse East European Jewry instead with a Dionysian spirit. However, both traditional Jewish Apollonianism and Hasidic Dionysianism were something quite different from the Apollonian and Dionysian mode of ancient Greece—or of other cultures which have been described as either Apollonian or Dionysian. What the Jewish Apollonians shared with their Gentile counterparts was the spirit of restraint, of measure, of "nothing in excess," a mode of life circumscribed by rules and precepts which must be obeyed in all circumstances. Into this Jewish Apollonian world, Hasidism injected a shrill note of Dionysian excess. From the viewpoint of the traditional Jew, the Hasidim were wild, uncontrolled, and unruly people, whose incomprehensible behavior, whether in the street, the synagogue, or the home, shocked and scandalized him. And since the ways of the Hasidim seemed to him nearer to those of the Gentiles than to those of the traditional Jews, he stamped them with the most severe mark of disapproval: they were, in his eyes, "un-Jewish."

For one thing, the Hasidim were boisterous, like the Gentile peasants. For a traditional Jew, quiet and subdued behavior was the inviolable rule. One suffered silently all blows, whether they came directly from the invisible hand of God, or from the all-too-tangible cruel fist of the Gentile peasant, bandit, or lord. At the utmost, if complete repression of all reaction was impossible, one broke into subdued sobs or poured one's heart out in tearful prayer sung to complaining and wailing tunes. The rare moments of joy were likewise expressed in a smile, a glance, a small gesture. The licit pleasures were tightly regulated in time and circumstance: the daily study of the Law; the weekly enjoyment of the Sabbath, consisting in a festive mood, a good meal, a glass of wine, a mild elevation of the spirit, and a nap in the afternoon; marital relations enjoyed on those two Friday nights every month on which one's wife was ritually pure. Nothing could be more foreign to the mentality expressed in and circumscribed by such measured deportment than the violently ecstatic, Dionysian behavior of the Hasidim.

To their opponents it had to appear as if the Hasidim had on purpose adopted patterns of behavior diametrically opposed to those accepted since times immemorial as traditionally Jewish. For the silent prayer they substituted loud, unrestrained shouting, screaming, and yelling. Their leaders, the Tzaddiqim, would often pray in such a powerful voice that all present in the synagogue would tremble with fear and break into tears. Their shouts were horrible and frightening to hear.[56] Not satisfied with giving ear-splitting expression to their emotions, the Hasidim would jump, leap, whirl, clap their hands wildly, run to and fro in the synagogue, and even turn somersaults in front of the Holy Ark as well as in the streets and marketplaces. This peculiar manifestation of exuberance in ecstatic acrobatics is referred to quite a number of times in the writings of both the Hasidim themselves and their opponents. Some of the Hasidim accompanied their somersaults with the exclamation, "For the sake of God and the Rebbe!" Others gave them a spiritual interpretation: "As soon as one is attacked by a sense of pride, one must throw oneself to the ground head over heels." [57] Their opponents pointed out with derision that while the traditional Jewish ritual demanded silent prayer, the Hasidim "roared like lions lusting after their prey," gesticulated madly, jumped like he-goats, alternately bent down to earth and shot up toward heaven, clapped their hands, turned their eyes right and left, and removed their shoes prior to reciting the Sh'ma'. As the ban issued by Elijah, the Gaon of Vilna, in 1772 states, the Hasidim would

> utter improper foreign words in a loud voice during the Eighteen Benedictions which traditionally were recited in total silence, behaving in a mad fashion and explain it by saying that in their thoughts they roam remote worlds . . . all their days are holidays. . . . As they recite their fake prayers, they scream and shout so that the walls shake. . . . They act as if they were wheels [i.e., turn somersaults], with their heads down and their feet up. . . . This is only one of their thousand ugly ways. . . ." [58]

This markedly Dionysian behavior pattern could have been that of the Khlysty, who in their secret nighttime services used to ejaculate such phrases as: *Dukh Bog, Dukh Bog, Dukh, Dukh, dukhota* (Spirit God, Spirit God, Spirit, Spirit, Spirituality) and *Oy Dukh, oy Dukh, Swyatoi Dukh* (O Spirit, O Spirit, Holy Spirit), as well as nonsense syllables. [59] Some would speak in tongues, shriek, jump, stamp, kick, hop, leap, run, whirl, and work themselves up into an extreme ecstasy which would end in total exhaustion. [60] Not only did the Hasidic behavior in the synagogue and at their get-togethers manifest a marked similarity to that of the Khlysty; some of the dances performed by the two sects were also strikingly similar, as Ysander has pointed out. [61]

As if this ecstatic indoor frenzy were not enough, some Hasidim went to the unheard-of extreme of running wild in the streets and marketplaces. There, too, some of them would turn somersaults, raise a tumult with their laughing, clowning, and jesting, relieve themselves in public, and even run about naked. [62] And within the synagogue itself, some Hasidim in their uncontrolled enthusiasm disregarded the traditional Jewish rules of strict modesty in dress. The *Praises* tell of a certain Rabbi Yudel who danced in the Bet haMidrash for two hours dressed only in a shirt. [63] Nakedness or scanty clothing in public is so un-Jewish that it can only be understood by reference to the customs of the dissenting Russian sectarians. Total or partial nakedness in public was a manifestation of Khlysty and Dukhobor extremism; it was based on such ideas as the imitation of Adam and Eve in Paradise but occasionally would lead to orgies of promiscuous intercourse at the close of religious gatherings.[64]

In order to achieve a state of ecstacy in prayer, the Hasidim occasionally and literally whipped themselves into a merry mood beforehand. One such scene was described by the Jewish philosopher Solomon Maimon (c. 1753–1800), who visited Mezhirich, the seat of the Maggid Dov Ber (c. 1710–72), the recognized successor of the BeShT as leader of the Hasidim. A Hasid came late to the prayers, the young Maimon reports, and excused himself by saying that his wife had given birth to a daughter during the night. When the Hasidim heard this, they thronged around him and wished him luck in a tumultuous fashion. The Maggid came out of his study and asked the reason for the commotion. When they told him, he said with great annoyance: "A daughter! He should be flogged!" The poor man protested; he could not understand why he should have to be punished because his wife gave birth to a daughter. "But it was of no avail, they took hold of him, laid him across the threshold, and gave him a thorough flogging. All, except the victim, reached a state of merry excitement, whereupon the Maggid urged them to commence praying: 'And now my brethren, worship God in joy!' " [65]

Another such incident was reported, again by a visitor, from the court of Rabbi Hayim Haykel (d. 1787), the Tzaddiq of Amdur in the Grodno district. One Sabbath morning during the prayers, the visitor saw that a group of men had gathered in the antechamber of the synagogue and were busy beating one of their ranks who was lying on the floor. When he (the visitor) asked them the meaning of what they were doing, they said that while they prayed they were overcome by the feeling that they lacked truly pious devotion, and sadness began to stir in them. This prompted them to administer a beating to one of their peers, so as to drive away mourning and gloom and allow only joy and jubilation to reign. Most remarkable was the reaction of the man who suffered the blows. Still lying on the floor, he said: "Who made you a judge over us? Can you not see that I hide my face and expose only my back? I myself offered my back to the beaters, I did it, and I shall suffer it." [66]

The two incidents, when read together, give the impression of a spontaneous (or perhaps established?) Dionysian ritual of obtaining merriment and a joyous elevation of the spirit by inflicting pain on a willing or unwilling victim.

Purim, which among the Mitnagdim was an occasion for the children to wear masks, carry around presents, and perform tame Purim-plays, became "the maddest and gayest of all holidays" among the Hasidim, with dignified patriarchs, their faces blackened with soot, dancing burlesque travesties and playing practical jokes on everyone they met in the streets.[67]

Family feasts were equally welcome for the Hasidim to engage in boisterous merrymaking. When a member of the Tzaddiq's family celebrated his (or her) wedding, the Hasidim would go all out to make it a truly memorable occasion. They would lose all sense of restraint and act up in carnival spirit. Some, with their beards hidden in scarves and kerchiefs, their hats turned backwards, the tails of their long caftans gathered up under their girdles, would jump on horses and amidst much shouting, flailing with whips, and brandishing of wooden swords would gallop for miles to meet the wedding party.[68]

Definitely Dionysian and entirely "un-Jewish" was the proneness of the Hasidim to violence, of which the communal beatings and floggings are examples. The traditional Jews, so often and for so long the victims of violence, feared and hated it in all its forms. Yet the Hasidim went counter to Jewish tradition in this respect as well. The BeShT had a violent temper, to which he often gave vent, and his followers took his behavior as the example to follow. Not content with hurling insults at their opponents and making sport of them, they also committed acts of violence against the leaders of the Kehilla (the Jewish community organization), whose power they greatly resented. "They set upon the rabbis and preachers with invective and abused them and beat them up murderously," wrote one of their opponents. Copying the methods of the gendarmes, the Hasidim, too, used clubs in beating the Mitnagdim. Occasionally one Hasidic group would physically attack another. This behavior led to criticism not only by the Mitnagdim but also by the more moderate Hasidic leaders. True, even their opponents, when they were in a position to do so, sentenced extremist Hasidic leaders to public flogging. The enmity between the two sects reached such heights that the Mitnagdim publicly burned the writings of the Hasidim, banned the Hasidic *minyanim*, or meetings, and excommunicated the Hasidim. The Hasidim, in turn, burned the writings of the Mitnagdim.[69]

Some of this inclination to violence remained with the Hasidim down to their final days in East Europe in World War II. Fights between admirers of various Tzaddiqim continued. When the "Umaner" Hasidim made their annual pilgrimage to the tomb of their leader, who was buried in the Ukrainian town of Uman, children of the "Skverer" Hasidim who were the majority in the locality would throw stones through the windows of the Umaners' synagogues and disturb them in their prayers with screams and jokes.[70] Numerous Hasidic anecdotes tell of two Hasidim who compete with each other by reciting fantastic tall tales, each about the greatness and the miracles of his own Tzaddiq, in boastful style and aggressive manner. Back in the heyday of Hasidism, the Tzaddiqim themselves engaged in often violent quarrels and hurled insulting or insinuating remarks at each other, in a manner reminiscent of that of the potlatching Dionysian chiefs in the American northwest coast.[71]

In the Dionysian atmosphere introduced into Jewish life by Hasidism, it was psychologically unavoidable that an outlet had to be found for the otherwise carefully hidden bitterness and suppressed resentment many Jews felt against a God who had condemned his "Chosen People" to centuries of exile, degradation, and suffering. Such an outlet was provided by the old Jewish tradition according to which evil spirits have the power to take possession of a person and then speak through his mouth in strange voices. The belief in spirit possession and the attendant practice of exorcism are well attested for Jewish antiquity in the apocrypha, the New Testament, Josephus, and the Talmud.[72] From the end of the Talmudic period, possession and exorcism were rare until the rise of Kabbalism, when both the belief and the practice again spread. It was on this basis that Hasidism built its belief in *dibbuqim*, as the spirits who take possession of people came to be called. When possessed by a *dibbuq*, a person could and would utter the most violent blasphemies or curses directed against people whom, "when himself," he would love and honor.[73] This provided a typically Dionysian and yet Jewishly safe outlet for all hostility directed against either God or man, because a person could not be held responsible for what he did or said while possessed by a spirit.

One of the ways in which a Tzaddiq could establish, maintain, or augment his reputation as a miracle-working holy man was by exorcising such evil spirits. The BeShT himself often pitted his powers against demons and exorcised them from possessed individuals or haunted houses.[74] The exact methods used differed from Tzaddiq to Tzaddiq, but they all had a distinctly Dionysian character, consisting of a contest between the power of the unclean spirit possessing the victim and the powers of holiness brought to bear against him by the Tzaddiq. The procedure often included bringing the victim into the synagogue, lighting candles, blowing the Shofar, opening the Holy Ark, marching around the victim with the sacred Tora scrolls, and, of course, powerful incantations and threats uttered by the Tzaddiq against the *dibbuq*. Sooner or later, the *dibbuq* was forced to leave the body of his victim and resume his painful wandering between heaven and earth.[75]

However, Hasidism found a way of giving vent to pent-up antagonism against God also directly, openly, and without the subterfuge of *dibbuq* possession. Several of the Tzaddiqim felt or claimed to have reached such a high degree of spiritual power that they dared to address reproachful and bitter words to God. The traditional justification of this behavior was found in the Talmudic stories which tell about "Pious Men" who would tell God in no uncertain terms what they wanted Him to do and He would listen to them. Such a saintly man was Honi the Circle-Drawer, who lived in the first century C.E., and whose power over God was so great that even the members of the Sanhedrin acknowledged it, saying to him: "You decree [on earth] below, and the Holy One, blessed be He, fulfills your words [in heaven] above." [76]

However, some Hasidic rabbis went much further than their Talmudic predecessors. Those early "Pious Men" are represented in Talmudic tradition, at the utmost, as individuals who because of their exceedingly great piety had unfailing influence on God. They are never presented as having dared to utter words of reproach against God, for it was axiomatic that man cannot argue with his Creator.[77] Yet this is precisely what several nineteenth-century Tzaddiqim presumed to do. They reproached God and dared openly to declare their disagreement with His acts or intention. Thus the story goes of Nahman of Horodenka, a friend and disciple of the BeShT, that while he and a group of Galician Hasidim sailed to the land of Israel (in 1764), a storm broke out and threatened to wreck their ship. Thereupon Nahman gathered his flock, took the Tora scroll in his arms, and addressed God: "If it has been decided in the Court of Law on High that, God forbid, we must perish, we declare as a Court of Law of a holy congregation, invoking the Omnipotent God and His Majesty, that we are in disagreement with this decision. . . ." All the Hasidim cried "Amen" and recited Psalms in a loud voice until the storm subsided and the city of Haifa came into view. Rabbi Levi Yitzhaq of Berdichev (1740–1809) taught that "the Tzaddiq was master over all the decrees issued by God, and had power to avert all the. dangers which threatened Israel." [78] Occasionally Tzaddiqim went so far as to administer verbal chastisement to God. One of these was Rabbi Israel Hofstein, the Maggid of Kozienice, whose reputation as a miracle-working "holy man" was so great that it even reached the Polish Christians, both ordinary people and noblemen and princes, among them the powerful Prince Adam Czartoryski. He often protested to God, saying, "When Tzaddiqim . . . see how humbled is the City of God . . . a mighty flame burns in their hearts and . . . they often begin to protest, saying, 'Why must our lot be less than that of the idol worshippers . . . ?' " [79] While not stated explicitly, the "mighty flame" burning in the hearts of the Tzaddiqim can be nothing but the flame of rage at the divine injustice against Israel.

Reb Mayerl, the Tzaddiq of Przemyslany, Galicia, was well known for his frequent quarrels with God. When something hurt him deeply, he would cross his arms, look spitefully toward heaven, and begin to argue with God: "Do You, my Father, wish by any chance that I sin against You? You can do to me what You will, Mayerl will remain Mayerl!" Or, when a sinful Hasid was in trouble, Reb Mayerl would hit the table and shout in anger: "Are you not ashamed of Yourself, Master of the World?! You created man of flesh and blood, of such weak stuff, and made him susceptible to every sin, whereas You should have created him strong and steadfast so that nothing should sway him; then You let him sin, although You could have safeguarded him from it—and now, on top of everything, You punish him? Are You not ashamed of Yourself?! " [80]

While this mode of behavior toward God was within the realm of the possible in Talmudic times, it was considered either sinful or most dangerous. Hence it was ruled categorically: "One must never throw words toward the

Above." Only two of the greatest prophets, Moses and Elijah, and the mother of a third one, Hanna, dared to disregard this injunction. One sage, Rabbi Levi, also did it, but was stricken with lameness as a punishment.[81] Despite these Talmudic warnings, Hasidic rabbis, as we have just seen, often hurled accusations against God, reproaching Him with injustice and cruelty toward His people Israel. The Dionysian feature in these accusations lies in the rebellious refusal to accept the will of God and in the enormous presumption of not only knowing better than God what is good for the people of Israel but telling Him what He ought to do. This was the ultimate in megalomaniac conceit ever achieved by the traditional Jewish mind.

In sketching the life and teachings of the BeShT, we referred to his fondness of wine and strong drink. This trait of the master was readily emulated by his followers who, like him, lived in a Gentile social environment in which drunkenness was rampant. Israel Zamosc (d. 1772), an early Enlightener and opponent of Hasidism, writes of them: "They all swim in wine and are drunk with brandy, the priest, the prophet, and the Ba'ale-Shem. . . . All their days are holidays, they eat to their fill, they drink and make merry. . . ." At the court of Rabbi Barukh of Tulczyn (or of Mezhibozh), a grandson of the BeShT who headed the Hasidic movement in Podolia for three decades (c. 1780–1811), the many visitors drank much wine and thus became stimulated to serve God "in joy." In a later generation, Rabbi Jacob Isaac, known as "the Jew of Przysucha," was so addicted to brandy that once, when the desire to drink overcame him and he had not a penny in his pocket, he announced in the Lubliner synagogue, "He who wants to acquire a share in the World to Come, let him give me some money so that I can buy a glass of brandy!" When nobody came forth, he went to the tavern anyway, left his belt as a pledge, drank his brandy, and said, "Now I have secured for myself a share in the World to Come!" Needless to say, the opponents of Hasidism, in describing the goings-on at the courts of the Tzaddiqim, did not fail to dwell on the communal meals the Hasidim took in the company of their adored rabbi, "swallowing masses of mutton and beef, emptying huge glasses of brandy until they are overcome by a disgusting belching." [82]

Both the Russian dissenters and the Hasidim were much troubled by a powerful libido which they felt was sinful and which they therefore, tried to eradicate, to suppress, or else to sublimate. The most ruthless form of getting rid of sexual desires and impulses was practiced by the Skoptsy, among whom the men were castrated while the women were subjected to a primitive and painful mastectomy. Other dissenting sects, such as the Khlysty, practiced abstention from sexual intercourse with their wives. The reverse side of the coin was that the Khlysty's communal dances included erotic and orgiastic traits and led to what they termed "communal sin" and blood rites.[83] Among the Hasidim, too, libido was both expressed in a sublimated form and suppressed, although the traditional Jewish valuation of life and wholeness of body kept them from the extreme of castration. We have heard of the BeShT's appreciation of female beauty, of his understanding of the passion a beautiful woman can arouse in the heart of a man, of his preoccupation with fornication, adultery, nocturnal and daytime spontaneous emission and the resultant impurity, and of his assertion that for fourteen years he had abstained from sleeping with his wife. Of various Tzaddiqim it is related that they were exposed to temptations by beautiful women who invited them to share their beds—temptations which their legends have them resist heroically, but which quite transparently sound like wish-fulfillment fantasies censored in the telling. A Hasid of Brody, Löb Melamed by name, who seems to have been a schoolteacher, tells of such a dangerous encounter in the handwritten glosses which he added to his copy of the *Shulḥan 'Arukh*. This copy reached the hands of Mitnagdim in Shklov who, to their consternation, found the notes replete with heresy and immorality. Among them was the following vignette:

> One day I was alone with a woman . . . the bed was made . . . and she asked me to be with her. I, however, did not listen to her but only looked at her body and her blinding beauty until I was overcome by great holiness and made myself stop. Likewise everybody who, when seeing a woman desires her, should nevertheless control himself and confine himself to looking at her closely and contemplating her. Thus he will pass the test and rise to a high degree. And enough said for him who understands.[84]

This fantasy of encountering an eager woman and resisting her advances, which, of course, is as old as the Biblical story of Joseph and the wife of Potiphar (Gen. 39:7 ff.), recurs in a legend about Jacob Isaac "the Jew of Przysucha" who was addicted to alcohol. One night, so the story goes, the daughter of his landlord entered his room and stood stark naked in front of him as if she wanted to seduce him to sin. Horrified, the young man jumped out of the window and wandered about all night in the snow and cold. Later the girl told him in tears that she could not understand what had come over her. He comforted her, saying, "I am sure the guilt is not yours but Satan possessed you in order to overcome me."[85]

A theory for sublimating sexual temptation and sin was formulated in the writings of the earliest Hasidic author, Jacob Joseph of Polonnoye, who puts these words into the mouth of the BeShT: "How are sinful thoughts to be cleansed? If they pertain to a female, he [the man who prays] should raise them up and unite them with their root which is *Ḥesed* [meaning in Hebrew both "mercy" and "shameful thing"] in accordance with the mysterious sense of the words, 'If a man take his sister . . . it is *ḥesed*' (Lev. 20:17)." The same line of thinking prompted Löb Melamed of Brody to say that it was "recommendable to imagine a naked woman while praying, in order to reach the known [high] degree," and that it was permitted "during devotion to let emissions of semen occur in order to rise up to the high degree in a purified state." [86]

These stories, sayings, and thoughts attest not only to a strong sexuality but also to a preoccupation with illicit sex and its dangers. They show an obsessive, Dionysian drive to get rid of sexual desire by psychologically induced emissions and by a complex process of elevating erotic fantasies into the realm of the divine.

Delving into the mysteries of the Zohar and other Kabbalistic works provided ample opportunity for gratifying the libido by sublimating it. Thus the teachings of a Tzaddiq could be replete with sexual and erotic elements while maintaining the pretense that he was discussing the spiritual and mystical longings, unions, pairings, and so on, between God and Israel. In this way Menahem Nahum, the Maggid of Chernobyl (1730–97), often made use of the erotic terminology of the Zohar, explaining the principle of union with the deity as the "mystery of copulation." The Community of Israel, he taught, was a female creature which received an efflux from the overabundance of the Creator; she always yearned for the Almighty, and, through this desire, she enticed Him to union with Israel. Their nuptials are brought about by means of the Tora. Thus, in the manner of the union between man and woman, there comes about the union with God through the strength of the desire and the love of Him. This union is analogous to the physical nuptials, that unification of female and male which alone can lead to birth. In this way the Community of Israel comes to constitute a single whole with the Creator. Without Israel, God cannot be called whole. [87]

Other Tzaddiqim sublimated their libido by reaching paroxysms of ecstasy in reciting the Biblical Song of Songs. One Tzaddiq who followed this route was Rabbi Barukh of Tulczyn. It is related of him that after returning from the *miqve*, the ritual bath, and following the onset of the Sabbath, he used to recite the Song of Songs with such enthusiasm that all those present thought they saw flames flashing around him. The Tzaddiq of Zhydaczov, Rabbi Hirsh, reports that in his youth he once hid in a chamber of Rabbi Barukh's house in order to listen to his recital of the Song of Songs. When the rabbi reached the words, "I am my beloved's, and his desire is toward me," and finally the words, "For love is strong as death . . . the flashes thereof are flashes of fire, a very flame of the Lord" (Song 7:11; 8:6), the young Hasid almost lost consciousness "from enthusiasm and desire." The Song of Songs, which in its mystical interpretation was taken to refer to the love between Israel and God, was calculated to bring about a total blurring of the boundaries between the *amor dei intellectualis* and the all-too-human sensual desires. [88]

Despite this clearly manifested preoccupation of the Hasidim with sex, it is doubtful whether the allegation of gross sexual misconduct leveled against them by their opponents had any factual basis. According to one such report emanating from Mitnaged circles, barren women, decked out in gaudy finery and heavily perfumed, would come to the house of the Hasidic rabbi, sit together with the men and drink wine, and then the Tzaddiq would seclude himself with them for the purpose of curing their barrenness. After examining the woman, the Tzaddiq would dismiss her with the blessing, "God give you pregnancy!" The author of the report makes no secret of his suspicion that on such occasions immoral acts would be committed and speaks with scorn of "the great fervor with which men would cleave to the wives of other men." [89]

In conclusion a word should be said on the enormously complex subject of the Hasidic attitude toward sin, though this can only be touched on here in the most cursory manner. It is generally taken for granted by students of Hasidism that the Hasidic doctrine of sin is a reflection, or an outgrowth, of Kabbalistic teachings. Some Kabbalists, such as Joseph Gikatila, taught that sin was an indispensable ingredient of existence. [90] Some of the Shabbataian heretics in Galicia, Podolia, and Poland went so far as to believe that the Messianic "end" could be hastened only by abolishing and disregarding all the halakhic rules, that is to say, by throwing oneself into a life of sin. Hasidism never embraced such a doctrine, but it admitted sin as part of the divine scheme. It countered the Shabbataian sectarian heresy by teaching that the "Evil Inclination," in trying to persuade man to commit a sin, makes it appear to him as if by sinning he would be fulfilling a commandment. [91]

On the other hand, the BeShT did teach that "it is an important principle that holy sparks are contained in everything that exists in the world, even in wood and stone, and also in every human act, *even in sin*. . . . When a man repents he carries the sparks which are enclosed in the sin he committed up to the higher world." And he also maintained that God "raises up sin and carries it aloft." These teachings were derived from the doctrine of Rabbi Yitzhaq Luria, the great sixteenth-century master of the Kabbala, according to whom when God created the world, holy sparks fell down and became enclosed in the material world which is the realm of the "husks" or impure shells; man's task is to liberate the sparks from their husks and, through prayer and contemplation, help them return to their divine root. [92] A disciple of the BeShT, Rabbi Jacob Joseph of Polonnoye, carried the teachings of his master further and recommended that one conjure up "unholy thoughts" while praying, in order thereby "to liberate the holy sparks from the husk." Rabbi Elimelekh of Lezhaysk (Lisensk) taught that the Tzaddiq, who is free of sin, does nevertheless occasionally commit a sin, thereby obtaining the possibility of attaching himself to the sinful and so helping them. Their opponents accused the Hasidim of resorting to such methods only for the purpose of blurring the distinction between what is commanded and what is prohibited, and of justifying their sinful desires. [93]

Related to the doctrine of sin was that of evil. According to the BeShT,

"Evil is but the lowest degree of Good," and "Inasmuch as Evil causes Good, it becomes the throne of Good" (i.e., the pediment upon which Good rests). He taught that the Shekhina comprises all the worlds and all the created things, the good as well as the evil ones.[94]

This Hasidic doctrine—that sin is part of the divine schema of things—has its counterpart in the teachings of Russian dissenting sects, although among the latter its explicit formulation came only in the late nineteenth century in the teachings of the "Old Israel" or "New Age" sub-sect of the Khlysty. Alexis Stchetinin, a young north Caucasian peasant, who founded and dominated the sect for a long time as its "Christ," taught that sin was needed for salvation. He held that a man must be immersed in the sea of sin but not let himself be drowned therein. He believed that the more a man sinned, the more he suffered, and the greater would be his salvation and future happiness.[95] In this form, the doctrine is quite close to the heretic Shabbataian ideas of the desirability and necessity of sin. However, such heretical antinomianism had no place in Judaism, and the Shabbataian heresy was summarily ejected from the body of Jewry.

Not so with Hasidism. Although its more extreme teachers occasionally came perilously close to antinomianism in their doctrine of sin and evil, they always managed to avoid the ultimate fateful step which would have carried them over into the realm of heresy. The gulf remained fixed between the heretic Shabbataian doctrine of the need to descend into the realm of evil in order to force open the prison doors from within, and the dangerous but still acceptable teaching of even the most daring Hasidic masters about the desirability of elevating sinful thoughts into the upper spheres of sanctity. Thus Hasidism, in its fashion, duplicated the notable psycho-cultural feats accomplished by Judaism in its past great encounters with Gentile cultures. It adopted, to use a Kabbalistic-Hasidic simile, the *kelim* or vessels of the Gentile environment, but filled them with, and used them to serve up, the same essentially and uniquely Jewish spirits. The shape of the vessels used by Hasidism was perhaps more strange and more foreign to Judaism than that of any it had borrowed and used in the past: the antics and delusions of Dionysian excess had to appear painfully discordant to the representatives of sedate, traditional Apollonian Judaism. But even the most fervent Hasidim did not deviate one iota from the essentials of Judaism and thus could and did remain one with the camp of their opponents.

6. *Other Gentile Influences and Parallels*

The influence of the Gentile environment on Hasidism was not confined to Dionysian elements. It extended into many other areas of religious expression. Take the concept of serving God with joy, which was perhaps the most radical departure of Hasidic doctrine from the dominant Apollonian Jewish tradition. Joy can be expressed in many ways—it can be wildly Dionysian abandon or quiet mirth. Hasidism knew both. Its wild ecstasies, discussed in the foregoing pages, had to be rare experiences—no man can maintain paroxysm for the duration. In their everyday life, the Hasidim could achieve joy only in its low-key variety, expressed in cheerful comportment and pious reliance on the powers of the Tzaddiq. However, even in this muted form the concept that joy was the way to God, and its doctrinal counterpart, that sadness ('atzvut) was a serious failing in the eyes of God, were daring innovations when considered from the perspective of traditional Judaism. Were these ideas original with the BeShT, or did he derive them from the religious atmosphere of his Gentile environment?

A glance at the mentality of the Eastern Christians among whom the BeShT lived inclines us to the second alternative. As a foremost student of Eastern Christianity expressed it, the Church of the East produced "a type of practical fervor which is unique in the history of Christianity. The sacramental and liturgical piety never absorbed or overcame a naïve, simple, almost childlike devotion to the humble, poor, and self-sacrificing Son of Man in Whom love and sympathy had reached the deepest abyss of human suffering. Humility, simplicity, and poverty in loving service, toil and self-denial were—in the minds of Eastern Christians—regarded as a genuine expression of the human communion with Christ." The hard struggle for existence was undertaken "in a spirit of childlike joy and obedience, with love for nature, with an assurance that the Lord of Glory was present with them in the form of a servant, poor, and still rich, crucified and still victorious, humble in His suffering and still an unceasing help in the struggle against foreign domination." [96] Christological elements apart, this description of a religious attitude bears a remarkable similarity to the main features of Hasidic doctrine as formulated by the BeShT and as it took hold of the Jewish masses to whom he ministered. One is therefore led to the conclusion that Hasidism was the specific Jewish variety of the generic religious posture which characterized East European Christianity, whether of the established churches or of sectarian dissident movements. This is not to say that Hasidic doctrine developed under the influence of Eastern Christian religiosity. But it does mean that the burgeoning of Hasidism from the ancient Jewish religious soil was facilitated by the religious atmosphere (or should one say with Teilhard de Chardin, the "noosphere"?) which had enveloped the Christian majority population of the area. Numerous concrete details can be adduced to substantiate this thesis.

Let us take first the formal similarity between the "court" of the Tzaddiq and those of the great Gentile lords of the nobility and the Church. The "court" of a Tzaddiq comprised, in addition to his family and employees, a varying number of devotees who constituted an impressive entourage, shared his meals, and lived, for shorter or longer periods, at the Tzaddiq's expense. The Tzaddiq was able to defray the cost of maintaining his court from the voluntary donations, the so.called *pidyon* or "redemption money" his Hasidim gave him when they came to visit him either in order to spend the holydays with him or to ask for his help, advice, or reassurance. This institution of the Tzaddiqs' entourage, as Raphael Mahler has pointed out, had its prototype in the Gentile environment:

> Even the term used to describe them, *yoshvim* (sitters), proved the extent to which the Hasidic order was grounded in the feudal system of the state—precisely the same expression (in Latin, *residentes*) was customarily attached to impoverished nobles in Poland who resided in the palaces of their magnate relatives and patrons, literally living at their expense.[97]

Before long, many of the "courts" of Hasidic rabbis resembled the courts of the Gentile high nobility, with their luxury, sumptuous clothes, fine food and drink. Rabbi Barukh (c. 1750–1811) used to visit the communities of his believers in a carriage drawn by fine horses; he had a palatial residence in which he was surrounded by an army of servants and secretaries, and he frequently gave luxurious parties where large quantities of food and drink were consumed. He even had a "court jester," none other than the famous Hersh Ostropoler who, like the jesters at royal courts, not only entertained the Tzaddiq and his entourage but occasionally alluded to things he found wrong in the Tzaddiq's behavior. Once the Tzaddiq became so enraged at the daring of his jester that he had him thrown down the stairs—the injuries Hersh suffered led some time later to his death. In his whole demeanor Rabbi Barukh emulated the manners and way of life of the great Polish lords and bishops.[98] Another Tzaddiq, Rabbi Mordecai (Motel) of Chernobyl (d. 1837), not only built himself a palace but imposed annual dues on his adherents, which were gathered by special collectors in his employ. Even more luxurious was the court which Rabbi Israel, a great-grandson of the Maggid of Mezhirich, maintained in Rushin in the Kiev *guberniye*.[99]

Similar to both the Gentile feudal system and some Russian dissenters' leadership was the dynastic development of Tzaddiqism. The Tzaddiqim divided up the country among themselves, jealously guarding the territory over which they held sway from incursion by other Tzaddiqim. Upon their death, they bequeathed their fief to their sons, together with their courts, "thrones," and "grades of Holiness." As time passed, the Tzaddiq dynasties became ramified "exactly like feudal dynasties, ruling by 'Divine Grace' over kingdoms divided up by legacies." Thus when Rabbi Mordecai (Motel) of Chernobyl died, his eight sons divided up his "kingdom," and their descendants held sway over Ukrainian Hasidism until World War I.[100]

The concept of society as a hierarchical structure (in which every class of people had its predetermined place, rank, and function) which underlay the feudal system of the Gentile environment was expressed by the other grandson of the BeShT, Rabbi Ephraim of Sudilkov (so named after the Volhynian town in which he served as rabbi and Maggid), in a simile:

> The Congregation has its heads, who possess the brains and the mind; and it has its eyes, those who supervise community affairs and their integrity; and it has its hands, those who implement its commandments and philanthropies; and it has its feet, the people of faith, who possess nothing but their faith. . . . Only when they all follow the head . . . are all the limbs sanctified . . . and are they like one complete man; and there the Shekhina resides.[101]

While these features of Tzaddiqism bear a resemblance mainly to the feudal order of the Gentile society in which it developed, others reflect the influence of the Christian religious environment. Tzaddiqist ideology assigned to the Tzaddiq as important a place in the divine scheme of things as the Catholic and Orthodox Christians did for their priests and the dissenters for their holy men and leaders. Like the priest in Catholicism and Russian Orthodoxy, the Tzaddiq in Hasidism was the mediator between God and the world. Rabbi Jacob Joseph, the foremost disciple of the BeShT, taught that the Tzaddiq not only cleared a path for delivering continued abundance to the world, but "was himself called such a path and vehicle, for the abundance passed through his hands. . . ." [102] This idea would have been most familiar to all Christians; to the Catholics and Orthodox it would have reechoed the saying attributed to Jesus in the Gospel (John 14:6): "I am the way, the truth, and the life," and for the sectarians it would have sounded like a claim often voiced by their own leaders.

Tzaddiqism reached the height of its development in the doctrine, and under the influence, of Rabbi Elimelekh of Lezhaysk (1717–87). The town in which he had his court is located on the west bank of the San River and still marks the boundary between the Catholic Poles and Galicians to the west and the Russian Orthodox Ukrainians to the east. While it would be far-fetched to seek an influence of the old Catholic custom of selling indulgences on the thinking of Rabbi Elimelekh, there is no denying that in raising the person of the Tzaddiq high above ordinary Jews, this Hasidic rabbi went so far as to attribute a redemptory effect to donations made to the Tzaddiq. In his influential book *No'am Elimelekh* or *Elimelekh's Graciousness* (printed in 1786), he assures his followers that "he who bestows of his possessions on scholars and Tzaddiqim will, through the ease so afforded them, sin the less readily," and that, by giving charity to the Tzaddiq, communion with the upper world was established.[103]

The centrality of the Tzaddiq as the intermediary between God and man is firmly established and forcefully expressed by Rabbi Elimelekh, according to whom all blessing from God can reach man only through the Tzaddiq, "who receives the abundance from on High and lavishes it upon all, even upon such as are not righteous or worthy of receiving thereof." Thus the Tzaddiq had, in effect, become God's vicar on earth, who provided livelihood to all, cured the sick, removed the curse of barrenness, rescued those in trouble, and performed all kinds of miracles. Most importantly, God desired the worship of the Tzaddiq because, for the duration of the Exile, the Shekhina, God's manifest Presence, dwelt within the Tzaddiq instead of the Temple which lay in ruins; and because God conferred rulership over the earth upon the Tzaddiq, who was like a king ruling through the reverence of God. In fact, the Tzaddiq decrees, and God fulfills. The Tzaddiqim are called "*Seraphim*," i.e., fiery angels, but rank even higher than the angels. Just as God is One, so the Tzaddiq, too, "is called One . . . and he is a part of God. . . . Because the Tzaddiq, in the strength of God, infused all the world with life, he was called Lord." Hence "he who speaks against the Tzaddiq . . . is blaspheming the Lord, for it is as though he were speaking of the Lord." [104]

Here again, as in several other features of Hasidism, Tzaddiqist thought could claim that it was harking back to Talmudic prototype. In Talmudic times there lived a few charismatic-magical-saintly "Pious Men," also known as "Whisperers," who were believed to have the power of acting as mediators between the divine and the human realms, and to guarantee the well-being of Israel or even of the whole world by the mere fact of their existence. [105] But, following the Talmudic period the belief in the power of these "Pious Men" faded away, and they no longer formed part of the living reality of Judaism. In Hasidic Tzaddiqism, 1,300 years later, the "Pious Men" not only came back, but attained a significance the like of which they had never possessed in antiquity. The Talmudic "Pious Men," although venerated, stood outside the official religious establishment in which the central position was occupied by the rabbis, that is, the teachers of the *Halakha* and the *Aggada*. It was the latter who molded Judaism and determined the Jewish religious duties. The "Pious Men" were eccentric outsiders, few in number—in fact, not more than one or two in a generation—who occasionally were asked to make use of their exceptional or miraculous powers, but whose role was entirely negligible compared to the solid stream of activity (consisting of establishing the religious Law, teaching moral precepts, and producing endless homilies) which was the domain of the hundreds of Talmudic teachers.

In Hasidism, the new "Pious Man," the Tzaddiq, became the central figure. True, he was heir to some extent to the work of the Talmudic teachers, which was continued through a long line of medieval rabbis. But the focus of his role was in his charismatic leadership—a role totally foreign to Talmudic teachers and medieval rabbi alike. The Tzaddiq claimed, as we have seen in the formulation of Elimelekh of Lezhaysk, to be something like a divine king, the manifestation and embodiment of God on earth, whom to oppose or contravene was blasphemy. According to Rabbi Nahman of Bratslav (1772–1811), non-belief in the Tzaddiq was tantamount to a rejection of the axiom of faith itself.[106]

The external similarity in semblance and demeanor between the Christian "holy men" and the Hasidic Tzaddiqim is illustrated by the story referred to above, according to which the appearance of the BeShT in front of a crowd of Christian peasants made them tremble and fall on their faces before him. While the story is told as proof of the greatness and saintly powers of the BeShT, it can be understood psychologically only in one way: the peasants recognized in him a holy man like those with whom they were acquainted from their own sectarian movements. Later Hasidic stories, too, tell of the awe this or that Tzaddiq inspired among Christian peasants.[107]

More significant is the similarity between the Hasidic concept of the Tzaddiq as God's vicar on earth, as a quasi-embodiment of the Lord among men, and the Russian sectarians' view of their leader as a "Christ." The most clearly expressed manifestation of this similarity is found in the belief in the transmigration of souls, which can also serve as an example of the difficulties involved in coming to a definite conclusion as to the origin of the various strands that went into Hasidic beliefs and practices. The belief in metempsychosis was a Kabbalistic doctrine, which figured prominently in the teachings of the sixteenth-century Kabbalists, and especially in those of Yitzhak Luria (1534–72) and Hayim Vital (1543–1620), leading masters of the Kabbala in Safed. Vital devoted one of his books to the subject.[108] Thus, there can be no doubt that the idea of the transmigration of souls was familiar to the Tzaddiqim from these sources. Yet the fact is that this belief played a more important role in the fantasy world of the Hasidim than in that of their Kabbalistic predecessors two centuries earlier. The Hasidim believed that the soul of the Prophet Habakkuk had transmigrated into the body of Rabbi Michel, the Maggid of Zloczov, and that the soul of King Solomon was reincarnated in Rabbi Barukh, grandson of the BeShT. Likewise, Rabbi Abraham Joshua Hershel of Opatov (known as *"der Apter"*) maintained that his soul had first been the soul of a High Priest, then of a Nasi (a prince in Israel), then of an Exilarch, and that he could well remember how he had served in the Temple of Jerusalem in his capacity of High Priest. According to legend, the soul of Rabbi Jacob Isaac, "the Jew of Przysucha," was "a spark" from the soul of the Biblical Mordecai who figures in the Book of Esther.[109]

To these examples of the welcome and prestige-conferring transmigration of the souls of famous men, who lived many centuries earlier, into the bodies of Tzaddiqim must be added the widespread Hasidic belief in *dibbuqim*— those souls of sinners who, for a variety of reasons, could find no rest and would therefore enter the bodies of Hasidic men or women, causing them much suffering and forcing them to act and speak irresponsibly and im-

piously, until exorcised by the sacred power of a Tzaddiq.[110] All these instances, when taken together, show that the mental world of the Hasidim
was considerably more "soul-ridden" than that of the Kabbalists. It is, of
course, entirely possible that the Hasidic belief in the transmigration of souls
was nothing more than a late outgrowth of Kabbalism alone, without any
other influence or impetus. However, it is rather unlikely that the proliferation of this Hasidic belief precisely in an environment in which the transmigration of souls occupied a central place in the doctrines of Russian dissenters should have been nothing but coincidence. For the fact is that in
some of the Russian sects it was a basic tenet that the soul of Christ was reincarnated in the body of the leader, who therefore was styled "Christ." The
Khlysty—one of the largest Nonconformist sects—believed that the Holy
Spirit, which had animated Christ, was thereafter "bequeathed by him to
successors worthy thereof," and that the reincarnated Christs who led the
Khlysty had special powers, such as foreseeing the future, predicting the
weather, crops, the success of fishing, or persecution by the government.
One of the important functions of these Christs was to serve as father confessors to their adherents, who relieved themselves of their sense of guilt by
confessing their sins to them.[111] This belief in the reincarnated Christ could
not have remained unknown to the Jews in the areas in which the Khlysty
sect was widespread.

The leaders of other Russian-Ukrainian dissenting sects, too, claimed to
possess divine powers and to be the representatives of God or Christ on
earth. The Ukrainian Dukhobor doctrine of the incarnate Christ was most
clearly formulated by the preacher Hilarion Pobirokhin of Tambov. According to him, God dwelt in the hearts of all Christians but was incarnate only in
the man of His choice. He was reincarnated in one man in each generation
and was still incarnate in one of the Dukhobors. Pobirokhin's successor,
Savely Kapustin (1790–1817) elaborated this theme by claiming that he was
the "Son of God," and by teaching that, after his own death, the Spirit of
Christ dwelling within him would transmigrate into his son, the chosen vessel. This doctrine had two consequences: it brought about the establishment
of the dynasty of Kapustinian "Christs" which existed until 1886; and it led to
a degeneration of the sect's leadership.[112] The parallel with Tzaddiqism is
too obvious to dwell on.

Remarkable, too, is the fact that a Tzaddiq should claim to be the reincarnation of precisely the prophet Habakkuk, one of the least significant
prophets of the Bible, when he could have chosen a great prophet such as
Isaiah or Jeremiah. Perhaps the explanation of this choice lies in the fact that
Habakkuk in its Russianized form, Avvakum, was the name of one of the
most powerful figures in the Russian *raskol* movement, who was not only a
servant of God but a prophet, who in his visions and ecstasies received the
counsel of God, and who died a martyr's death at the stake in 1681.[113]

Another such name which appears both among the Russian mystics and the Hasidim is that of Seraphim (lit. "fiery angels"). A founder of the Russian Starets movement chose for himself the name Saint Seraphim,[114] and according to Rabbi Elimelekh of Lezhaysk, the Tzaddiqim were called Seraphim. To say the least, it would seem that the general environment of Russian Orthodox and sectarian religiosity created an atmosphere in which the Hasidic belief in reincarnation could thrive as it had not in other times and other places.

In complete disregard of the Talmudic warning against "Gentile custom," some Tzaddiqim adopted specific Christian rites. Thus, on the eve of the Day of Atonement, Rabbi Levi Yitzhaq of Berdichev (1740–1809) "would crawl to the synagogue on all fours." The Hasidim of Bratslav adopted the Christian ritual of the confessional; they would go to their Tzaddiq, the famous Rabbi Nahman of Bratslav, "confessing on each occasion in speech to all that they have done," [115] just as laymen and monks confessed to their Starets. Many of the Tzaddiqim and Hasidim wore white garments, which were favored by the dissenters and considered reprehensible by the Mitnagdim.[116]

A reflection of the Polish Catholic environment, with its hierarchical structure of the clergy, can be seen in the development of a ranking order among the Hasidic rabbis, something completely foreign to traditional Judaism. Rabbi Barukh of Tulczyn and Mezhibozh endeavored to subject other Tzaddiqim to his rule and succeeded. Rabbi Jacob Isaac Horowitz of Lublin exercised his authority over other Tzaddiqim who, like parish priests in a bishop's diocese, had their own congregations. In this manner the "Seer of Lublin," as he was styled, spiritually dominated tens of thousands of Polish Hasidim. Like many a bishop, the "Seer" enjoyed "the blessings and the grace, an ample share of food and income, a dignified attire, and a pleasant dwelling in which all the chambers were good" and taught that this is how a leader of the Hasidim should live. In fact, he conducted his court so extravagantly that visitors came to regard his household as "the Kingdom of David." [117]

A different type of environmental influence was absorbed by Hasidism from the rich folklore of the Ukrainian and Polish peasants. The tendency to adopt songs and dances from the Gentiles had been manifested by the BeShT; subsequently his descendants, disciples, and successors followed the example of the founder. Rabbi Nahman of Bratslav, a great-grandson of the BeShT, presented much of his teaching in the form of folk stories. He composed long allegorical stories about kings, viziers, beautiful princesses, magnificent palaces and fortresses, merchants traveling into faraway lands, forests infested with bandits and wild beasts, ships sailing the seven seas, desert islands, and more of the like—all favorite themes in Ukrainian folklore. He greatly admired the folk melodies sung by the shepherds and composed numerous epigrams about song and dance. One of his sayings goes: "Every shepherd has his own peculiar melody, depending on the kind of grass and pasture lands he has, for every blade of grass has a song of its own. . . . And such is the power of melody, that through it one is united to the Blessed One." [118] The personification and individualization of "every blade of grass" betrays the same mentality that characterizes the Polish peasant. Dancing for Rabbi Nahman was a spontaneous, irresistible expression of joy: "When one is happy in the fulfillment of a precept . . . it affects one's feet, that is, one dances because of happiness." Such encouragement gave official doctrinal approval to the adoption by the Jews of the Ukrainian and White Russian peasant dance, the *prisiudki*, or deep knee-bending movement. In this dizzying dance, Rabbi Nahman "saw virtually the secret of inspiration by the divine spirit," [119] as did the Russian sectarians.

Music is the only aspect of Hasidic culture whose foreign roots have been investigated in considerable detail. Hasidic *niggunim* (tunes) have been collected, their types established, and their non-Jewish origins tracked down. Thanks to the work of A. Z. Idelsohn, pioneer of Jewish musicological research, and his successors in Jerusalem, we know which Hasidic school was influenced by which Gentile musical tradition. We know, for instance, that the *niggunim* of the Habad Hasidim and of those of Vishnitsa, White Russia, and Lithuania were influenced by East European folk songs, such as the Rumanian *doina*, or Russian motifs, and that the Bratslav Hasidim stood under the musical influence of their Ukrainian surroundings. In the Carpathian area the Hasidim of Maramarosh, Satmar, Munkacs, and Kalov sang tunes of Hungarian and Rumanian origin. Everywhere the local folk tunes—whether Russian, Ukrainian, Polish, Rumanian, Hungarian, or Turkish—impressed themselves upon Hasidic music. A different type of musical influence was that of Western European art music (operatic music, polyphonic voice division, mazurkas, waltzes, marches, etc.), which also found its way into Hasidic circles and left its mark. Even when these tunes were changed within the Hasidic tradition, as they often were, their origin is unmistakable. [120]

Earlier in this chapter I quoted sayings of the BeShT and of Nahman of Bratslav which show that they attributed holiness to the tunes sung by Gentiles. This view became standard among the Hasidim, many of whom made a point of going out to the fields, meadows, and mountains to learn the songs of the local shepherds and peasants. Even pothouse ditties were considered worthy of being learned and "sanctified." Often the original text was reinterpreted allegorically, or Hebrew explanatory phrases were added; in other cases the words were discarded altogether, and the tune was sung to meaningless filler syllables such as "oy, oy," "hey, hey," "ti-ri-ram," "ya-ba-bam," and so on. [121]

A famous example of this "sanctification" of peasant folk songs was supplied by the Tzaddiq of Nagykálló (Kalov) in Hungary, who was very fond of singing Hungarian folk songs. Once, wandering in the fields, the Tzaddiq heard a shepherd boy sing:

> The cock has crowed,
> Soon it will dawn,
> In forest green and meadow broad
> A bird walks up and down.
>
> What manner of a bird?
> What manner of a bird?
> Its mouth is gold, its foot is gold,
> It waits for me of old.
>
> Wait, O bird, just wait!
> Wait, O bird, just wait!
> If God has ordained me for you
> I'll be yours ere late.

The Tzaddiq felt that, unbeknownst to the boy, this was a sacred song, and he learned it from him. Then he changed the words and added two Hebrew lines, giving the song a Messianic meaning; and in this form it became a favorite of his and his Hasidim:

> The cock has crowed
> Soon it will dawn
> Yibbane hamiqdash 'ir Tziyon timalle
> [The Temple will be built, Zion will be filled]
> When will it come to pass?
> Wesham nashir shir hadash uwir'nana na'ale
> [There we shall sing a new song and joyously we shall ascend]
> Let it soon come to pass! [122]

It is well known that some Hasidim considered singing (and music in general) a high order of communication with God, higher even than prayer. Known, too, is the Hasidic idea that every tune contains *nitzotzot* ("sparks") from the great divine fire, and that, by adopting folk tunes and thereby endowing them with a sacredness, these tune-sparks can and should be lifted up from the sphere of impurity in which they were trapped to that of holiness. What has not been pointed out (at least as far as I am aware) is that this very doctrine was part of Russian sectarian mysticism as well. Skovoroda taught that Christ's voice resounded ceaselessly in every heart which contained a pure divine spark. Singing was a favorite form of religious self-expression among the Russian sectarians as well as the Polish Catholic peasants. Hasidism thus certainly emerged in an environment in which the Gentiles were wont to pour out in song their yearning for religious elevation. It is not at all improbable that the Gentile environment was the source of the Hasidic idea that singing cut a direct path to God, just as it was the source from which most of the Hasidic tunes themselves were taken.

With dancing the situation was much the same. We have seen that dancing was an essential expression of Gentile sectarian religious devotion. In Biblical times, dancing (like singing) was a common form of religious exercise among the Hebrews, but after the Babylonian exile (586 B.C.E.) it never again had this function. Thus, in the eighteenth century, the idea that dancing was a sacred, God-pleasing act was virtually a new notion which was adopted by the Hasidim from their Gentile sectarian neighbors. With the absorption of the idea went the adoption of specific Gentile dance patterns such as the Russian *prisiudki*.

One more area of Ukrainian and Polish folk life which influenced Hasidism must be pointed out: the important realm of folk medicine. Before the appearance of the BeShT, many a Jewish healer in East Europe performed magic cures with the name of God and was therefore dubbed "Ba'al Shem," i.e., "master of the Name (of God)," which epithet was appended to the personal name. One of the better known among them was Eliyahu Ba'al Shem, who lived in Chelm, Poland, in the seventeenth century and left behind a fascinating book of remedies. Another, who lived somewhat later, was Benjamin Binesh Ba'al Shem; he too made a collection of folk remedies in his *Book of Benjamin's Sack*.[123] Without wishing in any way to diminish the importance of the Jews as transmitters of folk medicine from the Near East to Europe, it must be pointed out that these Jewish medicine men often prescribed the ingestion of nostrums and potions containing parts of non-kosher animals (e.g., the snake, the fox, the hare, the raven, and even the pig) as remedies for all kinds of diseases and for barrenness, which are likely to have originated among Gentiles rather than Jews. This conclusion is confirmed by the fact that, while these Jewish remedy books are written in Hebrew, the names of the plants and animals they recommended as cures are given in the Yiddish vernacular and are derived from Latin, Greek, German, or Slavic originals. Moreover, the same non-kosher substances prescribed in Jewish folk medicines are also prescribed in, for instance, Polish, Ukrainian, Ruthenian, and Galician folk cures.[124]

The BeShT himself began his ministry as such a Ba'al Shem. He made use of plants and herbs, bloodletting, and other remedies he had apparently learned from village quacks and prescribed protective amulets and good-luck charms. Even later in his life, after he had become well known as the founder of Hasidism and had acquired the epithet "Ba'al Shem Tov" ("Master of the Good Name"), which elevated him above the many *Ba'ale Shem* (plural of *Ba'al Shem*) who preceded him, he still continued his work as a healer. On one occasion, he had a diamond ground up and gave it to a sick adherent to drink.[125] The Hasidic rabbis who followed in the BeShT's footsteps took over the practice of religio-magic healing which helped in establishing their reputation as miracle-working Tzaddiqim. Thus Rabbi Israel Hofstein, Maggid of Kozienice, became so famous as a holy man who healed the sick and cured the barren that his reputation reached Christian Polish circles, including the highest nobility. As their predecessors, the Ba'ale Shem, so the Hasidic Tzaddiqim, too, compiled remedy books or lists. One such was compiled by Rabbi Pinhas Shapira of Koretz (d. c. 1790), who was a friend and disciple of the BeShT and lived in Volhynia.[126] Instead of nostrums, or in addition to them, the Tzaddiqim also provided those who applied for their help with amulets and charms, which again conformed to old Talmudic custom on the one hand but also had its counterparts in the Gentile environment, on the other.

7. The Jewishness of Hasidism

Having tried to show in detail the extent to which Gentile influences are apparent in Hasidism, I should now try to put these influences in their proper perspective. The first point to be emphasized is that—as in the case of the earlier encounters between Jews and Gentiles—the influences of the environment on Hasidism remained confined to *form*, without ever touching the *essence* of the Jewish faith. All the ecstatic exercises and antics which the Hasidim seem to have adopted from the religious life of their Gentile neighbors are but *forms* of religious expression; the *content* they express is the same old Jewish belief in the "God of our fathers" which had motivated the Israelites, and their heirs, the Jews, ever since the days of Moses. It is also characteristic that the most extreme, self-destructive forms of Russian sectarianism—self-flagellation, castration, and self-immolation—never gained a foothold in Hasidism; such excesses were effectively barred by the Jewish essence of religiosity, whose guiding principle remained that all religious duty and observance must subserve the ultimate God-given purpose of individual and group survival, as succinctly expressed in the oft-quoted Biblical verse, "Keep My statutes and Mine ordinaces which, if a man do, he shall live by them: I am the Lord" (Lev. 18:5). The nearest Hasidim came to self-destruction was in their imagination, when some of them gave themselves up to the delusion that they no longer existed.[127]

Tzaddiqism is subject to the same observation. The luxurious and pomp-filled courts of the affluent Tzaddiqim certainly reflected the great manor houses of the nobility and the palaces of the Church dignitaries. The claims that the Tzaddiq was the vicar of God on earth, was endowed with miraculous powers as well as with almost superhuman wisdom, was the only channel through which the simple Hasid could approach God, and that all these qualities of the Tzaddiq were unfailingly passed on to his son or sons—all these features can be shown to have had their antecedents in one or the other of the established churches or sectarian movements. But again, all of them bear resemblances of form only to their Gentile counterparts and never impinge upon the essential Jewishness of the Tzaddiq, which was anchored deep in Jewish tradition and history and in the prototypal "Pious Men" of the Talmudic age.

The founders, leaders, and the followers of Hasidism undoubtedly learned to love nature from the Gentile peasants among whom they lived and expressed this love in forms adopted from them. Physically, the nature loved by both the Gentiles and the Hasidim was the same—the same fields and mountains, the same animals and plants. Yet the mental image the Hasid had of nature was very different from that of his Gentile neighbor: it was the image created in his mind by a nature perceived through the optical and conceptual filter of a thousand Biblical associations. Thus a tree meant something quite different for the Polish peasant who conceptualized it through the imagery of his animism and pagan-Christian folk belief, and for the Hasidic Jew for whom it was a Biblical-Talmudic concept, an object of many halakhic rules, and a subject of numerous legends in which trees act among themselves and react to God and man.

The conceptual background and basis was the factor which prevented the Hasidic Jews from becoming as addicted to alcohol as the Gentile peasants. They learned to imbibe, to find pleasure in the warm feeling that flowed through the body after drinking several glasses of vodka; but to become "dead drunk" was impossible for the Jew whose attitude to inebriation was fixed by age-old Jewish tradition reaching back to the Bible and the Talmud. Moreover, and most typically, the Hasidim found it necessary to justify the use of alcohol by a religious explanation—the vodka rapidly inflamed the senses and through alcoholic intoxication was supposed to lead to a spiritual enthusiasm. But we have no reports of Hasidim having drunk themselves under the table, nor of having indulged in solitary drinking. Drinking was a strictly communal activity, engaged in by Hasidic peer groups for the ostensible and approved purpose of facilitating the attainment of joy and the wholehearted turning to God.

The pivotal Hasidic doctrine which required that one serve God with joy and enthusiasm and attain "adhesion" to Him has, as we have seen, both its antecedents and its parallels in the established and sectarian Christianity of Eastern Europe. At this point Gentile influence came perhaps closest to affecting not only the form but also the content of Hasidism. To say the least, the turning to God carried the same emotional overtones among both sectarians and Hasidim. Yet a great difference still remained. The Christian who served God or Christ "in a spirit of childlike joy" and with "a childlike devotion," to use Hromádka's felicitous phrases, could do so with a total abandon which remained unattainable for even the most fervent Hasid. In rare moments of rapt enthusiasm the sparks of joy certainly penetrated the Hasidic heart; but it is doubtful whether even then they managed to drive out the shadows of sadness from its deepest corners. No wonder that, of all the enthusiastic sects of Eastern Europe, only Hasidism felt it necessary to proclaim formally and to insist that sadness ('atzvut) was a grave sin and that to rejoice was a *mitzva*, a religiously required good deed. One of the cardinal norms of serving God, according to the BeShT, was to overcome sadness. Worry and gloom, he taught, cause a "narrowing of the spirit" in man and an obstruction of the heart; while the service of the Creator of the World requires an "expansion of the spirit," that is, a mood fired by joy and hope. It was an important rule in the service of the Creator that one must beware of sadness. Crying was extremely detrimental, since man must serve his Lord in joy—only if one cries for joy is crying thoroughly beneficial. The Shekhina, the personified Divine Presence, "does not dwell in sadness but in joyful piety." [128]

One of the purposes of the convivial meetings of the Hasidim in their *kloyz* (prayer-room) was to "combat sadness." Rabbi Barukh of Tulczyn even found it necessary to give a materialistic twist to this basic Hasidic principle: "Sadness is detrimental to livelihood; therefore, one must endeavor to be joyful." Again, typically Jewish in their regulatory intent are the instructions given by Rabbi Shneur Zalman of Lyadi (1748–1812) concerning sadness and rejoicing: one must flee sadness caused by the workaday worries which deaden the heart, in order to preserve the ability to serve God in joy and with complete devotion; but one must beware of inducing joyful excitement in oneself by bodily measures, such as violent gestures and the like. [129]

The *mitzva* (religious commandment) of banishing sadness and of rejoicing forms the subject of a Hasidic folk song still heard in Israel:

> *No sadness, bakhurim, bakhurim*
> *The Rabbi commands us to rejoice.*
> *Our life is a vale of tears, of tears,*
> *It's a* mitzva *to forget the gloom.* [130]

Thus, despite all the emphasis on joy, or because of it, it is quite clear that rejoicing for the Hasidim was not a spontaneous attitude but rather an act of will, a therapeutic procedure in which one had to engage with purposeful determination. And there cannot be the slightest doubt that, despite the rabbi's command and all the other Hasidic directives, in the midst of all the singing and dancing and merrymaking and occasional foolery, the Hasidic Jews maintained the same posture toward God which had first been worked out in the Bible and was then again and again reworked and refined, but never redefined, from Talmudic times. Their God remained what He had always been: just and merciful, the Father in Heaven, the King of the World, whose many

demands—all well known and clearly explicated—are hard to fulfill, whose
inscrutable will keeps Israel in exile and servitude, but whom you had to
love "with all your heart, with all your soul, and with all your might,"
because there was no other choice. Ever since these words were first written
down in the Bible (Deut. 6:5) nothing has changed, because nothing could
change, in this relationship.

Another typically Jewish development set in among the Hasidim within a
very few years after the founding of the movement by the BeShT—the rapid
return to the valuation of Tora study. In the early years of Hasidism, the
Hasidic leaders and their followers exhibited strong antagonism against the
scholarly rabbis who considered halakhic study the supreme value in Judaism. Accordingly, the Hasidic attitude to studying itself was one of derogation. They considered concentration on Talmudic study not only useless but
even harmful for the joyousness of the spirit which was a prerequisite of true
piety.[131] However, the traditional Jewish value of studying proved too great
for the Hasidim to resist it for long. Soon after the death of the BeShT, some
of his disciples and successors returned to Tora study and devoted themselves to it like any traditional Mitnaged rabbi, with the one difference that
they added to the study of the Talmud and the halakhic codes also that of the
Zohar, the writings of Yitzhak Luria, and other Kabbalistic works. One of the
two grandsons of the BeShT, Rabbi Ephraim of Sudilkov, who became
famous for his excellence in Talmudic studies, said, "The Mitnagdim, the
more they study the higher they rise in their own eyes; the Hasidim, however, the more they study the lower they sink in their own eyes because the
more they learn to regard themselves unimportant and lowly." He also
emphasized that, of all learning, "only Tora-study is as endless as His Name,
because the Tora, God, and Israel are one." [132]

Great studiousness is attested also of other Tzaddiqim; in the new Hasidic
doctrine of Rabbi Shneur Zalman of Lyadi, Tora study was restored theoretically as well to the central position it had been denied in the system of the
BeShT. "The study of the Tora," wrote Shneur Zalman in his Tanya, "weighs
as much as the fulfillment of all other commandments, since the latter are
but husks while the Tora is both nourishment and husk·for the mind, inasmuch as in delving into study the mind becomes enveloped into the
Tora." [133] The Hasidic elaboration apart, we have here a return to the age-
old Mishnaic evaluation of Tora study as being higher than anything else a
Jew is commanded to do,[134] which was the main guideline of Jewish life from
Talmudic times until the emergence of Hasidism. Several other sayings
upholding the value of studying are found in the Tanya, including one we
would certainly not have expected from a Tzaddiq: "Tora study ranks higher
than the fulfillment of all other commandments, higher even than prayer
which unites one with the higher worlds." [135] Thus, the one movement in
the history of Judaism which started out by trying to shake off the claims of

studiousness became within a few decades yet another Jewish trend for which studying was a *summum bonum*.

As I was concluding this chapter, it came to me that similarities between the Jewish and other religions in external observance and on the folk level have existed and been noted elsewhere too. About the time Hasidism reached the height of its conquering march among East European Jews, Edward William Lane was engaged in studying the life of the Egyptians of his day and found that there was a striking similarity between what he called the "superstitions" of the Jews, the Christians, and the Muslims in Egypt and other countries in the East. They adopt, he said, "each other's superstitions, while they abhor the leading doctrines of each other's faiths." [136] Paraphrasing Lane's observation, we can say that in Eastern Europe the Jews and Christians adopted each other's forms of religious expression while certainly continuing to "abhor the leading doctrines of each other's faiths." As to the relationship between the Hasidim and the Mitnagdim, the opposite can be said. They shared the leading doctrines of Judaism while abhorring each other's forms of religious expression.

Looking back upon the five encounters between Judaism and other cultures surveyed so far, we can conclude with a general observation. Each of the five exemplifies the great vitality that characterized Jewish religious culture from its earliest. Each illustrates the historical law under which Jews made their way from country to country and from culture to culture and which reads: everywhere the Jews freely admitted foreign forms into the traditional structure of their culture, while retaining its essence throughout unscathed and unaltered. This is what I would answer the pagan who came to query Hillel, were he to reappear after two thousand years and ask me to explain to him, while he stands on one leg, the secret of Jewish survival. I would say: "The Jews were able to adopt the most disparate foreign cultural forms and yet retain unchanged the innermost content of their Jewishness."

9

Enlightenment: Triumph and Tragedy

1. Introductory

The second half of the eighteenth century saw the beginnings of three historic processes which, in the course of the nineteenth century, were to transform Jewish life to an extent that Jews had not known in their entire long history. One was the rise of Hasidism, which revolutionized Jewish religious life in East Europe—at the time the home of the great majority of European Jewry. The influences Hasidism absorbed from the Gentile environment and the nature of the transformation it brought about in the outlook of a major part of the Jewish people were discussed in the preceding chapter.

The present chapter deals with the other two great historic processes which began in the eighteenth century, when Ashkenazi Jewry was enabled for the first time to come face to face with modern European culture: the Jewish Enlightenment and the Emancipation of the Jews. The joint effect of this last, greatest, and, as we shall see, most fateful of Jewish encounters with the Gentile world was (to put it as briefly as possible) to transform the Jews, who for two millennia had constituted a separate religio-cultural entity in all countries of their Diaspora, into populations which, while still distinguishable from their Gentile environments, had in many places so much in common with them that their very group identity came under question. Their approximation of the Gentile mode was manifested in all areas and aspects of life from the most external to the most internal.

The two processes, Enlightenment and Emancipation, were preceded by individual initiatives, both Jewish and Gentile, some of them dating from the seventeenth or even sixteenth century. However, it was not until the late eighteenth century that they began to affect the religious, intellectual, social, and economic life of increasingly large segments of the European Jewish population. The movement for granting rights to Jews began in France in the first half of the eighteenth century and spread slowly across Europe, achieving its goal, the Emancipation of the Jews, at various times in various countries. It arrived most belatedly in Russia, where it had to wait for the 1917 Revolution. Enlightenment as an Ashkenazi Jewish movement began in the second half of the eighteenth century in Germany and spread, first rapidly to the West, then more slowly to the East; to this day it has not been able to overcome small pockets of ultra-Orthodox resistance, notably in the United States and Israel. In the general course of events, the two movements mutually reinforced each other. Neither could have brought about the profound transformation of Jewish life it effected without proceeding side by side with the other.

The typical Ashkenazi Jew of the pre-Enlightenment eighteenth century differed from his Gentile countryman in all conceivable criteria of group identification: in religion and language, in education, literacy, and occupations, in clothing and manners, in morality, temperament, and inclinations, in values, goals, and ambitions, in mentality and ethnicity. Because of these differences, and because of the emphatic ethnocentrism, or, rather, culturocentrism of the Gentile advocates of Enlightenment, when the latter first deigned to have a close look at the Jews what they saw appeared to them as an uncivilized, uncouth, and backward bunch of outlandish figures. Added to this was the disapproval the Enlighteners had for the typical Jewish occupations: moneylending, which was consistently stamped "usury," dealing in old clothes, and peddling—the only three means of support in which the Jews were universally allowed to engage. Hence the approach of enlightened liberalism to the Jews was rather ambiguous. It comprised the determination to give them rights and to wean them from their evil ways—their "uncultured" manners and appearance, their "superstitious" religion, and their "dishonesty" in business. In many cases the granting of rights was held out as the reward that would be given to the Jews if they undertook to "improve" themselves, or proved amenable to improvements imposed on them from the outside.

The pathetic aspect of the situation was that the Jews themselves, once they became acquainted with as much as the rudiments of Gentile cultural values and, in particular, with the Gentile stereotype of the Jew, began to be influenced by them and to share them. This brought about the emergence of a Jewish self-stereotype, which was (as we shall later see in the chapter on Jewish Self-Hate) largely a mirror image of the Jew as seen through Gentile eyes. The Jewish admission of cultural inferiority in relation to Gentile enlightened Europe was a particularly damaging development psychologically, which led, within a very few decades and long before the attainment of Emancipation, to large-scale defection from the ranks of Judaism and to conversion to Christianity.

The encounter between the Jews and modern European culture which is both the basis and the outcome of the Emancipation and the Enlightenment differed from all previous Jewish-Gentile encounters in several respects that will be discussed in the next chapter. One difference, however, must be noted right here because of its bearing on the way this chapter is structured. All those previous encounters took place between one Jewish and one Gentile culture group, and largely within one territorial unit: in Canaan; in Palestine and neighboring Alexandria; in Arab Spain; in Renaissance Italy; in Poland and the contiguous Ukraine. The Jewish-Gentile encounter which brought about the Enlightenment took place between several different Jewish populations, on the one hand, and many much more different Gentile populations, on the other; and its locale was the length and width of the European continent. There were great variations and even contrasts in the Gentile attitude to the Jews between one country and another, as well as in the Jewish condition, way of life, and mentality in various places. The confines of a chapter, even a lengthy one, would not permit a full presentation of all the local variations of this last great historic encounter. I had, therefore, no choice but to confine myself to a selection of those phases of the Emancipation and the Enlightenment which seemed to me most significant, either because they were "firsts" or because of their influence on the developments in other countries.

2. The Forerunners

In the seventeenth century, a time of most cruel suffering for East European Jewry, the Jews of the West enjoyed relative tranquillity, prosperity, and cultural productivity. The Ashkenazi Jews in the Polish orbit were forced to concentrate all their energies on how to survive massacres, destruction, and persecution and eke out a bare living. In these circumstances all intellectual endeavor, including original scholarly work even in the one field of the *Halakha*, inevitably suffered. At the same time, the Sephardim in Holland (to be discussed in the subsequent section) and the Italian Jews lived through a second Renaissance and continued to produce important Hebrew works in various fields of Jewish learning, as well as Spanish, Italian, and Latin books in the secular sciences. They also began to take a critical look at the forms in which Jewish religion was observed, at Jewish tradition, at the Jewish social condition, and at the attitude of the Gentiles to the Jews. Their findings and recommendations were presented in books and treatises written either in Hebrew or in the languages of the peoples whom they wished to influence in favor of the Jews. The authors of these writings, daring, and revolutionary for their time, must be considered the forerunners of that immense Jewish transformation which took place, under the leadership of the Mendelssohnian school, in the second half of the eighteenth century.

Their importance was fully recognized by Moses Mendelssohn himself and by his co-workers in the cause of Jewish Enlightenment. When these men embarked upon the great task of spreading a new type of scholarship, enlightened thinking, and European culture among the Jews, they searched for precursors in the not too distant Jewish past whose works they could hold up as precedents that would justify their own rational approach to Jewish problems. Inevitably, what they found were the writings of the Italian and Sephardi Jewish scholars of the seventeenth, and even the sixteenth century, and they immediately proceeded to present them to their contemporaries either in translations or in new editions. Thus they reprinted the encyclopedic work of Azariah de Rossi (c. 1511–78), the *M'or 'Enayim* (*Light of the Eyes*), [1] which when originally published in Mantua in the sixteenth century had evoked such sharp criticism among conservative rabbis. Now it was held up as a model of independent research. Such exponents of a critical approach to Jewish religion and its literary sources as Leon da Modena were "enshrined as examples to be followed." [2] The *Vindiciae Judaeorum* (London, 1656) of Manasseh ben Israel, the Dutch Sephardi contemporary of Modena, was considered of such importance by Moses Mendelssohn that he induced his friend, the physician and philosopher Markus Herz (1747–1803), to translate it from English into German. Manasseh ben Israel had argued that religion had no rights over its followers and must not resort to compulsory measures. This was considered most timely by Mendelssohn, and made a deep impression also on enlightened Christian clergymen.

Apart from such patently manifest influences, the Mendelssohnian Enlighteners could find inspiration in the entire Jewish world of medieval Spain and Renaissance Italy. There they saw Jews who had unhestitatingly participated in the cultural life of their Gentile environment, and yet remained devoted and committed Jews.

One of the earliest examples of a critical view of traditional Judaism is a book whose authorship is still in doubt, although it was surely written in Italy, either by Leon da Modena (1571–1648), the famous Venetian rabbi, preacher, scholar, and poet, or by a contemporary. [3] The book, entitled *Qol Sakhal* (*The Fool's Voice*), attacked Jewish traditionalism and uninhibitedly disputed Jewish laws which, the author felt, were in need of reform. He suggested streamlining of synagogue services, the abolition of many rites, the relaxation of the Sabbath and holyday observances, the abrogation, or at least simplification, of the dietary laws, the lifting of the prohibition against drinking wine with Gentiles, and other such reforms. The *Qol Sakhal* represents the most unrestrained and radical criticism of the slavish observance of the Jewish *Halakha* and *minhag* ("custom") to be written in Hebrew until the nineteenth-century Reform movement whose protagonists were to repeat many of its arguments.

Other early "enlightened" authors addressed themselves not to inner-Jewish religious, educational, or cultural reforms, but to the Gentile world, presenting a defense of the Jews and emphasizing the useful roles the Jews played, or could play, in the life of the state. One of these was Leon da Modena himself, who in his Italian book *History of the Jewish Rites* argued that many Jews had become abased in spirit and degenerated from true Jewish integrity because of the straitness of their Exile and because they had been excluded from land ownership and from many respected trades and occupations.[4] The implications and intentions of this and other such arguments are clear: remove the restrictions, and the Jews will regain their integrity and spirit.

Another scholar who argued along these lines was a younger contemporary and co-rabbi in Venice of Leon da Modena, Simone Luzzatto (c. 1583–1663).[5] His Italian book, *Discourse on the Status of the Jews*, is a treatise which defends the Jews by marshaling cogent arguments in their favor, such as their usefulness in commerce, the possible increase to be gained in state revenues by encouraging Jewish activities, the advantages Venice has reaped from her relationship with them, and so on. Luzzatto also stressed the loyalty with which the Jews observed the laws of the republic. This was the first apologetic work written by a Jew in which economic arguments were used systematically in favor of the toleration of the Jews. (Luzzatto's arguments were later to be used extensively by John Toland in 1714 in an English treatise advocating the naturalization of the Jews.)

Luzzatto distinguished between those Jews who held the Talmudic law of equal authority with the Bible, those who formed a philosophical and cultured class, the followers of the Kabbala, and the Karaites. More important, he was one of the earliest Jewish authors to attempt an unprejudiced psychological portrayal of the Jews. He stressed that underlying the apparent differences between Venetian, Constantinopolitan, Damascan, German, or Polish Jews, there was a common Jewish character. The Jews, he pointed out, were

. . . a nation of timid and unmanly disposition, at present incapable of political government, occupied only with its separate interests, and caring little about the public welfare. The economy of the Jews borders on avarice; they are admirers of antiquity, and have no eye for the present course of things. Many are uneducated, without taste for learning or the knowledge of languages, and, in following the laws of their religion, they exaggerate to the most painful degree. But they have also noteworthy peculiarities—firmness and endurance in their religion, uniformity of doctrinal teaching in the long course of more than fifteen centuries since the dispersion; wonderful steadfastness which leads them, if not to go into dangers, yet to endure the severest suffering. They possess knowledge of the Holy Scripture and its exposition, gentleness and hospitality to the members of their race—the Persian Jew in some degree suffers the wrong of the Italian—strict abstinence from carnal offenses, extraordinary carefulness to keep the family unspotted, and skill in managing difficult matters. They are

submissive and yielding to everyone, only not to their brethren in religion. The
failings of the Jews have rather the character of cowardice and meanness than
of cruelty and atrocity.[6]

In the next generation lived Isaac (Fernando) Cardozo (born of Marrano
parents in Portugal, 1604; died in Verona after 1681), physician, philosopher,
and polemicist, who was chief medical officer of Madrid, but had to flee from
the Inquisition, and settled in Italy where he openly embraced Judaism. He
composed verses in Spanish and wrote various Spanish scientific treatises,
but for our present subject most important is his great Spanish work, *The
Distinctions and Calumnies of the Jews.*[7] This book is a remarkable presentation on the one hand of the features which distinguished the Jews, and on
the other of the accusations brought against them. Among the former are
their selection by God, their separation from other peoples by their laws,
their compassion for the suffering of others, their philanthropy, chastity,
faith, and so on. The latter part amounts to a refutation of the Jewish stereotype which was prevalent in Cardozo's day among the Christians of Italy and
which included the allegation that they worshipped false gods, smelled bad,
were hard and unfeeling toward other peoples, had corrupted Scripture,
blasphemed holy images and the host, killed Christian children, and used
their blood for ritual purposes.

By the mid-eighteenth century the Sephardi *élan vital* had run its course.
This manifested itself both demographically and culturally. The Sephardi
birthrate declined and before the end of the century reached the point of
zero population growth. Thus in Holland, from 1780 to 1849, the number of
the Sephardim remained about 3,000, while that of the Ashkenazim increased from 30,000 to close to 60,000. The Dutch Sephardi community,
which in the seventeenth century produced many men of letters, scholars,
and authors of note, went in the eighteenth into an intellectual decline.
Faced with this situation, and aware of the danger of being submerged in the
growing Ashkenazi tide, the Sephardim withdrew into their pride and exhibited a mounting prejudice against their Ashkenazi brethren. The basis for
these sentiments was their unquestionably glorious ancestry and the fact that
they had assimilated in turn the Spanish, Portuguese, Italian, Dutch, and
French cultures, while the Ashkenazim still clung to their Talmudic tradition
and Yiddish tongue. In response to the awakening interest among the Gentiles in the Jewish condition, these late champions of Sephardi preeminence
took the road of emphasizing their own culture and refinement as against the
boorish backwardness of the Ashkenazim and asked for equal rights for themselves to the exclusion of the latter, whom they condemned in tones reminiscent of virulent anti-Semitic outbursts. Some of them, for instance, the
Portuguese Jews of Bordeaux who had begun to settle in that French port
city about 1550, went so far as to petition the authorities to expel the Ash-

kenazi latecomers from the city. In 1760 Jacob Rodriguez Pereira (Spain, 1715–Paris, 1780) actually obtained from Louis XV a decree of expulsion of the German and Avignonese Jews, which was put into effect the next year by the governor of Bordeaux, the duc de Richelieu.[8]

In these efforts Pereira was assisted by Isaac de Pinto (Bordeaux, 1717–Amsterdam, 1787), a man of Portuguese Marrano descent, possessed of both wealth and talent, a philosopher and economist of repute, whose devotion to the cause of his Sephardi brethren was matched only by his disdain for his Ashkenazi stepbrothers. Since, contrary to their expectations, the expulsion of the Ashkenazi Jews from Bordeaux weakened rather than strengthened the position of the remaining Sephardi élite, Pinto felt it proper and useful to write a treatise vindicating the Portuguese Jews and pointing out the wide differences between them and the meaner breed of Jews from other lands. An additional impetus for Pinto to speak out in defense of the Jews in general and the Portuguese Jews in particular was the article "Juifs" contained in Volume 7 of Voltaire's historical writings (published in Geneva in 1756), which depicted the Jewish character as evil ever since Biblical times, and which, as Pinto knew well, was widely read by influential French statesmen. Nevertheless, Pinto wrote his "critical reflections" on Voltaire only after the expulsion of the Ashkenazi Jews from Bordeaux. It was published in Amsterdam in 1762, under the title *Apology for the Jewish Nation*,[9] although in fact it is more a defense of the Portuguese Jews than of Jewry as a whole.

Pinto argues three points against Voltaire: that the Portuguese and Spanish Jews differ from the enlightened peoples of West Europe in nothing but religion, in fact, "vie with them in refinement, elegance, and show"; that they differ and hold themselves aloof from the other Jews; and that they are the descendants of the noblest families of the tribe of Judah, who had lived in Spain ever since the Babylonian captivity. Hence they deserve to be treated like, and to occupy the same positions as, Christian Frenchmen, or Dutchmen, or Englishmen.[10] To lend support to his argument, Pinto details the differences among Jews of various countries, which he explains as due to their having everywhere assumed, "like a chameleon," the character of the inhabitants of the country in which they live. As for the German and Polish Jews, Pinto does not deny that Voltaire's accusations against them are true, but he nevertheless defends them by attributing their dishonorable trades (usury) and other despicable actions to the overwhelming sufferings, slavery, and humiliations which they had to endure and are still enduring.[11]

Pinto was the last of the Sephardi and Italian Jewish scholars and authors (only a few of whom are discussed here) who served the Jewish cause according to their lights by pleading for improvements in Jewish religion and, either implicitly or explicitly, for an amelioration of their civic status. Mendelssohn hailed Pinto's pamphlet, which contained much of what was going to be said in the ensuing thirty years by his disciples or people under his influence.[12] However, before presenting the work of the German Jewish Enlighteners, we must have a look at the Dutch-Sephardi pre-Enlightenment scene of the seventeenth century, and at the Gentile propagation of Jewish enfranchisement in the eighteenth.

3. Dutch Interlude

The Netherlands, which in 1581 achieved independence from Spain, held three great attractions for the Marranos. One was the possibility afforded to them by the tolerant Dutch state to return openly to the religion which their fathers had been forced to abjure in Spain and Portugal. The second comprised the great economic opportunities available at the time to all inhabitants of the Netherlands, which in the seventeenth century became the first commercial state and the first maritime power in the world. The third was the cultural flowering which accompanied the great material prosperity. The Jews, who after 1593 began to arrive as Marrano refugees from the Portuguese Inquisition, made important contributions on all fronts.

The Dutch Sephardi interlude of the seventeenth century can be taken as a prime example of the cultural-historical law which can be formulated as follows: Whenever the Jews enjoyed even a modest measure of liberty in the midst of a Gentile society whose culture they found attractive, they experienced a cultural upswing both in Jewish learning and in many of those fields in which their neighbors excelled. This law operated in all the great Jewish-Gentile historic encounters discussed in preceding chapters, and it again proved valid in seventeenth-century Holland.

The Portuguese Jews who settled in the Netherlands beginning with the last years of the sixteenth century never attained considerable numbers. At its zenith (c. 1670), the community numbered 4,000 families.[13] Yet in the seventeenth century there were among them dozens of outstanding physicians, surgeons, and pharmacists; and many of them were artists, illuminators and engravers, poets and playwrights in Spanish and Portuguese. Their achievements in Jewish studies were the more remarkable since many of the Marranos who found refuge in Holland had received only a Christian education and began studying Jewish subjects at an advanced age, admittedly helped by the fact that Holland became in that period a celebrated center of Hebrew printing.

However, even after having settled in Amsterdam and returning openly to Judaism, these ex-Marrano intellectuals could not divest themselves of the Spanish and Portuguese cultures they had imbibed in their childhood and youth. Together with their Spanish or Portuguese mother tongue, they retained their interest in Spanish or Portuguese poetry and literature, and to a lesser extent also in the fine arts. Thus Jacob Israel Belmonte (Madeira,

1570–Amsterdam, 1629), one of the founders of the Amsterdam Jewish community, wrote a Spanish poetic account of the Inquisition in 100 octaves which he called *Job*. One of his sons, Moses Belmonte (1619–Amsterdam, 1647), inherited his father's poetic talent, wrote original poems in Spanish, translated the Songs of Solomon and the Sayings of the Fathers into Spanish, and also was an engraver. Isaac Nuñez (Don Manuel) de Belmonte (b. Amsterdam, ?–d. there, 1705) was the agent general and resident of the king of Spain in Amsterdam; he, too, was a poet and founded in 1676 the poetic society Academia de los Sitibundos and in 1685 the Academia de los Floridos. His official position in the Spanish court did not prevent Nuñez from writing a poem on the martyr Abraham Nuñez Bernal, who was burned at the stake by the Inquisition of Cordova in 1655. This martyrdom, together with that of Isaac de Almeida Bernal, was commemorated and bemoaned in a work published in the same year in Amsterdam under the title *Elogios que Zelozos Dedicaron a la Felice Memoria de Abraham Nuñez Bernal que fue Quedamo Vivo, Sanctificando el Nombre de su Criador* (*Eulogies Which the Zealous Dedicated to the Blessed Memory of Abraham Nuñez Bernal Who Was Burned Alive, Sanctifying the Name of His Creator*), which contains, among other items, poems by nine Sephardi Jews. Books such as this, and the poetic societies, testify to the role of seventeenth-century Amsterdam as a prime center of Spanish Jewish poetry.

The *autos-da-fé* of the two Bernals were not the only cases in which the fate of Marrano martyrs shook the Amsterdam community and moved it to express its pain in poetry. In the 1640's and 1650's, hundreds of Marranos were accused of Judaizing by the Spanish and Portuguese Inquisition, and dozens of them were burned alive in Cuenca, Granada, Santiago de Compostela, Cordova, Lisbon, and elsewhere. All of them had close relatives in Amsterdam who heard about the martyrdom of their kin with pain and rage and frequently expressed their feelings in Hebrew and Spanish verses.

Some of the Spanish and Portuguese poetic output of the Amsterdam Sephardim found its way into their synagogue. In 1624 a dramatic Portuguese poem in praise of Judaism, *Dialogue of the Mountains*, was recited at Shavu'ot in the Amsterdam synagogue. It was written by Reuel Jesurun (Lisbon, c. 1575–Amsterdam, 1634), whose original Marrano name in Portugal had been Paulo de Pina.[14] Poetry, incidentally, ran in the Jesurun family. A contemporary of Reuel was David Jesurun, who escaped from the Inquisition and settled in Amsterdam, where he continued to write poetry in Portuguese.

Seventeenth-century Sephardi Jewish life in Amsterdam was innovative in other respects as well. In 1678, the city saw the publication of the first Jewish periodical, the Ladino-language *Gazeta de Amsterdam*. It was followed in 1686–87 by a Yiddish semi-weekly, whose Tuesday edition was entitled *Dinstagishe Kurant* while its Friday issues bore the title *Freitagishe Kurant*.

Both were short-lived. From 1728 to 1761, also in Amsterdam, a Hebrew monthly bulletin entitled *P'ri 'Etz Ḥayyim* (*Fruit of the Tree of Life*) was published by the members of the Sephardi Bet Midrash (study house) "Arbol de las Vidas" ("Tree of Lives"). Not until 1750 was a Jewish periodical to appear in another place: it was the *Qohelet Musar*, of which only two issues were published by Moses Mendelssohn and Tobias Beck.

The two best-known names among seventeenth-century Dutch Jews are those of Manasseh ben Israel (1604–57) and Baruch Spinoza (1632–77). Both were of Marrano descent, but right there the similarity between them ends. Manasseh was a prolific author who published works in no less than five languages—Hebrew, Latin, Portuguese, Spanish, and English—on Jewish, and emphatically pro-Jewish, subjects. He functioned as rabbi and yeshiva head in Amsterdam, was a renowned orator, and set up the first Hebrew printing press in Holland. He was of a strongly mystical turn of mind, a Kabbalist, convinced (as were many contemporary Christians) of the early coming of the Messiah, and maintained close relations with Christian mystics in Holland, Sweden, Germany, and France. However, he secured for himself a place in the annals of Jewry by his successful advocacy of the readmission of the Jews to England, which was tacitly allowed by Cromwell in 1656 shortly before Manasseh's death. The treatise Manasseh wrote in order to secure a favorable response to his *Humble Addresses to the Lord Protector*, entitled *Vindiciae Judaeorum*, was published in London in 1656 and was to play a role, as we saw, in Mendelssohn's efforts for Jewish Emancipation.

Spinoza, of course, belongs not to Jewish history but to modern philosophy, of which he is considered the greatest figure. His relationship to the Jewish community was an unhappy one; his heretical views earned him excommunication from the Amsterdam Jewish community at the age of twenty-three, even before he published any of his writings. From that time until his death at the age of forty-four, he had no contact whatsoever with Jews, living in the most modest circumstances on his earnings as an optical lens grinder and on small stipends he received from Christian patrons. He saw only two of his works published during his lifetime: his analysis of Descartes' philosophy (1663) and his *Tractatus Theologico-Politicus* (1670), which brought him general opprobrium from the contemporary Christian world. In the *Tractatus*, Spinoza is throughout preoccupied with the Bible, which he treats critically, anticipating in many respects the approaches developed in the nineteenth century by the schools of Kuenen and Wellhausen. Spinoza lived out his life in complete intellectual isolation, communing only in spirit with those great minds whose works influenced him: Descartes, Giordano Bruno, Hobbes, and the Jewish philosophers Maimonides, Gersonides, and Ḥasdai Crescas.

One cannot speak of Spinoza without at least mentioning his greatest work, the *Ethics*, which is primarily responsible for his preeminent position in modern philosophy. The *Ethics* is an enormously complex and difficult book which defies summation. Nevertheless, one of its basic thoughts can be pointed out—its emphasis on loving God. As Spinoza puts it: "The love of God must occupy the mind to the utmost." For Spinoza, the power of the most perfect intellect was the power of the *amor dei intellectualis*, "the intellectual love of God," which constitutes man's true happiness. Whether the age-old Jewish precept of "Thou shalt love the Lord thy God with all thy heart, and with all thy soul, and with all thy might" (Deut. 6:5) had anything to do with this fundamental Spinozan idea could be debated at length. The Biblical passage refers to three factors which must lead to the love of God: heart (that is, reason), soul (that is, emotion), and might (that is, willpower). In Spinoza's formulation of the love of God, there are three corresponding factors: happiness, intellect, and power. Can Spinoza's "intellect" be equated with the Biblical "heart," his "happiness" with the "soul" of the Bible, and his "power" with its "might"? Can there be here a connection of which, perhaps, Spinoza himself was unaware? [15]

Spinoza had a profound influence upon European philosophy of the seventeenth and eighteenth centuries, and the late nineteenth-century scientists took a renewed interest in his thought. Among the Jews, although Mendelssohn opposed Spinoza, he was nevertheless influenced by him and made use of some of his arguments. In the nineteenth century, all Jewish philosophers felt compelled to take a stand on Spinozism and discussed his philosophy extensively. The judgment of the Jewish historian Graetz was that Spinoza "against his will has contributed to the glory of the race which he so unjustly reviled. His powerful intellect, logical acumen, and strength of character are more and more recognized as properties which he owed to the race from which he was descended." [16] In the twentieth century, dozens of weighty studies have been published about Spinoza, and he has come to be called "the philosophers' philosopher." The influence of his thought shows no sign of decreasing.

In addition to these towering figures, the seventeenth-century Amsterdam Sephardi community produced a fascinating galaxy of minor luminaries. Among them were philosophers and philologists, physicians and mathematicians, cartographers and cosmographers, historians and dramatists, poets and poetesses. The typical seventeenth-century Dutch Jewish intellectual was born a Marrano in Portugal or Spain, left the place where he lived in order to escape the persecution of the Inquisition, and settled in Amsterdam where he openly embraced Judaism and became a rabbi, merchant, or communal leader, but was primarily preoccupied with an intellectual pursuit. A listing of the works produced by this remarkable community would include books on subjects as diverse as ethics, the ebb and flow of the tides, Hebrew grammar, Kabbala, the immortality of the soul, the history of the Dutch-Portuguese war in Brazil, Biblical dramas, cartography, cosmography, reproductions (models) of the Jerusalem Temple and its holy vessels, and so on. Frequently, the upbringing these men had received in their Iberian homes was a strictly Catholic one, but when the fact of their Jewish descent became known to them, they gradually developed a secret longing for the religion of their fathers. Desire was translated into practice, and before long they aroused suspicions of secret Judaizing, at which point they decided that fleeing the Inquisition was the better part of wisdom. This, in a nutshell, was the early life story of the philosopher Uriel Acosta or da Costa (Oporto, 1590–Amsterdam, 1647) and many other Sephardi Jews whose presence in Holland made that country the most important Jewish intellectual center in the seventeenth century. Most of the works these Iberian refugees produced in Holland were written in Spanish or Portuguese, their unforgotten mother tongues; but they also ventured into Hebrew, which was quite an achievement for people who, in their childhood and youth, received no Hebrew or Jewish education at all. Other, or often the same, authors also wrote in Latin.

Sephardi Dutch Jews had a major share in the overseas expansion of Holland which took place in the seventeenth century. They led in the establishment of commercial relations with the Barbary states of North Africa and with Turkey, which at the time dominated the entire eastern Mediterranean. They took part in setting up the Dutch West Indies Company and settled by the thousands in Brazil, whose northeastern parts were under Dutch control from 1624 to 1654. By about 1640, fully one-half of the civilian European population of Dutch Brazil was Jewish.[17]

The first Ashkenazim arrived in the Netherlands in 1620, about twenty years after the first Portuguese Marranos. They came from Germany and by 1635 had their own congregation. In the second half of the century came many Jews from Poland and Lithuania who established their own communities, but were soon ordered by the authorities to amalgamate with the Germans. Long before the end of the century, the Ashkenazim outnumbered the Portuguese. Nevertheless, the Sephardim retained their élite position. Toward the end of the eighteenth century, influenced by ideas of the French Revolution, members of both communities began to work for the Emancipation of the Jews. In 1795, when the French took possession of Amsterdam, prominent Ashkenazi and Sephardi Jews together founded the "Felix Libertate" ("Happy Through Freedom") society for the purpose of attaining full civil rights for the Jews. Although the rabbis and the all-powerful *parnasim* (board members) of both the Ashkenazi and Sephardi communities opposed these initiatives, the society's efforts were crowned with success, and in 1796 the National Assembly declared complete civic Emancipation. The internal strife among the Jewish traditionalists and modernists continued, and it took outside intervention, in the form of successive royal "règlements," to regulate the relationship between them. In the meantime the numerical prepon-

derance of the Ashkenazim continued to increase; by 1810, their number in
Holland had reached 50,000, as against 3,000 Sephardim, all of whom were
concentrated in Amsterdam and The Hague. In 1849, there were in Amsterdam 22,426 Ashkenazim and 2,747 Sephardim.

The Sephardi numerical decline was accompanied by a decline in cultural
and communal activity. Toward the end of the seventeenth century, Daniel
Levi (Miguel) de Barrios (Montilla, Spain, 1625–Amsterdam, 1701), the
Spanish Jewish poet and historian, wrote a book in Spanish entitled *Triumph
of Popular Government* in which he enumerated and discussed the work of a
large number of Sephardi scholars in Amsterdam. He also described the
Sephardi scholarly and charitable institutions which functioned in the city,
giving their Hebrew names in a neat phonetic Spanish transliteration, in
which (e.g.) what we would transliterate as *Reshit Hokhma* appears as *Resit
Joxma*. The eighteenth century was a time of rapid decline for the Dutch
Sephardim, the last representatives of Sephardi cultural preeminence; in its
second half, Jewish cultural leadership became concentrated in Ashkenazi
hands.

4. The (Helping) Hands of Esau

The European Enlightenment, which within a remarkably short time had
transformed the entire intellectual physiognomy of the continent, must also
be credited with placing the question of Jewish rights on the agenda of the
scholarly societies and political forums throughout Europe. One of the basic
tenets of the Enlightenment was that religious intolerance was an evil, contrary to the "spirit of the times"; consequently the feeling spread that something ought to be done about the Jewish condition which, as many came to
recognize, was dismal. So for once, Esau—who to the Jewish mind personified the Gentile world in its role of the eternal oppressor of Israel—lifted
up his hands not to strike Jacob but to help him. However, the hands were
still Esau's, and even while trying to help they inflicted hurt.

The idea that the Jewish condition must be improved was not born with
the Enlightenment. We have heard of the Jewish authors who put it forward
in the seventeenth century. Before the end of that century Gentile authors,
too, were expressing the same thought. The English philosopher John
Locke, in his *Letter Concerning Toleration* (1689), touched upon the question of Jewish rights as a side issue when he wrote: "Neither Pagan nor
Mahometan nor Jew ought to be excluded from the civil rights of a commonwealth because of his religion. . . . If we allow the Jews to have private
houses and dwellings amongst us, why should we not allow them to have
synagogues?" [18]

Twenty-five years after Locke, but still well before the French Enlightenment got under way, the Irish-born British deist John Toland (1670–1772) spoke up in the cause of the Jews. Toland became acquainted with Simone Luzzatto's *Discorso*, translated it into English (the translation remained unpublished), and incorporated its economic argument into his own treatise entitled *Reasons for Naturalising the Jews in Great Britain and Ireland on the Same Footing with All Other Nations*. This treatise, anonymously published in London in 1714, was a plea for facilitating the naturalization of foreign-born Jews and thereby attracting them to England. The burden of its argument was to demonstrate the usefulness of the Jews to the country.[19] However, it was not until 1740 that Parliament passed an act permitting Jews (not in England itself but in its colonies) to become naturalized after a residence of seven years. In 1745 and 1746, a similar bill passed the Irish House of Commons but failed to pass the Irish peers in 1747. Both houses of the British Parliament passed the so-called Jew Bill in 1753 allowing Jews to become naturalized; but it had to be repealed within the year because of the popular outcry against it. Thereafter it took another hundred years until all Jewish disabilities were gradually removed in England.

In France, the eighteenth-century advocates of rights for the Jews based their approach to the problem on two arguments. One was that the "spirit of the times" required that the state mete out equal treatment to all the people living within its boundaries, irrespective of religion. The second was the economic argument which had been adumbrated in the preceding century by Jewish leaders such as Simone Luzzatto in Italy and Manasseh ben Israel in Holland. Their plea for easing the restrictions imposed upon the Jews because such improvements in the Jewish condition would redound to the advantage of the state was amplified and sharpened by the eighteenth-century Enlighteners, who argued more boldly that the state would derive great economic benefits by enabling the Jews to function with the *same rights* and obligations as other groups.

In stressing their philosophical-ethical and economic arguments for Jewish rights, the French *philosophes* manifested modern thinking. On the other hand, these enlightened thinkers remained unaware of the hold that medieval convictions still exercised over their minds when it came to the "faults" of the Jews. In particular, they were convinced that the Jews were deceitful, superstitious, addicted to usury, and, to use a new term for a very old idea, clannish. These traits attributed to the Jews were part of an age-old stereotype whose beginnings had gone far back even beyond the Middle Ages to Roman times, and which was to survive the French Revolution. What was new in the approach of the French *philosophes* was that they evenhandedly apportioned the blame for these axiomatic Jewish faults to the Jews themselves on one hand, and, on the other, to the state which had kept them in degradation for centuries. New also was their belief that despite all the regrettable Jewish characteristics, the Jews were still capable of being redeemed, or at least ameliorated and made "useful" to the state, if only a more friendly and constructive attitude were taken toward them. These, in simplest terms, were the theoretical foundations for the spread of the idea of granting equal rights to the Jews among the leaders of the European Enlightenment.

The advocacy of this idea was facilitated by the presence in France of a relatively small group of Jews whose appearance, demeanor, and way of life could be taken as indicating the direction in which all Jews could develop if only given a chance by the state. This was the Sephardi (Portuguese) Jewish community in Bordeaux, which numbered some two hundred families who had retained their proud Sephardi tradition and yet were well advanced in assimilating to French language, culture, and way of life. As early as 1723, these Bordelese Sephardim received the right to practice their religion; by the middle of the century, occasional meetings with some of them had convinced the Christian liberal leaders of both the desirability and the feasibility of granting equal rights to them as well as to the other Jews in the country.[20]

Most of these other Jews lived at the time in Alsace-Lorraine, a territory which had been under German rule for eight centuries until 1681 when Louis XIV gained control over it. Thereafter, both the Christian majority and the Jewish community rapidly developed pro-French sympathies. However, the Jews retained their Yiddish and were considered a foreign element by the French and an inferior branch of the Jewish people by the Bordelese Sephardim. There was also a small Jewish population of mixed origin in Paris; and in 1791, when Avignon was annexed to France by the French National Assembly, a poor and much harassed Jewish community added yet another element to French Jewry.

One of the first among the Frenchmen whose thinking about the Jews was influenced by encounters with educated and enlightened Sephardim and Italian Jews was the marquis d'Argens (1704–71), whose writings were extremely popular in his day. In line with the literary fashion of the times, d'Argens published in 1736–37 critical observations of the contemporary society, in the form of letters written by a fictitious Jew from Constantinople to whom he gave the name Aaron Monceca. In these letters, the stereotyped conviction of the age that all Jews were usurers finds ample expression; but, at the same time, recognition is given to the outstanding intellect of the Sephardi and Italian Jews, whose "decisions on matters of the mind are often of much greater value than those of the best of the academicians." D'Argens' encounters with these Jews impressed upon him the possibility of the Jews' entering into European society, although he envisaged this development as conversion to Christianity.[21] Years later, when d'Argens served as chamberlain to Frederick the Great of Prussia, he met, and was impressed by, Mendelssohn, and obtained for him the privileges of a "protected Jew" by saying to the king: "A *philosophe* who is a bad Catholic begs a *philosophe* who is a bad Protestant to grant the privilege to a *philosophe* who is a bad Jew. There is too much philosophy in all this for justice not to be on the side of the request." [22]

Within a generation of d'Argens' *Lettres Juives*, it had definitely become fashionable in France not only to plead for Jewish rights but also to allocate the blame for the usury, deceitfulness, and "superstitious" religious practices and beliefs of the Jews to the unjust treatment they had received at the hands of the state and the other powers that be—or, as the Jews would have put it, at the hands of Esau. Among those who went on record in this sense were Abbé Antoine Guénée, Jean Baptiste de Mirabaud, Jean Baptiste Nicolas de Lisle de Sales, [23] and, above all, Jean Jacques Rousseau (1712–78). In speaking of the Jews, Rousseau sounded a theme which was to become a favorite sermon topic for modern rabbis, who used their newly won knowledge of world history to find encouragement for the Jews in a comparison between their fate and that of other peoples of antiquity:

> The Jews present us with an outstanding spectacle: the laws of Numa, Lycurgos, and Solon are dead; the far more ancient ones of Moses are still alive. Athens, Sparta and Rome have perished and all their people have vanished from the earth; though destroyed, Zion has not lost her children. They mingle with all nations but are never lost among them; they no longer have leaders, yet they are still a nation; they no longer have a country and yet they are still citizens. . . .[24]

Not only did Rousseau demand equal civic rights for the Jews. He was also a Zionist in the sense that, uniquely among French writers of the eighteenth century, he expressed the hope that the Jews would be restored to their land. He did this in his influential *Émile* (1762)—influential incidentally also on the *Haskala* movement—in which he wrote that the Jews should have a free state of their own, with schools and universities, where they could speak and argue without danger. [25]

In the political arena, the liberal French statesman Malesherbes (1721–94), while he served as minister of the Maison du Roi, having brought about the recognition of Protestant marriages by the civil authorities, turned his attention to the Jews. In 1788, he summoned an informal commission of "Portuguese" and "German" Jewish notables to make suggestions for the amelioration of the Jewish condition. The commission was composed of Portuguese Jews from Bordeaux and Bayonne, who were best able to articulate in French the desires and requests of the Jews, as well as Herz Cerf Berr (1730–93) for Alsace, and Berr Isaac Berr (1744–1828) for Lorraine. Malesherbes put a number of questions to the commission, and the memorandum the Portuguese members wrote in reply, describing the state of the Jews, was to influence the questions put by Napoleon to the Assembly of Jewish Notables and to the French Sanhedrin eighteen years later.

The presence in Alsace and Lorraine of an unassimilated German Jewish community gave the impetus to the Royal Society for Arts and Sciences, which had its seat in Metz, to offer a prize in 1785 for the best essay on the topic "Are There Means to Make the Jews More Happy and More Useful in France?" Of the three entries which shared the prize, one was submitted by the Jesuit priest and politician Abbé Henri Grégoire (1750–1831), the second by the Protestant Thierry, and the third by the Polish Jew Zalkind Hourwitz, of whom more will be said in the next section. Grégoire's essay, entitled *On the Physical, Moral, and Political Regeneration of the Jews*,[26] was in no way original—it advanced the by then standard enlightened arguments that the persisting medieval oppression of the Jews was responsible for their faults. But it revealed Grégoire as a staunch champion of civil rights for the Jews, for which he continued to fight for many years. As a member of the National Constituent Assembly he made a formal motion for the emancipation of the Jews, and on the day his bill was put on the agenda (October 1, 1789), he exclaimed, "Fifty thousand Frenchmen arose this morning as slaves; it depends on you whether they shall go to bed as free people." [27] His efforts were seconded with similar eloquence by two liberal noblemen, Count Mirabeau and Count Clermont-Tonnerre.

Mirabeau (1749–91), the famous French politician, diplomatist, and orator, who in 1791 was to become president of the National Assembly, had been favorably impressed by enlightened Jews he had met in Holland, England, and Prussia, and above all by Moses Mendelssohn. He had discussed the problem of the Jews in his book *On Moses Mendelssohn, On the Political Reform of the Jews*,[28] and again in his 1788 memorandum to Frederick the Great of Prussia, *On the Prussian Monarchy*. In the Assembly debate of December 24, 1789, Mirabeau emphasized that the very fact that the Jews were requesting equality was a proof of their desire to give up their Jewish separatism.[29]

Count Stanislas de Clermont-Tonnerre (1757–92) was an energetic participant in the 1789 National Constituent Assembly, in which he urged that "the Jews should be denied everything as a nation, but granted everything as individuals." Every Jew, he said, "must individually become a citizen; if they do not want this, they must inform us and we shall then be compelled to expel them. The existence of a nation within a nation is unacceptable to our country." [30] These words summarized most poignantly the attitude of many enlightened French leaders toward the Jews: they were determined to do for the Jews what they thought was best for them, i.e., to give them citizenship, but it was a gift they were prepared to force upon the Jews on pain of expulsion. In effect, they said, Either you become what we want you to, or else out with you!

The man who spoke most incisively of the Jewish rights in the Assembly and indicated most unreservedly where the responsibility for the abject plight of the Jews lay was none other than Robespierre:

> Jewish vices are rooted in the lowly status to which you have reduced them. . . . It is our misdeeds as a nation, which we must atone for by restoring to them those inalienable human rights of which no human power may deprive them. . . . Let us restore them to happiness, to a fatherland, to propriety, by restoring to them the dignity of human beings and of citizens. . . .[31]

As a result of these efforts, the Portuguese and Spanish Jews—as well as the Avignonese who had moved from the papal domain to Bordeaux and other places in France—were declared full citizens in 1790; and in 1791 the same rights were extended to all the Jews in France, including those of Alsace-Lorraine. Thus France became the first country in Europe to emancipate fully all the Jews living within its borders. In the same year of 1791 the "Pale of Settlement" was set up in Russia, which restricted the Jews to residence in the western border provinces. The coincidence of two such diametrically opposed moves dealing with the Jews in the same year is a stark testimony to the contrasting attitudes toward them found in Western and Eastern Europe, traces of which are still in evidence to this very day.

In Germany, at the initiative of Moses Mendelssohn, the Christian historian, economist, and diplomat Christian Wilhelm von Dohm (1751–1820) wrote a treatise entitled *On the Civic Improvement of the Jews*.[32] Dohm's basic argument in favor of improving the situation of the Jews was identical to that put forward by French *philosophes* for more than a decade: the oppression to which the Jews had been exposed had corrupted their character so that they had become not only a politically incapacitated but a morally degenerate group. The Jews had wisdom and a sharp intellect, were assiduous and persevering; and if they were also addicted to material gain and usury, this was but the result of their oppression and of their self-imposed segregation. Hence, these flaws of character could, and should, be eradicated by putting an end to their oppression, by educating them to identify themselves more closely with the state, by abolishing the economic restrictions imposed on them, and by encouraging them to participate in the culture of their Gentile environment. This would redound to the benefit of the state, whose enlightened government aimed at justice and the increase of its population. While Dohm's book expressed the opinion prevalent at the time among many enlightened Christians and Jews in Berlin, its publication provoked stormy debates which helped make the Jewish question the issue of the day.

The 1782 "Toleranzpatent" of Austrian Emperor Joseph II, extended to Galicia in 1789, served as a model to be followed in certain respects in Prussia and Russia. Its overall intent was to put the legal status of the Jews on an

equal footing with that of others, but in effect it amounted to a ruthless intrusion into their communal and private lives. Joseph showed his goodwill
toward the Jews as soon as he ascended the throne by abolishing the poll tax
and the Jew's badge (1781); and his 1782 edict laid down the principle of
gradually removing the restrictions under which the Jews lived in Austria,
and of encouraging them to take up handicraft and agriculture. Its aim was to
bring about the Enlightenment of the Jews, by demanding that they assimilate to their environment, adopt the language of the country, establish and
attend schools with modern pedagogical principles, advance into high schools
and universities, be admitted to places of amusement, adopt family names,
serve in the army, and so on. On the other hand, Jewish residential restrictions, a crucial Jewish disability, were expressly maintained. Subsequently,
under the long reign of Francis II (1792–1835), his uncle Joseph's liberalism
was reversed, and the Jews were made subject to a great number of renewed
and entirely new restrictions. However, even this reactionary monarch was
sufficiently influenced by the spirit of the times to take active interest in a
scheme to improve the spiritual condition of the Jews (1795), and to plan the
establishment of a rabbinical seminary. In 1797 he issued a "patent" for
Bohemia, which stated that his ultimate object was to remove all Jewish
disabilities—truly an echo of Joseph II's avowed intentions. At the time,
however, the only measure enacted was a law requiring that every rabbi take
a course in philosophical studies. This law was subsequently (in 1820 and
1826) extended to other provinces of Austria, but remained for long a dead
letter. In 1829, a rabbinical seminary, known as the Istituto Rabbinico Lombardo-Veneto, was actually established in Padua (then under Austrian rule),
the first modern scholarly institution of its kind. It enjoyed a wide reputation, primarily due to the brilliant work of Samuel David Luzzatto
(1800–1865), and continued to function until 1870. The Jews of Vienna obtained permission to build a "temple," a modern Jewish house of worship. A
rather tyrannical measure was the requirement that every Jew who wished
to marry had to pass an examination in religion, based on the textbook *Bene
Zion* (1810) written by Herz Homberg, a narrow-minded rationalist who
denounced his contemporary rabbis as blind fanatics and the Talmud as
the source of all Jewish troubles, and whose book was repugnant to most
Jews.

The late eighteenth century saw the beginnings of political modernization
also in East Europe, where the majority of the Jews lived at the time. This
led to Gentile demands for the assimilation of the Jews, their adjustment to
the general population, the discontinuation of their self-government, and the
abandonment of their traditional mode of life. These demands were either
presented to the Jews as preconditions for granting them equality, or were
expressed in legal fiats, or both. The state took it for granted that the Jews
wanted to attain equal rights with the non-Jews; hence they were not con-

sulted about the measures prescribed for them. In fact, in the entire movement for changing the status of the Jews the state approached the issue quite
openly and ruthlessly from the viewpoint of what it considered beneficial for
itself. The concept of Jewish "usefulness" which we met in France, and
which had been introduced in German lands and in Austria as early as the
seventeenth century, now became pivotal. The Jews were divided into two
categories: those who were "useful," and those who were "useless" or even
"harmful" for the state; and the enactments handed down stated unequivocally that their purpose was to increase the usefulness of the Jews. Among
the efforts initiated to achieve this goal there were apparently constructive
measures, such as attempts to transfer Jews to new, productive occupations,
mainly agriculture, and the imposition on them of secular education and the
duty to learn the language of the country (or another European language,
e.g., German in Russia). On the other hand, many of the new enactments
were restrictive or even destructive, such as those curtailing the business activities of the Jews, increasing their taxation, and imposing new levies on
them. Worst of all, they included undisguised attempts to reduce the
number of the poor Jews (the overwhelming majority) by restrictions on their
marriages, high marriage taxes, and even expulsions.[33]

The partitions of Poland (1772, 1793, and 1795) brought 1 million Jews
under the rule of the three countries which absorbed the Polish provinces:
Prussia, Austria, and Russia. This meant a certain differentiation in their fate,
although by and large the attitude of each of the three states, all ruled by
"enlightened" absolute monarchs, was similar. The Jews, like the peasant-
serfs, were still considered the property of the king and the nobles, who
could treat them or mistreat them at will. In all three states the Jews were
allowed to reside only in certain restricted areas, their numbers were arbi-
trarily limited, they were shifted from village to town, excluded from certain
occupations, and often harsh steps were taken for the avowed purpose of
reducing their "harmfulness."

Much more could be said about the Russian government's attitude toward
the Jews and its reformist interventions in Jewish life, but limitations of
space do not allow this here. Instead, we must proceed to a brief presentation of the role the Jews themselves played in the early moves toward their
Emancipation.

5. The Voice of Jacob

Compared to the outspoken and well-meant but mostly crude, ill-in-
formed, and inconsiderate demands of Gentile statesmen and intellectuals
for Jewish civil rights, the voices raised by the Jews themselves in the early
phases of the struggle for their equality were timid and muted, although as

time passed they were to grow louder and more confident. The absence of Jews from the ranks of the initial fighters for Emancipation was the inevitable consequence of the pre-Enlightenment and pre-Emancipation Jewish condition. Before these movements began, an Ashkenazi Jew who knew the language of the country and was familiar enough with the ways of the Gentiles to be able to address them on Jewish rights was a rarity. Even rarer was one whose vision reached beyond the immediate local Jewish disabilities to encompass a general concept of Jewish rights, let alone rights equal to those of the Gentiles. Hence the initiative had to come, as it did, from Gentiles, from the hands of Esau. What the Jews themselves could do in the early decades of the emancipatory movement was to respond positively to the moves made by the Gentile leaders, and to present all the arguments they could think of in favor of their own Emancipation.

The Jewish contribution to the cause of Emancipation came, of course, only from the Jewish champions of Enlightenment. One had to be enlightened to have, first of all, a positive attitude toward the changes in Jewish life the Emancipation was imagined and hoped to bring about. And, secondly, only enlightened Jews had the mental aptitude to marshal arguments in favor of Emancipation in the language of the Gentiles and in the manner and style of the discourses produced by Gentile advocates of Emancipation.

An early Jewish plea for equal rights and freedom, which for long was to remain an isolated phenomenon, is contained in a pamphlet published in 1753 by Levi Israel in Hamburg. Following the type of presentation popularized by Montesquieu's *Lettres Persanes* (1721), Levi Israel cast what he had to say in the form of a correspondence between a Jew and a Christian philosopher. This pamphlet was written immediately after the 1753 Nationalization Bill of England to which it refers as an example to follow.[34]

Moses Mendelssohn (1729–86), whose name has repeatedly appeared already, is generally recognized as the father of the German Jewish movement of Enlightenment and foremost advocate of Jewish civil rights. At the age of fourteen Mendelssohn, who was crippled by a deformed spine, went on his own to Berlin and applied himself to studying German, French and Latin, as well as philosophy, poetry, and mathematics. By twenty-five he was considered by Lessing to have the makings of "a second Spinoza." In the next sixteen years Mendelssohn wrote several philosophical works, including the celebrated *Phaedon* (1767) which established his reputation and earned him the epithet of "the German Socrates." Publicly challenged by the Zurich preacher Lavater to a defense of Judaism, Mendelssohn embarked in 1770 upon the second, Jewish period of his activity. He produced letters, statements, memoranda, and scholarly opinions, all in the defense of Judaism and in the service of the cause of Jewish civil rights. Convinced that the Jews would be given such rights only if they become enlightened, he began to publish works of Jewish content, foremost among which were his German translation of the Pentateuch with a Hebrew commentary (published from 1780 on) and his *Jerusalem*. He also enlisted the help of other *literati*, both Jewish and non-Jewish, in his struggle for Jewish Emancipation and Enlightenment. In 1781, he prevailed upon Christian Wilhelm von Dohm to come out in writing for the civic improvement of the Jews; a year later, he persuaded Markus Herz to translate into German Manasseh ben Israel's *Vindiciae Judaeorum*. Only when the Preface Mendelssohn wrote to the latter work produced a minor avalanche of attacks and counterarguments, including demands that he answer them, did he finally decide to present in full his own views on Jewish religion and his plea for Jewish Emancipation.

He did this in his book *Jerusalem, Or, On Ecclesiastical Authority and Judaism*, which was published in Berlin in 1783, when he was fifty-four and had only three more years to live. At the time of its appearance, and for decades thereafter, this book was considered an epoch-making work. Today one is more aware of its limitations and its consonance with the spirit of the times. While there can be no doubt that *Jerusalem* is a powerful plea for the granting of rights to the Jews in the name of tolerance and the secular concept of the state, it was not able to bridge effectively the gap between traditional Judaism and modernism, nor to reconcile the conflict between the preservation of the specific Jewish values and the acquisition of the modern European (German) culture. Mendelssohn and his co-workers for the *Haskala* were mainly responsible for launching the Jewish people on the perilous road to assimilation which led a sizable portion of German Jewry to conversion to Christianity (among them four of Mendelssohn's own six children), and most of the rest into the twilight zone of cultural assimilation from which for several generations many Jews continued to pass over into the majority religions.

All this was not, could not have been, envisaged by Mendelssohn. He was convinced that Enlightenment and Emancipation would enrich Jewish life and exhorted his following (which, by the time his *Jerusalem* was published, was considerable): "Adapt yourselves to the mores and the constitution of the country into which you have been placed; but also cling steadfastly to the religion of your fathers. Carry both burdens to the best of your ability." [35]

Of lasting interest, and relevant to present-day conditions, is Mendelssohn's poignant comment on the Gentile tendency to attribute to the Jews at all times precisely those acts and traits which happen to be currently most abhorred. In reading his words, written nearly two hundred years ago, one cannot help being reminded of the resolution passed in 1975 in the United Nations General Assembly by the automatic majority wielded in that body by Communist, Arab, and Third World nations, which equates Zionism (or Judaism) with their latest *bête noire*, racism. It was in 1782, in his Introduction to the German translation of Manasseh ben Israel's *Vindiciae Judaeorum*, that Mendelssohn wrote:

> It is remarkable to observe how prejudice has taken on the shape of all centuries in order to oppress us and to place difficulties in the way of our civil acceptance. In those superstitious times it was the sacra which [they said] we wantonly desecrated; crucifixes which we pierced through and made bleed; children whom we secretly circumcised and tore apart for the delight of the eyes; Christian blood which we needed for sacrificial feasts; wells which we poisoned, etc.; unbelief, stubbornness, secret arts and devilishness of which we were accused and because of which we were tortured, robbed of our property, driven into misery, even when not actually executed.—Now [that] times have changed, those calumnies no longer make the desired impression. Now it is precisely superstition and stupidity which are attributed to us; lack of moral sentiment, of taste and refined manners, inability in the arts, sciences and useful crafts, especially those in the service of war and the state, unconquerable inclination to cheating, usury and lawlessness, which took the place of those ruder accusations, in order to exclude us from the number of useful citizens and to push us away from the motherly bosom of the state.[36]

The foremost disciple and co-worker of Mendelssohn in the cause of the *Haskala*, Naphtali Herz (Hartwig) Wessely (1725–1805) had spent his childhood in Copenhagen, where his father was purveyor to the king of Denmark, and where there was a Portuguese Jewish congregation. He had read widely in the Hebrew scientific works of the Middle Ages, written by Sephardi Jews, and of the Renaissance, written by Italian Jews, including the writings of the seventeenth-century Italian Jewish physician, thinker, mathematician, astronomer, and Talmudist Joseph Solomon Delmedigo (1591–1655). Years later, when he wrote his famous Hebrew epistle *Words of Peace and Truth* (Berlin, 1782), he outlined an extraordinarily rich course of study for Jewish youths, comprising history, geography, sciences, astronomy, and religious philosophy—because, he felt, these were prerequisites for a thorough understanding of the Bible and Judaism. The Portuguese community of Trieste and Italian rabbis in Ferrara and Venice were the first to respond to him positively, and thereby save him from excommunication by German and Polish rabbinical authorities. What was especially vexing for the Orthodox was that Wessely not only advocated educational and social reforms (he was enthusiastic about the measures outlined in the "Toleranzpatent" of Joseph II) but also stressed, for the first time in modern Jewish literature, the value of material things in life.[37]

One year after the publication of Mendelssohn's *Jerusalem*, his followers in Königsberg launched the Hebrew periodical *HaM'assef* (*The Gatherer*). Its first issue (September 1784) stated that its aims included—in addition to the dissemination of secular knowledge and the development of a taste for beauty—the diffusion of information "among all readers who cannot read the languages of the Gentiles, so that they should know the situation of the people of God in their days, and the things that occur among them, and what God puts into the hearts of kings for their benefit. . . ." However, after announcing this ambitious program, *HaM'assef* in fact dealt little with the problems of Jewish Emancipation. Evidently, the editors shared the view of most enlightened Jews that the only way for the Jews to work for Emancipation was to spread Enlightenment.[38]

Mendelssohn had a certain influence on the course of the Jewish Emancipation in France through the impression he made on Mirabeau, and possibly also through the marquis d'Argens. To them now must be added the name of a Jewish Mendelssohnian, Zalkind Hourwitz (1740–1812). Born in Lublin, Hourwitz lived for some time in Berlin, where he associated with Mendelssohn, then went on to France, and finally settled in Paris. He soon mastered French, and when the Metz Royal Society of Arts and Sciences announced its essay competition he submitted an entry which won one of the three prizes. His essay, entitled *Apology for the Jews*,[39] contained little that was original, emphasized that certain tenets of Judaism constituted an obstacle to the admission of the Jews to full equality, and was less restrained than his Christian colleagues in deprecating the Jews and describing them as debased by their own traditions. In 1790 Hourwitz was a member of the Jewish delegation, headed by the advocate Godard, to the General Assembly of the Paris Commune, and in 1806–8 he cooperated with the commission which prepared the decisions of the Paris Sanhedrin (discussed below).

Soon after the French Revolution, ideas of Jewish Emancipation spread to the countries nearby. In 1796 a group of Dutch Jews submitted a petition to their States General, asking for Jewish Emancipation—a step vigorously opposed by the rabbis of both the Portuguese and the Ashkenazi communities, who feared that political Emancipation would lead to a disintegration of Judaism. Despite this opposition, in the very same year, the Dutch National Assembly passed a law conferring citizens' rights on all Dutch Jews. In countries opposed to France, Napoleon's Sanhedrin—unquestionably the greatest Jewish event of the period—evoked little response. An Austrian police survey conducted in 1806 found that the Jews of Austria took no interest whatsoever in the Sanhedrin's proceedings.[40]

In view of the oppression of the Jews in Russia, it is remarkable that in 1784 the Jews of White Russia (a part of Poland annexed by Russia) petitioned the empress Catherine for the amelioration of their condition. They did not, of course, ask for anything as bold as Emancipation, but to be permitted to continue leasing various revenues from the landlords as they had done for generations; to be given a few years of grace in case a landlord wished to raise the rents; to receive protection against the arbitrary demolition without compensation of Jewish-owned buildings in cities for the purpose of making room for squares and streets; to have representation in the courts in cases involving Jews and Christians; to be allowed to try purely Jewish and religious matters in their own Jewish courts; and to be protected in the observance of their religion. After the Russian Senate had considered this petition, most of the requests were granted in 1786.

This petition is typical in that it reflects not only the injustices to which the East European Jews were exposed at the time but also the limited scope of vision as to what they wished to achieve for themselves. Evidently they felt that they had to confine their requests to being confirmed in the *status quo ante*, and to a few very minor improvements. To ask for more, they must have known, would have been futile and could even be dangerous. As far as the adjudication of internal Jewish issues by their own Jewish courts was concerned, this request was granted in a modified form: instead of permitting the establishment of special Jewish courts, religious matters were placed under the jurisdiction of the rabbis and the Kehilla. However, even this arrangement could be utilized by the Jews only as long as all of them recognized the authority of the same rabbis and same Kehillot. In the controversy between the Hasidim and the Mitnagdim this proved not to be the case, and in the last years of the eighteenth century both sides felt compelled to bring their complaints to the secular authority, which they did in the form of denunciations and often false accusations.

In Poland, where only the rabbis and the members of the newly developed small Jewish middle class were articulate, writers belonging to this class, beginning in 1786, published several pamphlets proposing a highly assimilationist program for the betterment of the Jewish position. The rabbis, as could be expected, opposed any such development and argued vociferously for the maintenance of the *status quo.* One of them, Rabbi Herschel Josefowicz of Chelm, even took the highly unusual step of publishing a pamphlet *in Polish* in which he criticized the suggested reforms. However, his fears were premature. At the Quadrennial Sejm of 1788–92 all plans for improvements in the condition of the Jews and the peasants were summarily rejected, and the rights of the Jews were even curtailed. On the other hand, Tadeusz Kosciuszko, the leader of the anti-Russian Polish revolt, declared in his 1794 speeches that he considered the Jews equal to other classes of Poles. The Jews responded enthusiastically and participated in the revolt; when it drew to its bloody close, all the Jews of Praga, the historic suburb of Warsaw, were massacred by the Russian army.[41]

6. Women and the Salons

The women of the Jewish élite, newly liberated by the heady atmosphere of the Enlightenment, were to play a leading role in the Jewish-Gentile rapprochement which was the great ambition of the Central European Jewish upper crust in the decades preceding the Emancipation. Before the Enlightenment, if the religious knowledge of the average Jew, which was his sole cultural possession, was limited, that of the average Jewish woman was minimal, being confined to rules pertaining to the kitchen and to sexual life. She could, of course, read Hebrew, but she did not understand the prayers she read, and, moreover, *Halakha* did not obligate her to pray or to go to the synagogue, since such duties fell under the general rule of "positive commandments ["do's"] occasioned by time" from whose observance women were (and, of course, are) exempt. Because of their ignorance of Hebrew and their consequent inability to understand the Bible in the original, or any other great sourcebook of Jewish religion—which, incidentally, women were not supposed to study—they were provided with a special women's literature in Yiddish; this, taking account of the women's supposedly limited intelligence, combined uplift with entertainment. The most popular was the so-called *Tzene-rene* (from the Biblical Hebrew *Tz'ena ur'ena,* "Go out and see," Songs 3:11), by the Polish Jacob ben Isaac Ashkenazi (1550–1623?), a paraphrase-translation of the Pentateuch and the Five Scrolls richly studded with commentary, legend, allegory, epigram, and ethical observation, culled from two thousand years of Hebrew literature.

With the switch from Yiddish to German, this traditional Yiddish women's literature became inaccessible to the modern Jewish woman. Since Hebrew remained the closed book it had been, the only language she could read and understand was German. And since at the time no literature of Jewish content in German yet existed, the modern Jewish woman—even if she retained some interest in matters Jewish—had no choice but to read German literature written by German Christians and intended for Christian German readers. Soon quite a class of rich Jewish women emerged, wives and daughters of Jewish bankers and other members of the Jewish élite, who not only were entirely at home (more than their menfolk) in German letters but could discuss them intelligently, wittily, and charmingly. This, coupled with the psychologically understandable desire to gain admission into the circle of German intellectuals, was the background for the emergence of that spectacular and paradoxical phenomenon, the German Jewish salon. Spectacular, because of its success as the only place in pre-Emancipation days where Jewish and Gentile intellectuals could freely meet and mingle; and paradoxical because at the time when these salons flourished in Berlin, Vienna, and elsewhere (beginning in the 1780's), the Jews in general were still devoid of all rights and were looked down upon by members of German and Austrian society. The salons became the stage on which the wives and daughters of the new Jewish financial aristocracy, charming, elegant, educated, and eager for the attention of the German nobility and army officers, competed with their Christian counterparts. Presided over by the womenfolk of the Berlin Jewish bankers Ephraim, Itzig, Cohen, and Mayer, these salons were frequented by Prussian officers, diplomats, and courtiers, who often entered into dalliances and love affairs with the lovely daughters of Israel. At the same time, the very cities in which the salons formed recognized intellectual and social centers were still forbidden territory for the average Jew. Even Moses Mendelssohn, whose greatness as a *German* philosopher was recognized in the highest academic circles, had to wait until 1763, when he was thirty-four years old, to be granted the privileges of a "protected Jew" which allowed him to stay in Berlin permanently.

The German Jewish salon, like many another feature in the eighteenth-century Jewish Enlightenment, had Sephardi and Italian antecedents. In describing the Jewish-Arab encounter in medieval Spain, I mentioned that the gatherings of *literati* in the home of Ḥasdai ibn Shaprut were probably the first example of the Jewish literary salon. However, those early gatherings, in keeping with the exclusively masculine orientation of the Arab environment, were presided over and attended by men only. The first Jewish literary parties hosted by a woman and attended by both men and women were those which took place in the home of Sarah Copia (Coppio) Sullam (1592?–1641), the Venetian Jewish poet. Sarah's beauty and charm and her musical, well-trained voice, no less than her elegant Italian verses and bold spirit, attracted Christian Venetian scholars, lords and ladies, as well as Jews to her salon to participate in the sophisticated and cultured conversations. Leon da Modena, who was a leading member of this circle, dedicated to Sarah his Italian adaptation of Solomon Usque's Spanish tragedy *Esther* and, upon her death, wrote a Hebrew epitaph for her.[42]

It was possibly in emulation of these examples that Moses Mendelssohn made his house into a center for scientific and literary intercourse. In the Mendelssohn home—the first German Jewish salon—his friends could expect to meet distinguished strangers who, in turn, were attracted by the fame of the "German Socrates." Mendelssohn's daughters and their young companions also participated in these gatherings, and in later years one of them, Dorothea Mendelssohn Veit, presided over a salon of her own.

However, the most important salon of the period was that of Henrietta Herz (1764–1847), wife of Mendelssohn's friend and disciple, the physician and philosopher Markus Herz. Henrietta Herz, née de Lemos, was undoubtedly one of the most remarkable women of the period. A queenlike Spanish beauty—her physician father was of Portuguese Jewish descent—she married Markus Herz, who was twice her age, at the age of seventeen and under his tutelage completed the education begun by her father. She acquired fluency in ten languages including Hebrew, was interested in the sciences, and had a literary judgment deferred to by authors of repute. Her Berlin salon was a gathering place for the most outstanding men and women of the period—artists, writers, philosophers, scholars, scientists, and members of the aristocracy, including Jean Paul Richter, Friedrich Schiller, Mirabeau, Rückert, Niebuhr, Schlegel, Johannes von Müller, Moses Mendelssohn, and Solomon Maimon. It was also frequented by Alexander von Humboldt, whom Henrietta taught Hebrew, and his brother Wilhelm; by Ludwig Börne, who at the age of seventeen came to live with the Herzes and fell desperately in love with the thirty-six-year-old Henrietta; and above all by Friedrich Schleiermacher, with whom she had an especially close (but Platonic?) relationship, and who, fourteen years after the death of her husband, succeeded in persuading Henrietta to convert to Christianity (in 1817). She herself wrote novels and carried on an extensive correspondence but destroyed all this material before her death in 1847.

Mendelssohn's oldest daughter, Dorothea (1763–1879), married the banker Simon Veit and had four sons by him. Her Berlin salon, like those of her friends Henrietta Herz and Rachel Levin Varnhagen, was a meeting place of intellectuals, politicians, and industrialists. Admired by the philosopher and romantic writer Friedrich von Schlegel, who was nine years her junior, she dissolved her marriage and went to live with him. In 1802 she converted to Protestantism and in 1808, together with Schlegel, to Catholicism, after which their union was legalized by the Church. They settled in Vienna, where their home became a social and intellectual center.

The Viennese counterpart of Henrietta Herz was Fanny von Arnstein (1757–1818). Daughter of the wealthy Berlin Jewish banker Daniel Itzig, in her youth she and her eight sisters and four brothers made the Itzig house a social center and were close to the children of Moses Mendelssohn. Upon her marriage to the banker Nathan Adam von Arnstein, her salon at the Arnstein mansion in Vienna and her villas at Schönbrunn and Baden became the most dynamic literary gathering places of Austria. Among the frequent visitors were Wellington, Talleyrand, Hardenberg, Capo d'Istrias, the Varnhagens, the Schlegels, Justinus Kerner, Karoline Pichler, and Zacharias Werner. For over a generation she exercised an influence upon Austrian arts and letters. She was so well liked in Viennese society that when, during her widowhood, one of her admirers, Freiherr von Weichs, challenged Prince Karl von Lichtenstein and killed him in a duel, her reputation and popularity remained unscathed.

Her sister Cecilia, wife of the Austrian Jewish financier Freiherr Bernhard von Eskeles (1753–1839), who was a partner in the banking house of Arnstein and Eskeles, also had a salon in Vienna which came into prominence during the Congress of Vienna and was the meeting place of diplomats and writers.

Rachel Levin Varnhagen (1771–1833), daughter of a wealthy Jewish jeweler, while still a young woman made her home in Berlin a meeting place for the intellectual élite of the city. Liberated from a tyrannous father by his death in 1806, she went to live in Paris and various German cities. After two unsuccessful engagements to Christians, impoverished and at odds with her family, she converted to Protestantism in 1814 and married a Prussian diplomat, Karl August Varnhagen von Ense, who was fourteen years her junior. While he was stationed in Vienna, the Varnhagen salon was frequented by the Prussian delegates to the Vienna Congress; thereafter, her reestablished Berlin salon became a meeting place for Heine, Börne, Gutzkow, and other authors close to the young Germany movement.

In Paris, the Jewish salon was a relatively late development; but once it flourished, it outdid both its Berlin and Viennese counterparts. In the luxurious *hôtels* of the wealthy Jewish Parisian bourgeoisie, many of them lining the broad avenues near the Parc Monçeau, Jews and Gentiles alike were entertained in great style by charming and often celebrated *salonnardes*. Outstanding was Madame Arman de Caillavet, daughter of the wealthy Jewish banker from Austria, Auguste Lippmann, and Frédérique Koenigswarter, who was herself of a baronial Jewish family. The Caillavet salon was attended by such luminaries of the French litarary world as Anatole France, the younger Dumas, and a host of other artists and intellectuals. Another salon of distinction was presided over by Geneviève, the daughter of the composer Fromenthal Halévy (of *La Juive* fame), who married Émile Straus, the Jewish attorney of the Parisian house of Rothschild. These salons effectively competed with the anti-Semitic salons of the aristocracy, and their hostesses served as models for leading characters in Proust's *Remembrance of Things Past*.[43]

The tradition of maintaining literary salons continued among wealthy Jews in Berlin into the early twentieth century, but the golden age of the German Jewish salon lasted only a short time; essentially, it was a pre-Emancipation phenomenon. While it flourished, a very few rich, exceptionally well educated, and spirited Jewish women cast their spell upon Gentile intellectuals in whose eyes the fact that they were of exotic birth was a strong added attraction for attending such gatherings. However, whatever rapprochement was achieved in these salons between Jewish and Christian intellectuals could not prevent the emergence of the anti-Semitic wave which swept over Germany in the first half of the nineteenth century.

7. Outer Opposition: Anti-Semitism

When the movement for the Emancipation of the Jews began, the history of anti-Semitism, or to use a more precise term, Judeophobia, was already more than two thousand years old. As could be expected, among the eighteenth-century Enlighteners, too, were men whose dislike of the Jews proved stronger than their idea that all men must be equal before the law.

A favorite strategy of the eighteenth-century anti-Semites in their attacks on the Jewish character was to quote the Biblical prophets, whose writings are full of denunciations of the contemporary Hebrews. This was resorted to by François J. A. Hell, by Foissac (probably a pseudonym for Jean Baptiste Annibal Aubert Dubayet, who subsequently became minister of war under the Directory), and others.[44] Most influential of the enlightened anti-Semites was Voltaire, who considered the mental traits of the Jews a fixed constituent of their being from Biblical times to his own day, equal in this respect to physical features.[45] In 1771 he put these words into the mouth of Memmius, an imaginary correspondent of Cicero: "They [the Jews] are, all of them, born with a raging fanaticism in their hearts, just as the Bretons and the Germans are born with blond hair. I would not be in the least bit surprised if these people would someday become deadly to the human race." [46]

Voltaire's writings are interspersed with derogatory remarks about the moral conditions of the Biblical Hebrews. In addition to being extremely cruel and fanatical, they were, according to him, guilty of cannibalism; they were a band of unrestrained barbarians given to atrocities and to sexual immorality, including intercourse with animals; they sold their own sons and daughters into slavery; they were cheats and knaves, dishonest and greedy; and they strove for dominion over the whole world. All these traits, which Voltaire claimed to deduce from Biblical passages, characterized the Jews down to his own time.[47]

The idea that the Jews were innately evil was so widespread among the leaders of the French Enlightenment that even Mirabeau, a staunch friend of the Jews, felt it necessary to refute what he termed "a prevalent opinion that the Jews were bad by nature." He asserted that history proved that "the Jews, considering them as men and as citizens, were greatly corrupted only because they were denied their rights." [48]

It was a curious inconsistency of the age that another contradictory idea was also widespread, namely, the age-old tenet [49] that the Biblical Hebrews were the teachers of the Greeks. So many contemporaries of Voltaire subscribed to this belief that he found it necessary to deny it emphatically and at length. He says that, in fact, "never was a smaller nation more uncouth; all their stories were plagiarisms, just as all their ceremonies were visibly an imitation of the Phoenicians, the Syrians, the Egyptians." In several of his works Voltaire returns to this point, arguing that the Biblical Jews borrowed from one or the other of these peoples—or from the Chaldaeans, the Persians, the Indians, the Arabs—the names of their God, their cosmogony, their ritual (including circumcision), even the name "Israel" itself, as well as the names of their angels and of the devil, and the stories contained in the Bible. The greatest number of features, however, they "plagiarized" from the Greeks: "If one only wants to take the trouble of comparing all the events of the Greek fable and ancient history, one will be amazed by not finding a single page in the Jewish books which are not a plagiarism." [50]

The "originality" of the Bible apart, even the friends of the Jews held that
the Jewish character was bad and that it was formed by influences which
went back to the early rabbis. Montesquieu, who in 1721 termed Judaism
the "ancient trunk which produced two branches which have covered the
whole earth," i.e., Christianity and Islam, and noted with satisfaction that
the situation of the Jews was improving because the spirit of intolerance was
abating in Europe, nevertheless held that there was a Jewish character which
was identical in two countries as widely separated as France and Persia.
"Know," he has Usbek write in *Lettres Persanes*, "that wherever there is
money there are Jews." [51] And elsewhere, writing prior to 1748, he states
that the works of the rabbis, which represented the spirit of slaves, fashioned
the continuing low taste and character of the Jews: "The moral causes more
than the physical ones form the general character of a nation and determine
the quality of its spirit. One can find a great proof of this among the Jews
who—dispersed in all the earth, come at all times, born in all countries—
have had many authors of whom however one can barely name two who had
some commonsense. . . ." Because of the Jewish slavery in Assyria, says
Montesquieu, ignorance became entrenched among the rabbis, whose "miserable written works" were regarded by the Jews as "the perfect models after
which they have ever since formed their taste and their spirit." [52]

Such samples of what the greatest French minds of the eighteenth century
thought of the Jews should suffice to show what prejudices the liberal Enlighteners had to overcome before the French National Assembly was willing
to grant civil rights to all the Jews who lived in the country. A quarter of a
century later, after the fall of Napoleon, a wave of anti-Semitism swept over
Europe, reaching its greatest heights in Germany. In many German cities
anti-Jewish riots broke out, several Jews were murdered, others expelled or
maltreated, synagogues attacked, and the old Jew-baiting cry, "Hep, hep!"
could be heard everywhere. It seemed as if the clock of history had been
turned back (as was to happen again in the 1930's with infinitely more tragic
consequences), and the Jews were reliving the horrors of the Middle Ages.
Worse than that, there was a new, modern note in this renewed persecution
of the Jews which ominously prefigured what was to become a horrible reality in Hitler's Third Reich. For the first time in history, as far as we know, a
German went on record suggesting the systematic extermination of the Jews.
The author of this idea was a certain Hartwig Hundt, who in 1819 published
a pamphlet entitled *The Jew Mirror*, in which he wrote, among other things,
that in order to prevent the increase of the Jews, ". . . the men should be
emasculated, and their wives and daughters be lodged in houses of shame.
The best plan would be to purge the land entirely of this vermin, either by
exterminating them, or as Pharaoh and the people of Meiningen, Würzburg,
and Frankfurt did, by driving them from the country." [53]

8. Inner Opposition: Orthodoxy

After having overcome the Hellenistic rift, throughout the long centuries of their Exile the Jews of every Diaspora community had stood solidly united in their relationship to, and view of, the Gentile authority on whose good graces their existence depended. Whatever their internal dissensions, this traditional unity toward the outside world was not only a great source of strength but also a force making for cohesion and solidarity. Enlightenment and Emancipation put an end to this state of affairs and brought about a deep internal fission in the Jewish community whose traces are still with us. One camp comprised those who went along, willingly and joyfully, with the new developments, acquired as much as they could of the national variety of European culture, made efforts to spread it among their co-religionists, advocated religious reforms, fought for Emancipation, and did what they could to strengthen the hand of the liberal Gentile statesmen, politicians, rulers, and influentials in their attempt to have laws passed or decrees issued for equal Jewish rights. Against them were arrayed the traditionalists, the unwavering adherents of halakhic Judaism, who saw only evil in both Enlightenment and Emancipation and embarked on a fierce struggle against them. They fought on the home front, shoring up the traditional defenses of Jewish Orthodoxy, and also on the "foreign" territory of the Gentile authorities, trying to stop them from taking any step that would bring about a rapprochement between Jews and Christians. Thus the leaders of the Lithuanian Jewish council collected money to send representatives to Warsaw in order to "forestall the danger so that, God forbid, no new reform be introduced." [54]

On that earlier occasion, when Hellenism introduced such a rift in the Jewish ranks of antiquity, the struggle between the Pharisees and the Hellenists ended with the victory of Pharisaic Judaism. While numerous elements of the Hellenistic Jewish culture became incorporated into rabbinic Judaism as it subsequently developed, long before the completion of the Talmud Hellenism had become but a faint memory of a cultural challenge met and overcome. The conflict between modernist and Orthodox Jews which began about 1775 has not ended to this day. But, to judge from the numerical strength of the two camps two centuries later, the balance has tilted more and more in favor of the pro-Enlightenment forces, at least in the sense that relatively few Jews today still adhere to the position that was represented and fought for by the early opponents of the *Haskala*.

Those anti-*Haskala* forces were led by the same men who for two millennia had been the leaders of Jewry in all parts of the Diaspora—the rabbis. There were, of course, from the very outset some rabbis who went along with, and even led, the movement for Jewish Enlightenment; but, at least until the middle of the nineteenth century, the overwhelming majority were in the opposite camp. The position of these rabbis—let us refer to them as "Orthodox," although the term in the sense of "strictly tradition-abiding" came into use only later—was clear-cut and had great inner consistency. Judaism for them was a way of life determined by the *Halakha*, the traditional Jewish law as explicated in the *Shulḥan 'Arukh* (the great sixteenth-century Jewish code), and as adjusted and applied to conditions and problems which developed subsequently by the great halakhic luminaries, rabbis whose word commanded obedience solely on account of their religious-scholarly authority. The basic principle guiding the work of these later rabbis was that their decisions must conform to the Law as laid down in the *Halakha*, which could neither be changed nor amended. All that a rabbi could do was to interpret the *Halakha* so as to be applicable to new situations. The general tendency was toward more and more stringent restrictions; that is, the area of the forbidden was gradually enlarged—this was always considered sound and safe rabbinic practice—while even the most outstanding rabbi would never presume to declare allowed something that had been forbidden of old.

The working of the principle involved can be illustrated by a simple example which presents a prohibition still observed by Orthodox Jews. When electricity was introduced, the Orthodox rabbis decided that it was forbidden to operate an electric switch on the Sabbath. Their argument ran as follows. There is a Biblical-Talmudic prohibition against lighting fire on the Sabbath; hence it had for long been forbidden to light a candle on the Sabbath, even if it could be done as effortlessly as by striking a match. To turn on an electric light was declared essentially the same act as lighting a candle—therefore it was forbidden. By the same token, the turning off of an electric light was equated with the putting out of fire—another forbidden act. A further extension of this prohibition was the inclusion of the switching on and off of all appliances which worked with electricity. What the rabbis did allow was the use of automatic electric timing devices, which can be set on Friday afternoon to turn on lights or appliances at a pre-set hour on the Sabbath and to turn them off thereafter, or vice versa. Modern Orthodox Jewish households are equipped with such time-clocks. Religious kibbutzim in Israel use them to activate the electric milking machines early Saturday morning and to turn them off after the milking is completed. The principle adhered to throughout is that whenever the *Halakha* allows it, use can be made of modern technological conveniences; when not, the Orthodox Jew must simply forego them, even if this involves hardship, rather than violate the *Halakha*.

The minutiae of living in accordance with the *Halakha* had been fully developed and scrupulously followed by almost all the Jews until the Enlightenment. Connected with them was the stricture that the Jew was duty-bound to study, and allowed to study, only the *Halakha* and such subjects as had a bearing on it or were necessary for its full understanding. This was the basis of what is often referred to as "East European Talmudism"—the over-riding concentration on Talmudic study, the valuation of Talmudic study above all else, and the bestowal of status and prestige on the basis of ex-cellence in Talmudic knowledge above any other achievement. Mention must be made in passing of the fact that precisely the most outstanding Tal-mudic authorities of the eighteenth and nineteenth centuries had, neverthe-less, considerable familiarity with those areas of secular knowledge which they considered conducive to a better understanding of the *Halakha,* such as astronomy, anatomy, geography, and that the desirability of acquiring such knowledge was clearly stated by some of them.

From this background, it is readily understandable that the work of the *Maskilim* provoked bitter opposition on the part of the Orthodox rabbis. *Haskala* was anathema for them on several counts. First, it advocated the acquisition of secular knowledge for its own sake, and especially of those branches of secular knowledge which had nothing to do with Jewish life and which, moreover, were vehicles of non-Jewish and hence anti-Judaistic or anti-halakhic ideas, such as German literature, philosophy, and his-toriography. Second, the *Maskilim* proposed to introduce changes into the sacrosanct area of the *Halakha* with a view to declaring some of its rules non-obligatory. This was perceived as a most dangerous and intolerable assault on the central fortress of Jewish life. Third, beyond the *Halakha* itself, the *Maskilim* dared to tamper with the Jewish *minhag* (custom), which, while having no halakhic sanction, was considered by the Orthodox no less impor-tant and no less part and parcel of an essentially Jewish life. The *Maskilim* advocated, for instance, the adoption of German garb and of German speech, to mention only two things which, while not impinging on the *Halakha* but merely on the *minhag,* were considered no less sacrilegious in the eyes of the Orthodox, who were deeply attached to their traditional caftan and Yid-dish as hallowed signs of Jewishness. Above all, the burden of the *Haskala's* message was that Jews should participate in the cultural life of their Gentile environment, which was a frontal attack on the most basic tenet of traditional Judaism: the duty of the Jew to keep himself apart from the Gentiles, as it is written, "And ye shall not walk in their statutes" (Lev. 18:3).

There is nothing more traumatic for a convinced observant Jew than to see the *sacra* of his religion touched by impious Jewish hands. Of the hands of Esau nothing else can be expected; their brutality has been part of Jewish life for two thousand years. But that Jews themselves should discard the *Halakha* and, worse still, openly preach that from now on Jews should live in the manner of Gentiles, cuts the traditional Jew to the quick. In instinctive defense of himself and the *k'lal Yisrael,* the Community of Israel, which he sees thereby endangered, he resorts to the one traditional weapon of the

Jew, crying out and raising his voice, the Voice of Jacob, to warn the faithful and denounce the sinners.

Of the many rabbinical opponents of the Enlightenment, we can only discuss the three most important ones. All three, interestingly and characteristically, were rather exceptional figures in that, in addition to being the most outstanding halakhic authorities of their age, they also took an active interest in secular sciences. Their opposition therefore was not to non-religious knowledge as such, but to the Berlin *Haskala*, which, they feared, would diminish the total Jewish commitment to the traditional Jewish religious way of life.

The oldest of the three was Ezekiel Landau (1713–93), rabbi of Prague and all Bohemia. His vast erudition and great personal qualities won for him the respect of the Austrian authorities and the admiration of the Jews. Although a student of the Kabbala and well versed in mystical literature, he was an opponent of Hasidism. While he had a positive attitude toward secular scholarship (he gave approbation to books on history, grammar, natural sciences, and other subjects), he saw great danger for Judaism in the spread of the modern Jewish and German culture which came from Berlin and opposed Mendelssohn's German translation of the Bible and the study of sciences and languages as advocated by Wessely. "A rabble of unclean birds," was the way he contemptuously referred to the group whose members edited and wrote for *HaM'assef*.

A few years younger than Landau was Elijah, the Gaon of Vilna (1720–97). Elijah did not occupy any rabbinical position, and the great fame and respect he enjoyed was due solely to his unexcelled mastery of all fields of traditional Jewish learning. In addition, he studied secular sciences in which he saw an aid to the understanding of the *Halakha* and to which he made original contributions. And he encouraged his pupils and friends to study the sciences from which, he was convinced, Judaism could only gain. He also delved into the Kabbala and wrote a multi-volume commentary on the Zohar, as well as ten other Kabbalistic works. His studies of the Hebrew grammar resulted in a book on that subject. His scientific writings include treatises on mathematics, geography, and astronomy, as well as one on the phases of the moon, the seasons, and planetary movements. (Of all this, and the dozens of rabbinical books he wrote, nothing was published in his lifetime.) He was interested in the study of music which, he felt, was necessary for an understanding of the Biblical cantillation and the "secrets of the Levites' songs"; and he took a great interest in medicine. Despite his interest in the Kabbala, Elijah was an unrelenting enemy of Hasidism, issued repeated warnings against it, and ordered the popular Hasidic book *Testament of R. Israel Ba'al Shem Tov* to be burned in public. As for the secular sciences, while he exhorted his disciples to take an interest in them, he opposed the Berlin *Haskala* and philosophy, in which he saw a threat to traditional Judaism.

In the next generation when the reform measures of Francis II posed a new threat to Jewish Orthodoxy, a bevy of oustanding rabbis joined the fight against them.[55] They were headed by Moses Sofer (or Schreiber, 1762–1839), rabbi of Pressburg (Pozsony, today Bratislava), the recognized leader of Jewish Orthodoxy in Europe, who spearheaded the fight against both Enlightenment and Emancipation. His one hundred volumes of rabbinic writings are a monument to his great traditional learning, but he also studied the Kabbala and the secular sciences of astronomy, astrology, geometry, and general history. Like the Gaon of Vilna, he advocated the study of sciences as aides for a fuller compliance with the *Halakha*. In one of his annual sermons, he said:

> It is not possible to know the Tora without knowing all the other sciences. It is not possible to accept testimony about the new moon if we do not know all the particulars about the movement of the sun and the moon and their courses . . . nor the law of *T'refa* [impure meat], if we do not know anatomy; the songs of the Levites, if we do not know the science of music; the divisions of the Land of Israel without a knowledge of the earth and the science of measuring, geography.[56]

Despite his wide learning, Moses Sofer was a most determined opponent of all cultural assimilation and social rapprochement with the Gentiles. In his annual sermon of 1809, he warned, "The more we mingle with them and wish to approach them and adopt their customs, the more God puts hatred between us and them." And a few years later, he returned to the same topic: "It is not good for us to mingle with the Gentiles. We mix with the Gentiles and learn their ways, [but] their company is not fitting for us. . . . Only if Israel remains a people dwelling alone, and sanctify themselves and cleanse themselves from the defilement of intermingling in the exile, will the nations walk in their light. . . ." [57]

The anti-innovationist position was expressed most uncompromisingly by Moses Sofer who, using a Talmudic saying which in the original context meant something entirely different, coined the pithy dictum: *Ḥadash asur min haTora*, in the sense of "Innovation is forbidden by the Tora," and taught that the introduction of any new feature, even a halakhically least important one, was strictly prohibited.

Once a young Jew decided to enter a secular educational institution, as thousands did by the early nineteenth century, he had to overcome, in addition to a host of objective problems, the determined resistance of his own father. When Rabbi Israel Salanter (actually Israel Lipkin, d. 1883), a foremost Orthodox rabbi at Kovno, fell ill, he went to Germany for medical treatment. But on learning that his son had gone to Berlin to study medicine, he performed the traditional ritual of seven days' mourning [58] which was the Orthodox Jewish way of demonstrating that a next-of-kin had left the fold and

was therefore considered dead. The relationship between many a father and
son ended in this abrupt way, in places, as late as the turn of the century.

In general, the position of the Orthodox rabbis was clear-cut and unequiv-
ocal: the *status quo* in Jewish life had to be maintained because it had been
sanctioned by many centuries of Jewish tradition. Therefore any change
which impinged upon it must be opposed and combated; *all* innovation had
to be fought simply because it was innovation.

(I cannot resist mentioning in parentheses that this traditional Jewish objection to innovation as such has its exact parallel in the orthodox Muslim
dread of all *ibtidā'* [i.e., innovation] which again must be combated—and
still is by the conservative *'ulamā*, the Muslim equivalent of Orthodox rabbis, simply because it is new.)[59]

9. The Problem of Nationalism

Emancipation, even in its earliest stage when it was merely a subject for
discussion, brought with it a host of new problems for the Jews. One of the
most puzzling of these, because they had never before encountered the likes
of it, was nationalism, or more precisely, national integration. Prior to the
Emancipation, the Jews had lived for more than two millennia among peoples as varied as the ancient Babylonians, the Romans, the Arabs, and practically all the nations of Europe. In all these Diasporas the question of
whether or not the Jews belonged to the same nation as the majority population never arose. It did not, and indeed could not, for two reasons. First,
because the concept of nationhood as it emerged with the French Revolution
was new; it had its ideological base in the writings of Rousseau, who stressed
the value of the moral unity of the masses bound together in pursuit of a
common purpose—the good of the whole—and emphasized the necessity of
supreme loyalty to *la patrie*, the fatherland. No concept like this had existed
in earlier times, although group loyalties of different types had. Second,
whatever bonds in pre-Enlightenment times united the inhabitants of a
given territorial entity were counterbalanced or even overshadowed by the
existence of various estates into which the population was divided, and each
of which had its specific corporate status. In the Middle Ages, the numerous
small units—feudal domains, towns, ducal and Church states—were all
characterized by isolation, provincialism, and mutual competitiveness, not to
mention the differences and tensions among the estates, such as the nobles,
the burghers, villeins, the serfs or peasants, and the clergy, which co-existed
side by side in the same territorial unit but were separated and lined up
against one another by disparate traditions and clashing interests. In these
circumstances, it was taken for granted by both Gentiles and Jews that the
Jews constituted a separate corporate body, since evidently they belonged to

none of the other social aggregates. Underlying all this was the religious difference. Since in pre-Enlightenment times religion was a dominant concern, their Jewishness created a much greater gulf between the Jews and the Gentile population groups than differences in estate ever could between the Gentiles themselves. In most places the religious difference went hand in hand with differences in language, garb, traditions, and mentality, all of which set the Jews entirely apart from the Gentile population. Also, the Jews enjoyed considerable internal autonomy, had strong in-group loyalty, and a unique religio-cultural configuration. Under these conditions the Jews, while dependent upon the interests or whims of the prince, lord, bishop, or whoever was in control of the territorial unit in which they lived, and while expected to fulfill their assigned tasks faithfully and satisfactorily, were never considered anything else than tolerated aliens. Their otherness was accepted by both sides like something in the order of a natural phenomenon.

All this was suddenly changed by the Enlightenment. The Rousseauan idea of *la patrie* rapidly captivated the Western world and led to an unparalleled social upheaval, especially in Western and Central Europe. The concept that all the people who lived within the confines of an independent sovereign state constituted, or ought to constitute, one nation sharing all duties and privileges as citizens equal before the law, was enthusiastically embraced by more and more statesmen. Before long they came to feel that, once the egalitarian structure of society was substituted for the corporate one, it was an anomaly and an anachronism to leave the Jews in their special status as the only remaining corporate body within the state not sharing the rights and duties of the others. Hence, as Baron pointed out, "emancipation was an even greater necessity for the modern state than it was for the Jews." [60]

The changing position of the state as to what kind of human aggregate the Jews constituted is reflected in the terminology used to describe the Jews in the official documents dealing with their status. The early decrees, issued from 1657 to the 1780's by the Netherlands, England, Italy, Germany, Austria, and so on, refer to them as "the Hebrew nation" or "the Jewish nation." From 1796 on, these terms are no longer encountered and the Jews are referred to as "the Hebrews," "the Jews," "the Israelites," "the Jewish community," "adherents of the Jewish faith," "confessors of the Mosaic religion," "persons professing the Jewish religion," and the like. Evidently, in this period the Gentile authorities of Western and Central Europe no longer considered the Jews a nation but a religious group. Then, from 1848 on, all references to the Jews are omitted in civil rights legislation, and the laws, instead, speak only of the equal rights of people professing any religion, or of the equality of all citizens before the law. [61]

As for the Jews themselves, they had considered themselves a nation ever since Biblical times. The verse, "Who is like Thy people Israel, a nation one in the earth?" (2 Sam. 7:23), was often recited by the Jews and supplied the

Biblical sanction for both their nationhood and their uniqueness, just as another Biblical statement, which described them as "a people scattered abroad and dispersed among the peoples" (Esth. 3:8), provided the Scriptural validation of their Diaspora. That they were a nation separate, unique, and different from all the other nations of the earth they did not have to be taught by the Gentiles. Ever since Biblical times they had known that mankind fell into two parts, Jews and Gentiles, and that it was the wont of the latter, the *Goyim*, to hate and oppress, or, in the best of circumstances, to tolerate the Jews, God's own chosen people.

What was entirely new for the Jews in the eighteenth century was that soon after the Gentiles had embraced the idea of nationhood, they began to bandy the double-edged program of Jewish Emancipation and Enlightenment. On the one hand, the Jews were to be given the same rights as achieved in that very same age by all the Gentiles; on the other, they should become like the Gentiles in their manners, clothes, speech, education, and occupations. This had never been experienced by the Jews in their entire history, and they were therefore unprepared to meet it. Many of them, at first blush, mistook it for a new form of the old Gentile demand that had been the bane of Jewish existence throughout the long exile: the demand that the Jews convert to whatever the religion of the locally dominant majority happened to be. Consequently, their reaction to it was the old one: No, a hundred times no! Even when it was understood that this time the demand was not for a change of their religion but for a change in everything else that was traditionally Jewish except religion, the initial answer of the majority was still no, although with less determination and defiance. However, before long the culture of the modern world began to exert a magnetic influence upon the Jews, especially in Western and Central Europe. In many cases the Jewish Enlighteners, the *Maskilim*, who set out to learn German, or French, or English, in order to be able to enjoy the treasures whose medium was one of these languages, ended up by being assimilated totally into the Gentile environment. They either converted to Christianity or, if they did not take this ultimate step, in practice severed all ties with their Jewish background. For these men, German, or French, or English nationalistic sentiment came as a natural consequence of their cultural assimilation.

The early Mendelssohnian Enlighteners, of course, could not have foreseen these developments. Their blueprint for the enlightened Jew called for the enrichment of the Jewish mind by the addition of a new dimension, that of modern European culture, while retaining all or most of the traditional Jewish culture. Steeped as they were in Jewish lore and tradition, and in many cases religiously observant as well, the basic Jewish identification of these men was never in doubt. Thus these early *Maskilim* were the nearest duplication the Ashkenazi world ever produced of the position routinely taken for centuries by Sephardi and Italian Jewish intellectuals, who had been equally at home in both the Jewish and Gentile worlds. Little wonder that Mendelssohn and his co-workers resorted to Sephardi writings as prototypes and precedents for what they wished their contemporary co-religionists to do and to be.

However, those Sephardi precursors lived in a pre-nationalistic age and thus were of little help to the *Maskilim* trying to come to terms with modern nationalism. The Jewish Enlighteners were faced with the newly formulated Gentile assumption that the Jews were not, or were no longer, a nation but a religious community. Inasmuch as this was not yet a fact, it was a demand: the Jews were expected to become Germans (or Frenchmen, etc.), just like the Christian majorities from whom they were supposed ideally to differ only in religion. Within two or three decades of the inception of the *Haskala*, leaders of Western Jewry were ready to embrace this position. Of the two principles laid down by Mendelssohn in his *Jerusalem* as the guidelines for enlightened Jewish life, the first, the adaptation to the mores of the country (in which nationalism and patriotism were main features) became the dominant concern; the second, to "cling steadfastly to the religion of the fathers," appeared to be too heavy a burden and must be drastically lightened. This was the ideological position which was given explicit and official formulation by the Assembly of Jewish Notables and the Grand Sanhedrin, convoked at the initiative of Napoleon in Paris in 1806 and 1807.

The story of these decorous Jewish conclaves is a thrice-told tale, but it is nevertheless instructive to point out that their resolutions, passed by rabbis and Jewish lay leaders, came to form the basis of the new relationship of the Jews to all countries which granted them Emancipation. Of the twelve questions which the French government handed down to the Assembly, all but one were answered precisely as they were expected to be and as the meetings were pressured into answering. Both the Assembly and the Sanhedrin duly passed nine decisions resolving that (1) polygamy was, in accordance with the old ban of Rabbenu Gershom (1000 C.E.), forbidden to Jews; (2) Jewish divorce was only valid if it followed civil divorce; (3) Jewish marriage had to be preceded by civil marriage; (4) marriages between Jews and Christians were valid, although they could not be solemnized with religious forms; (5) every Israelite must consider his non-Jewish fellow citizens as brothers and aid, protect, and love them as though they were co-religionists; (6) the Israelite was required to consider the land of his birth or adoption as his fatherland and had to obey its laws, love it, and defend it when called upon; (7) Judaism did not forbid any handicraft or occupation; (8) it was commendable for Israelites to engage in agriculture, manual labor, and the arts as their ancestors in Palestine were wont to do; and (9) Israelites were forbidden to exact usury from either Jew or Christian.

The only point in which the Assembly's and Sanhedrin's decisions did not completely coincide with the emperor's wishes was that touching upon

Jewish-Christian intermarriage (point 4 above). Napoleon was all for intermarriage as a means for the rapid assimilation of the Jews. Just before the
convocation of the Jewish Assembly he had even toyed with the idea of forcing every third Jew and Jewess to marry a Christian, which typically auto-
cratic plan was turned down by the more sedate French Imperial Council.[62]

It is interesting that while the Assembly drew the line at any approval of
intermarriage, there was at least one German Jewish reformer who anticipated Napoleon's idea by two years in a treatise entitled *A Friendly Word to
the Christians About the Total Settlement of Their Quarrel with the Jews*, in
which he suggested that the Jews should be forced to teach their sons a
handicraft, to marry their daughters to Christians, and, to boot, to eat *T'refa*
food.[63]

The significance of the Assembly and the Paris Sanhedrin for the inner development of West and Central European Jewry—as contrasted with the
changes brought about by the Emancipation in its external, social, political,
and economic position—lies in the new development they represented in
the relations between the Jews and the state. For the first time in their history, the Jews not only were told by the state what overall, general attitude
they were expected to have toward it, but were required to enter into a solemn undertaking to fulfill those expectations. Most importantly, they had to
promise to love *la patrie* and their non-Jewish fellow citizens. The all-too-
willing consent of the Jewish representatives to shoulder this new duty of
love shows to what extent they were ready to substitute the new French nationalism for their old Jewish one and for the old Jewish emotional commit-
ments which traditionally included several loves: the love of the stranger
who dwelled in their midst, the love of Zion and the Holy Land, the love of
the people of Israel, and, above all, the love of God. What all this amounted
to was that, for the first time in their history, the Jews allowed a new and
foreign concept to penetrate the innermost adytum of their Jewish consciousness.

There is little doubt that at the time of their adoption by the Paris Sanhedrin, these ideas did not represent the consensus of the Jewish majority in
Western Europe, let alone in the east of the continent. Yet, within a relatively short time they had spread and, what is more, become internalized, so
that they came to represent for most thoughtful Jews in the West, even in
countries in which there was no sympathy for Napoleon or anything he stood
for, the prevalent mode of accommodation to the modern world with its na-
tion-states, its Enlightenment, its ideal of equality of all citizens, and its powerful nationalistic sentiments. In those countries of Western and Central
Europe in whose national character patriotism and nationalism came to occupy a central place in the nineteenth century—and I am thinking here in
particular of France, Germany, and Hungary—these sentiments were enthusiastically adopted by the Jews. If the Gentiles were fervently patriotic, the

Jews were even more so, or at least were given to more frequent, more emphatic, and more flamboyant asseveration of their patriotism. In the writings of Jewish journalists and authors, in the synagogue sermons of rabbis, and even in the works of Jewish scholars, references to the total devotion of the Jews to their *patrie*, or *Vaterland*, or *haza*, cropped up with monotonous regularity, often coupled with an emphatic denial that Judaism was anything but a religion, and the complementary assertion that the French Jews (for instance) were Frenchmen, equal in every respect except their religion to non-Jewish Frenchmen. Not infrequently this trend degenerated into a veritable Jewish self-hate (which will be discussed in a later chapter), because it was felt that any trait in respect of which the Jews differed from their compatriots was *eo ipso* evil and contemptible. But even where that did not happen, the feeling of total self-identification with the Gentile majority led almost everywhere in Western and Central Europe to social and cultural assimilation and, in some circles, to a theoretical abnegation of the value of Jewish survival.

A change in this position took place only in the late nineteenth century under the impact of a series of traumatic events which shook this Jewish complacency to its foundations: the Russian pogroms (from 1881 on) and the subsequent arrival of masses of Jewish refugees in the West; and the emergence of virulent forms of Jew-baiting in countries with which the Jews felt most closely identified, signaled by such events as the 1882 blood-libel of Tiszaeszlár, the attacks on German Jewish communities (in the 1880's), the Dreyfus affair (1894), the violent anti-Semitic riots in French cities and in Algeria (in 1898), and the like. These developments not only constituted the background for Herzl's Zionist solution of the Jewish problem, but also supplied the motivation for many Jews all over Europe to embrace Jewish nationalism.

In East Europe, where most of the Jews lived and where the culture of the Gentile environment had little attraction, the traditional concept of Jewish peoplehood underwent an inverse modification to that it evinced in the West. Here circumstances did not lead the Jews toward Gentile nationalisms, but to an increasing emphasis on a Jewish nationalism of their own. What happened was that they progressively pried loose the concept of Jewish nationhood from its age-old religious matrix and claimed instead to be a national minority like the several other such minorities in Russia, even though, unlike those others, the Jews were not concentrated in a definite territory but were "scattered abroad and dispersed" among all the other peoples of the czarist empire. On the other hand, in support of their claim that they were a national minority, they could point to the fact that they differed from both the dominant Russian nation and the various minorities in their Jewish religion, their Yiddish language, and their Jewish mores and traditions, and that for many generations they had enjoyed internal autonomy. This development, however, did not surface until about a century after the

Jews of West Europe had begun their move into the nationalisms of the countries which gave them, or which they hoped would give them, equal rights. It was only in the 1880's that the Russian Jews began to demand not only equal rights but also recognition as a national minority.

The Jewish philosopher and revolutionary Chaim Zhitlowsky (1865–1943) and the historian Simon Dubnow (1860–1941) were the fathers of the ideology of "Galut nationalism," whose basic tenet was that the Jews the world over constituted a nation and that they must be recognized as such by the states in which they lived. They demanded autonomy for the Jewish people so as to enable it to regulate its economic, social, and cultural life. Both were a-religious, and Zhitlowsky went so far as to maintain that it was possible to be a Christian by faith and a Jew by nationality. Although these autonomist plans never came to fruition, Galut nationalism did become a significant factor in the struggle against assimilationist views among the East European Jews. Jewish nationality was the basis also of the Bund, a Jewish Socialist mass organization which was founded in 1897 in Vilna and after World War I became the largest Jewish party in Poland.[64] The East European Jewish demand for national minority rights was energetically supported by the American Jewish Congress and the Comité des Délégations Juives at the Paris Peace Conference of 1919. The work of these two Jewish bodies can be considered a decisive factor in the inclusion of guarantees, not only to the Jews but to all minority groups, in the international treaties signed by the newly independent states (Poland, Czechoslovakia, Yugoslavia, Lithuania, Latvia, and enlarged Rumania) which were carved out at the Peace Conference from the territories of Russia, Germany, and Austria-Hungary. In Russia itself the Jews became recognized as a national minority soon after the victory of the Revolution.

The support Western Jewish representative bodies gave to the East European Jewish struggle for rights as national minorities points up, on the one hand, the global solidarity which by that time had become entrenched in Jewish consciousness; and on the other, the deep cleavage that had developed between the Western and Eastern European Jews with reference to their relationship to the countries in which they lived. In the United States, England, France, Germany, and so on, the Jews were fully integrated and were considered by the Gentiles as well as by themselves not only citizens but nationals. They were Americans, Englishmen, Frenchmen, etc., of the Jewish faith, exactly as limned in the resolutions of the Paris Sanhedrin. Nothing could have been more repugnant to them than to ask for or be offered rights as a national minority. Yet the members of the Western Jewish delegations to the Peace Conference agreed with the East European Jews that in East Europe the Jewish position was radically different and that there the Jews were well advised to ask for recognition as a national minority. The difference, often amounting to a contrast, between the Jewish position in the

East and the West inevitably impressed itself upon the Jewish mentality and
influenced the Jewish response to the Zionist movement.

10. Jews of the East and the West

One of the outcomes of the Enlightenment was a marked increase in
inner-Jewish religious and cultural diversity. Originally, religious observance
was the general rule in each Jewish community. Laxity, such as the few
"Court Jews" permitted themselves, was rare and exceptional. By and large,
each Jewish community was characterized by religious homogeneity—assured by adherence to the *Halakha* and observance of the local Jewish
minhag, compliance with which was considered as binding as with the
Halakha. Because of the variety in local *minhag*, the religious profile of one
Jewish community could differ considerably from that of another, especially
if the geographical distance between them was great. But in the essentials of
both credo and ritual, and, more importantly, in the unquestioning acceptance of religiosity as the natural condition of Jewish life, there were neither
intra-community nor inter-community differences. Whatever differences did
exist between one Jewish community and another—in speech, *minhag*, material culture—were brought about largely by the absorption of Gentile influences, which varied from place to place and from country to country, and
which managed to penetrate even the most ghettoized and isolated Jewish
community. However, beneath these surface differences the same essential
Jewishness lay everywhere.

Within a given Jewish community there was in many places a thin upper
crust, consisting of wealthy merchants, suppliers, leaseholders, physicians,
etc. These people occupied an exceptional position within, or on the margins
of, the community, inasmuch as they differed culturally from the poor and
downtrodden Jewish masses; they had access to the upper classes of Gentile
society and the opportunity to get acquainted with, and be influenced by, its
way of life, outlook, and intellectual interests. But their number until the
Enlightenment was so small that their existence made no appreciable difference in the cultural uniformity that characterized the overwhelming majority in each and every Jewish community.

Here we must mention a new development that came about after the
Spanish expulsion of the Jews. As a rule, when the Sephardi refugees settled
in cities where there was an indigenous Jewish community, they kept themselves apart and aloof from it. In such places, therefore, there was, after
1492, no overall Jewish religious and cultural uniformity but rather a dichotomy, the old Jewish community constituting one largely homogeneous
group, and the Sephardi newcomers another—often with considerable tension between the two. Similar phenomena could be observed elsewhere in

the wake of sizable Jewish migrations, except that the newcomers would, in contrast to the Sephardim, occupy a lower position in relation to the old-established Jewish community. However, even these dual (or plural) configurations which developed in various places could not materially impinge upon the overall basic religious unity that characterized the Jewish people as a whole until the Enlightenment.

Of course, even before the Enlightenment, in every community some people were ignorant of Jewish Law and lore and others well versed in both. But each end of the spectrum belonged to the same cultural continuum, in which the generally recognized measure of status was that of scholarly excellence in Talmudic study. Whether one rose high in such proficiency or not, the community as a whole was united by unquestioningly upholding this Jewish learning as the one supreme value.

With the Enlightenment, the Jewish unity came to an end. A wide gap opened up between those who continued in their old, traditional Jewish way of life, and the increasing number of those who acquired Enlightenment, and whose cultural orientation thereupon turned away from religious Judaism toward secular Europe. Within a few decades after the inception of the Jewish Enlightenment, in any large Jewish community these two disparate Jewish groups existed, between which there was no cultural continuity and in many cases not even a religious one. Before long this led, in addition, to a split between the Jews in Western and Central Europe on the one hand and those of Eastern Europe on the other. At a time when the Jews of the West had become generally enlightened and either had been or were about to be emancipated, the great majority of the Jews of the East were still traditional; Emancipation for them lay still decades ahead in the future.

The dividing line between these two Jewries did not necessarily follow political boundaries. It ran along the eastern frontier of Germany, but farther south it cut across Austria and Hungary. To the west of this line, the Western Jews, even if psychologically averse to assimilation, had adjusted to their Gentile environment: they spoke its language, attended its schools, and shared its culture, including material equipment, manners, mental postures, attitudes, and values. To the east of it, a sharp distinction continued to exist between Jews and Gentiles, with the Jews speaking a different vernacular, wearing different garb, exhibiting different manners, and having in general little in common culturally with the Gentile majority. Moreover, in the East the Jews considered themselves, and were considered by the Gentiles, a separate national minority, which status was legally recognized after World War I. All in all, that specific mixture of religion, tradition, and ethnicity which is usually meant by the term "Jewishness" was much more evident in the East than in the West.

A concomitant of this rift between Eastern and Western Jews was the emergence of mutually derogatory stereotypes. The tradition-bound Jews of

East Europe looked down upon their Western brethren because of the latter's "un-Jewish" appearance, speech, manners, and, above all, lack of religiosity. In the language of the Polish and Russian Jews, all these objectionable features were summed up in the term *Datch* (with a long *a*), which is the Yiddish form of the German word *Deutsch*, meaning "German." The *datchisher Yid* wore a short jacket, trimmed or shaved his beard, uncovered his head, spoke German, knew little or nothing of Talmudic literature, did not observe the *Halakha*, and was suspected of being, God forbid, an *epikoyres*—unbeliever. He certainly was a *poshe Yisroel*, a sinner in Israel, with whom one should have no truck.

From the other side of the dividing line, the Jews in the West who had acquired the language and culture of their Gentile environment, even if only in a rudimentary way, tended to look down upon their co-religionists to the East who had not gone through this process of acculturation but had instead preserved the Jewish religio-ethnic culture of former generations. We have heard of the contemptuous attitude displayed in the eighteenth century by Isaac de Pinto, an acculturated Sephardi Jew of Portuguese descent, to the Ashkenazi Jews, some of whom had settled in his home town of Bordeaux. By the time this Sephardi disdain of the Ashkenazim subsided, it was replaced by a no less intensive enlightened Ashkenazi dislike of unenlightened Ashkenazim. It was especially strong among those Ashkenazi Jews who themselves were located to the west of but not far from the dividing line between the Jewish West and East. Thus the dislike and contempt of the German Jews was directed toward those Jews who lived to the east of Germany—the "Ostjuden." The same attitude set the acculturated German- and Hungarian-speaking Jews in the western parts of Austria and Hungary, including the capitals of Vienna and Budapest, against the Yiddish-speaking Jews of the eastern territories of the Hapsburg Empire, contemptuously referred to as "Galizianer." It was another heritage of the Enlightenment that in German-speaking countries, as well as in Hungary (where all educated Jews knew German in addition to Hungarian), contempt was the prevalent attitude toward the Yiddish language, which was regarded as gibberish, a common and vulgar tongue, even by those religiously most Orthodox Jews whose own parents had known no other spoken language.

The cruder outcroppings of this contempt often felt by Jews toward co-religionists of a different background are discussed more fully in Chapter 17. Here let me only refer to a small incident which I remember from my own youth that illustrates the animosity even Orthodox Jews in Hungary had for Yiddish as late as 1930. In that year, I still clearly remember, my grandmother gave me a smart slap because I had the temerity to use a Yiddish expression in conversation with her. The daughter of a man who had migrated from Kurland to Transylvania, she had received a good Hungarian and German education. Throughout her life she remained very religious, wore a *sheitel* (wig), and observed all the commandments as expected of a good Jewish woman. It was she who had taught me the Sh'ma' prayer in Hebrew. But when it came to Yiddish, she had an almost instinctively hostile reaction. (Both she and my grandfather, a scion of Moses Sofer, died in the early 1940's in the Budapest ghetto; may they rest in peace.)

The East-West rift within the body of Ashkenazi Jewry ultimately was healed as a result of several historical developments. First, the gap between Western Jewish assimilationism and East European Jewish traditionalism began to diminish in the second half of the nineteenth century. By that time it had become evident that Western Jewry, far from disintegrating under the impact of assimilation, was able to work out various syntheses between European culture and Judaism, ranging from the Reform movement to the Frankfurt Neo-Orthodoxy. It also developed the Science of Judaism, which led to a new appreciation of the history, literature, and ethics of Judaism. Incidentally, all these adjustments to the "spirit of the times" were products of German Jewry. In the East, too, modern influences penetrated sufficiently to create an increasing interest in Jewish issues along lines other than traditional Orthodoxy and Talmudism. Mention has been made of Galut nationalism, the movement for Jewish autonomy, and the Bund. These were significant departures from the old established East European Jewish outlook, which resulted in a new spirit and a corresponding weakening of the hold exercised over the Jewish masses either by the *Halakha* or by Hasidism. Even in the late eighteenth century, an increasing number of young Jews had begun to go from East to West in search of a European secular education; some of these, in the course of time, returned home bringing along, and disseminating, Western ideas. Governmental interference, too, brought about changes which could not be resisted. In this way, the distance which had separated Eastern and Western Jewry in the early years of Enlightenment was reduced from both sides.

By the nineteenth century, Enlightenment, in one form or another, was accessible to most Jews who learned of its existence and were attracted to it. Even in the remote villages of Poland and Russia, those who wanted it could learn the Latin alphabet and, at the price of considerable struggle, could teach themselves to read and understand German (sufficiently similar to Yiddish not to defy a determined and sustained effort). This is how Solomon Maimon (1754–1800), who was destined to become an important German philosopher, and many others like him, began their acquisition of European culture. By the early 1800's, as Jacob S. Raisin, quoting Solomon Maimon, put it, thousands of young Russian Jews flocked to high schools and universities "like starving persons suddenly treated to a delicious meal." [65]

Another factor working in the same direction was the outbreak of bloody pogroms which in the late nineteenth and early twentieth centuries swept over parts of Russia. The emigration of large numbers of Jews from both West and East to America created a new Jewish community. Before long, this had become numerically the largest as well as the most influential in the Jewish world, and here East-West differences paled in the face of the challenges of the New World. The Zionist movement, created by a Western Jew, Theodor Herzl, and organized along West European lines, had the strongest response in the East and provided Eastern and Western Jews with a great cause to unite and fight for. East-West differences were further confused when, during World War I, the Western Jews of England and France found themselves in one camp with the Russian-Polish Jews of the East, while other parts of Western Jewry, those of Germany and Austria-Hungary as well as the typically Eastern Jews of Austrian Galicia and Hungarian Carpatho-Ruthenia, were in the other camp; and when the German, Austrian, and Hungarian Jews who had migrated to America fought in the armed forces of the United States against their brothers who had remained in the old countries. Following World War I, the Jews of the West took an active part in aiding, defending, and speaking up for the Jews of the East in the latter's struggle for national minority rights.

Since those days, the community of fate among all parts of the Jewish people has remained a basic tenet and a powerful motivation for Jewish action all over the world. Finally, with the foundation of the State of Israel, the differences between immigrants from Eastern, Central, and Western Europe, as well as between them and American 'olim, have tended to diminish in view of the much greater cultural differences between all of these on the one hand and the immigrants from the Muslim countries on the other. East-West differences in Israel mean those between Jews from the Middle East and Jews from the Western world,[66] and the problems created by these differences still rank immediately after the problems of Israel's security in the face of continued Arab hostility.

The Jews in the Muslim world did not experience anything like the major changeover from Talmudic study to secular subjects, because the great movement of European Enlightenment had not reached the Middle East until after World War I. Consequently, there was nothing in the environment that could have enticed away studious young Middle Eastern Jews from the one and only traditional intellectual field, that of the Talmud. Moreover, the general cultural stagnation which characterized the Muslim world until the twentieth century [67] extended into the life of the Jewish communities as well. The Jewish condition in the Muslim world was certainly not favorable to attaining excellence even in the traditional Talmudic field, and widespread poverty severely limited the number of those young men who could devote any time at all to Talmudic studies. Thus the Middle Eastern Jews had become in the last few hundred years relatively impoverished even in this one field of traditional Jewish specialization. Nevertheless, the Jews in the Muslim world constituted, as they did in the West, an exceptionally literate and educated element when compared to their Gentile environment. In 1860 a French Jewish charitable organization, the Alliance Israélite Universelle, was founded. It established schools in several major Muslim cities and brought an echo of the European Jewish Enlightenment into the life of some of the largest Middle Eastern Jewish communities. Indeed, more parents wanted, as a rule, to enroll their children than could be absorbed by the limited capacity of the schools.

The establishment of universities and colleges with a Western-type secular education in the more advanced Middle Eastern countries came in general too late for the Jews to take advantage of it. Middle Eastern higher education began to function on an appreciable scale only after World War II, when most of the Jews were already leaving the Muslim countries to settle in Israel, France, and elsewhere. But even if they had stayed, two factors make it doubtful whether they could have penetrated the newly developing professional fields in considerable numbers. First, they were an oppressed, or at least disadvantaged, community, whose members could not count on being readily admitted to locally or government-controlled universities in any of the Muslim countries. Secondly, just as the Middle East as a whole never produced a movement like that of the European Enlightenment, so the Middle Eastern Jews never experienced anything like the European Jewish Enlightenment; hence the idea of switching from traditional Talmudic to modern secular studies remained, on the whole, foreign to them.

These considerations also explain the wide educational gap that became apparent as more than a million Jews immigrated from the Middle East and Europe to Israel after 1948. In contrast to the European Jewish immigrants, those who arrived from the Middle East had, with a few exceptions, nothing more than a very elementary education which forced them into the lowest rungs of unskilled labor after their settlement in Israel. Despite the persistent demands voiced by the Sephardi and Oriental Jewish leaders in Israel to have this gap closed, and the efforts to the same end made by the Israeli political and educational leadership, today, a generation later, it still exists and is only now beginning to narrow appreciably. It has become more and more apparent that the urge to education has been markedly increasing in the Oriental sector of Israel, and that its transition from the traditional religious to more modern educational goals has been taking place with less tension and community friction than might have been expected. Thus there can be little doubt that Israel as a whole is heading toward becoming one of the most highly educated countries in the world, in accordance with the age-old Jewish tradition of perceiving the highest human value and the greatest good in developing the mind through persistent study.

11. In Summary

The Jewish Enlightenment began as the program of a small group of German Jews led by Moses Mendelssohn. The basic idea of its protagonists was to familiarize Jews with European (and, in the first place, German) culture. They were neither against the traditional observance of Jewish religion, nor against a continuing study of the Talmud, but felt that European culture contained great values which should also be made accessible to Jews. Consequently, they advocated learning European languages (and, again, German in the first place) as the key to opening up the cultural treasures of Europe.

However, as it developed, the *Haskala* had unforeseen consequences. The first *Maskilim* were yeshiva students or graduates, who, by the time they began to take an interest in German literature and philosophy, had been thoroughly grounded in Talmudic studies. Many of them used their knowledge of the two languages, Hebrew and German to write works in Hebrew inspired by German culture. Thus sprang up the Hebrew *Haskala* literature in which novels, plays, poems, philosophical treatises, grammars, textbooks of geography, history, and more were produced, all of them bearing the signs of valiant struggle against the inadequacy of the ancient and venerable Hebrew language for expressing the modern concepts of eighteenth- and nineteenth-century science and literature.

Soon a change began to make itself felt. Younger people, and especially those who grew up in *Maskil* households, tended to learn more and more of the German subjects and less and less of the traditional Hebrew-Jewish studies of Bible and Talmud. Before long an entirely new phenomenon emerged, one that had not existed in Jewish history since Hellenistic times—a class of educated young Jews who knew woefully little of what had for centuries constituted the only cultural and religious basis of Jewish life, but were instead well versed in the secular culture of the non-Jewish environment in which they lived. Thus, again for the first time since the days of Hellenism, the Jewish community in some localities was no longer culturally and religiously homogeneous. The *Haskala* irrevocably disrupted the age-old cultural continuum based on Talmudic learning. There were now two separate, unconnected fields of cultural endeavor: the traditional one, and the new one represented by the *Haskala*. Further, the two were sharply antagonistic. The *Haskala*, to the tradition-minded, meant submission to the forbidden enticements of the non-Jewish world, the world of the *Goyim*. The *Maskilim*, in turn, viewing traditional Jewish religious observance in the light of their newly acquired modern European outlook, found much in Jewish religious law and custom objectionable. As soon as they got used to contact with Gentiles, even the traditional Jewish garb, the style of hair and beard, the language and speech mannerisms, the behavior, gestures, and facial expressions—all appeared to them outlandish, inferior, and contemptible. Indeed, the very forms of traditional religious observance, and especially those of communal prayer, appeared to them barbarous. Hence, one of the outgrowths of the *Haskala* was religious reform, which began among German Jews, and much of which centered, tacitly but unmistakably, on making the services in the synagogue similar to those in the Christian churches while retaining what they considered the essence of Judaism. For the traditionals, for whom the minutest religious custom was as important as the Ten Commandments, all this was, of course, anathema. Putting aside the struggle between the Hasidim and their opponents (the *Mitnagdim*), which for a generation had divided them into two enemy camps, they united against the new common danger, that of the *Haskala*. Thus, whenever the *Haskala* penetrated or even as much as appeared on the horizon, the battle cry of the traditionals was sounded and they spared no effort to prevent its entry, block its progress, and combat it. Despite all efforts, however, the *Haskala* spread, making irreparable inroads into the formerly solid and closed ranks of the devout.

Apart from breaking up Jewish religious unity, and rapidly weakening "Jewishness," *Haskala* had another quite phenomenal outcome. It enabled the *Maskilim*, or their children, not only to become consumers of the best in European culture but to penetrate the ranks of the select few who spearheaded cultural production in the Central and West European countries. Even before Emancipation gave them equal rights as citizens in one European country after the other, Jews had begun to take an intensive part in the European cultural scene. Before long the percentage of Jews among writers, poets, dramatists, musicians, artists, scientists, and economists became much higher than their proportion in the total population and even in the urban sector. In trying to explain this remarkable phenomenon, some students speak of the long-pent-up Jewish talent which, having been confined for centuries to the "four cubits of the *Halakha*"—the one area of Talmudic and related religious studies—now burst forth into all the fields of European cultural endeavor that the Enlightenment and the Emancipation suddenly threw open to it. A more likely explanation seems to be the transference of the age-old Jewish habit of Talmud study and of producing works of halakhic and religious import to the newly opened-up fields of secular culture. For centuries scholarship had been the highest Jewish value. Aspired to by all, and actually achieved by a remarkably high proportion, it was the only road to distinction open in a traditional Jewish community. Hence, when new fields became accessible in which studiousness and self-application promised rewards, an uncommonly large number of young Jews entered them, predisposed as they were by centuries to take the road of learning to prominence. The subject matter of study was new and very different; instead of continuing the well-trodden path of Talmudic study, they had to choose one of many fresh disciplines to master and excel in. But the method leading to achievement and renown in the new fields was the same old familiar one—study, an activity at which they had been singularly adept for centuries.

Hand in hand with this transference of method went the transference of the valuation of study. Just as under the old system to study the Talmud was the highest value, so now to study one of the new specializations came to be considered a top-ranking activity. "Study!" remained the constant admonition to a son from his parents; compared to the overriding importance of studying, the specific subject matter studied was of secondary significance.

To the present day this Jewish zeal for studying has not abated; nor has the supreme value set on those professions or specializations which are acquired by studying, by excercising one's brain power. When a Jewish mother in America, or any other Western country, speaks proudly of "my son the doctor," or "my son the professor," or "my son the lawyer," she is actually expressing her pride in having a son who has used his brain and talents to study diligently and become a member of a distinguished and prestigious occupation. (The disproportionately high percentage of Jews in the academic professions in all Western countries will be touched upon later in a different context.)

Looking back at the Jewish Enlightenment from a distance of two hundred years, one cannot escape the conclusion that it led the Jewish people to both triumph and tragedy. There can be no question but that the Enlightenment was a triumph for the Jewish mind. It has made the Jews a part of the modern world. It enabled them to achieve Emancipation and to make full use of the opportunities opened up by it. Thanks to the Enlightenment, wherever Jews live today they form an intellectual élite within the general population—and this is true, albeit to varying extents, even in the Communist countries. In the free world they have become something of a leaven and a catalyst, their work and their presence stimulating and enriching all fields of cultural endeavor. All this could not have come about without the Enlightenment. Nor would Marxism, psychoanalysis, or relativity have been created and many other great breakthroughs achieved. Without the Enlightenment, Herzl would have been a yeshiva student and perhaps an outstanding Orthodox rabbi, but Zionism would not have come into being, nor could it have been organized into a European-style political movement, nor could the State of Israel have been born. And, like Israel, the entire modern physiognomy of all the Jewish people outside Israel is derived from, and is an outcome of, the Enlightenment. These are the great landmarks of its triumph.

Its tragedy lies in the fearful price it exacted from the Jewish people. In its wake hundreds of thousands of Jews have left the fold; as many, or more, became marginal people with an ambivalent attitude toward Jewishness. The inner unity of the Jewish people was disrupted. The peace of mind which had been the great strength of a believing, God-fearing, and God-loving Jew was lost. Neuroses became a Jewish affliction, just as alcoholism afflicted certain Gentile peoples. The pathology of Jewish self-hatred was born. Suicide, almost nonexistent among the Jews in pre-Enlightenment times, rose in some places to rates twice or three times as high as among the Gentiles.[68] And, worst of all, that inner core and essence of Jewishness which had been preserved intact through millennia of exposure to Gentile cultures, proved for the first time in Jewish history no longer impregnable to outside influences, thereby putting Jewish existence itself in jeopardy.

It is always difficult to strike a balance between the positive and the negative outcomes of a historical event or process. The final word can never be said because as long as a people is alive, the consequences of its past flow on and stretch forward into its future. However, judging from the present condition of world Jewry, and comparing it with its situation two centuries ago, one can say that an overall improvement has taken place. The threats to Jewish existence, both internal and external, are unquestionably greater today than they were two hundred years ago. But the position of world Jewry today is much stronger, and so are the forces it can muster to meet the present and foreseeable challenges.

10

The Trend of Millennia

A survey of the works produced by Jewish authors—partly in response to inner Jewish developments and partly under the impact of the successive historic encounters reviewed in the preceding chapters—indicates an overall trend in which Jewish religious and cultural ethnocentricity gradually loosened. In antiquity, everything the Hebrews and the Jews created was religious in character. They produced nothing of significance of a secular or non-Jewish nature, nothing that, at the very least, did not center on Israel, or Jews, or Judaism. As time passed and they were exposed to new influences in new Gentile environments, they gradually began to bring forth cultural products which had nothing to do with Jews or Judaism but were contributions to the general culture of the Gentile world in which they lived. In comparison to what they created in the Gentile style and cultural context, their specifically Jewish cultural products decreased both in number and in variety. Ultimately, under the impact of the Enlightenment, the non-Jewish cultural output became predominant. This process, which signified a gradual widening of the interests encompassed by the Jewish mind, led by the second half of the nineteenth century to the achievement of a position in the forefront of global intellectual development, and an undisputed leadership in opening up new scientific, intellectual, and social horizons to the world.

To recapitulate from this viewpoint the main cultural events of the six great historic encounters discussed previously, we found that the first one—that between the Israelites and Canaan—resulted in the development or adaptation of certain theological concepts and certain style elements used for their formulation, such as poetic phraseology and imagery. These were incorporated into the Bible, the most original and most authentically Israelite religious creation.

The second one, between the Jews and Hellenism, produced, in the main, a large number of literary works written by Jews in Greek in the fields of history, drama, epic, philosophy, and apologetics, all of which (with the exception of the works of one insignificant author) were Jewish to the core in that their purpose was to glorify and defend Jewish history, Jewish religion, and Jewish Law.

The third encounter—that between the Jews and the Muslim Arabs— brought about for the first time a branching out and away from Judaism as the only theme treated in Jewish writings. The most important of the works, whether written in Hebrew or in Arabic, were still Jewish. They consisted of codes of Jewish Law, commentaries to the Bible, responsa deal- ing with Jewish religious problems, Hebrew grammar, Hebrew poetry, and Jewish religious philosophy. But works of secular import also made their ap- perance: treatises on medicine, mathematics, geometry, astronomy and as- trology, and the like—all written in Arabic and identifiable as "Jewish" only inasmuch as their authors were Jewish. Even Hebrew poetry, for more than two thousand years (at the time) the exclusive domain of Jewish religious expression, was penetrated by a secular non-Jewish and un-Jewish spirit when Hebrew poets, among them the authors of the greatest Jewish re- ligious poems, began to write also secular poetry, including war songs, na- ture songs, and erotic love songs.

With the next encounter—that of the Italian Jews with the culture of the Renaissance—the balance shifted in favor of the secular Italian as against the religious Jewish subjects. To be sure, the Renaissance Jews still created Jew- ish works in all fields of traditional literary activity, but most of what they wrote, and certainly the most important books they produced, were on secu- lar subjects, even if written, as some of them were, in Hebrew. Their life, with which their literature and their other cultural activities were closely in- tertwined, was also more Italian-secular than Jewish. They participated in the intensive preoccupation of the Renaissance with medicine, with the arts and crafts, with music and the dance, with the theater, technology, political affairs, with pastimes and sports, and they even had their share in crimes, gambling, and sexual license. The Jewish core of their life and being, which they nevertheless preserved beneath all these activities and interests, had perceptibly shrunk. Also for the first time in Jewish history, one could witness a Jewish intellectual élite whose mind was no longer unquestionably Jewish-centered.

The fifth encounter, that of East European Jews with Russian and Ukrain- ian sectarianism, does not quite fit into this series pointing to a successively diminishing Jewish core in relation to the widening horizon of Jewish gener- alism. Hasidism was a remarkably Jewish phenomenon which, whatever foreign religious forms it adopted, managed to digest and assimilate them thoroughly and thus reduce them to insignificant accretions. Yet, in relation to the East European Talmudism which had dominated the Jewish mind in Poland and the neighboring countries for at least two centuries, and against which it was a rebellion, Hasidism nevertheless represented a step away from traditional Jewish values and in the direction of one definite type of Gentile folk piety.

In the sixth and last encounter discussed—that between the Jews and the European Enlightenment—the Jewish core not only experienced its greatest shrinkage ever but seemed to be in danger of disappearing altogether. While the Jewish Enlightenment started out as a Jewish-centered movement, its followers became rapidly less and less Jewish—a process which found its most poignant expression in their literary and other works. These new intellectual products became important contributions to the national cultures of the countries to which the Jews assimilated with no traces of Jewishness left in them. Had it not been for the determined stand of the Orthodox rabbis and the efforts of the emerging Reform-Jewish leadership, it is doubtful whether Central and West European Jewry would have survived the nineteenth century until new vigor was infused into it by Zionism.

The psychological motivation behind this trend from Jewish cultural particularism toward secular intellectual generalism was the increasing enchantment of the Jewish mind with the culture of the majority. With each successive encounter between Jews and Gentiles (with the possible exception of that which endowed Hasidism with certain alien features) the Jewish mind came a step closer to the mind of the Gentile host people. The steps of this rapprochement became each time bigger and bigger, resulting in a larger accretion of common features between the Gentile and the Jewish mentality. In fact, the Hellenized Jews had more in common with the pagan Hellenistic peoples than the Biblical Israelites had with the Canaanites. Similarly in the Arab orbit, the culture and outlook of the Jews were more Arab-colored than those of their Hellenized ancestors were Greek-tinged. Again, the Jews of fifteenth- and sixteenth-century Italy were more imbued with the Renaissance spirit than were the Jews in Spain with that of either the Arabs or the Spaniards. Hasidism to some extent at least, fits into this series of geometric progression; in it, for the first time since the early and largely formative Canaanite period, some Gentile forms of religious worship were incorporated into Judaism. This progressively greater Jewish adjustment to every successive new environment—provided it was attractive enough to evoke a positive response—has, I believe, been amply demonstrated in earlier chapters.

With the Enlightenment, a new factor appeared on the Jewish horizon. This was a difference of formerly unknown magnitude between the *Halakha*-centered, traditional, pre-Enlightenment Jewish culture and the a-religious, enlightened, rational-culture of eighteenth-century Europe. No such fundamental difference had existed between the Jewish culture and the Spanish Arab culture, nor between the culture of the Jews and that of Renaissance Italy. For one thing, in those two previous encounters the language spoken by the Jews was the same as the one spoken in their Gentile environment. Linguistic identity (or near-identity, if we wish to take dialectal differences

into consideration) carried with it many other common cultural features on
the folk level which formed the basis for the impact the great tradition of the
Gentile culture made on the Jews. Common between Jews and Gentiles was
also the basic approach to religion. And, despite the irreconcilable differences between Judaism and Islam and between Judaism and Christianity,
common to all three, until the Enlightenment, was the fact that religion was
the supreme mistress of life, so secure in her commanding position that she
could tolerate minor lords under her: philosophy, poetry, art, sciences,
linguistic studies, and the like. A man who devoted himself to the service of
one of these was not considered, in consequence, less faithful to his religion,
whether he was a Muslim, a Christian, or a Jew. Hence the Jews could
remain devoted to Judaism while adopting philosophical teachings and scientific methods, art forms, and literary genres from the Muslims and the Christians, and while cooperating with them to the fullest and the best of their intellectual capacity in every religiously neutral field.

In the two centuries immediately preceding the Enlightenment, European Jewry—with the exception of its small Sephardi contingent—had been
withdrawn into the "four cubits of the *Halakha.*" This Jewish retrenchment
had reached such an extent that even the study of the Bible was neglected.
And the enormously rich Jewish output in a dozen non-halakhic fields (discussed earlier) was not only ignored but its perusal was forbidden, although
in many cases it was the work of the very same masters whose Talmudic
commentaries or codes were part of the approved curriculum. Thus, to mention only one example, the *Mishne Tora* of Maimonides was diligently studied, but his *Guide* was anathemized. After several generations of such drastic
self-confinement and utter self-limitation, even most rabbis had become ignorant of Jewish culture with the sole exception of halakhic literature.

If this was the state of Jewish learning, one can easily imagine the antagonism that pervaded these traditional Jewish circles against all secular culture.
As the Yiddish language had attained a position of quasi-sanctity, it was used
to the exclusion of the vernaculars of the Gentiles. One had to speak Polish,
or Ukrainian, or Russian sufficiently to be able to communicate with the
Gentiles, on daily contact with whom the livelihood of most Jews depended.
But to be too fluent in a "goyish" language was frowned upon, and to read
anything written in one of them, whether a book or a newspaper, was absolutely forbidden and considered an irreligious act, a sin.

It was from this background that the fathers of the German Jewish Enlightenment emerged. Having managed to learn German and begun to read
German literature, they were bedazzled, nay, intoxicated, by the sight and
sound and taste of the new world that opened up before them. This was no
longer a world dominated by another religion like the Muslim and Christian
worlds in Spain, or by a religious humanism like Renaissance Italy, but a
world of individualism and secularism permeated by a political and scientific

outlook. Thus the acquisition by the Jewish Enlighteners of the new European culture—which comprised, as an integral part, an attitude of indifference to religious doctrine and practice—inevitably had to mean the adoption also of this dominant Gentile attitude to religion. At the beginning, the German Jewish Enlighteners were blissfully unaware of the danger this meant for Judaism. They advocated the acquisition of European culture with the retention of an improved and modernized version of Jewish culture and religion. This was the approach epitomized in the slogan of the *Maskilim*: "Be a Jew at home, and a man [meaning a man of European culture] abroad." The founders of the Jewish Enlightenment, like the founder of Christianity some seventeen centuries earlier, even emphasized the importance of observing all the *mitzvot*, the religious precepts of Judaism. But soon their disciples came to be convinced that in order to be truly enlightened and cultured Europeans, they must relate to Judaism in the same way that the contemporary enlightened Christians related to Christianity.

This Jewish change of attitude to Judaism had two sources. It was based, first of all, on an inner subconscious process set in motion by the acquisition and internalization of the cultural values of the European Enlightenment, which imperceptibly instilled in the Jewish mind the typical enlightened attitude to religion—all religion, including its own.

Secondly, it was brought about by the persistent and overt demands of the Gentile environment. For two millennia the Gentile world had perceived the Jews as a group separate and different from itself on account of its religion. This difference was felt to be an irritation, which in turn gave birth to the demand that the Jews cease to be different by converting to the religion of the majority. The methods resorted to in putting this demand to the Jews differed from place to place and from age to age. They ranged from making their lives uncomfortable and letting them feel the majority's scorn, through inflicting physical harm to their body and property, to expulsion and forced conversion under the threat of death. Yet, withal, the most disparate acts undertaken against the Jews had always one and the same ultimate aim: to make them give up their religion and embrace instead that of the local majority.

The Jewish reaction to these attempts was, throughout, one of resistance. True, the Jews were ready, and often eager, to adopt many things offered by any Gentile environment which they found attractive; but religion was never one of them. The Jewish-Gentile encounters in Hellenistic Alexandria, in Arab Spain, and in Renaissance Italy are all examples of this attitude and of the process of cultural adaptation in which it found its expression. In all the three, the Jewish intellectual leadership, despite its near-total assimilation to the culture of the environment, remained totally Jewish, retaining its unshakable commitment to Jewish religion, tradition, ethnicism—in a word, to Jewishness.

In the age of Enlightenment, for the first time in their history, the Jews were faced with a Gentile demand that differed fundamentally from those they had previously encountered. This time they were not asked to give up their religion, but to assimilate to the culture of their environment in all other respects. Since, as a result of the Enlightenment, religion had lost its all-embracing significance for the European intellectuals, they now came with a new variant of the age-old demand addressed to the Jews. The call, "Be like us!" was still there; in fact, it was there even more emphatically than in the past, but the measure of similarity was no longer religious but cultural. "Be like us" now meant, "Be like us in language, in garb, in occupation, in manners; as for your religion, we don't care whether or not you continue to adhere to it, provided that your attitude to your religion and the way in which you practice it are similar to our relationship to our religion."

On the surface it seemed paradoxical, but psychologically it was inevitable, that the abandonment of the Gentile demand for Jewish conversion, coupled with the demand for cultural assimilation, should have achieved what all pressure and coercion of former ages could not—large-scale, voluntary baptisms (albeit in most cases not from conviction but from practical considerations) and even larger-scale dereliction from the duties of Jewish religious observance. As long as the exigencies of history placed the Jew in the midst of peoples who believed in their religions as firmly as he did in his, he could resist all Gentile pressure to abandon his faith and convert to that of the majority. Underlying both the pressure and the resistance was the common premise, subscribed to by both sides, that religion was a supreme good, and faithfulness to it a supreme duty. This unassailable premise, coupled with the Jewish conviction that Judaism was the only true religion, gave the Jews the strength to resist. Indeed, it made it psychologically inevitable for them to fight all pressures and demands, and in many cases even to face death rather than to convert to an alien faith.

The Enlightenment confronted the Jews with a culture which not only attracted them irresistibly by its glitter but comprised, as one of its fundamentals, a new attitude to religion—ranging from lukewarm to hostile, from practical indifference to opposition in principle, from enlightened deism to philosophical atheism. Thus, assimilation to the culture of the Enlightenment undermined the belief of the Jew, not in Judaism but in the value of religion as such. At best, religion was reduced to an abstract belief in God and to a humanistic ethic. On this level, it was difficult to maintain a distinction between a reductionist Judaism and a reductionist Christianity. This is why the last of the great historic encounters of the Jews with the Gentile world was fraught with dangers such as Judaism had never before known.

It is an interesting postscript to this acceptance by the Jews of the enlightened Gentile indifference to religion that in the twentieth century, again at least partly under Gentile influence, the Jews in America have turned around and returned to a considerable measure of religious observance. It has been noted by students of the American Jewish religious scene that "in duplicating the 100-percent community-cum-church posture of the non-Jewish American, the Jew vouchsafes himself as an all-rightnik in the American host community. Operating with the morally dubious notion that one's neighbors will respect one more if one is religious, the Jew seeks to insure that acceptance. . . ." [1] In this manner the Gentile environment, which in the 1780's alienated the Jew from his religion, has changed sufficiently to have surrounded the Jews in the 1950's and 1960's with an atmosphere which now requires him to return to his religion. This is certainly one of the factors accountable for the thriving Jewish congregations in American suburbia.

Apart from religious indifference, there were other problems during and after the inception of the Jewish Enlightenment to which conversion to Christianity seemed the logical solution. Within one or two decades of the beginning of the Jewish Enlightenment, many in the younger generation of German Jews became aware that to maintain any connection with Judaism would prevent them from making as much headway in German society as they would like. In almost all walks of life, but especially public office, including positions in the government-controlled universities, it soon proved either extremely difficult or altogether impossible for a Jew to make a career as long as he remained Jewish. The baptismal certificate was the admission ticket not only to European culture, as Heine put it, [2] but to many a coveted office, however excellent otherwise the qualifications of the aspirant. Since the typical enlightened attitude toward religion weakened both the emotional and the credal hold of confessional affiliation, conversion in the circumstances became nothing more than paying the price for the admission ticket. Consequently, many Jews underwent what Milton Himmelfarb has called "prudential baptism" or "expediential conversion." [3] A wave of voluntary adoptions of Christianity, such as had never before been known in Jewish history, swept through German Jewry. By 1823—only thirty-seven years after the death of Mendelssohn—one-half of the members of the Berlin Jewish community had converted, and in other parts of Prussia many more followed the same path.

This German Jewish movement into Christianity was paralleled in England by the large secession of leading Sephardi families. [4] During the whole of the nineteenth century, according to the figures compiled by a historian of the Evangelical mission to the Jews, the number of Jewish converts to the three main branches of Christianity—Catholicism, Protestantism, and the Greek (Russian) Orthodox Church—reached 204,500. Other estimates run from a low of 100,000 to a high of 250,000. Whatever their exact number, the converts included many who were outstanding in fields whose very existence had been unknown to them or their fathers but a generation earlier,

including the sciences, the arts, literature, journalism, historiography, politics, law, acting, exploration, social movements, political economy, medicine, linguistics, mathematics, astronomy, Oriental studies, industry, finance, ecclesiastic history, and theology. Many became university professors;
some, judges in the highest courts, members of parliaments, and even
bishops in the Catholic Church. Among them were men of world renown,
such as Heine, Disraeli, Marx, Börne, Ricardo, Anton Rubinstein, Rachel
Felix (the French actress), to mention only a few of the many who won fame
and died before the end of the nineteenth century.[5]

Thirty-five years after the end of the nineteenth century, the German
children and grandchildren of these converts were suddenly faced with the
Nuremberg Laws, which set up various categories of people of partly Jewish
descent. The number of German Jews at the time was 503,000, but more
than 2 million more were stamped "non-Aryans," which led many to utter
despair and even suicide. These figures give us some idea as to the magnitude of the demographic loss by attrition sustained by German Jewry in the
wake of the Mendelssohnian Enlightenment and that brief moment of German liberalism which transformed the Jews into German citizens of the Jewish faith. In other countries the rate of defection may not have been this
high, but wherever Jewish Enlightenment spread, assimilation followed and
conversion was considerable.

To return for a moment to the motivations for the early post-
Mendelssohnian conversions, by the nineteenth century, numerous Christian missions to the Jews were active in several European countries, and
their work may have resulted in sincere conversions. A consideration of the
social conditions of the Jews in various countries, however, points rather to
utilitarian and self-seeking motives. In a list of more than a hundred prominent converts in the nineteenth century, there are many from Germany,
Austria, and Hungary, countries in which conversion was the price Jews had
to pay for an academic or other career, but few (eight) from England, and
only two from France, where conversion was not a necessary prerequisite for
a public career.[6] This seems to indicate that motives other than religious
ones were the main factor in such conversions.

Enlightenment had, of course, some quite different consequences aside
from the large-scale defection from Judaism. To mention only its effects in
the intellectual and spiritual realms, it led to the beginnings of the *Wissenschaft des Judentums*, the scientific study of Jewish history, literature,
and religion. It gave rise to the Jewish religious Reform movement, to the
crystallization of neo-Orthodoxy, and to Conservative Judaism. Above all, it
enabled the Ashkenazi Jewish mind, which for centuries had been confined
to concentration on the single domain of the *Halakha*, to strike out into all
areas of human creativity and thus to reassert its intellectual powers.

However, despite these developments which in themselves were of enormous significance, demographically the Enlightenment caused great damage to the Jewish body politic. Its net effect was a large-scale reduction of the substance of world Jewry by an inestimable proportion. It also brought about a large-scale brain drain, in that it removed from the Jewish fold many (again the proportion is not known) of the best minds for whom the success of their intellectual pursuit was more important than their Jewish affiliation. If we go along with Thorstein Veblen's famous hypothesis that it is the marginal position of the Jewish intellectual in relation to the Jewish and the Gentile cultures which has enabled him to achieve preeminence,[7] then this merging or submersion of eminent Jewish intellectuals in the Gentile society is a loss for the world as well. In any case, Jewry managed to survive the effects of Enlightenment, just as it did the genocidal attack that was launched against it from the same country in which the *Haskala* started some 150 years earlier. That it survived, and that today, after both Enlightenment and Holocaust, it is more vital and vibrant than it was for many a generation, is the most eloquent testimony to the ability of the Jewish mind to cope with and adapt to the most unforeseen exigencies.

III

JOURNEY INTO
THE JEWISH MIND

11

Jewish Intelligence

We now come to the question which most readers of this book will probably consider the central issue in a study dealing with the Jewish mind. Is it true, as persistent rumor has it, that the Jews are more intelligent than the Gentiles? And if so, why?

In trying to answer these questions we must proceed step by step. First, then, what about the rumor? Superior Jewish intelligence is part of the Jewish self-stereotype. No person knowing Yiddish (and until one or two generations ago most Ashkenazi Jews knew Yiddish) can be unaware of the two expressions: *Yiddisher kop* (lit. "Jewish head"), meaning cleverness, and its opposite, *Goyisher kop* ("Gentile head"), denoting stupidity. Cleverness, or intelligence, takes an honored place among the qualities Jews like to attribute to themselves. The same rumor is mooted by Gentiles as well. Those of them who are free of the taint of anti-Semitism simply refer to it as a fact, without any emotional overtones, unless it be a twinge of envy or a note of grudging admiration. The anti-Semite will find it possible to speak of Jewish intelligence only in terms of negative connotations such as shrewdness, sharpness, craftiness, cunning, slyness, and the like. He will see in these traits examples of the many Jewish features which are blameworthy and thus justify his Judeophobia. Characteristically, however, even the fiercest enemies of the Jews, including the Nazis, have never alleged that the Jews were stupid or obtuse. All people who know Jews, whatever their reaction to them otherwise, subscribe to the rumor of their intelligence.

1. What Is Intelligence?

Before proceeding any further and presenting the data bearing on Jewish intelligence as compared to that of Gentiles, two technical issues have to be cleared out of the way. First, what is intelligence? And second, what is the I.Q.?

Most of us have some notion as to what intelligence is, or at least, as to who among our acquaintances is intelligent and who is not. Some people strike us as being "intelligent," others as dull. While in many cases the impression we get of the presence or absence of intelligence in an individual is strong, it is at the same time also vague. Were one to ask the proverbial "intelligent" reader to define intelligence, one would, in all probability, get nothing more than a series of synonyms, such as "cleverness," "smartness," "understanding," "comprehension," "mental alertness," "keenness of discernment," and the like. (For a full list of such terms consult Roget's *Thesaurus*, in which it takes up no less than three columns.) While each of these terms denotes concepts or traits which undoubtedly have something to do with intelligence, they do not satisfy the experts' requirement of precision and, above all, comprehensiveness.

The first scholar to study those mental functions whose sum total was considered to comprise intelligence was the French psychologist and pioneer psychometrist Alfred Binet. Binet first suggested in 1895 that the general mental ability of individuals could be tested by administering a series of tests of memory, mental imagery, imagination, attentiveness, mechanical and verbal comprehension, suggestibility, aesthetic appreciation, moral sensibility, the capacity to sustain muscular effort, and visual judgment of distance. The story of how Binet devised his tests, how they were revised by him, his collaborators, and successors, and how they were supplemented by an increasingly voluminous battery of tests which were applied to millions of persons is a fascinating one but has no direct bearing on our subject, and therefore we must desist from recounting it. What is of more immediate interest for us is that, in the course of the three-quarters of a century that have elapsed since Binet's seminal work, new and clearer understandings have emerged as to what intelligence is and what the factors are which determine its level as far as can be ascertained by tests.

At present it is agreed by most experts that intelligence consists of a group of distinct but interconnected mental qualities which vary from individual to individual. Opinions vary as to the number and identity of these separate mental qualities, and the ways and degrees of their interconnectedness. A few examples will illustrate both the differences and the consensus as to what intelligence consists of.

Barely a decade after Binet, Charles Spearman distinguished between two factors involved in intelligence: (1) a general factor (designated as g); and (2) specific factors (s), which come into play in certain types of mental activity.[1] In 1931, L. L. Thurstone argued that intelligence is comprised of several independent abilities, which he termed Primary Mental Abilities (PMA) and for whose measurement he devised the method of multiple factor analysis. The PMA consist of spatial visualization, perceptual ability, verbal comprehension, numerical ability, memory, word fluency, and inductive and deductive reasoning. He also found certain correlations among the PMA, noting, for instance, that verbal comprehension often went together with word fluency.[2]

A much more complex "structure of intellect" theory was put forward by J. P. Guilford,[3] while Sidney Cohen suggested that, in functional terms, intelligence can be reduced to three different skills which are:

(1) The ability to pay attention or concentrate;

(2) The ability to form a permanent memory trace—in the form of changed RNA molecules or in the form of protein manufactured under the direction of RNA; and

(3) The ability to develop a retrieval system by which the memory is scanned and focused.[4]

Without committing himself to discerning the precise component factors comprised in intelligence, David Wechsler, who devised two of the most widely used intelligence scales, defined intelligence as the "aggregate or global capacity of the individual to act purposefully, to think rationally, and to deal effectively with his environment."[5]

Before leaving the subject, it will be useful to add that, according to many experts, intelligence itself is so elusive that only its reflection as mirrored in intelligence tests can be seen as a reality. This was expressed as early as 1923 by Edwin Boring of Harvard when he said: "Intelligence as a measurable capacity must at the start be defined as the capacity to do well in an intelligence test. Intelligence is what the tests test."[6] The same view was echoed almost half a century later from across the Atlantic by P. E. Vernon, who wrote that intelligence tests "measure the average efficiency with which testees cope with the kinds of problems the tester chooses to include."[7]

Clearly, the definition of intelligence is far from being a simple thing. Nevertheless, this brief discussion should give us a better understanding of what is meant by it and enable us to proceed to the question of how intelligence can be measured and on what basis one can compare the intelligence of the average Jew and the average Gentile. The instrument which has been developed for such measurement is the I.Q. test.

2. What Is the I.Q.?

Psychologists in general agree that tests can be devised to measure intelligence—or at least certain aspects of it. In fact, a large number of tests have been developed to measure this or that aspect of intelligence. However, the results these tests yield differ from the results of the usual measurements with which we are familiar. If we want to measure the weight of a person, we have him stand on the scale. His weight as given by the scale is an absolute figure, which has nothing to do with the weight of other people in his society. An intelligence test does nothing of the kind. All it tells is how far below or above the average (or mean) of his society a given individual stands in mental ability. In other words, the result is not an absolute figure (as is the weight shown by a scale) but a relative one. This position, relative to the average, is called the Intelligence Quotient, or I.Q. for short.

On the basis of mass testings it has been found that the intelligence of children increases with age up to about eighteen years; accordingly, tests containing increasingly difficult items have been devised for each year level. If a child does as well on the test devised for his age level as does the average child of the same age, he scores 100, and his "mental age" is considered to equal his chronological age. If his test score equals that of the average score of a higher age group, he is considered advanced beyond his age, which is expressed in a score higher than 100, and vice versa. Thus the I.Q. of children, and subjects up to about eighteen years of age, is obtained by dividing the mental age by the chronological age and multiplying the result by 100 (to eliminate decimals):

$$\frac{\text{Mental Age (M.A.)}}{\text{Chronological Age (C.A.)}} \times 100 = \text{I.Q.}$$

For example, if an eight-year-old child is found to do as well as an average ten-year-old, then his mental age is ten and his I.Q. is $\frac{10}{8} \times 100 = 125$. On the other hand, if a ten-year-old child has the mental age of an eight-year-old, then his I.Q. is $\frac{8}{10} \times 100 = 80$.

Tests have shown that, while a child's I.Q. *can* undergo considerable changes, in the majority of cases the I.Q. does not change much after five years of age. The correlation between the I.Q. of a person at the age of seven and his I.Q. at any time thereafter until the age of senescence is .8 or better, which in simple terms means after the age of seven the I.Q. changes very little if at all. The individual's relative standing in intellectual capacity among his peers will remain practically the same throughout his life. This indicates one of the important features of the I.Q.: because of its stability, it has great predictive value. That is, the I.Q. score of a seven-year-old predicts, with a high degree of reliability, how the child will perform in school in the years to come. The same is true for college entrance tests, whose value as predictors, states the president of the Educational Testing Service at Princeton, "is no longer a subject of legitimate dispute. The studies have been widespread, they number in the thousands, and the results are consistent." [8]

When it comes to adults, such as college students, the I.Q. no longer measures how far below or above his own age group a given individual

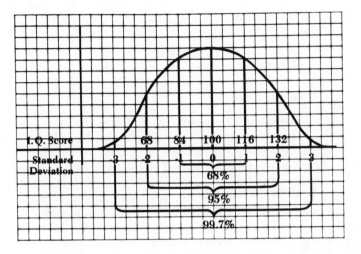

FIGURE 1. Graphic Representation of the I.Q. Frequency Distribution in a Normal Population

stands in mental ability, but his relative standing among all other adults irrespective of age. Thus, if an adult takes an I.Q. test and scores 100, his score equals that of the average of all adults; half of the population for which the test was standardized has a score lower than his, and the other half higher. If he scores 84, this means that only 16 percent of the same population had a score lower than his, while 84 percent scored higher. On the other hand, if he scores 116, then 84 percent of the population had a score lower than his, and only 16 percent a higher one.[9]

A simple visual device to show the distribution of persons with various I.Q.'s in a given society is a graph in which the horizontal coordinate shows the I.Q. and the vertical the numbers of persons in percentages. The normal distribution of the I.Q. in the population produces the typical bell-shaped curve, known as the normal distribution curve, shown in Figure 1. A glance at the figure reveals that the great majority of persons have an I.Q. of 84 to 116; on the revised Stanford-Binet Test, 68 percent of the population have I.Q.'s falling between these figures, and 95 percent between 68 and 132. This means that there are only 5 percent whose I.Q. is either lower than 68 or higher than 132.[10]

When group tests are administered for the purpose of comparing the I.Q. of one group (whether expressed as the mean or shown in a distribution curve) with that of another, a basic problem arises. Such a comparison can be meaningful only if one can make sure that the differences shown between the scores of the two groups are, in fact, due to differences in intelligence alone, and not to differences in other factors which can influence test performance.

We shall consider this problem after we have had a chance to acquaint our-selves with some of the results yielded by comparing the I.Q. scores of Jews and Gentiles.

3. The Findings

The results of numerous intelligence tests comparing Jewish and Gentile subjects have been collated in *The Myth of the Jewish Race*. It was found that the cumulative evidence of these tests shows that "Jewish groups, when compared with similar non-Jewish groups, score higher on tests measuring general intelligence and especially verbal intelligence." [11] Only a few com-ments need be added to this conclusion, which has been confirmed by addi-tional studies carried out too late to be taken into consideration. [12]

The Lesser, *et al.*, study of 1965 [13] requires some critical comment. The subjects of this study were groups of eighty first-grade children aged six years and two months through seven years and five months, from four cul-tural groups: Chinese, Jewish, Negro, and Puerto Rican. Each group was subdivided into forty middle-class and forty lower-class children. In each group and sub-group the number of boys and girls was equal. Although this study suffers from the absence of a white non-Jewish group which would have placed it in the proper perspective against the general American back-ground, its findings are valuable in themselves. Four tests were adminis-tered: a verbal ability, a reasoning, a number facility, and a space concep-tualization test. It should be noted that the reasoning test consisted of visual tasks: picture analysis, picture arrangement, and jump peg tests. The nu-merical and space tests were also based entirely on pictures, while the verbal test was based partly on pictures. Thus the visual element played an impor-tant role in each of the four tests. The statistically most significant differences found were those in verbal ability, in which the Jewish children scored sig-nificantly higher (90.4) than the Negro (74.3) and Chinese (71.4) children, who, in turn, scored significantly higher than the Puerto Ricans (61.9). In the other three tests the Chinese and the Jews were very close to one another, and both were significantly higher than the Puerto Ricans and Negroes who were also very close to one another (see Table I).

However, the value of these test results as indications of the mental abili-ties of the four ethnic groups as a whole is diminished by the composition of the groups tested: one-half of the testees from each ethnic group belonged to the middle class and half to the lower class. In each of the four ethnic groups, the middle-class children scored higher on all tests than the lower-class children, which in itself is an eloquent testimony to the influence of en-vironment, as against heredity, on the test scores. Since most of the Jews in the United States belong to the middle class, while most of the American

TABLE I. *Mean Test Scores of 80 Children (40 Middle-Class and 40 Lower-Class) from Each of Four Ethnic Groups*

ETHNIC GROUP	MENTAL ABILITIES			
	VERBAL	REASONING	NUMERICAL	SPATIAL
Jews	90.4	25.2	28.5	39.8
Chinese	71.4	25.9	28.1	42.7
Negro	74.3	20.4	18.4	34.4
Puerto Rican	61.9	18.9	19.1	35.1

TABLE II. *Mean Test Scores of 40 Middle-Class Children from Each of Four Ethnic Groups*

ETHNIC GROUP	MENTAL ABILITIES			
	VERBAL	REASONING	NUMERICAL	SPATIAL
Jews	96.7	28.8	33.4	44.6
Chinese	76.8	27.7	30.0	44.9
Negro	85.7	26.0	24.7	41.8
Puerto Rican	69.6	21.8	22.6	37.4

Source: Both tables are based on Gerald S. Lesser, Gordon Fifer and Donald H. Clark, *Mental Abilities of Children from Different Social-Class and Cultural Groups,* Monographs of the Society for Research in Child Development, University of Chicago Press, no. 102, 1965, Vol. 30(4): 54–58.

Negroes and Puerto Ricans, and probably also the Chinese, belong to the lower class, the test results tell us little about the mean mental abilities of all children from each of the four ethnic groups. What it does validly indicate is the relative mental ability of the middle-class children from the four ethnic groups separately, and of the lower-class children of the same four groups separately. It remains for the reader to interpret the data in the light of his knowledge of the class structure of each of the four groups. One must conclude that the mean score of *all* Jewish children is much closer to the mean of the forty middle-class Jewish children tested than to the mean calculated from the test results of the forty middle-class plus forty lower-class Jewish children (see Table II).

One additional point in this test requires comment. In each of the three non-Jewish groups and in each of the four tests (with some statistically insig-

nificant exceptions), boys scored higher than girls. In the Jewish group, on
the contrary, the girls scored higher than the boys.

These findings were partly corroborated and partly supplemented by the
results of a large-scale study of 2,295 twelfth-grade students of upper-middle-
and lower-middle-class background. Since this study, carried out by
Margaret E. Backman and reported in 1971, included 1,236 Jewish, 488
Negro, 150 Oriental students, as well as 1,051 non-Jewish whites, it is one of
the few studies which fulfill the requirement stated above. The findings were
that the pattern of mental abilities of the Jewish students tested was distinguished by high mean scores on verbal knowledge and mathematics, and low
mean scores on visual reasoning and memory. In other mental ability factors—English language and perceptual speed and accuracy—little difference
was noted between the scores of the Jews and the non-Jews. "Verbal knowledge," it should be noted, is a general factor but primarily a measure of general information (see Table III).[14]

A review of data such as these led Christopher Jencks, the noted Harvard
sociologist and a strong "environmentalist" (the meaning of this term is discussed below), to conclude, "Jewish children . . . do better on I.Q. tests
than Christians at the same socio-economic level."[15] As for adults, Carl
Senna, another convinced environmentalist, states, "As a group . . . Jews
have (so far as we can determine) always had a higher average I.Q. as compared to Christians."[16]

4. What Goes into the I.Q.?

In the course of the many decades during which I.Q. tests have been administered to thousands of subjects and their meaning discussed, a general
consensus has developed that the scores achieved by a testee depend on his
heredity, as influenced by the environment in which he has lived until the
moment of taking the test. In fact, the finding that the intelligence of every
individual is determined by a combination or interaction of his biological
(i.e., genetically inherited) potential and his experiences or training, including such factors as prenatal or intrauterine influences, the sum of which is referred to as "environment," has become a commonplace in human genetics,
psychology, and psychometrics and is considered axiomatic in standard
texts.[17]

However, this overall agreement cannot mask the continuing sharp differences between the "hereditarians" and the "environmentalists." These
designations, to be sure, are misleading. No hereditarian denies that the
I.Q. is influenced by the environment, and similarly no environmentalist denies that the I.Q. is influenced by heredity. The difference between the two
schools lies in the relative weight they give to the two factors. The heredi-

TABLE III. *Test Scores of Twelfth-Grade Students of Upper-Middle and Lower-Middle-SES from Four Ethnic Groups*

GROUP	MENTAL ABILITIES					
	VKN [1]	ENG [2]	MAT [3]	VIS [4]	PSA [5]	MEM [6]
Jews	57.1	50.8	58.6	46.0	51.0	47.8
Non-Jewish Whites	51.9	51.1	52.1	51.8	49.5	50.9
Negroes	46.0	47.5	47.3	45.1	50.9	50.4
Orientals	49.0	52.5	59.1	49.4	50.3	51.6

[1] VKN—Verbal Knowledge—a general factor, but primarily a measure of general information.

[2] ENG—English Language—grammar and language usage.

[3] MAT—Mathematics—high school mathematics with a minimum of computation.

[4] VIS—Visual Reasoning—reasoning with spatial forms.

[5] PSA—Perceptual Speed and Accuracy—visual-motor coordination under speeded conditions.

[6] MEM—Memory—short-term recall of verbal symbols.

Source: Margaret E. Backman, "Patterns of Mental Abilities of Adolescent Males and Females from Different Ethnic and Socioeconomic Backgrounds," in *Proceedings, 79th Annual Convention, APA,* 1971, pp. 511–12.

tarians attribute up to 85 percent of the I.Q. variance to heredity, and as little as 15 percent to the environment. The environmentalists, on the other hand, deny that heredity plays such an overwhelming role and allocate a much higher share to environmental influences, although they do not generally commit themselves to precise or even approximate percentages.[18] A balanced position is taken by Theodosius Dobzhansky (1900–1975), the distinguished geneticist, who states:

> Researchers have securely established that *individual* differences in I.Q. scores are genetically as well as environmentally conditioned. The evidence comes from more than 50 independent studies in eight countries. But how much of this variation is due to genetics, or heritability, as scientists call it, is unknown.

He goes on to explain that "genes *determine* the intelligence (or stature or weight) of a person only in his particular environment. The trait that actually develops is *conditioned* by the interplay of the genes with the environment." [19] Despite recent attempts at debunking the I.Q. in general,[20] this summary remains a valid judgment of the factors that go into the I.Q.

5. *What Is the Meaning of Group Differences in the I.Q.?*

We are now ready to tackle the question of the meaning of frequently reported differences in mean I.Q. scores between one racial or ethnic group,
or class, and another. The most frequently studied of these differences is the
one between blacks and whites in the United States, which amounts to 10 to
20 points. For instance, tests administered to almost two thousand randomly
selected white children yielded a mean I.Q. of 101.8, while a similar number
of black children in the Southeastern United States had a mean score of 80.7,
or a deficit of 21.1 points. For blacks in the Northern states, the differences
would be half of this value, i.e., about 10 points.[21] The hereditarian explanation of such racial differences in I.Q. is that, as stated above, up to 85 percent of it is due to heredity. The environmentalist objection to this position
is based on the argument that, as far as different racial groups are concerned,
no meaningful comparison can be made between their I.Q. scores. This is for
the simple reason that all I.Q. tests are "culture-bound," that is, they pre-
suppose familiarity with a definite culture, which in the case of the American
I.Q. tests is the culture of the white middle class in the United States. Testees who have a good grounding in knowledge, skills, and abilities which are
derived from and developed in an average white middle-class home and
school do well on the tests. The black testees are not as thoroughly at home
in this culture as white testees, and therefore it is this circumstance, and not
a genetic "deficit" in intelligence, which is reflected in the 10- to 20-point
difference in the mean scores. The very fact that black children in the North
of the United State score 10 points higher than black children in the Southeast, they say, proves their point. Their position is that the differences in the
mean I.Q. test scores are due primarily not to heredity, but to class, or
socio-economic status (SES).

With this issue in mind, numerous tests have been carried out in Europe
and the United States probing the question of the relationship of the I.Q.
and social class or status. The results have confirmed and reconfirmed what
had been known since the time of Binet, that "children from 'high' or 'favorable' socioeconomic backgrounds tend to secure higher scores on the usual
intelligence tests (both individual and group) than do children from lower or
less favorable socioeconomic backgrounds."[22] The cultural differences between the environment of the middle-class child and that of the lower- or
working-class child have been studied and analyzed, and it was found that
the home and family life as well as the neighborhood and community life are
more varied, enriched, and stimulating in the case of the middle-class child
than in that of the lower-class child; that the middle-class attitude toward education is more positive than that of the lower class; and that the school itself, with its rewards and punishments, is more in keeping with the values
the middle-class home inculcates into the children than with those of the

lower class. All these factors together explain much of the differences in the
I.Q. scores between middle- and lower-class children.[23]

To illustrate the issue involved by at least one concrete example, let me
mention that in the 1960 revision of the Stanford-Binet Test, given to children under the age of six, two of the three questions ask the child to indicate
the difference between "a slipper and a boot" and "wood and glass." To what
extent these questions are culture-bound becomes evident if one considers
that children in, say, a traditional Indian village have never seen slippers,
boots, or glass, and therefore cannot but be stymied by these two questions.
It is certainly impossible to draw any conclusion as to the I.Q. of such a child
from its inability to answer them.

Such environmentalist arguments are countered by the hereditarians, who
point to I.Q. studies in which all the background variables were carefully
equalized, and in which the differences in mean I.Q. scores between races
and ethnic groups, while somewhat reduced, remained nevertheless significant. Beyond this point the argument on both sides becomes too technical to
summarize here, and all that can be said is that it is still far from settled.
Dobzhansky, an unquestionably objective geneticist, admits that "researchers have found a consistent 10 to 20 point disparity in average I.Q.
scores between blacks and whites in the U.S.," but he cautions that since
"nobody, not even racists, can deny that living conditions and educational
opportunities are disparate in races and classes," he "remains unconvinced"
as to the existence of a "strong genetic component" in these score differences
between blacks and whites. Moreover, he warns that what the differences in
I.Q. between whites and blacks mean is simply a matter of a higher
frequency or percentage of individuals with a higher I.Q. in one group than
in the other; the fact remains that "an individual's potentialities are determined by his own genetic endowment, not by his class or race." [24]

In this connection it is useful to show how I.Q. differences between two
hypothetical groups can be plotted on a coordinate system and thereby made
apparent at a glance. In Figure 2, which represents two such hypothetical
populations, the average I.Q. of Population I (solid line), when measured by
any one of the usual statistical methods (mean, median, or mode), is lower
than that of Population II (broken line). At the same time the overlap between the two curves shows that, despite the marked difference between the
two populations, Population I comprises a certain number of individuals
whose I.Q. equals, or is higher than, the I.Q. of a certain number of individuals in Population II.

To sum up, it has been found that intelligence is the sum total of mental
abilities which can be measured by tests; that the I.Q. test scores give no
absolute measure of intelligence but merely the relative standing of a child
or youth in relation to his age group or of an adult in relation to the average
of the population of which he is a member; that the I.Q. is a function of the

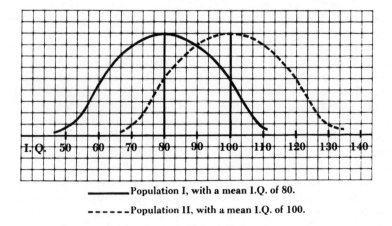

_____ Population I, with a mean I.Q. of 80.

- - - - - - Population II, with a mean I.Q. of 100.

FIGURE 2. Comparison Between Two Hypothetical Populations

combined effect (or interaction) of heredity and environment; and that we are still far from scholarly consensus as to the extent to which differences in mean I.Q. scores between racial and other culturally disparate groups such as classes reflect environmental (or cultural) and genetic (i.e., racial) differences, respectively. Mindful of these findings and considerations, we are now equipped to approach the question of differences in intelligence between Jews and Gentiles. We shall begin by focusing on the differences in the frequency of exposure to nutritional and sociogenic brain damage between Gentile and Jewish children.

6. Brain Damage: Nutritional and Sociogenic

Recent research has shown that the environment can influence not only the functioning but the very structure of the brain. The functional effect of malnutrition—a most important environmental influence in the prenatal and early postnatal phase of development—has been found to be intellectual retardation and behavioral disorders in children. The addition of nutritional supplements to the otherwise deficient diets of pregnant women was found to raise the I.Q. of their children significantly at the ages of two, three, and four years compared with children whose mothers had not received the nutrients. Experiments on animals have shown that in early infancy malnutrition or undernourishment causes retardation of brain growth, as well as a deficiency in the level of brain DNA (which is presumably a measure of brain cell number), and that neither of these deficits can be made up subsequently even by the richest diet.[25] On the basis of the extensive literature on the subject, Ashley Montagu could claim that the damaging effects of such mal-nutrition "constitute one of the best-supported findings of contemporary social biology." [26]

Further corroborating evidence was presented in November 1975 at the annual meeting of the Society for Neuroscience in New York City on the basis of large-scale studies carried out in various parts of the United States. One of the most striking findings was that the average deficit in brain weight among four-year-old malnourished children (whose normal average brain weight is 1,400 grams) was 125 grams, or about 9 percent. Although in a nor-mal population there is no correlation between brain weight and in-telligence, this deficit in malnourished children is so great that the chances that it represents a normal variation were held to be less than one in a million. It was estimated at the meeting that more than 1 million infants and young children in the United States in 1975 either have suffered brain dam-age due to malnutrition or are faced with the risk of such damage. [27] At a symposium of the International Brain Research Organization held in New Delhi in October 1974, it was reported that "nearly 60% of all pregnant women living below poverty in the United States are evidently consuming calories at such a low level that brain development in their unborn children will likely be deficient." [28]

For the world at large it has been estimated that 350 million children run the risk of brain damage as a result of protein starvation, which affects the developing countries most, but from which the poor in the industrial socie-ties also suffer. [29] The problem is compounded by the transgenerational effect of brain damage due to malnutrition. It has been established that mal-nourished female animals, such as rats, if allowed to produce offspring, pass on their brain weight deficit and their lowered DNA to the next generation. The behavioral effect is similarly passed on to the next generation.

The relevance of these findings for our subject is as follows. Ever since an-tiquity, the specter of hunger has accompanied man on his painful road through history; over and over again, catastrophic outbreaks of famine deci-mated the population in this or that area. Even when there was no acute famine, the majority of the people, who were always and everywhere poor, had an inadequate diet. The request in the Lord's Prayer, "Give us this day our daily bread," [30] which has its antecedents in the Hebrew Bible in the Book of Proverbs, "Feed me with mine allotted bread," [31] readily sprang from hungry lips ever since Christianity dominated the Western World.

The Jews, prior to the Emancipation, were certainly not better off in this respect than the Christians or the Muslims among whom they lived. But they had as one of their most important religious commandments the *mitzva* of charity, of helping the poor, and, in the first place, of feeding the hungry. The great anonymous prophet of consolation whose words form the last chapters of the Book of Isaiah expressed most poignantly what the prophets who preceded him had also taught—the true fast which is acceptable to the Lord is "to deal thy bread to the hungry." [32]

Jewish historians have often pointed out that the practice of charity, and most of all the feeding of the hungry poor, was such a fundamental religious duty for the Jews that no Jew, not even a penniless stranger passing through a village which had as few as one or two Jewish families, was ever allowed to go hungry. Without wishing to idealize the relationship between the few well-to-do Jews in a locality and the many poor ones, it was always considered a prime duty of the rich to keep hunger away from the poor. Nor do I wish to imply that malnutrition or undernourishment did not exist among the Jews, but its ravages were mitigated by the unquestioned observance of the supreme Jewish duty of charity, because, as all Jews were constantly reminded, "charity delivereth from death." [33] Thus, if malnutrition did cause brain damage among the Jews, it probably did so to a lesser degree than among the Gentiles.

To this must be added the great Jewish concern and sensitivity for all physical debility (a subject which is dealt with elsewhere in this book). This expressed itself also in the very special consideration given to pregnant women—both physical and magical means were employed to the fullest possible extent to secure their well-being. Part of these ministrations was to provide them with the kind of food they desired and to insist that they eat well. In poor families this often meant that the husband and older children had to go hungry so that more food should be available for the expectant mother. While this reduced the likelihood of antenatal brain damage, early postnatal brain damage was likewise minimized by the mother's great solicitude for the infant and small child, expressed above all in her insistence that he eat, eat, and eat! If the child cried, it meant that he was hungry and was given to eat—this has remained the typical attitude of the Jewish mother down to the present day. The combined result of these features was that brain damage caused by malnutrition was probably less frequent and less severe among Jews than among Gentiles.

Even more recent than the concern of anthropologists and geneticists with brain damage caused by physical malnutrition is their attention to "sociogenic brain damage," that is, the damage which can be inflicted on the developing brain of the infant and young child by social malnutrition, an impoverished social environment, and inadequate stimulation. We must leave aside the many difficult methodological problems involved in moving from inadequate stimulation (which is observable in poor socio-economic conditions) to inadequacies in the "behavior syndrome" which comprises deficits in behavior, intelligence, learning, and motivation (subject to observer interpretation), and thence to brain damage (which cannot be directly observed but only inferred from behavior). [34] Confining ourselves to the purely functional level, there can be no doubt that the amount and kind of stimulation the infant and child receives is a factor in the development of his or her intelligence, learning capacity, and motivation. The cause and effect relationship between early stimulation and score level on I.Q. tests has been convincingly demonstrated and often commented upon.[35]

On this count, too, Jewish tradition, which dominated Jewish life everywhere until the Enlightenment and in a modified form has continued to influence it subsequently, gave the Jews an advantage over their Gentile neighbors. It has often been pointed out—more than once in this book itself—that learning was upheld by Jewish tradition as a supreme value. In most places Jewish children at the tender age of three or four were sent into school, the *Ḥeder*, where they began to be taught the Hebrew alphabet. But long before that, in fact from the very moment of its birth, the child, and especially the boy, was surrounded by an atmosphere of great attention, even appreciation. Children were considered a blessing, a source of joy and pride for the parents. A couple with children was said to be "blessed with children"; childlessness was considered a shame and an affliction. If a couple had no children within ten years of their marriage, they were supposed to divorce. Children were much petted and pampered, and a great deal of affection and care was lavished on them. Especially during the first months of the infant's life, it was constantly surrounded with warmth and attention. At first it slept with the mother, then in a cradle or swinging crib near her bed. If the baby woke up and cried, it was picked up, carried about, and crooned to. All its wants were attended to by the mother and the frequent female visitors, but the father would also play with it. The baby was carried about a great deal, so that it got used to constant attention, rocking, swaying, singsong. The mother used to talk to the baby constantly, sing to it, pet it, address it with endearments; the father, too, would sing to it and talk to it in baby language. If the baby started crying, it was immediately attended to, given the mother's breast, fussed over, cuddled, and comforted. If the child learned to speak before it was weaned, it was taught to say the "before-meal blessing" before taking the breast.[36] Thus from its second year on, the stimulation of the infant was gradually transformed into teaching. The child's development, both physical and mental, would be watched eagerly and every sign of precocity observed with great satisfaction, commented upon with praise, and encouraged. As soon as the child could walk, the father would pay more attention to him and sometimes let him sit in his lap to "study" the Talmud with him. Before long, the boy-child would be sent to the *Ḥeder* where he was expected, and forced, to study eight or nine hours a day.

This brief sketch of the amount and kind of attention the Jewish child got in the first few years of its life gives an idea of the nature and intensity of stimulation to which it was exposed. Most importantly, there was no layer or sector in the Jewish community so poor that it could not provide its children with this type of attention. It was the rule to which there were no exceptions. On this basis one may generalize and say that throughout the long centuries of the Jewish Diaspora, not only has sociogenic brain damage not occurred among the Jews, but they have enjoyed an exceptional measure of sociogenic brain stimulation. The home environment in which the Jewish child was (and still is) exposed to this extraordinary stimulation requires a brief examination.

7. The Jewish Home Environment

In order to appreciate the role of the Jewish home in the intellectual development of children, a word has to be said about the importance which modern psychology attaches to the home environment in general in the individual's mental development. Studies carried out in recent years have produced a consensus among psychologists that the home environment, in which the child spends the first years of his or her life, is a more important factor than the school in influencing its intellectual development. The most significant variables in the home environment which affect the child's intellectual performance have been summarized by Benjamin Bloom. Among them are the parents' intellectual aspirations for the child, the parental reinforcements of different types of intellectual performance by the child, the opportunities for learning provided both inside and outside the home, the value placed by parents upon the child's intellectual performance, and work habits emphasized in the home.[37] In a word, the crucial factor is the parents' intellectual orientation, which indelibly impresses itself upon the mind of the child and determines to a great extent the direction of his intellectual development.

Whatever studies have been made comparing the average Gentile and the average Jewish home with respect to the factors listed have all yielded one typical result: the quality of the home environment maintained by the Jewish family differs from that in the Gentile family even if both belong to the same socio-economic stratum. Hence, Jewish and Gentile children of the same socio-economic background, and educated in the same school, can still score different means on I.Q. tests and have different scholastic achievements, not because of any differentiating genetic factor but because of differences in the home environment. As for the nature of these differences, they can be summed up in one brief statement: The Jewish home, more than the Gentile home, is a place in which learning is highly valued. This single factor underlies all the other differences.

The valuation of learning above all other achievements is, as we have seen, an age-old Jewish trait. For centuries, learning meant nothing but Talmudic-halakhic study, which was the magic key to material and psychological well-being in This World and to unsurpassed rewards in the Other. With

Enlightenment modern disciplines came to be substituted for the traditional religio-legal curriculum, but this in no way affected the value of learning as such. The same pride which a Jewish mother of the eighteenth or nineteenth century felt when she thought or spoke of her son the great Talmudic luminary filled the heart of her granddaughter in the twentieth when she could refer to "Mein Sohn der Doktor." In practice this translated into the higher intellectual aspirations which the Jewish parents had (and still have) for their children than the Gentile parents.

In the modern world, the road to intellectual achievement led through the gates of academic professions. This was almost intuitively grasped by the millions of East European Jewish immigrants who arrived in America until the introduction of quotas in 1924. They came with nothing but Yiddish as their language, with a rudimentary Jewish and almost no secular education, and with no skills to speak of, so that they were forced by the thousands into sweatshops. But they came also with an irrepressible urge for education— unachievable for themselves, since the seventy-hour work week squeezed the last drop of strength out of them—but possible, desirable, and, indeed, an absolute must, for their children. The rise from the lower into the middle class via intensive application to study was a phenomenally rapid one, accomplished from one generation to the next. It could be achieved because even the poorest home of the most ruthlessly exploited sweatshop worker was a place permeated by the age-old Jewish emphasis on learning, often the last vestige of a formerly all-pervasive tradition of *Yiddishkayt* (Jewishness), and because both father and mother did everything they could to enable their children to study, to stimulate them to study, and, if necessary, to drive them, push them, force them to study.

The same environment surrounds the Jewish child to this day in the parental home. As the parents have risen on the socio-economic ladder, the physical environment they can create for their children has improved, and the means they employ to motivate them to study have changed, becoming more refined. But their intention remains the same. From the earliest age the infant and child is surrounded by the latest and presumably best educational toys, and no effort is spared to create for him the most stimulating surroundings. The parents play with him, fondle him, talk to him, and reward all manifestations of intellectual ability they can discern in him. The typical Jewish child knows the alphabet and can even read long before he enters school, and he usually keeps well ahead of the national average in his mastery of the three R's. Unwittingly he internalizes the parental expectations and, to the enormous satisfaction of his parents, begins, while still in the lower grades of the elementary school, to indicate an inclination toward this or that academic profession. Needless to say, the parents will do everything possible to send their child to one of the best schools, to supplement the school curriculum with private tutoring, and to create in the home the best of circumstances conducive to doing all homework in the most satisfactory manner.

Beyond all this, most Jewish homes have magazines and books around, as well as a set of an illustrated encyclopedia, so that the child becomes early habituated to reading out of interest and for his own pleasure. Thus, even if the theoretical genetic component of the mean I.Q. of Jewish children differed but little or not at all from that of Gentile children from the same socioeconomic background, by the time they reach the age of seven (after which the I.Q. has been found to change very little) their mean I.Q. scores would tend to be higher than those of the Gentile children, because of the differences in the home environment.

8. Hereditary Factors

So far, the environmental factors in the development of Jewish intelligence have been stressed. I emphasized the relatively smaller amount of nutritional and the absence of sociogenic brain damage in the case of the average Jewish child, and the role of the home environment in transmitting and inculcating intellectual interests, a devotion to learning, and preference for academic careers. But such factors are purely environmental ones, which means that they must be present in each generation in order to affect it, and that, if they are eliminated, the very next generation will no longer manifest those intellectual features which resulted from them and which characterized its ancestry for hundreds of years. In fact, something like this has recently begun to appear on the American scene among children who are growing up in thoroughly assimilated Jewish homes from which the traditional Jewish push toward intellectual achievement is absent. Teachers are now encountering some Jewish students—for the time being, relatively few—who are beset by the same problems in mastering the arts of reading and writing as a proportion of Gentile students, and whose I.Q. test results depress the Jewish mean and bring it closer to the national average.

In addition to such environmental influences, however, there is the distinct possibility that genetic factors have also been at work in the development of Jewish intelligence. It has been argued that conditions in the often hostile Gentile environment in which the Jews have lived for two thousand years were such as to favor the survival of the most intelligent among them. As the German anthropologist Hans F. K. Günther (whose anti-Semitism, incidentally, enabled him to prosper under the Nazi régime) put it in 1930:

> Life as a "guest people" among "host peoples," the "typical parasitism" . . . must have pushed selection among the Jews of all African and European areas in one and the same direction: only for those Jews was it possible to leave

behind a larger number of offspring who were able to adapt to the specific conditions of life among foreign peoples, who possessed those talents of empathy
into a foreign psychology, prudent demeanor, adroit speech, versatile calculation of all conditions of the environment which made it possible to thrive
among other races often inclined to utter rejection.

Among the mental traits necessary for thriving in these circumstances,
Günther enumerates "a special measure of intelligence," and in particular,
those talents "required in a predominantly urban environment and in trading
with merchandise and in money transactions." These selective pressures
seem to explain "the considerable average intelligence which distinguishes
the Jewish people." [38]

There can be no doubt that the Jews were subject to severe economic restrictions, had to put up with humiliations, were frequently attacked by
mobs and victimized by potentates, periodically expelled from cities and
whole countries, captured and held to ransom, and exposed to untold other
hardships and perils. Other things being equal, those who were mentally
better equipped to weather all this had a better chance, not only to survive
but to have children, secure *their* survival, and thus perpetuate their genes.
In the course of generations, these circumstances brought about a gradual
shift in the balance between those of higher and those of lower intelligence;
the mean intelligence of the Jewish community tended to increase. If such a
process actually did take place—and it seems reasonable to assume that it
did—then it was an environmentally induced genetic development, akin to
the Darwinian survival of the fittest, and its effects would persist even after
the conditions whose pressure had brought it about in the first place had
disappeared. As Maller put it as early as 1931, "It is reasonable to assume
. . . that the trials and ordeals of the Jews throughout the centuries placing
a premium on mental acumen in the struggle for survival operated as selective factors in raising the average intelligence of the Jews as a group." [39]

Other students of Jewish intelligence, thinking along similar lines, have
suggested that the immense value attributed by the Jews to Talmudic learning contributed indirectly but, in the course of centuries, cumulatively to the
development of Jewish intelligence. Their argument, briefly, is as follows.
Until the Enlightenment, the Jews considered Talmudic scholarship the
greatest of all achievements. The appreciation of this scholarship was inculcated into the children to such an extent that, generally speaking, all the
boys who had the mental capacity endeavored to achieve—and many actually
did achieve—scholarly status. The most distinguished among the many
budding scholars obtained coveted positions as rabbis of Jewish communities
or as heads of yeshivot (Talmudic academies). Wealthy Jews sought out the
promising young rabbinical scholars to be their sons-in-law. A rich man's
daughter, on her part, considered it a great distinction to be chosen as the

bride of such a young luminary. Thus excellence in Talmudic study (which this argument considers a mark of high intelligence) enabled a young man to attain a better economic situation, marry earlier, have more children, give them better care, and thereby save more of them from infant and child mortality than other young men. This course, which was followed for many centuries, resulted in an increase in the percentage of the most intelligent element among the Jews, which statistically meant a higher mean intelligence among the Jews than among the Gentiles.[40]

This argument has recently been combined with the contention that among the Gentiles, contrariwise, the most intelligent had the least chance to produce offspring. Throughout the Middle Ages, the greatest, fastest, and, indeed, nearly the only advancement possible for the intelligent sons of the lowly born was offered by an ecclesiastic career. The priesthood attracted the most ambitious and talented sons of the lower estates and the most intellectual ones from the others. Since priestly celibacy was the rule, this meant that the most intelligent portion of the population had no offspring (or had only a few illegitimate children), and this inverse selection, in the course of the centuries, lowered the average intelligence level of the Gentile populations.[41] Among the scholars who subscribe to this hypothesis of a Jewish genetic selection for intelligence are Norbert Wiener, J. B. S. Haldane, and Lewis S. Feuer.[42]

The trouble with this hypothesis, as with many others of a similar nature, is that no historical data are available which could substantiate it. All one can say, based on a general knowledge of Jewish history, is that it looks sound, and that it is quite probable that such a historic process of Jewish genetic selection for intelligence (as measured by excellence in Talmudic studies) actually did take place, although of course the people involved remained unaware of it. And if so, then it was an added factor in the modification of the Jewish gene pool in the direction of higher intelligence; added, that is, to the effect of persecution which also favored the survival of those mentally better endowed. So we have these two environmentally induced genetic factors, over and above the effect of the environment on each new generation, which jointly can be considered responsible for the superior Jewish scores on I.Q. tests.

9. Intra-Jewish Differences

So far in this chapter I have discussed the differences between the Jews and the Gentiles in mentality and intelligence and the factors which make for these differences. Because attention was focused on this subject, I treated and presented the Jews as if they were one single human group characterized by one single set of mental traits. But now that we have established that such differences indeed exist and manifest themselves in the generally higher mean I.Q. scores achieved by Jews, it is time to have a closer look at the intelligence of the various Jewish ethnic groups which make up the totality of the Jewish people, and at the variance found among them.

The fact is that, as a result of two thousand years of Diaspora life, considerable physical and intellectual disparities have developed among the Jews dispersed in the far corners of the earth. As far as the physical differences are concerned, these are due, in the main, to interbreeding between Jews and Gentiles in every place in which Jews have settled and lived. This is why many Russian Jews looked (and their descendants still look) like Russians, German Jews like Germans, Yemenite Jews like Yemenites, Persian Jews like Persians, and so on. And this is why, beneath such phenotypical similarities, striking similarities are found to exist also genetically between the Jews and the Gentiles—especially in countries where the Jews have lived for many generations. [43]

A like phenomenon can be observed also in the Jewish psychology, except that here the issues involved are much more complex. Physical similarities, after all, are primarily the function of the genes and, to put it in the simplest terms, depend on the proportion of the genes members of a given Jewish group received from their Jewish and Gentile biological ancestors respectively. No such simplification is possible when considering mental traits. First of all, the mind is the product, in addition to heredity, of the environment. Thus, whatever the proportion of the Jewish to the Gentile genes in the genetic makeup of the individual, the functioning of his mind reflects the combined effect of the inherited genetic potential and of the environmental influences through which it was realized. Secondly, the environment itself is complex: it contains a Jewish and a Gentile component, with the proportion between the two varying from place to place and from time to time. So far we already have four independent variables which are always present and which can affect the mind of the individual Jews in varying proportions. To them must be added the fact that the influence of the Gentile environment on the Jewish mind can result in imitation or opposition, or else in a combination of, or alternation between, these two reactions. For instance, the Moroccan Jews were influenced by the bellicose behavior of the Moroccan Muslims directly, which produced in them a similar stance; while the Yemenite Jews, faced with a rather similar Yemenite Muslim pugnacity, developed a reaction of self-effacing humility.

The common feature characterizing the Moroccan Jews and the Yemenite Jews, as well as the Jews in every other locality, is a definite interrelationship between their mentality and that of the Gentile group around them. Each of the great historic encounters between Jews and Gentiles discussed earlier in this book can serve as an example to substantiate this general observation. It can be observed, for instance, that when there was a flowering in the culture of the Gentile environment, it was paralleled by an efflorescence in Jewish cultural activity. Decline in the former was accompanied by decline in the latter, unless special circumstances were at work—for example, the arrival of a Jewish contingent from a high-culture environment in a place of low culture, with a resulting transplantation of cultural attitudes from the first place to the second.

The process of global Jewish dispersion, which began in antiquity, reached its peak just before and during World War II. After the end of the war, with the establishment of the State of Israel, this process began to be reversed. An "ingathering of the Exiles" was set in motion, and several Jewish ethnic groups or communities were transplanted, either totally or nearly so, to the land of their fathers. As a result of this great movement of return, as well as of the Nazi holocaust and some other factors, the Jewish people has undergone a vast demographic transformation in the last forty years. Except for Soviet Russia, in no East and Central European country has a sizable Jewish community remained. In France, half of the Jewish contingent consists of North Africans. Most of the centuries-old Jewish communities of the Middle East—of Afghanistan, Iran, Bukhara, Turkey, Yemen, Iraq, Syria, Lebanon, Egypt, Libya, Tunisia, Algeria, and Morocco—have been ingathered in Israel, where their numbers, stationary for many centuries, have begun rapidly to increase. Today (1976) the so-called Oriental Jews make up about 60 percent of the Jewish population of the Jewish State.

Because of this ingathering of the Exiles, Israel is the obvious place to study the cultural and psychological differences among various Jewish ethnic groups. Many studies have, in fact, been carried out, and their findings throw light on the variance exhibited by the Jewish mind as a result of influences absorbed from the Gentile environment in the countries of the Diaspora. Some Israeli studies discuss the psychology of one or another ethnic group, such as that of the Moroccans, the Yemenites, the Polish, or the German Jews; most of them, however, concentrate on differences between two overall categories: Jews born in Europe and America and their Israeli-born offspring on the one hand, and those born in Asia and Africa and their Israeli-born offspring on the other. This procedure is influenced by the Israeli statistical office, which consistently uses these two categories in its numerous demographic studies of the population of Israel. While methodologically one can fault this dichotomy, which disregards the considerable differences that exist within the Asian-African and also within the European-American group, the findings are nevertheless instructive.

Before presenting some of them, however, a general outline of the differences in socio-economic status (SES) between the European-American and the Asian-African Jews in Israel must be sketched. The latter all come from Muslim countries, whose population was and still is generally characterized by low literacy, low educational level, low income level, low housing standards, high incidence of poverty and disease, high fertility and high mortality, patriarchal rule, subordinated position of women, fatalistic religious outlook, strong familism and factional loyalties, strong traditionalism, emphasis on honor, and a vacillation between outbursts of temper and quiet resignation.[44] The Jews who had lived for a thousand years in this Middle Eastern Muslim environment, even though in many cases relatively isolated in their separate quarters, were greatly influenced by these cultural traits. They arrived in Israel with a psychological profile similar in many respects to that of the Muslim majority. In the modern Israeli environment, this meant that the Middle Eastern Jews (or, as they are usually referred to, Oriental Jews) came to occupy in general socio-economically low positions. They concentrated in unskilled and low-paying occupations, lived in slums or at least inferior sections of the towns, did not do as well in school as the European-American Jews (the Ashkenazim), went on but rarely to higher education, and continued to have many children, most of whom now survived thanks to the superior medical and health services available in Israel. In the first ten years or so after the arrival of the Oriental Jews in Israel, until about 1960, the attitude of the Ashkenazim to this group was largely negative, which caused resentment among them and led to increasingly vocal demands for improvements in their socio-economic status.

Up to this point there is a certain similarity between the situation of the Oriental Jews in Israel and that of the blacks in America; but there were also special circumstances as a result of which the Jews' position has improved more rapidly than has that of the blacks. There has never been any official discrimination in Israel against the Oriental Jews, nor any ideology advocating their segregation in residence or schooling. The intermarriage rate between the Ashkenazim and the Oriental Jews has been high—it reached around 15 percent of all Jewish marriages in 1965 and has continued to increase since. The efforts at equalizing their SES have been much more energetic. Nevertheless, for the time being, the effects of the disparate ethnic-cultural backgrounds and SES persist and are reflected in psychological tests.

One of the early studies which show the approximation of Ashkenazi standards by Oriental Jews was carried out and reported in 1953 by Dr. Gina Ortar. Various intelligence tests were administered to three groups of children aged six to sixteen: one Ashkenazi group, one Oriental group consisting of children of old immigrants to Israel, and one group of children of new Oriental Jewish immigrants. Comparison was made among those children of these three groups whose general level of intelligence was identical. The Ashkenazi children were found superior in command of language, the Oriental children in command of numbers. Abstract thinking ability was weaker in the new immigrant Oriental children than in the other two groups, but the children of Oriental Jewish old-timers in Israel were found equal in this respect to the Ashkenazi children. Among the Ashkenazi children, who were of a higher socio-cultural background, there was a greater percentage of talented children than among the Orientals, whose socio-cultural background was lower.[45]

The findings of this study remained typical for the many that followed. In each, the poorer showing of the Orientals was found to be paralleled by a poorer showing of subjects from a lower SES. Since, however, most Oriental subjects are of a lower SES, it is difficult to separate the two factors—ethnic background and socio-economic status—as to their causative function in influencing test performance.

This was borne out by a large-scale study again directed by Gina Ortar and reported in 1967. Tests administered to all elementary school graduates (who numbered c. 44,000 at the time) showed that the two main environmental factors affecting pupils' achievements were the father's country of birth and his level of education, which are closely related to ethnic background and SES respectively. It was found that pupils whose fathers were born in Europe did better than those whose fathers were born in the Middle East; but within each of these two groups, those whose fathers had had a higher education did better than those whose fathers had had a low level of education. Since most of the Middle Eastern fathers had had only low education, the ethnic and educational factors reinforced each other in creating differences between the achievement levels of children from European and Middle Eastern backgrounds.[46]

Several years later, a study of fifty-eight ethnically varied three-year-old children in Israel showed that high family density and low maternal schooling, either alone or in interaction, related to poor motor performance for the boys. Also, significant differences were found between boys and girls.[47] In early childhood, not ethnicity but family size and the parents' educational level were found to be the significant variables on which the patterns of intellectual stimulation depended. This was brought out in a study of Israeli children aged twenty-eight to thirty-four months.[48] Of course, it so happens that large numbers of children and low parental educational level are both usually found in Middle Eastern Jewish families, while the opposite is true for European Jewish families. Hence the precise formulation of the findings is that ethnicity influences intellectual stimulation, motor performance, and mental ability in general, through the intermediacy of parental educational level and family size.

Another Israeli study of ethnic and class differences as factors influencing mental ability had 357 first-grade boys and girls as its subjects. The children were divided into four groups: Western lower class, Western middle class, Middle Eastern lower class, and Middle Eastern middle class. They were given the task of grouping objects into rational classes. The children of lower-class background were less able to employ the most abstract grouping style and to achieve the required conceptual breadth than their middle-class peers. Also, children of Middle Eastern background gave fewer descriptive responses, the style most commonly employed by all children, and failed to cope with the requirements of grouping as well as did the children of Western background. Girls emerged superior to boys on all measures.[49] The researchers' conclusion was:

> Lower-class membership adversely affected the child's ability to successfully encompass all the objects under one class label, although he tried to meet the demands of the task. Membership in the Middle Eastern group, on the other hand, adversely affected the child's ability to deal with the fundamental requirement of grouping per se.[50]

In yet another Israeli study 320 first-graders born in Israel of immigrant parents from Europe and the Middle East (Iraq, North Africa, Yemen) were tested. Each group was divided into middle and lower class. It was found that the social class factor had an impact upon the levels of scores in verbal, reasoning, numerical, and space mental abilities. Similarly, the cultural background (i.e., ethnicity) influenced both the levels and the patterns of scores. That is to say, these findings confirm that both ethnic (cultural) background and SES have a bearing upon mental abilities as reflected in test score levels.[51]

Dina Feitelson has for many years studied the problems in learning reading encountered by lower-class children in Israel whose parents had immigrated to Israel from Middle Eastern countries. Her own work and a survey of studies of similar phenomena in other countries—especially in the large urban centers of the United States—led her to the conclusion that there is a typical, culturally deprived lower-class home environment which impedes the child's learning ability. Such a home lacks certain types of manipulative play and work materials usually provided to preschool children of middle-class families, such as crayons, paper, scissors, paste, play dough, etc. The absence of these prevents the child from developing deftness and coordination in the use of his hands. Also, the home in which the culturally disadvantaged child spends his early years lacks construction toys and the various form boards and puzzles which among middle-class children help to develop a series of skills essential to the successful acquisition of reading. Thirdly, the culturally disadvantaged child has much less language experience, a poorer command of his mother tongue, and a smaller vocabulary than the middle-class child, who is exposed to an "elaborate " language code.

Additional differences between the middle-class and the culturally disadvantaged child are: the latter, in general, is unable to defer gratification, has a short attention span and a poor ability to concentrate, all of which hamper successful involvement with a prolonged learning task such as reading. He is unable to deal with the sense of failure which develops as soon as he becomes aware that his progress lags behind that of others. Once the child starts going to school, the home environment of the culturally retarded continues to be a hindrance in that he does not receive the requisite help from his parents, siblings, or relatives.[52] While children of Oriental Jewish immigrants in Israel had in most cases such a culturally deprived home environment, the opposite has been true, both in Israel and all over the world, for the Ashkenazi Jews, whose major concern has been to provide their children with as stimulating a home environment as possible.

These differences in the home environment significantly influence achievement in both school and later life. Israeli studies have shown that Jewish children of Middle Eastern background evidence lower levels of academic achievement and are less represented in institutions of higher learning than their peers from Western backgrounds, and that among adults Middle Eastern Jews are less represented in executive managerial positions and occupy lower positions in the civil service than Jews of Western backgrounds.[53] Such differences in achievement seem to be related to differences in perceptual articulation. A more articulated perception is characterized by a tendency to perceive figures as clearly distinguished from their background, an ability to impose structure on relatively unstructured perceptual fields, and the experience of oneself as possessing an identity distinctly independent of one's social environment. These traits bear on achievement: "the ability to analyze and organize the perceptual field appears to be essential to the successful execution of complex social tasks. . . . Thus perceptual articulation may account, in part at least, for the intersubgroups differences in social task achievement,"[54] noted in Israel between Jews of Western and Middle Eastern background.

Studies done outside Israel have shown that people from cultural or ethnic groups which foster individual autonomy show more articulated perceptual functions than do people from societies that stress conformity and dependence on authority—such as may be found in tradition-oriented groups.[55] The typical Middle Eastern Jewish family in Israel, in contrast to the Western family, is more tradition-oriented, with an authoritarian, patriarchal structure that tends to foster subordination to authority and the restriction of emotional autonomy.[56] Such a lack of autonomy in childhood correlates with a lack of articulation in perceptual functioning. On the other hand, it was found that individuals reared in a kibbutz, which strives to cultivate emotional autonomy and self-reliance, had a higher level of perceptual articulation than non-kibbutz subjects of Western origin. The I.Q.'s were equal in every paired group compared (104–110 I.Q. for the Middle Eastern–Western comparison and a mean I.Q. of 114 for the kibbutz–non-kibbutz comparison). A positive correlation was found between measures of perceptual articulation and level of achievement on a series of psychological tests. As the authors conclude,

The relationship found . . . between level of perceptual articulation and task achievement on the one hand, and between perceptual articulation and group membership on the other . . . points to perceptual articulation as a possible intervening variable which could contribute to the relationship between group membership and level of task performance.[57]

Kibbutz versus non-kibbutz differences are a favorite subject of Israeli psychometrics. One study carried out among Israeli soldiers who entered their compulsory training and service period in the Israeli Defense Forces from 1961 to 1964 concentrated on the differences between subjects born and bred in a kibbutz (about 4 percent of the total) and others. It was found that the kibbutz-soldiers were markedly superior to the others in intelligence as measured by both verbal and non-verbal tests; superior in education, in knowledge of Hebrew, and in personal qualities which were assumed to influence their chances of success in the army. They were also found to be superior to the others in their qualification for command tasks, and a much higher percentage of them actually achieved commanding positions in the army. The author concludes that kibbutz education and the communal way of life must be partially responsible for these differences.[58] Incidentally, kibbutz children, despite their common upbringing, were found to exhibit considerable individuality and variability.[59]

Summing up the results of the Israeli studies, the findings show that:

1. The Oriental Jews differ from the Ashkenazi Jews in that they achieve, in general, lower scores on I.Q. tests, have a lower level of perceptual articulation, a poorer motor performance, a lower achievement level in school, a lower command of language but a better command of numbers, and achieve fewer executive and managerial positions and lower civil service positions.

2. These differences are explained by Israeli social psychologists as being the outcome of the culturally deprived home environment in which most Oriental Jews grow up, of the greater density in the home (larger number of children and more persons per room), of the lower parental education level, and of the authoritarian, patriarchal character of the Oriental Jewish family. (We note in parentheses that no Israeli scholar attributes the differences to "racial" factors.)

3. The early childhood environment as the major factor in Oriental-Ashkenazi differences in intelligence is confirmed by differences found between kibbutz-bred and non-kibbutz-bred subjects. The culturally enriched environment provided by the kibbutz for its children, the cultivation of emotional autonomy and self-reliance, all produce individuals who have a higher level of perceptual articulation than Ashkenazi non-kibbutz subjects and are superior to the latter in intelligence and qualifications for leadership.

All of which boils down to a clear-cut sequence. The culture of the non-Jewish environment impresses itself upon the culture of each Jewish community. A combination of Jewish cultural tradition and Gentile cultural influence determines the way the Jewish family is structured and functions, including such features as the educational level of the parents, the extent of parental authoritarianism, the number of children, the cultural stimuli provided the children, and the life-goals inculcated into them. These factors, in turn, influence the intellectual development of the children.

Thus "Jewish intelligence" is a catchword which has little concrete meaning unless one defines quite stringently the identity of the Jewish group with whose intelligence one is concerned. Intra-Jewish differences, which can be considerable, vitiate any general pronouncement about "Jewish intelligence." Likewise, Jewish-Gentile comparisons must be handled with the utmost caution. Since the Jews are everywhere a highly urbanized, middle-class group, comparisons are meaningful only between Jews and urban middle-class Gentiles in one and the same country or geographical area. And if such comparisons show differences between the two, these must be attributed to the formative power of the specific Jewish historical experience and cultural tradition, which even today, two centuries after the Enlightenment, sets the Jews apart from the Gentiles.

12

Giftedness and Genius

The preceding chapter discussed, for the most part, the statistically ascertainable differences between the mean I.Q. of Jews and Gentiles, as well as between the I.Q. of European (Ashkenazi) and Middle Eastern (Oriental) Jews. Its findings, and especially the consistently higher Jewish than Gentile scores on tests measuring verbal intelligence, laid the foundation for proceeding now to an analysis of the special phenomenon of giftedness among the Jews, and of that rarest of all mental configurations which deserves the designation of genius.[1]

A note of caution must be sounded before we open our investigations. Giftedness stands at the upper limits of that dimension of mental function which can be tested and measured. Or, to be more precise, certain types of giftedness still fall within the measurable range while others do not. By administering the Stanford-Binet Test to some 160,000 pupils in grades 1 through 9 in California, the famous Terman study found that 1,444, or less than 1 in 100 (0.925 percent), scored an I.Q. of 135 to 200 (with a mean of 151). Subjects with such high I.Q.'s were considered by Terman, and are generally considered, to be gifted. Giftedness, in this context, is a general finding; it means that the subjects did extremely well on the tests, and that they were expected to do very well in school and in adult life. This expectation was, indeed, borne out in follow-up studies carried out in the course of forty years after the original study.[2] The tests did not show in what specific area one child (and, later, one adult) was more gifted than the other. If two of the original subjects became, say, painters, the tests did not, because they could not, show which of the two was "greater" or more gifted. That is to say, even when dealing with mere giftedness, the I.Q. tests are limited as instruments of measurement.

When it comes to genius, we are faced with a phenomenon which is totally beyond the ken of psychological testing. The achievement or performance of a genius cannot be reduced to quantitative expression. The dividing line between "very gifted" and "genius" is a matter of subjective judgment; it cannot be drawn between two numerical values. As Otto Klineberg put it, "There is no simple criterion by which we can recognize the man of genius." [3] Nevertheless, there is in most cases a practically unanimous consensus as to who is a genius and who merely a talent, even if a great one. All agree that Rembrandt was a genius, Ingres a talent; Mozart a genius, Ravel a talent; Proust a genius, Zola a talent. Talents can be compared albeit with difficulty; geniuses cannot. Each genius is a phenomenon *sui generis*. It is therefore futile to ask who was a greater genius, Michelangelo or Leonardo, Bach or Beethoven, Shakespeare or Goethe.

This being the case, when speaking of Jewish talent as compared to Gentile talent we shall be able to base our conclusions on some statistical data, which we shall have to supplement with subjective judgment. When, however, we consider geniuses, everything said about them will of necessity be devoid of all statistical basis, will be of a subjective nature, and will, in the best case, reflect the consensus of critical opinion.

1. Medieval Scholarship

Thanks to George Sarton, we are in a position to give a rough estimate of the proportion of Jewish participation in scientific advancement in the Middle Ages. In his monumental five-volume *Introduction to the History of Science*,[4] Sarton surveyed the development of the major sciences from Homer and the Biblical Hebrews to the end of the fourteenth century. The subjects he covers include translations, education, philosophic and cultural background, mathematics, physics, technology, music, chemistry, geography, natural history, medicine, historiography, law, sociology, and philology. The cultures surveyed for the Middle Ages are, in the main, those of China, Japan, India, the Muslim-Arab world, the Jews, and Christian Europe. Because of the vast amount of material dealt with, Sarton divides it into half centuries, beginning with the first half of the fourth century B.C.E. and closing with the second half of the fourteenth C.E.

In several of the parts dealing with the Middle Ages (which take up the bulk of his opus), Sarton not only surveys the scientific and intellectual progress of the period covered but also presents a comparison between the achievements of various groups, or cultures. These comparisons are most instructive, despite the omission of any reference to the relative numerical strength of the populations whose scientific achievements are compared. We learn from them what was the absolute number of outstanding scientists among, say, the Japanese and the Hindus in a given fifty-year-period but are given no indication as to their proportion relative to the total number of the populations. This shortcoming notwithstanding, Sarton's comparisons can serve as a basis for an attempt to evaluate numerically the intellectual achievements of the Jews in the Middle Ages.

Sarton's comparative figures start with the 1150–1200 period. In that half century he found five Japanese scientists, fourteen Chinese, six Hindu, one Iranian, forty-three Muslim, two Samaritan, twenty-five Jewish, and eighty Christian. For the first half of the thirteenth century, the figures are as follows: Japanese 4, Chinese 14, Hindus 3, Muslims 42, Samaritans 2, Jews 23, Christians 96; and in the second half: Japanese 6, Chinese 23, Indians 5, Muslims 41, Samaritans 1, Jews 47, Christians 143.[5] Regrettably, these comparative summaries are not continued by Sarton in the two volumes which deal with the fourteenth century.

All in all, in the 150 years from 1150 to 1300, Sarton found 626 outstanding scientists in the whole world; of these 95 were Jews (and 5 Samaritans). The 95 Jewish scientists make a little more than 15 percent of the total. The numerical proportion of the Jews to the total population of the countries in which there was scientific work in the period in question—Japan, China, India, the Muslim countries, and Christian Europe—is almost impossible even to estimate. The total number of the Jews at the time was about 1.5 million. But what was the number of the total population of the countries listed? We can only guess: perhaps 300 million. If so, the Jews constituted one-half of 1 percent of the general population. This would give an estimate of thirty times as many Jewish scientists as would be expected on the basis of the proportion of Jews in the countries in which scientific work was pursued.

A more realistic idea of the Jewish participation in science will be obtained if we omit those countries in which no Jews lived at the time—that is, Japan, China, and India. Considering only those parts of the world in which Jews did live, we find that they produced 546 great scientists, of whom 95 were Jews (and 5 Samaritans). That is, about 17.6 percent of these scientists were Jewish (or 18.3 percent if the Samaritans are added to the number of Jewish scientists). The total population of the Muslim and Christian world in which all the Jews lived at the time can be estimated at 150 million. This gives 1 percent for the Jews in the general population, and about eighteen times as many Jewish scientists as would be expected on that basis.

This remarkable record becomes even more striking if one considers individual countries. In Spain, from 1150 to 1300, there were 35 Jewish, 30 Muslim, and 20 Christian scientists. In France, from 1200 to 1300, there were 47 Christian and 16 Jewish scientists. In Germany and Central Europe, from 1250 to 1300, 11 Christian and 3 Jewish scientists. In Egypt and Syria in the same fifty years, 13 Muslim, 4 Jewish, 1 Samaritan, 3 Arabic Christian, and 3 Syriac Christian scientists.[6] In order to appreciate the significance of these figures, it has to be pointed out that in each of the countries mentioned the Jews constituted a very small percentage of the total population, and that, consequently, the number of Jewish men of science is many times higher than expected. In Spain, in 1300, of an estimated total population of 5,500,000, the Jews numbered 150,000, or 2.7 percent; yet 41.2 percent of all the preeminent scientists were Jewish. In France, of the total population of circa 14 million, not more than about 100,000, or 0.715 percent were Jews; but of all scientists, 25.4 percent were Jewish. In Germany and Central Europe, in a total population of about 12 million, only about 100,000 were Jews, or 0.83 percent; while of all scientists, 21.4 percent were Jews.[7] Because of lack of estimates for Egypt and Syria no corresponding calculations can be made.

The later Middle Ages and the modern period until the Enlightenment were a time of deep troubles for most Jewish communities, in which Jewish talent was submerged almost everywhere. The only centers of Jewish intellectual activity were Spain until the 1492 expulsion, Italy from the fifteenth through the seventeenth centuries, Safed in the sixteenth century, and Holland in the seventeenth. In other places and times, Jewish scholarly work was confined to "the four cubits of the *Halakha.*" With the Enlightenment all this suddenly changed.

2. *Post-Enlightenment Upsurge and Reaction*

In the wake of the Enlightenment, and even before they attained full Emancipation, a rapidly increasing number of Jews in Central and Western Europe made use of their newly won half-freedom to break out of the confines of traditional Jewish occupations and to penetrate the innermost recesses of Gentile national, economic, scholarly, literary, artistic, and cultural life. The suddenness with which Jews began to appear and make a mark in numerous such areas, of whose very existence their fathers had in most cases no idea at all, is nothing short of astounding. It seemed as if a huge reservoir of Jewish talent, hitherto dammed up behind the wall of Talmudic learning, were suddenly released to spill over into all fields of Gentile cultural activity. In England, France, Germany, Austria, and Hungary, within a few years after they were first allowed to sit on the benches of general secular schools, Jews were found among the leaders of industry, of literature and journalism, of music and the performing arts, of all fields of the sciences, and even in painting and sculpture, two areas from which they had been most strictly debarred by their own religious tradition. To substantiate this general statement by examples would necessitate an interminable list of names with *Who's Who*-like biographical sketches, and an evaluation of the work of the persons so identified within the perspective of their chosen fields of activity. This, frankly, appears an unattractive task, and so, instead of undertaking it, I refer the interested reader to the three or four most competent books which deal with "the Jewish contribution to civilization," and in which the sudden abundance of names after 1800 indicates the magnitude of this Jewish breakthrough.[8]

There is, however, one domain whose rapid penetration by Jews testifies not only to their having developed within a few decades the talent, acumen, and ability to hold their own among the best of the Gentile minds, but also to the trust the Gentiles placed in the commitment of their new Jewish fellow citizens to the well-being of the state and in their loyalty to the great causes and overriding interests of the country as a whole. I refer, of course, to politics which, because of this added consideration, differs qualitatively from, say, painting, music, journalism, or industry, and in which, therefore, one would have expected a slower, more gradual opening of doors before the Jews. After all, their fathers or grandfathers were still considered members not of the German, French, or whatever nation but of the "Jewish nation," a foreign element, even if they were not new immigrants from another country. But the fact is that the very children of those "foreign" Jews who themselves had spent most of their lives in pre-Emancipation thralldom did attain political positions ranking up to the highest and did so in numbers far above the proportion of the Jews in the general population. To mention only one very small but important category of political office, that of cabinet minister, from the mid-nineteenth century on Jews were found in it first in Western, then in Central, and finally even in Eastern Europe. In France, within sixty years of the Emancipation, there were three Jewish members of the cabinet, two of whom, Michel Goudchaux and Achille Fould, were ministers of finance, and the third, Adolphe Crémieux, minister of justice. Within the ensuing century, sixteen more French Jews served as cabinet members, two of them as prime ministers. In England, in addition to the baptized Disraeli, ten professing Jews served as cabinet members until 1970. In Italy with its very small Jewish community (less than one-tenth of 1 percent of the total population), there was one Jewish prime minister and six Jewish ministers from the 1890's on, one of them under Mussolini. Jews attained cabinet membership also in Australia, Austria, Germany, Holland, Hungary, the United States, and even in Communist Russia (where their title was commissar). If we add baptized Jews, the list increases considerably. No more eloquent testimony could be found to the total identification of an upwardly mobile Jewish intellectual sector with the interests, ideas, aims, and ethos of the general society in the Western countries, and, in particular, with the political trends which vied for leadership and governmental control in them.

By the second half of the nineteenth century, Jewish preeminence in most fields of intellectual activity as well as in politics, industry, and finance was so apparent that it contributed to the emergence of a new theme in anti-Semitic literature—the myth of Jewish domination. The anti-Semites accused the Jews of every conceivable political misdeed, including treason and spying for the ubiquitous enemy beyond the borders. One of the favorite variants of this theme was the Jewish domination of the country, secretly but nonetheless effectively, in politics, in economy, and later in the arts and literature, which domination was always presented as a national bane and as the fountainhead of every national or sectional ill.

The underlying premise in all these accusations was the tacit assumption that the Jews were mentally equipped to best the Gentiles; in other words, that they were intellectually superior. Only this assumption can explain how even the most prejudiced anti-Semite could come to believe that the Jews in his country who constituted a minute fraction of the total population were able to obtain and maintain a stranglehold over the political, economic, and intellectual life of the entire nation. The more the anti-Semite believed in the Jewish domination and exploitation of his country, the more he subscribed—subconsciously—to the tenet of Jewish intellectual superiority. One will, of course, search in vain for an open acknowledgment of Jewish preeminence in anti-Semitic literature. The anti-Semite's intention is to bury the Jew, not to praise him. But quite often, the ostensibly and crudely negative features with which the portrait of the Jew is painted mask a grudging admission of his intellectual superiority. A statement by the French arch-anti-Semite Édouard Drumont can serve as an example. In his *La France Juive*, published in 1886, Drumont wrote, "The Semite [read: the Jew] is mercenary, greedy, scheming, clever, cunning; the Aryan [read: the Frenchman] is enthusiastic, heroic, chivalrous, unselfish, frank, trusting to the point of naivety." [9] One does not have to be a psychologist to read between the lines: the three adjectives which refer to mental capacity (as against special mental traits such as mercenariness and greed), "scheming, clever, and cunning," describe manifestations of intelligence; while "naivety" is a transparent euphemism for the lack of it. What Drumont is saying, once the emotionally laden expressions are peeled away, is that the Jews are more intelligent than the French.

Also before the end of the nineteenth century appeared the most famous and infamous anti-Semitic tract, *The Protocols of the Elders of Zion*. This forgery, concocted by an unknown author in Paris working for the Russian secret police, the Okhrana, was based on earlier French anti-Semitic writings. It purported to contain the records of a secret conference held by leaders of world Jewry, and to demonstrate that the Jews held the whole world in their grip, controlling and exploiting it with their secret international organization, their money, and their ruthless cunning. After being circulated privately and put into the hands of the czar, the *Protocols* was first published in Russian in 1905, and from 1919 on was translated into many languages. In the United States it was sponsored, until 1927, by Henry Ford. [10] Arabic translations were issued in several Arab states and President Nasser of Egypt, in one of his more ebullient moments, publicly vouched for their authenticity. A new Spanish edition of the *Protocols* was published in 1975 in Argentina. As in Drumont's portraiture of the Jew, so in the *Protocols*, the underlying premise is that the Jews possess the superior brain power to carry out their schemes of global domination.

Lagging behind the anti-Semitic writings were objective scholarly studies either devoted in their entirety to the phenomenon of Jewish intellectual preeminence or incidentally throwing light on it. Of the latter, one of the most significant is the large-scale longitudinal study of giftedness, referred to in the opening paragraph of this chapter, which was carried out from the early 1920's under the direction of Lewis M. Terman, and to which we turn next.

3. The Terman Study

In 1921–22, Terman and his associates canvassed closed to 160,000 pupils in grades 1 through 9 in the schools of Los Angeles, San Francisco, and Oakland and, using several methods, located among them those who were the "most intelligent." The group thus selected consisted of 1,444 subjects, i.e., less than 1 percent of the total, with I.Q.'s (Stanford-Binet) ranging from 135 to 200 (with a mean of 151). At the time, the Jewish population of the three cities was estimated at 5 percent of the total. Yet "the proportion of Jewish blood" in the group selected by Terman was 10.5 percent, or about twice that expected. In reporting these findings, Terman remarked that the actual percentage was probably greater than this since there was reason to believe that the fact of Jewish descent had in some cases been concealed.[11] In a follow-up study, carried out by Terman and Oden twenty-five years later on the same group of subjects, it was again stated that there were twice as many Jews in the gifted group as would be expected on the basis of their percentage in the general population.[12] In a special chapter in this follow-up study, entitled "Subjects of Jewish Descent," it was pointed out that the 10.36 percent (or, counting the deceased, 10.41 percent) Jews in the group comprised only those whose parents were both of Jewish descent but excluded all those who were reported having a non-Jewish parent or grandparent.[13]

There were minor differences between the Jewish and the non-Jewish subjects. The childhood I.Q. showed a mean of 1.2 higher for Jewish than for non-Jewish boys, and of 9 *lower* for Jewish than for non-Jewish girls. On the Concept Mastery test (data for fifty-six Jewish men and forty-five Jewish women in 1940), the Jewish men averaged 5.3 points higher than the non-Jewish; the Jewish women almost equaled the non-Jewish. These differences were considered "not reliable," and the authors add that "any significant difference in achievement of Jewish and non-Jewish subjects will therefore have to be accounted for by non-intellectual factors." As to occupational status and income, 57.5 percent of the Jewish men were in Census Group I, which included the professions, as against 43.9 percent of the non-Jewish men. On the other hand, in Groups III to VI combined there were 15.0 percent Jewish men as against 30.6 percent for non-Jewish—a highly reliable difference (CR = 3.59). In 1940, the monthly income of the employed Jewish men averaged nearly 25 percent above that reported by non-Jewish men. In civilian employment in 1944, the income of Jewish men rose to approximately 42 percent above that of the non-Jewish men. [14]

In addition to these objective data, "three judges, working independently, examined the records of 730 gifted men who were 25 years old or older, and rated each on life success. The criterion of 'success' was the extent to which a subject had made use of his superior intellectual ability." [15] On this basis the men were classified into three groups, the top 20 percent, the middle 60 percent, and the lowest 20 percent. Among the most successful 150 men, designated as the "A" group, the Jewish element was considerably greater than in the gifted group as a whole; it was three times as high in this top group as in the lowest group, designated the "C" group. The authors stress that this finding was in line with the fact that "the educational tradition was stronger in the families" of the A group than in those of the C group. [16]

Significant in this connection is the fact that in childhood,

during the elementary school years, the A's and C's were almost equally successful. Their average grades were about the same, and the average scores on the achievement tests were only a trifle higher for the A group. In high school the groups began to draw apart as a result of lower grades in the C group, but it was not until college that the slump of this group assumed alarming proportions. The slump cannot be blamed upon extracurricular activities, for these were almost twice as common among the A's as among the C's. Nor can much of it be attributed to intellectual deterioration. Although the intelligence survey of both 1922 and 1940 averaged higher for the A's than for the C's, the difference was not great. [17]

This leaves the family background as the operative factor. "More than three times as many A fathers than C fathers had graduated from college, and a similar difference was found between the siblings of the A's and C's. More than twice as many fathers of the A's were in the professional classes." [18] These differences point strongly to the importance of the family background in influencing how much use subjects made of their superior intellectual ability.

There were several additional significant differences between the A's and the C's. The A's had better mental health, as indicated by assessing symptoms of nervousness and emotional instability; they displayed leadership qualities far more often; they had a higher marriage rate, a 50 percent lower rate of divorce, and the score on the marital happiness of their wives was significantly higher. More than half of the A wives were college graduates, as against only one-quarter of the C wives. The A wives were reliably superior on the Concept Mastery test. In job achievement and occupational interest the A's were superior to the C's. In Perseverance, Self-confidence, Integration, and Absence of Inferiority Feelings, the A's were rated far higher than the C's by themselves, their wives, and their parents. The field workers rated the A's much higher than the C's in Appearance, Attractiveness, Alertness, Poise, Attentiveness, Curiosity, Originality, and to a somewhat lesser degree in Speech and Friendliness. [19]

The findings of this study are quite remarkable testimony to the role played by Jewish educational and intellectual tradition in enabling children to attain high "life success" by realizing to the fullest their intellectual abilities. It is this cultural tradition, and certainly not any innate "racial" difference between Jews and Gentiles, which explains why even among the most gifted top 1 percent of the 160,000 California children encompassed by the Terman study, the Jewish children outnumbered (relatively) and outperformed the others. As the authors remarked, "Jewish subjects in the gifted group differ very little from the non-Jewish in ability, character, and personality traits, as measured either by tests or by ratings, but . . . they display somewhat stronger drive to achieve, form more stable marriages, and are a little less conservative in their political and social attitudes." [20]

These general observations can only be properly understood and evaluated if we keep in mind that the Jewish children constituted more than twice as high a percentage in the gifted group as did the Jews as a whole in the total population of cities canvassed for the Terman study. So, while the gifted Jews as a group differed very little from the gifted non-Jews as a group, the incidence of giftedness in children among the Jews was at least twice as high as among the non-Jews. In trying to explain this higher incidence of giftedness, as well as the higher percentage of Jews among the most successful 150 men within the group as a whole, we must first of all quote the authors themselves, who came to the conclusion that "the typically gifted child is the product of superior parentage, superior not only in cultural and educational background, but apparently also in heredity. As a result of the combined influence of heredity and environment, such children are superior physically to the average child of the general population." [21]

Applying this general observation to the disproportionately high representation of Jews in the gifted group, we are led back to what we found in the preceding chapter. Leaving aside physical traits, which do not concern us here, the Terman study confirms our finding that both the higher mean I.Q.

of the Jews and the higher percentage of gifted individuals among them must be attributed to the combined effect of environment and environmentally induced selectivity.

4. Early Views of Jewish Preeminence

Many authors have gone on record with observations and comments on Jewish intelligence and on the preeminence of Jews in numerous fields of intellectual endeavor. In general, modern Jewish authors dealing with the subject have shown considerable restraint, as if apprehensive lest they be reproached for a pro-Jewish bias. Cecil Roth's statement in the Preface to his book *The Jewish Contribution to Civilization* is typical in this respect:

> The Jew is distinguished, perhaps, by a slightly greater degree of intellectualization, possibly by a freshness of outlook, natural in one whose approach tends to be external; and, in consequence, by a faculty for synthesis and for introducing new ideas. He is apt to show, in fact, certain characteristics inevitable in persons who belong, through the circumstances of their history, to a single sociological group. To say more is hazardous.[22]

To which we may add that to say no more neglects a large body of incontrovertible evidence.

In the past, Jews were not this reticent in evaluating themselves. Compare the following words of Menahem Nahum of Chernobyl, a leading Hasidic rabbi of the late eighteenth century: "All nations, with the exception of Israel, lack understanding; and because they lack understanding no country can forgo Jewish leadership, for which reason every king, even in countries in which it has come to expulsions and forced conversions, has a Jew at his side." [23] For a Hasidic rabbi, of course, Judaism was the supreme value; and "understanding" (that is, intelligence) was a trait possessed, of all peoples, only by Israel because of divine dispensation. But even the infatuation with French culture and the ardent French patriotism which characterized the enlightened French Jews of the nineteenth century, for example, could not undermine their traditional Jewish conviction that the Jews were superior to all other peoples, including the French. Thus Heber Marini, coupling his Jewish pride with the anti-clericalism which was the political stance of the French Jews in general, made the point that Jews displayed a "natural superiority" to many Frenchmen. Although this was not because of any inherently superior personal qualities, but because of their liberal Jewish background, which protected them from the "exaggerated devotion bordering on fanaticism" engendered by a Catholic upbringing.[24] A similar "environmentalist" explanation of Jewish superiority was put forward by the philosopher and logician Adolphe Franck, a leader of the Alliance Israélite Univer-

selle, president of the Société des Études Juives, and an Academician of
stature. According to Franck, Jewish superiority derived in part from Jewish
education: ". . . the place which all the Christian peoples have given to the
Church or let the Church take, has been given by Judaism to science, to
religious instruction." [25]

The explanations of Jewish preeminence most frequently invoked in the
nineteenth century were racial. Race was the answer to all questions pertaining to both physical and psychological differences that were felt, perceived,
or imagined to have existed between the Jews and the Gentiles in any country. What interests us in the present context is that mental traits were
unhesitatingly attributed to heredity, and that the terms "race" and "racial"
were used uninhibitedly by both Jews and Gentiles, who spoke glibly of *la
race juive*. Few indeed were those who, like Theodore Reinach (1860–1928),
branded this view as "an old and hackneyed opinion." [26] Rather, the position
taken by Jules Caravallo, an official of the Alliance Israélite Universelle, is
typical. Reporting on the findings of various authorities, and especially of
Alfred Legoyt (a non-Jewish French government statistician), Caravallo concluded that their consensus was that the Jews constituted a distinct racial
type; that the Jewish cranial dimensions were found "without exception to be
superior to the dimensions of the corresponding Christian cranium"; and that
it seemed to be reasonable to accept "a superiority of the Jewish heads over
the Christian heads." Then, in a curious combination of the scientific approach and religious outlook, Caravallo went on to say that the Jewish race
was created by God "to live, to struggle, to triumph definitively one day by
the physical privilege of race, by its cerebral development, and by the privilege of a well-tempered spirit." These racial and mental privileges, however,
entailed special duties: "If God has given us a brain more vast, He has imposed upon us the duty to perfect it by greater meditation, by more work,
by a firm and courageous march towards the triple pole, the supreme goal of
our activity: the beautiful, the true, the good." The Alliance, it should be
noted, awarded a gold medal to Legoyt's *mémoire* and had it printed and
widely distributed to libraries. [27]

The simplistic view which attributed Jewish intellectual preeminence to
the racial factor of superior cranial dimensions soon gave way to more insightful and complex explanations. The most penetrating of these was presented in 1886 by Joseph Jacobs (1854–1916), a British-Jewish scholar, to the
Anthropological Institute of Great Britain and Ireland, in a paper remarkable
for its breadth and intuitive grasp of the numerous factors bearing upon and
responsible for Jewish excellence. A complicated procedure of counting eminent Jews, calculating their proportion to the total Jewish population, and
comparing these figures with the ones for English men of genius arrived at
by Sir Francis Galton in his well-known book *Hereditary Genius* (published
in 1869) led Jacobs to the conclusion that "the average Jew has 4 per cent

more ability than the average Englishman." Next, Jacobs proceeded to his
analysis of the causes of Jewish superiority. He referred, first of all, to the
fact that the Jews tended to concentrate in cities, "always more conducive to
the life intellectual." Within the cities, they engaged primarily in commerce,
an occupation requiring "head work" rather than muscular exertion. They
were, moreover, always characterized by "care in education." In addition,
the Jews, because of their religion, were in the position of dissenters in relation to the Gentile majority, and "dissenters seem more intellectual because
they have early to think out their differences from the generality."

Jacobs also touched upon the effects of adversity on the Jewish mind: "Persecution, when not too severe, has probably aided in bringing out their best
powers: to a high-spirited race, persecution, when there is hope of overcom-
ing it, is a spur to action." Jewish solidarity, too, has added its share: "The
solidarity of the Jews and the aid they willingly give to young men of promise
assists in developing whatever talent there may be in the community." After
mentioning the effects of "the happy home-life of Jews," Jacobs observed
that "the practical and undogmatic character of their religion, together with
the absence of a priesthood, have contributed to give the *corpus sanum* and
thus the *mens sana*. Jewish reason has never been in fetters . . ." Finally,
he spoke of the Darwinian effect of persecution: ". . . the weaker members
of each generation have been weeded out by persecution which tempted or
forced them to embrace Christianity and thus contemporary Jews are the
survival of a long process of unnatural selection which has seemingly fitted
them excellently for the struggle for intellectual existence." [28] We can sum
up the factors which, according to Jacobs, have contributed to Jewish preeminence. They are urbanism, commerce, education, dissent, solidarity, a
happy home life, undogmatic religion, and persecution.

Three years after the publication of Jacobs' paper in the *Journal of the Anthropological Institute*, Cesare Lombroso (1835–1909), the famed Italian
Jewish alienist and founder of the science of criminology, touched upon the
question of Jewish genius in his book *L'Uomo di Genio* which rapidly became
very popular and was translated into all major European languages. Its English translation, *The Man of Genius*, was published in 1891. Lombroso
believed that the national character depended on heredity and climate, and
accordingly he maintained that, "owing to the bloody selection of medieval
persecutions, and owing also to the influence of temperate climate, the Jews
of Europe have risen above those of Africa and the East, and have often surpassed the Aryans." After listing a large number of Jewish musicians, poets,
novelists, linguists, physicians, philosophers, naturalists, economists, jurists,
statesmen, mathematicians, and astronomers, Lombroso commented on the
seminal role of Jews in revolutions, politics, religion, and science. "Jews, indeed, initiated Nihilism and Socialism on the one hand, Mosaism and Christianity on the other. Commerce owes to them the bill of exchange, philoso-

phy owes to them positivism, literature the Neo-humourism." One of Lombroso's favorite ideas was that there was an interrelationship between genius and insanity; he pointed out that "The Jewish elements in the population furnish four and even six times as many lunatics as the rest of the population." After citing some statistical data from Italy and Germany, he concluded his cursory treatment of the Jewish genius by stressing that race is the basis of both genius and insanity: "Education counts for little, heredity for much." [29]

5. Fritz Lenz and Rabbi Dreyfuss

In no other country at any time in the course of their long and sorrowful history have the Jews experienced anything even remotely like the systematic genocide organized by Hitler's Germany. The 6 million Jews who perished under the Nazi onslaught constituted some 70 percent of the Jews of Europe and some 40 percent of all the Jews in the world. The "scholarly" support that the Nazis received from representatives of the German academic community has repeatedly been analyzed and exposed in its incredible inhumanity. [30] It has also been pointed out to what extent these academic lackeys of the Nazi régime had built upon the German anti-Semitic literature parading in the mask of scholarship which was abundantly available from the nineteenth century on. [31]

Nevertheless, during the Weimar years there were also German geneticists and eugenicists who discussed the physical and psychological characteristics of the Jews in a detached manner. Foremost among these was Fritz Lenz, whose two-volume textbook on human heredity (written jointly with Erwin Baur and Eugen Fischer) enjoyed a popularity in Germany never equaled in this country by any comparable American text. It went into several successively augmented editions, the fourth of which was published in 1936, after Hitler's rise to power. Like many of his German colleagues, Lenz believed that races were characterized by physical as well as mental traits— that certain physical features went hand in hand with certain mental characteristics, and that both the physical and mental makeup of a "race" were the result of genetic selective processes. Thus he says that "the Frisians, who belong for the most part to the heavily-built blond race, are seldom musical" because "the heavily-built blond, like the slender blond, has been selected rather for his visual than for his auditory aptitude." [32]

Lenz's attitude to the "Jewish race" was unsympathetic but correct. He was opposed to anti-Semitism as an unscientific position. He considered "Judophobia . . . for the most part the outcome of a feeling of 'insubordination,' " by which he meant that "the spirit which animates many of the anti-Semites is 'the envy felt by a non-possessing class' " toward the Jews, who "form an upper stratum," while the Germans form its opposite.[33] Lenz considered the Jews a "mental race," that is, possessing "mental racial peculiarities . . . more marked even than the bodily" and explained this apparent paradox by his favorite method of invoking hypothetical processes of selection. Since the Jews were excluded for thousands of years

> from the labours of primal production (agriculture) not only by their own inclinations, but also in great measure by external forces, they naturally turned to commerce and similar occupations. The result was that, in the main, only those Jews could found a family who had special aptitude for acting as intermediaries in dealing with the goods produced by others, and in stimulating and guiding others' wishes.

Having thus taken care of the problem of the basic features of the Jewish "mental race" by invoking genetic selection, Lenz used the same method to explain the Jewish physical similarity to the host peoples:

> If the peculiarities of the Jews are less conspicuous in the bodily than in the mental domain, this may arise from the circumstance that Jews whose bodily aspect was markedly exotic were less successful than those whose bodily type resembled that of their hosts. The instinctive desire not to look singular would also operate by sexual selection, by a preferential choice of a partner in marriage who did not look too much unlike the hosts. . . . Thus the type has become less conspicuous thanks to the working of such a process of selection. . . .[34]

Next, Lenz proceeds to a portraiture of the Jewish character. He finds that the Jews are characterized by shrewdness, alertness, diligence, perseverance, an "amazing capacity for putting themselves in others' places (empathy) and for inducing others to accept their guidance." They are voluble, hasty ("Jewish haste"), sociable, more importunate, and more sensitive than the Teuton. The German Jews, on the average, "greatly excel in intelligence and alertness" when compared to the average German. In elementary schools, "the Jewish children on the average shape much better than the Gentiles." "In the higher schools, where the pupils represent a selection for talent, the proportion of Jewish children is many times as large as the proportion of Jews in the general population." In the Vienna Commercial Academy, to which only the most select students are admitted, the Jewish students possess a "better intellectual endowment" than the Gentile. However, Lenz cautions that "the brilliant achievements of youthful Jews depend rather upon precocity and quick-wittedness than upon creative talent," for which reason "they seldom fulfil the promise of their early years." Nevertheless, "Jews form an immoderately large proportion of undergraduates at the universities." In Prussia, for instance, in 1911–12, of every 10,000 male Catholics 5 were university students, as against 13 Protestants and 67 Jews per 10,000 of their respective male population. In "the domain of mental life the Jews are more prominent as intermediaries and interpreters than in the primary work of production. On the other hand, it is absurd to deny that the Jewish race has produced persons of outstanding genius. Enough to mention the names of Spinoza and Einstein." [35] The Jews, Lenz continues, are further characterized by a strong family sense,

> [a] strong sense of tribal interdependence, their readiness to render mutual aid, and their feeling for humanity at large. Next to the Teutonic, the Jewish spirit is the chief motive force of modern Western civilization. The emancipation of the Jews has had an effect like that of one of the waves of Nordic blood upon the Indo-Germanic civilization. Were it merely through the origination and diffusion of Christianity as one of the main roots of western civilization, the Jewish spirit has been decisively effective in universal history. [36]

This is certainly high praise coming from a German geneticist who was a sworn believer in the superiority of the German ("Teutonic") race. In fact, Lenz finds two Jewish characteristics which he feels the Germans could and should emulate with advantage. One is the Jews' "sense of mutual fellowship"; and the other, their "power to resist the seductive charms of alcohol." Their sobriety is "obviously . . . based on their hereditary mental endowment" and "might set an example to the Germans," who in this respect "manifest a weakness of which a part cause, unfortunately, is beyond question their racial heritage."

In concluding his analysis of the Jewish "mental race," Lenz explains that "in respect of many heredity factors," Jews and Teutons (i.e., "persons of a predominantly Nordic race") are extremely alike:

> Jews and Teutons are alike distinguished by great powers of understanding and by remarkable strength of will; Jews and Teutons resemble each other in having a large measure of self-confidence, an enterprising spirit, and a strong desire to get their own way—the difference being that the Teuton is inclined to seek his ends by force, the Jew rather by cunning. As far as business efficiency is concerned, the Jews are, on the whole, excelled by some of the Nordics, such as the Hanseats, the Scots, and the Yankees. . . . The Teutons of Nordic descent are like the Jews inclined to diffuse themselves as a ruling caste over foreign populations. They, too, prefer, whenever they can, to have the hard physical toil of life done for them by others—for that is a universally human characteristic, and differences in this respect are only differences of degree. [37]

Lenz even goes so far in his presentation of the similarity between Jews and Germans that he attributes to it the "frequent outbreaks of enmity between Germans and Jews" (read: the frequent anti-Semitic attacks by Germans against Jews); it is "the similarity in their respective gifts which leads to a strong competition like that which has again and again led the ruling groups of the Teutons into conflict with one another, each striving to establish power over the others." [38]

One last point must be mentioned. Lenz offers an ingenious explanation for the Jewish fondness for Lamarckism. Lamarckism is, of course, the well-known and now discredited theory, first propounded by Jean de Monet, Chevalier de Lamarck (1744–1829), which held that the evolution of plants and animals can be explained by the inheritance of acquired characteristics. Darwin and early evolutionists after him accepted this theory, until August Weismann (1834–1914) disproved it. Lenz observes that the advocates of Lamarckism are mainly, and its opponents only to a very small extent, of Jewish descent. Why? Because the Jews "wish that there should be no unbridgeable racial distinction." If Lamarck was right, and acquired characteristics can be inherited, then "by living in a Teutonic environment and by adopting a Teutonic culture, the Jews could become transformed into genuine Teutons. This enables us to understand why the Lamarckian doctrine should make so strong an appeal to the Jews whose fate it is to exist everywhere among the Gentiles as a sharply differentiated minority." And Lenz quotes Paul Kammerer, a Jew and a Lamarckian (who committed suicide in 1926 after his proof of the inheritance of acquired characteristics was shown to have been false), to the effect that "the denial of the racial importance of acquired characters favors race hatred." [39]

Despite his nationalistic conceit, Lenz was a serious scholar whose work represented the best that German science produced until his time in genetics. His disquisition on the similarities between the Jewish and the German character was the result of his own investigations, supported by some earlier scholarly work on the subject such as that of Luschan whom he quotes. No such original work in national psychology could be expected of a practicing rabbi in charge of a busy congregation. If therefore we find that J. H. Dreyfuss, the Grand Rabbin of Paris, sermonized on the similarities between the Jewish and the French mentality, he must have been echoing views which had been put forward by contemporary anthropologists and with which he was familiar. In any case, similarities very much like those found by Lenz between Jews and Germans were pointed to by Rabbi Dreyfuss in an 1891 sermon as existing between the Jews and the French. "The moral affinities between the two races" were, according to him, remarkable:

> Both Jews and Frenchmen, Dreyfuss declared, were "respectful of family ties and traditions," both were "permeated with the same ardour for work, the same care for saving money, the same provident solicitude for the future." Both were "preoccupied with the development of material resources, less for the legitimate satisfactions of well-being which they allow than for the intellectual

and moral enjoyment of which they can be the source and for the good which they make possible." There was also a broader, more historical level of comparison. A real similarity existed between the "mission" of Israel and the "historical role" of France. Dreyfuss referred to the French as "this elect people of modern times, spreading abroad the blessed notions of liberty, equality, and fraternity." There was a direct parallel between this elect people and the elect people of the ancient world. Against the French there was arranged on the international level the same kind of "jealousy" for having been divinely chosen which Israel had endured. The one and the other had to suffer in bringing their message to the world around them.[40]

While Rabbi Dreyfuss can perhaps be suspected of an apologetic tendency in emphasizing those Jewish traits where the Jews could be shown to be similar to the French, such an intention can certainly not be assumed to have actuated Fritz Lenz, whose general attitude to the Jews was, to put it mildly, less than friendly. Yet, as we have seen, he found even more similarities between the Jews and the Germans than the French rabbi did between the Jews and the French. These two testimonies (which could easily be amplified by many others, and which were a frequent theme, especially in the patriotic Jewish press in France, Germany, Austria, and Hungary) should suffice to show that, according to observers of widely differing backgrounds and orientations, the Jews in those countries which had emancipated them and whose cultures they absorbed in the wake of their Enlightenment developed also a certain psychological affinity with the national character of their Gentile environment. This is aptly epitomized in the oft-quoted Jewish saying, "Wie es sich christelt, so jüdelts sich," which can only be freely translated as, "Like Christian, like Jew."

6. Marginality and Eminence

In 1919, the prominent American economist and sociologist Thorstein Veblen (1857–1929), best known for his book *The Theory of the Leisure Class* (1899) and his concept of "conspicuous consumption," published a short but remarkable article entitled "Intellectual Pre-eminence of Jews in Modern Europe." [41] He began by presenting a brief résumé of the manifestations of observable Jewish intellectual preeminence. "Men of Jewish extraction," he stated, "continue to supply more than a proportionate quota to the rank and file engaged in scientific and scholarly work"; and, more importantly, "a disproportionate number of the men to whom modern science and scholarship look for guidance and leadership are of the same derivation." The Jews—in general, that is, not only the scientists and scholars among them—differ from the Gentiles "in distinctive traits of temperament and aptitude." Although racially they are hybrids and evince great variations, nevertheless there is something distinctly Jewish in these cross-bred individuals. As for their intellectual preeminence, that "has come into bearing within the gentile community of peoples, not from the outside," and "the men who have been its bearers have been immersed in this gentile culture in which they have played their part of guidance and incitement." While the Jewish "homebred achievements" were considerable, they were distinctly Jewish; only in contact with Gentile cultures did the Jews achieve true greatness as "creative leaders in the world's intellectual enterprise." (In the next section we shall return to this phenomenon.) A concomitant of this is that among great men of science there have been many "renegade Jews."

Having thus presented his facts, Veblen proceeds to their explanation, arguing that the first prerequisite for constructive work in modern science is "a skeptical frame of mind." In this respect, "the intellectually gifted Jew is in a peculiarly fortunate position" because he has no secure place either in Jewish tradition, which he has left behind, or in the Gentile world, in which he is not totally at home. The "safe and sane" Gentile scientist enjoys a peace of mind which is not given to the Jew. On the other hand, this supplies the Jewish scientist with "the prerequisite of immunity from the inhibitions of intellectual quietism." He will unavoidably enter fields of learning in which Gentile interests predominate; but because of his skeptical frame of mind, "the nationally binding convictions of what is true, good, and beautiful in the world of the human spirit" will be recognized by him as being "only contingently good and true." As Veblen sees it, the force of circumstances over which the gifted Jew has no control supplies him with that ingredient of skepticism which is the prerequisite of truly creative work in science. Thus the Jew becomes a disturber of the intellectual peace and is likely to become intellectually an alien. Spiritually, however, "he is more likely to remain a Jew; for the heart-strings of affection and consuetude are tied early and they are not readily retied in after life."

Translated into more modern terminology, Veblen finds that the marginal position occupied by the intellectually gifted Jew in Gentile society enables him to have a more critical and more skeptical look at the entrenched values of truth, goodness, and beauty; and this, in turn, gives a freer play to his talents than can be enjoyed by the Gentiles. The apparent plausibility of this argument has been weakened in the course of the close to six decades that have passed since it was put to paper. If Jewish marginality is a precondition of Jewish skepticism, which, in turn, is a prerequisite of Jewish intellectual preeminence, then a reduction in Jewish marginality—which has indubitably taken place at least in America since Veblen wrote—should have resulted in a reduction of Jewish intellectual preeminence. Yet precisely the opposite has been the case. The children and grandchildren of Jewish newcomers—who in their old European home countries were certainly marginal enough to be prompted to emigrate—became Americanized, that is, integrated into American culture; they absorbed and internalized the American cultural values and, at the same time, produced more intellectually preeminent individuals than they had in Europe. Hence either marginality is not a prerequisite of Jewish skepticism *vis-à-vis* established cultural values, or, if it is, then skepticism is not a prerequisite of high-level work in modern science.

I shall, however, go along with Veblen's argument to this extent. Inquisitiveness and argumentativeness—both related to "a skeptical frame of mind"—have been Jewish mental characteristics for many centuries, nurtured by a concentration in halakhic study with its method of *pilpul*, questioning and arguing over apparently contradictory statements contained in the Talmud. As long as the Jewish intellectual horizon was boxed in by the "four cubits of the *Halakha*," as it was in the Ashkenazi majority of Jewry until the Enlightenment, the outlets for these old Jewish gifts were limited and remained outside the Veblenian global "intellectual enterprise." Once these barriers were removed, Jewish inquisitiveness and argumentativeness spilled over into all the newly opened up fields of scientific and scholarly inquiry, and especially into those which were of dominant interest among the Gentiles of the immediate environment.

While Veblen stresses the marginality of the Jew as the main enabling factor for the development of his intellectual preeminence, Chaim Weizmann—one of the founding fathers of the State of Israel—explains the same phenomenon by emphasizing what could be termed the double exposure of the Jewish mind to Talmudic study and to modern scientific training. Weizmann touches upon the issue in his autobiography:

> Our great men were always a product of symbiosis between the ancient, Talmudic learning in which our ancestors were steeped in the Polish or Galician ghettos, or even in Spain, and the modern Western universities with which their children came in contact. There is as often as not a long list of Talmudic scholars and Rabbis in the pedigrees of our modern scientists. In many cases they themselves have come from Talmudic schools, breaking away in their twenties and struggling through to Paris or Zurich or Princeton. It is this extraordinary phenomenon—a great tradition of learning fructified by modern methods—which has given us both first-class scientists and competent men in every branch of academic activity, out of all relation to our numbers.[42]

I should add that Weizmann himself belonged to the category he describes. Born in 1874 in Motol near Pinsk, he attended a traditional *Ḥeder*, entered high school in Pinsk at the age of eleven, and after graduation studied at the polytechnic institutes of Darmstadt and Berlin and at the University of Freiburg. He became an outstanding chemist, although he devoted most of his life to the service of Zionism, and was the first president of Israel when he died in 1952.

A third explanation is offered by Lewis S. Feuer, a modern specialist in the sociology of ideas and a psychologist of renown. Feuer considers science in general the fruit of a "hedonist-libertarian" spirit; its great enemy is the spirit of "masochist asceticism," whose medieval Christian heritage still informs the Christian world to some extent. The Jewish Enlightenment was a revolt against ghetto Judaism, which "had become contaminated with strong ingredients of the masochist asceticism." In fact, in the late eighteenth century, "despite all difficulties, the greatest scientific movement that has ever seized and transformed a people began" among the Jews. For, he adds, "the psychological revolution among the Jews in the nineteenth century was the most rapid and thoroughgoing emotional revolution the world has ever seen." The Jewish revolt against "the masochist asceticism of ghetto Judaism," says Feuer, "took many forms—psychoanalysis, Zionism, Socialism. All these modes of thought were linked, however, with the common denominator of the hedonist-libertarian ethic, which in its variant forms was the philosophy of the Jewish renaissance, the philosophy of the Jewish scientific intellectual." [43]

This, then, is Feuer's explanation of Jewish intellectual preeminence: more than the contemporary Gentile world, the Jews succeeded in revolting against, and liberating themselves from, the shackles of medieval (in the case of the Jews, ghetto) masochist asceticism and embracing the hedonist-libertarian ethic. It is this differential which is reflected in the Jewish preeminence among the scientific intellectuals.

The explanations of Jewish intellectual preeminence range from racial, through combinations of environmental and genetic, to purely psychological ones. If I am not ready to go along with any one of them, the reason for this is, first of all, an *a priori* consideration. My reaction to any effort to explain such a complex phenomenon as the intellectual preeminence of an ethnic group by a single cause is one of unease and wariness. Even simple phenomena are often the results of a combination of several factors. And the more complex the phenomenon, the greater the likelihood that it is the product of numerous factors in interaction and combination.

This points to Jacobs' approach as the most satisfactory. Jacobs gave recognition to the selective (that is, genetic) effect which centuries of persecution had on the Jewish mind. But he also emphasized the role of other environmental factors in producing Jewish intellectual preeminence, namely, urban residence, concentration on commerce, emphasis on education, the necessity to understand and justify a dissenting position in religion, group solidarity, devotion to the family life, and an undogmatic religion. [44] This type of "multifactorial" approach is used in the next section in analyzing the probable bases of Jewish intellectual excellence.

7. A Factor Analysis of Jewish Excellence

The title of this section is reminiscent of the multi-factorial theory of intelligence of which L. L. Thurstone was the leading exponent, and which claims that intelligence is multi-faceted, comprised of several independent but intercorrelated Primary Mental Abilities. However, this is not the sense I have in mind. I do not intend to analyze the various Thurstonian abilities comprised in Jewish intelligence, but rather the various factors which have been responsible for producing Jewish intellectual excellence. In so doing, I shall try to isolate, and discuss as concretely as possible, those causes which seem to be the most significant propellants toward the preeminence achieved by Jews in so many different fields.

To begin with, we must recapitulate the findings of the preceding chapter concerning the high scores of Jewish subjects on I.Q. tests, and the reasons to which they were attributed. It was found that: (1) the Jewish cultural tradition of the value of learning created an atmosphere conducive to the utmost mental effort and to a maximal realization of intelligence potential; (2) the harsh circumstances of life in a generally inimical Gentile socio-economic environment favored the survival of the more intelligent among the Jews; and (3) quite possibly, the valuation of learning as reflected in the traditionally established marriage preference also contributed to an increase in mean intelligence by providing the most intelligent with the best chances of surviving and passing on their genetic specificity to their offspring. The combination of these three factors—the first of which is purely environmental, while the second and third are environmental in their origin but genetic in their effect—seems to supply the most complete explanation not only of the generally higher Jewish I.Q. scores, but also of a number of other related phenomena (such as preference for urban residence and occupational choices) in which Jews differ from Gentiles to varying extents.

The same factors undoubtedly provide part of the explanation for the Jewish preeminence in scientific and literary fields. They certainly constitute the general background, or rather, the ground, for Jewish excellence. Down to the present day, the average Jewish home is a place where it is most unlikely that any exceptional promise shown by a child could be overlooked or where everything possible would not be done to help develop its talent. Hence, even assuming that Gentile and Jewish children were born with an identical mean genetic potential for genius, the Jewish children stand a better chance of realizing their potential and developing it to the fullest. Such an assumption, however, is purely hypothetical since in actuality the I.Q. test scores show the results of the interaction between heredity and environment, and there is no way to separate the two to establish either an identity or a differential between the genetically determined mean I.Q. potential of two groups (whether of infants, children, or adults). Whatever differences show up in the I.Q. tests between the mean scores of Jewish and Gentile children (or adults) are always the end results of the combined effect of heredity and environment.

The findings presented and discussed in the preceding chapter also constitute a basis for explaining the Jewish tendency to concentrate in those occupations for which the completion of graduate studies is a prerequisite. It stands to reason that Jewish students who have a higher mean I.Q. and do better in scholastic achievement should tend to go on to college and then to graduate studies more frequently than their Gentile peers who, on the average, do less well at school. In addition, the same environmental and, to a lesser extent, hereditary factors which we found responsible for the higher scores of Jewish children on I.Q. and scholastic achievement tests continue to operate in the last high school years. These channel them into college, prompt them during the college years to continue in graduate studies, and, after having acquired an advanced degree, instill in them a strong achievement orientation throughout their careers. The higher percentage of college students and graduates and of professionals among the Jews than among the Gentiles (or the general population) is well attested in statistical studies.

The next point to emphasize is that, at least since the nineteenth century, almost the only route to great intellectual achievement has been via college. Before a person's mind can manifest its excellence, he must first familiarize himself with what has been achieved by others in his chosen field of specialization. This is less true in creative than in scholarly and scientific fields, but even in the arts and in literature a knowledge of what has been produced by others is generally a prerequisite for outstanding work in any field. By the mid-twentieth century, the amount of work that had gone before was so great in each area of specialization that systematic guidance—such as can best be provided by institutions of higher learning—was practically indispensable. This being so, one must assume that the higher the percentage of college graduates in a given human group, the higher the percentage of outstanding talents and geniuses emerging from that group. On this basis, we would expect a higher percentage of preeminent individuals among the Jews than among the Gentiles.

Related to the emphasis on education both in the traditional context (in which it meant Talmudic schooling) and in the modern sense of college attendance is the very old Jewish preference for urban residence. Prior to 1800, the Gentile population of all countries was overwhelmingly rural, while the Jews have been, ever since ancient times, a predominantly urban people. The statistical material bearing on Jewish urbanization has been summarized in an earlier book of mine, where it was shown that in the early twentieth century between 75 and 94 percent of all Jews in East, Central, and West Europe, in the Middle East, and in America lived in cities.[45]

Among the attractions of urban living for the Jews until the Enlightenment was the availability of yeshivot. In a city a Jewish youth could devote himself to Talmudic study—the highest avocation for the traditional Jews—while in a village he could not advance beyond the *Ḥeder* stage (the study of the Bible with commentaries and the rudiments of the Talmud). For this reason, Jewish village families would very frequently send their boys to a city to study in a yeshiva at the tender age of ten or twelve.

In addition to the yeshiva, the direct attraction of urban living included other Jewish amenities, or rather religious necessities, which existed only in the city: a synagogue with a daily *minyan* (quorum of ten male adults), a *miqve* (ritual bath), a *shoḥeṭ* (ritual slaughterer), a sufficient choice of suitable prospective marriage partners, a Jewish cemetery and a *Ḥevra Qadisha* (charitable society which took care, in the main, of burials), and the like. Studies carried out in America among blacks and whites and elsewhere have shown that urban life provides a stimulus effect, absent in the rural environment, which is reflected in the higher mean I.Q. scores of urban versus rural subjects.[46] The difference in rural-urban distribution between Jews and Gentiles, therefore, must have been an important contribution to raising the Jewish intelligence.

Closely related to urban residence was the concentration of Jews in those few occupations which were permitted to them by the Gentiles. In the Christian world, these were, in the main, moneylending, peddling, and dealing in old clothes; to which can be added the leasing and managing of taverns, especially in East Europe. All of these were commercial activities, and all required the use of one's brains. Here, then, was yet another factor which put a premium on intelligence, rewarding it with an advantage in chances of survival.

Thus the specific and unique circumstances in which the Jews have lived for two millennia in the Diaspora converged to force them into a cerebral mold, to impose upon them a higher mean intelligence than that found in their Gentile environment. The higher mean intelligence became the baseline from which those of special gifts could rise more frequently to the greatest heights of intellectual power. Given these conditions, it was inevitable that the leap from giftedness to genius should be made by the rare Jewish individuals capable of it precisely in those Jewish societies which were surrounded by, impinged upon, stimulated, and challenged by the larger Gentile environment. A glance at the ten greatest Jews of all times will bear out this generalization.

Moses (thirteenth century B.C.E.) was culturally half Egyptian—a fact which is much more important for understanding his greatness than the Freudian fantasy of his Egyptian descent.

Isaiah (and the other Hebrew prophets who were his near-contemporaries in the eighth century B.C.E.) lived in a Jewish society permeated by political, cultural, and religious influences from all directions across the narrow borders of the country.

Jesus (c. 4 B.C.E.–30 C.E.) lived in the shadow of imperial Rome in a largely Hellenized Jewish Palestine.

Maimonides (1135–1204) was as much at home in Arab philosophy and medicine as in the Jewish *Halakha*.

Spinoza (1632–77) was nurtured by both Jewish and Gentile thinkers whose works were available to him in his Dutch homeland.

Marx (1818–83) was exposed to early West European Socialist thought and movements, while retaining a quasi-Biblical messianic fervor.

Freud (1856–1939) was the product of Viennese and Parisian medical-psychiatric education.

Bergson (1859–1941) was a great French philosopher with a merely residual Jewish conscience.

Herzl (1860–1904) matured in an assimilant Jewish environment permeated with Hungarian and German culture.

Einstein (1879–1955) was saturated with German scientific thinking.

Conversely, no such Jewish genius of world stature arose in times when, or in places where, the Jews lived in isolation without contacts with the outside world, or when and where such contacts did take place but the surrounding larger environment was intellectually stagnant. In such circumstances, Jewish giftedness remained confined within the "four cubits of the *Halakha*"—a limited domain which enabled its foremost students to manifest giftedness and acumen, as did the many rabbinic luminaries from Talmudic times to the Enlightenment, but not to make the leap to the peaks of genius.

To sum up, then, we found the following factors to be mainly responsible for Jewish excellence and genius:

First of all, two probably selective factors—the pressure of the Gentile persecution, or at least discrimination, which made for the survival of the most intelligent; and the advantages enjoyed by the best scholars in mating and procreation. The latter was a direct outcome of factor three: the religio-cultural tradition of considering learning the highest value. Factor four, derived from, or correlated with, the third, was the extremely stimulating character of the home environment. The fifth was the age-old preference for urban living and the actual concentration in towns and cities. The sixth consisted of being forced by the Gentiles to eke out a livelihood in commercial occupations in which intelligence is a *sine qua non*. And the seventh was the challenge of the Gentile cultural atmosphere. Exposure to these factors for many generations tended to raise the level of general Jewish intelligence, to increase the percentage of the gifted among the Jews, and to produce among them a remarkable number of men of genius whose works and words changed the world.

8. *The Jewish Nobel Prize Record*

While it would be giving too much credit to the Nobel Prize Committee to assume that, in selecting the recipients of the prizes, it infallibly comes up each time with a man of genius, there can be no doubt that in general the laureates are men of extraordinary accomplishments. One would, perhaps, not be amiss in saying that the Nobel Prize winners as a group greatly surpass the level of the average gifted individuals, even that of the extremely talented, and that they approximate the heights of genius. On the other hand, one must not lose sight of the competitive nature of the awards, which means that a man crowned with the prize in one year may be a much more outstanding scholar or writer than another who receives the prize in the same field in another year. In saying this, and only this, I am purposely abstaining from the argument that the committee allows itself to be influenced in its choices by political considerations. In any case, the Nobel Prize winners constitute what is unquestionably the most élite group among men of unusual intellectual achievement. Hence there is at present no better yardstick for measuring Jewish intellectual preeminence than the record of Jews among the laureates.

The first Nobel Prizes were awarded in 1901. By that time, Jewish Emancipation was an accomplished fact all over Europe except for Russia where the majority of the Jews still lived. In Central and Western Europe, enlightened Jews had taken an increasing part in the life of the Gentile environment and had produced many prominent men in various fields. But it was to take another few years before the achievements of any one of them were judged to be of Nobel caliber. The first prize went to a Jew in 1905. Thereafter, the percentage of Jews among the winners showed an increasing trend. By 1930, 11 of the total of 153 prizes awarded to individuals, or 7.5 percent, had gone to Jews. Four more were given to Jews who had left Judaism, and five to half-Jews, adding up to a total of twenty. The last two figures indicate the extent of assimilation and attrition among the most outstanding Jewish scientists in the early twentieth century to which Veblen referred. If we add their number to the eleven Jews, we get 13 percent as the proportion of Jews and persons of Jewish or half-Jewish background among the Nobel Prize winners.

In the forty-two years from 1931 to 1972, no less than 18 percent of the winners were Jews. In the thirty years from 1943 to 1972, Jews were awarded forty-three prizes, or more than twice the number they won in the first thirty-year period of the prize (twenty). In the seventy-five years of prize awards, the Jewish record as against the total shaped up as shown in Table I.

As the table shows, the higher the number of total Nobel Prize winners in a field, the higher the percentage of Jews among them. The number of win-

TABLE I. *Number and Percentage of Jews Among*
Nobel Prize Winners, 1901–75

FIELD	TOTAL NUMBER	NUMBER OF JEWS	PERCENTAGE OF JEWS
Economics (1969–75)	11	4	36.36
Physiology or Medicine	115	28	24.35
Physics	103	20	19.42
Chemistry	88	10	11.36
Literature	72	5	6.94
Peace *	59	4	6.78
Total	448	71	15.85

*Only Peace Prizes awarded to individuals are listed. In addition, Peace Prizes were given to institutions and organizations.

ners in Economics is an apparent exception, because this prize was first awarded only in 1969; that is, it has a record of only seven years as against the seventy-five years of the prizes in the other fields. If we multiply the numbers of the total and Jewish prize winners in Economics by $10^5/_7$ in order to equalize them with the numbers of the total and Jewish prize winners in the other fields, we get 118 for the total, and 32 for the Jewish prize winner. Had prizes in Economics been awarded for seventy-five years, the rule stated in the first sentence of this paragraph (as far as one can extrapolate from the seven years in which the prizes in Economics were awarded) would still have held good.

Why should Jews win relatively more Nobel Prizes in those fields in which the total number of prizes awarded is greater? The basic rule of the Nobel Prize Committee is to award one prize annually in each of the five, and since 1969, six, fields. If in a given year the committee finds that no individual has made a contribution outstanding enough to deserve the prize, it can withhold it that year. Conversely, if it finds that two or even three individuals have made outstanding contributions in one field, it can divide the prize among them. Over the years, these variations have resulted in the differences in the numbers of prizes awarded in each of the six fields shown in the table. It seems reasonable to argue that the larger the number of Nobel Prize winners in a given field, the larger the total number of individuals

TABLE II. Number and Percentage of Jews Among Nobel Prize Winners by Countries* and Fields 1901–75

COUNTRY	TOTAL							JEWS							
	PHYSICS	CHEMISTRY	PHYSIOLOGY OR MEDICINE	LITERATURE	PEACE	ECONOMICS	TOTAL	PHYSICS	CHEMISTRY	PHYSIOLOGY OR MEDICINE	LITERATURE	PEACE	ECONOMICS	TOTAL	PERCENT OF JEWS IN TOTAL
U.S.A.	33	20	45	7	15	5	125	10	2	16	–	1	3	32	25.60
England	18	18	14	5	6	1	62	3	1	2	–	–	–	6	9.68
Germany	16	23	11	6	4	–	60	3	4	3	2	–	–	12	20.00
France	9	6	5	11	7	–	38	1	2	2	1	1	–	7	18.42
Russia	6	1	2	3	1	1	14	1	–	–	1	–	1	3	21.43
Switzerland	–	4	4	2	3	–	13	–	–	1	–	–	–	1	7.69
Holland	5	2	3	–	1	1	12	–	–	–	–	1	–	1	8.33
Denmark	3	–	4	3	1	–	11	2	–	–	–	–	–	2	18.18
Italy	2	1	2	5	1	–	11	–	–	–	–	–	–	–	–
Austria	2	1	4	1	2	1	11	–	–	2	–	1	–	3	29.27
Total	94	76	94	43	41	9	357	20	9	26	4	4	4	67	18.76

*Only countries whose citizens or residents won ten or more prizes are listed.
Sources: Encyclopedia Americana; Encyclopedia Judaica and its Yearbooks.

devoting themselves to that field, which in turn can be taken to indicate a greater relative importance of that field within the general cultural configuration of the Western (or Westernized) world. If so, the higher percentage of Jewish Nobel Prize winners in those fields in which the total number of prizes awarded is higher shows that the same fields are more attractive to both Jews and Gentiles, or, as I put it a few years ago, "the greater the stimulus provided by the cultural atmosphere and attainments of the Gentile environment in a given field, the higher the level of Jewish performance in that field." [47] (See Table II.)

While there is no complete correlation between the total number of prize winners in a country and the percentage of Jews among them (the small numbers involved would, in any case, make any such correlation statistically not meaningful), nevertheless there is generally a tendency for the percent-age of Jewish winners to be higher in those countries in which the total number of prize winners is higher. This is clearly the case in the United States, Germany, and France, three out of the four countries with the high-est total number of prizes (ranging from 38 to 120). The low percentage of Jews among England's 61 winners, and their high percentage among Russia's 13 and Austria's 10 winners, are exceptional cases whose explanation must be sought in the special circumstances of Jewish life and the general intellectual climate in these three countries.[48] In any case, the country-by-country record of the Jewish Nobel Prize winners again points to the tendency of the Jews to direct their attention and talent, and to manifest their genius, in those fields which represent cultural foci in the intellectual and scientific en-deavor of their host peoples. A discussion of this phenomenon leads us into the subject of special Jewish talents which will be taken up next.

As far as the significance of the Jewish Nobel record goes, I leave it to the reader to draw his own conclusion from the fact that the Jews, who constitute less than half a percent of mankind, have won more than 15 percent of the prizes generally recognized as the highest accolade of modern times.

13

Special Talents

1. Three Basic Questions

With the presentation of the Jewish record in the august company of Nobel Prize winners we have actually begun to discuss the question of special talents possessed by Jews. If Jewish scientists figure most prominently among the winners of the prize in Physics, Chemistry, and Physiology and Medicine, this can be, and indeed has been, taken as indicative of special Jewish talents in these fields. These findings lead us to three general questions. First, are there, in fact, special fields in which the Jews show special talent, and if so, which are those fields? Second, assuming that the answer is affirmative, what are the factors which can be considered responsible for these special Jewish talents? And, third, have the Jews manifested the same special talents throughout their long history, and in all countries of their Diaspora, or have they shown different talents in various times and places?

For methodological reasons it is best to dispose of the third question first. If one reviews Jewish history from the viewpoint of cultural achievement, one soon finds that at various times and various places Jewish talent has expressed itself in various fields. The early chapters in this book contain numerous examples to illustrate this general observation. This means that Jewish talent, far from being a constant, is a greatly variable entity correlating to the different cultural environments in which the Jews have lived during the last two millennia.

We saw, for instance, that in environments in which philosophy was an important intellectual activity, the Jews manifested what certainly must be considered special talents for this most abstruse mental exercise, as exemplified by Philo of Alexandria, Maimonides, and Spinoza, to name only three who are among the greatest figures of world philosophy. In many other places and times, we would search in vain for Jewish thinkers. Do, then, "the Jews" have a talent for philosophy? When put in this general form, the

343

question is unanswerable. The answer can only be specific, relating to certain times and places: in Hellenistic Alexandria they certainly had such talent, and so they had in medieval Arab Spain and in seventeenth-century Holland (as well as in several other places). But, just as clearly, they did not manifest any such talent in, say, Yemen, Iraq, or Kurdistan.

Analogous observations could be made on the outcropping of Jewish talent in every field which is generally considered the domain of human giftedness, including, in the first place, the arts to which a major part of this chapter will be devoted. Instead of adducing more examples, however, it seems more important to add a clarifying comment on the nature of the relationship between Jewish talent and the environmental influences to which the Jews have been exposed throughout their history. For Jewish talent to find expression in a specific field, a number of conditions had to be present. If the field in question was part of the Jewish cultural heritage, its cultivation would inevitably attract the talented among the Jews; but this attraction could be translated into actual creativity only if the environmental conditions were not too prohibitive. In sixteenth-century Poland, for instance, there was considerable Jewish creativity in rabbinics—the most important traditional field of Jewish intellectual concentration—but in the seventeenth century, when waves of cruel persecution swept over Polish Jewry, this creativity markedly declined.

If the field in question was cultivated by the Jews' Gentile neighbors, there had to be, first of all, enough contact between the two for the Jews to become aware of the existence of the field. Secondly, the field had to be so attractive to the Jews that the talented among them would be motivated to seek it out and try their hand at it. This was the case with philosophy, poetry, medicine, and mathematics in Arab Spain, with music, dance, and the theater in Renaissance Italy, and with practically every cultural specialization in post-Enlightenment Europe. On the other hand, painting and sculpture in Renaissance Italy, although the Jews were familiar with it, did not attract them, for reasons to be discussed later, and thus whatever potential talent they possessed in these fields remained unrealized.

Finally, if a field existed neither in Jewish tradition nor in the culture of the Gentile environment, it remained of course unattended by Jewish talent. Thus the Jews who lived in Arab countries, which from about 1400 stagnated culturally,[1] suffered a cultural decline, while those Jews who lived in culturally more fertile and more stimulating environments in Europe forged ahead.

At no time was the Jewish dependence on the cultural stimulus of the Gentile environment more apparent than after the Enlightenment. Among the enlightened Jews there was an upsurge of talent in every field embraced by eighteenth- and nineteenth-century European culture. Areas formerly closed to them either because of Gentile reluctance to admit them, or because of their own religious views, or because of a combination of both these factors, now irresistibly attracted them. At the same time, however, the unenlightened Jews, whether in East Europe or in the Middle East, showed no traces whatsoever of any of those talents which their enlightened co-religionists so splendidly displayed. Had a student of Jewish culture concentrated on this issue in, say, the period between 1850 and 1900, he would have concluded that the Jewish people consisted of two disparate branches: a talented minority, living in the countries of Central and Western Europe, and a majority lacking talent, which lived in East Europe and the Middle East. And at the time this conclusion would have been generally correct (with some exceptions). Within two generations, however, it was vitiated by the emergence of talent which followed the spread of secular learning and mundane interests among the formerly unenlightened Jews. In sum, the answer to our third question is that the Jews have manifested different talents in various times and places, and that the talents they did manifest had a distinct correlation to the cultural activities in which the Gentiles of their environment were engaged.

We are ready now to tackle the first of our three questions. Since Jewish talent has varied so greatly with time and place, it is well nigh impossible to enumerate the fields in which "the Jews" have shown special talent. To illustrate this once more: Is virtuosity on the violin a special Jewish talent? It certainly is in the twentieth century in the Western world, where most of the greatest violin virtuosos have been Jews of East and Central European origin. But the Middle Eastern Jews down to the present time, and the Ashkenazi Jews until the nineteenth century, have produced no violin virtuosos. Can then a talent which appeared within a certain subdivision of the Jewish people at a certain time be considered a special "Jewish" talent? Hardly.

Can one, nevertheless, point to any special talent which has accompanied the Jews throughout their long history and manifested itself in all places of their Diaspora? If we confine ourselves to those fields usually taken to be the domains proper of talent—the arts, music, literature, philosophy, and the sciences—the answer must be no. While in each of these fields the Jews excelled in some places and at some times, in none of them were they preeminent in all places and at all times. Even in the religious field, in which lay the greatest strength of the Jews in antiquity, their *creativity* in later periods was intermittent (see below), as everyone familiar with the history of Jewish religion will have to admit. If, however, one takes talent in the widest possible sense of the term, as meaning exceptional ability or giftedness in any field of activity, one can indeed locate areas in which the Jews, more than other peoples, have excelled always and everywhere.

The most important of these areas is undoubtedly the Jews' ability to preserve their identity. The various factors (religious, historical, social, and cultural) which instilled into them the *will* to do so have been often and ably discussed. But the will to preserve group identity, however strong, is no guarantee of success. In addition to it, there must have been, as indeed there was, great talent which enabled the Jews to translate this will into fact, into the unique phenomenon of actual group survival for two thousand years in a widely scattered Diaspora, often in precariously small aggregates. Wherever historical circumstances, or, as they themselves would say, the will of God, placed the Jews, their talent for ethnic self-preservation came into play, and they survived. This was the general rule everywhere, which is only underlined by the extremely few exceptional cases (such as that of the Chinese Jews of K'ai-feng Fu) [2] in which wholly unusual circumstances brought about the total assimilation and disappearance of small and isolated Jewish communities.

In looking at Jewish history one often gets the impression that, in many ages and places, the best Jewish talents were invested in the pursuit of this paramount quest for group survival. Occasionally, at least, individual survival had to be sacrificed for the sake of the survival of the group. Until the emergence of racial anti-Semitism in the nineteenth century, Jews could assure their personal survival even in the most inimical environments at the price of giving up their religion and embracing the faith of the locally dominant majority. As is well known, there were those who actually took this step. Others, given the choice between apostasy and death, chose to die; and, while they did so because of religious conviction, their death strengthened the will of the rest to carry on and spurred the Jewish talent to greater efforts, to a search for new ways to achieve and secure group survival, this oldest and greatest of Jewish aims. Jewish ingenuity did not find it difficult to attribute the quest for group survival to the will of God. Is it not written in the Book of Isaiah (6:13) that even though the great oak of Israel cast off its leaves, its holy seed must grow back into a new stock?

Next to the talent for survival, religious talent is the one which most constantly accompanied the Jews, from Moses son of Amram to Moses son of Mendel. Not in the sense of religious creativity, which, I must repeat, was intermittent, but as expressed in the very special aptitude for an incessant preoccupation with the religious dimension of life. Certainly throughout the European Diaspora, and probably in the Middle East as well, religion played a more focal role in the lives of the Jews than in those of the non-Jewish peoples among whom they lived; it was more of a cohesive force, and more of a motivation in everyday existence. However one looks at it, this did require extraordinary religious talent.

Thus the answer to our first question is that the Jews have, indeed, possessed special talents in a few selected fields, of which the talent for group survival and the talent for religious preoccupation are the outstanding examples. These two talents, at least, have been manifested by the Jews throughout their history and in every place, and it is due to them that the Jewish people, scattered all over the world, has survived to the present day.

This leaves the second of the three questions posed at the beginning of this chapter: What are the factors which can be considered responsible for the special Jewish talents? This question is the most difficult to answer. In many cases the factors responsible for the emergence of special Jewish talents elude us; in others, we can only venture more or less informed guesses as to their nature. In the following pages these issues are discussed in some detail in connection with a presentation of special Jewish talents as seen by three scholars of greatly disparate orientation, and as manifested in the major fields of artistic, musical, and literary activities.

2. The "Semites"; or, The Desert and Monotheism

In the nineteenth century, several leading historians contrasted the "Aryans" with the "Semites"—two designations which, at the time, were taken to refer to races with fixed character traits unchanged since early history. Some of the things they had to say about the special talents of these two human groups strike us today, to say the least, as singular. As a rule, the "Aryans" were taken to be exemplified by the Christian population of the country of which the investigator was a national, England, France, and Germany in the first place; the "Semites" were considered as being embodied in the Jewish populations of the same countries, as well as of Eastern Europe, and also, with increasing vagueness, in the Biblical Hebrews, in other ancient Near Eastern peoples, and the contemporary Arabs, about whom relatively little was known at the time.

Such generalized, impressionistic, and almost always inductive comparisons eminently lent themselves to serving as excuses for anti-Semitic diatribes. The list of nineteenth-century scholarly, semi-scholarly, and popular works which present the "Semitic" Jew as possessed of an assortment of evil talents is an ominous one, not so much because of what such works say about the Jews as because of what they reveal about the Gentiles' attitude to that small, newly emancipated Jewish element which so fervidly strove to be accepted by them. I shall refrain from adding examples of these West European manifestations of anti-Semitism, ranging from scholarly to demagogic, to those already cited earlier in this book, and shall instead present some of the opinions about the talents of the "Semites" or the Jews held by serious scholars who were free of the taint of anti-Semitism. Let us refer, first of all, to that French school of environmentalists (to which also the Italian Jewish Cesare Lombroso adhered to some extent) which considered geography and climate major factors in psycho-cultural development. Ernest Renan, to whom reference has repeatedly been made, was the most influential among those who applied the views of this school to the Semites, including the Biblical Hebrews. He was, however, anticipated by some three centuries by the Spanish physician Juan Huarte de San Juan (d. 1592), famed as the founder of modern psycho-technology and vocational guidance, who suggested an environmentalistic explanation of the specific traits of the Jewish mind. According to Huarte, the influences which once and for all molded the Jewish character were the wanderings of the Children of Israel in the hot climate and infertile environment of the desert, and the limited diet of manna on which they subsisted for forty years. Despite all subsequent experiences, including persecutions, slavery, and the like, the Jewish character has remained as it was formed in that ancient period.[3]

Coming now back to Renan, his general approach to the interrelationship between environment (or "nature") and culture is summed up in his statement to the effect that "all of nature is reflected . . . in the consciousness of primitive peoples in the form of gods as yet unnamed." [4] Accordingly, Renan attributed the origin of monotheism to the desert:

> There are monotheistic races just as there are polytheistic races, and this difference is derived from an original diversity in the manner of envisaging nature. In the Arab or Semitic conception nature does not live. The desert is monotheistic. Sublime in its immense uniformity, it revealed from the first day the idea of the infinite, but not that feeling of fecund activity with which an incessantly creative nature has inspired the Indo-European. This is why Arabia has always been the highway of monotheism. Nature does not play any role in the Semitic religions: they are all of the head, all metaphysical and psychological.[5]

Two years later (in 1855), Renan returned to this subject and emphasized:

> The Indo-European race, preoccupied with the variety of the universe, did not by itself arrive at monotheism. The Semitic race, on the contrary, guided by its firm and sure views, from the very first extricated the Divinity from its veils and, without reflection or reasoning, attained the most purified religious form which humanity has known. Monotheism in the world had been the work of the Semitic apostolate. . . .

Renan believed that the Semitic race had arrived at the notion of divine unity

> by a primitive intuition from its first days. . . . In place of a nature animated and alive in all its parts, it conceived, if I may say so, a nature dry and without fecundity. How great is the distance from this rigid and simple conception of a God isolated from the world and of a world fashioned like a vase between the

hands of the potter to the Indo-European theogony, animating and divinizing nature, conceiving life as a battle, the universe as a perpetual change. . . .

Building on his own momentum, Renan found that "the intolerance of the Semitic peoples is the necessary consequence of their monotheism," and that they were inferior in all non-religious respects to the Indo-Europeans:

> An incomplete race by its very simplicity, it has neither plastic arts, nor rational science, nor philosophy, nor political life, nor military organization. The Semitic race has never comprehended civilization in the sense which we attach to this word: one finds in its bosom neither great organized empires, nor public spirit, nothing which would recall the Greek city, nor anything that would resemble the absolute monarchy of Egypt and of Persia. The questions of aristocracy, of democracy, of feudalism, which comprise all the secrets of the history of the Indo-European peoples, make no sense for the Semites. Semitic nobility is entirely patriarchal: it is not derived from conquest, it has its source in the blood. As for supreme power, the Jew, like the Arab, accords it strictly to God alone. . . . Judaism, Christianity, Islam, here is their work, a work always directed to the same goal: to simplify the human spirit, to ban polytheism, to write at the head of the book of revelations the word which rendered human thought such a great service in effacing the mythological and cosmogonical complications in which profane antiquity lost itself: "In the beginning God created the heaven and the earth." [6]

While the followers of Renan accepted and even developed the theme of monotheism derived from the monotony of the desert with its harsh, rigorous, unmerciful conditions,[7] in recent decades this whole approach has been completely discredited. No serious scholar will today consider a view which attributes any major psycho-cultural feature to the influence of the physical environment as anything but an unfounded assumption. Nevertheless, since the introduction of monotheism into the consciousness of mankind is the greatest single achievement of the ancient Hebrews, a brief comment on Renan's thesis seems justified. First of all, one must take exception to representing monotheism, as Renan does, as if it had been the work of the "Semitic race" or "Semitic peoples," when, in fact, the Biblical Hebrews alone were responsible for it. To attribute this specifically Hebrew achievement to the "Semites" in general is as if an art critic would maintain that Impressionism, which flourished in France in the days of Renan, was developed by the Indo-Europeans. All the Semitic peoples, who comprised large cultural entities such as the Babylonians, Assyrians, Syrians, Canaanites, Arabs, etc., were strictly and richly polytheistic; only among the numerically insignificant Hebrew tribes did monotheism arise. To say that "Arabia has always been the highway of monotheism" is about as true as would be to assert that, say, Spain was the highway of Impressionism. In fact, Arabia has remained the last domain of polytheism in the ancient Near East until Muḥammad in the seventh century C.E. introduced his Jewish-inspired monotheistic faith.

As erroneous as attributing monotheism to the "Semites" is the attempt to see in it the influence of the desert. First of all, the monotony, or "immense uniformity," of the desert is nothing but a figment of scholarly fancy fondly indulged in by savants living amidst the rich verdure of a more humid northern clime. In reality, the Syro-Arabian desert, of which they spoke, is characterized by great variations of terrain, interspersed with green, lush oases, and by great seasonal variations, in fact, contrasts, between the dry summers when the earth (outside the oases, that is) is parched, yellow or brown, and the rainy winters when the desert literally turns green with grass and shrubs. This, and not the sandy expanses, such as the great Rubʿ al-Khali of southern Arabia, is the desert in which and around which the polytheistic Arabs had lived for many centuries in pre-Islamic days.

The Arabs, yes, but not the Biblical Hebrew fathers of monotheism. They lived, as exemplified by Abraham, the first Hebrew, in the fertile stretches of Mesopotamia and Canaan where there was enough vegetation all year round to keep their sheep and goats alive. Moses, the greater traditional master of monotheistic thought, spent his formative years in the luxurious court of Pharaoh in the most lavishly fertile riverain land in the world, Egypt. Finally, the highest development of Biblical religion, that of universal ethical monotheism, was the achievement of the great Hebrew prophets of the eighth century B.C.E., who lived in Judah and Israel, that is, not in the desert but in a "sown" land. Thus the construct of the desertic derivation of monotheism is factually untenable.

These factual details apart (and there are many more in the passages quoted which need correction, such as the erroneous generalizations that the Semites had no empires and no philosophy), and if we substitute "Hebrews" for "Semites," we have here a remarkable pen picture of what undoubtedly is the greatest achievement of the Hebrew genius: "the most purified religious form which humanity has known," the notion of the one and only God, the creator and wielder of supreme power.

Whatever the factors which went into its making, whatever the circumstances of its origin, this great and entirely unique [8] religious insight stamped the Jews once and for all with a special character, made them a "people dispersed and separated" (Esth. 3:8) for all times from the Gentiles whether the latter were polytheists, or the adherents of one of the two daughter-religions of Judaism, Christianity and Islam. If it is at all permissible to speak of a specific Jewish genius, a genius which accompanied them from their earliest origins to the century of Enlightenment, it is the genius for religion,[9] or, if you will, religious virtuosity. Not even the briefest sketch of the role religion played in the Jewish life from the days of Abraham to the present can be given within the confines of the present study, but one thing can, and has to, be said: Jewish religion more than anything else has kept the Jews alive to the present day, formed their minds and their personalities, determined their values and aspirations, spurred, and provided the outlet for their talents. It was his stubborn adherence to his ancestral faith which set the Jew apart from the Gentiles, although in many cases not to the extent of completely isolating him, or preventing his participation in the cultural endeavors of his non-Jewish environment.

In occupying the preeminent positions they did in a rich variety of cultural activities, the Jews manifested many talents, all of which, however, were circumscribed by age and place. The only area in which the Jews manifested genius throughout their history is that of religion. In most places and times, the Jewish religious genius expressed itself in nothing more than a total devotion to religious precepts, in living a life dominated by religion, in a willingness to endure sufferings and humiliation for the sake of their religion, and, if need be, to die for it, for "the sanctification of the Name." Occasionally, it consisted in producing doctrines destined to change man's knowledge of God and his relationship to the divine, and to become the bases of global religious movements or quasi-religious transformations. Mosaic tribal Yahwism, the universal ethical monotheism of the great Hebrew prophets of the eighth century B.C.E., and the teachings of Jesus based on the latter are among the supreme manifestations of the Jewish religious genius. Next to them ranks the Jewish influence manifested in Islam, followed half a millennium later by the Kabbala, and, after another five centuries, by the Hasidic movement. In modern times, the teachings of Marx and Freud gave rise to two great quasi-religious movements which transformed the conceptual outlook and the world view of man to no lesser degree than did the teachings of Jesus. Few indeed are the regions of the world today in which man's life is not dominated, or influenced, by at least one of the great Jewish-born or Jewish-based doctrines of Christianity, Islam, Marxism, and psychoanalysis or the psychological schools which grew out of it.

I shall refrain from speculating on the factors which may have had a bearing on the emergence of the Jewish religious virtuosity in antiquity and on its persistence through the ages. Unless one is satisfied with vague surmises and unprovable assumptions, such as the influence of the desert on the mind of the early Semites, such attempts are, I believe, a priori doomed to failure. Jewish religious talent is best regarded as a given, much like the genes which make the male lion grow a mane. What is more tempting, because it holds out more of a possibility of yielding results, is to try to correlate some of the other Jewish talents with this prime factor of religious virtuosity. Before doing so, however, let us continue with the presentation of a couple of additional scholarly views on special Jewish talents.

3. Views of Jewish Talents

We begin with Joseph Jacobs, with whom we are by now familiar. He has proffered some observations—actually not more than suggestions—on the factors which produced a special giftedness among the Jews in a number of fields. Attributing the musical preeminence of the Jews to "the home character of their religion which necessarily makes music a part of every Jewish home," he observes that music was "the only direction in which their artistic sensibilities could be gratified." The prominence of Jews in philology, Jacobs says, is "in part due to their frequent change of country, and also to the fact that they have had an additional sacred language besides the vernacular"; that is, he considers philological ability a direct outcome of polyglottism. The leadership of the Jews in finance was, according to Jacobs, "thrust upon them: the world forced them to become financiers centuries before finance became a power," and, moreover, "their finance has something to do with their decided leaning for mathematics." As for metaphysics, in which Jacobs finds the Jews prominent, here, too, "we can trace the influence of their mathematical tendency in the abstract nature of their thought." Altogether, Jacobs says, "the productions of Jewish intellect strike one as being predominantly *abstract* [emphasis in the original]," which, in turn, he explains as resulting from the Jews' "long life in cities and exclusion from Nature on the one side, and from the education which lies in handicrafts on the other." He concludes his brief comments on special Jewish talents by observing that "we may expect great mathematicians and philosophers from them, but not, I think, great inventors, biologists, or painters, till they have had time to throw off the effects of their long seclusion from Nature." [10]

While Jacobs is, in general, correct in naming the fields in which the Jews have shown special talent, some of his explanations are, to say the least, open to serious doubt. As for musical talent, surely it must have been present among the Jews before it became such an integral part of their religion that the "home character" of the latter made music a part of every Jewish home. If polyglottism leads to eminence in philological research, why have no other polyglot peoples, of whom there is no dearth, produced outstanding philologists? In pointing to external pressure as the factor which forced the Jews to specialize in finance (and commerce), Jacobs is undoubtedly right. Their forced concentration in this field provided the opportunity to whatever financial talent the Jews possessed to come to full fruition. While it is difficult to follow Jacobs when he attributes Jewish prominence in metaphysics to a "mathematical tendency," the general observation that the Jewish intellect has an abstract bent is certainly valid, although exclusion from nature and from handicrafts cannot explain it (quite apart from the fact that both "exclusions" were by no means general).

For our next sample we return to yet another scholar whom we have already met. Fritz Lenz, who considered the Jews a "mental race," observed in connection with special talents evinced by them that they "have produced noted scientists in the domains of physics, mathematics, medicine, and psychology." In the first two, "their successes have been rather in the abstract than in the concrete field; here their strength lies in their highly developed sense for numbers, and in their gift for formal logic." These Lenz considers hereditary factors, to which the Jews owe also their remarkable skill at chess. The chief concern of the Jews is "with all the factors of mental activity. Most of those who have given special attention to the problem of sexual life have been Jews (Freud, Adler, etc.)." In medicine,

> the field of social hygiene has been mainly worked by Jews. The fondness of the Jews for the art of healing dates from classical times. In part this devotion to medicine may doubtless arise from the circumstance that the Jew dreads pain, illness, and death, more than does the Teuton, but a powerful factor may also be that the success of the physician so largely depends upon his capacity for exerting a mental influence over his fellow human beings.

Other scientific fields preferred by the Jews are economics, philosophy (especially its psychological aspects), the history of art, the history of literature, and Germanistics. In the arts, "a disproportionately large number of great musicians have been Jews," while there have been few distinguished Jewish painters, and scarcely any great Jewish sculptors and architects. "The visualizing and technical ability of the Jews is comparatively small. The faculties of ear and tongue are in them more developed than the faculties of the eye." This trait, Lenz feels, seems to be connected with the lack of beauty in the Jewish body; a sense of form appears to have played a comparatively small part in the selective processes that produced the typical Jewish physique. If the Jews have contributed much to modern expressionism, the reason is that modern expressionism "is rather an art of mental expression than an art of configuration—a quasi-musical gift." The explanation of the intense Jewish participation in the acting profession is that "their marked imaginative insight (empathy), their power of putting themselves in others' places, makes the Jews born actors. . . . The Jewish aptitude for expression by words and gestures is also helpful to them as actors."

The Jews have a "talent for living among purely imaginative ideas as if they were concrete facts." This faculty "is advantageous, not only to the actor, but also to the barrister, the trader, the demagogue." Also in revolutionary movements "hysterically predisposed Jews play a great part, being able to give themselves up unreservedly to utopian ideas, and therefore able with a sense of inward sincerity to make convincing promises to the masses." Marx and Lassalle in the nineteenth century, and Eisner, Rosa Luxemburg, Leviné, Toller, Landauer, Szamuely, and Trotsky (Lenz observes) were all

Jews; and he adds that the explanation of such a great number of Jews among revolutionary leaders is to be sought in "the peculiarities above described, peculiarities which by no means tend towards destruction," as the anti-Semites believe, because "even when the Jew destroys, it is usually with the aim of rebuilding." [11]

There is no point in entering into a detailed analysis of Lenz's presentation of special Jewish talents, but two general comments must be made. One is that the portrait painted by Lenz, although richer, is fundamentally similar to that sketched by Jacobs a generation earlier. Lenz's list of fields of special Jewish talents includes ability for abstraction, sense for numbers, gift for formal logic, concern with all mental activity, developed faculties of the ear and tongue (rather than those of the eye), a talent for handling ideas as if they were facts, empathy, and a capacity for exerting mental influence. These basic traits are responsible, according to Lenz, for the Jewish prominence in mathematics, physics, medicine, psychology, philosophy, economics, art history, history of literature, Germanistics, music, acting, law, and revolutionary leadership.

Our second comment pertains to both Lenz and Jacobs. The purport of each is to describe the talents of the Jews in general; but the features they discern are valid only for those Jews who lived in their immediate environments, the German Jews, the English Jews, or, perhaps, the enlightened and partly assimilated element in European (Ashkenazi) Jewry as a whole. With the possible exception of musicality, all the talents enumerated by either Lenz or Jacobs could surface only in a modern Western cultural environment, or in the similarly stimulating atmosphere of medieval Arab culture. Where does one find, for instance, manifestations of any of these talents among Yemenite, Kurdish, Persian, Bokharan, or Afghan Jews?

The phenomenon of Jewish special talents as a correlate of the Gentile cultural environment can be observed in a number of greatly disparate historical contexts, as it was earlier in this book in the chapters dealing with the great encounters between Jews and Gentiles. In each of those historic encounters the Jews, stimulated by cultural developments which were taking place in the Gentile environment, manifested outstanding talents in certain fields, while in other places and at other times they showed no signs of the same talents.

These considerations vitiate not only the hypothesis of the existence of special talents among "the Jews" in general, but also the Lenzian concept of the Jews as a "mental race." Instead of accepting such a sweeping generalization, one is forced to be specific and to speak only of Jewish talents as manifested within a definite Gentile cultural environment. The talents attributed to the Jews by Jacobs and Lenz are not Jewish talents as such, but rather talents emerging in one particular Jewish community under the impact of a specific cultural and intellectual ambience on the traditional Jewish inclination to learning, scholarship, and mental activity. Or, to put it differently, what one can legitimately speak of is the relationship, including similarities and differences, between the special talents of the Jews and the Gentiles within a given cultural context.

We are now in a better position to scrutinize the effects of a religion-dominated past on the participation of Jews in various fields of cultural activity. Whether these effects are positive or negative, that is, whether they foster or inhibit a certain type of cultural specialization, can be observed only within specific local correlations between Jews and their Gentile environment. The baseline in each case was the Jewish religio-cultural tradition. From it, under the impact of the Gentile environment, the talented contingent in the Jewish community departed to varying degrees. Everywhere, however, the outcropping of special Jewish talent was a function of the interplay of these two factors—the Jewish tradition and the Gentile environment.

In the following pages of this chapter the reader will look in vain for the names of outstanding Jewish figures in painting, sculpture, architecture, music, literature, and poetry. While a brief section is devoted to each of these fields, it would have been cumbersome and tiring to include name lists which are often meaningless. Hence, I chose to forego the mention of any names and, instead, refer the reader to the readily available sources in which he can find extensive lists and biographies of Jews outstanding in the fields mentioned.

4. Painting and Sculpture

Two passages in the Bible spell out the prohibition of making statues and pictures. The first is contained in the Ten Commandments, the second of which reads as follows:

> Thou shalt have no other Gods before Me. Thou shalt not make unto thee a graven image, nor any manner of likeness, of anything that is in heaven above, or that is in the earth beneath, or that is in the water under the earth; thou shalt not bow down unto them, nor serve them; for I the Lord thy God am a jealous God, visiting the iniquity of the fathers upon the children unto the third and fourth generation of them that hate Me; and showing mercy unto the thousandth generation of them that love Me and keep My commandments.[12]

A more explicit enumeration of the things whose representation is forbidden is contained in a passage in Deuteronomy:

Take ye therefore good heed unto yourselves—for ye saw no manner of form on the day that the Lord spoke unto you in Horeb out of the midst of fire—lest ye deal corruptly, and make you a graven image, even the form of any figure, the likeness of male or female, the likeness of any beast that is on the earth, the likeness of any winged fowl that flieth in the heaven, the likeness of any thing that creepeth on the ground, the likeness of any fish that is in the water under the earth.[13]

The intent of these two passages when taken together is unmistakable. They prohibit the sculptural, and secondarily also the pictorial, representation of human beings, animals, birds, "creeping things," and fish for idolatrous purposes. Yet the rabbis who occupied themselves with the interpretation of these passages took them, in most places and most times, to be general prohibitions of the making of any statue or picture of all living things—irrespective of the purpose such likenesses were supposed to serve. This effectively prevented Jews, again in most places and most times, from engaging in sculpture and painting. Moreover, according to historians of Jewish culture and art, as a consequence of this blanket prohibition whatever talent Jews may have had for sculpture and painting became stifled, or at least diverted into related but not prohibited fields. Thus it came about that throughout the Middle Ages and until the Enlightenment, Jewish artistic activity was confined to the minor arts and to art-crafts: the embellishment of silver and bronze ritual objects such as *Rimmonim*, crowns, shields, and pointers for the Tora scrolls, the Eternal light, *Qiddush* and *Havdala* cups, spice containers (for the *Havdala*), Ethrog boxes (for Sukkot), Hanukka lamps; the application of decorations and figures embroidered in gold thread on the Tora wrappers, the curtains of the Holy Ark, the bags used for keeping and carrying the prayer-shawl and the phylacteries, etc.; the painting of decorative motifs on the interior walls of synagogues; the decoration of the Book of Esther, the Passover Haggada, prayer books, etc., and private religious documents such as the *ketubba* (marriage contract) with multicolored miniature ornaments and even pictures showing houses, animals, and human figures; colored paper-cuttings to be hung on the east side of the main room of the home to indicate the direction toward which one has to turn when praying; the ornaments of tombstones with floral and animal motifs in relief; ceramic plates for the *Havdala* and the Passover Seder with garlands, griffins, and other motifs. In all this, the influence of the Gentile environment is palpable, occasionally to the extent of causing the Jewish artist to take a timid step across the border of the forbidden territory of "graven images" and "likenesses." However, the representation of animals and people in miniature could be excused by arguing that if a living being is shown in a picture or relief at a fraction of its true size, this difference in itself excludes the work from the prohibited category of "likeness."

While the names of a few Jewish craftsmen are known, by and large all this was folk art, the Jewish equivalent of the arts and crafts which flourished among the simple Gentile folk. None of the works enumerated in the preceding paragraph evinced any true artistic ability; all of them were primitive attempts to embellish objects used in Jewish religious life, in the synagogue or in the home. None was art for art's sake. The major arts practiced by the Christian artists and developed by them to great heights had no counterpart among the Jews, and for this unquestionably the Biblical prohibition is responsible.

From the point of view of artistic development, the Diaspora environment in which the Jews lived fell into two sharply differentiated categories. One was the Hellenistic world, whose European part was drawn into the Christian orbit; the other was the Middle East in which, since the seventh century, Islam has been the dominant religion. Hellenism bequeathed to Christianity its love of the plastic arts and its use of painting and sculpture as handmaidens of religion. In a world in which painting and sculpture were among the foremost expressions of the religious sentiment, the rigorous abstention of the Jews from these major visual arts appeared in Christian eyes as a willful abnegation of basic religious values. From the Jewish aspect, since the practice of painting and sculpture was associated with first pagan and subsequently Christian idolatry, the Jewish objection to the great arts which served the Church became an essential part of the Jewish rejection of Christianity.

In the Muslim world, the situation was entirely different. Here the Jews lived in an environment which (with a few local exceptions) shared with them the view that the pictorial and sculptural represenation of living creatures, and especially of man, was a sin in the sight of God. According to Muslim law it is forbidden to copy living beings, those that have a *rūḥ* (= Hebrew *ruah*, spirit); only the images of plants and objects, that is, things apart from living creatures, can be represented in pictures.[14] That Islam derived these prohibitions from Judaism is well known but not relevant for our present purposes. What is important is that in the Muslim orbit the Jews had no occasion, as they had in the Christian world, to reject painting and sculpture because these arts did not form part of the cultural world of the Muslims. Whatever arts the Muslims did cultivate were licit for the Jews as well; hence, in this respect the Jews and Muslims were one, and their aniconism contrasted sharply with the iconolatry of Christianity.

Apart from the express prohibition of "graven images" and "likenesses," the very nature of the Jewish concept of God's incorporeality must have had a share in making the Jews less interested and less adept in the major arts. Painting and sculpture deal with form, and form, in a sense, is the antithesis of essence which can only be penetrated with the intellect. As Karl Schwarz, the well-known German Jewish art critic and art historian, pointed out in his book *The Jews in Art,* the characteristic Jewish disposition is mental rather than artistic.

> The inclination to a mental penetration of all phenomena, the mystical thinking, and the intellectual speculation, inhibited the development of the sense of form and the perception of its rhythmic harmony. Moreover, as among almost all Orientals, so among the Jews, the sense of color is much more strongly developed than the sense of form.

This is why, says Schwarz, the Jews "satisfy the sense of solemnity by lighting many candles, but do not know how to mark off a room from profane structures by a special way of building." In synagogue architecture there is, in most cases, a complete lack of feeling for space. In tombstones, too, effect is achieved not through overall form but small-scale decorative ornamentation.[15]

There is certainly some truth in the observation that in relation to the intellectual penetration of phenomena, the sense of form was underdeveloped among the Jews. Of all the ancient Near Eastern peoples, the Biblical Hebrews and their heirs, the Jews, stand entirely apart in the paucity of structural and other tangible remains they left behind for archeology to unearth and study. Their uniqueness in this respect parallels their exceptional position as a monotheistic people in the midst of polytheistic nations, and as believers in an invisible God whom one cannot and must not visually represent as against believers in many gods whose images were objects of worship in pagan piety. A people worshipping a God who has no form, whose very essence is antagonistic to form, cannot relate to form in the same positive manner, cannot develop the same sense of form, cannot devote itself to a study of the harmonies and the enjoyment of the beauties of form as can those peoples who are used to seeing their gods represented in beautiful, appealing, touching, moving, or awe-inspiring visible and tangible forms. The underdevelopment of the sense of form—indeed, of the aesthetic sense in general—was but one of the minor prices the Jews had to pay for their unswerving adherence to their unique concept of God.

Aside from the religious factor, there may have been another purely practical factor which prevented Jews from engaging in the practice of the major arts despite the example of their Christian neighbors. It seems likely that the Jews, who were so frequently driven out of their places of residence and always had to reckon with the possibility of expulsion, felt disinclined to invest either their talents or their money in large works of art, such as life-size paintings or statutes, which they would not have been able to take along in case they suddenly were forced to leave their homes. Small art objects were portable and could be saved; large ones would have had to be abandoned, or rapidly sold for a fraction of their worth. Moreover, religion intruded even here. Religious Jews had to be ready to leave their homes under short notice not only in case of expulsion by Gentile authorities, but also in case of the arrival of the Messiah, whom they expected any day to come and lead them back to the Holy Land. When the news of the pseudo-Messiah Shabbatai Zevi reached Amsterdam, most of the Jews quickly sold whatever they could not carry along, chartered ships, and waited for his signal to set sail. The same scene could be observed all over the Jewish world. In the early nineteenth century, Rabbi Moses Sofer of Pressburg warned his congregation not to build houses because such a major and lengthy undertaking would make it appear as if they had given up hope in the imminent coming of the Messiah. In brief, neither the social nor the religious atmosphere in which the Jews lived was conducive to the development of the major arts of painting, sculpture, and architecture.

One can perhaps carry this argument a step further and maintain that this religiously and socially conditioned turning away from the visual arts led to a general neglect of the visual aspect of existence in favor of the oral and vocal one. The fact is that also beyond the artistic sphere, the Jews of the long Exile remained passive and unproductive in the visual field. They created little that was original in any domain of material culture: they developed no styles of their own in dwellings, in furniture, in utensils, in clothing. In all this they were content to copy what the Gentile environment had to offer, occasionally with minor modifications, and but rarely with original contributions.

The neglect of the visual aspects of existence brought about, or was correlated to, a neglect of visual ability. After hundreds of years of this kind of life, the traditional lack of interest in things visual led to a decreased visual ability—not genetically conditioned, of course, but transmitted and reinforced anew in each generation culturally, i.e., environmentally. This has been shown in numerous studies (several of which were quoted earlier), in which the Jewish subjects were found to achieve lower scores on tests measuring visual ability, visual reasoning, space conceptualization, etc., than Gentile subjects. The relatively short time that has passed since large Jewish population aggregates have entered the mainstream of modern European culture has evidently not been enough to bring about a significant change in the Jewish home environment which would be required before the Jewish subjects could achieve higher scores on such tests.

All this does not mean that individual Jews could not develop talent in the fine arts. Of course they could and did. Prior to the Enlightenment there were only a very few Jewish painters, among Sephardi Jews who were exposed to Italian, Dutch, and English artistic influences. After it, the number of Ashkenazi Jews who suddenly made their appearance in the major arts was impressive.

There can be no doubt that, down to the nineteenth century, the Biblical prohibition of three-dimensional "graven images" was felt to be a more stringent one than that of "likenesses" of a two-dimensional nature. The latter was occasionally disregarded, or liberally interpreted, and examples of pictorial art used in synagogue decoration survive from antiquity from places in which Jews lived in iconolatrous pagan or Christian environments. The murals of the Dura Europos synagogue from the third century C.E., depicting Abraham, Moses, David, and other Biblical figures, are a prime example of this kind of pictorial representation. Others are the pictures in the fine mosaic floor found in the ruins of a sixth-century synagogue at Bet Alpha in the eastern Jezreel Valley in Israel, which also show numerous human and animal figures. More recent (medieval or later) examples of Jewish miniature art were referred to above. With these historical antecedents, soon after the Enlightenment painting became an artistic expression practiced by Jews in a manner resembling the styles developed by Gentile painters. From the early nineteenth century on, the number of the Jews in painting and the graphic arts grew rapidly. Many of them ranked with the best non-Jewish artists, and before long in several Central and West European countries there were considerably more Jewish painters in proportion to the total number of the Jews than Christian painters in relation to the total Christian population.

Compared to this rapid penetration of Jews into painting and the graphic arts, their entrance into sculpture was slower and much less frequent. From the Middle Ages we hear occasionally of Jewish medalists, artists who fashioned coins, medals, and medallions—an activity they continued into the twentieth century. But not until the second half of the nineteenth century did the first modern Jewish sculptor appear. Karl Schwarz surveyed the entire course of Jewish sculpture in all lands of the Diaspora until 1935 and found only 32 names worth mentioning, as against 106 Jewish painters (beginning with the early nineteenth century, and not counting several dozen graphic artists), including some of the greatest names in the field.

Among the younger generation of artists today Jewish painters and sculptors are well represented, although there is little that is specifically "Jewish" in their work. Since the modern development of painting and sculpture among the Jews was a product of the assimilation that set in in the wake of the Enlightenment, it was almost inevitable that these artists should share the cultural and artistic outlook of their neighbors and join in those artistic styles and trends which developed among the Gentile majority.[16]

5. Architecture

Throughout history, architecture on a monumental scale has been confined to two types of structures: temples for gods; and palaces for kings, including the Egyptian Pyramids, which were palaces to be inhabited by Pharaohs after their death. From antiquity almost no Jewish royal palaces have survived, and in the Diaspora the Jews had neither kings nor potentates powerful enough to have palaces built for themselves. This leaves the temple as the only type of large structure in which Jewish architecture could have proved its mettle. Unfortunately, no traces have been left of Solomon's temple built in Jerusalem by Phoenician architects, nor of its replacement by the Jewish returnees from Babylonia under Zerubbabel, nor of the restructuring of the latter by Herod. Remains of ancient synagogues, which have been preserved in Palestine and elsewhere, show that they were built in the style of Greek and Roman temples. Ever since that time, the overall rule was that the synagogues everywhere reflected the architectural styles of the religious buildings of the Gentiles among whom the Jews lived.

In the Roman period, the synagogues built in both Palestine and the Diaspora followed patterns of Greco-Roman basilicas. After the Arab conquest of Spain, the Jews of the Iberian peninsula built synagogues which looked like mosques, although sometimes they were also partly Gothic.[17] In medieval Germany the Jews built their houses of worship after the twin-nave plan used by the austere churches of the Mendicant orders. This type of religious building was carried east to Bohemia and thence to Poland, where it was used as model for both churches and synagogues. In the sixteenth century the Polish synagogues adopted the square, centralized plan which had evolved under the influence of the Italian Renaissance on Polish architecture. After the expulsion of the Jews from Spain and Portugal, those who settled in Holland built synagogues similar in floor plan to the mosques; however, they also took the houses of Protestant dissenters as a model in building galleries, most of which were used for seating the women. This Amsterdam pattern became standard for Sephardi Jews and was adopted ultimately by the Ashkenazim as well. In nineteenth-century Europe, when the Church reverted to medieval Romanesque and Gothic styles, the Jewish synagogue architects first tried a less ecclesiastical, attenuated version of the Romanesque style; then, in a romantic attempt at recovering the ancient Jewish spirit, they turned to the Orient, and for decades a pseudo-Moorish style became dominant in synagogue architecture.[18]

The same observation can be made of the decoration employed for the purpose of embellishing the interior and, to a lesser extent, the exterior of synagogues. In the Greco-Roman period, murals and mosaics depicting human and animal figures such as were characteristic of the pagan temples were used on the walls and floors of synagogues.[19] In the Arab orbit, the floral and geometric patterns on doors, windows, and in the form of friezes, characteristic of the mosques, appear in synagogues. Moreover, the use of inscriptions running along the whole length of the walls under the ceiling, or framing doors and windows, is also emulated, except that mostly Hebrew inscriptions are used instead of Arabic (although the latter can be found, e.g., in the famous El Transito synagogue in Toledo, built in the fourteenth century).[20]

Inside the synagogues, they imitated the raised mosque pulpit called *minbar* (pronounced *mimbar*) in Arabic, which is approached by a long straight flight of stairs, except that they placed the corresponding structure, a highly elevated *bima* (parapeted platform used for the reading of the Tora) on the longitudinal axis of the hall facing the Ark. Occasionally, the *bima* was placed closer to the western than the eastern wall of the synagogue in whose center the Ark was (and still is in all synagogues to the west of Israel) located. In the Middle Ages, the Ashkenazi Jews designated the *bima* by the term *al-membra* (derived from the Arabic *al-mimbar*) which, in German lands, became *al-memor*.

As far as the seating arrangements were concerned, in Muslim lands (Spain, North Africa, and the Near East) the worshippers sat around the four walls of the synagogue on the floor, which was covered with mats, following the prevalent Muslim custom in the mosques. In the Christian countries, where the Christian worshippers sat on chairs or benches in their churches, the same seats were used in synagogues.[21]

There is a lot more to be said about the influence of Gentile architectural styles and decorative patterns on synagogue architecture,[22] but these few remarks should suffice to show that the Gentile environment everywhere and at all times indelibly impressed itself upon the form of the buildings erected by Jews to serve as their house of prayer.

The absence of original Jewish architectural activity for nearly two thousand years (from the fall of Judea to the Romans to the Enlightenment) is eloquently illustrated by the fact that the article "Architecture and Architects" in the *Encyclopaedia Judaica* contains two parts only—one dealing with antiquity and the other with the modern period. As a connection between these two parts, the article states that, with the exception of the synagogue, "it is impossible to point to the development of a distinctive Jewish style of building." [23] But even in synagogue architecture, nothing that could be considered originally "Jewish" has developed to the present time. In the twentieth century, when church architecture in Europe and America struck out into new directions, synagogue architecture too began to experiment with modern styles, again with the result that only the emblem—the cross or the two tablets of the Law—gives a clue as to whether one faces a Christian or Jewish house of worship.

6. Music

The inhibiting effect Jewish religion had on the development of Jewish fine arts was duplicated, although not quite to the same extent, by its role in impeding the Jewish musical expression. Not quite, because the prohibition of all "graven images" and "likenesses" was Biblical, or at least taken to be Biblical in post-Biblical times, while the prohibition of instrumental music was definitely post-Biblical in its origin. In the retrospect of the Talmudic age, all "graven images" of the Biblical period (with the exception of the Cherubim [24] and some other sculpture of lesser importance) were considered idolatrous and hence forbidden; while the many musical instruments used in the temple service were regarded as part of the legitimate religion, and their prohibition was merely a rabbinical ruling issued as a measure to make manifest that the Jewish people was in a state of perpetual mourning over the destruction of the Temple. Because of this difference in provenance, in later ages it was considered a lesser sin to disobey the prohibition of instrumental music than to transgress the taboo on painting and sculpture.

There is another parallel as well between the traditional Jewish position on fine arts and on music. The prohibition of fine arts, as we have seen, channeled Jewish talent into the minor arts of silver jewelry, embroidery, manuscript illumination and illustration, and the like. Quite similarly, the prohibition of instrumental music resulted in a concentration on vocal music, on singing, which came to play an exceedingly important role in Jewish life.

In various Biblical passages, and especially in the Psalms, a great many musical instruments are mentioned by name. Further, the early rabbis who lived before the destruction of the Temple by the Romans (in 70 C.E.) personally witnessed the Temple services and heard enough of the ritual music which formed part of them to leave behind some traditions concerning the instruments used in it. After the destruction of the Temple, these Biblical references and rabbinic traditions came to form the basis of the prohibition of instrumental music in the synagogue as well as outside it. Subsequent religious developments made this prohibition both general and almost total. They allowed for two exceptions: the Shofar and (among Ashkenazi Jews) the "klezmer" and its equivalent among Sephardi and Oriental Jewish communities.

The Shofar is the ancient ritual horn which was used in Biblical times on various festive occasions. [25] The forms of its ritual use crystallized in Talmudic times and seem to have remained unchanged ever since. The most frequently used Shofar was a ram's horn, although wild goats' horns and other horns (except for a cow's horn) were also used. [26] It is blown once every day (except for the day preceding *Rosh haShana*) of the penitential month of Elul; a hundred times on each of the two days of *Rosh haShana*, the Jewish New Year; and then one single time at the conclusion of *Yom Kippur*, the awesome Day of Atonement. In addition, it is blown on the occasion of the announcement of an excommunication.

The sound range of the Shofar consists of no more than two or three notes which are organized into three brief phrases termed *t'qi'a*, *sh'varim*, and

SHOFAR-CALLS

Source: The Jewish Encyclopedia, s.v. Shofar.

FIGURE 1

t'ru'a, respectively. That these phrases go back to pre-exilic days is shown by the fact that they are basically the same in the religious-musical traditions of the most diverse Ashkenazi, Sephardi, and Oriental Jewish communities (see Figure 1). It is a specified religious duty to listen to the sounds of the Shofar, which are considered awe-inspiring in the highest degree. Upon hearing them one is supposed to be induced to repentance—repentance being the great central theme of the solemn Days of Awe—and to becoming aware of the transitory nature and frailty of human life and of the incomprehensible greatness of God. They are believed to frighten and confuse Satan and to force him to cease his two customary nefarious pursuits of seducing men to sin and accusing them before God of having sinned. Most important, they are believed to awaken the compassion of God, who on these solemn days sits on His Throne of Judgment and decides the fate of every man. Thus, while from a purely musical point of view the Shofar is an insignificant and primitive instrument, emotionally it occupies a most important place in Jewish consciousness as a tonal bridge linking man and God.

The "klezmer" is quite a different thing. While the Shofar is Biblical in origin, the klezmer is not more than a few hundred years old. Its very name is a relatively recent Yiddish contraction of the Hebrew *kle zemer,* meaning "instruments of music," which was changed so as to denote not the instruments, but the person playing them (plural, *klezmerim*). The typical East European klezmer of the nineteenth century played the fiddle, although occasionally some klezmerim would also use the flute, the horn, the bass violin, and the drum.[27]

The one occasion on which the klezmerim were indispensable was the traditional East European Jewish wedding, at which they would play their repertoire of traditional folk tunes. Purim, too, was an occasion for the klezmerim to sound off, in the houses of the better-to-do where traditional Purim-plays would also be performed, mostly by children.

The klezmerim fiddled gypsy-fashion; they learned to play their violins one from the other without ever learning to read notes. Their reputation was, if not exactly low, a far cry from the respect enjoyed by an expert *ba'al t'qi'a*, or Shofar-blower.

To complete the picture, and since in modern music all kinds of noise-producing instruments have found a place, one might add that on Purim, whenever the name of Haman was reached by the reader who recited the Scroll of Esther in the synagogue, the children were allowed to break into an infernal noise with the rattles bought or provided for them by their parents for this one day in the year.

In the Muslim world, the same instruments, such as the *rabāb* (a one-stringed boxlike violin), the *'ūd* (a many-stringed lute), etc., were used by both Muslims and Jews. Arabs and Jews, who shared the religious abstention from representational art, also shared the religious limitation in instrumental music. In fact, in some places the religious prohibition of instrumental music was more strictly observed by the Muslims than by the Jews, with the result that Jewish musicians would be invited to perform in Muslim houses on festive occasions. This was the practice in Persia, for example.

As this brief sketch shows, the practice of instrumental music was severely limited among the Jews until the Enlightenment. Vocal music, on the other hand, was ubiquitous, although religious tradition approved only of the male voice. An old Talmudic rule had it that *Qol ba'isha 'erva* or "The voice in woman is a nakedness," [28] meaning that it was forbidden to listen to the singing of women because of its eroticism. Consequently, the traditional Jewish synagogue service—as it developed in Talmudic times and was conducted, until the Enlightenment, in every community all over the Diaspora—comprised only male voices, which were utilized extensively.

The traditional Jewish service consisted of nothing but singing or chanting. All the prayers and benedictions were sung or chanted either in unison by the whole congregation (the men, that is; the women, who sat secluded in an adjoining room or in a gallery, were never supposed to raise their voices), or by the cantor, or in responsive singing in which the cantor and the congregation sang alternately. In those services in which reading from the Bible was a part, this, too, was done in the traditional form of cantillation. The only exception from this general rule was the silent recitation of the so-called Eighteen Benedictions by the congregation, which were thereafter repeated by the cantor in their traditional melody. Children's voices, in the form of choirs to accompany the cantorial solo, came into vogue only after the Enlightenment in imitation of the Christian usage. In some of the Reform temples women, too, are admitted to the chorus, following the more widespread use of the organ by liberal congregations—another instance of Jewish emulation of Christian custom.

Whatever religious rituals were performed in the home were also sung. These included prayers, benedictions, the after-meal grace, and so on. In brief, one can say that the traditional Jew never spoke to God, he always sang to Him.

An important part of traditional religious life was the study of the Talmud to which every Jew tried to devote as much time as his circumstances allowed. Whether studying alone or in a group, at home, in the synagogue, or at the *Bet haMidrash* ("House of Study"), it was always done in sing-song, in the same chanting in which it was taught to children in the *Heder* and to youths in the yeshiva.

After the late eighteenth century the Jews of Eastern Europe were split into Hasidim and their opponents, the Mitnagdim. While the melodic repertoire of the two parties differed considerably, singing and chanting played the same role in the lives of both. The melodies sung in various parts of the Diaspora differed from place to place and frequently showed the influence of the Gentile environment, but common to Jewish communities all over the world was a life full of tunes and melodies. Singing was the most widespread folk art, unfailingly practiced by every Jew every day, and not confined to religious life. On the contrary, it expressed the simple people's hopes, joys, anguish, and despair. Women, too, could indulge in it when alone, or within the family circle.

Cantorial singing and folk tunes, of which each Jewish community developed its own traditional style and repertoire, are a richly variegated musical art form, but their relationship to the great musical traditions of the West is like that of the Jewish embroiderers', silversmiths', and miniaturists' works to those of the major Western arts of sculpture and painting. In both music and the visual arts, the Jews were condemned by their religious tradition to remain confined to a few minor fields, while being barred by the same tradition from the major ones. What works of genius remained unborn as a result, we shall never know.

As far as the arts were concerned, the Jews thus adhered to a typically Middle Eastern religio-cultural tradition everywhere, even in the West, until the onset of the Enlightenment.

As early as the seventeenth century, well-to-do Jews in Central and Western Europe began to have their children, and especially their daughters, instructed in singing and instrumental music. This trend increased considerably in the eighteenth century with the onset of Enlightenment. Gradually the influence of European music penetrated even the synagogue, and cantors began to compose new, "modern" synagogue melodies. Since among the Enlighteners music came to be regarded an important path of Jewish integration into European culture, as soon as the obstacles of personal advancement were removed, Jewish musicians entered the mainstream of Gentile musical life. By the twentieth century Jews constituted the majority among the greatest violinists, and a very high proportion of the foremost pianists, and had a fair share in the ranks of outstanding composers and conductors.[29]

7. Literature

That writing is a special Jewish talent is a story as old as the Bible. The Hebrew Scripture contains some of the greatest prose and poetry of world literature. It is taught today in many college courses under the title "The Bible as Literature." Less known is the literary quality of the Hebrew *Midrash*, the rich homiletic and legendary literature produced by Jews from circa 400 to 1200 C.E. In the later Middle Ages, which for the Jews ended only with the Enlightenment, their sole literary achievement of the highest quality was Hebrew poetry, a remarkable feat for a people whose colloquials were languages other than Hebrew. In the Middle Ages began the Jewish trend of writing literary works in the languages of the Gentiles, especially scientific, scholarly, and philosophical studies (primarily in Arabic). At the same time, some Jewish authors wrote poetry, prose, and plays also in German, Italian, Spanish, and Portuguese. But it was not until the Enlightenment that the Jewish literary talent burst upon the European scene and that the output of a splendid galaxy of Jewish poets and novelists began to appear in all the major, and several of the minor, European languages, as well as in the home-grown Jewish tongue of Yiddish. Since the nineteenth century Jewish writers have figured prominently in all the major Western literatures, often taking the lead in new literary developments.

A prerequisite for this literary flowering was the ability to learn new languages, which the Jews possessed in ample measure. Leaving aside the more remote past, in the last few centuries prior to the Enlightenment many if not most of the Jews in Eastern Europe had a working knowledge of four languages: Yiddish, which was their mother tongue and colloquial; Hebrew, which they learned in childhood so as to be able to read and understand the prayers and the Bible; Aramaic, which was acquired somewhat later and kept alive by a ceaseless study of the Talmud; and the local idiom of the non-Jewish population, such as Polish, Ukrainian, Russian, or Lithuanian, which was necessary for maintaining contact with the Gentiles upon whom the live-lihood of most Jews depended. With the spread of the Enlightenment the acquisition of a new language, one of the media of modern European cul-ture, became indispensable; and, given the polyglottism of many genera-tions, it was accomplished with great ease. Thus, within a generation, cul-tured (in the new sense) East European Jews had mastered German, which also became the literary language of the educated Ashkenazi Jews in general all over Central and Western Europe with the exception of France and En-gland, where they acquired the national tongues.

Once this was accomplished, and in cases almost simultaneously, the age-old Jewish literary talent began to make use of the new media which the Enlightenment put at its disposal. However, in order to write in German, French, or English, the Jewish writer had to acquire more than fluency in the language itself. He had to acquaint himself with the treasures of the lan-guage, with the works important and influential in it; he had to saturate him-self with its style, immerse himself in its spirit. This, in turn, meant that the works created by Jewish writers in German, French, English, or any other European language belonged largely to those national literatures, even though they bore more or less clearly marked Jewish characteristics.

This, of course, leads us right into the middle of the much-debated prob-lem of what constitutes "Jewish" literature. To talk for the moment only of the novel, is a novel written by a Jewish author *eo ipso* part of Jewish litera-ture? Or, if written in, say, German, is it part of German literature? And conversely, does a novel written by a Gentile author dealing with a Jewish theme belong to Jewish literature? Where shall we place the Jewish Franz Werfel's novel *The Forty Days of Musa Dagh*, which deals with the tragedy of Armenians in Turkey? Or the Christian Thomas Mann's *Joseph and His Brethren*, which uses not only the Biblical story of Joseph but also many of its Midrashic embellishments? Or the Christian John Hersey's *The Wall*, which tells of the heroism of the Jewish defenders of the Warsaw ghetto? And what about the half-Jewish Marcel Proust's *Remembrance of Things Past*, whose hero is a French Catholic intellectual of Jewish descent who feels himself Jewish but moves in the circle of French aristocrats? The mere enumeration of these examples suffices to show the impossibility of imposing a taxonomical Jewish-Gentile dichotomy on the novel. Shall we add just one more example from poetry? There is the famous poem *Die Lorelei*, written by Heinrich Heine who converted to Christianity but retained a strong emo-tional commitment to Judaism. This poem had become part of German liter-ature, more than that, of German folk-consciousness, to the extent that the Nazis, unable to spirit it away, designated it a German folk song, "author un-known." This poem is certainly as far from being considered part of Jewish literature as any piece of writing conceivably can be.

Since our subject is the Jewish mind, we don't have to be concerned about literary works written by Gentiles even if their themes are decidedly Jewish. For the same reason literary works written by Jews, however non-Jewish in theme, character, and intent, *are* our concern because they are products of the Jewish mind. From this standpoint, the *Lorelei* and the *Musa Dagh* and the thousands of works written by Jewish authors in many languages and devoid of all Jewish identification appear as so many examples of the Jewish literary talent, even if they are in no way parts of Jewish literature.

Literature written by Jews differs from other literatures in the same way that the Jews themselves differ from other peoples. Other peoples live in one country, form one nation, speak one language. The Jews live in many countries, are parts of many nations, speak many languages. Likewise, the literature of other peoples is written in the national language by individuals who are members of one nation. This is the general rule. Jewish literature cannot be described in this manner. The term "Jewish literature" is not at all analogous to French literature, or American literature. Strictly speaking, there is no such thing as Jewish literature. There is only: (a) literature written by Jews in European (and other) languages; (b) literature written by non-Jews dealing, in one way or another, with Jews; (c) literature written by Jews and dealing with Jews. In addition, of course, there is Hebrew literature, written in the national tongue of the Jews, from the Bible down to the latest Hebrew writings in Israel and in the Diaspora, and dealing, in its recent development, with all those subjects which are found in the literatures of other nations. Finally, there were, and to some extent still are, the literatures produced by Jews in their specific languages apart from Hebrew: in Aramaic, Ladino, Yiddish, Judeo-Arabic, Judeo-Persian, and Neo-Aramaic.

Such observations could be made also of other fields in which Jewish talent has expressed itself in the Diaspora. A work of art or a piece of music does not become "Jewish" merely because it was created by a Jew; again, the product of a non-Jewish painter, sculptor, or composer may have a so-called Jewish theme, but again, this alone does not make it "Jewish art" or "Jewish music" any more than a Rubens goddess is Greek art or Ravel's *La Valse* is Viennese music. With art and music there is the additional problem that they cannot be clearly identified with a national entity by means of language, as can literature. Hence national boundaries are blurred among all peoples. In the case of the Jews, this blurring of boundaries is more pronounced. Most of the art and music produced by Jews since the Enlightenment belongs to the trends developed in their Gentile environments. Thus Jewish artists have participated in many countries in Impressionism, Pointillism, Symbolism, Expressionism, Cubism, Futurism, Dada, Surrealism, etc., and Jewish architects in the Bauhaus and other modern developments. Similarly, Jewish composers participated in the writing of atonal music and other modern musical trends in various countries. It is usually quite clear to which school these artists and composers belong; whether their works belong to

French, or German, or American art, is questionable, but there is no doubt that they do not belong to Jewish art.

This leaves as unquestionably Jewish only those works of art, music, and literature created by Jews which are informed by Jewish tradition, Jewish mood, Jewish spirit, or which have Jewish themes. Works of this kind form only a small part of the total Jewish artistic, musical, and literary output. This is the onus of the Diaspora and, from the standpoint of Jewish national consciousness, its tragedy. When Shakespeare writes about Julius Caesar, it is English literature. When Racine writes of Iphigenia, it is French literature. But the work of a Jewish author dealing with a non-Jewish theme is not Jewish literature; if it is written in English, it is English literature, if in French, French literature, no matter what Jewish sensitivity he brings to the subject. Only if he chooses a Jewish subject does his work become Jewish literature, although even in that case it belongs also to the literature of the language in which he wrote it. Thus the literature produced by Jews in the Diaspora in the languages of their Gentile environments, even if it has a Jewish subject matter, is a hyphenated literature—American-Jewish literature; French-Jewish literature; and so forth.

Only in Israel have the Jews rid themselves of this hyphenated condition of their art, music, and literature. However, even there, the work they produce is only in small part "Jewish." What it is in every case is Israeli. Thus there is a modern Israeli art, Israeli architecture, Israeli music, and Israeli Hebrew literature. In all this, the Israeli output is the taxonomical equivalent of the art, etc., of any other nation. There is, to be sure, a hyphenated art in Israel as well; but it is produced by the Arabs—their art is Israeli-Arab art, their music Israeli-Arab music, and so on.

What is of special interest for us in the present context is that whatever language the Jews acquired or developed was used without delay as a literary medium. This holds good even for languages which were only spoken but not written by Jews. Thus the Kurdish Jews had a rich folk poetry in Neo-Aramaic, transmitted orally for generations, until my late teacher and friend Professor Joseph J. Rivlin had it written down, collected, and published.[30] In a literate environment, Jewish talent enriched the literatures of all those countries in which the Jews assimilated linguistically and received stimuli from the literary development of the Gentile environment. Moreover, in the major languages of Western literature, especially English, French, German, and Russian (as well as in some of the minor languages such as Hungarian and Czech), Jewish authors struck out in new directions and frequently formed the *avant garde* of new trends. In some of these literatures (notably German and subsequently American), their share in the total literary output exceeded by far the numerical proportion of the Jews in the general population. A relatively recent development on the American literary scene is the appearance of many novels with a Jewish theme written by leading Jewish authors.

While I have spoken only of the novel, Jewish talent has sought out numerous other literary fields. In all the major literatures of the Western world Jews have figured as poets, playwrights, essayists, critics, and have played a prominent role in journalism. They have also contributed to the servicing of literature as publishers, editors, theatrical directors and producers, film makers, and the like. Especially in pre-Hitler Germany and Hungary, and in post-World War II America, Jews had a major share in the literary, musical, artistic, and theatrical life of the country.

We can now try to answer our initial question as to the factors which can be considered responsible for the manifestation of special Jewish talents in certain times and places. It appears that the following conditions had to be met for this to take place:

1. The absence of traditional religious inhibitions, or at least the kind of disregard for them which developed especially following the Jewish Enlightenment.

2. The presence of a sense of settledness, of security, of permanent, residential rootedness.

3. Positive influences from the non-Jewish environment, and a general atmosphere appreciative of the specialty engaged in.

4. The possibility of working in the chosen field, including the admission of the Jewish aspirant to schools, academies, and other professional institutions.

This, of course, presupposes something about which no concrete information is available—that the incidence of individuals with a potential talent in the various fields is at least as high among the Jews as among their Gentile neighbors. Only if this is indeed the case can the actualization of Jewish talent be contingent on the circumstantial and environmental factors enumerated above. However, it would seem to me that the end result of the process—that is, the actual appearance of talented Jews in the arts, in architecture, music, literature, and other fields, wherever the listed conditions were met—permits us, nay, forces us, to conclude that underlying this ample outpouring of Jewish talent since the Enlightenment there must have been a large generalized reservoir of Jewish creative ability. But, again because of specific traditional and circumstantial factors, this remained untapped up to that fateful turning point in Jewish history.

14

Personality and Character

The last two chapters made it clear that—with the notable exception of Jewish religious genius—the talents possessed by Jews have expressed themselves in those fields of specialization which were and are well developed and had importance in the cultures of their Gentile environments. The same general observation can be made with reference to the personality, or character traits, exhibited by the Jews. Here, too, the mold of the environment would inevitably impress itself upon the Jew and remarkable similarities could be, and indeed were, observed between the Gentile and the Jewish personality.

1. The Problem of the "Jewish Personality"

In trying to give a simple definition of personality, one can scarcely do better than say that it consists of the patterns of behavior characteristic of a particular person.[1] These patterns of behavior are organized in such a way as to enable the individual to get along in the society of which he is a member. Because of the pressure (or influence) of the social environment to which the individual is exposed from the moment of his birth, his personality structure comprises traits in which he is similar to others in his society. The sum total of these similar traits constitutes what has variously been called "modal personality," "basic personality structure," "typical personality," "configurational personality," "social character," or "national character."[2] While the precise connotation of each of these terms differs, all are based on the observation that people who grew up in one culture share a number of character traits. For reasons which will become obvious as the discussion proceeds, I prefer to use the term "modal personality," as being most suitable in presenting and analyzing the common features found in the personality of a given Jewish group.

Each individual's personality, of course, is made up of features in which he is like all other men, as well as features in which he is like no other man.

Understandably, however, the "culture and personality" school concentrates not on these features, but on the area which lies between these two categories. This consists of the traits in which members of a given human aggregate are similar to one another and differ from persons outside the group. The hypothesis which has most dominated the culture and personality field—derived from the work of such thinkers as Max Weber, Abram Kardiner, Erich Fromm, Talcott Parsons, and David Riesman—holds that the efficient functioning of a society depends upon the existence in its members of "congruent personality or motivational structures, sometimes referred to as social character. This congruence is thought to be produced by the shaping of personality by society's socialization institutions." [3] Almost all theories developed by students of culture and personality hold that the socio-cultural environment in which the individual develops has a profound effect on the course of his development. While the precise nature of these influences is still far from being adequately understood, there is general agreement on the existence of a correlation between the character of the culture, and in particular its socialization (or enculturation) institutions, on the one hand, and the modal personality "produced" by them, on the other.

Applying this approach to the Jews, one can, first of all, observe that within a given socio-cultural environment they exhibit certain personality traits that are like those of the Gentiles among whom they live, while in other traits they differ from them in varying degrees. On the other hand, it can also be observed that the basic personality of two Jewish aggregates— say, that of the French Jews and of the Rumanian Jews—contains a set of features in respect of which they differ, while in another set of traits they are similar to each other. On the basis of such observations, one can theoretically assume that the modal personality of a Jewish group will, in certain respects, be (1) like other Jewish groups; (2) like the non-Jews of its environment; and (3) like neither.

As far as the genesis of the modal personality is concerned, there is no consensus among psychologists. While they agree on the factors which go into it, they differ over the weight to be assigned to these factors. All agree, however, that the cultural milieu in which the individual grows up and which is mediated to him in the early life stages by the mother is an important molding force of the personality. In the case of the Jews, the cultural milieu is that of the specific local Jewish subculture, which consists of Jewish as well as non-Jewish features. Hence the environmental factor itself produces, or contributes to the development of, both "Jewish" and "non-Jewish" personality traits. Some psychologists put greater stress on non-environmental factors in personality development and emphasize the importance of biological-genetic factors in the development of special characteristics.[4] Whatever the weight given to human biology, in this respect too the situation among the Jews is, generally speaking, more complex than among the Gentiles, since the genetic antecedents of the Jews involve, as a rule, a larger number of strains and a greater variance.[5]

Another point to be stressed is that within the area of one common culture great variability in personality has been found to exist. Hence when one speaks of the English, or Spanish, personality one actually focuses on the *mode*, which may comprise considerably less than the absolute majority of the population in question, and which neglects the non-modal personality types in it. For the Jews this variance factor is even more pronounced. Jewish communities in modern times represent the end result of many migrations which frequently brought together in one locality elements of diverse antecedents. On analysis, they will probably be found to display greater personality differences than the Gentile population of the same place.

This internal personality variance within a given Jewish community is correlated to the degree of heterogeneity in its historical background. To take two extreme cases: the American Jewish community, composed as it is of immigrants from a large number of countries and their children and grandchildren, exhibits great personality variance. It is only in the third generation that this variance tends to become submerged as a result of an inner-Jewish mutual assimilation and amalgamation and of the overall Jewish tendency to assimilate to the dominant American culture and personality. On the other hand, the variance in the Yemenite Jewish personality can be expected to be small because, until their transplantation to Israel in 1948–49, the Yemenite Jews had been an isolated community, practicing inbreeding, and exposed for hundreds of years to the same Muslim Arab external and Jewish internal socio-cultural environment. Thus, in general, the extent of personality variance will be found to reflect the degree of socio-cultural homogeneity in each local Jewish community.

These considerations also lead us to expect great personality variances among the various constituent aggregates of the Jewish people. Exposed as they were to many greatly disparate environmental-cultural influences in various parts of the world, the Jews simply had no choice but to develop considerable variances between the modal personality of one Jewish community and another. In a later section of this chapter (on variance), a few comments will be made about such differences exhibited by the Jewish personality in societies as disparate as those of Lithuania, Galicia, Yemen, and Morocco. Here we shall be satisfied with the general conclusion that the above considerations, which represent little more than a random sampling of the issues involved, make it clear that it is absurd to speak of the "Jewish personality" in general terms. What we shall try to do, therefore, is to confine the discussion of the Jewish personality to certain selected times and places. Even this modest but more realistic attempt encounters great difficulties because of the discouraging paucity of data.

2. Historical and Modern Views

To begin with, a few historical vignettes. Now and then Biblical statements lift for a few and tantalizingly brief moments the veil of obscurity which generally covers the personality of the ancestral Hebrews.

The Children of Israel, following their Exodus from Egypt, are described as quarrelsome, disobedient, stubborn, rebellious, and "stiff necked." [6] Their courage is alluded to in words put into the mouth of the pagan seer Balaam: "None hath beheld iniquity in Jacob, neither hath one seen perverseness in Israel. . . . Behold a people that riseth up as a lioness, and as a lion doth he lift himself up. . . ." [7] Rebelliousness seems to have remained an Israelite character trait five centuries after the Exodus, when Isaiah and the Psalmist repeatedly reproach the people for it,[8] as well as in subsequent generations when Jeremiah and Deutero-Isaiah scold them for the same sin.[9] Crookedness or a "froward heart" is another shortcoming for which the Hebrews are repeatedly blamed.[10] Indications of the Jewish tendency to separatism are found in Biblical references from the thirteenth and fifth centuries B.C.E.[11]

In Talmudic times, the Jews had the reputation of being a rash, impetuous, overhasty people,[12] a trait attributed in Genesis to Reuben.[13] Most frequently, however, the Talmudic teachers emphasize compassion as a Jewish characteristic; the Jews are described as "the merciful sons of merciful fathers," in which trait they imitate God.[14]

A search of Biblical and Talmudic literature would undoubtedly yield up more features, but since our interest is focused on modern times, I must move ahead to have a brief look at four authors who, in the late nineteenth and early twentieth century, expressed themselves on the Jewish personality. One was a historian, the second an anthropologist, the third a sociologist, and the fourth the founder of psychoanalysis. All four were committed Jews, which did not mean that they looked at the Jewish personality uncritically. On the other hand, all four of them were guilty of generalizing in that they spoke of "the Jewish character" as if the Jews were one single socio-cultural entity.

Joseph Jacobs, with whom we are by now familiar, spoke of the Jewish personality—in general—as characterized by versatility, flexibility, enthusiasm, stiff-neckedness, optimism, cheerfulness, *"Hutzpa"* (cheek), gracefulness, charitableness, tact, pity, worldliness, vulgarity, idealism, and rationalism. In addition, he felt that the Jews were sensitive to public opinion, had a historic sense, were cosmopolitan, played the role of intermediaries, and had strong ethical conceptions and religious feelings.[15]

Before World War I, when most American Jews were immigrants, Maurice Fishberg (1872–1934), the pioneer Jewish anthropologist, commented upon a number of Jewish personality traits which he attributed to the parvenu or upstart status of the Jews in European and American society. However, he found that the parvenu personality occurred among American Gentiles to the same extent as among the Jews:

> One has to consider the large number of upstarts in the United States who do not at all differ from the Jewish upstarts. Their arrogance, ostentation, and self-assertion, their lack of manners, want of tact and distinction are notorious. They also crave for display, jewels, horses, and anything that may excite comment; and will go to any extreme to gain recognition in European "noble" society, or give away their hard-earned fortunes to some scion of European family with a title.[16]

Elsewhere Fishberg remarks on the adaptability and power of regeneration manifested by East European Jews in France, Switzerland, England, the United States, and so on. He finds that the Jews, in general, are prone to "hysterical mood"; that because of the preponderance among them of "the morbid, melancholy phases of life, full of grief, sorrow, and sadness," those plays are most successful on the Yiddish stage which illustrate these tendencies; and that in sickness, "the hysterical element often predominates" among both patients and their relatives. Due to the "cumulative effects of repeated psychic injuries," the Jew has become "a temperament Mensch," characterized by an "emotional temperament." However, "nowadays they have been acquiring many of the habits and manners of life of their Christian neighbors, and they are also learning that self-possession and calmness are usually of more benefit than alarm and excitement."

The nervous disposition of the Jews, Fishberg goes on to say, is the result of their concentration in "precarious occupations," such as commerce, banking, speculating, and small trading, which entail a large amount of care and anxiety. On meeting with reverses, such people often lose their mental balance. The majority of the Jews are what are known in the vernacular as "bundles of nerves." There is in them a "disproportion between the inadequately developed physique and the constantly active mind, with its restlessness and ceaseless mental activity." The "fatigued, weary, and exhausted brain" of the Jew is "easily deranged under the least exciting cause." The psychic trauma to which the Jew has been repeatedly subjected in the last eighteen centuries has greatly contributed to his nervous disposition. At the same time, "he is ambitious and persevering, possessing an enormous amount of 'push,' which he cannot always bring into play while struggling against adverse circumstances," and this taxes the nervous system to its limits. Added to this is the effect of "the massacres which have not ceased during the twentieth century," and which greatly affected the mental balance of the survivors.[17]

A less depressing picture of the mental state of the Jew was painted by Arthur Ruppin (1876–1942) some two decades after Fishberg. Ruppin was a well-known Jewish sociologist, demographer, and Zionist leader. He enumerates several factors which he holds responsible for the Jewish mental specificity—again, like Jacobs, speaking of the Jews in general. He points out that the Jews, being a very old people, have left the stage of the dominance of the instincts behind them to a greater extent than the peoples with a newer culture. They are more rational, clearer in their thinking; but they lack the impetus which intractable instincts can provide to a group. In addition, the Jews have specialized in commerce, and their religion has made the study of the Talmud a prime duty. City life forces people into intensive interaction, into an exchange of goods and ideas. It demands constant mental alertness. Commerce, too, requires great mental agility. This was especially pronounced in the last five hundred years, during which the attitude of the Christian majority to the Jews has been almost always hostile and they have been considered a harmful foreign people. Such a situation demanded of the Jew an increased measure of caution and cleverness in his contacts with his neighbors. The great mental agility of the Jews, which enabled them to have a quick grasp and orientation in all things, was often detrimental when it came to a deeper comprehension of things.

For the Jew, the world has no longer any secrets. He rationalizes and categorizes everything, until all mystery disappears and everything is "comprehensible." On the other hand, the ready mastery of reality enables the Jew to perform great scholarly feats. While the Jews have produced many men of genius (Ruppin mentions Spinoza, Herschel, Heinrich Hertz, Marx, and Einstein as proving his point), what is most characteristic about them is their abundance of talent. Even their fantasies and illusions are essentially rationalistic: "They are not—like, e.g., the German mysticism—detached from the law of causality which governs knowledge, nor based on 'seeing' (intuition), but are widenings, transfigurations, or distortions of reality." This is generally true despite such counter-examples as the Hasidic movement with its mysticism, and the fine feeling for the mysteries of nature and art found precisely among the richest and best educated Jews in Western Europe.

Another Jewish feature can be seen in the difficulty Jews have in obeying authority. One reason for this is the Jewish mental alertness: the Jew is always on the lookout for objects on which he can sharpen his mind. This is why he prefers those occupations which keep his mind in a state of tension and is repelled by activities which would force him to engage in monotonous, mechanical tasks, or make him an appendix of a machine. Thus his spirit drives him to probe into the appropriateness of commands, to discuss them. Another factor is that throughout the Middle Ages, which for the Jews of East Europe continued into the twentieth century, external oppression made all the Jews equal; among themselves they learned neither how to command nor how to obey. This seems to be one of the reasons why the Jews enter so rarely into personal service (as butlers or maids).

Quoting Werner Sombart and Fritz Lenz, Ruppin agrees that the Jews possess an extraordinary ability to adjust to the most diverse conditions and have a high degree of efficiency and purposefulness. Their prime concern is with accomplishment; their concern with the work or the thing as such is secondary. The great number of successful Jewish actors, musical virtuosos, journalists, and lawyers can be seen as proving that the Jews have a great capacity for empathy, for putting themselves into the place of others and interpreting the works and thoughts of others for themselves or for third parties. This Jewish talent seems to derive from the general Jewish ability to effect rapid and correct combinations. This enables them to conclude from the behavior of a person what motivations influence him most and how one can get him to make a desired decision.[18]

Sigmund Freud (1856–1939) was never sufficiently interested in his contemporary Jews to analyze them in a special study. But he did have a strong sense of Jewish identity, and occasionally he made brief but insightful comments on the Jewish personality. In his last book, *Moses and Monotheism*, Freud propounded the theory that Moses was an Egyptian, that he was killed by the Jews, and that the religion he gave them was, after a time, rejected by the Jews but came back to life centuries later as the religion of Moses.[19] These theories are not susceptible to historical proof and are destined to remain ingenious exercises of Freud's octogenarian mind. What Freud correctly evaluated was the seminal role of Moses in shaping the character of the Jewish people. As he put it, "We venture to say that it was this one man Moses who created the Jews." [20] In this connection, Freud describes the Jewish character:

> [The Jewish people] has met misfortune and ill-treatment with an unexampled capacity for resistance, it has developed special character-traits and incidentally has earned the hearty dislike of every other people. We should be glad to understand more of the source of this viability of the Jews and of how their characteristics are connected with their history.
>
> We may start from a character-trait of the Jews which dominates their relation to others. There is no doubt that they have a particularly high opinion of themselves, that they regard themselves as more distinguished, of higher standing, as superior to other peoples—from whom they are also distinguished by many of their customs. At the same time they are inspired by a peculiar confidence in life, such as is derived from the secret ownership of some precious possession, a kind of optimism: pious people would call it trust in God.
>
> We know the reason for this behaviour and what their secret treasure is. They really regard themselves as God's chosen people, they believe that they stand especially close to him, and this makes them proud and confident.[21]

Freud attributes the proliferation of ritual prescriptions and proscriptions imposed by his religion upon the Jew to the Jewish sense of guilt:

> Driven by the need to satisfy this sense of guilt, which was insatiable and came from sources much deeper, they must make those commandments grow ever stricter, more meticulous and even more trivial. In a fresh rapture of moral asceticism they imposed more and more new instinctual renunciations on themselves and in that way reached—in doctrine and precept, at least—ethical heights which had remained inaccessible to the other peoples of antiquity. Many Jews regard this attainment of ethical heights as the second main characteristic and the second great achievement of their religion [the first being the idea of a single God].[22]

Indirect references to the Jewish character are also found in the comments Freud made on his own relationship to Judaism. In his "Autobiographical Study" he only stated briefly, "I have never been able to see why I should feel ashamed of my descent or, as people were beginning to say, of my 'race.'"[23] But in his 1926 address to the B'nai B'rith, he not only admitted that "Jewry and Jews" had an "irresistible attraction" for him, but also explained that his Jewishness was a powerful formative influence in his life and thought:

> What bound me to Jewry was (I am ashamed to admit) neither faith nor national pride. . . . But plenty of other things remained over to make the attraction of Jewry and Jews irresistible—many obscure emotional forces, which were the more powerful the less they could be expressed in words, as well as a clear consciousness of inner identity, the safe privacy of a common mental construction. And beyond this, there was a perception that it was to my Jewish nature alone that I owed two characteristics that had become indispensable to me in the difficult course of my life. Because I was a Jew I found myself free from many prejudices which restricted others in the use of their intellect; and as a Jew I was prepared to join the Opposition and to do without agreement with the "compact majority."[24]

The most outspokenly positive evaluation Freud ever gave of Judaism is contained in his 1938 comment on anti-Semitism, which is at the same time a brief but poignant psychological portrait of the Jewish personality as Freud saw it shortly before his death. In this statement, which he wrote under the guise of anonymous Gentile authorship, Freud says:

> In some respects, indeed, the Jews are our superiors. They do not need so much alcohol as we do in order to make life tolerable; crimes of brutality, murder, robbery and sexual violence are great rarities among them; they have always set a high value on intellectual achievement and interests; their family life is more intimate; they take better care of the poor; charity is a sacred duty

to them. Since we have allowed them to cooperate in our cultural tasks, they
have acquired merit by valuable contributions in all the spheres of science, art
and technology, and they have richly repaid our tolerance. So let us cease at
last to hand them out favours when they have a claim to justice.[25]

This passage not only betrays a considerable familiarity on Freud's part with
the Jewish character but also shows that he shared the "particularly high
opinion" of the Jews which he recognized the Jews had of themselves.

3. Two Special Cases: Sephardim and Italian Jews

As with so many other aspects of the Jewish mind, so with personality the
Jewish Enlightenment represents the great divide. Before the Enlightenment, in most places, and within the Ashkenazi majority in every place, the
barriers of the physical and/or mental ghetto in which the Jews lived had not
only isolated them from the culture of their Gentile environment but also
precluded the amount of social contact which is a prerequisite for the adoption by a minority of personality features from the majority. Added to this
was another factor: the general attitude of the Gentiles toward the Jews was
one of hostility and contempt, which was reciprocated in kind by the Jews.
This mutual relationship was certainly not calculated to facilitate the emulation of Gentile character traits by the Jews, whether consciously or subconsciously. The Gentile and Jewish value systems, too, were so different, in
fact, so antagonistic, that personality influences across ethnic lines were, to
all intents and purposes, blocked.

Only in a few instances was this cultural and emotional isolation absent in
pre-Enlightenment times, so that Gentile character traits could be incorporated into the Jewish personality. The Spanish Golden Age and Renaissance
Italy are the outstanding examples.

In Arab and early Christian Spain, as we have seen, there was a unique
cultural and social symbiosis between the Jews on the one hand and the
Muslim Arabs and Christian Spaniards on the other. This resulted among the
Jews in a considerable assimilation of personality traits characterizing the
Arabs and the Spaniards among whom they lived. One example will have to
suffice—the famous Spanish pride. Pride in descent, in nobility, and in purity of family line was a highly emotion-laden value among both the Spanish
Muslims and Christians. The Arabs had brought along this trait from their
Arabian homeland, where it had been their characteristic feature from pre-
Islamic days. The concept of nobility and the emphasis on purity of descent
gave rise among them to an intense preoccupation with, and knowledge of,
familial and tribal genealogy. Arab pride is the basis of the honor syndrome,
including self-respect, a dominant concern in Arab life.[26] The Christian-

Spanish counterpart of this syndrome was the great pride in noble descent, in being a grandee, or at least a *hidalgo* (a contraction of *hijo de algo*, that is, "son of something"), and in one's *limpieza de sangre*, "purity of blood." These traits are eloquently expressed in the demeanor of the Spaniard, which expresses pride, dignity, and a pervasive sense of self-importance, and which is artistically stylized in the typical flamenco dance in which the two partners strut around each other with feet stamping, arms raised, shoulders pressed back, head lifted, and the face bearing an expression of *grandezza* and disdain.

This Spanish pride was internalized in toto by the Sephardi Jews. Their emphasis on purity of descent led them to add the abbreviation S.T. after their name, standing for "S'faradi ṭahor" or "pure Sephardi." [27] In their writings, even as late as in the eighteenth century, they liked to refer to their nobility of descent; and in their pride, they refused to intermarry with non-Sephardi Jews down to the present century. Even before the Spanish Exile (1492), their own spiritual leaders reproached them for their haughtiness. [28] Pride in noble descent assumed such proportions that some members of the high-ranking families, on being called up to the Tora in the synagogue, refused to read their portion if the man who was to follow them was not of the same rank as themselves. The members of the noblest families grouped together into exclusive organizations among the Muslims, and this, too, was emulated by the Jews. [29] In general, the Sephardi Jews considered themselves a superior class, the nobility of Jewry; and for a long time other Jews, on whom they looked down, accepted this claim without question.

Among the Muslims and the Christians in Spain, great dignity in behavior was a foremost manifestation of self-pride. This, too, was adopted by the Sephardi Jews. As Meyer Kayserling, a lifelong student of the Sephardim, put it:

> This sense of dignity which the Sephardim possessed manifested itself in their general deportment and in their scrupulous attention to dress. Even those among them whose station in life was low, as, for example, the carriers in Salonica, or the sellers of "pan de Espana" in the streets of Smyrna, maintained their old Spanish "grandezza" in spite of their poverty. [30]

The relationship of the Sephardim to other Jews in Greece was eloquently described in 1935 by a Salonican Sephardi author, Joseph Nehama, who largely shared their evaluation of themselves and deprecation of other Jews. Being a Sephardi, Nehama was sensitive to prestige differences within the Sephardi community; the Castilians were the highest-ranking sub-group, to whom other Sephardim, such as the Aragonese, Catalans, and Majorcans, had to, and did, defer. Nehama describes the behavior of the Castilians who settled in Salonica:

The Castilians were soon giving the tone to everything, to the entire population, their customs and their manners. The task was easy for them. They were
by far the most numerous and they exercised a considerable ascendancy in all
domains. Who could have contested their superiority? These proud hidalgos
were versed in all the sciences. Munificent, of the grand manner, they had
been admitted into the entourage of the Court and the grandees of Spain, and
they had preserved their sentiments and demeanor. They themselves had often
worn the cape and the sword, they had occupied the most eminent positions.
They had known honors and dignities. They looked down from above on other
people and had the habit of command. Imbued with the sentiment of honor,
perquisite of the Spanish feudal aristocracy, they were courteous, brave, respectful of the given word, and persevering in their enterprises. The contrast
between them and the other people was all too manifest. The Aragonese,
Catalans, Majorcans bowed and let themselves be eclipsed. The Portuguese
themselves were, in their great majority, of Castilian origin, and it was not for
them, however rich and lettered, to deny a supremacy in which they had a
share. Italians, Sicilians, Calabrians, Apulians put up some resistance. They
even tried to combat the Castilians' influence. Above all those of Otranto had
pride in their origin. For a long time they married only among themselves and
followed meticulously their own customs.

Next, Nehama describes the relationship between the Sephardim and the
Ashkenazim:

> The last to yield were the Ashkenazim. They did not mingle with the Sephar-
> dim, nor married their daughters who, in any case, would have been refused to
> them as if they belonged to another race. Sephardim and Ashkenazim did not
> eat at the same table, they did not touch each other's dishes, for they mutually
> considered impure the meat prepared according to the others' rites which to
> eat would be a grave sin. Customs, prayers, liturgies, everything differentiated
> them. The Sephardi looked down from on high upon the poor little Jew from
> the north, accustomed to misery and oppression, who cowered, made himself
> humble and hugged the wall; who had always lived with doors and windows
> closed, shut up in the *Judengassen* [Jewish streets] in sullen isolation, who
> shunned all social contact, all friendship with the non-Jew; who, always de-
> spised and unwanted, lived here and there as a veritable nomad, always ready
> to take off, with his bundle and his wanderer's staff.
>
> The Ashkenazi, in turn, regarded the Sephardi with distrust. He did not con-
> test his superiority, but considered him some sort of miscreant. He did not
> want to let himself be subjugated, he bridled and kicked.
>
> After ten centuries of separation, these two brothers in Israel had ceased to
> recognize each other. Their encounter did not take place without hurt. They
> were not far from considering each other strangers.

The Sephardi superiority expressed itself, among other ways, in the
linguistic assimilation of the other Jews to the "Castilian," i.e., Ladino, colloquial of the Sephardim:

The proud Castilian witnessed this rapid triumph with real pleasure. Was there in the world, in their eyes, a language more harmonious and nobler than theirs? It was honored all over Spain, where an army of writers and of scholars, sustained by the princes, had raised it to literary dignity. The Sephardim who established themselves, in a period of 150 years, in all the vital points of the earth, adopted it, as they did in Salonica. This is how it happened that Tunis, Nice, Amsterdam, London, Hamburg preserved for a long time the Spanish of Castile, this one living relic of the lost fatherland. . . .

As one can see, the influx of the first waves of immigrants, among whom the Castilian refugees dominated, changed the aspect of the old city of Salonica within twenty years, and imparted [to] it a clearly Jewish and Spanish character.[31]

A trait not mentioned by Nehama which the Sephardim adopted from the Spaniards was extreme rigorism in the religious organization and management of their communities. Just as the Spanish Inquisition would not tolerate any deviation from the established religious creed and observance, so the *Ma'amad* or presidium of the typical Sephardi congregation, consisting of a lay president and the rabbinate, would rule with an iron hand over the religious life of the community. The president and the *Ma'amad* were not only the absolute religious authority; they had the right to observe the religious conduct of individuals and, in a truly inquisitorial fashion, to call before them, to investigate, and to punish those suspected of heresy or of violating the law. The proceedings against Uriel Acosta and Spinoza in Amsterdam are celebrated cases of such Sephardi inquisitorial severity.[32]

The other pre-Enlightenment example, that of Gentile influence on the Jewish personality in Renaissance Italy, can be dealt with more summarily. Here too, as in the Spanish Golden Age, we witness an intensive participation of the Jews in the cultural and social life of the Gentile environment. As in Spain, so in Italy, cultural and social contacts led to an adoption of Gentile personality traits by the Jews. Some of these can be briefly referred to.

Under the influence of the Renaissance environment, the Jews manifested a strong inclination to superstitious beliefs, in magic, sorcery, witchcraft, the efficacy of amulets, palmistry, physiognomy, and so on. Belief in the influence of the stars led to fatalism among Christians and Jews alike. If gambling is an instinct, it certainly requires a special cultural milieu to manifest itself. Such a milieu was provided by the Renaissance, and accordingly we find that many Jews, among them highly talented scholars and poets, and leading rabbis, were incurable gamblers. The same can be said about crime—both inclination and environmental influences must be present to make a man a criminal. Under the influence of the Renaissance ambience, criminality penetrated the Jewish community, with the result that bandits, gangsters, informers, robbers, and murderers, including hired killers, were found among the Jews just as among the Christians. The "spirit of the times" favored the free expression of one's passions, which led to a display of vengefulness, aggression, and violence among both Christians and Jews. The other side of the coin was the display of great courage. Sexual license, too, was characteristic of the mores of both Jew and Gentile. Early signs of religious laxity—which was to become a widespread Jewish characteristic after the Enlightenment—could be noticed under the influence of the Christians' similar attitude to their religion. The love of luxury and ostentation was yet another Renaissance trait which the Jews adopted.[33] Thus the Jews of Italy not only shared Renaissance culture but also displayed a personality which in many ways mirrored the character traits of Renaissance man.

4. Variance

Situations such as those of the Spanish and Italian Jews, however, were exceptional in pre-Enlightenment times. In the Ashkenazi lands of Central and East Europe, as well as in the Muslim world from the later Middle Ages on, the rule was a high degree of isolation of the Jews from the Gentiles. In those circumstances, the Jewish personality absorbed fewer influences of the non-Jewish environment and was more the result of inner-Jewish psychological developments. Consequently, the differences between the Jewish modal personality in one country and another were neither as pronounced, nor the number of variants as great, as after the Enlightenment.

One of the most significant pre-Enlightenment differences in personality was that between the Lithuanian and the Southwest Russian (Podolia, Ukraine, Galicia, South Poland) Jews. The Lithuanian Jew, the "Litvak," was considered sharp-witted, hard-headed, stubborn, of a logical bent of mind, rational, cool, dry, stressing the value of study and insistent on fulfilling all the minutiae of the commandments, scrupulous and just, and a firm believer in a God who was like him in all these respects. When Hasidism arose (in the second half of the eighteenth century), it could make little headway in Lithuania, and the "Litvaks" remained among its fiercest and most determined opponents. In contrast to them, the Jews of the Polish-Galician-Ukrainian region were considered warm-hearted, soft and pliable, inclined to mysticism, stressing the values of good deeds, compassion, helpfulness, "love of Israel," and, in general, the works of the heart rather than those of the mind. The teachings of Hasidism, with their emphasis on the love of God and man and on serving God with joy, found a wide and enthusiastic reception among them and helped to crystallize a concept of God centered on the divine equivalents of these features.

Pre-Enlightenment, too, are the traits characterizing the Oriental Jewish communities. In the Muslim world, there was no Enlightenment. The modal personality of the Jews in the age-old Jewish communities of that area was the outcome of inner developments and of the gradual influences over many centuries of the Muslim social environment within which the Jews occupied special niches and with which they maintained some contact throughout. Not much is known about the Jewish personality in the Middle East before the dramatic and traumatic large-scale transplantation to Israel of entire Jewish communities from Muslim lands, primarily in the years 1948–52. However, from studies made among them in Israel, it is possible to reconstruct a picture of what they were like in their old countries, since many of their personality traits remained unaffected by their settlement in Israel—at least for a number of years.

There can be no doubt that the same piety, modesty, undemanding demeanor, quietness, and peaceableness which characterized first-generation immigrant Yemenite Jews in Israel had been their personality traits for many generations back in Yemen. These traits, together with their intelligence, capability, diligence, willingness to work, cleanliness, and conscientiousness, and their developed artistic taste in silver filigree work, embroideries, and music, have made the Yemenite Jews the most liked of all the Oriental Jewish communities among both Ashkenazim and Oriental Jews. These traits surely developed among the Yemenite Jews in response to environmental conditions through many centuries. They had lived in Yemen as a clearly identified religious community ever since pre-Islamic times. There was a time when Jews were the rulers of the country. After the victory of Islam, however, they were reduced to the status of pariahs, untouchables, whose contact defiled. Oppression, often in a most humiliating form, was their fate. In order to survive in these circumstances, they had to develop a humble, self-effacing personality. They had to learn to bear silently and without any outward reaction the jeers of the Muslim Yemenites, their abuse, and their vilification. When a Jew encountered a Muslim in the street, he had to move aside, even if it meant stepping into the putrefying refuse that lay around everywhere in the sewerless alleys of the Yemenite towns, lest his inadvertent touch should render the Muslim impure. In the midst of such treatment, the Yemenite Jews nevertheless managed to eke out a living by engaging in a large variety of crafts, among which the making of silver filigree jewelry was their exclusive specialty. They also maintained an almost general literacy in Hebrew among the men and even produced some religious writings down to the last years prior to their emigration to Israel. No wonder that these conditions had imprinted the Yemenite Jews with the traits for which they were still known in Israel thirty and more years after their transplantation.

The Moroccan Jews, briefly alluded to above (page 307), exemplify an opposite type of psychological adjustment to adverse conditions. They had lived in Morocco for many centuries in the midst of two mutually hostile major population elements, the Arabs and the Berbers. The balance between these two was kept by close ingroup cohesion and loyalty and by an ever-present readiness to resort to the force of arms in defense of one's own group. Woe to any group which could not maintain the reputation that it was able and willing to stand up and defend itself and every one of its members with the sword, the dagger, the gun. In these circumstances, a show of pugnacity and ferocity was just as important as the actual manpower a group could muster. The Jews, located, and often caught, between Arabs and Berbers, had to learn that they too must resort to the same type of behavior or become ruthlessly victimized. The possibility of being aided by Berbers against Arabs, and by Arabs against Berbers, enabled them to use violence or the threat of violence whenever endangered by attack from either of the two major ethnic groups—a course of action entirely impossible for the Yemenite Jews who lived within the locally homogeneous population of the Zaydi Muslim Arabs in the hill country of Yemen.

It was this particular background which produced the bellicose fierceness for which the Moroccan Jews are still known in Israel decades after their arrival from Morocco. They are notorious for their uncontrolled temper, which can flare up at the slightest provocation. *"Maroko—sakin"* ("Morocco—knife") is an oft-quoted saying in Israel. Other traits attributed to them are quarrelsomeness, self-righteousness, chronic dissatisfaction, untruthfulness, greed, and unreliability. These features, for which the Moroccans are famous in Israel, and which they themselves recognize in their own character, must be a contributing factor in making the Moroccans (and, by extension, the North African Jews in general) the least liked ethnic group in Israel.

Among the Ashkenazi Jews, the modal personality of each community has developed since, and as a consequence of, the Enlightenment and the Emancipation. As I have repeatedly emphasized, one of the basic tenets of the Jewish Enlighteners was that the Jews must acquire European culture; and the same demand was put to the Jews by Gentile potentates and influential leaders, whether in or out of the government. Culture and personality impress themselves jointly and inseparably upon those who wish to acquire a culture they consider superior. Thus within a short time after the Jewish Enlightenment was set in motion, the Jews of, say, Germany not only learned the German language, acquired a taste for and a knowledge of German literature, adopted the German fashion in clothing, entered German schools, universities, and occupations, took up the arts, the music, the sciences, and the other specializations cultivated by the Germans, and tried to penetrate German social life; they also, consciously or unconsciously, first imitated and soon internalized those character traits which were valued in German society. This was the process which resulted in that unique phenomenon, the Germanized Jew whose offspring after his arrival in Palestine in the 1930's impressed the other Jews of the Yishuv as a peculiarly un-Jewish creature. He was formally polite, punctual, meticulous, exacting, precise, humorless, thorough, serious, hardworking, as likely as not a university graduate, a highbrow who loved German literature, music, art—in brief, a typical *Jecke* (Yekke), more German than Jewish, at least in comparison to the non-German Jews, the product of 150 years of assimilation to the German personality.

In a like manner the Jews became assimilated to the modal character of the Gentile population in every country in which Enlightenment had spread among them and in which they acquired the culture of the Gentile environment. This is the basis of the observations, invariably made by sensitive outsiders, that the French Jews are as impatient as the French Christians and have as much *esprit*; that the Hungarian Jews display the well-known Hungarian traits of patriotism and of polite charm (in contrast to the German formal politeness); that the Italian Jews are, like the Italians, characterized by an effusive liveliness; the Polish Jews, like the Poles, by a warm sentimentality; and so on.

The absorption of Gentile character traits proceeded in the Ashkenazi world at a rate unprecedented up to the Enlightenment. This process was not an automatic or unplanned one, as had been the influences which had penetrated the ghetto, the *mellah*, or the *hara* almost imperceptibly through many generations. It was the inevitable by-product of a purposely effected assimilation to those whom the Enlighteners considered the carriers of a superior culture. By recognizing the latter, the Jewish Enlightener put himself into a situation where he not only embarked on the difficult course of acquiring the culture of his Gentile neighbor, but also (no matter whether wittingly or unwittingly) tried to absorb his values and imitate his behavior. This, of course, had to lead to an assimilation of Gentile character traits.

This was the road traversed primarily by those Jews for whom Enlightenment meant a throwing off of the yoke of the commandments, a liberation from what they came to perceive as the shackles of the *Halakha*. That the assimilant German Jew should, within two or three generations, become more German than Jewish in his behavior, mannerisms, and character is something that should not make us wonder. After all, he wanted to become German in all this, just as he wanted to become German culturally; and he succeeded. What is more remarkable is that the German Orthodox Jews, who insisted on retaining their Jewish religious observance with an uncompromising rigidity, should also have absorbed as much as they did of the German character. These men did accomplish the seemingly impossible: they united in themselves Jewish Orthodoxy and German personality. For the non-German Jews who encountered them, especially in Israel after 1933, they were as much *Jeckes* as their non-religious compatriots—the designation *Jecke* refers to the German-like features of the Jew; whether he was religious or not made no difference.

Similarly, the Enlightenment caused Jews to absorb great chunks of the

Gentile personality in all countries in which they were enabled to participate in the economic, cultural, and social life. This is how French Jews became like the French, English Jews like the English, etc. And this is how the variance in Jewish modal personality grew to such an extent that today it is no longer possible to speak of "the Jews" as a single group with reference to personality.

5. *Profile of the American Jew*

All that has been said above must not be construed as meaning that there are no differences between the Jewish and the Gentile modal personality in a given locality, or that there are no differences between them in respect of the traits mentioned. As soon as one ceases to look at the German (or French, or whatever) Jews from the outside, from which viewpoint one's attention is focused on the differences between the Jews of one country and another, and looks instead from the inside, as it were, comparing the German Jews with the Germans, the French Jews with the French, and so forth, differences become palpable. However long the period during which the Jews assimilated to the modal personality of the Gentile environment, the assimilatory process could not result in a total elimination of all differences between the Gentile and the originally rather alien Jewish character. The very fact that the Jews maintained their identity as a separate group—whether they defined their identity and separateness in religious or ethnic terms—precluded total personality assimilation. A smaller or larger measure of differences remained, and wherever studies focused on them they showed up. Several dozen such studies have been made, especially in the United States.

One of the most readily noticeable, although very rarely studied, expressions of differences between the Jewish and the Gentile personality is in patterns of gestures. David Efron compared the gestural patterns of East European Jews and southern Italians, both in New York City, and found that the gestural behavior of the traditional East European Jews was more confined than that of traditional (i.e., non-assimilated) southern Italians. In contrast to the Italians, who might make gestures of full arms' length, the Jews' gestural motions were confined to the lower arm, with the upper arm, in general, remaining at the side of the body. There was a great deal of head movement among the traditional Jews but little among the Italians. The Jews' gestures were made sequentially, while those of the Italians were made simultaneously, with both arms and hands. The Jewish gestures had an irregularity of tempo and abruptness as against the more even flow of the Italians'. The Jews stood more closely together in conversational groups, and one often touched the body of his interlocutor, which was not the case among the Italians. The Jew tended to gesticulate in an up-and-down direction in front of his body and toward the interlocutor, while the Italian's motions tended to take place on either side of his body. However, assimilated Jews and assimilated Italians in New York City differed from their respective traditional groups and appeared to resemble each other in gestural behavior.[34] A study of patterns of gesture among Levantine Arabs was published ten years after this one,[35] but no comparison between Arab and Jewish gestures is available.

If old gesture pattern differentials can persist after years of life in an environment as new and intrusive as the American, then one can expect personality traits, which lie deep beneath the behavioral surface, to be even more resistant to external influences. That differences in such traits do in fact exist and persist has been shown in a series of studies carried out since the 1920's among American Jews and elsewhere. Only a brief résumé of some can be given in the present text.

In 1929, H. E. Garrett reported that the Laird Personal Inventory B2, which he administered to Jewish and non-Jewish college students, showed no significant differences between them in personality and college achievement.[36] A year later, J. Rumyaneck found, on the basis of a study in the Netherlands, that the Jews were much more emotional than the Gentiles; that they were quickly offended, of a critical temperament, anxious and suspicious, and less good-natured.[37] In 1935, Keith Sward and Meyer Friedman reported their findings on Jewish temperament, based on a large-scale study involving well over a thousand subjects. The Benreuter Personality Inventory and the Heidbrecher questionnaire for introversion and inferiority feeling were administered to freshmen at the University of Minnesota, high school seniors in Pittsburgh, and father-mother-offspring triads at Western Reserve University. All belonged to urban families, and the non-Jewish control groups were carefully matched. The results were that the Jewish average scores rated consistently higher in sense of inferiority (although the differences were not statistically reliable). The Jews showed greater variability in temperament. They had higher neurosis averages (again the results were consistent but not statistically reliable) and feelings of inadequacy.[38] In a subsequent report, Sward gave an analysis of 125 items on the Benreuter and found that the Jews were characterized by four distinguishing patterns: (1) gregariousness or strong social dependence; (2) submissiveness; (3) drive and over-reaction; and (4) feelings of insecurity (emotionality or instability).[39]

In 1938, M. Sukov and E. Williamson administered the Rundquist-Sletto Test and the Bell Adjustment Inventory to Jewish and non-Jewish students and found that the Jewish students had, on the average, a more marked tendency toward maladjustment.[40]

In 1942, Abraham P. Sperling published the results of his study of eighty Jewish and eighty non-Jewish students at City College, New York. No significant differences were found in general adjustment score or in work efficiency, emotional stability, superiority-inferiority, social acceptability, objectivity, and family relations. However, the tests showed that the Jews were significantly more extroverted and ascendant, more liberal, and achieved a higher theoretical and social score on the scale of interest values, but were less religious than the non-Jews. The Jewish group was indicated to be educationally accelerated by about three-quarters of a year over the non-Jewish group and, on the Thurstone Intelligence Test, scored higher by a critical ratio of 2.4 (which, however, was deemed not large enough to be statistically reliable).[41]

A. M. Shuey returned to the same subject in 1944, reporting on the results of a Bell Adjustment Inventory administered to 490 Jewish and non-Jewish students. The results largely tallied with Sperling's. The Jewish students appeared on the average to be probably more gregarious, more liberal and radical, slightly less stable emotionally, more aggressive, less timid, and less religious. The non-Jewish instructors of the same students rated the Jews higher in aggressiveness, and somewhat higher in alertness and enthusiasm.[42]

Aggressiveness in Jews often takes the form of a desire for superiority, which, in turn, appears to be a contributing factor to a more intense motivation. This was observed by a psychoanalyst,[43] and in a psychometric study of 6,774 freshmen at Northwestern University from 1921 to 1941. In the latter, with aptitude scores held constant, the grade point averages of Jewish men definitely, and of Jewish women probably, were significantly higher than those of non-Jewish students. These findings were considered "compelling evidence" of the higher motivation of Jewish students.[44] A nationwide sample survey confirmed these results. In it, thematic apperception measures were administered to three religious groups, and it was found that high achievement motivation scores were most prevalent in Jewish men, less in Catholic, and least in Protestant men.[45]

Whether or not high achievement motivation is the outcome of aggression deflected into a quest for superiority, there seems to be no doubt as to the prevalence of a higher achievement motivation among the Jews. In fact, one suspects that high parental expectations could be an equally effective factor in providing the impetus for such motivation. Parental expectations have been observed to be especially high among Jews; consequently, Jewish boys find high-status occupations more attractive, which, in turn, motivates them to make efforts toward attaining the qualifications (in college) required for such positions. The result is that they do in fact have a better chance to achieve good positions.[46] To a higher degree than their non-Jewish colleagues, Jewish college students expect, and work for, scientific, literary, and social service careers; and, to a lesser extent, mechanical, computational, artistic, and musical careers.[47]

Summarizing the findings of several studies on Jewish character and outlook, Nathan Hurwitz enumerates the following traits characteristic of American Jews. They subscribe to a democratic philosophy, have a worldly orientation, a utilitarian attitude toward life, rationalistic and empirical approaches toward the environment, an emphasis on moderation, and a high regard for literacy; they show strong family unity and solidarity, foresight, calculability, and flexibility. As for the sources of these specific Jewish traits and values, the same author believes they lie in four historical features: (1) religious tradition, (2) business ethic, (3) urban adaptation, and (4) minority group status.[48]

A somewhat more complete picture of the American Jewish modal personality can perhaps be ventured on the basis of the studies surveyed. It seems to be made up of the following features in respect of which there appears to be a difference in degree between the American Jew and non-Jew:

> The Jew is less religious, more liberal, more radical, and more inclined to a democratic philosophy.
>
> He has greater foresight, calculability, and flexibility and more of a worldly orientation, with a utilitarian attitude to life and a rationalistic and empirical approach toward his environment.
>
> He is more gregarious, has a stronger feeling of family unity and solidarity, and a stronger social dependence.
>
> He has higher drive, motivation, enthusiasm, alertness, and "interest values"; he is ascendant, academically advanced, has a high regard for literacy, and is oriented toward literary, scientific, and social service careers, and to a lesser extent also toward mechanical, computational, artistic, and musical vocations; he scores higher on intelligence tests.
>
> He tends to overreact, is more emotional, and less stable emotionally.
>
> He has feelings of inadequacy, inferiority, and insecurity, is more neurotic.
>
> He is more sensitive (quickly offended), anxious, suspicious, and less good-natured.
>
> He has a critical temperament, and also is characterized by greater extroversion, moderation, and submissiveness, but less timidity.
>
> He has a greater variability in temperament.
>
> He is more inclined to a deferment of gratification (as will be shown in Chapter 18).
>
> He is internally more maladjusted, despite an apparently good social adjustment record (as shown in Chapter 15).

Finally, a cautionary comment. The above differences between Jews and non-Jews diminish if one compares the Jews not to the non-Jewish population in general, but to its middle-class sector, to which most Jews belong.

6. Intensity, Sensitivity, and Impatience

Our sketch of the American Jewish personality requires a few additional comments. A careful analysis of the traits enumerated discloses that many of them are derived from, or cluster around, three basic features in which the Jews of America, and of other English-speaking and non-Mediterranean countries, differ from their Gentile countrymen: the Jewish personality is characterized by greater intensity, greater sensitivity, and greater impatience. Cuddihy's recent book on the Jewish "ordeal of civility" [49] dwells at length on one manifestation of the first of these features. Yet what he, from his Gentile point of view, perceives as the traditional Jewish lack of civility is, in fact, nothing but one expression of the greater Jewish intensity in the display of emotions, in reactions to the most varied situations and especially to emergencies, in goal-oriented activities, and in innumerable other contexts. Many other observers have spoken and written of the Jewish loudness, vulgarity, rudeness, and "pushiness"—all these are but more specific manifestations of the Jewish intensity. The same is the basis of the relationship of Jewish parents to their children, the motive force behind the attitude and behavior of the Jewish mother so often pilloried by modern Jewish writers, and the key to strong attachment of Jewish children to their parents. [50]

Jewish sensitivity is evidenced in many varied fields, among them the reaction to physical pain and to emotional stress, but also the ready response to suffering and distress experienced by others—the latter expressed both in private personal encounters and in the establishment of institutions such as hospitals, orphanages, old people's homes, and the like. These institutions are a hallmark of Jewish communal life everywhere. Jewish sensitivity is also expressed in the manifold activities Jews engage in for the purpose of alleviating Jewish suffering in other countries (e.g., Soviet Russia), and of aiding in every possible way Jewish populations wherever they are endangered (especially in Israel). Quite a different kind of sensitivity is the one which underlies Jewish talent in many fields. In the arts, in literature, in music, in medicine, in psychiatry and psychology, and so on, apart from the specific gifts each of these activities requires, there is a general overall prerequisite, that of sensitivity, of which the Jews have an ample supply and which undoubtedly contributes to paving their way to preeminence in many of these pursuits.

As for impatience—a trait which, as we have seen, characterized the Jews in antiquity—it has been in modern times proverbially attributed to Jews in many places. In pre-Nazi Germany, Gentiles among themselves would talk of *jüdische Hast* ("Jewish haste"), but when speaking to a Jew they would refer to it as *unvornehme Hast* ("unrefined haste"). In America, too, the observation that Jews are (or seem) always in a hurry has often been made and has been related to Jewish "pushiness." Wherever he goes, whatever his goal, the Jew seems to be in a greater hurry to get there than the Gentile.

As for the genesis of these traits, we can only guess. They are, perhaps, a residual Mediterranean heritage; or they may have been produced in reaction to the conditions in which the Jews have lived in the countries of their

Diaspora; or, most probably, both of these factors may have contributed to them. The fact remains that the contrast between the greater Jewish and lesser Gentile intensity, sensitivity, and impatience is most pronounced in non-Mediterranean Europe and in the English-speaking world. Some of these differences all but disappear (or, rather, never arose) between the Jews and the Gentiles in the Muslim orbit and in Latin lands. The intense display of emotions, for instance, has been characteristic of both Arabs and Jews. The same sensitivity to physical pain has been observed among both Italians and Jews.[51] Both the French and the Jews are characterized by the same impatience.

On the popular level it has often been observed that "the Jews are like the Gentiles, only more so," which refers to the Jewish tendency to emulate the Gentiles but at the same time to overdo things. This has been found among assimilant Jews in Europe but has been documented extensively in American Jewish religious, social, and business life. One almost feels as if the Jews had a compulsion to outdo the Gentiles in all those activities and behavioral features they find attractive enough to emulate. Thus the Jews are impelled by a number of factors to replicate the Gentile forms of religious life, especially in suburbia; but once they do so, with them everything must be bigger and better. Their suburban Jewish centers, synagogues, or temples with religious schools affiliated and with recreational and adult educational facilities are as a rule larger and more luxurious than the Christian churches and their appendages. Having adopted from the Gentile confirmation the idea of making the Bar Mitzva and Bas Mitzva into an impressive celebration (which has no basis in Jewish tradition), they make it a more sumptuous affair than its Gentile original. As for weddings, an observer of the American Jewish scene commented, "I haven't seen any statistics comparing the size of Jewish weddings with those of non-Jews, but I would guess they are generally considerably larger." [52] In imitation of the Gentile commercialization of Christmas in which gift-giving is a central feature, they took to celebrating Hanukka as an important holiday (whereas in Jewish tradition it is a very minor half holiday), with lavish presents given to children throughout its eight days. Having for long been excluded from Gentile urban and country clubs, they set up such facilities as a rule with more luxurious premises than those of the Gentiles. Challenged by the Y.M.C.A.'s and Y.W.C.A.'s, they built their own Y.M. and W.H.A.'s with finer buildings and richer programs.

On the personal level, when it comes to the amenities the American economy makes available to the middle class, Jewish Americans acquire more of them, use them more frequently, and display them more ostentatiously than Gentiles. Studies exist which show this with reference to housing; it certainly could be shown to be true in furniture, clothing, the use of cosmetics, and the like. The traditional Jewish concern with children, as expressed in the modern vulgar-popular context, means that the Jews pamper their children more than the Gentiles. If the daughter of a middle-class Gentile family is a pampered girl, her Jewish classmate is a Jewish princess.

Again, the participation of Jews is characterized in political life by a greater intensity than that of non-Jews. It was observed that in the 1964 elections, 81.0 percent of all eligible Jews went to the polls as against 62.8 percent of the population as a whole. Estimates of the number of Jewish Freedom Marchers ran as high as 50 percent of the white total, and of Peace Corps workers 33 percent.[53]

Even before World War I, Maurice Fishberg remarked: ". . . the difference between the Western Jews and their Christian neighbors is only one of degree. They are going more rapidly on the frenzied path of modern life." And he added that in respect of reduced birthrate, "as in many other respects, the Jews are merely the *avant-coureurs* [forerunners] showing whither modern society is travelling." [54]

If we consider greater frequency a manifestation of greater intensity, then the extraordinarily high Jewish participation in the cultural life of America also attests to the prevalence of this Jewish characteristic. Leaving aside the proportion of Jews among culture producers which, after all, is a question of talent, and focusing only on cultural consumption, it appears that the share of the Jews exceeds many times their percentage in the population, even in the major urban areas. Thus it was estimated that about half of the ticket purchasers to Broadway plays are Jewish, that 80 percent of all contemporary art in America is owned by Jews, and that three-quarters of the members of Artists' Equity in New York are Jewish.[55]

Many more such items could be listed, but these should suffice to prove the point: American Jews have carried to an extreme the Jewish tendency to imitate the Gentiles which has characterized Jewish life in the Western world since the Enlightenment and have done so with what can best be described as a heightened intensity. When the same tendency is carried over into the fields of literature, the arts, and sciences, the result is a more intense participation in these activities whether measured quantitatively or qualitatively. Moreover, in those areas where originality is valued, the greater intensity of the Jewish mind is reflected in an incessant striving for greater originality.

7. *Galut-Jew,* Sabra, *and Kibbutznik*

Two generations of life in their own country sufficed to produce marked personality differences between the Israeli Jews and the generalized image they developed of their co-religionists in the Diaspora. The *sabras,* as the native Israeli Jews are called, [56] early developed a strong ego image and a contrastingly dim view of the Diaspora Jew. This dichotomy was prevalent in pre-state days (prior to 1948) but after the achievement of independence it became much more emphatic. The *sabra* youth looked at Diaspora Jewry with a mixture of incomprehension and contempt: now that the Jews had their country to which every Jew could come, those who chose to remain in the Diaspora had to have something wrong with them. This was brought out clearly in a 1965 study of 512 students aged fifteen to twenty-two in Tel Aviv. The *sabra* was seen as tough and strong, representing an Israeli version of Superman, and thus a most positively loaded self-image. The figure of the Diaspora Jew appeared in the responses as its exact opposite. His appearance was described in such terms as lean, meager, weakly, sickly, sad-eyed, bearded, pale. His personality was perceived as closed, strange, anxious, distrustful, isolated, religious, rigid, self-conscious, despised, quiet, modest, taciturn, shameful, perplexed, polite, disciplined, sad; he was seen as an individual who did not enjoy himself, revealed traces of crises, etc. The stereotype of the Diaspora Jewess was almost identical with this image—in both, the negative features predominated. The researchers remarked that these stereotypes "mirror a caricaturic conception of the East-European ghetto Jew of the turn of the century" and saw in them a heritage of the East European immigrants of the first quarter of the twentieth century, "transmitted through literature and education to the present Israeli generation." [57]

The negative attitude of the *sabras* toward Diaspora Jewry reached such an intensity that the Israeli Ministry of Education felt it necessary to introduce special courses into the school curriculum on "Jewish consciousness," centering on the importance of the Diaspora in Jewish history and life. [58]

The difference between the personality of the *sabra* and the Galut (or Diaspora) Jew, as perceived by the *sabras* themselves, was summarized by Ferdynand Zweig, who described the *sabra* as follows:

> . . . a buoyant, extrovert type with a heightened sense of living and purpose, centered around the new nation and the New State, and in complete anti-thesis to the model of the Ghetto Jew. . . . A Jew transformed into an Israeli is a sturdy, robust and lusty fellow, non-emotional, with rough edges and no complexes. . . . He styles himself on a peasant's mentality. . . . He rejects complexity and intellectuality, and he likes to think of himself as a simple, straightforward man without far-fetched ideas and claims. He rejects emotionality, softness, familism, possessiveness and the bourgeois mentality. . . . He hates verbosity and long-winded phrases, and has little time for big talk, for juggling with words and abstractions. [59]

On the basis of his analysis of the *chizbat*—a special type of humor popular in Israel—Elliott Oring found that it reflected a series of antithetical personality traits which are believed or felt to characterize the *sabra* as against the

Galut-Jew: the *sabra* is secular in his outlook, the Galut-Jew "sacred," i.e., religious; the *sabra* is "primitive," the Galut-Jew civilized. Other antithetical pairs of features are: boorish—cultured; dirty—clean; unintellectual—intellectual; unemotional—emotional; strong and violent—weak and nonviolent; audacious—retreating; terse—loquacious; uses slang—is poetic and literate; devoted to his age set—familistic; unregimented—regimented; has braggadocio—has humility.[60] Needless to say, the *sabra* self-image, as shown in the features he attributes to himself, is all positive; even traits such as primitive, boorish, and dirty are felt to be desirable as against their opposites, which characterize the Galut-Jew and which are throughout negative.

Just as the *sabras* consider themselves the élite of the Jewish people, so they consider the kibbutzniks, those of them who live in a kibbutz, as the élite among the *sabras*. One would imagine that there would be no significant differences in personality between those *sabras* who live in kibbutzim and those who live outside them, and especially those who live in other types of agricultural settlements, such as the *moshav* or the *moshava*.[61] Until recently, most persons living in either kibbutzim or other villages were the offspring of Jewish immigrants who had come from East Europe. They all were equally suffused with Israeli nationalism and with pride in being *sabras*. That differences did nevertheless develop was due primarily to the unique child-rearing practices adopted by the kibbutz movement. In addition to the insistence on owning all property in common, performing all work on a joint basis, defraying all expenses of each individual from the common treasury, adhering to the principle of "From each according to his ability, to each according to his needs," and taking their meals in the communal dining room, the founding fathers of the kibbutz developed a method for the communal upbringing of the children.

In most Israeli kibbutzim the children are, to this day, brought up in communal children's homes, grouped into age classes, and under the care of nurses for whom this activity is full-time professional work. The mothers breastfeed their children, and both parents spend an hour or two every day visiting with them, so that the collective child-rearing system does not impair the parent-child relationship, while it undoubtedly reduces the child's reliance and dependence on his parents. The effects of this system on the children's personalities have been frequently studied by Israeli experts and repeatedly been discussed by American psychologists. While these authorities do not agree on all points, their findings comprise enough common ground to enable us to base some generalizations on them.

Kibbutz upbringing stresses the equality of the sexes, and the absence of separation of sexes (in dormitories and showers), and "emphasizes self-control, postponement of gratification, especially in the sexual area, and devotion to ideals and common objectives." Among the ideals inculcated in kibbutz children, the principles of economic justice and equality predominate.

These influences tend to produce a kibbutz personality in which idealism, perseverence, industriousness, and devotion to duty are important features.[62]

Some observers have found that young kibbutz children tend to manifest signs of emotional disturbance. By the age of ten or eleven, however, these problems seem to disappear, and the children's intellectual development equals or surpasses that of non-kibbutz children. Also, the kibbutz children were found to be better in ego strength and overall maturity, although they showed more anxiety. They evinced more positive attitudes toward the family, less intense sibling rivalry, less clear-cut identification with the parent of the same sex, and less superego development.[63] The superiority in intelligence and personality traits in adult life exhibited by kibbutz-bred individuals has been commented upon above.

The personality of the kibbutz member is certainly not typical of the entire Jewish population of Israel, nor does it even come near to being modal, since the population of all the kibbutzim constitutes not more than about 3 percent of the Jewish population of Israel. But the kibbutz is a cherished concept in Israel (and, beyond its borders, among Jews all over the world), whose importance exceeds by far its numerical strength. The kibbutz members are considered the élite of Israel, in the sense of being people who realize in their lives a high social and ethical ideal which is beyond what other, ordinary people can attain. Therefore, the kibbutz personality is an important factor in the Israeli consciousness, a type of individual of whom the country as a whole is proud. The personality differences between the kibbutz members and non-kibbutz Israelis, who as recently as two generations ago shared a common East European Jewish socio-cultural background, show the difficulties one has to face in trying to delineate the modal personality of even a narrowly defined Jewish sub-group.

8. Religiosity and Identity

Sociologists looking at the Jews as a minority group amidst a large Gentile majority are apt to ask two questions very frequently: How does Jewish religiosity compare with that of the Gentiles; and to what extent do Jews feel their Jewish identity? Religious observance and self-identification are, after all, the two basic criteria which separate the Jew from the Gentile. Once a Jew abandons all religious observance and has no feeling of Jewish identity, he has ceased to be a Jew, no longer considers himself as a Jew, and, before long, he or his offspring will be considered non-Jewish by others as well. This is the road of assimilation, of submerging oneself in the Gentile social environment, which has been taken by many Jews since the Enlightenment. Prior to it, the question of Jewish religiosity and identity did not arise, aside from a few exceptional cases. Internally, Jewish religion and the Jewish community had such a hold on the individual Jew that his Jewish observance and identification were his natural condition—matters determined once and for all by the very fact of his birth, to which due reference was made in the daily recital of the benediction: "Blessed art Thou, O Lord, our God, King of the Universe, who hast not made me a Gentile." As far as identification was concerned, the external world, the world of the Gentiles, had imposed its own will upon the Jews. It forced them from the outside to remain within the confines of the Jewish community, the Jewish people, the Jewish way of life.

Among the Jewish communities of the Middle East, living in a world untouched by the influence of the European Enlightenment, the traditional hold of Jewish religiosity and the Jewish community remained unbroken until the great upheaval of the establishment of Israel and the transfer of most Oriental Jews either to Israel or to France. The typical distinguishing features of a minority in the Muslim world were, and remained, first, a different religion, and second, a different language. In the Arab countries, the Jews constituted Arabic-speaking religious minorities, although their Arabic vernacular differed from the dialects of the Muslims in the same localities. There were other Arabic-speaking religious minorities as well, such as the Copts in Egypt, the Greek Orthodox in Iraq, Syria, and Lebanon, and the like, but these did not feel (nor were they felt by the Muslim Arab majority to be) as different as the Jews. These Arabic-speaking Christian minorities, to varying extents and degrees, were considered Arabs; they were "Christian Arabs." In no Arab country, on the other hand, were the Arabic-speaking Jews considered Arabs to any extent or degree; and never were they referred to as "Jewish Arabs." This is the more remarkable since the purely religious differences between Islam and Judaism were much smaller than those between Islam and Christianity, and it was considered less objectionable for a Muslim Arab man to marry a Jewish than a Christian woman. Notwithstanding all this, the Jews as an ethnic group were considered more alien in the Arab world than the Christians. In Persia, the Persian-speaking indigenous Jewish population was considered even more of an alien group because the Jews were the only sizable non-Muslim minority, and because Shīʿite Islam, the dominant sect in Persia, was on the whole less tolerant of other religions than Sunni Islam to which almost all Arabs belonged.

In a few places in the Middle East, the Jews differed from the majority population not only in religion but also in language. In the cities of western Turkey, there were Sephardi Jewish communities whose members spoke Ladino, the ancient tongue the Sephardim had brought along from Spain when they were expelled in 1492. In southeastern Turkey and in contiguous areas of Iran and Iraq, in the region known as Kurdistan, lived the Kurdish

Jews who spoke (like the Nestorian Christians in the same area) dialects of Neo-Aramaic; while the Muslim Kurds, who were the majority population there, spoke Kurdish, an Iranic language related to Persian. As expected, the otherness of these Jews—distinguished from the local majority by both religion and language—was felt to be most pronounced.

In these circumstances, neither a relaxation of religious observance nor a weakening of the sense of Jewish identity was possible. Apart from the religion-dominated nature of Middle Eastern culture—of which the Jews formed a subdivision of their own and in which one simply could not give up one's religio-ethnic identity—such a move was unthinkable for the Jews for another reason as well. They considered themselves, their religion, their traditions, their way of life, and their values superior to those of their Muslim neighbors, an evaluation which in itself precluded even the thought of religio-ethnic apostasy.

In this respect, the conditions among the Oriental Jews until their emigration from the countries in which they had lived since their exile from Palestine resembled quite closely those which prevailed among the Ashkenazi Jews until the Enlightenment. It was only after the Enlightenment that the movement away from Judaism and Jewry began, that assimilation proved both feasible and attractive to many, and that Jewish religious observance and self-identification became matters of individual choice and hence issues for sociological interest and sociometric studies.

Most of these studies have American and Israeli Jews as their subjects, while little information is available about the Jews of any other country. Since, however, Israel is a country with a Jewish majority, the questions of both Jewish religiosity and identity assume there an entirely different aspect from the one characterizing these Jewish traits in the Diaspora. In Israel, as far as religious observance is concerned, the Middle Eastern majority of the population is only now going through that process of secularization which, among the Ashkenazi Jews, had been accomplished one or two or more generations ago. The process is accelerated because of the generally prevalent desire among Middle Eastern Jews to assimilate culturally and behaviorally to the Ashkenazi Jews, which includes the emulation of the latter's pattern of a-religious behavior. It is partly at least necessitated by the fact that in Israel, in contrast to the Diaspora, all activities which cannot be disrupted on the Sabbath must be performed by Jews. These include the operation of water works, electricity, police and fire duties, armed services, at least a partial maintenance of inter-urban and intra-urban public transportation, and the like. In all this, the prevailing usage is calculated to instill the idea that these secular necessities take precedence over the traditional religious laws of the Sabbath rest; and, by extension, that religious life in general must yield to secular life.

In the modernizing sector of the Middle Eastern Jewish communities, and in the great majority of the Ashkenazi Jews in Israel, Jewish religious consciousness has in fact been eclipsed and replaced by Israeli national consciousness. For the modern Israeli Jew, Jewishness is expressed, not in observing religious precepts, but in living a Hebrew-Israeli life. For him, the full and only adequate expression of Jewishness is his living in Israel, his participation in all aspects of the country's national life, its culture, economy, society, defense, politics, and his total emotional commitment, if not to the present, then to the future of Israel. The religious aspect of life is, for the average Israeli, a decidedly minor issue; this is manifested in the overall secularization of the Sabbath and the annual celebrations, all of which have been largely transformed from holydays into holidays, devoted not to communion with God, to ritual and ceremonial, but rather to recreational and cultural activities; in the rarity of attendance at services in synagogues; in the widespread disregard of the dietary laws and most of the other ceremonials (with the exception of circumcision, weddings, and funerals), and in the paucity of thoughts about God.

In the Ashkenazi population of Israel, that is, those of European extraction, Jewish religiosity, in general, is weak. In a study of Israeli high school students in the 1960's, 25 percent were found to be religious,[64] while in a sample of 560 students of Tel Aviv University in 1967 and 1969, the religious constituted only 4 percent.[65] The majority of high school students in Israel, and an even greater proportion of the university students, are Ashkenazim. Despite their religious indifference, 68 percent of the high school students and 56 percent (1967), 66 percent (1969), and 67 percent (1970) of the university students gave responses showing a strong Jewish identification. True, Jewish identification was most general among the religious students (100 percent of whom showed strong Jewish identification), less frequent (54 percent) among the non-religious, and least frequent (39 percent) among the anti-religious;[66] still it is noteworthy that such a proportion of the non-religious and even anti-religious students should have a strong sense of Jewish identification.

Moreover, the religiousness of the sample studied showed an inter-generational decline: 25 percent of the students reporting their parents to be religious or traditionalist identified themselves as non-religious, while only 2 percent moved in the opposite direction. It has also been found that a higher percentage of non-religious or anti-religious students whose parents were religious or traditionalist or observed certain religious customs had a stronger Jewish identification (56 percent) than such students whose parents were non-religious or anti-religious (46 percent). While the difference is not significant, it indicates a diminishing trend in Jewish identification as the religious background recedes. On the other hand, the traumatic experience of the Six

Day War of 1967 strengthened the students' Jewish identification,[67] which seems to indicate that Jewish identification is more susceptible to the influence of events, experiences, and changes in the environment than Jewish religiosity.

A secularizing trend can be observed among the Jews of America, the largest Diaspora community, which in the 1970's comprises some 40 percent of the Jewish people and some 50 percent of all the Jews outside Israel. A study reported in 1961 found that, as measured by frequency of attendance at religious services in a house of worship, the American Jews were far less observant than other religious groups. Only 13 percent of the Jews attended services "regularly" (i.e., once a week or more often), as against 39 percent of the Protestants and 72 percent of the Catholics. Moreover, 15 percent of the Jews stated that they never attended services, as against 8 percent of the Protestants and 4 percent of the Catholics. The 51 percent of the Jews who reported attending synagogue "seldom" (a few times a year or less) constitute the typical Jewish pattern of "High Holy Day" (New Year and Day of Atonement) attendance.[68]

This trend away from the synagogue is much more pronounced among native than among foreign-born Jews. In New York City in 1963–64, it was found that 23 percent of the foreign-born Jews attended synagogue at least once a week; but only 5.8 percent of the native-born Jews had such a frequency of attendance, as against 80 percent of the Irish for church attendance, 57.3 percent of the Italian, 64.5 percent of the other Catholics, and 26.9 percent of the white Protestants. The returns show clearly that the younger generation of Jews (the native-born) finds synagogue attendance an onerous duty and consequently tends to reduce it to the barest minimum. No less than 23.8 percent of them visits the synagogue once a year or less, and 16.6 percent never; while among the Protestants only 11.6 percent, and the Catholics only 3.9 percent, never went to church.[69]

Observances which come around only once a year prove more resistant to neglect. In the conservative Jewish community of Providence, Rhode Island, for example, 79 percent of the Jews surveyed reported that they attended a Seder celebration (the festive meal with lengthy prayers and songs on the first, and possibly also second, evening of Passover) each year; and 74 percent stated that they light the Hanukka menora.[70] The observance of the laws of *kashrut* (the system of dietary laws of which the separation of meat and milk is an important part) is, again, a hard everyday discipline, which few Jews observe. In Providence, only 32 percent said that they used separate dishes in the home for milk and meat. Even this relatively small percentage of observers is on the decline, as can be concluded from the fact that 53 percent of the first generation, 25 percent of the second, and 16 percent of the third reported using separate dishes.[71]

In his analysis of the relative pattern of the retention versus neglect of Jewish observances, Marshall Sklare discerned five criteria. The highest degree of retention, he finds, occurs when a ritual:

(1) "Is capable of effective redefinition in modern terms," such as Passover and Hanukka, which are interpreted as symbolic of "man's unquenchable desire for freedom." Although the dietary laws, too, were reinterpreted as having hygienic significance, this had little appeal for people who live in a publicly safeguarded sanitary environment and who, in addition, tend to regard food prohibitions as primitive taboos.

(2) "Does not demand social isolation and the following of a unique lifestyle." This criterion excludes from retention a large number of rituals and customs, which are, however, observed by those Jews, such as the Hasidim and other ultra-Orthodox groups, whose purpose is precisely the opposite—to isolate themselves as completely as possible from the Gentile environment.

(3) "Accords with the religious culture of the larger community while providing a 'Jewish' alternative when such is felt to be needed." Hanukka as the Jewish counterpart to Christmas provides the best example. I would add the lavish Bar Mitzva and Bas Mitzva celebrations as Jewish counterparts to the Christian confirmation.

(4) "Is centered on the child." Passover and Hanukka had traditional elements which could be, and are, emphasized as being directed toward the children in the family and are utilized for acquainting and involving them with attractive Jewish rituals. This criterion, of course, presupposes that the Jewish parent wishes to transmit his Jewish identification to his children.

(5) "Are performed annually or infrequently." The modern American Jew finds it difficult to maintain daily or weekly religious routines which would tax his patience. Hence Passover, Hanukka, the High Holy Days of New Year and Yom Kippur, etc., are observed by more Jews than the Sabbath, the daily prayers, the laws of *kashrut,* and the like. [72]

The result is a narrow selection from among the many traditional Jewish religious observances, and the retention of those rituals that can be fitted into the strongly secularized atmosphere of the Jewish home, and which, moreover, do not too blatantly set the Jew apart from his Gentile neighbor. In other words, the benign neglect of religion which characterizes the general environment has been taken over by the American Jew, except that, in accordance with his proclivity for intensity, he carries the reduction of the role of religion in his life a step further than the Gentiles.

Compared to the lukewarm attitude to religion which is a general American Jewish characteristic, there is a surprisingly strong trend among American Jews toward the maintenance of their Jewish identification. The difference between the prevalence of these two features, religious observance and Jewish self-identification, is an eloquent testimony to the effect that Jewishness is more than observance of Jewish religious precepts and belief in

Jewish religious teachings. If it were not so, there would be no Jews left who, while devoid of all belief and observant of no practice, nevertheless have a strong sense of Jewish identity.

What precisely is this sense of Jewish identification is rather difficult to define, more difficult even than the definition of self-identification in general. Some twenty-five years ago Bernard Lazerwitz proposed a series of traits as criteria of minority group identification: a person who identifies himself with the minority group to which he belongs adheres to the view that the preservation of the group is of utmost importance; desires to participate in the life of his group; resists temptation to join other social groups; comes to the aid of his group whenever it may be threatened or attacked; feels that his group has a unique and valuable contribution to make to overall society; gets satisfaction from participation in various activities of his group; and has internalized the values and standards of his group.[73]

While there is no doubt that all these traits are applicable to the Jews, the Jewish case is complicated by an additional set of factors; to wit, there is an inevitable inner connection between what the Jews feel to be the nature of the Jewish community and the manner in which they conceive their Jewish identification. For those who consider Jewishness a matter of religion, Jewish identification is a religious one. For those who see Jewishness as a nationality, Jewish identification is a question of nationality. The historically conscious Jew identifies himself with the history and fate of the Jewish people. For those who value Judaism above all as a set of cultural and humanistic values, Jewish identification means adherence to these values. The Zionist in the Diaspora feels a strong identification with Israel, while conversely, the Jewishly conscious Israeli has the same feelings about the Diaspora. These diverse Jewish identifications are reflected even in the work of scholars who adopt one or the other of these points of view in approaching and discussing the issue of Jewish identification.[74]

In whatever manner or fashion Jewish identification is defined, there can be no doubt that it is a feeling inculcated, to begin with, in the parental home into the infant, child, and adolescent [75] and, partly concurrently and partly subsequently, by the wider social environment, the experiences to which one is exposed, the information one absorbs, and the manner in which one's own reactions shape up and one's convictions develop under the impact of these factors. It is a syndrome comprising the conviction that one is a member of a group, the Jews, however defined, or, at least, of being closer to Jews than to other people. It is the belief that one possesses mental features, resulting from history, tradition, upbringing, and from one's own manner of absorbing these factors, in respect of which one is similar to other Jews. And, as a rule, it is the almost instinctive desire to pass on this sense of Jewishness to one's children.

I know of no studies of Jewish identity outside America and a few other countries of the modern Western world. Yet my reading of Jewish history and studies of Jewish culture in other countries and other times leaves me in no doubt that in the past the Jews were entirely suffused with a consciousness of their Jewish identity, even though the very concept did not exist among them. Wherever he lived, and whatever his status in the Gentile society, the Jew was a Jew, first, last, and always. His Jewishness was something that filled his entire being "as the waters cover the sea" (Isa. 11:9).

Jewish identity and Jewish religiosity were, of course, inseparable. This was eloquently manifested in the *ḥerem*, the excommunication, with which the Jewish community traditionally punished a Jew who had offended by "throwing off the yoke" of religion. The transgression was a purely religious one, but the punishment was social. The culprit was excluded by the ban from the community; he was publicly deprived of his Jewish identity.

Jewish identity was first put in question by the Enlightenment. For the first time since Abraham, Jewishness was no longer a matter of castelike inevitability, but became instead an issue of individual choice. As is only too well known, many of the children and grandchildren of the original eighteenth-century Enlighteners made use of this newly won freedom and opted out of Judaism. Ever since, the denial of Jewish identity has been a possibility open to those Jews who wished to avail themselves of it. The number of those who have done so during the last two centuries is considerable. But in view of the enticements that assimilation and merging into the Gentile majority offered, what is notable is not that many did leave the fold but that the number of those who did was not greater. For the fact is that while the renegades did make a dent in the Jewish body politic in the Central and West European countries, they did not inflict major demographic damage, and the Jewish population as a whole continued to increase. True, the replenishment of the losses in the West came from the great Jewish population reservoirs of the East; but by the time that Eastern contingent was largely exterminated by the Nazis, the movement out of Judaism in the West had all but ceased.

The greater tenacity of the hold Jewish identity exercises over the Jews than Jewish religious observance is illustrated in a study of the integration of North African Jews in France carried out in the late 1960's. This study found that while the observance of Jewish ritual manifested a rapid decline after the arrival of the North African Jews in France (although it had begun in North Africa), the Jewish self-identification of the young generation increased. Only 10 percent of those interviewed observed the prohibition of writing, and only 12 percent that of using a vehicle, on the Sabbath; 28 percent of the young generation, as against 8 percent of their fathers, never went to the synagogue; not more than 28 percent of the young generation as against 45 percent of their fathers ate only kosher food when taking a meal outside the home. On the other hand, when asked, "If you ask yourself,

'What am I?' what would be your answer?" no less than 75 percent of the adults and 84 percent of the youngsters answered "a Jew," or "a North African Jew," or "Jewish and French"; and only 25 percent and 16 percent respectively replied "French," "North African," or "Pied-noir." [76]

In a study carried out in 1970 among Jewish students at Oxford University, a definitely élite group in British Jewry, it was found that "religious attitudes [were] the least important factor in Jewish identification." Only 28 percent of the respondents stated that they "believed in the existence of God," while 41 percent stated that they did not, and 31 percent expressed uncertainty. The percentage of those attending synagogue services or observing *kashrut* was very small. On the other hand, 56 percent said that they had at some time belonged to a Jewish or Zionist youth movement, 48 percent were members of the Jewish Society in Oxford, 75 percent believed that "Israel makes mistakes but in general has [my] sympathy," with an additional 7 percent assenting to the proposition that "Israel is entirely in the right and has your full support." Although 18 percent considered intermarriage "desirable," 52 percent had no strong opinion on the subject, and 26 percent considered it undesirable, nevertheless 75 percent asserted that they intended to bring up their children as Jews. The researcher concludes that "Judaism as a creed or code of conduct no longer seems to represent the primary form of Jewish identification," but Jewish identification persists; it "subsists chiefly in common patterns of social behaviour and outlook, although here too . . . a dissolving process is at work." It is especially in their political outlook and behavior, and notably in relation to Israel, that the students displayed their Jewish identification most strongly.[77]

These results were paralleled by those of a study of Jewish identification in America. The Sklare-Greenblum study of Lakeville (the fictitious name of a suburban Jewish community in the Midwest) showed, first of all, a rapid decline of religious observance from one generation to the next, which the authors term "declining sacramentalism." The rules of *kashrut* were the most neglected among the rituals: only 5 percent of the respondents bought kosher meat, and only 9 percent ate no bacon or ham. As for synagogue attendance, no more than 5 percent of the respondents attended services on every Sabbath, while 35 percent never attended. Within the field of religion, emphasis has definitely shifted from ritual to morality, as shown by the fact that while only 29 percent considered themselves "very religious" in ritual observance, 62 percent gave themselves the same rank in moralism.

Against this weakening of the hold of religious observance, Jewish identification, as expressed in organizational affiliation, remained strong. At various phases of the life cycle, 68 to 93 percent of the respondents belonged to a Jewish organization. The same tendency was manifested in the pronounced preference Jews had for other Jews as close friends: 89 percent of the respondents (87 percent of their parents) reported that most or all of their friends were Jews. In conformity with these patterns, 93 percent of the respondents gave highest ranking to ethical and moral life as "essential" to being a good Jew, and 85 percent felt it "essential" that one should accept being a Jew and not try to hide it. As against these high-ranking essentials, only 31 percent felt that it was essential (and 44 percent that it was "desirable") for a good Jew to belong to a synagogue or temple; 24 percent held that it was essential (and 46 percent that it was "desirable") to attend services on High Holy Days. Attendance at weekly Sabbath services was considered by no more than 4 percent as essential and by 46 percent as desirable; only 1 percent thought that the observance of the dietary laws was essential, and only 11 percent that it was "desirable." The traditional ideals of Jewish learning and charity, too, showed a decline, but a far smaller one than ritual observance; 48 percent felt it was essential to know the fundamentals of Judaism, and another 48 percent felt it was "desirable" to have such knowledge. As for charity, 39 percent felt that it was essential and 49 percent that it was desirable to contribute to Jewish philanthropies. On the other hand, 58 percent felt it was essential, and 37 percent that it was desirable, to help the underprivileged improve their lot.[78]

The significance of Jewish self-identification as a value in modern American Jewish life is poignantly illustrated in a study carried out among mostly Conservative Jews and reported in 1971. This was predicated on the fact that attendance at High Holy Day services ranks very high among those religious activities which are most widely carried on by Jews. As we have seen, data indicate that the majority of Jews attends synagogue at least once a year, on New Year or Yom Kippur. Since Jews "in very large numbers make every effort to participate in such services . . . an analysis of the factors leading to such attendance might very well cast light on what it means to them to be Jews." [79] The results, quite surprisingly, showed that the overwhelming majority of the Conservative, Orthodox, and Reform Jews questioned stated that the most important goal they looked forward to obtaining from attending High Holy Day services was Jewish identification.

To understand why this is surprising, we must point out the difference between the High Holy Days and the other Jewish holydays. All other Jewish holydays are basically of a commemorative character, that is, their observance serves to indicate that the individual Jew, in this day and age, recognizes his dependence on his traditional and historical Jewish antecedents. This is a strong element in the so-called Pilgrim Festivals, which commemorate the Exodus from Egypt (in the Passover feast), the Giving of the Law at Mount Sinai (in *Shavu'ot* or Pentecost), and the forty years wandering in the desert (in *Sukkot* or Tabernacles). As for Purim, the Ninth of Av, Hanukka, they are purely historical holydays. In contrast to these observances, the High Holy Days of New Year and Yom Kippur commemorate no historical event but are "Days of Awe" in which the Jew individually and personally stands before God, repents of his sins and confesses them, cleanses his soul, and, contritely aware of his fragility as a weak and mortal vessel, throws himself upon the mercy of his Divine Father. This ever since Biblical times had been the traditional meaning of the High Holy Days, which made them the most emotion-laden time in the life of the Jew, so that strong men shed tears like children while reciting the old prayers in the synagogue. This being the case, one would have expected that the prime motivation of those Jews whose Jewish observance is largely reduced to attending High Holy Day services would be personal, religious, and psychological—to "straighten out" one's relationship with God, to obtain forgiveness for one's sins, to go through something of a cathartic process, to achieve peace of mind, and the like. Answers such as these were, indeed, given by some of those questioned in the study, but they ranked low in frequency. In fact, not before the ninth rank (out of a total of thirty) did any reference to God appear in the responses.

The results of this study, whose value is greater than would be indicated by the small number (ninety) of those questioned, indicate that in the modern American environment what Jews primarily seek in attending High Holy Day services is an expression not of their religious feelings but of their urge for Jewish self-identification. As Rabbi Lasker, who carried out the study, concluded, "Inasmuch as Jews express themselves positively as Jews by joining synagogues and attending High Holy Day services, they share a desire to identify themselves with the Jewish People and to carry on a Jewish tradition." [80]

15

---◆◆◆◆---

Health: Physical and Mental

1. Physical Health

Intense concern with health is a two-thousand-year-old characteristic of Jewish culture—or, more precisely, of individuals brought up in a Jewish cultural milieu.

The main traditional prayer, formulated in Talmudic times and still recited three times daily by all Orthodox Jews (and let us not forget that until a hundred years ago almost all Jews were Orthodox), contains these words as one of its "Eighteen Benedictions": "Heal us, O Lord, so that we be healed, save us, so that we be saved, for You are our praise! And bring full recovery from all our afflictions, for You are God, King, Faithful and Merciful Physician. Blessed are You, O Lord, Healer of the sick of His people Israel." This benediction, as the entire prayer of which it forms part, is referred to in the Talmud as an established prayer, and its wording is based on Jeremiah 17:14. The same Talmudic passage states that if somebody is sick in one's house, one is allowed to insert into this benediction a personal request for his recovery.[1] Another indication of this ancient Jewish preoccupation with health is the Talmudic saying which has become an oft-quoted Jewish proverb: "The Holy One, blessed be He, provides the remedy before the affliction."[2]

Nor did the Jews, even the most religious among them, confine themselves to invoking divine help in case of illness. Quite to the contrary. Stringent and down-to-earth measures were taken to ensure health and well-being. In Talmudic times it was accepted as a general rule that the purpose of all the religious commandments was "to live through them, but not to die through them," that all commandments (except those prohibiting idolatry, incest, and bloodshed) might be violated in case of danger to life, that to fast or undergo other ascetic exercises, even including the abstention from wine, was a sin, and that a scholar was not allowed to live in a city where there was no physician. In the Jerusalem Temple itself, a special room was set aside to serve as the office of a physician who looked after the health of the priests.[3]

Well known is the important role that dietary laws play in Jewish religious observance. Some students of Jewish religion have tried to interpret these laws, or some of them, as having a prophylactic intent. The prohibition of pork, for instance, was explained as intended to prevent trichinosis. Although these interpretations cannot be accepted, there is another, lesser known, category of rules, prescriptions, and precautions enjoined by the Talmudic teachers in connection with food intake for the explicit purpose of proving physical well-being. On this basis alone, quite apart from ritual permissibility, the rabbis prescribed what one should and should not eat, when, how, and how much one should eat, what kinds of food should be combined in one meal, and so on.[4]

Many other measures to preserve and promote health were recommended by the Talmudic rabbis and their medieval heirs, such as where, how, and in what position one should sleep, how to avoid contagions, how to preserve food and drink, what rules to observe in connection with sexual intercourse (cf. Chapter 18 on "The World of Values"), how to guard oneself against physical injury, and the like.[5]

Moreover, the health and well-being of the individual were not just his own private affair but the concern of the community as a whole. Hence if somebody said, "It is no one's affair if I wish to expose myself to danger," he committed a sin. Since life was considered as belonging to God and not to man, such a transgression was punishable with stripes.[6] On the other hand, if a person becomes ill, that, too, is a matter of concern for the entire community. The Talmud makes it a duty for every Jew to visit the sick, whether Jewish or Gentile, in order to express sympathy, cheer him up, help him, and relieve him in his suffering.[7] This duty was considered by the rabbis as a salient example of *imitatio dei:* just as God visited Abraham when he was sick (this is how they interpret Gen. 18:1), "so you too must visit the sick." [8]

The *Hasidim* (or "Pious") of the pre-Talmudic period, a strongly religious quietist sect, who were the chief force in the Maccabean uprising of 168 B.C.E., made the visiting of the sick a special obligation. Matthew refers to it (Matt. 25:36); in the Talmud, as we have just seen, it is a basic charitable duty; and the *Shulhan 'Arukh* devotes a full chapter to it. Above all, special societies which bore the Talmudic name of *Biqqur Holim* ("Visiting the Sick") have existed right up to the present time and have carried on the ancient tradition of visiting and helping the sick.

As might be expected in a culture in which this mentality prevailed, and in which the visiting of the sick was considered one of the things which "have no limits" [9] (i.e., cannot be overdone), medical science was bound to attract much attention. By Talmudic times medicine was a highly developed specialization,[10] and it remained so throughout the Middle Ages and thereafter.

Whether in the Muslim or the Christian realm, Jewish doctors were sought out and employed as personal physicians by kings, princes, popes, and Church leaders, were consulted by all who had access to them, and pioneered in many fields of medical research. The concentration of Jews in the medical profession in modern America can thus be seen as a continuation of this old Jewish tradition. Such a tradition could not fail to influence the life of the people as a whole. When Dr. Ignaz Philipp Semmelweis (1818–65), the nineteenth-century Hungarian pioneer of hygiene and fighter against puerperal fever, was ridiculed by his colleagues because he advocated that obstetricians should wash their hands before touching a woman in labor, the Jews had had a religious custom for two thousand years which required them to wash their hands frequently (especially before meals) and to perform other ablutions. As a result of their better hygiene, infant and child mortality was less frequent among the Jews than the non-Jews, which prompted Arab parents who lost several children to hand over the next child born to them to a Jewish family to be taken care of for a number of years.[11]

These are some highlights from the background against which one must view the continuing Jewish concern with health. They show that it is based on a two-thousand-year-old traditional preoccupation with physical well-being, which comes to expression most prominently in the parents' (and especially the mother's) solicitude for their children. Zborowski and Herzog in their reconstruction of Jewish life as it was in the East European small town, the *shtetl*, until its destruction by the Nazis give a graphic picture of the forms in which this concern found expression. The child is constantly reminded not to hurt itself, not to get into a draft, not to get chilled. It is bundled into layers of clothes, even in the summer, to keep warm and stuffed with as much food as it will take.

> Nothing is worse than illness. . . . Illness of one member upsets the whole household, arouses the anxiety of everyone, from parents to distant relatives and neighbors. With sighs, advice and money, all participate in efforts to cure the ailment. . . . The women take command, the men are helpless. Their only contribution is the recital of prayers and psalms. . . . The mother will first try her own remedies, perhaps compresses or tea with raspberry syrup. The neighbors will join in with advice . . . bringing in nostrums handed down through generations.

A "universal method is the enema administered either by a member of the household or a 'professional' . . . the enema woman who devotes herself exclusively to this art. . . ." If all this fails, "the *feltscher* or *feltscherkeh* is called — a man or woman who has a rudimentary knowledge, not of medicine but of medicines. . . . In extreme cases, with both reluctance and fear, the doctor is called." If he, too, gives up hope, "the last resort is the Tsaddik with his amulets and prayers. During any illness, of course, prayers are offered, charity distributed, appeals taken 'to the graves.' " [12]

Preoccupation with illness was so great that some observers got the impression that "demonstrating that one is really ill and needs help is a value in Eastern European Jewish culture." [13] The use of amulets, incidentally, is known to have been customary among Jews since Maccabean times at the latest. [14] Among Hasidic Jews in Europe, and even more so among the generally tradition-bound Jews in Muslim countries, amulets have continued in use almost until the present time. Most of these amulets are small plaques—ranging in size from less than 1 square inch to something like 3 by 4 inches—are made of silver, tinned copper, brass, or iron, have a great variety of shapes (including crude imitations of a hand or a foot), and all carry Hebrew inscriptions, scratched in or carefully engraved. The inscriptions vary from lengthy and complex magic formulas, replete with divine, angelic, and demonic names, to simple requests of half a dozen words. Among the purposes for which such amulets were obtained (usually from artisans who copied them, often introducing spelling errors in the process) were curing of diseases, protection against the evil eye, promotion of fertility, prevention of miscarriage, protection of mother and child in childbed, and general benefits. A frequently encountered purpose is the promotion of health. [15] A very small and simple circular amulet in my collection, originally worn as a pendant, reads like the outcry of every sick person: "El na r'fa na l'Miriam bat Esther"—"God, please, heal, please, (Num. 12:13) Miriam the daughter of Esther," and on its reverse: "For the name of Miriam daughter of Esther."

From the nineteenth century the death rate of the Jews in all countries of Europe and Canada (with a few local exceptions) has been lower than that of the general population, and so has infant mortality. Three factors seem to be responsible for these differences. One was the concentration of Jews in the cities, in which the hygienic conditions and health services were better than in the rural areas; the second was the specific Jewish demographic profile, which included such features as a higher educational level and a concentration in certain occupations. The third consisted of the numerous commandments of ritual purity which were observed for religious reasons but which, incidentally, also amounted to hygienic measures: the frequent washing of the hands, other ablutions, dietary laws which excluded certain types of food and prescribed methods of preparing meals. Religious commandments were also responsible for the rarity of venereal diseases and (as we shall see in the next chapter) for the absence of alcoholism among the Jews. Nor must one overlook the traditional concern for health in general and for the health of children in particular, and the relatively larger number of Jewish physicians. [16] That the resulting lower mortality did not bring about a higher natural increase among the Jews than among their Gentile neighbors was due to the fact that the Jews had a lower birthrate. The question of birthrate does not concern us here, but a few findings as to the differential infant mortality rates are relevant.

In 1911–16, when the Jewish immigrants lived in as crowded conditions in the American cities as other newcomers and had a much lower income than the native-born whites, their infant mortality was 54 as against 94 for the native whites, 127 for the foreign-born whites, and 154 for the blacks. The differences between the Jews and others were of similar magnitude with reference to neonatal mortality due to respiratory diseases, while infant mortality caused by gastric, intestinal, and respiratory diseases was less than half among them as compared to native white Americans.[17] Commenting on these phenomena, researcher Odin W. Anderson surmised that "a closer examination would probably reveal a pattern of infant care of a high order embedded in the Jewish culture."[18]

Indeed so. Another surmise, by a researcher who investigated Jewish "illness behavior," is that "it is probable that the concern of Jewish mothers makes their children highly sensitive to 'abnormal symptoms' and may in fact induce a tendency toward 'hypochondriasis.' "[19] Jewish (and Italian) patients studied related to the investigator how their mothers were overprotective and overconcerned about their children's health and participation in sports, how they were constantly warned about colds, injuries, fights, and how their parents responded with sympathy, concern, and help whenever a child came to them crying and complaining. The conclusion reached by the investigator was that the Jewish parents, by their overprotective and worried attitude, fostered a complaining and tearful behavior in the children. The children learned to pay attention to pain and to look for help and sympathy, which were readily given. "In Jewish families, where not only a slight sensation of pain but also each deviation from the child's normal behavior is looked upon as a sign of illness, the child is prone to acquire anxieties with regard to the meaning and significance of these manifestations."[20] Accordingly, Jewish (and Italian) patients in hospitals responded to pain in an emotional fashion and tended to exaggerate experiences of pain, in contrast to "old Americans," who tended to be more stoical and objective in response to their pain experience. Also, in another study conducted among U.S. army inductees, Italians and Jews of East European extraction reported the greatest number of symptoms and illnesses.[21] A difference observed between the Jews and the Italians was that while the Italians primarily sought relief from pain and were relatively satisfied when such relief was administered, the Jews were mainly concerned with the meaning and significance of their pain and its consequences for their health.

Differences between Jews and others were found also in stress situations and among persons with disabilities. A comparison of the reactions of Jewish, "old American," Irish, and black aged male amputees showed that the loss of a limb was more serious for the Jewish than for the non-Jewish patients. On the part of the Jewish patients there was crying and overt expression of emotion.[22]

Additional data on Jewish-Gentile differences in attitudes toward health and illness were gathered in a study of more than 1,300 students in two American universities. It was found that the Jewish students had a significantly higher tendency to visit a physician than either the Protestant or the Catholic students. Moreover, among the Jews but not among the Christians, the higher the father's income the higher the student son's tendency to visit a physician. The Jewish students also had a higher tendency than the others to take self-medication and to absent themselves from classes because of illness. These marked differences had nothing to do with religious attitudes; on the contrary, while the overwhelming majority of the Christian students did attend church regularly, only 6 percent of the Jewish students reported similar attendance at Jewish religious services.[23] Hence the Jewish concern with health is a more persistent feature than Jewish religious observance.

The Jewish concern with health is the subject of many Jewish jokes which show a full awareness of the difference in this respect between Jews and Gentiles. One of the few collected by Theodor Reik reads: "When a Goy [a Gentile] has much thirst, he drinks a few pints of beer. When a Jew has much thirst, he goes to the doctor to be examined for diabetes." [24]

Mechanic asks why do assimilated or non-affiliated Jewish college students, mostly of upper-middle-class social background, reflect traditional Jewish patterns of illness behavior, but "fail to reflect the strong alcohol patterns observed among more traditional Jews?" He speculates that attitudes toward alcohol may be more easily affected by college associates and outside groups in general, "but the more subtle patterns of perceiving symptoms of evaluating health are not so easily affected." [25] While he may be right in this assumption, I believe there is another factor to be considered. Attitudes toward health are inculcated by Jewish mothers into their children from the earliest age on. By the time a young Jew reaches college, or even high-school, age, these attitudes have long been internalized to an extent which renders him practically immune to influences emanating from the peer group. As we shall see, no comparable immunizing indoctrination takes place in the Jewish home against alcohol because, in contrast to illness, which was considered an ever-present danger, the possibility that their child could become an alcoholic lay entirely beyond the Jewish parents' horizon.

2. Mental Health

The discussion on physical health was confined to the attitudes of Jews and Gentiles toward illness, since an analysis of actual differences in morbidity between Jews and non-Jews belongs not to the realm of the Jewish mind, but to that of comparative genetics and physiology.[26] With mental health the situation is radically different. Here, the differences in the actual incidence of various types of disorders between Jews and Gentiles, as well as between one and another division of the Jewish people, can throw light, directly and immediately, on characteristics of the Jewish mind whose malfunctioning is of as much interest to us as any of the numerous aspects of its normal functioning. A study of mental disturbances is, of course, a highly specialized field with which we can deal only in its sociological aspects.

Statistical information on the frequency of psychosis and neuroses among the Jews is available from the late nineteenth century on. While the data are often contradictory, their general import unmistakably is that, at least until the years of World War I, the incidence of both types of disorders was considerably higher among the Jews than among their Gentile neighbors. Thus the earliest available returns show that in Denmark, in 1863, of every 10,000 Christians there were 5.8 insane, while of every 10,000 Jews there were 33.4 insane, or 5.7 times as many. In Italy in 1870, there were 5.63 insane among 10,000 Catholics, as against 26 insane among 10,000 Jews; that is, insanity among the Jews was 4.6 times as frequent as among the Catholic Italians. In Prussia in 1871, of every 10,000 Catholics there were 8.84 insane, among Protestants 8.47, and among Jews 16.79, or about twice as many. On the other hand, in Berlin in 1880, as against 14.0 insane Catholics per 10,000 of population, and 18.1 Protestants, there were only 13.9 Jews. In New York City, until the end of the nineteenth century, the proportion of Jews admitted to insane asylums was about the same as their proportion in the general population.[27] Thereafter, the proportion of psychotics among the Jews declined. In 1917–18 it was found that of all the insane from New York City committed in that year to state hospitals, 16.5 percent were Jews, while in 1918–19 their number amounted to 14.5 percent of the total, although in that period the Jews made up an estimated 20 percent of the city's population.[28]

Maurice Fishberg convincingly argued some seventy-six years ago that in order to get a clear picture of the incidence of psychoses among the Jews as compared to the non-Jews, one must compare the Jews, who are a predominantly urban population, not with the general non-Jewish population but with the *urban* one. Insanity, as the figures quoted above illustrate, has a much higher incidence in the cities than in a country as a whole. Compared to that of other urbanites, the insanity rate of the Jews is not higher. Moreover, while most Gentile urbanites are relative newcomers to the cities, the Jews had been living in them for eighteen centuries.

The evil effects of the strained, nerve-shattering city life has thus been deeply rooted in their bodies and minds, and is kept up by hereditary transmission. With each new generation the nervous vitality of the Jews lessened, and one of

TABLE I. *General Population and Psychiatric Population (Including Ambulatory Psychoneurotic Patients) in New Haven in 1950 in Percentages by Religious Affiliation*

GENERAL POPULATION	CATHOLICS 57.5	PROTESTANTS 33.0	JEWS 9.5	TOTAL 100.0
Psychoneurotic disorders	46.2	29.8	24.0	100.0
Alcohol and drug addiction	68.5	31.5	0.0	100.0
Schizophrenia	60.8	29.4	9.7	99.9
Affective disorders	55.1	34.0	10.9	100.0
Disorders of senescence	55.9	37.4	6.8	100.1
Psychoses with mental deficiency	61.5	25.3	13.2	100.0
Epilepsy	71.5	25.7	2.9	100.1
Other organic disorders	53.8	43.4	2.8	100.0
Total psychiatric population	57.0	31.0	12.0	100.0

Source: Jerome K. Myers and Bertram H. Roberts, "Some Relationships Between Religion, Ethnic Origin and Mental Illness," in Marshall Sklare (ed.), *The Jews: Social Patterns of an American Group,* Glencoe, Ill.: The Free Press, 1958, p. 553. Originally published in *The American Journal of Psychiatry,* 1954, 110(10): 759–64. The order of the diseases listed has been changed here to make comparison with Table III easier.

the results of this mode of life is that most of the diseases which increase with the advance of civilization, especially the neuroses and psychoses, are more common among them than among others.[29]

As we shall see, this gloomy view of the Jewish mental stability was disproved by more recent studies.

As far as neuroses are concerned, these were so frequent among the Jews in the late nineteenth and early twentieth century that some observers, including physicians, claimed that most of them were neurasthenic and hysterical. As statistics became available, they showed that the incidence of neuroses was indeed much higher among Jews than among non-Jews. Especially hysteria in the male was found to be, as Fishberg put it, "a characteristic privilege of the children of Israel."[30]

By the middle of the twentieth century, several more sophisticated studies had been carried out in America which showed that the Jews had a higher incidence of psychoneuroses than the non-Jews, but a lower rate of psy-

TABLE II. *Psychiatric Population Prevalence Rates of Patients per 100,000 Populations in New Haven by Religious Affiliation (Based on Table I)*

	CATHOLICS	PROTESTANTS	JEWS
Neuroses and character disorders	140	158	442
Alcohol and drug addictions	45	36	0
Psychoses and affective disorders	481	414	496
Organic disorders	120	136	68
Total patients' rate	786	744	1,006

Source: Leo Srole, *et al., Mental Health in the Metropolis: The Midtown Manhattan Study,* New York: McGraw-Hill, 1962, p. 301.

choses. This was found, for example, in New Haven (1950), where the Jewish population at the time amounted to about one-tenth of the total population while almost one-fourth of those in treatment for psychoneurotic disorders were Jews. On the other hand, in epilepsy and other organic psychoses the Jews accounted for less than 3 percent of all the patients; that is, their rate was about one-third of the expected. The figures for these and other psychiatric disorders are presented in Table I.

The New Haven data were subsequently recalculated by Srole and associates so as to arrive at the rates per 100,000 estimated population among Catholics, Protestants, and Jews. The results, as given in Table II, show that the Jewish rate of neuroses and character disorders was about three times as high as that of the Catholics and Protestants; and that the Jewish rate of psychoses and affective disorders was somewhat higher than that of the two other religious groups, but about half as high as that of the others in organic disorders, while alcoholism and drug addiction were entirely absent among the Jews.

Quite similar findings were made about the same time in New York City. Here, among patients admitted to hospitals and diagnosed as suffering from psychoneuroses, the rate of the Jews was twice as high as that of either the Catholics or the Protestants. It was also significantly higher than that of the non-Jews in manic-depressive psychoses, but significantly lower in those psychoses which accompany old age (senile psychoses, and psychoses with cerebral arteriosclerosis) or are of organic origin (especially general paresis), and somewhat lower in dementia praecox. The figures in Table III summarize the results of the New York City study and show the annual rates of first admissions with various psychiatric disorders per 100,000 of the population

TABLE III. *General White Population (1952) in Percentages and Annual Rate of First Admissions from New York City to Mental Hospitals (1949–51) per 100,000 Population by Religious Affiliation*

GENERAL WHITE POPULATION	CATHOLICS 51.5	PROTESTANTS 16	JEWS 29.7
Psychoneuroses	(c.) 5.9	(c.) 5.5	11.7
Alcoholic psychoses	9.7	10.4	0.4
Dementia praecox	41.2	41.7	35.5
Manic-depressive psychoses	4.0	5.5	8.8
Senile psychoses	17.0	36.0	12.2
Psychoses with cerebral arteriosclerosis	24.7	36.7	18.7
General paresis	1.9	2.1	0.4
Involutional psychoses	12.4	14.6	16.6
Total of above eight categories	116.8	152.5	104.3
All psychoses of organic origin	53.3	85.1	31.8
All functional disorders	63.5	67.4	72.6
Total of above two classes	116.8	152.5	104.4

Source: Based on data contained in Benjamin Malzberg, "Distribution of Mental Disease According to Religious Affiliation in New York State, 1949–1951," *Mental Hygiene*, 1962, 46(4); as reprinted in edited version in Ailon Shiloh and Ida Cohen Selavan (eds.), *Ethnic Groups of America: Their Morbidity, Mortality and Behavior Disorders*, vol. I, *The Jews*, Springfield, Ill.: Charles C. Thomas, 1973, pp. 289–91.

belonging to each of the three religions. Both the New Haven and the New York studies showed a total, or almost total, absence of alcoholic psychoses among Jews.

On the basis of a review of studies and reports from New York, Massachusetts, Illinois, and other states, I. D. Rinder concluded that, as revealed by official statistics of hospital admissions, the Jews averaged "about one half of the mental illness of non-Jews." As for psychoses, with one probably insignificant exception, the Jews again had "consistently lower rates." However, in psychoneuroses, the Jewish rates exceeded those of the non-Jews. This was found to be the case in New Haven especially among the lower-middle-class and working-class Jews (who, however, form a rather small proportion of all Jews); they had two to three times their proportionate share of psychoneurotics.[31] The last-mentioned finding is in accordance with the general observation that "the upper classes comprise a somewhat smaller proportion of the psychiatric population than they do of the total community, whereas the lowest class in each religious group contributes about twice its proportionate share." [32]

The results of these studies were borne out by the Midtown Manhattan mental health study which was carried out by L. Srole and associates (c. 1954) and reported in 1962. This study found that relatively fewer Jews than non-Jews (per 100,000 population) were treated in mental hospitals (692 Catholics, 446 Protestants, and 398 Jews), which indicates a lower incidence of psychosis among the Jews. On the other hand, the relative number of Jews treated in psychiatric clinics on an out-patient basis for various forms of "mild impairment" (i.e., neuroses) was almost four times as high as that of the non-Jews (108 Catholics, 103 Protestants, and 380 Jews).[33]

Standardizing the sample for age and socio-economic status, statistically significant differences remained between the Jews and the two other religious groups. The Jews had the lowest prevalence of those well and impaired but were more heavily concentrated in the sub-clinical range of mild and moderate symptom formation (cf. Table IV).

Speculation about the causes of the high rates of neuroses and low rates of psychoses among the Jews began even before the statistical bases of these phenomena were firmly established. In the late nineteenth century there were some who, like Georg Buschan, saw in the tendency to psychosis a racial characteristic which they traced back to the Biblical Hebrews. Others, like A. Pilcz, attributed it to the Jews' acute struggle for existence and their peculiar occupations as merchants, speculators, stockbrokers, etc.[34] As for the causes of neuroses among the Jews, in addition to the urban character of the Jewish population and their "peculiar occupations," Fishberg found them in "the repeated persecutions and abuses to which the Jews were subjected during the two thousand years of the Diaspora. . . . Their effect on the nervous system of the Jews could not be other than an injurious one. Organic as well as functional derangements of the nervous system are transmitted hereditarily from one generation to another." Another etiological cause, according to Fishberg, is the age-old Jewish custom of marrying close relatives. "Being very neurotic, consanguineous marriages among Jews cannot but be detrimental to the progeny," because such marriages increase the chances of "perpetuating a nervous strain in families." Also the traditional Jewish educational system contributed its share: the Jewish child studied in the Ḥeder from a very early age, spending the greater part of his day there, which was "an important factor in the production of nervousness among the Jews. As is

TABLE IV. *Mental Health Classification of Respondents in Midtown Manhattan by Religious Origin as Standardized for Age and Socio-Economic Status (Percentages)*

MENTAL HEALTH CATEGORIES	CATHOLICS	PROTESTANTS	JEWS
Well	17.4	20.2	14.5
Mild symptom formation	34.5	36.4	43.2
Moderate symptom formation	23.4	19.9	25.1
Impaired	24.7	23.5	17.2
N = 100% $t = 2.6$ (.01 level of confidence)	(832)	(562)	(213)

Source: Srole, et al., Mental Health in the Metropolis, p. 305.

well known, the intellect of the Jewish child is very precocious, and, on this account, the nervous system suffers severely." [35]

Several years after the publication of Fishberg's work, Dr. Israel S. Wechsler discussed the causes of neuroses among the Jews and suggested that the makeup of their character is "nervous" because of the "psychic conflict" in which they have lived for centuries. The Jews experienced an "intense emotion of fear" of being attacked, they were in "a perpetual state of anxiety," to the extent that "to be afraid, then, to be sensitive became the abnormal-normal state of the Jew." Emancipation "often tended to intensify these anxieties and bring them to the surface." Added factors were the Jewish economic distress and the "excessively fond ties" within the Jewish family. Moreover, the Jew "has developed an intense individualism with a powerful ego ideal and an equally ardent striving for the socialization of all his impulses, for the sublimation, or translation, or shunting of all those inner strivings into socially valuable activities." Thus, between his equally strongly developed individualism and gregariousness "there rages eternal conflict," which "furnishes an additional source of the neuroses." [36]

These early students of Jewish psychopathology took it for granted that the number of persons in treatment, whether in hospitals, clinics, or private practice, was an accurate reflection of the incidence of mental impairment among various ethnic groups. Before long, however, this very premise came under question. It was inevitable that, with advances in data-gathering techniques, the issue should be raised whether or not in each of the ethnic groups compared there was an identical degree of willingness to seek out psychiatric help; in fact, whether or not in each of them there was the same degree of awareness of mental impairment. Among the first to deal with this question were Bertram Roberts and Jerome Myers, who argued in 1954, on the basis of their New Haven study, that "among Jews it is generally accepted that there is no conflict between religious doctrine and psychoanalytic theory. . . . The Jews exhibit a high level of acceptance of psychoanalytic psychiatry with a minimum of disturbance of their social values." [37]

Similarly, on the basis of his survey of the literature, I. D. Rinder concluded that the Jews, more than others, were disposed by their cultural values which encourage intellectuality to a greater awareness of psychiatric symptoms and a greater acceptance of psychotherapy; hence they "are more likely to become a voluntary treatment statistic in the area of the psychoneuroses." [38] Or, as Roberts and Myers put it, "the acceptance of psychoanalytic psychiatry is an important factor accounting for the extra-ordinarily high rate of psychoneurosis among Jews." [39] It can be added that among the Jews there is a greater readiness to accept also psychiatric treatment other than psychoanalytic. One of the findings of the Midtown Manhattan study was that the Jewish respondents suggested much more frequently (49.2 percent) than Protestants (31.4 percent) or Catholics (23.8 percent) that psychotherapy should be sought in response to certain hypothetical psychiatric problems. [40] In addition, one must take into account the greater Jewish concern with health in general, of which the willingness to seek psychiatric help is but one sub-variety. These considerations render it possible that the proportionately higher number of Jews under treatment for "mild impairment" does not in itself prove that they have a higher rate of neuroses; all it may show is that a higher percentage of those Jews who suffer from neurotic symptoms seek professional help than is the case among the non-Jews.

Other researchers, taking the statistical data at their face value, have sought to locate the etiology of the Jewish neuroses. Rinder has speculated that "the traditional Jewish emphasis upon sobriety, the control of hostile aggressive impulses, etc., means that these avenues of behavioral expression, hence symptom formation, are less readily available to one socialized in this cultural community," and that therefore "the closing off of other behavioral alternatives . . . may contribute substantially to the high Jewish rate of psychoneuroses." [41] A different explanation was offered by Paul Barrabee and Otto von Mering. Among patients in the Boston Psychiatric Hospital belonging to various ethnic groups, but all of a lower-class background, they observed that in the case of Jewish boys more frequently than in other ethnic groups, "membership in the ethnic group can be a source of stress." Although "the Jewish boy can select avenues to success that by-pass his Jewishness . . . since this implies a restriction in his freedom of choice, he often cannot shake off a diffuse sense of deprivation about his ethnic membership." [42] The explanation for the higher Jewish rate of neuroses and the lower rate of psychoses that follows (rephrased here in simplified language) is that given by Srole and his co-workers, who conducted the Midtown Manhattan study.

The historical experience of the Jews in the Diaspora has created in them anxiety about the instability of their conditions of life—anxiety which is communicated to Jewish children within the family. In a considerable percentage of individuals, the actual circumstances of their adult lives aggravate this anxiety to the extent of resulting in mild symptoms which prompt them to seek treatment in mental hospitals as out-patients. This would explain the high relative number of Jews treated for various forms of mild impairment (or neuroses). On the other hand, the same anxiety as generated in the Jewish family may function preventively to immunize the Jewish children against the potentially disabling forms of more severe mental disorders.[43]

Furthermore Srole, *et al.*, suggest the possible presence in the Jewish family unit of "an impairment-limiting mechanism that operates to counteract or contain in some degree the more pathogenic life stresses." This mechanism, they feel, "may be part of a larger survival-ensurance process rooted in the Jewish family and religious tradition," which is expressed in the explicit emphasis on health, in the psychological and material support given the sick individual by family and kin, and in the readiness to call upon outside "healing resources." [44]

In Chapter 11, the influence of the Jewish home on the *intellectual* development of children growing up in it was discussed. Here we must add a few comments on the influence of the Jewish home on the *emotional* development of the Jewish child, and especially on his mental health.

Among the emotional assets with which the Jewish family endows its children is, first of all, the security they derive from overtly and profusely demonstrated parental affection. This is expressed in the parents' concern about the child's health, in their obvious delight at any manifestation of ability on his part, in providing him with as much food as the circumstances of the family permit and more, and in surrounding him with warmth, sympathy, and encouragement. Related to parental affection is the unfailing readiness of the parents to support their child through the long years of his education, and, in fact, their insistence that the best or only way in which he can reciprocate their love is to persevere in his studies and make good in school and career. It is in the parental home that the Jewish child is provided with the verbal and intellectual skills which will open to him various avenues of accomplishment, as well as with the motivation to succeed and the values to strive for.

On the other hand, the same parental home is the source of much of the emotional stress with which many Jews are beset throughout their lives. While motivating the child to succeed, the parents also entertain very high expectations about him and instill into him a high level of aspirations, which manifest themselves in the child in the feeling that he must succeed, that he owes it to his parents to achieve what they expect of him and what he has come to expect of himself. This syndrome can backfire and lead to a rebellion against the parental (and self-) expectations, which explains the dispropor- tionately high number of Jews in such counter-culture groups as the hippies. Most of them, however, do not follow this path but, having inescapably in- ternalized the parental values and motivations, tend to develop a strongly achievement-oriented personality.

In many cases, as the child grows, his achievement orientation becomes intensified because as a member of a minority group he either actually does suffer from disabilities in relation to his Gentile peers or believes he does. In his efforts to overcome these real or imagined disabilities, he is apt to be- come an over-achiever with all that this implies in stress and personality problems.

As a result of their upward-striving motivation, the Jews in the Western world, and especially in America, have actually been characterized by an ex- ceptional upward mobility. Numerous studies have found that the upwardly mobile have higher incidences of neuroses, including such symptoms as hos- tile rejection of parents and family, etc., than the non-mobile. Thus the suc- cess of the Jews in social mobility may in itself be socio-psychologically dys- functional.[45]

The pathogenic effect of the Gentile environment on the developing per- sonality of the Jewish child was a subject of concern to researchers particu- larly before and during World War II. Harold Orlansky, who reviewed the field in 1946, called attention to those views according to which, from the age of four or five, when the child first understands that he is a Jew, "normal development as a free individual is impossible: the child's personality must insulate itself against public scorn and rejection, either directly experienced or anticipated." The result of this, and of the feeling of guilt which develops as a reaction to anti-Semitism, is an inferiority complex, which in turn is compensated for by feeling more dominant than the Gentiles. In addition, there is also a reaction in the form of a desire for aggression. The latter offers an added psychological explanation for Jewish preeminence in business, art, intellectual life.[46] While the assumption of such a direct psychogenic chain reaction (anti-Semitism→feeling of guilt→inferiority complex→domi- nance→aggressiveness→preeminence) appears simplistic, it can be viewed as an example of the tendency to derive the specifics of the Jewish personal- ity from one external source—anti-Semitism. The fallacy in this argument will become evident when we come to consider the pathological symp- tomatology of the Oriental Jews, who grew up in a no less anti-Semitic envi- ronment and yet have developed no feeling of guilt, no inferiority complex, no dominance or preeminence, but, on the other hand, do develop a stronger aggressivity than the Ashkenazi Jews. It would seem that the way in which Jews react to the emotional assault represented by an anti-Semitic environment is contingent upon the quality of the Gentile modal personality. The latter influences the Jewish modal personality, which then reacts in different ways to the impact of anti-Semitism.

A more recent study of the pathological features in the Jewish personality must be mentioned, albeit briefly. In 1968, the psychologist Louis A. Berman singled out the pathogenic family and existential insecurity as "sources of strain in Jewish living" and argued that the Jewish pattern of neurotic behavior is characterized by hypersensitiveness, hyperactivity, motor inhibition, neurotic aggressiveness, paranoid attitude, moral masochism, and certain obsessive-compulsive symptoms.[47]

As this brief review indicates, a leitmotif in the studies dealing with neuroses and psychoses among Jews is anxiety and such related phenomena as strain, tensions, depression, reactions to persecutions and abuses, fear of attacks, and the like. The question to which we now turn is whether this etiology is valid for all the divisions of the Jewish people, as Fishberg thought and as Rinder and others implied, or only for the Ashkenazim (European Jews) who were exposed to largely common influences in the European Diaspora. What about the Oriental Jews who experienced different formative influences in their Muslim environment? In search for an answer to this question we have to turn to psychiatric studies which were conducted in Israel, and several of which were concentrated on the differences in symptomatology between Ashkenazim and Oriental Jews. Some of these differences were touched upon in an early (1952–53) study, which showed that immigrants from Europe had a significantly higher rate of essential hypertension and peptic ulcer, while Oriental Jewish immigrants suffered from a very high rate of intestinal infections. Another early report on mental illness in Israel pointed out that, in contrast to the fully developed psychiatric symptoms found among Ashkenazi Jews, the Oriental Jews tended to express their psychoses in hypochondriacal physical complaints.[48]

Before reviewing the more recent findings on the differences in symptomatology between the Ashkenazim and the Oriental Jews in Israel, I should stress that marked disparities were found to exist in the *rates* of mental illness between these two major origin groups of Israeli Jews. Israeli statistics usually divide the Jewish population of the country into those born in Asia and Africa on the one hand and those born in Europe and America on the other. The Israel-born descendants of these two groups are as a rule considered as forming a third group. For the sake of simplicity, and in order to conform to the terminology used throughout this book, I shall continue to refer to the first group as "Oriental Jews" or "Orientals," to the second as "Ashkenazim," and to the third as "Israel-born." All the rates which follow refer to incidence per 100,000 population in the fifteen-year-old and older age group.

In 1958, the rates of first admission for neuroses were twice as high among the Orientals as among the Ashkenazim and the Israel-born. The highest rate was that of the Iranian immigrants (65), who had particular adjustment problems as well as an apparently greater tendency to paranoid reactions. The general Israeli rate for neuroses was 30. The 1966 returns showed a higher overall rate, but the differences between the two immigrant groups had disappeared—both now had a rate of about 40.

For personality (character, behavior) disorders, in 1958, again the Orientals showed remarkably high hospital incidence rates (36–48), as did the Israel-born (50), while the Ashkenazi rate was about half as high (15–25). By 1966, the Oriental rate had decreased to 25, and the Israel-born rate was 23.

Similar changes were found in the rates for schizophrenia. In 1958, the Oriental rate of first admissions was 57–80 (among them that of the Yemenite immigrants was the lowest and that of the Turkish the highest). The Ashkenazi rate was 39, and that of the Israel-born 81. By 1966 the Oriental rate had decreased to 51, the Ashkenazi rate increased to 45, and the Israel-born decreased to 67, but the latter was still the highest.

The one mental disorder which showed markedly lower rates among the Orientals than among the Ashkenazim was depression. In 1958, the Ashkenazi rate was 48, while the Oriental rate was half as high. The rate of the Israel-born was even lower. Similar rates (and differences among the three groups) were found in 1966. In paranoia, the Oriental rate was somewhat lower than that of the Ashkenazim.

In 1966, the differences in the rates of the various disorders almost balanced one another, so that the overall rates for all psychoses of a functional, non-organic nature (schizophrenia, effective, psychotic episode, paranoiac) were quite close in the three groups: for the Orientals they were 100, for the Ashkenazim 121, and for the Israel-born 107. The total rates of first admission in 1966 were 218 for the Orientals, 226 for the Ashkenazim, and 188 for the Israel-born.[49]

It should be noted in passing that the above Israeli rates of total first admissions were considerably higher than the corresponding rate for American Jews which, as we have seen, was 104.4 in 1949–51.

Based on the Israeli data, the general conclusion was reached that the Oriental Jews more often showed schizophrenic and personality disorders, while the Ashkenazi patients had higher rates of affective psychoses. Also, the pathology of the Oriental Jew was found to be "essentially extroverted and hysterical with a marked proclivity to magical beliefs and illusions," while the Ashkenazi Jew had an emphatically greater tendency to depression and suicide.[50]

A study of an Israeli child-guidance clinic population found marked differences between the psychopathology of boys of Middle Eastern (Iraqi and Yemenite) and European (German and Polish) parentage. The four groups studied were socio-economically and educationally matched. It was found that the psychopathological expression of Middle Eastern boys tended toward overtly expressed maladaptive and aggressive behavior, while among the European boys ideational and self-directed symptomatology predominated. Differences were also found between the Iraqi and Yemenite boys, with the former manifesting more explicit and direct expression of aggression, and between the Polish and German boys, of whom the former exceeded the latter in avoidance of and withdrawal from social contact.[51]

The results of this study were confirmed and amplified by another carried out somewhat later and based on interviews and observations of 350 patients in Israeli mental hospitals. Fifty-three male and fifty-three female Ashkenazi patients (of Russian, Polish, and Rumanian extraction) were compared with fifty-seven male and fifty-seven female Oriental Jewish patients (of Iraqi, Yemenite, Persian, Moroccan, Algerian, Tunisian, Libyan, Egyptian, Greek, and Turkish origin). Apart from certain basic analogies in their symptomatology (attention-demanding, psychotic belligerence, schizophrenic excitement, hysterical conversion, paranoia, withdrawn and anxious depressive states), the two groups showed differences which were "as extensive although subtler" than the similarities. The Middle Eastern subjects showed greater aggressivity than the Ashkenazim, manifested greater belligerence and greater resistance to the attendants, demanded more attention, and evinced "more chronic, disruptive, disorganized, and deteriorated aspects," had higher rates of schizophrenia, some with catatonic and hebephrenic traits, but were more sociable than the Ashkenazim. Among the latter, there was a greater prevalence of depression symptoms, with delusions of guilt, flattened affect, and suicidal attempts, and more complete withdrawal as part of their depressive syndrome; while laughter, unrealistic plans, delusions of grandeur, and sexual arrangement played a more noticeable part in their manic syndrome. They also evinced "more intellectualized, controlled, withdrawn syndromes and acute, bizarre disorders," and a "guilt-evoking forward striving nature," as compared to the Middle Eastern subjects. The Orientals showed less insight than the Ashkenazim, whose syndromes were more obsessive, and the paranoid syndrome of the Orientals was characterized by more hallucinatory activity. They tended to respond socially even when depressed and blamed for their depressive anxiety states not themselves—as did the Ashkenazim, in a guilt-ridden manner—but others, in the form of outside hexes (e.g., the evil eye) put on them. They were extroverted, with tendencies toward projection, somaticization, hysteria, and magical beliefs. As "possible etiological explanations for these differences" between the Oriental Jews and the Ashkenazim, the author suggests "varied cultural backgrounds, war experiences, socioeconomic and educational levels, criteria for hospitalization and treatment regimes."[52]

As for the relationship between cultural background and psychiatric symptomatology, only a few indications can be given. The symptomatology of the patients seems to be a pathological reflection of several of the traits discerned in the modal personality of the Jews hailing from two largely disparate cultural environments. The American Jewish modal personality (as sketched in Chapter 14) can be taken for the present purposes as being representative, in a generalized form, of the Ashkenazim when contrasted with the Oriental Jews. In particular, the following traits seem to form the psycho-cultural background of the formation of the Ashkenazi psychiatric symptoms: the considerable drive and achievement motivation, the upward-striving orientation, over-reaction, emotional instability, feelings of inadequacy, inferiority, and insecurity, internal maladjustment, deferment of gratification, which means a constant exercise of self-control, and a tendency to self-blame. In their psychoneurotic and psychotic over-proliferation, these features can lead to depression, self-blame, delusions of guilt, and other self-directed symptoms.

The Oriental Jewish symptomatology, on the other hand, is expressive, extrovert, uncontrolled; it places the blame on others and uses projection and somaticization as defense mechanisms. These features are congruent with the Middle Eastern modal personality, which comprises exaggerated self-assertion and self-importance, flamboyant behavior and speech, the tendency to blame others for one's own shortcomings, weaknesses, and failings, a preference for quick and easy achievement (i.e., instant, as opposed to deferred, gratification), lack of correlation between thoughts and words, on the one hand, and acts and the reality to which acts must conform, on the other, aggressiveness, quarrelsomeness, irascibility, and uncontrolled temper.[53] This is the emotional reservoir from which the Middle Eastern psychotic personality draws its nourishment. Thus the symptomatology of the Oriental Jewish psychotic personality presents a pathologically distorted image of a number of selected features of the Middle Eastern personality, exactly as that of the European psychotic does with reference to the normal (or modal) personality of the Western Jew. Just as there are palpable differences between the two personalities in general, so there are between their psychotic distortion. This confirms what has been suggested by Myers and Roberts in their study of New Haven psychiatric patients from different ethnic groups: ". . . it appears that there is some kind of cultural determination in the formation of symptoms."[54]

This being the case, one would expect that the symptomatology of the Ashkenazi patients in Israel should generally conform to that of the Jews and non-Jews in Western countries, while that of the Oriental Jews should show a parallel similarity to the general Muslim symptomatology. As far as the available studies allow us to draw conclusions, this indeed appears to be true. In America, while differences in incidence have been noted, the typology of the Jewish and Gentile psychoses has been found to be analogous. The same parallelism cannot be assumed with similar certainty for the Oriental Jews because of the paucity of psychiatric data for Muslims. However, the available studies do definitely point in the direction of Muslim-Jewish analogy. Thus two cross-cultural inquiries reported in 1963 and 1967 show differences, *inter alia*, between Euro-American and Middle Eastern (i.e., Muslim) psychotic symptomatology. The 1963 study presents the differences between Euro-American and Near Eastern patients with reference to schizophrenia. As we have just seen, in Israel the incidence of schizophrenic disorders was found to be significantly higher among the Orientals than among the Ashkenazim. This conforms with the findings of the cross-cultural inquiry mentioned, according to which certain schizophrenic disturbances of reality contact, such as visual and tactile hallucinations, were most frequently reported in peoples of Africa and the Near East. Also, the catatonic and hebephrenic types of schizophrenic process, which in Israel were found to be a "specifically and idiosyncratically Sepharadi [i.e., Oriental Jewish] factor," were found to be either least frequently reported in Euro-Americans, or most frequently reported outside the Euro-American sphere.[55] Incidentally, among American Jews schizophrenia was found to be less frequent than among non-Jews.[56]

The second cross-cultural study presents differences in depressive psychosis between Muslim and Christian patients. It found that suicidal ideas did not at all figure in the Muslim symptomatology, and guilt feelings were "particularly uncommon . . . as might be expected from the lesser Muslim concern with sin and introspection." It also appeared that "adherents of Muslim religion are apt to project their bad internal objects into the outer world," because "ideas of influence or possession, not a common feature in classical depression, are a common feature in these depressive samples." Further, agitation and excitement were more frequent symptoms in Muslim depressives than in others.[57]

These general surveys, which of necessity are lacking in depth, are supplemented by a specific study on depression and guilt in patients in an Arab psychiatric clinic in Cairo, reported in 1969. Confirming earlier studies of Iraqi and Turkish patients, the investigation found that the Cairene depressives tended to attribute their sufferings to God or to other people, and that the illiterate among them "did not seem to direct any aggression against themselves and most projected the responsibility for their distress on to God or other people. Acts of sorcery were frequently blamed by the illiterate as methods whereby the malicious intentions of other people could produce the symptoms." This tendency, several investigators surmised, was "possibly a manifestation of the general projective tendencies" of Arab culture.[58] We might add that this, precisely, is what students of Oriental Jewish psychotics also found.

All these findings seem to point to the following conclusion: the Ashkenazi Jews are similar to the Christians among whom they have lived for many hundreds of years in that both share exposure to religious influences, which can have "an ego-restricting effect" and "foster a sense of wrong-doing and feelings of guilt in states of depression," [59] accompanied by low somatic symptoms and high suicidal tendencies. The Oriental Jews, on the other hand, are similar to the Muslims among whom they have lived for many hundreds of years in that both share exposure to religious influences which are less concerned with guilt, sin, and introspection and therefore create, in states of depression, a tendency to blame outside forces or individuals such as the evil eye, magic, etc., for whatever impairment they perceive in themselves, as well as a tendency to high somaticity and low suicidal tendencies. That is to say, the influence of the socio-cultural environment is evident in both the well and the ill Jewish personality. Therefore, the picture painted of "Jewish psychoses" in Western countries is not applicable to the Oriental Jewish psychotic symptomatology.

3. "On the Fence"

Before leaving the subject of mental health we must dwell for a short while on the psychological problems of marginality, manifested in a specific syndrome by some acculturated Ashkenazi Jews. This takes up again a subject discussed in Chapter 12 (under "Marginality and Eminence"). There the focus was on the relationship between the marginal position the Jewish intellectuals occupy in their Gentile environment and their outstanding achievements in various fields of scholarly, artistic, and other intellectual activity. Here we shall concentrate on the emotional problems that marginality can, and actually does, produce in a certain proportion of Jews in the modern Western world.

For most of the Jews, to be sure, the fact that they are both Jews and members of the nation within whose territorial boundaries they live causes no emotional problems. As Kurt Lewin pointed out some thirty years ago, "every individual belongs to many overlapping groups: to his family, his friends, his professional or business group, and so on." [60] In the emotionally healthy and balanced Jew there is no conflict between his being a Jew and, say, an American or a Frenchman; nor does he feel any discomfort or embarrassment over the emotional attachments which tie him to his country on the one hand and to the Jewish community, of which the State of Israel is a central part, on the other. As Justice Brandeis put it in a famed statement, double loyalty does not lead to ambiguity, to which Kurt Lewin added that "not the *belonging to many groups* is the cause of the difficulty but an *uncertainty* of belongingness." [61]

Until the Enlightenment and the Emancipation, problems of ambiguity and uncertainty as to the Jew's position in relation to the Gentile world did not, because they could not, arise. In all countries of the Diaspora the Jew was a tolerated alien. Nor was there, prior to the rise of nationalism, such a concept as national loyalty. Occasionally, some Jews were in a position of serving a feudal master in one capacity or another (e.g., in Arab Spain or in Italy), in which case, of course, personal loyalty to their overlord was both expected of them and given by them. This kind of relationship between a Jew and a non-Jewish ruler has its Biblical prototype in the person of Joseph, who faithfully served Pharaoh, his country, and his people, saving the whole land from starvation. The loyalty—more than that, the devotion—of Joseph to his king could not be doubted. But at the same time Joseph was nothing but a Hebrew; even as viceroy of Egypt, he was not an Egyptian. While individual Jews repeated the feat of Joseph in one country, city, or principality after another, the loyalty of the average Jew remained undivided with his people, the Jewish community scattered over many lands. In a word, until the Enlightenment and the Emancipation, a Jew was a Jew and nothing else.

This, by and large, remained the position of the Jew in the Muslim world until the very end of his sojourn there as a compact minority set apart from the dominant majority by age-old traditions. The exclusively Jewish identity of the Jews in Arab and other Muslim countries was never in doubt. The traditional contempt in which the Muslim held the Jew as *dhimmis* (protected but underprivileged people) was countered by the Jewish pride in being superior to the Muslim in religion, education, culture, and values. The phenomenon, and the very concept, of Jewish marginality was unknown, except perhaps in those limited circles into which, as a result of the educational work of the Alliance Israélite Universelle, some French culture, and with it rudiments of French consciousness, were introduced and which constituted no more than a small fraction of the Middle Eastern Jewish population. Among the Arab upper and middle classes, the French *mission civilisatrice* did cause more personality disruption with occasional marginal and ambivalent symptomatology.[62] Among the Jews, the superimposition of French orientation merely increased the feeling of otherness that had dominated their relationship to the ignorant, illiterate Arab majority and thus, in effect, contributed to their commitment to Jewishness in contradistinction to the Muslim Arab majority.

For the Ashkenazi Jews, the Enlightenment brought an entirely new development. It induced them to acquire, especially in Central and Western Europe, the language and culture of the country in which they lived, while Emancipation made them equal citizens of the countries of their residence. Therewith the question of Jewish identity arose, and both the Jews themselves and the Gentiles among whom they lived answered it in different ways. The answer which was favored by many Jews both in Europe and in America was that the Jews were nationals of the countries of which they were citizens and differed from the non-Jewish citizens of the same countries only in their religion. Thus, in America, this solution held, they were Jewish Americans just as there were Protestant Americans and Catholic Americans.

However, despite this neat taxonomical solution, many Jews in the Western world (and even more so in the Communist orbit) feel that their position differs essentially from that of other religious minorities. To refer again to the American example, these Jews feel that their relationship to the white Anglo-Saxon Protestant (WASP) majority is not the same as that of the white Catholic American minority; they feel that they differ from the majority more and in more ways than do the Catholics. Most of the Jews can digest this fact, consider it as part of their existence, and live with it, as they live with the many other circumstances of their existence. Many even consider their Jewishness an asset and feel that being Jewish endows their lives with a special added flavor. But then there are some for whom their Jewishness does become a source of problems, tensions, and stress which can contribute to the development of a neurotic personality.

The most typical forms these problems take cluster around the issue of marginality. "Marginality" denotes the state of belonging to two cultures without being able to identify with either.[63] The trouble with the marginal man is that his attitude toward the two cultures to which he belongs and with neither of which he can identify creates in him a stress which affects his personality and the way he relates to his social environment. One type of marginal Jew in America (and the same situation obtains in other Western countries as well) tries to "pass"; that is, he strives to assimilate to his non-Jewish environment. But this cannot be successfully accomplished because, however strenuously he tries to dress, speak, and behave like the Gentiles whose company he seeks and acceptance he craves, they will nevertheless consider him a Jew. Thus he becomes frustrated, and his Jewishness, even if it is nothing more than the awareness of the fact that he was born to Jewish parents, becomes for him a source of irritation, a burden which he would like to lay down but does not know how. This, in turn, results in an alienation from other Jews (in extreme cases including members of his own family), and in a critical or even hostile attitude to Judaism, the Jewish people as a whole, and, more recently, the State of Israel. This is an extreme and acutely pathological form of marginality, a mental state which can easily produce neurotic symptoms, one of which, as Jessie Bernard put it, is the desire "to tear down the Gentile world" as well. "Since they could be neither Jew nor Gentile, they must destroy everything these stood for." Because they are outsiders, they become revolutionaries and radical extremists.[64]

In Chapter 17 on "Jewish Self-Hate," the phenomenon of Jewish Judeophobia will be treated in its social and cultural context. Here I must say a few words about its psychiatric aspect. That Jewish self-hate is a psychopathological manifestation has been strikingly illustrated by the case of Otto Weininger (cf. page 463). Ludwig Lewisohn, in his well-known novel *The Island*

Within (1928), portrayed it as a kind of psychosis. From a different angle, Milton Steinberg in his popular *A Partisan Guide to the Jewish Problem* treated it as a mental disease afflicting Jewish individuals.[65] The historian Salo Baron coined for these self-hating Jews the term "inverted Marranos" because, while they are recognized by their environment as Jews, they deeply resent this fact and, being unable to alter it, develop a hatred of their Jewish heritage and involuntary allegiance. They "usually become self-haters of a pathological kind," who "not only destroy their own peace of mind" but "are a menace to the equilibrium of the general, as well as Jewish society around them." [66] In addition to these "inverted Marranos," Ernst M. Wolf discerned four more major forms of expression of Jewish self-hate: (1) the Jewish inferiority complex, (2) Jewish "escapism," (3) Jewish "snobbishness," and (4) "Jewish anti-Semitism." [67]

As early as 1946, Harold Orlansky, on the basis of studies available at the time, summed up the American Jewish personality as comprising these traits—inferiority feelings, self-hatred, neurosis (?), striving for dominance, radicalism, as well as a great deal of ambivalence, with "submissive and aggressive tendencies which may wage constant emotional war" within the individual.[68] While this type of general portraiture must be qualified as applicable only to a certain percentage of American Jews, it is nevertheless useful in pinpointing some of the relatively frequent Jewish neurotic phenomena within the specific socio-cultural framework of Western democracies.

Less ambitious but more realistic is a recent paper published in England, in which it was suggested on the basis of a study of forty-six Jewish and seventy-one Protestant depressives (with matching control groups) that "depression among Jews may be related to mental stress arising from 'marginality' and that single Jewish males may be particularly vulnerable to depression." [69]

The more frequently encountered classical type of Jewish marginality was described as early as 1928 by Robert Ezra Park. It emerged, says Park, when "the walls of the ghetto were torn down and the Jew was permitted to participate in the cultural life of the peoples among whom he lived," in other words, after the Emancipation and the Enlightenment. A new type of personality appeared,

> a cultural hybrid, a man living and sharing intimately in the cultural life and traditions of two distinct peoples; never quite willing to break, even if he were permitted to do so, with his past and his traditions, and not quite accepted because of racial prejudice, in the new society in which he now sought to find a place. He was a man on the margin of two cultures and two societies which never completely interpenetrated and fused. The emancipated Jew was and is, historically and typically the marginal man, the first cosmopolite and citizen of the world.

The effects of marginality, says Park, are profound and disturbing on the more sensitive mind, causing a permanent crisis, "spiritual instability, intensified self-consciousness, restlessness, and *malaise*." [70]

To this we may add that frequently the stress of marginality and its malaise are intensified by the futile efforts made by the marginal Jew to be so completely part of each of the two worlds that the members of neither should know that he also belongs to the other. This involves a double standard of speech and behavior, and even a formal conforming with two different sets of values. When with his Gentile friends, colleagues, or associates, he will talk and behave like a WASP; when with his parents or other relatives, he will use Yiddishisms and Jewish mannerisms. Consequently, he is unable to "feel sufficiently rooted in either of these groups to be clear and confident about his views and about his personal relations to either side. He is therefore compelled to remain in a rather vague and uncertain but permanent inner conflict." [71] He is condemned to the stressful position of "sitting on the fence" and beset by the unrelenting anxiety of maintaining what in effect amounts to a dual personality.

Studies carried out by Victor Sanua have a direct bearing on the issue of Jewish marginality. Sanua showed that, over successive generations, two disparate processes take place in the personality of American Jewish high school students. On the objective test (the Thurstone Neurotic Inventory), they achieve progressively better scores moving from first to third generation, which shows that as far as "social adjustment" is concerned, having learned patterns of overt behavior, they appear more adjusted. But on scores from the projective test (the Rorschach Multiple Choice Test), which measures "inner adjustment," each successive generation manifests a greater internal malaise, in areas in which there are no conventionally learned "right answers." Comparing the results with scores achieved by boys from matched Protestant families, Sanua found that the latter obtained better adjustment scores than every Jewish generation group. These findings indicate that the greater the Americanization of the Jewish boys the greater their maladjustment. [72] Reviewing Sanua's work, Rinder adds that the personality thus described resembles the "heightened self-consciousness" which sociologists have found characterizes the marginal man. In a certain percentage of persons afflicted with this malaise of marginality, the condition "may become clinical and warrant later treatment." In others, however, it "may become channellized as social, economic, artistic, aesthetic, etc., drive. The crucial question is whether this maladjustment will overwhelm the individual and become pathology, or whether he can harness and utilize it as his private version of a divine discontent." [73] Here we have the kernel of a hypothesis that explains the high incidence of both Jewish neuroses and Jewish talents as alternative derivatives of maladjustment in the Jewish marginal man.

16

Three Problem Areas: Alcoholism, Overeating, and Drug Addiction

1. Alcoholism

In view of the lasting influence exerted on the Jewish mind by Biblical and Talmudic myths in general, the mythical references to drinking and drunkenness contained in those ancient sources constitute the best starting point for a discussion of the Jewish attitude toward the use of alcohol.

MYTHS ON INTOXICATION

According to the Book of Genesis, Noah was the first vintner as well as the first man to get drunk, which he did with disastrous consequences. The Biblical version of what happened was apparently bowdlerized by a sensitive editor, but the full story is told with unabashed explicitness in the Talmud and the Midrash. Satan, these later sources divulge, offered his partnership to Noah in tending his vineyard, and upon Noah's consent, he killed a lamb, a lion, an ape, and a pig one after the other and watered the vines with their blood. Hence, if a man drinks one glass of wine he becomes meek like a lamb; if he drinks two glasses, he is filled with courage like a lion; if he continues to drink, he soon begins to jump around foolishly like an ape; and if he drinks still more, he vomits and soils his clothes like a pig. Despite this implied warning, Noah did drink too much and uncovered himself in his drunkenness. When Noah's youngest son, Ham, saw his father's nakedness, he (according to the Biblical version) "told his two brethren without," or (according to the Midrash) took a string, wound it around his father's genitals (just as Dionysus did to Agdistis), and unmanned him. According to another Talmudic tradition, Ham committed sodomy on his drunken father. Whatever the exact nature of the deed, when Noah awoke he cursed Ham in his son Canaan and all his descendants, condemning them to eternal slavery.[1]

Noah's drunkenness, like the acts of all typical heroes of myth, had fateful consequences not only for himself but for his descendants many generations later. Interpreting the word *wayitgal*, which in the Biblical context means "he was uncovered," in its other possible meaning, "he was exiled" (hence the term *galut*), Talmudic sages opined that his drunkenness "caused Noah and generations after him to be exiled: the ten tribes of Israel were exiled only because of wine, as it is written, 'Woe to them that rise up early in the morning, that they may follow strong drink, that tarry late into the night, till wine inflame them!' The tribes of Judah and Benjamin were exiled only because of wine, as it is written, 'But these also reel through wine, and stagger through strong drink.' " Hence Rabbi Yoḥanan warned, "One should never have a passion for wine." [2]

Nor were emasculation (or being sodomized) and exile the only calamities brought about by drunkenness; it also led—and hence can lead—to incest. Some generations after Noah, Abraham's nephew Lot escaped from Sodom with his wife and two daughters. Lot's wife looked back and turned into a pillar of salt, but Lot with his daughters found refuge in a cave. Thinking that God had destroyed the whole world, and that therefore "there is not a man in the earth to come in unto us after the manner of all the earth," the daughters resolved to make their father drunk with wine and lie with him. They carried out their scheme in two consecutive nights, and in due course the elder gave birth to a son whom she called Moab, meaning "from father," while the younger called her son Ben-Ammi meaning "son of my kinsman." The Biblical text is at pains to exonerate Lot, who in the entire story of Sodom is presented as an upright man, and therefore emphasizes twice that in both cases, "he knew not when she lay down, nor when she arose." Nevertheless, the horror of the event was not lost on the later generations: "Drunk as Lot" has remained a household expression among Jews to this day. The sin of Lot was that he did not resist drinking too much wine and became so intoxicated that unawares he committed one of the three most horrendous sins known to Jewish tradition (the other two being idolatry and bloodshed).

As if these two object lessons of the pernicious consequences of drunkenness were not enough, the Talmudic sages attributed the very fall of Adam to wine. Rabbi Meir said, "The tree of which Adam ate was a grapevine, for nothing brings as much woe over man as wine." [3]

To top it all, Talmudic legend has it that even Ashmodai, the king of the demons, suffered his downfall because of drunkenness. To capture Ashmodai, Benaiah, the chief officer of Solomon, replaced with wine the water of the cistern with which Ashmodai used to quench his thirst. At first, Ashmodai would not drink, citing Biblical verses which warn against wine; but ultimately he could not resist his thirst, drank deep, and fell asleep. Benaiah, who had watched from a tree, thereupon chained him with the chain Solomon had given him upon which the Name of God was engraved. When Ashmodai awoke he was powerless, and Benaiah brought him to Solomon, who kept him imprisoned for a long time.[4]

The parts of these myths (about Noah and Lot) contained in Genesis were studied by Jewish children at an early age in the *Heder* and were listened to thereafter once a year in the synagogue by every Jew. The Talmudic myths became known to those who continued to study the Law in a yeshiva. In any case, until the Enlightenment no Jew could remain unfamiliar with the mythical validation of the dangers of inebriety.

MORALISTIC WARNINGS

Myths apart, inebriety is often decried in explicit or implicit statements in both the Bible and the Talmud. Aaron and his sons throughout all generations were warned not to drink wine or strong drink when going into the Tent of Meeting "that ye die not"; and even lay persons suspected of entering drunk the sacred precincts were admonished and derided. Drunkenness could easily lead to fornication, and both were sharply condemned by Hosea: "Harlotry, wine and new wine take away the heart."[5] His contemporary, Isaiah, as we have just seen, also has sharp words against intoxication. The Book of Proverbs contains numerous warnings against inebriety, which is a sign of foolishness, leads to poverty, woes, ravings, wounds, and confusion, and, in the case of kings and princes, to perversion of justice.[6] The early second-century B.C.E. author of the Book of Wisdom of Ben Sira talks about inebriety in the same vein.[7] Similarly, the first-century C.E. Alexandrian Jewish philosopher Philo warns, "Let us . . . never drink so deep of strong liquor as to reduce our senses to inactivity."[8]

But the Talmudic sages were not satisfied with mythically elaborating and sharpening the lessons contained in the Biblical stories about drunkenness. They sought support for their anti-intoxication views in the legal, ethical, and prophetic writings contained in the Bible. The Biblical law provides that if a couple has a delinquent son they can bring him to the elders of the city, saying, "This our son is stubborn and rebellious, he doth not hearken to our voice, he is a glutton and a drunkard," whereupon "all the men of the city shall stone him with stones that he die."[9] In discussing this law, the sages of the Mishna and the Talmud ruled that, as far as the son's drinking habit is concerned, if he drank a *log* of wine, or even as little as half a *log* of Italian wine, and drank it undiluted with water, he is subject to the death penalty.[10] Since a *log* was the equivalent of the volume of six eggs, the sages were certainly most strict in setting the upper limits of the permissible use of wine.

The dangers of inebriety alluded to in the Biblical wisdom literature in poetic language are made explicit by the sages. A passage in the Book of Proverbs which reads:

> Look not thou upon the wine when it is red,
> When it giveth its color in the cup,
> When it glideth down smoothly;
> At the last it biteth like a serpent,
> And stingeth like a basilisk . . .

was explained by Rava: "Look not thou upon the wine, for its end is blood." And Rabbi Yitzḥaq added, "Wine reddens the faces of the godless in This World and pales them in the World to Come." [11]

IN PRAISE OF WINE

Side by side with the Biblical and Talmudic warnings against the baleful consequences of over-indulgence in wine and "strong drink" (which was the generic term for all intoxicating beverages apart from grape wine), the same sources contain numerous statements which praise the effects of wine and even recommend its use, as long as it is done in moderation. In an old parable which preserved a piece of very early Israelite folklore, the vine says, "My wine cheereth God and man"; while the Psalmist's praise, "Wine maketh glad the heart of man," has become an oft-quoted adage. [12]

The careful distinction between moderate drinking, which is recommended, and overindulgence in alcohol, which is decried, parallels the similarly twofold ancient Jewish view of sex, which meticulously holds apart the recommended pleasures of legitimate marital sexuality and its sinful and hence pernicious and forbidden forms, sharply condemned as incest, fornication, etc. This similarity aside, the physical consummation of love was poetically compared to, or viewed as, the drinking of wine: "How much better is thy love than wine," we read in the Song of Songs, and "I have drunk my wine. . . . Drink, yea drink abundantly, O beloved . . ." [13]

The same two books of Hebrew wisdom literature, Proverbs and Ben Sira, which so sharply condemn inebriation, have high praise for the pleasures wine gives to man. Proverbs presents Wisdom as saying, "Come, eat of my bread, and drink the wine which I have mingled; forsake all thoughtlessness, and live and walk in the way of understanding." And, characteristically, directly after King Lemuel's mother warns him not to drink lest he pervert justice, she goes on to say, "Give strong drink unto him that is ready to perish, and wine unto the bitter in soul; let him drink and forget his poverty, and remember his misery no more." [14] Similarly Ben Sira, after warning of the pitfalls of wine, continues: "Wine-water is life to man, if he drinks it in moderation. What is life without wine which from the beginning was created for joy?" and more of the same. Later he sums up his double vision of wine and other gifts of nature:

> The head of all needs for the life of man
> Is water and fire and iron and salt,
> The fat of the wheat, milk and honey,
> The blood of the grape, pure oil and clothes.
> All these do good to the good
> But turn to evil to the evil. [15]

As to the pleasure of moderate enjoyment of wine, the Talmudic teachers were as eloquent as the Biblical authors, if not more so. The myth of Noah shows that moderate drinking of wine was believed to have beneficial effects: one glass makes a man meek like a lamb; two, brave like a lion; only too much is harmful. This insight is summed up by the Talmudic saying, "A little wine strengthens, much irritates," while another saying emphasizes only the good effect: "Wine makes strong and glad." According to Rabbi Yoḥanan, whenever a scholar dreams that he drinks wine, this has a good meaning for him. Rabbi Y'huda ben B'thera believed that there was no festive rejoicing without wine, and Rava said, "Wine and spices make me wise [or alert]." Some Talmudic teachers even thought that wine can cure heart ailments, while others held wine to be the greatest of all medicines. [16] It was considered also a great comfort for the bereaved, for which reason ten cups of wine were given to the mourners with "the meal of consolation." [17]

THE PRACTICE OF DRINKING

Despite the many warnings, it seems to have been the practice in Biblical times to become drunk in the course of a festive meal. When Nabal, the husband of Abigail who later became one of David's wives, held a feast in his house "like the feast of a king," he became "very drunken." When Absalom, plotting his revenge against Amnon, invited him to a sheep-shearing feast, he took it for granted that Amnon would get drunk, which did indeed happen, thus giving Absalom the opportunity to have him killed. King Elah's drunkenness at a banquet in the house of a courtier in Tirzah enabled Zimri to kill him. Prior to a battle with Ahab, king of Israel, Ben-Hadad, king of Aram, and thirty-two kings who were with him got drunk "in the booths" and subsequently suffered a bloody defeat at the hands of the Israelites. [18]

Deuteronomic law considered the drinking of wine or of "strong drink" a part of the pilgrimage ritual. It provided that if a householder lived too far from the Temple, he should turn the tithe into money, go with it "to the place which the Lord thy God shall choose and thou shalt bestow the money for whatsoever thy soul desireth, for oxen, or for sheep, or for wine, or for strong drink, or for whatsoever thy soul asketh thee; and thou shalt eat there before the Lord thy God, and thou shalt rejoice, thou and thy household." [19]

Nor was the drinking of wine confined to men, as we can gather from the words of Zechariah prophesying the triumph of Judah: "How great is their goodliness, and how great is their beauty! Corn shall make the young men flourish, and new wine the maids." [20]

That wine was drunk all over Israel in antiquity is attested also by the widely scattered remains of ancient wine presses. These graphically illustrate what was meant when Rab-shakeh, an Assyrian general, described the Judah as "a land of corn and wine, a land of bread and vineyards, a land of olive trees and honey." The use of wine was certainly universal in ancient Israel, although we cannot know how many drank it moderately and how many excessively. It formed an integral part of the sacrificial ritual of the Temple in the form of drink offerings or libations; the amount was specified for each species of animal sacrificed. [21] Only Nazirites and the Rechabites abstained from wine and strong drink, the former as a result of their special vows, and the latter in observance of the restrictions imposed upon them by their forefather. [22] On the other hand, for the people at large wine was such an important part of the meal that a banquet was called "drinking of wine." [23]

As in Biblical, so in Talmudic times, the common practice among the Jews was to drink wine with their meals. Some of the stories quoted when speaking of charity show that wine with the meals was considered a basic requisite even for impoverished persons (cf. page 527). The Talmud contains so many details about the making of wine, the different varieties of wine, the drinking of wine, and expertise on wine that it leaves no doubt as to the daily use of wine by practically the entire Jewish community.

The practice of frequent but moderate drinking has been carried on by the Jews from Talmudic to modern times. Of the latter, only a few data can be cited. A study carried out by the *Jewish Chronicle* in England in the 1960's showed that "the great majority of its readers took alcoholic drink regularly"; similar results were obtained by American studies, which demonstrated that the proportion of abstainers was considerably smaller among Jews than among other denominations. [24]

THE RITUAL USE OF ALCOHOL

The Bible and the Talmud contain ample material to hammer into the Jewish mind the conviction that while wine in moderation is good, too much of it is inherently evil and dangerous. Since until the Enlightenment the Bible and the Talmud were by far the most potent formative influences upon Jewish thinking, attitudes, and values, one need not wonder that these sources acted as an effective deterrent against inebriety. Another equally important factor was the place wine has in Jewish ritual.

The unique position of wine in Jewish religious life, and, in fact, in Jewish food and drink patterns, is indicated by the fact that of all foods and drinks, there are special benedictions in the Jewish ritual only for wine and bread. Benedictions must, of course, be recited prior to the ingestion of any kind of food or drink, but all of these are generic. One and the same benediction is to be recited before enjoying any "fruit of the tree," another for all "fruit of the earth," and a third one for all foods that do not fall in either of these categories. But prior to drinking wine one must recite, "Blessed be Thou, Lord our God, king of the world, creator of the fruit of the vine," while before eating bread one recites, "Blessed be Thou, Lord our God, king of the world, who bringeth out bread from the earth." There can be no doubt that these two special benedictions have impressed upon the Jewish mind the uniquely sacred nature of bread and wine, which are raised above the level of other ordinary food and drink. For the traditional Jew, partaking of bread and wine means performing a small act of communion with the Creator.

To this must be added the fact that the brief Friday and holyday evening ritual of reciting the benediction over a cup of wine and then drinking it carries the name *Qiddush*, or Sanctification. No other Jewish religious ritual is designated by this term. The *Qiddush* is primarily a home ritual, but it is also performed every Friday evening in the synagogue at the close of the service, by the cantor. After returning home, the cantor, like all Jewish family heads, will have to perform the *Qiddush* before supper; since one is not allowed to perform the same rite twice, after he finishes the benediction over the silver cup of wine, a child, specially selected for the honor, takes a sip of it. As soon as the master of the house arrives home, he must perform the *Qiddush*, drink a mouthful of wine, and give of the "cup of blessing" also to all members of the family and guests who partake of the Friday evening meal.[25] Immediately after follows the blessing over the bread, and then the festive Sabbath meal.

Next morning, the second Sabbath meal is again preceded by a *Qiddush*, and again all those present partake of the *Qiddush* wine. At the conclusion of the Sabbath, the *Havdala* ("Separation") ritual is performed, in the course of which again a benediction is recited over a cup of wine. Thus the enjoyment of the Sabbath—the greatest pleasure of traditional Jewish life—is marked by the measured drinking of three cups of wine, and the Jewish child at a tender age learns that some religiously sanctioned drinking of wine is a licit pleasure in which he is encouraged by his parents.

Historical conditioning and prescriptive religio-cultural background thus combine to explain the drinking behavior of the tradition-bound Jew. In addition, the annual holidays have their *Qiddush* and cup of wine. At the Seder ceremony, held in the home on the first night of Passover in Israel, and on both the first and second nights in the Diaspora, the ritual requires each participant to drink four cups of wine. Only on Purim, the singular Jewish holiday which early developed a merry, somewhat carnival-like character, was inebriety condoned or even prescribed, although this particular prescription was as a rule not taken too seriously. Thus mythical deterrents on the negative side, combined with traditional approval of moderate drinking, and the frequent ritual use of wine on the positive side, made wine a regular part of the God-centered life of the traditional Jew and effectively removed it from the realm of dangerous excess or frenzy. One may say that the ritual use of wine immunized the Jews against drinking to the point of intoxication and thus against alcoholism. It should be added that the same attitude was transferred from wine to other intoxicating beverages. When and where no wine was available, other fermented drinks were used in its stead. In Talmudic times there was a shortage of wine in Babylonia, and consequently other drinks, such as a fig beverage, or beer made from barley, or other fruit juices, were used as substitutes.[26] In this manner, the control Jewish culture had over wine drinking was extended to all other intoxicating beverages as well.

Before discussing the special relationship that developed among the Hasidim to wine and other alcoholic beverages, a brief comment must be made on yet another aspect of Jewish drinking. In Talmudic times, the rabbis introduced a prohibition of drinking wine intended for pagan rituals. Subsequently, in accordance with the principle of "erecting a fence around the law," this prohibition was surrounded by a wider one—that of drinking any wine prepared by Gentiles, and even of touching it. Other alcoholic beverages prepared by Gentiles (such as beer) are allowed; however, the sages of the Talmud forbade these to be drunk at banquets, or in the company of Gentiles, because such commensality could lead to intermarriage.[27] These rules are observed by Orthodox Jews to this day, and they help to explain the inverse correlation between traditional observance and frequency of intoxication.

Hasidic Inebriety

We have seen that a basic doctrine of Hasidism was that God must be served with joy, with enthusiasm, and with the intention of attaching oneself to Him with love. In the oppressive poverty and inimical social environment in which the Jews lived in East Europe where Hasidism spread from the late eighteenth century on, it was certainly not easy for a Jew to put himself in the proper mood for turning to God with joy. Thus the Hasidim took a leaf out of the book of the Christian Orthodox, Catholic, and sectarian groups who were their neighbors and took to drinking the hard liquor in which the Gentiles indulged and which in many cases was available only from the local Jewish tavern keeper. Before long, a mildly intoxicated Hasidic Jew became a common sight in the East European *shtetl*. Alcohol, the Hasidim felt, elevated the human soul to a higher level and brought the Hasid nearer to his Tzaddiq, the miracle-working rabbi. However, drinking for the Hasidim was always a group activity; a Hasid never drank alone.[28]

Drinking among the Hasidim became so much a part of their lives that it even entered the mystical lore which was the form much of their teachings took. There is a parable attributed to the Ba'al Shem Tov, the founder of Hasidism, which tells about the lost son who is in foreign captivity and enters the local tavern with his captors. His captors drink for the sake of drinking, and the son drinks too. But he is drinking only to disguise his true happiness, which consists in the knowledge that he guards a secret message, a letter from his father, that he carries with him everywhere, carefully hidden, and that informs him of the impending release from captivity. The meaning of this parable is that while waiting to be liberated from the captivity of matter, man has no choice but ostensibly to cooperate with it.[29] But the simple Hasidim, no doubt, read a closer-to-home meaning into it. While the Jews wait for the advent of the Messiah whose coming was promised to them by their Divine Father, while they are in the captivity of the Exile, they must conform to the customs of the Gentiles, even to the extent of drinking with them in their taverns.

Their custom of drinking added yet another feature to the comportment of the Hasidim for which their opponents, the Mitnagdim, derided them—they were not only ignoramuses, unable (or, even worse, unwilling) to devote themselves to the study of the Law, and therefore unreliable in their religious observance, but also drunkards! Yet, in reality, the Hasidim were far from being drunkards. True, they drank considerably more than the Mitnagdim, who mostly drank only wine and even that in great moderation; and they did indulge in a few daily glasses of *bronfn* (or by whatever other name the plum or potato brandy went). But they never drank themselves into a stupor, which was a frequent pattern among their Christian peasant neighbors.

Statistical Data

No statistical data are available about the drinking patterns of the Hasidim. But had they been habitual or even occasional drunkards, this would have left its mark on Polish Jewry down to the early twentieth century, for which some statistics are extant. However, in Warsaw in 1925, the rate of alcoholic transgression was 1 per 3,566 among the Jews as against 1 per 52 among the Christians; in other words, the Gentile rate was 68.6 times higher than the Jewish. In Lodz, in 1926–28, the rate of arrest for inebriety was 40 times as high among the Christians as among the Jews. A similar picture emerges from the data gathered in the Prussian mental institutions in 1898 to 1900. Among the Protestant inmates, 7.5 percent suffered from *delirium tremens,* among the Catholics 5.1 percent, among the dissidents 12.3 percent, and among the Jews 1.1 percent.[30] Since in East Europe a major part of the Jews adhered to Hasidism, these figures indicate that alcoholism must have been extremely rare among them.

In New York in 1925, the rate of admission with alcoholism to public and private hospitals was 0.1 for Jews as against 5.9 for non-Jews—a 59-fold difference, reminiscent of the differences noted in Warsaw and Lodz. These figures are duplicated in other parts of the United States and in Canada.[31]

For recent years figures are available from Israel which are especially valuable because they include information as to differences in alcoholism between Ashkenazi and Oriental Jewish communities. In 1964, of all cases in mental hospitals in Israel, only 0.3 percent presented alcoholic problems. Of all new admissions to mental hospitals in 1966, 2 percent were alcoholic cases. Among those born in Europe and America, the rate was 3; among those born in Asia and Africa, it was 7; among the Israel-born, it was 1. If these figures are typical, then it appears that alcoholism is more frequent among the Oriental Jews, less frequent among the Ashkenazim, and least frequent among the *sabras*, whether of Oriental or Ashkenazi extraction. As to the overall rate of 2 percent of the admissions, it should be mentioned that in some countries this is up to 25 percent. It should also be added that the rate of women was negligible in all Israeli groups.[32]

The above returns can be compared with those available from New York State for the years 1929–31, when the rates of first admissions with alcoholic psychoses to the New York State hospital system per 100,000 of foreign-born national groups were as follows: Irish, 25.6; Scandinavian, 7.8; Italian, 4.8; English, 4.3; German, 3.8; Jewish, 0.5. Other studies show similar differences. The second striking finding is that the Jews have the smallest percentage of abstainers—13 percent, as compared to 21 percent among the Catholics, and 41 among the Protestants. Also, they rank highest among occasional drinkers—64 percent, as against 52 percent of the Catholics, and 46 of the Protestants.[33]

A recent study confirms these findings. Summarizing the results of a national study of drinking behavior and attitudes, Don Cahalan, *et al.*, found in 1969 that the proportion of drinkers was highest among Italian and German Catholics and Russian-Polish-Baltic Jews (9 percent of the Italian Catholics, 10 percent of the Jews, and 12 percent of the German Catholics were abstainers, as against 50 percent or more of English, Scotch, Welsh, Scotch-Irish, and Irish conservative Protestants). On the other hand, the Jews had a relatively low rate of heavy drinking (10 percent): the percentage of heavy drinkers was 25 for Jewish men, and 0 for Jewish women, this despite the fact that 96 percent of the Jewish men and 89 percent of the Jewish women were "drinkers"—i.e., were not abstainers.[34]

The emerging picture parallels that of the Jewish mental disorders. Just as more Jews than Catholics and Protestants were found to have mild or moderate symptom formation, so more Jews than Catholics and Protestants are mild or moderate drinkers. And just as fewer Jews than Catholics and Protestants were found to have serious mental impairment, so fewer Jews than Catholics and Protestants are heavy drinkers or alcoholics. This parallelism tempts us to apply the explanation given by Srole and his associates to the Jewish psychosis-neurosis pattern. They argued that the frequent incidence of mild impairment immunizes Jews against serious mental impairment, through a "this-far-and-no-farther" control mechanism. Similarly, one can assume that the religiously and culturally sanctioned, or even imposed, moderate drinking pattern immunizes the Jews against alcoholism and does so very effectively.

ASSIMILATION AND ALCOHOLISM

Can the age-old Jewish pattern of moderate, ritually anchored, and ethically approved drinking hold up under the stress of modern life, peer group conviviality, and all the other Gentile influences to which the Jews have in recent decades become exposed in the Western world? The available studies, while containing no definitive answer to this question, do indicate that the traditional Jewish resistance to alcoholism is weakened to the extent to which Jews become assimilated to their Gentile environment. Or, to put it differently, when Jews cut loose from their moorings in traditional Jewish life, they become more prone to adopt the alcohol patterns of their Gentile peers.

As early as 1908, Cheinisse called attention to the fact that among the recently immigrated East European Jews who were patients in the Rothschild hospital in Paris there was not a single alcoholic, but that among those Jewish patients who had arrived in Paris at least five years earlier "the alcoholic contagion had already opened a small fissure." [35] Subsequent studies by Snyder and others have borne out Cheinisse's observation. A similar trend could be observed among the Jews in the United States. In 1949–51, of all Jewish first admissions 1.5 percent were intemperate users of alcohol as against 8.7 percent of the non-Jews (which is a ratio of 1 to 5.8). When broken down into foreign-born and native-born, the percentage of the former among the Jews was 1.2, while that of the latter was 2.7; that is, under the influence of the American environment, the Jewish intemperance rate more than doubled. No corresponding increase was found among the non-Jews. In fact, the rate for the foreign-born non-Jews was 9.8, and that for the native-born non-Jews 7.9, a decrease of almost 20 percent.[36]

Snyder, who made an intensive study of alcoholism among New Haven Jews and Jewish college students, found that Jewish student drinkers were consistently below the general student population "in incidence and in proportions at various frequencies of intoxication." That is to say, fewer Jewish than non-Jewish students ever got drunk, and those Jewish students who did get drunk did so less frequently than the non-Jewish students. But he also found that Orthodox Jewish men were less frequently intoxicated than non-observant Jewish men, and that the same difference was manifested among the Jewish students. Only 9 percent of the Orthodox Jewish students were drunk twice or more; 18 percent of the Conservative Jewish students had the same frequency, 35 percent of the Reform Jewish students, 35 percent of the Irish Catholic students, 39 percent of the Jewish secular (i.e., religiously non-affiliated) students, and 39 percent of the British Protestant students. These data indicate that as religious observance declined among the Jews and secularism increased, their alcohol pattern more and more approximated that of the Christians and signs of an increased rate of alcoholism were emerging.[37]

Another finding which points in the same direction was that the longer the families of the Jewish students had resided in America, the more the frequency of intoxication increased among them. Of the foreign-born Jewish students, only 18 percent were drunk twice or more; of American-born Jewish students both of whose parents were born abroad, 25 percent; of those Jewish students one of whose parents was foreign-born and the other American-born, 32 percent; and of those who were children of two American-born parents, 38 percent.[38] These data clearly show the erosive influence of the American environment on the traditional cultural patterns as reflected in drinking behavior. Assimilation to American culture, whether measured by abandonment of formal (Orthodox) religious observance, or by the passing of time (the generations) which, in general, means greater acculturation, leads to the weakening of the age-old Jewish immunity to alcoholism and the adoption of the environmental drinking habits.

The same phenomenon was observed by Howard Jones in 1963. He found that for the religious Jew frequent but, of course, moderate drinking is a religious duty which is taken very seriously. The less observant the Jew, the more frequently drunkenness occurs. Also, the more Orthodox the Jew, the more wine tends to predominate over spirits in his drinking, and the more his drinking takes place within the family rather than outside it. But the more the Jew tends to leave behind the traditional way of life and to become assimilated to the prevalent Gentile pattern, the more his drinking also tends to approximate that pattern.[39] This was the finding also in the London area, where a recent study among middle-class Jews showed that alcoholism appeared to be more likely for Jews with few ties to their family and Jewish background.[40]

By the 1970's, alcoholism had spread among American Jews to such an extent that Jewish and non-Jewish agencies began to recognize it as a Jewish social problem. At a conference on alcohol abuse and the Jewish community held under the auspices of the Federation of Jewish Philanthropies in New York in March 1976, Commissioner Jerome Hornblass of the New York City Addiction Services Agency (A.S.A.) called attention to the growing problem represented by Jewish alcoholics. His data showed that among those with a strong commitment to Jewish religion or to Jewish causes (such as the welfare of Israel, the problem of Soviet Jewry), alcohol and drug abuse were virtually unknown. However, in those Jewish circles where this was not the case, the pattern of addiction was quite similar to the one manifested among non-Jews. Most susceptible among all groups are those in the middle- and lower-class economic brackets, who experience severe social and family problems because they live near or below the poverty line. The extent of the problem among the Jews could not be accurately estimated because the Jewish families regarded addiction with extreme guilt and shame and were unwilling to bring it to the attention of mental health organizations. Again, those who enter treatment programs often fail to report religious affiliation. On the basis of unquestionably incomplete data, it was nevertheless estimated that 6 percent of all the clients of the A.S.A. administration were Jews, or about 16 percent of the white clients. Rabbi S. Zimmerman of the East 55th Street (Manhattan) synagogue estimated that the Jews constitute 40 percent of all members in Alcoholics Anonymous groups in Manhattan.[41]

Data such as these indicate that the Jew who has lost the emotional support represented by Jewish traditions, observances, and values becomes as prone to alcohol abuse and addiction as his non-Jewish neighbor of the same socio-economic status. Whether the actual incidence of alcoholism among Jews will reach the frequency it has among non-Jews remains to be seen.

EXPLANATIONS AND CONCLUSION

Several of the students of alcoholism and the Jews have put forward explanations of the resistance to this disease, which until quite recently was an entirely unique Jewish phenomenon. Immanuel Kant, while not a student of the subject, observed it and offered an explanation: the civic position of the Jews (like that of women and ministers) was weak and needs to be preserved.

> All separatists, that is, those who subject themselves not only to the general laws of the country but also to a special sectarian law, are exposed through their eccentricity and alleged chosenness to the attention and criticism of the community, and thus cannot relax in their self-control, for intoxication, which deprives one of cautiousness, would be a scandal for them.[42]

Charles R. Snyder explained the Jewish disinclination to alcoholism by saying, "Where drinking is an integral part of the socialization process, where it is interrelated with the central moral symbolism and is repeatedly practiced in the rites of a group, the phenomenon of alcoholism is conspicuous by its absence." [43] Another student of alcoholism, Peter B. Field, shifts emphasis to some extent: ". . . some father-centered ethnic groups with a high degree of lineal social solidarity—such as the Jews and the Chinese— have very low rates of alcoholism and drunkenness. . . ." [44] And a third one, Robert F. Bales, while concentrating on attitudes toward drinking in Irish culture, contrasts these with the Jewish attitudes and finds that among the latter, the laity participates in "the sacred act of drinking," that "the Jewish child is introduced to the relevant sacred ideas and sentiments at an earlier age and in more familiar surroundings than is the Irish child," and that in Jewish culture,

> where wine is not accessible, "strong drink," i.e., beer or mead, and later on, spirits, under the name of "wine of the country"—or any beverage other than water, such as syrup or the juice of fruits, have been used, and are deemed fit substitutes for wine in the rituals. Thus, by cultural definitions, the attitudes applying to the wine used in the ritual are also expected to apply to other alcoholic beverages in the Jewish culture, whereas in the Irish culture they are not. [45]

It should be mentioned in passing that at least one student of Jewish drinking patterns considered the possibility that the Jews had some sort of genetic immunity to alcoholism. [46] But the recent spread of alcoholism among the Jews of course makes short shrift of any attempt at a genetic explanation of Jewish drinking patterns. Nor can the relatively frequent references to intoxication in the Bible and the Talmud support such an argument. The typical pattern of Jewish sobriety cum frequent moderate drinking developed in post-Talmudic times and began to suffer inroads after the Enlightenment and the Emancipation. The latter development also militates against the rationalistic explanation of Kant, since loss of self-control through intoxication remained as calamitous after the Emancipation for the assimilated Jew as it had been prior to it for his co-religionist isolated in the ghetto.

The explanation of the phenomenon of Jewish sobriety until the Enlightenment and its gradual decline thereafter is actually very simple. Jewish religion, as we have seen, encouraged Jews to drink frequently in moderation but made it a sin to become intoxicated. Until the Enlightenment all Jews were conditioned by their Jewish cultural environment to obey the precepts of their religion. Hence it would be as unlikely for a Jew to become drunk as it would be for him to eat pork, or drink *nesakh*-wine. The approach to wine conformed to the general Jewish religious approach to many things, including food, sex, clothing—to do a certain thing in one way was forbidden, was a sin; to do the same thing in another way was commanded, was a *mitzva*. The use of wine was an integral part of this pattern, which required a constant awareness of the often minute differences between the prohibited and the permitted. The Jew liked and practiced sex but was not allowed to have it at all times and had to abstain from incest and fornication; he liked fine clothes (every age had its elegance) but was not allowed to wear *sha'atnez*; he liked good food but would not touch *t'refa,* nor many of the varieties eaten by the Gentiles; and he drank wine but would not over-indulge, nor drink wine prepared by a non-Jew. The common feature in all this was the encouragement to act in a prescribed, limited manner, and the corresponding prohibition of acting in a proscribed, unlimited manner.

It is, therefore, *a priori* futile to ask why the Jews did not fall victim to alcoholism and to search for an answer in the special relationship of the Jews to wine and strong drink. While such a special relationship, as has been shown above, did indeed exist, it alone cannot supply the explanation to the Jewish moderation in drinking. The ultimate explanation is the domination of the Jew by his religious tradition. Alcohol was merely one of many things concerning which the Jew behaved as his religion dictated.

This explanation also answers the question as to why the Jewish moderation in drinking has begun to break down. The culprit, as in many other phenomena that have emerged in the last three or four generations, was the Enlightenment, which brought in its wake, by way of assimilation, the urge to be like the Gentiles, and the loosening of restraints in all areas. In fact, the remarkable thing is not that the Jewish moderation pattern has finally broken down in the Western world among the Jewish members of the "now generation," but that this breakdown has not occurred sooner. It seems that for several decades after the penetration of Western culture into the Jewish world the age-old restraints have still worked, carried on through some kind of inertia. By the turn of the century, the signals of relaxation could be perceived. By the sixties, they were loud and clear. By the seventies, what with the well-known Jewish proclivity to being in the vanguard of new cultural (as well as counter-cultural) developments, the emergence of a serious alcohol problem among the Jews had become inevitable.

2. *Overeating and Obesity*

A phenomenon related to the Jewish concern for health is the incidence of obesity among Jews. However, the historical documentation of Jewish eating habits, which are the prime factor in obesity, is all but lacking. A number of passages in the Biblical Song of Songs can be interpreted as indicating that corpulence was considered an aesthetically pleasing trait, as indeed it has remained in the traditional Middle East down to modern times. The beloved whose "neck is like the tower of David," and whose "two breasts are like two fawns," or the lover whose "legs are as pillars of marble" and whose "aspect is like Lebanon" [47] can certainly not be imagined as a slim wisp of a girl or boy. Biblical tradition attributes a love of plentiful and varied food to the ancestors of the Israelites who were liberated from the Egyptian slavery. During their wandering in the desert, although well supplied with the miraculous manna, the Children of Israel were dissatisfied and wept, remembering not the sufferings of slavery but the rich diet they had in Egypt:

> And the Children of Israel also wept on their part and said: Would that we were given flesh to eat. We remember the fish which we were wont to eat in Egypt for nought; the cucumbers, and the melons, and the leeks, and the onions, and the garlic; but now our soul is dried away, there is nothing at all, we have nought save this manna to look to.[48]

Moses took the people's dietary complaints to God, who thereupon sent them quails to supplement the manna, but the next day He punished them with a plague which killed many people. The place where this event occurred and where "the people that lusted were buried" was thereafter called *Kivrot haTa'ava*, or "Graves of Lust." [49]

In later times, both Jews and Arabs shared the appreciation of ample dimensions in women. An ancient Arab poet, singing the praises of his beloved, exclaims enthusiastically, ". . . and her hips, Allah be praised, cannot pass through the tent door!"

Poetic imagination and exaggeration aside, until the emergence of modern American urban sedentary civilization, throughout history the problem people everywhere faced was not how to escape obesity, but how to find enough food to keep body and soul together. The Middle East was no exception. Corpulence, in such circumstances, had to be rare, and if it occurred it was confined to some members of the leisured classes. A Biblical story says of a king of Moab, Eglon by name, that he "was a very fat man." [50] A Talmudic reference to two rabbis, Yishma'el ben Yose and Ele'azar ben Shim'on, mentions that they had such enormously protruding bellies that as they stood facing each other with their bellies touching, a pair of oxen could pass through between them, and that their wives were even more corpulent.[51]

Although these were undoubtedly exceptional cases and are presented in anecdotal exaggeration, the Talmudic rabbis (perhaps making a virtue out of necessity) advised frugality in diet. They recommended that, while one should try to have a dwelling beyond one's means and dress according to one's means, one should eat less than one can afford. In any case, the general diet in Talmudic times consisted mainly of bread, vegetables, and fruit, as well as milk; meat and fish were consumed only on the Sabbath and special occasions.

It is against this background that we must understand the Middle Eastern attitude to corpulence. Where most people are thin because they do not have enough to eat and must earn a living "with the sweat of their brow," corpulence is a visible sign of affluence and hence a valued trait. In the

Middle East, this is how obesity has been looked upon down to modern times among both Jews and Muslims. A complementary view is one which deplores thinness. I remember well a Moroccan Jewish friend in Jerusalem who, when I first met his wife, said to me in a whispered aside, "Alas, she is thin!"

The same attitude prevailed in the *shtetl*. Corpulence was rare, and therefore an asset in women. When a prospective bride was looked over by a *shadkhan* (matchmaker) or the groom's mother and aunts, her own mother carefully instructed her to sit up straight with her chin pushed down against her chest so that it should appear as if she had a double chin, which attractive feature would be duly reported back to the groom.

The great concern of Jewish mothers with feeding their children is probably a result of the dire poverty in which most of the Jews lived for hundreds of years both in Eastern Europe and in the Middle East. In the *shtetl*, whenever there was acute scarcity of food, which was quite a common occurrence, it was "natural" to feed the children first, while the parents, especially the mothers, would go hungry. Thus to give food came to be symbolic of maternal love, just as the first expression of a mother's love for her child was to give him her breast. The children were given as much food as they wanted and, if they did not want to eat, efforts were made to arouse their appetite by giving them what they liked. Food may be used as a reward, but it is never withheld from a child as a punishment; "even if the mother is angry, or is 'not speaking' with any member of the family, she is still concerned about feeding them. She will silently bring out the food and never ceases to worry if they do not eat properly." [52] Growing up in such a Jewish house, the child inevitably observed and absorbed the eating habits of his parents. He saw that his mother kept the best for the father, who needed good food to keep up his strength. She insisted on his eating, just as she insisted on "honoring" with food the guests who would drop in on the Sabbath and holidays. The mother herself would eat constantly, nibbling (*nashn* in Yiddish) and tasting while she cooked and rarely sitting down to a real meal except on special occasions. Eating was incidental for her, but feeding others was most important. [53]

The preparation for the Sabbath, which occupied the mother from early Friday morning, consisted (apart from cleaning the home) exclusively of cooking and baking, although purchases for the Sabbath such as the chicken and the fish which were the Sabbath staple for those who could afford them were made the day before, on Thursday. But even in a poor house, where the woman had to skimp with the food all week, the Sabbath meals had to be as rich as possible. Thus the earliest memories a child retained from the Sabbath in his parental home were those of a succession of fine, ample, and leisurely meals, in the course of which he was allowed to have a taste of wine as well. As he left infancy behind, he began to be aware also of other features of the Sabbath—the festive clothes, the candles, the spirit of solemnity, the learned discussion between the courses, the singing, the synagogue; but these subsequent impressions could not blot out from his memory the earliest sensation and enjoyment of that most elemental of human pleasures, tasty food and drink.

The mother's insistence on feeding her children, her constant admonition, "*Iss!*" (Eat), and her frequent mention of corpulence as a trait indicating not only health but in the case of girls also beauty may have something to do with Jewish obesity. The number of studies on the incidence of obesity among various ethnic groups, including Jews, is small, but they show that a higher percentage of American Jews than of Gentiles are obese or are compulsive eaters. A 1940 study of obese children found that slightly over 50 percent of the cases were of Jewish origin.[54] Another comparative research led to the conclusion that "the Jewish child remains an infant, so far as taking food is concerned, much later than other children."[55] A third researcher, on the basis of his own limited observations, commented that a pattern of compulsive eating, analogous to addictive drinking, may be common in the American Jewish group.[56] To these can be added the observation that Jewish mothers show great anxiety lest their children fail to eat enough, even though the children were eating quite satisfactorily in the opinion of pediatricians, and that they even exhibit a tendency to resort to forced feeding when confronted with persistent refusals to eat on the part of their children.[57]

Jewish wit, which is not only a mirror image of Jewish wisdom but often sheds a light on the working of the Jewish mind, has much to say about feeding as the prime concern of the Jewish mother. The Jewish poet Heinrich Heine (who was the greatest lyricist produced by German literature as well as a great satirist) describes in his *Germany: A Winter's Tale*, written in 1844, how his mother received him when he came to visit her after an absence of many years:

> My boy! It's all of thirteen years!
> Let me look at you, are you fatter or thinner?
> Thirteen years: You must be hungry for sure,
> Now, what would you like for dinner?

In the sequence the poet describes the goose his mother gave him to eat.[58] Theodor Reik, who quotes these lines, tells a modern American-Jewish anecdote which contains a precise parallel to them: "A Jewish gangster walked into an ambush and received serious bullet wounds. With his last strength he climbed the stairs to his mother's apartment and rang the bell. 'Mama!' he cried, when she opened the door. But she, unaware of the son's state, said: 'Eat first, talk later.' " Generalizing, Reik remarks: "Jewish jokes ascribe to mothers an inclination to stuff their children, and worry that their sons do not eat enough or not the right food. It is as if Jewish mothers tried to make the nutritional symbiosis of babyhood and with it the dependence of the children on them permanent. Their main solicitude is thus directed toward food." In the eyes of the Jewish mother, moreover, food was the universal remedy; chicken soup was the cure-all for all ailments and illnesses from a cold to cancer, and from bronchitis to a broken leg.[59] A visit to his childhood home in Brownsville brought back to Alfred Kazin's memory a scene he had often witnessed: how mothers rammed great meals down the throats of their helplessly kicking offspring, cursing them meanwhile: "Eat! Eat! What will become of you if you don't eat! Imp of darkness, may you sink ten fathoms into the earth if you don't eat! Eat!"[60]

Jewish religion, as followed by all Jews from antiquity to the Enlightenment, and as it still is followed by Orthodox Jews in all parts of the Diaspora and in Israel, places extraordinary emphasis on food observances. It is not entirely without basis that Jewish Orthodoxy was uncomplimentarily described as "stomach Judaism." The origin and historical development of Jewish dietary laws are beyond the scope of this study, but the place they occupy in Jewish life must be dealt with briefly. Since every morsel of food and every drop of drink a Jew ingests is regulated by his religious law, there is no other aspect of that law of which he would be reminded so frequently as the food prescriptions. Whenever the Jew eats or drinks anything, he either obeys or disobeys a religious commandment. Whatever secular occupation rivets the attention of an Orthodox Jew, he can divert his thoughts from his Jewish religious duties no longer than it takes him to go from one meal or snack to another. If Napoleon was right in saying that an army marches on its stomach, it is equally true that the Jewish people, in preserving its separate religio-ethnic identity, marched from century to century on its stomach.

It has been pointed out more than once by historians that the Jewish religious prohibition of commensality with Gentiles maintained a most effective barrier between the Jews and their environment everywhere and at all times. Sharing a common meal is one of the oldest, most primitive, and therefore most basically human acts of establishing friendly relations—more than that, bonds of mutual trust and obligation—among people. This is the underlying motivation of the ancient Biblical custom of offering a hospitable meal to a guest and sharing it with him, and one of the bases of the sacrificial ritual in which part of an animal is offered up to God before the rest of it is eaten by man. In both cases a bond is established between him who gives and him who partakes of the food. These were the psychological connotations of the bond of commensality from which Jewish religious law excluded the Gentile.

Factors such as these have made eating a much more significant act in the life of the Jews than it was in that of the non-Jews. The non-Jew eats in order to satisfy his hunger, to enjoy the taste of good food, and to spend a sociable hour with friends. For the Jew eating means all this—but also more. Inas-

much as he is observant (and I cannot refrain from pointing out again and
again that until the Enlightenment all Jews were observant), each time he
eats he observes a religious law and thus obeys the will of God. Prior to
major meals the hands have to be washed and bread is broken to the accom-
paniment of appropriate benedictions, and after them a longer grace has to
be recited. Light snacks, and even a draught of water, must be preceded by
a benediction. Nothing at all can be ingested without the recital of at least a
short blessing. Moreover, unless one eats at home or in the house of trusted
and like-minded friends, before ingesting anything the possibility of its not
being *kosher*, that is, ritually permissible, must be carefully considered and
excluded. The law which requires that after having eaten a meat dish one
must let six (or eight) hours pass before one is allowed to have a milk dish
(i.e., any milk product) means that even before sitting down to eat one must
be mindful of religious rules. In sum, the dietary laws make religious consciousness and observance ever present in the life of the Jew.

In the wake of the Enlightenment the inevitable happened. More and
more West European Jews broke away from obeying the dietary laws, which
thereupon became a barrier between Jew and Jew as well. Faced with a *de
facto* neglect and disregard of this entire province of Judaism, nineteenth-
century Reform rabbis had to make a choice, as Rabbi Kaufmann Kohler,
president of the Hebrew Union College, put it in the early 1900's "whether
the religious consciousness of the modern Jews should be allowed to suffer
from a continual transgression of these laws, or whether the laws themselves
should be submitted to a careful scrutiny as to their meaning and purpose
and be revised—that is, either modified or abrogated by the rabbinical authorities of the present times." [61] Eventually, Reform Judaism came to consider the entire complex of dietary laws obsolete, within the general framework of its renunciation of the binding authority of the rabbinical codes.

Two generations later the chafing of Reform-minded Jews at the dietary
laws continued, as can be seen from a statement by John K. Rayner, of the
London Liberal Synagogue: "To create the impression that this [the concern
with eating habits] is one of Judaism's chief preoccupations is to debase it in
the eyes of Jews and non-Jews." [62] This contrasts sharply with the enlightened Orthodox Jewish view, which holds that by observing the dietary laws
and reciting the prescribed benedictions before and after meals, the Jew introduces an element of sanctity into the otherwise entirely mundane, physical, and animalistic act of eating.

In either case, the Jewish tendency to overeat and to be overly preoccupied with food continues. Jews still seem to spend a greater proportion of
their income on food than do other groups in America, though not in France.
As Seymour Leventman put it, "The 'gastronomic syndrome' lingers on in
the passion for bagels and lox, knishes, blintzes, rye bread, kosher or kosher-
style delicatessen, and for good food in general." In the third generation of

American Jews there is even a revival, "especially among college educated young Jewish housewives, of interest in traditional Jewish cooking evidenced by the successful sales of Jewish cookbooks." [63] And the continued, or revived, interest in Jewish food is, of course, accompanied by a relatively high incidence of overweight and obesity among Jews.

3. Drug Addiction

Only a few brief comments can be added here on drug addiction, which among Ashkenazi Jews is an entirely new phenomenon, although individual cases are known to have occurred in the past. [64] Among Oriental Jews, as can be concluded from the Israeli data, drug addiction (especially the use of marijuana) was part of their cultural heritage which they shared with the Muslims in the countries of their birth and brought along to Israel. Most of the Jewish offenders against the Israeli Dangerous Drug Laws in the 1960's were immigrants from the Middle East. The rate was 10 per 100,000, which was half as high as that of the Israeli Arabs. However, the Oriental Jewish addicts did not pass on their habit to the next generation in Israel.

Following the Six Day War of 1967, drug addiction in Israel developed into a problem among the young generation of Jews of Western extraction. The habit was introduced into these circles by students and volunteers who flocked to Israel under the impact of the Six Day War, or somewhat later, and settled there or stayed for several months. A certain percentage of these volunteers had brought along a drug habit from their home countries, and from them the contagion spread to some of their age group. Another factor was that as a result of the Six Day War the usual routes for smuggling hashish were disrupted, and many Arab suppliers in the West Bank and East Jerusalem, which came under Israeli rule, were left with amounts of hashish and no marketing possibilities. This resulted in a drop in the prices of illegal drugs in Israel, and the country became a low-price source for hashish, which is more expensive than marijuana. At one point, the price of hashish in Israel was one-tenth of its price in the United States and Canada. Consequently, the first admissions of drug addicts to Israeli hospitals doubled between 1966 and 1970 (from twenty to thirty-nine), and the increase was sharp especially among the younger Israel-born Jews. It was estimated that in 1970 there were more than four hundred hard-core addicts in Israel. [65]

In America and England, drug abuse spread to Jews just prior to the Six Day War. In 1965, a Synanon estimate showed one hundred Jews among five hundred addicts, which, of course, is a very high proportion. Similarly in London from 1965 on, the proportion of Jewish drug addicts was higher than the proportion of Jews in the general population. [66]

A volume entitled *Judaism and Drugs*, published in 1973, contains studies dealing with the history of drugs and drug addiction among Jews, and with the halakhic and Jewish attitudes to the drug problem and its ethical implications.[67] One of the contributors to the volume, Norman E. Frimer, after discussing the epidemic proportions drug use has assumed among American students, remarks that in the area of drug usage the Jewish student

> possesses by and large few positive marks of differentiation. . . . The Jewish student on many a campus, like his Gentile compeer, is deeply involved in the drug culture. This claim can amply be documented in a number of national studies on the subject surveying not only the college scene but also that of the high school. In fact, a very recent [1971] and comprehensive analysis of drug patterns in several major New York campuses reveals that Jewish collegians are over-represented in the culture. For regardless of the drug considered, they are heavier users than Catholic or Protestant users.[68]

A significant correlation has been found between drug abuse and the relaxation of religious bonds and the subject's distance from his religio-cultural background.[69]

The available data definitely point to a higher Jewish susceptibility to drugs than to alcohol. The reason for this seems to be the absence of religious preoccupation with drugs, which contrasts sharply with the important position wine occupied in Jewish tradition, myth, and ritual. By the time the young Jew became exposed to Gentile influence, in college or at his place of work, he had a clearly formed negative attitude toward drinking to inebriety. No such attitude had been formed in him toward drugs. While the Gentile proclivity to heavy drinking formed an occasional or even frequent subject of conversation and of derogatory parental comment in the Jewish home, the phenomenon of drug addiction was never discussed because it was entirely unknown—until the 1960's, that is—to Jewish parents, and largely so to their children. Hence when the Jewish youngster did become exposed to the example of Gentile drug abuse, he had no psychological defenses against it.

An added factor was the almost total absence of halakhic concern with drugs, which again contrasts with the position of the *Halakha* on drinking. While the average Jewish parent knew about the halakhic proscription of heavy drinking, he certainly was unaware of the few obscure rabbinic statements warning against the use of drugs. Only a very scholarly Jew would, for instance, know that Rabbi Samuel ben Meir (1085–1158), a commentator on the Talmud, warned: "Do not drink drugs because they demand periodic doses and your heart will crave them." [70] Thus the Jewish youngster, not being forewarned, was not forearmed and easily fell victim to the lure of drugs.

This, of course, does not explain the higher incidence of drug addiction among Jews than among non-Jews. Perhaps those who crave a release from the tensions and anxieties of Jewish existence, but because of their conditioning cannot or will not take to liquor, are more likely to resort to drugs as an alternative means of relaxation and reprieve. In any case, the most recent (1976) data show that "an extraordinary 16.5 percent of the Jewish youth queried in a study in New York City admitted to being current users and former users of illegal drugs, more than double the 8.2 percent Catholic and 7.2 percent Protestant of the total sample. . . ." [71] The magnitude of the problem is indicated by the increased attention it receives from Jewish welfare agencies.

In one respect, at least, Jewish drug addiction parallels Jewish alcoholism: both are virtually unknown among Orthodox Jews and among Jews who have a strong Jewish commitment and identification.

17

Jewish Self-Hate

1. Parasitism

Parasitism, in the Soviet Russian legal vocabulary, is a crime for which a person can be sent to jail—the crime consists simply of not being engaged in an income-producing occupation. Many a Russian Jew who has applied for an exit permit so as to be able to go to Israel, and has thereupon been dismissed from his job, is subsequently accused of parasitism, although his only crime is his inability to secure a new job.

Jews had encountered the charge of parasitism a long time before the concept was adopted by the Soviets. In the nineteenth century, numerous Gentile thinkers and scholars, politicians and agitators, had characterized the Jews as a "parasitic people." A few examples will suffice to indicate the tenor of their pronouncements. Pierre Joseph Proudhon (1809–65), the influential French Socialist theoretician and philosophical anarchist, wrote: "The Jew is by temperament an anti-producer, neither a farmer nor an industrial, nor even a true merchant. He is an intermediary, always fraudulent and parasitic, who operates, in trade as in philosophy, by means of falsification, counterfeiting, and horse-dealing." [1] And Alphonse Toussenel (1803–85), the French Socialist leader and anti-Semitic author, stated in his book *The Jews, Kings of the Epoch: A History of Financial Feudalism*: "I call by the despised name of Jew every dealer in money, every unproductive parasite living off the work of someone else . . . note well that not one Jew has done anything useful with his hands since the beginning of time." [2]

A generation later, another French Socialist writer, Auguste Chirac (1838–1903), wrote of "parasitism" (which term, however, in the French Socialist writings of the period had become the equivalent of capitalism) that the Jews constituted its "first and most complete incarnation." [3] The same sentiment was echoed from across the English Channel by the founder of biostatistics, Sir Francis Galton (1822–1911), who said, "The Jews are specialized for a parasitical existence upon other nations, and . . . there is need of evidence that they are capable of fulfilling the varied duties of a civilized nation by themselves." [4]

The allegation of Jewish parasitism was not confined to Europe. In North America, Professor Goldwin Smith of Toronto called the Jews intruders and parasites, while accusing them also of "tribal exclusiveness and cosmopolitanism." [5]

Forty years after Galton, his disciple and biographer Karl Pearson (1857–1936), in trying to prove the undesirability of Jewish immigration into Britain, warned, "They [the Jews] will not be absorbed by, and at the same time strengthen, the existing population; they will develop into a parasitic race." [6] By the time Pearson said this, the allegation that the Jews were a parasitic "race" or people had become a commonplace in anti-Semitic literature.

Needless to say, Germany proved a fertile soil for the outcropping of scholarly judgment on Jewish parasitism. Thus M. Haberlandt, a leading German anthropologist of the early 1900's, expressed his amazement at the Jewish ability to combine the "popular conceit" (Volkswahn) of being the "chosen people" with "a typical parasitism." [7] A special twist was given to the concept of Jewish parasitism by the German anti-Semitic author Theodor Fritsch, who in his book The Riddle of Jewish Success rants about the "crooked thinking" of "the Hebrew," whose brain is "a provocation-machine [Vexiermaschine] with a perverse way of thinking," and who is "the born bacillus of decomposition." [8] A colleague of his, Arno Schickedanz, goes one step further and creates a scientific designation for the Jew: he is the "homo parasiticus." [9]

But enough of this sorry list of irrational Jew-hate masquerading in scholarly guise. What interests us in the present context, and what is pathetic from the standpoint of Jewish psychology, is that the relentless reiteration of the allegation of Jewish "parasitism" made it accepted as a fact even by Jewish thinkers, writers, poets, and communal leaders who incorporated it into their Jewish self-stereotype. Theodor Herzl (1860–1904) commented on this phenomenon in his first published Zionist writing, The Jewish State:

> . . . even Jews faithfully parrot the catchword of the anti-Semites: we are supposed to be living off the "host nations," and if we had no "host nation" surrounding us, we should have to starve. This is one of the points at which the undermining of our self-respect through unjust accusations manifests itself. [10]

In Herzl's analysis, the factors making for the acceptance by Jews of hostile anti-Semitic stereotypes were suffering, depression, and discouragement: "There are more misconceptions in circulation about the Jews than about any other people. And our age-old sufferings have made us so depressed and so discouraged that we ourselves parrot and believe these canards." [11]

In the early twentieth century, quite a number of Jewish nationalist authors went on record with statements on Jewish parasitism and related unsavory features which showed that Herzl's censure went unheeded. Aharon David Gordon (1856–1922), the ideological leader of the Palestinian Jewish worker's movement and father of the "religion of labor," wrote that in the Diaspora the Jews were characterized by parasitism and were a fundamentally useless people. David Frischmann (1860–1922), the Hebrew and Yiddish writer and editor, stated that the Jewish life was a dog's life that evoked disgust. Mikha Yosef Bin-Gorion (Berdyczewsky, 1865–1921), the Hebrew essayist and novelist, wrote that the Jews were "not a nation, not a people, not human." And Yosef Hayim Brenner (1881–1921), the Hebrew novelist and Palestinian Jewish labor leader, described the Diaspora Jews as "gypsies, filthy dogs, inhuman."

These early Diaspora-haters were followed by Abraham Schwadron (1878–1957), an outspoken critic of the contemporary Jewish scene, who referred to the Diaspora Jews as "slaves, helots," as a people of "the basest uncleanliness, worms, filth, parasitic rootlessness." [12]

Surprisingly, even the leading German Jews in America could not escape the reproach of parasitism. It was hurled at them from the pulpit of Temple Emanuel by their own spiritual leader, the renowned Dr. Judah L. Magnes (1877–1948), in his Passover 1910 sermon: "Insofar as it is Reformed, your Judaism and mine has something of a parasitic nature. . . ." [13]

The communal counterpart of these individual criticisms was represented by the position taken by Jewish organizations. It was in 1929 or 1930 that, as a young student in Breslau, Germany, I first became aware of the way in which anti-Semitic stereotypes could insinuate themselves into the Jewish mind. The National Socialist Party was engaged in a concerted effort to increase its following in Germany, and I learned to my surprise that among my colleagues at the Rabbinical Seminary there were two who sympathized with, and supported, the Nazi Party. They belonged to the Verband National-deutscher Juden (Association of National-German Jews), which was founded in 1921 by Max Naumann and whose platform acknowledged the truth of some anti-Semitic charges and demanded that the Zionists be deprived of German citizenship. The Verband had its own youth movement, which had approached the Hitlerjugend and tried—in vain, of course—to identify and ingratiate itself with the Nazi Party. After the Nazis popularized the old German anti-Semitic slogans, "The Jews are our misfortune" (coined by the historian Heinrich von Treitschke in the 1870's), [14] and "Out with the Jews!" Jewish opponents of the Verband would have it that its members joined the Nazis in their street parades carrying banners which read, "We are our misfortune," and "Out with us!" The term "parasites" did not appear in this context, nor did the Naumannites actually ever parade with such slogans. But the acceptance by *any* Jewish group, even a small and insignificant one, of any part of the Nazi anti-Semitic doctrine speaks volumes about the inability of some Jews to escape the impact of vicious anti-Jewish propaganda.

Nor did the solid center of Jewish organizational life remain entirely immune to the influence of anti-Semitism. As Yehezkel Kaufman pointed out in a penetrating and bitter article, even the Zionist movement itself, dedicated though it was to a reaffirmation of the strength and soundness of Jewishness, succumbed to the anti-Semitic "suggestion" of the basic contemptibility of Jewish life in the Diaspora.[15] The emotional basis as well as the propagandistic purpose of the Zionist derogation of pre-Zionist and non-Zionist Jewish life was, of course, to emphasize the value of Zionism by showing, as sharply as possible, the contrast between its aims and the Jewish condition in the Galut. Jewry in the lands of its Exile had to be painted in the darkest possible colors for the Zionist achievement and program to shine the brighter. But even if we recognize these motivations, the fact remains that Jewish life in the Galut was characterized in Zionist writings not so much as a life of oppression, poverty, powerlessness, suffering, and persecution, but rather as repulsive in itself. Instead of emphasizing the misery inflicted upon the Jews by their anti-Semitic environment, they presented Jewish degradation as if it were the result, not of external pressure but of the nature of Jewish society and Jewish character. Thus the implication, more than that, the conclusion, was that Galut Jewry had earned its fate and deserved to be hated: its way of life, its occupations, its attitudes, its very personality were such as to provoke the justified contempt of its Gentile environment. There was only one way to escape this moral degradation: to leave the Galut and to make one's "ascent" (*'aliya*) to the Land of Israel.[16]

But even after the *'aliya*, the memory of the Galut degradation rankled, and the pathetically internalized allegation that the Jews in the Diaspora were a parasitic people was not easy to get rid of. One of my earliest memories from Tel Aviv, after my own *'aliya* in early 1933, is of a celebration by the *Histadrut*, at which Jewish workers marched down Allenby Street carrying a huge banner reading, "A parasitic people has become a people of workers." At the time there was no Hebrew word available for "parasite" or "parasitic," and so the inscription incorporated, in Hebrew transliteration, the foreign word itself which gave in capsule the anti-Semitic view of the Jews: " *'am shel parazitim* . . ."—"a people of parasites. . . ." [17]

For decades the concept of the parasitism of Diaspora Jewry infested Hebrew literature and the mind of the *sabras*, the home-bred Jewish youth of Palestine and Israel. Much has been written about this phenomenon, which amounted to an emphatically negative stereotype of life in the Galut. It included not only the parasitism of the Jews, who were seen as nonproductive middlemen, engaged in nothing but underhand wheelings and dealings, *luftmenschen* (literally "air people," i.e., persons eking out a living from the exact opposite of productive work), but also the accusation of cowardice, of spineless servility, of having neither shame nor honor. Even the holocaust was seen in this dismal light: a few brutal and inhuman Nazi troopers riding herd over masses of cowardly, cringing, and whining Jews and driving them to their death "like sheep being led to slaughter."

An article by Professor Benjamin Akzin, a leading Israeli legal authority, can serve as the last and most recent example of the persistence of the concept of Jewish parasitism. One of the three major social ills which endanger the very existence of the State of Israel (the other two being the social gulf between the Ashkenazi and the Oriental Jews, and the lack of devotion to the state and to the national vision the state is destined to realize), parasitism, Akzin says, has reached the dimensions of a mass epidemic. Its four major manifestations are: (1) The parasitism of those who spend their working hours trying to do as little as possible; (2) the parasitism of those who do not want to work at all and live on aid and charity; (3) the parasitism of those who engage in criminal activities and form a large "underworld" sector; and (4) the parasitism of corruption and fraud.[18] To call attention to the prevalence of crime and social ills is, of course, an entirely proper undertaking for a public-minded jurist. What is unusual in Dr. Akzin's article is that he identifies the four greatly disparate types of phenomena he discusses as four categories of parasitism. No such generic designation would have been used by a jurist in discussing the same unsavory behavior patterns and activities in a Gentile society. Such phenomena have frequently been reported, for example, from the American scene in *The New York Times*, but I cannot recall a single instance in which it would have designated them as parasitism. One must, therefore, conclude that the use of this term by Akzin (and others) echoes—subconsciously, of course—the old Gentile allegation of Jewish parasitism which has been accepted as true by some Jewish leaders, thinkers, and authors, and which is still being directed against Jews in Soviet Russia.

2. Collective Guilt and Collective Excellence

The negative stereotype of the Galut-Jew, and the negative image of Galut life in general, has a long history behind it. One very ancient feature that went into its making was the traditional Jewish view of the Exile itself as a divine punishment for Israel's sins. The fact that the archetypal sin, that of Biblical idolatry, has with the passage of time receded more and more into the distant past and that, ever since the Roman Exile of 70 C.E., the Jews have been singularly devoted to God, could in no way eliminate, or even diminish, the consciousness of having sinned, of being sinful in the collective sense as a people. The very permanence of the Galut, the failure of the Messiah to appear and redeem Israel, the persistence of the sufferings—all this proved the Jews guilty in their own eyes day after day. As Moritz Lazarus (1824–1903), the outstanding German Jewish philosopher and founder of the discipline of *Völkerpsychologie*, put it: The core question of the Jew is, "Why do they persecute us?" And the answer is always, "Because we have sinned." [19]

Fortunately for the equilibrium of the Jewish mind, this feeling of collective guilt has been counterbalanced by an equally strong conviction of collective superiority. Despite its national sin, Israel has remained God's Chosen People; it was a God-fearing and God-loving people, whose heart was full of compassion, whose mind was honed to a keen edge by constant study, and whose hand was always extended in charity. This, at least until the Enlightenment, was the balance that kept the Jew from despairing over his condition and fate, and from falling victim to the opposite human failing, the one which the Greeks called *hybris*. One of the gravest effects of the Enlightenment was to disturb this balance by making light of the traditional Jewish values and intensifying the negative features in the Jewish self-stereotype. It is the latter at which we must have a closer look in the present context. But before doing so, a word is in place about the psychology of self-hate in low-status minority groups in general.

Studies carried out among such groups—e.g., blacks, Irish, French Canadians, and Jews—have shown that each of them tends to develop negative self-stereotypes. [20] The negative features in this self-stereotype can be so strong that they assume the character of self-hatred. Kurt Lewin's explanation of the phenomenon was that in low-status minority groups, the desire arises for the respect and rewards enjoyed by the higher-status majority. This supplies the impetus to leave the low-status group and become part of the higher-status majority. When the way to accomplishing this is found barred, frustration is generated which, in turn, gives rise to aggression. The aggression cannot be directed against its logical target, the high-status majority, because it is powerful and still remains the ideal, albeit unattainable. Therefore it is directed instead against one's own low-status minority group which one is prevented from leaving, and, ultimately, against oneself. Thus a hatred of one's own group, and of oneself as a member of it, is developed. [21]

In view of the unquestionable soundness of this explanation, it is nothing short of remarkable that prior to the Emancipation, that is, at a time when the status of the Jews as a minority group was much lower than after it, Jewish self-hatred was almost unknown. Although Jewish consciousness was ridden by the collective guilt feeling of being a sinful people, or at least the offspring of a sinful people, this did not generate self-hate. The general mode, and mood, of Jewish self-evaluation was positive; more than that, it was an attitude of admiration for the qualities on which the Jews had prided themselves for centuries. They considered themselves the people chosen by God to observe and study the Tora, a peace-loving people, a people whose heart was filled with compassion, a people of high morality, a people of believers who loved God and whom God loved, a people unique in the world and standing high above all other nations. If they nevertheless continued to live in Exile, contemned and persecuted by the Gentiles, this was explained as a divine punishment for sins committed by their forefathers while still living in the Land of Israel, and alternatively, as the inscrutable will of God. In a manner most typical of the religious mind, the contrast between the misery of the Exile and the unexcelled qualities attributed to the Jewish people was never allowed to rise to the level of consciousness. On the contrary, the objectively dismal Jewish condition was covered over by the brilliant self-stereotype. The external reality, however cruel, could not touch the Jewish soul, which lived in an entirely different world—a world of inner, higher reality.

This being so, the Jewish people as a whole constituted a striking exception to the Lewinian rule about the inevitability of the development of a negative self-stereotype, and even self-hatred, in low-status minority groups. Throughout their long history until the Enlightenment, there was no other minority group in Europe as deprived of rights, as exposed to persecution, as limited in personal freedom as the Jews. Yet self-hatred did not, could not, develop among them because they firmly believed that they, to put it in the simplest terms which would have been used by the Jews themselves, were better than the Gentiles. Because of this conviction, the desire to leave their own group and to be accepted into the majority, which Lewin considers the first stage in the psychological process leading to self-hatred, simply did not exist among them. Hence Lewin's rule, that low-status minority groups develop self-hatred because of their frustrated desire to acquire the respect and rewards of the higher-status group, must be amended by adding that this entire mechanism comes into play only if the members of the low-status minority group recognize and accept as a fact that they are indeed a low-status group in relation to the majority. The Jews never recognized this, and therefore no self-hatred could develop among them. None, that is, until the Enlightenment. For the most damaging outcome of the Enlightenment, which its protagonists did not foresee, was that it convinced the Jews that their own culture was inferior, that modern European culture was superior to theirs, and that they must acquire European culture for their own benefit.

Once this idea penetrated Jewish consciousness, the psychological processes leading to a negative self-stereotype and self-hatred were set in motion. The acquisition of European culture was believed to be the key to the modern world, whose rewards were now desired. Finding themselves barred from full (or even partial) acceptance into European society despite their laboriously acquired European culture, the Jewish Enlighteners felt frustrated, and the Lewinian law began to operate: frustration led to aggression, not toward the Gentile majority whose values were continued to be admired and desired, but toward their own group and themselves. This, in its barest outline, is the genesis of the new post-Enlightenment phenomenon of Jewish self-hatred.

As an example of the extremes to which a Jew could be led when caught up in the syndrome of this self-hate and of the adulation of the superior Gentile personality, let me refer to Otto Weininger (1880–1903), the precocious philosophical genius who had himself baptized in 1902 on the very day he received his doctoral degree and created a stir with the publication of his book *Geschlecht und Character* (*Sex and Character*) in 1903. Weininger was one of the most unrestrained and venomous anti-Semitic authors of his time. In his book he defined Judaism as a Platonic idea, that is, a tendency of the mind, or a psychological structure to which any individual may be subject, irrespective of his race or religion. He coupled this definition of Judaism with his philosophic postulate of Maleness and Femaleness as Platonic ideas. Masculinity, he asserted, is positive, it is Being, it is the expression of all that is great, noble, valuable. It is embodied in the Aryan. Femininity is negative, is Non-Being, is guilt, is man's lower self, and is embodied most typically in the Jew. The Aryan believes in some Absolute, strives for eternal being, and therefore is Something; the Jew, utterly without faith, is Nothing. "The Aryan, like Man, knows extremes of good and evil, of brilliance and stupidity. The Jew, like Woman, is utterly devoid of genius, and hence always mediocre and imitative." Weininger, moreover, held that "the bitterest anti-Semites are to be found among the Jews themselves; and their anti-Semitism bears witness to the fact that not even they themselves consider their kind lovable." [22] Weininger's intense Jewish self-hate rapidly turned against himself, and within a few months after the publication of his opus, at the age of twenty-three, he committed suicide.

3. Sephardi Pride and Prejudice

In its efforts to escape the most destructive forms of self-hatred—which, if carried to their logical extreme, can lead to self-annihilation as in the case of Weininger and several other self-hating Jews—the Jewish ego usually managed to create an escape hatch for itself. First it latched onto the patent fact that the Jews, after the Enlightenment, were comprised of several discrete, and greatly disparate, groups. Next, the group to which ego belonged was conceived as possessed of desirable qualities in general seen as identical with, or very similar to, the features characterizing the high-status majority. This, in turn, opened the door to a criticism, often in the sharpest and most condemnatory terms, of the *other* Jewish groups to which ego did not belong. Typically, these other groups were castigated most ruthlessly for possessing precisely those qualities in which they were most different from the high-status Gentile majority. Thus the potentially self-destructive self-hatred was safely channeled away from the self and from the Jewish group with which one identified oneself, and directed instead toward other Jewish groups in relation to which one felt distant and superior, and whose "otherness" was perceived as a source of painful irritation.

What are the criteria used to distinguish between ego's own Jewish ingroup and the other Jewish groups which he can criticize with psychological impunity? In pre-Enlightenment days, it was mostly descent and learning which served as the basis of differentiation. When, before their expulsion, Sephardi Jews came in contact with Middle Eastern Jews, and later with both Middle Eastern and Ashkenazi Jews, they drew the line clearly and proudly between the Sephardi ingroup and these other Jewish outgroups. Thus Maimonides wrote to his son Abraham:

> My son, let your pleasant company be only with our brothers the Sephardim who are called Andalusians, because they have brains and understanding and clarity of thought. . . . And beware of some of the people who dwell in the West in the place called Jerba and in the Barbary States, for they are dull and have a crude nature. And beware most particularly of the people who dwell between Tunis and Alexandria of Egypt, and also of those who dwell in the mountains of Barbary, for they are to me more ignorant than the rest of mankind, although they are very strong in their faith, and God is my witness that I regard them like the Karaites who deny the Oral Law, and they have no clarity of thought at all. . . .[23]

A few decades later, another proud Sephardi, the poet Judah Alharizi (1190–1235), visited Kurdistan and, like Maimonides, referred with scorn to the ignorance in matters Jewish he found in the community of Mosul: "And when I reached the city I saw its community—each man asleep in the bosom of stupidity . . . —for when the Jews were exiled from Jerusalem—the pious were exiled to Damascus and Egypt . . . —and the lost ones came to the land of Ashur [i.e., Kurdistan]. . . ."[24]

In the seventeenth century the Cretan-born astronomer, mathematician, and philosopher Joseph Solomon Delmedigo (1591–1655), who lived for several years in Poland as the personal physician to the Lithuanian Duke Radziwill, paints a similarly dismal picture of the cultural backwardness of the Polish Jews, reproaching them in particular with their ignorance of secular sciences:

> The country is wrapped in darkness and teams with ignorant people. Although it is covered all over by Yeshivot and schools, compared to the great number of people the prevalence of study is small. . . . The Jews of Poland are

enemies of science, and assert that God has as little liking for grammarians, poets and logicians as for mathematics and astronomy. . . . In all the provinces I traversed I found not even one of my people who devoted himself to scholarly research.[25]

With the inception of the Enlightenment, the Sephardim felt increasingly uncomfortable about being considered part of the people whose bulk consisted of unenlightened Ashkenazim, German, and East European Jews. Thus Isaac de Pinto, whom we have already met in a different context (page 228), in his argument against the article *"Juifs"* which appeared in the Geneva 1756 edition of Voltaire's historical writings takes pains not only to explain that a Portuguese Jew and a German Jew are two entirely different beings, but also to adduce evidence (mythical, to be sure) to show that the Portuguese Jews were descended of the noble tribe of Judah and have ever since kept themselves apart from the other Jews. While Pinto's primary interest in writing his tract against Voltaire was to defend the Portuguese Jews of Bordeaux, he did not wish to cause any harm to the Ashkenazi Jews and refrained from saying anything detrimental about them. But he could not escape the influence of the negative stereotype of the Jew which prevailed among the French Enlighteners. Hence he adopted the procedure referred to above. While admitting that the Ashkenazi Jews, in contrast to the noble and enlightened Portuguese Jews, had their faults, he attributed these to their oppression and persecution. "Is it astonishing," he asks, "that, deprived of all the advantages of society, . . . condemned and humiliated on all sides, often persecuted and always insulted and degraded," the German and Polish Jews are what they are?[26]

4. A Miscellany of Critics

Historical data show that the differences and dislikes which had existed among Jewish groups prior to the Enlightenment were insignificant compared to those which developed in its wake. With the Enlightenment, and the absorption by many Jews of the culture of their Gentile environment, the former Jewish religio-cultural unity, which had characterized Ashkenazi Jewry, was replaced by a great cultural diversity. Within one or two generations, there emerged greatly disparate Jewish communities readily identifiable, and eagerly identifying themselves, as French Jews, English Jews, German Jews, and so forth. This development went hand in hand with the outcropping of a feeling of estrangement or otherness among these newly arisen cultural subdivisions of the Jewish people. Most hurtful, however, was the antipathy that developed between those Jews who had assimilated to any one of the European cultures and those who remained anchored in their old, traditional religious culture, that is, between the "enlightened" and the "non-enlightened" Jews.

The enchantment of the Jewish Enlighteners with the values of European culture was so great that they unreservedly accepted the Gentiles' views of the Jews. They began to see the Jews through Gentile eyes and to apply Gentile yardsticks in evaluating them. This meant that the Enlightener, with a typical low-status minority mentality, equated Gentile features with "good," and Jewish traits with "bad," and consequently judged his fellow Jews according to the extent they had replaced their traditional Jewish with newly acquired Gentile features. Mendelssohn himself was not immune to this Gentile-inspired Jewish self-stereotype, as becomes evident from many of his statements about the unenlightened Polish Jews and the Yiddish they spoke, which he considered "a tongue of buffoons, very inadequate and corrupt," from which "a reader capable of elegant speech must recoil in disgust." [27] Mendelssohn's faithful co-worker in the cause of Enlightenment, Naphtali Herz Wessely, had the same negative view of Yiddish. It was, he wrote, a language "mutilated and confused," as well as "desolate and arid." It was because the Jews did not speak "a correct language" that they were remote from all wisdom and the virtues which comprised the law of men. [28]

Much of the ire of the *Maskilim* was directed at Hasidism in particular. The enmity the enlightened felt toward the Hasidim was expressed not only in literary form but also in thoroughly un-Jewish acts of denunciations. They wrote against the Hasidim in Hebrew, as well as in their newly acquired languages such as French and German, and knew no restraint in heaping vitriolic vilifications on the new sect, including the use of such expressions as "a damaging cancer spreading by the hour." [29] In general, the numerous petitions submitted by the opponents of Hasidism to various governmental authorities make dismal reading. [30]

One of the sharpest critics, not of Hasidism but of traditional Judaism in general, was Lazarus Bendavid (1762–1832), a Berlin Jewish philosopher, follower of Mendelssohn, leading Kantian, much-sought-after expert accountant, and unpaid principal of the Jewish Free School from 1806 until its closing in 1825. In his German book *Something on the Characteristic of the Jews*, Bendavid not only pleaded for the abolition of the Jewish ceremonial laws, thus becoming an early advocate of Jewish religious reform, but also presented a depressing picture of the Jewish character. The Jews had all the slavish shortcomings: they envied and hated their Christian oppressors; they practiced the most miserable ceremonies, adopted from the Greeks, Romans, and Christians, in order to regain the grace of God and through it dominion over their country. Motivated by a false piety, they submissively obeyed their uneducated and superstitious rabbis. The isolation from the Christians produced among them a confused language mixed with foreign elements, and a one-sided development of a purely formal, insubstantial acuteness, a hollow cunning which made of them mockers, misogynists, and scheming businessmen. Even Enlightenment, says Bendavid, did not help much. All it achieved was to bring to the fore a striving for external frillery at the expense of inner development; it took the form of surface polish and rank luxury. The rich Jewish youth was deeply corrupted, because it doubted everything—it jeered at Jewish ritual as well as the Jewish moral law. Neither did conversion to Christianity, to which many had hurried, bring about improvement; on the contrary, the convert became a scoffer of two religions, totally rootless, and destined to psychological destruction.

Having given unrestrained vent to his hatred of various types and kinds of Jews, Bendavid suggests that the dismal Jewish condition can be remedied by a vague ethic. Judaism must be transformed into "a true natural religion," with a belief in God and immortality, and in "the progress of the souls of the deceased toward perfection." But first of all, "the mischief with the shameful, nonsensical" ceremonial law must be stopped. To achieve this, Bendavid calls upon the government to intervene by force. Otherwise, while some would leave Judaism, "the others would even more tightly crawl together and indulge in their tomfoolery with greater zeal." [31]

It is remarkable that the man who wrote these things—a respected philosopher whose work was crowned by the Academy of Berlin and who had a major share in popularizing the teachings of Kant—found nothing in his philosophy to mitigate the brutality of his attack on Jews and Judaism.

Even some of the scholars who devoted their lives to studying Judaism displayed a sharply critical attitude toward their unenlightened co-religionists. Isaac Marcus Jost (1793–1860), the first modern Jewish historian, accused the "Talmudists"—those Jews who, in accordance with old Jewish tradition, concentrated on the study of the Talmud—of having "stood outside the present-time, living in an imaginary world." [32]

The same is the approach of the great Jewish historian Heinrich Graetz (1817–91), whose work is of such fundamental importance that it requires closer examination. As evidenced in his multi-volume *History of the Jews*, Graetz had a deep feeling for the Jewish struggle for survival, for the uniqueness of the Jews, their sufferings in Exile, and the courage of their martyrs. He was a strong Jewish nationalist, was imbued with a Messianic fervor, and held that the basic ideas of Judaism were eternal, changing only their external form. But, like Jost, he was the captive of a rather naïve rationalism, which rendered him unable to understand the Kabbala and Hasidism; he despised both as malignant growths in the body of Judaism. Above all, he was a late product of the *Haskala*, and the typical hostile attitude of the *Maskilim* toward traditional East European Jews and their Yiddish tongue comes through in his attacks on pre-*Haskala* Jewry. Graetz's hatred of Yiddish-speaking Talmudic East European Jewry was undoubtedly due in part to the circumstances of his own youth. He was born and grew up in East

Europe, where he was a yeshiva student until the age of nineteen, had to acquire European languages and secular knowledge by private study, and gained admission to a university (that of Breslau) only at the age of twenty-five.

Pre-*Haskala* Jewry, Graetz writes in his *History of the Jews*, had become "despicable in its own eyes; admirable only by reason of its domestic virtues and ancient memories, both, however, disfigured beyond recognition by trivial observances; scourging itself with bitter irony." He quotes Mendelssohn's "just" remark, "My nation has become so estranged from culture that the possibility of improvement is doubtful." Graetz considered even the physical appearance of the pre-Enlightenment Jews repugnant, as indicated by his comment that Mendelssohn was "the incarnation of his race . . . stunted in form, awkward, timid, stuttering, ugly, and repulsive in appearance," and that this Jewish "race-deformity" had only one saving feature: "a thoughtful spirit." To Graetz, the method used by most expounders of the Talmud was "distorted, hair-splitting, and perverse" and "made the crooked straight and the straight crooked." The Hebrew used by the pre-Enlightenment Jews was an "ossified, distorted, over-embellished Hebrew style . . . which had debased the Hebrew language into the mere mumbling of a decrepit tongue." As for Yiddish, "the German vocabulary in use among Jews was antiquated and misleading," and "almost all, with the exception of a few Portuguese and Italian Jews, had lost pure speech, the first medium of intellectual intercourse, and a childish jargon had been substituted, which, a true companion of their misfortunes, appeared unwilling to forsake them. . . ." In this connection Graetz again refers to Mendelssohn, who "felt disgust at the utter neglect of language" and "saw that the Jewish corrupt speech contributed not a little to the 'immorality of the average man.' " Graetz himself felt that "it was one of the consequences of the debasement of language that the German and Polish Jews had lost all sense of form, taste for artistic beauty, and aesthetic feeling." The Polish Jews were "barbarous" and had an "aversion to civilization." Even the Jewish mind had deteriorated:

> The perverse course of study [i.e., the concentration on the Talmud] pursued by the Jews since the fourteenth century had blunted their minds to simplicity. They had grown so accustomed to all that was artificial, distorted, super-cunningly wrought, and to subtleties, that the simple, unadorned truth became worthless, if not childish and ridiculous, in their eyes. Their train of thought was mostly perverted, uncultivated, and defiant of logical discipline.

Using "twisted methods and thoughts," which became "repugnant" to Mendelssohn, the commentaries and super-commentaries encumbered the ancient Revelation with "close layers of musty rubbish." Mendelssohn, says Graetz, formed "a striking contrast to the caricatures which German and

Polish Jews of the time presented." The Polish Jewish schoolmasters, whom he must have remembered from his own childhood, "with rod and angry gestures, instructed Jewish boys in tender youth to discover the most absurd perversities in the Holy Book, translating it into their hateful jargon, and so confusing the text with their own translation that it seemed as if Moses had spoken in the barbarous dialect of Polish Jews." More, "the neglect of all secular knowledge, which increased with every century, had reached such a pitch that every nonsensical oddity, even blasphemy, was subtly read into the verses of Scripture."

A more scathing and more unfeeling caricature of pre-Enlightenment Jewry could not have been drawn by the most rabid anti-Semite; yet Graetz was not only a great Jewish historian but, as indicated above, a deeply committed Jew. His venomous picture of traditional Judaism shows to what extent he was influenced by the post-Enlightenment adulation of German *Kultur* which, by contrast, made the great tradition of Judaism appear contemptible in his eyes.[33]

Accordingly, the awakening Jewish desire to absorb German *Kultur* was for Graetz a reaching out from darkness toward light. Mendelssohn, he says, began to take an interest in German civilization because "a fresh breeze was wafted from the Prussian capital into the narrow chambers of his Rabbinical studies." At the same time, with the accession of Frederick the Great, "literary dilettanteism, French customs, and contempt for religion began to grow into fashion among Berlin Jews," and "an impulse towards culture, the spirit of innovation, and imitation of Christian habits began to manifest themselves" among them. This is how they began to advance from their cultureless state toward culture, from their depravity of mind and, worst of all, morals, toward what Graetz considered the high German mentality and morality. And this was the great mission of Mendelssohn: "to purify the morals and elevate the minds of his brethren."

The results of Mendelssohn's work were soon felt, says Graetz: "As if touched by a magic wand, the Talmud students, fossils of the musty schoolhouses, were transfigured, and upon the wings of the intellect they soared above the gloomy present, and took their flight heavenwards." Evidently, we are gratified to learn, the corrupt Talmudic study of centuries did not cause permanent damage to the Jewish mind. On the contrary, Graetz now suddenly discovers that

> . . . the acumen, quick comprehension, and profound penetrativeness which these youths had acquired in their close study of the Talmud rendered it easy for them to take their position in the newly discovered world. Thousands of Talmud students . . . became little Mendelssohns; many of them eloquent, profound thinkers. With them Judaism renewed its youth. . . . In a very short time a numerous band of Jewish authors arose who wrote in a clear Hebrew or German style upon matters of which shortly before they had had no knowl-

edge. . . . They found their level in European civilization more quickly than the Germans, and—what should not be overlooked—Talmudic schooling had sharpened their intelligence.[34]

One is somewhat surprised to find that, according to this great Jewish historian, Talmudic study both "blunted the minds" and "sharpened the intelligence" of those who devoted themselves to it; but then it is a historian's privilege to look at the same phenomenon through two different spectacles.

From Mendelssohn, Wessely, and Bendavid, the heritage of Jewish self-hate was passed on not only to Jewish historians such as Jost and Graetz, but also to outstanding Jewish intellectuals, writers, statesmen, politicians, journalists, and others who left their mark on the countries in which they lived. While six of these—Paul Reé, Otto Weininger, Arthur Trebitsch, Max Steiner, Walter Calé, and Maximilian Harden—were singled out for analysis by Theodor Lessing in his German book *Der jüdishe Selbsthass (Jewish Self-Hate)*,[35] he did not include the most famous and most influential of all Jewish self-haters, Karl Marx (1818–83).

The hostility of Marx, scion of a long line of rabbis, to Jews and Judaism cannot be explained on the basis of his theories of history and society alone. Marx stated in an 1842 letter to Arnold Ruge that "the Israelite faith" was "repugnant" to him; termed Lassalle (in one of his letters to Engels, who, like Marx, was Jewish) "the Jewish nigger"; and consistently equated Jews with capitalistic exploiters. The Jewish historian Simon Dubnow attributed Marx's anti-Semitism to "the natural hatred of a renegade for the camp he deserted"; his biographer, Werner Blumenberg, saw in it the "self-hatred to which others among the newly emancipated Jews were also liable";[36] and Sir Isaiah Berlin explained it as the manifestation of the "well-known condition of self-hate of men forced into an alien culture," evidence of which he found also in the diaries of Walter Rathenau and the "tormented essays of Simone Weil."[37] The fact remains that Marx was merely one more example of the Jewish self-hate engendered by the internalization of the anti-Semitic stereotype of the Jew. Since Marx, however, considered the capitalistic exploitation of the workers the greatest human crime, he put the emphasis on that component of this stereotype which accused the Jews of plutocratic domination of the poor Gentile working classes. This is the more indicative of the entirely emotional, non-rational basis of Marx's Jew hatred since, in contrast to the Gentile anti-Semites, who had no precise knowledge of the Jewish occupational structure, Marx could not have been unaware of the desperate economic plight of the overwhelming majority of the contemporary Jews.

The pathetic aspect of Jewish self-hate consists not of the fact of self-criticism itself—moral indignation over the shortcomings of one's own people has many times led to embittered outbursts and denunciations, of which the great Hebrew prophets are the classical examples—but of the *manner* in which the Jewish critics of Jews from Mendelssohn on uncritically accepted the anti-Semitic stereotype of the Jew and so tragically internalized it.

They spoke volubly and glibly about the deficiencies of the Jews, which in reality existed only if Jewish life and religion, society, and tradition were measured by a theoretically inapplicable Western Gentile yardstick. They found the Polish Jews with their long beards and long caftans uncouth and repulsive, because people in civilized Western society wore both beards and coats short. Even more damagingly, they considered the traditional Jew, who was saturated with a knowledge of the Bible and the Talmud, a primitive and uneducated creature because he knew nothing of the philosophers and poets of eighteenth- and nineteenth-century Germany. They were so deeply influenced by the dominant trends in the German variety of Enlightenment that they saw in traditional Jewish life, as lived by the contemporary Polish Jews, nothing but a manifestation of decay, degeneration, perversity, and even immorality. And even in the twentieth century, they considered the occupational structure of the Jews in the Diaspora, imposed upon them by the authorities whose yoke they were forced to bear, as "parasitic," because this was the favorite anti-Semitic epithet applied by Proudhon, Galton, Pearson, and others of their ilk. This is the ultimate tragedy of living as a low-status minority among a high-status majority—the internalization of a hostile stereotype into a devastating self-stereotype, a self-alienation compared to whose trauma the Marxian alienation of the working class is but a minor emotional discomfort.

5. The French Infection

Late nineteenth-century French Jewry supplies an example of an educated and assimilated community many of whose intellectual leaders tried to combat the negatively weighted stereotype of the Jew which was part of the dominant view of "racial" characteristics and differences. Yet, at the same time, being an integral part of French society and inescapably influenced by French ideas, these French Jewish *literati* themselves echoed the prevalent French view of the Jews. Ernest Renan (1823–92), one of the most influential French savants of the second half of the nineteenth century, wrote the oft-quoted sentence, "I am . . . the first to recognize that the Semitic race [of which he considered the Jews the foremost representatives], compared to the Indo-European race, represents essentially an inferior level of human nature." [38] Although Renan never uttered anything even faintly anti-Semitic, his negative view of the Semitic race, which was seconded by several other important French scholars—anthropologists, sociologists, and physicians— was utilized by anti-Semitic authors such as Édouard Drumont, Edmund

Picard, and others,[39] who made good use of these scholarly authorities for their own anti-Jewish purposes. Exposed to the views which had become prevalent in their environment, before long the Jews themselves became convinced that they did indeed possess the negative traits so widely attributed to them. Since, however, the avowed intention of the Jewish spokesmen nevertheless was to defend the Jews, their utterances present a peculiar mixture of praise and criticism. Thus a Jewish columnist, writing in a Jewish yearbook, claimed that the Jews had "moral virtues" and "intellectual qualities," while admitting "their shifty looks" and their "few significant defects." [40] And another Jewish writer, echoing Renan's ideas, went on record in L'Univers Israélite to the effect that "one can then believe that the Semites, thanks to their intelligence and their facility for adaptation . . . will not take long to strip themselves of their horrible faults and rejoin their Aryan cousins on the heights where they bask in a glorious light of purity and holiness." [41] The "horrible faults" of the Semites (i.e., the Jews) are accepted as an incontestible fact; their improvement, on the other hand, is spoken of merely as a pious hope.

Similarly Alfred Naquet, a Jewish member of the French Chamber of Deputies, rising to the defense of the Jews, "contended that modern French Jews were the equal of other Frenchmen, because, in the course of time they had clearly lost that 'inferiority which I find in all Oriental people,' an inferiority from which the Jews had suffered, but from which they had been freed due to the action of what he called 'Aryan fertilization.' " [42]

Again, Camille Dreyfus, freethinker and political editor of La Nation, in a series of articles he wrote against anti-Semitism and in which he argued that there was no such thing as a Jewish race, burst out, "Were those grandmothers so chaste, that a drop of blue Aryan blood never mixed itself with the cursed blood of the Semites which flows in my veins?" [43]

One can quite clearly see what went on in the mind of these authors. They were committed Jews and set pen to paper because they were impelled by their Jewishness to defend the Jews against anti-Semitic attacks. But even while doing so, they could not help revealing the extent to which they had internalized certain features in the anti-Semitic stereotype of the Jews. Hence the "shifty look" of the Jews, their "significant defects," their "horrible faults," their "inferiority," and their "cursed blood."

The latter part of the nineteenth century was a period in which French Jewry produced a number of outstanding individuals who came to occupy important places in the French scholarly world. Yet the thoroughness and detachment on which these men prided themselves did not prevent them from accepting, without any scientific investigation, the premise of Jewish decadence, degradation, and contemptibility in a manner reminiscent of the Jewish journalists and popular writers—with the one difference that the scholars more emphatically blamed the Gentile environment for the sorry

Jewish condition. Among them was Theodore Reinach (1860–1928), renowned Orientalist, Jewish historian, professor at the École des Hautes Études Sociales, and chevalier of the Legion of Honor, who wrote in his *History of the Jews*, "Hatred, persecution, legal restrictions have everywhere engendered in the Jews physical and moral decadence, all of the vices of oppressed and deprived races. . . ." [44] In the first edition of this work he went even further, stating that as a result of the treatment meted out to the Jews by the Church, "Israel was withering away . . . it came to deserve the contempt under which it fell. . . ." [45] In the second and subsequent editions the offending judgment was omitted; it was replaced by a vague reference to "the greatest depression of Israel" which coincided with the period of the Renaissance of Europe.

His elder brother Salomon Reinach (1858–1932) was an archeologist, philologist, and historian of note, whose major work, *Orpheus, Histoire Générale des Religions* (first published in French and in an English translation in 1909), followed the Voltairean tradition of radical rationalism and classified both Judaism and Christianity as "barbaric." As for the Talmud and "those backward Jews who follow its rules," he had nothing but contempt, and he was convinced of the "inferiority of the East European Jews." [46] The two Reinachs, as well as their oldest brother, Joseph (1856–1921), the well-known French statesman and historian, while extremely critical of Jews, were intrepid fighters for the Jewish cause. All three were confirmed Dreyfusards, who demanded a new trial for the convicted captain, took part in Jewish affairs, and contributed importantly to Jewish scholarship.

Others, too, took this two-pronged approach. Léon Kahn (1851–1900) was a historian of French Jewry, editor of *L'Univers Israélite*, and was active in many Jewish associations in Paris. Yet he too followed the anti-Semitic line when he wrote that, because of oppression, the Jew had become a creature in whom "there was room for nothing else . . . but hypocrisy, cowardice, and vice. But comes the idea of liberty, of equality, of fraternity [and] all these miasmas piled up in him disappear under [the influence of] the purity of the restorative breath of air." [47] Similarly Julien Benda (1867–1956), the well-known writer and philosopher, considered his Jewish origin a troublesome burden and went on record characterizing "the narrowly Hebraic Jew" as a person "enslaved by the passion for small and daily lucre, patient, fearful, thrifty, hardworking, blind preserver of a bundle of customs which has lost its end and justification." [48] What is noteworthy in these and many similar utterances is the unquestioning acceptance even by Jewish scholars and historians of the allegation that the Jews were hypocrites, cowards, full of vices, morally depraved. Once this repulsive stereotype of the pre-Emancipation Jews is subscribed to as a fact, loyalty to Judaism comes into play and blame for the Jewish condition is laid at the Gentiles' doorstep. A critical examination of the question whether this stereotype is borne out by historically ascertainable facts had to wait for a new spirit to assert itself in Jewish scholarship.

Some examples nevertheless can be found of Jewish scholars and writers who managed to rid themselves of the disease of self-hate and develop a Jewish national consciousness and a pride in Judaism and their own Jewishness. Bernard Lazare (1865–1903) is the outstanding case in point.

Son of a Jewish businessman of Nîmes in Provence, Lazare had become an unbeliever even before going to Paris in 1886. There he devoted himself to literature and criticism and became attracted to the anarchist movement. The growing manifestations of anti-Semitism and the arrival of Jewish refugees from czarist pogroms and persecutions impelled Lazare to express his view on the Jewish question. He discussed it for the first time in 1880 in two articles in his own short-lived *avant-garde* journal *Entretiens politiques et littéraires*. Utilizing the approach typical of the Jewish Enlighteners, Lazare distinguished between two kinds of Jews: the *israélites* and the *juifs*. The former—assimilated into French society, much refined, long established in France, and making up the group to which he himself belonged—had his full sympathy. The latter—comprising the German and East European Jews— were the object of his unrestrained scorn. He portrayed the *juifs* in the manner of the traditional anti-Semitic caricature: their goal in life was money, the making of a quick fortune; they were "coarse and dirty, pillaging Tartars," "contemptible people," "cosmopolitan," "with no ties to any nation, no affection for any nation . . . [like] the Bedouin moving his tent about with complete indifference," and more of the same. Anti-Semitic charges, he felt, were substantially correct when applied to these *juifs*. The French *israélites*, however, had nothing in common with these people and should have nothing to do with them. In fact, they should "kick out these lepers who corrupt them . . . vomit up the rottenness that wants to creep in." He went on to denounce the *"solidarité juive"* to which some Jewish agencies appealed in their endeavor to help the Jewish refugees from the east and proclaimed that "we must abandon them," because, as things stand, "we are confused with them. . . ."

At this early stage of Lazare's thinking, he saw the remedy for anti-Semitism, so unjustly directed even at the decent and patriotic *israélites* of France, in assimilation. The Jews must vanish entirely, must "lose themselves in the mass of the French nation." Prophesying what he wished would happen, Lazare envisaged (in an article published in *Le Figaro* in 1893) that the merging of the Jews into the French nation was only a matter of time, for they "were destined to disappear totally." [49]

In 1892 Lazare began working on a book on anti-Semitism which was published in 1894 in two volumes. [50] While the central argument in this book was similar to the contention Lazare expressed in his 1890 articles, namely, that "the general causes of anti-Semitism have always resided in Israel itself," his attitude had undergone a perceptible change. A historian of the period feels that this change was due partly to the anti-Semitic crisis which was building and to the influence of Maurice Barrès (1862–1923), the fiercely chauvinistic French nationalist author and politician, who influenced several other French Jewish nationalist writers.[51] It seems likely that Lazare's growing knowledge of Jewish history, with which he familiarized himself in preparing his book on anti-Semitism, was an additional factor in bringing him to a more positive appreciation of Judaism. He discerned that "national consciousness" or, as he also puts it, "national pride," was the basic factor in Jewish survival, and recognized that Judaism was characterized by a revolutionary spirit, "a constant agitation," which imbued Jews with a predisposition to bringing about a radical transformation of the oppressive societies in which they lived. And he discovered that all Jews had "received the impress of the national genius [of Judaism] acting through heredity and early training." Even if a Jew abandons all religion and faith, he retains these Jewish characteristics, says Lazare, and mentions Heine, Marx, Börne, Lassalle, Moses Hess, Robert Blum, and Disraeli as examples. "The emancipated Jew being no longer bound by the faith of his ancestors" is still shaped by the revolutionary "Jewish spirit" and has become in modern nations "a veritable breeder of revolutions."[52] This, coming from a man with Lazare's revolutionary outlook, was the highest praise that could be accorded to any people.

Having thus placed the Jewish question in a revolutionary social and political framework, the next step for Lazare was to recognize that, "from the Jewish point of view, the most powerful obstacle to Jewish liberation was a psychological one." It was not so much his cultural backwardness as his profound demoralization which prevented the Jew's real emancipation. In an article entitled "The New Ghetto" (which he published late in 1894 in La Justice), Lazare speaks of the hostile atmosphere of suspicion, hatred, and prejudice which has replaced the old physical ghetto and constitutes a psychological wall built by the anti-Semites between themselves and the Jews.[53] From this time on, Lazare became an intrepid fighter for Jewish nationalism. He joined the incipient French Zionist movement, fought for the rehabilitation of Dreyfus, edited the French Zionist journal Zion, and, above all, used his sharp pen in defending Jewish nationalism and attacking its enemies. He became a fearless champion of the Jewish cause, and in a complete reversal of his earlier position, he came to see in assimilated French Jewry a group "in an advanced state of decomposition," which had "become rotten in contact with the Christian world." He emphasized with pride that "we have always been the old, stiff-necked people, the intractable rebel nation; we want to be ourselves, what our forefathers, our history, our traditions, our culture, and our memories have made us, and we will know well how to win that right which is ours, not only to be men, but also to be Jews."[54]

A part of the Jewish "national consciousness" which from 1894 so com-

pletely filled Lazare's whole being was the recognition that, far from the contemptible and dishonest commercial wheeler-dealers he thought them to be
in 1890, the Jews were a people of workers. It was, he said in 1899, nothing
but an anti-Semitic myth that the Jews were a people of capitalists and
merchants. In fact, "no people has a larger proportion of poor than the
Jews." The Jews were "the proletarian people *par excellence.*" [55] He came to
the conclusion, again in sharp contrast to his early view, that "the Jews could
best work for humanity by being themselves, by remaining true to their
traditions." [56] In his notes for a planned study on Jewish thought and history
which his early death prevented him from completing, he manifested an empathy with the wounded Jewish soul that is reminiscent of Shylock's great
outburst:

> What things of history has the Jew not felt? What has he not experienced? To
> what shame has he not been subjected? What pain has he not suffered? What
> triumphs has he not known? What defeats has he not accepted? What resigna-
> tion has he not shown? What pride has he not displayed? And all that has left
> profound traces in his soul, just as the flood waters leave their sediments on the
> valley floor. [57]

Among the factors which contributed to Lazare's metamorphosis from a
Jew-hater to a man of proud Jewish national consciousness were his meetings
with Herzl. Herzl refers for the first time to a meeting with Lazare in a diary
entry dated July 17, 1896, in which he characterizes Lazare as an "excellent
type of a fine, clever French Jew" and mentions that he discussed with him
his Zionist plans. Lazare must have made a strong impression on Herzl,
because four days later he singles out Lazare as having been present at the
Russian Jewish students' club which Herzl addressed and which drew a
crowd. Still in July 1896, Herzl, in a letter, asked Lazare to take care of the
French edition of his *The Jewish State.* In October of the same year Herzl
suggested to Zadoc Kahn, chief rabbi of France, that Lazare be appointed
editor-in-chief of the Zionist daily he wanted to have launched in Paris. By
March 1899 disagreements had developed between Lazare and Herzl; Lazare resigned from the Vienna Zionist Actions Committee but accepted
membership in the expanded Central Committee of the Zionist Organization. At a chance meeting between Lazare and Herzl on April 30, 1900,
Lazare assured Herzl that "he had never ceased being of one mind" with
him and told him of his plan to go to Constantinople, whereupon Herzl
asked him to try to win Ambassador Constans for the Zionist cause. The two
made an appointment to meet a week later in Vienna. The last entry in
Herzl's *Diaries* about Lazare dates from January 23, 1902: "In the Paris
propaganda sheet *Pro Armenia* Bernard Lazare has published a mean, malicious article against me, on the occasion of the exchange of Zionist Congress
telegrams with the Turkish Sultan. . . . What interest can he possibly have,

apart from the nice gesture, in defending the Armenians?" [58] While the relationship between the two men ended on this sour note, there can be no doubt that Herzl and the Zionist movement had an important role in the latter phase of Lazare's conversion to Jewish nationalism. On September 2, 1903, the thirty-eight-year-old Lazare died of cancer. On July 3, 1904, Herzl, aged forty-four, died of a heart ailment.

6. Between East and West in Israel

A special sub-variety of self-hatred emerged in Israel among members of some Middle Eastern Jewish communities. Within a few years after Israel achieved independence, hundreds of thousands of Jewish immigrants found themselves living side by side with people from entirely different backgrounds. The culturally dominant group was that of Ashkenazi Jews of European origin, who were in positions of leadership and whose first reaction to the encounter with Middle Eastern Jews was a shock of otherness. Some twenty-five years ago I analyzed the mutual stereotypes which rapidly developed between these two major divisions of the Jewish people in Israel. I found that the European Jews considered the Middle Eastern Jews unstable, emotional, impulsive, unreliable, and incompetent; given to habitual lying and cheating, laziness and boastfulness; inclined to violence and having an uncontrolled temper; superstitious, childish, and dirty; and, in general, primitive and lacking in culture. The Middle Eastern Jews, for their part, resented that the Ashkenazim exercised authority over them, that they insisted on punctuality, that they were irreligious, that they discriminated against the Middle Eastern Jews, and that they regarded them as inferior, second-rate, low grade. [59]

In the course of years these mutually derogatory stereotypes underwent certain modifications. The Ashkenazim learned that the Oriental Jewish character was not as negative as it seemed in the first flush of the early encounter, and that the features in respect of which the Orientals differed from them were not necessarily "bad." Ideas of "cultural pluralism" became accepted by the Ashkenazi leadership of Israel, and there was more and more talk about, and action for, safeguarding the traditional cultural values of the various Jewish communities. On the Oriental Jewish side, demands were increasingly voiced for equal rights, the elimination of all discrimination, and recognition that Israel has become *de facto* a country with an Oriental Jewish majority population. [60]

While this went on at the political level, some Oriental Jewish groups, and especially the North Africans, could not escape becoming infected with self-hatred. Just as the European Jews in the post-Enlightenment era willy-nilly accepted and parroted the Gentiles' negatively weighted stereotype of the inferior and contemptible Jew, and did so precisely at a time when the Gentile attitude toward the Jews was becoming more liberal and less negative, so the North African Jews internalized the emphatically derogatory Ashkenazi stereotype of the Oriental Jew while among the Ashkenazim this stereotype was on its way out, or at least was modified by a more objective understanding of the Oriental Jewish personality.

A study of self-rejection among North African immigrants to Israel, published in 1966, showed that they internalized to a considerable extent the earlier, heavily negative stereotype other Jews in Israel had of them. North African Jews were mentioned "most frequently as least desirable neighbors not only by the European and Near Eastern respondents, but by themselves as well." In fact, about the same percentage of North Africans, Europeans, and Near Easterners rejected members of the North African group as neighbors (Europeans, 32 percent; Near Easterners, 38 percent; North Africans, 33 percent). Among the negative features of the North Africans, mentioned in approximately equal proportions by European, Near Eastern, and North African respondents as reasons for not wanting to have North Africans as neighbors were (in descending order of frequency among North African respondents) aggressivity, undesirable personal traits, lack of culture, dirtiness, and bothersome children. The younger the age group of the North African respondents, the higher the percentage of those who exhibited these symptoms of self-rejection; it increased from 18 percent among those sixty years old or older, to 40 percent in the eighteen-to-twenty-four-year age group. These findings were interpreted by the author of the study "either as a response to the ambivalent status of the North Africans as the major target of ethnic hostility in Israel, or as an attempt on the part of immigrants from North Africa to conform to one of the prevailing normative patterns of the society." A complementary feature found was that North Africans displayed a disproportionate desire for Europeans as neighbors. In fact, the more residential contact they had with Europeans, the more positive was their attitude toward these neighbors.[61]

Similar findings were reported in 1972 on the basis of studies conducted in Glasgow (Scotland), Oxford, and Haifa, which showed that children aged six to eleven were sensitive to subtle social influences, which led to a "devaluation" of their own group as compared with an outgroup conceived in some sense to be "dominant" or "superior." In Israel, both European Jewish and Oriental Jewish children preferred photographs showing European Jewish young men to those showing Oriental Jewish young men. The results were taken by the researchers as showing that children assimilate negative ingroup evaluations.[62]

These childhood attitudes persist into adulthood not only among Moroccan Jews (as mentioned above) but among Oriental Jews in general. Thus it was found that, while Jews of European origin in the Israeli army preferred to have social contact with their own kind, Jews of Middle Eastern origin did not.[63] On the other hand, it was also found that the higher valuation of the outgroup was a *class* phenomenon, confined to working-class people but found among both Ashkenazim and Sephardim; both had a more favorable stereotype of the outgroup than of their own group. In the middle class, however, among both Ashkenazim and Sephardim, the auto-stereotypes were more favorable than their hetero-stereotypes.[64]

My own experience with Oriental Jewish adults and youths in Israel was that frequently they were ashamed of their origin and tried to appear as if they were of Ashkenazi extraction. For example, if one asked a North African Jew his place of origin, one would typically get the answer "Paris," or "France." Several further questions would be needed until one elicited the admission that he was, in fact, from Algeria or Morocco.

The self-hate of the Oriental Jew in Israel is the outcome of his higher valuation of the Ashkenazi Jews, who represent the dominant cultural and socio-economic entity in the country, and to whom he attempts to assimilate. In a Christian environment, such as that of the United States, a parallel psychological process can motivate Jews to make strenuous efforts to move toward and merge into the Christian majority. One manifestation of this tendency was the New Left movement, in which much Jewish self-hate found expression.

7. The New Left

The New Left was a left-wing radical trend which, in the 1960's, attracted many students and other young people in the United States and Western Europe, and in which Jews played a prominent role. The Jewish participation in the New Left was explained by some analysts as a result of the rationalistic, child-centered, and psychologically understanding home environment of the Jewish middle-class family, which produced children intolerant of rules and restrictions and insistent on the rapid achievement of an ideal society. Another explanation emphasized the historical background of American Jews, which led them, more than the Gentiles, to embrace liberalism, socialism, and communism. The Six Day War of 1967 brought about a crisis and a split in the ranks of the Jewish New Leftists: some became most virulent enemies of "Zionist imperialism," while others began to organize distinctively Jewish and pro-Jewish New Left splinter groups and to claim support from the Jewish establishment for their activities.[65] According to Bernard Lewis, who devoted some attention to this phenomenon, the Jewish members of the New Left (mostly American children of survivors of European ghettos and death camps) unconditionally identified themselves with left-wing Marxism, black anti-Semitism, Arab anti-Israelism, and Russian anti-Zionism. Whenever there was a divergence between a Jewish and an anti-Jewish position, they could be counted on to support the latter. This extreme manifestation of Jewish self-hate provided, or appeared to provide, "an opportunity of freeing oneself from ancestral and, more immediately, parental bonds, and passing from the minority to the majority," while "the curious phenomenon of Jewish supporters of black anti-Semitism" could be understood as their acceptance, or rather demand, of "a share of guilt for the enslavement of the African in America"—a way in which they "tacitly assert their membership of the dominant even if guilty majority." [66] By the mid-1970's, the New Left as a whole, both in America and in Western Europe, was largely a thing of the past. [67]

This specific form of Jewish anti-Semitism is but the most recent manifestation of basically the same psychological mechanism which emerged with the Enlightenment, when the values of the Gentile environment were internalized by the *Maskilim* to the extent that they almost automatically adjudged every feature in which the Jews differed from the Gentiles as bad, inferior, and contemptible. Ernest M. Wolf pointed out several years before the emergence of the New Left that this form of behavior, which espouses the cause, and, I would add, the values of the Jews' worst enemies and leads the Jews to echo some of the prejudices which anti-Semitic non-Jews harbor, "is obviously a very striking and virulent form of contempt of the larger self," akin to "the psychoanalytic device of 'identification with the aggressor.'" [68] There is in it, also, a considerable measure of that Lewinian "negative chauvinism" which infects persons ashamed of their membership in an underprivileged group (or, what amounts to the same thing, in a group which they consider underprivileged). Such a person "will place those habits, appearances, or attitudes [and, I may add, causes and values] which he considers to be particularly Jewish *not* particularly high; he will rank them low. . . ." [69]

These late outcroppings of Jewish self-hate notwithstanding, by the beginning of the last quarter of the twentieth century the Jewish psyche seems largely to have got rid of this uninvited hanger-on of the Enlightenment. There can be no doubt that the Jews were able to purge themselves of it because, within the last generation, history has bombarded them with a sequence of events the like of which no other people has had to experience. First, the horror of the holocaust. Then the reestablishment, after two thousand years, of a sovereign State of Israel. Then the four wars Israel had to fight against an enemy outnumbering it fifty to one, and side by side with this, the plight of Russian Jewry. And finally, as late as the fall of 1975, the equation of Zionism with racism by a resolution in the global debating society of nations rammed through by the unholy triple alliance of Communist, Arab, and Third World countries. These events reinforced Jewish solidarity all over the world and at the same time effectively reduced to insignificance the last vestiges of Jewish self-hate.

18

The World of Values

The concept of values is the key to the innermost chambers of the human mind. The term "values" has been described as referring to "interests, pleasures, likes, preferences, duties, moral obligations, desires, wants, needs, aversions and attractions and many other modalities of selective orientation." [1] That is to say, values are standards of desirability, and as such they establish norms. While oppositions or contradictions among values are not unusual, nevertheless the different kinds and levels of values compose a cultural value system. Each culture has a distinctive value system, which, in turn, patterns the behavior of its carriers. Within each society there are, of course, diverse value sets of group and individuals, varying according to sex, age, personality, and social role. Still, it is possible to abstract from these diverse sets the overall value system of large and complex socio-cultural entities, such as a people or a nation.

When trying to distill the basic values or value system of the Jews one runs into the same kind of difficulty which we have already encountered in studying the Jewish personality. The greatly differing Gentile societies in whose midst the Jews have lived in many parts of the world have exerted manifold influences on them, which made their impact not only on the culture and personality of the Jew, but also on his values. One will, therefore, have to expect a certain measure of congruence between the value systems of Jews and Gentiles in every locality, and especially in those places where the Jews have lived for many generations. On the other hand, the old, tradition-sanctioned values, which were developed in Biblical and Talmudic times, when the Jews formed compact populations in the Land of Israel and in Babylonia, still inform the Jewish mind to this day. The literary residues of those old Jewish values are embedded, in the first place, in the oldest holy books of Judaism, the Bible and the Talmud, which for more than fifteen centuries were the main subject of study in all parts of the Jewish world, were considered the expression and interpretation of God's will, and which therefore had the greatest formative influence on the Jewish mind. Because of the unparalleled sway the Bible and the Talmud exercised over all Jewish generations until the Enlightenment, I shall devote what may seem a disproportionately large part of this chapter to a presentation of Biblical and Talmudic sources relating to values and shall speak much more briefly of their medieval and subsequent formulations. At the same time we must not lose sight of the fact that while studying the Talmud with indefatigable zeal, the Jews in every age had to conduct themselves in accordance with the rules laid down in the latest available Jewish law code recognized as authoritative. These codes, of course, were but updated formulations of the *Halakha*, the traditional Jewish Law, as it could be extracted or distilled from the voluminous legal argumentations contained in the Talmud. The latest of them, still considered authoritative by Orthodox Jews, is the *Shulḥan 'Arukh (Set Table)* completed in 1565 by the Sephardi Joseph Caro in Safed, Palestine, and adapted for Ashkenazi use by Moses Isserles of Cracow who was Caro's contemporary. When, in the wake of the Enlightenment, halakhic ignorance assumed disquieting dimensions, a Hungarian rabbi, Solomon Ganzfried (1804–86) of Ungvár, prepared in 1864 a digest of the huge tomes of the *Shulḥan 'Arukh* and called it *Qitzur Shulḥan 'Arukh* or *Abridgment of the Set Table*. This handbook achieved wide popularity and was translated (from the original Hebrew) into several languages, among them English. However, the continuity and immutability of the *Halakha* are such that every legal decision and instruction found in this nineteenth-century work is essentially identical with the teachings of the sages contained in the Talmud completed thirteen centuries earlier.

Needless to say, a legal system such as the Jewish *Halakha*, which is considered by traditional Jews as going back ultimately to divine revelation on Mount Sinai, is held to have a built-in validity for all times. To observe all its minutiae is God's will; to study it is a supreme value. This being the case, beneath all the values the Jews of the Diaspora adopted from their diverse cultural environments, they retained everywhere a basically identical value system which went back to Biblical and Talmudic times and which remained a common characteristic of Jewish life as long as it was dominated by its own traditions.

A full analysis of the Jewish value system would require a major study of its own. What we can do in the present context is to discuss three values which are among the most central and most important in traditional Jewish life, and which, therefore, can be assumed to have had the most significant formative influence on the Jewish mind and personality. They are the *family* (including sex), *education*, and *charity*. Tenets relative to these values had at a very early time—long before the onset of the Talmudic era—received religious sanction and therewith been made into intrinsic ingredients of Jewish belief and observance. But it was only in Talmudic times that they were explicitly and concretely formulated as essential parts of religious conduct.

In a famous Mishnaic passage, the sages taught, "These are the things whose fruits one enjoys in This World, while the principal remains preserved in The World to Come: honoring father and mother, charity and peace making; and the study of the Tora which weighs as much as all the rest." [2] Having come to this conclusion on the basis of their own priorities, the sages found ingenious interpretations to Biblical verses in order to give their views a Scriptural foundation. [3] For our purposes, I shall take the liberty of reinterpreting somewhat this second-century passage and (1) consider the honoring of father and mother within the general context of Jewish family relations; (2) treat peacemaking, as well as hospitality, which is added in a Talmudic amplification of the Mishna quoted above, [4] under the general heading of charity; and (3) discuss "the study of the Tora" in the wider sense of education in general. I shall, moreover, reverse the order of (2) and (3) and discuss the family first, education second, and charity third, for the simple reason that the influence of family comes first in human life, that of education second, and that the practice of charity can be engaged in, at least to a full extent, only after reaching adulthood.

1. The Family

The basic features which characterize the Jewish family to this day go back to early Biblical times and are rooted in the ancient Near Eastern environment in which the Hebrews lived and of which they formed part. Anthropologically speaking, this family can be (and has been) [5] defined as patrilineal, endogamous, polygynous, patrilocal, extended, and patriarchal. In simple terms this means that among the Biblical Hebrews each individual belonged to that kin group to which his father, his father's father, and so on, belonged, because descent was reckoned *patrilineally*, in the father's line. The preferred wife for a man was a close relative, such as a cousin, if possible on his father's side; that is, marriages took place, ideally, *endogamously*, or within the kin group. A man was allowed to marry two or more wives simultaneously, in other words, marriage was *polygynous*. When a man married, he brought his wife into the house of his parents where the young couple remained living; this is what is meant by the term *patrilocal*. Since, in this manner, three generations would live in the same household, the family was *extended* (in contrast to our modern family, which consists only of father, mother, and minor children and which is termed *nuclear* or immediate family). And finally, in Biblical society the male head of the family was an almost absolute ruler over all his dependents and descendants, his wife or wives, his sons, his daughters-in-law, and his grandchildren; in a word, the family was *patriarchal*. Each of these features is amply illustrated in the Biblical stories about Abraham, Isaac, Jacob, and his twelve sons, as anyone familiar with the Bible will readily recall.[6]

CHILDREN AND PARENTS

In the Fifth Commandment, the old popular tradition which assigned a ruling position to the father in the family was modified to the extent of giving the mother an equal place of honor: "Honor thy father and thy mother that thy days may be long upon the land which the Lord thy God giveth thee." [7]

Upon this Biblical basis the Talmud built an elaborate superstructure, spelling out in detail the significance of the respect one must show to father and mother, and the manner in which one must express it. According to Shim'on ben Yohai, the famous second-century Palestinian teacher, the duty of honoring father and mother was even greater in the eyes of God than the obligation of honoring Him. Lest anyone be taken aback by this teaching, Rabbi Shim'on, as was the wont of the Talmudic sages, adduced Biblical passages in its support: "So great is the duty of honoring father and mother that the Holy One, blessed be He, considers it more important than honoring Him, for it is written, 'Honor thy father and thy mother,' and it is written, 'Honor the Lord with thy substance.' " Since some students of the Law may have missed the point in the juxtaposition of the two Biblical quotations, Rabbi Shim'on went on to explain that these verses show that the fulfillment of commandments which aimed at honoring God, such as the offering up of sacrifices, giving the tithe, building a booth for the Feast of Tabernacles (*Sukkot*), helping the poor, and the like, was obligatory only for him who had "substance," that is, property, from which to defray these expenses; but as to father and mother, "whether one has or has not, one must honor them, even if one must go begging at the doors." [8]

Moreover, the sages taught, when people honor their parents, God says, "I count it for them as if I dwelt among them and they honored Me." And they found Scriptural passages also to support their view that the Bible itself equated the fear of father and mother with the fear of God.[9]

When Rabbi Y'huda the Prince codified the Mishna (c. A.D. 200), he included in it precise instructions as to how children must honor their mother after the death of the *pater familias*: she must be assured the same living conditions which she enjoyed while her husband was alive, and not even the slightest change must be introduced into her circumstances. Thus she was to retain not only the same home, but also the same pillows and cushions, the same silver and gold vessels, and so forth.[10] When the time came for Rabbi Y'huda himself to die, on his deathbed he enjoined his sons: "Be careful to honor your mother. Let the lamp remain lit in its place, let the table remain set in its place, and let the couch remain standing in its place." [11] Characteristically, these cautions touch upon little things, the frills of existence; the more basic features of honoring a widowed mother, such as providing her with food and clothing and approaching her with a respectful deference, are not mentioned because they were taken for granted; it was generally understood that these things were covered by the Fifth Commandment.

What the Law prescribed, myth and legend rendered psychologically almost impossible to disobey. Talmudic literature contains a spate of stories about filial devotion which strike us as exaggerated, but which must have represented an ideal to be striven for in the eyes of the contemporaries among whom they originated and their descendants whose minds for fifteen centuries were nurtured on the Talmud. Interestingly, the protagonists in these stories are as often Gentiles as they are Jews, as if to signify that filial devotion is an ideal form of behavior which can be attained even by Gentiles ignorant of the noble Biblical precepts. One of these stories, transmitted in variant Palestinian and Babylonian versions, tells of a Gentile, the chief magistrate of Ashkelon, Dama ben Nethina by name, who had in his possession a rare jaspis. One day, the jaspis, which was the stone of Benjamin in the ceremonial breastplate (ephod) of the High Priest, got lost, and the sages went to Dama and offered him 100 dinars for the jaspis he owned to serve as a replacement for the lost stone. (This detail, incidentally, places the story prior to the destruction of the Temple of Jerusalem, which took place in A.D. 70.) Dama agreed, but when he went to fetch the stone he found that the key to his strongbox was under the pillow of his father who was asleep. He did not want to disturb his father, and when he returned empty-handed the sages thought he was holding out for a higher price; they raised their offer to 200 and finally went as high as 1,000 dinars. After his father awoke, Dama went and fetched the jaspis, and the sages wanted to pay him the last price they had offered. But he refused to accept more than the original 100 dinars, explained the reason for the delay, and said, "I will not make a profit from honoring my father." The Talmudic sources also relate that all his life Dama never sat on the stone on which his father used to sit, and that after the death of his father he honored him as a god.

The honor and respect with which Dama surrounded his mother was perhaps even greater. On one occasion Dama, dressed in his gold-embroidered silken toga, was sitting among the Roman high officials, when his mother, who was not quite right in her mind, came up to him, tore his toga off his shoulder, spat in his face, and hit him over the head with her slipper. As she did this, she dropped the slipper, whereupon Dama picked it up and returned it to her. Rabbi Ḥanina, upon hearing of the exemplary behavior of the pagan Ashkelonite, said, "If a person who is not commanded to honor his father and mother behaves thusly, how much greater a duty it is for one who is commanded to honor them." [12]

In the same context the Babylonian Talmud goes on to tell stories about sages who knew no bounds in honoring their parents. Rabbi Abimi, we read,

had five sons, each of whom was an ordained rabbi, and yet when his old father, Rabbi Abahu, would come to visit him and knock on his door, he would
cry, "Yes, yes, I'm coming," and would run himself to the door to open it.
One day his father asked him for a drink of water, and while he was fetching
it, his father fell asleep. Thereupon he bowed down and stood before him
with the water in his hands until his father awoke. In the next sentence the
Talmudic text indicates the reward Rabbi Abimi received for his filial piety—
while he was thus waiting on his father, the interpretation of a formerly
baffling Biblical passage came to him. [13]

And the stories go on. Of Rabbi Tarfon (Tryphon) it is related that whenever his old mother wanted to climb into bed he would bend down so that
she could step on his back. Once he told this to his colleagues in the House
of Study, whereupon they said: "You have not yet reached one half of the
duty of honoring your mother. Has she thrown a purse of gold into the sea in
your presence and have you refrained from rebuking her?" [14]

According to the Palestinian Talmud, Rabbi Tarfon's mother took a walk in
her courtyard on the Sabbath, and her sandal broke. Thereupon her son
placed his hands on the ground before her feet so that she stepped only on
them, and not into the dust or mud of the yard. Once he fell ill, and when
the sages came to visit him, she said to them, "Pray for my son, for he
honors me overly." When they heard what he did, they said, "Even if he
would do a thousand times more, he would not have reached even half of the
honoring of a parent required by the Tora." [15]

Rabbi Joseph, upon hearing the footsteps of his mother, would say, "I am
getting up in front of the Shekhina who approaches," [16] thus equating his
mother with the personified Presence of God on earth.

In true hyperbolic fashion, Rabbi Yoḥanan, who had been an orphan since
birth, said, "Happy is he who has never set eyes on his parents," because (as
Rashi explains) "it is impossible to fulfill the duty of honoring them properly
and one is apt to suffer punishment for its neglect." [17]

The same feeling motivated Rabbi Z'ira, another orphan, to exclaim: "O, if
I could have a father and a mother! I would honor them and merit a share in
the Garden of Eden!" [18]

Of Rabbi Asi it is related that his old mother asked him for jewels,
whereupon he provided her with them. Then she asked him to find her a
husband, and he said he would try. "But he must be as handsome as you
are!" said his mother. Thereupon Asi felt constrained to leave her and moved
to the Land of Israel. Undaunted, his mother set out to follow him but died
on the journey. [19]

Since the Bible commands children both to fear and to honor their
parents, the Talmudic sages felt it necessary to define the meaning of these
two commandments. To fear the father, they said, means that one must neither stand nor sit in his place, nor speak in his stead, nor contradict him, nor

join with a scholarly opinion contrary to his. Honoring the father means to feed him, to give him to drink, to clothe him, to cover him, to provide him with shoes, and to help him go in and out of the house.[20]

The Ten Commandments promise long life as a reward for him who honors his father and mother. As we have seen above, Talmudic teachers felt that this was an insufficient reward for so great a *mitzva* (commandment) and found a way of interpreting the relevant Biblical verses so as to derive from them a divine promise of rewards both in This World and in the World to Come. Moreover, they found it possible to extend the reward for honoring father and mother to the children of the person who fulfills this great commandment, and even to his remote descendants. The Biblical exemplar whose progeny was thus rewarded was, according to the Talmudic teachers, none other than Esau. In the days of these sages, the Romans, whom they identified with Edom, and hence considered the descendants of Esau (just as Jacob was called Israel, so his brother Esau was called Edom), ruled Palestine and, as far as the sages knew, most of the world. This was a situation they could not easily accept. Did not their father, Isaac, bless Jacob and thereby make him, and in him his children, overlords over all peoples?

> Let peoples serve you,
> Let nations bow to you,
> Lord of your brothers!
> Let your mother's sons bow to you,
> Let your curser be cursed,
> Let your blesser be blessed! [21]

How then could now the sons of Esau-Edom be lords over the sons of Jacob-Israel?

Searching the Bible, the sages found what they were looking for: a Scriptural justification of the dominance of Rome in their contemporary world. They found, or rather concluded, that throughout those twenty years which Jacob spent in Paddan-aram, serving Laban for his wives and building up his fortune, Esau remained at home, thus fulfilling the great commandment of honoring his parents. Daily he went hunting, exposed himself to great dangers, so as to be able to provide his old father with the game he liked. He never entered his father's tent except in festal dress, for he said to himself, "My father is a king; it is not according to the honor of father that I come before him in anything but royal clothes." This was the ineradicable merit that Esau acquired for himself, enjoying great prosperity as long as he lived, and for his descendants who ultimately became the overlords of Israel and received dominion over the world. It was with reference to this mythical story that Rabban Shim'on ben Gamliel, president of the Great Sanhedrin, said, "All my life I served my father, and yet I did not serve him one hundredth as much as Esau served his." [22]

Let us conclude this section with one quotation to indicate the extent to which these Biblical and Talmudic traditions of honoring one's parents remained part and parcel of everyday life for the tradition-bound East European Jews down to the present time. A Jew from the *shtetl*, the East European Jewish small town, recalled:

> You cannot imagine the respect I felt for my parents. . . . There is a Jewish expression for it which explains it so well, *derekh erets* [lit. "way of the land," but meaning respectful demeanor] . . . . It is not fear. If it were fear, then the respect would be asked of the child, and my parents never asked for anything.[23]

Parents and Children

It is characteristic of the great value set by the Talmudic teachers on the close, harmonious, and warm relationship within the family that they not only considered the children duty-bound to honor their parents, but also vice versa. An instruction to this effect is transmitted in the name of two teachers, Rabbi Ami and Rabbi Asi: "One should always spend less than one's means on food and drink, dress according to one's means, and honor wife and children beyond one's means because they are dependent on him, and he is dependent on Him who spoke and the world was."[24]

A father's duties toward his children comprised, of course, much more than merely honoring them. He was responsible for their moral, mental, and material well-being. Foremost among the paternal duties was to teach one's son Tora and a trade (and, according to some sages, even the art of swimming), and to provide him with a wife and his daughter with a husband.[25] Rabbi Meir emphasized that a man should teach his son a clean and easy trade, while another, less known sage warned against letting one's son become a donkey driver, a camel driver, a shipper, a cattleman, or a grocer because these occupations were considered either dishonest or dangerous.[26] Needless to say, a father had to provide for his children, and especially so if they were engaged in the study of the Law (Tora).[27]

A daughter required special parental attention and supervision. From earliest Biblical times, the father was the guardian of the sexual morality of his daughter, and even of his widowed daughter-in-law.[28] Special Talmudic precepts obliged the father to provide his daughter with suitable clothes and to give her a dowry when she married.[29]

Since it was held that three were partners in the creation of each child, God, the father, and the mother,[30] children were considered a divine trust. This concept is beautifully illustrated by a story about the death of the two sons of Rabbi Meir, the famous second-century sage, and his learned wife, Beruria.

One Sabbath afternoon, while Rabbi Meir sat in the House of Study and held forth, his two sons died in their home. Their mother laid them out on the bed and covered them with a sheet. When the Sabbath ended, Rabbi Meir returned home and asked his wife, "Where are my sons?" "They went to the House of Study," she answered. He said, "I looked for them and did not see them." She handed him the *Havdala* cup, he performed the ceremony of saying farewell to the Sabbath, and then repeated his question. She said, "Occasionally they would go to such and such a place, and soon they will be back." She set food before him, and after he ate, she said: "Rabbi, I have a question to ask of you. Some time ago somebody left a trust with me, and now he came and asked me to return it. Shall I return it or not?" Rabbi Meir answered, "My daughter, if somebody holds a trust, does he not have to return it to its owner?" Thereupon she took him by the hand, led him upstairs, and removed the sheet from the bodies. When he saw their two sons lying dead, side by side, on the bed, Rabbi Meir cried and said: "My sons, my sons! My masters, my masters! My sons in conduct and my masters whose Tora lighted up my eyes!" His wife said: "Rabbi, have you not said just now that we must return the trust to its master? Thus, the Lord gave, and the Lord took away, may the name of the Lord be blessed." In this manner, said Rabbi Ḥanina, she comforted him, and his pain subsided.[31]

I presented this moving story in full to give an example of the kind of atmosphere which pervades Rabbinic literature and which had such a seminal influence upon Jewish family life throughout history.

In all this we have not yet touched upon what according to Jewish religious tradition is the most fundamental element in the relationship between parents and children: that of love. From the stories contained in the Bible we know that the Hebrew father had strong emotional ties to his children, and that, occasionally at least, he "loved not wisely but too well." Jacob "loved Joseph more than all his children, because he was the son of his old age,"[32] which preference almost cost Joseph his life at the hands of his jealous brothers. After he believed Joseph dead, Jacob loved Benjamin, his youngest.[33] David loved his son Absalom with an intensity which could not be diminished even by Absalom's rebellion against him, and which made him mourn excessively after Absalom's death.[34] An important element in fatherly love was compassion, which became proverbial in early Israel: "Like as a father hath compassion upon his children, so hath the Lord compassion upon them that fear Him."[35] Incidentally, the first half of this verse is recited frequently in Jewish prayers, so that the image of the compassionate father is deeply embedded in traditional Jewish consciousness.

Nevertheless, the love between mother and children eclipsed that between father and children. The mothers of Israel, Sarah, Rebekah, Rachel, and Leah, played very important roles in the life of the patriarchal family and decisively influenced their husbands and children. It was at Sarah's initiative that Abraham "went in unto" her slave-girl Hagar, and that he later sent her away together with Ishmael, the son she bore to him.[36] Sarah's influence upon him was so strong that even after her death he "sent away" all the children by his later concubines, so as to ensure that Sarah's son, Isaac, would become his only legitimate and full heir. The whole life history of Jacob was determined by the fact that his father Isaac loved his brother Esau, while his mother "Rebekah loved Jacob." [37] It was Rebekah who managed to obtain her husband Isaac's blessing for her beloved son Jacob and subsequently dispatched Jacob to her brother Laban in distant Haran.[38] From the days of David comes a tantalizingly brief tragic vignette of Rizpah, a concubine of King Saul, whose sons were hanged by the Gibeonites, and who in an almost incredible display of motherly love guarded their bodies as they hanged from their gallows for several months, "and she suffered neither the birds of the air to rest on them by day, nor the beast of the field by night," until finally David had them buried.[39]

Just as a mother's love for her children continues after their death, so does the love of a son for his mother. After the death of his mother Isaac continued to mourn her for a long time, in fact, until the day he married Rebekah: "And Isaac brought her into his mother Sarah's tent, and took Rebekah, and she became his wife; and he loved her. And Isaac was comforted for his mother." [40] In a Psalm attributed to David, who lived some eight centuries after Sarah, the death of the mother still appears as the greatest grief a man can suffer: "I bowed down mournful, as one that mourneth for his mother." [41]

Motherly love figures prominently in the poetic imagery of the Hebrew prophets. In Jeremiah's words, Rachel, who in the intervening centuries attained the symbolic position of the mother of the entire Hebrew nation, commiserates with the bitter fate of her children: "Thus saith the Lord: A voice is heard in Ramah, lamentation and bitter weeping: Rachel weeps for her children, she refuseth to be comforted for her children, because they are not." [42] As long as the mother is alive, none can comfort as she. The mother, therefore, is taken as the prototype by God when He holds out the promise of His redemption: "Rejoice ye with Jerusalem . . . that ye may suck, and be satisfied with the breast of her consolations . . . ye shall be borne upon the side, and shall be dandled upon the knees. As one whom his mother comforteth, so will I comfort you. . . ." [43]

The Talmudic teachers, while scrutinizing every word of the Bible most closely, did not miss the general implications of the Biblical narratives either. In connection with the story of Joseph and his brothers there is a tradition attributed to Rav which reads: "Never should a father favor one of his children over the others: for it was because of a coat weighing two *Sela*'s which Jacob gave Joseph in excess of his other sons that Joseph's brothers became jealous of him, and the matter resulted in our forefathers' descent into Egypt." [44]

A hyperbolic story of a mother's adulation of her son is contained in the Palestinian Talmud. One day the mother of Rabbi Yishma'el went to the sages and said to them, "Reprimand my son Yishma'el because he does not give me due honor." Upon hearing this, the faces of our masters turned pale, and they said, "Can it be that Rabbi Yishma'el does not honor his parents?" And they asked his mother, "What did he do to you?" She answered, "When he returns from the House of Assembly I want to wash his feet and drink of the water, and he does not let me." They said to him, "Since this is her will, it is her honor." [45]

HUSBAND AND WIFE

The relationship between husband and wife, like that between parents and children, was considerate, respectful, and loving. The husband, of course, dominated his wife, as he did in all ancient Near Eastern societies, and the grand myth of Genesis 3 explains, among other things, why this should be so: it was the consequence of Eve's sin for which God condemned her, and in her all her daughters, to subservience to their husbands. [46] The language of the Ten Commandments makes it clear that a man's wife was considered his property, along with such other assets as his house, field, slaves, and animals. [47]

Yet from a very early time it was taken for granted that a husband owed his wife three obligations—he had to provide her with food, clothing, and cohabitation. These were the inalienable rights of the wife, which he had to give her; otherwise she could leave him. [48] Since Biblical law made the wife the subordinate partner of the couple, the sages of the Talmud concentrated on recommendations directed to the husband to the end of making him as pleasant and attentive toward his wife as possible. They knew no bounds in emphasizing the value of the wife for the husband. Thus Rabbi Tanhum in the name of Rabbi Hanilay said, "A man who has no wife lives without joy, without blessing and without goodness," to which Palestinian teachers added, "and also without Tora and without moral protection." [49] Rabbi Hama b. Hanina said, "As soon as a man takes a wife, his sins are stopped." [50] Rabbi Ele'azar capped it all by announcing succinctly, "A man who has no wife is not a man, as it is written 'male and female created He them, and blessed them, and called their name Adam' i.e., 'man' "; only with his wife does a man deserve the name "man." [51]

The Talmudic teachers extolled the devotion a man must have for his wife and children: "He who loves his wife as much as himself, and honors her more than himself, and trains his sons and daughters in the right way, and marries them as they approach maturity, about him the Bible says, 'And thou shalt know that thy tent is in peace, and shalt visit thy habitation and miss nothing.' " [52]

Even if a woman was quarrelsome, her husband surrounded her with attention. "His wife used to vex Rabbi Ḥiyya; nevertheless when he would find something, he would wrap it in his scarf and bring it to her. Rav said to him: 'But she vexes you, O master!' He answered: 'It is enough that she brings up our children and that they [i.e., wives, in general] save us from sin.' " [53]

A common saying among the sages was, "If your wife is small, bend down and whisper into her ear," [54] meaning, of course, that a man should be kind to his wife. In general, a man must never be imperious in his house, but must always speak in a friendly tone to all members of his family. [55] He who honors his wife will be rewarded with riches. [56] According to Rabbi Akiba, the personified Presence of God dwells in a pure and loving home. [57] Rabbi Yoḥanan said, "He who divorces his wife is hated by God," and, according to Rabbi Eleʿazar, "If a man divorces his first wife, even the altar sheds tears." [58] The ideal thus was for man and wife to remain together for life. According to Rabbi Yoḥanan, "If a man's first wife dies, it is for him as if the Temple had been destroyed in his lifetime," while others added that the world becomes dark for him, his steps become shortened, and his mind collapses. [59] They also taught, "The man dies only for his wife, and the woman dies only for her husband," [60] meaning that the death of a person afflicts most deeply the surviving spouse.

FAMILY COHESION

In addition to the love and respect which characterized the relationship between parents and children and between man and wife, and which could not fail to impress every student of the Bible and the Talmud, the same sources contain ample data reflecting the importance of the family as a whole. Even if he stopped studying, the Jewish youth and adult listened to the reading of the Pentateuch in the synagogue every Sabbath morning and thus heard the stories and laws repeated year after year. He listened and heard again and again that the ancient Hebrew family was a large kin group—exemplified by the family of Jacob, which consisted of no less than seventy souls at the time they went down to Egypt—that the married sons lived together with their father, and that even after they had wives and children of their own they continued to recognize their father as the head of the family. He learned, from reading or listening to the historical accounts and the laws of the Bible, that members of a family were united by the strongest ties of blood and kinship; that if one was murdered, his closest kinsmen had the duty to avenge his death by acting as his *go'el*, literally "redeemer," or "avenger" of blood. He would also learn that, from early times down to the days of King David, the family determined what was right and wrong, made its own laws, and administered justice, including capital punishment.[61] He would understand that a man was required to purchase the freedom of his relative sold into slavery, that the property of a deceased kinsman which had been alienated because of poverty had, likewise, to be redeemed,[62] and that, if a man died childless, his brother was required to marry the widow.[63] And he would learn that the family was the religious unit, whose members originally joined together for the offering up of sacrifices, and that some of the family celebrations which he could still observe in his own parental home went back to Biblical times.[64]

These readings gave him a true sense of the age-old traditions of Judaism in general and taught him what was meant by a tightly knit family life. Thus he could fully appreciate what the Psalmist meant when he sang, "Thy wife shall be as a fruitful vine in the innermost parts of thy house, thy children like olive plants round about thy table. Behold, surely thus shall the man be blessed that feareth the Lord." [65] Or when he praised brotherly love: "Behold, how good and how pleasant it is for brethren to dwell together in unity." [66] If he was of an analytical bent of mind, he observed that all the larger social units among the ancient Israelites—the clan, the tribe, and even the nation as a whole—were considered extensions of the family; but even if he was not, he knew, because it was a most elementary part of the tradition imparted to him in childhood, that the Hebrews, and the Jews, as they came to be called from the end of the Biblical period on, were the patrilineal descendants of Abraham. If he later proceeded to a study of the Talmud, he would read that according to Rava, "the family of the father counts as the family, the family of the mother does not count as family," [67] which taught him that descent was reckoned patrilineally also in Talmudic times. Then he would come across the many warnings issued by the Talmudic sages to the effect that a man should marry a woman from a good Jewish family lest his children do not turn out well, because, as one statement has it, "most sons resemble their mother's brothers." [68]

THE HOME

The Jewish home, which from Biblical days on was central to much religious observance, became by Talmudic times enveloped in a veritable aura of sanctity. The Mezuza on the doorpost signified that the home as a whole was dedicated to the observance of the Law.[69] The everyday routine of the household, under the aegis of the mother, became the expression of one of the most ubiquitous religious observances—that of the dietary laws. The daily prayers could be recited in the home as well as in the synagogue, and some of them, such as the "bed-time Sh'ma'," could be said only in the home, as could numerous benedictions before and after meals and on other occasions. The Sabbath was celebrated more in the home than in the synagogue. Only some of the features of its home observance can be indicated briefly: the kindling of the Sabbath candles by the mistress of the house, who mystically became identified with the Queen Sabbath; the blessing of the children by the father, who lovingly placed his hand upon their bowed heads and recited the age-old words, "May God make you like Ephraim and Manasse" for his sons, and "May God make you like Sarah, Rebekah, Rachel, and Leah" for his daughters; the joint singing of the *Z'mirot*, Sabbath songs, by the whole family; the solemn *Qiddush*, Sanctification, over the silver cup of wine of which the children too were allowed to take a sip; the festive clothes worn and the exceptionally fine meal consumed; the spark of love—carefully hidden, of course, from the children—arcing between husband and wife in anticipation of their marital union traditionally confined to Sabbath nights; and finally the hour of spiritual union next day between the father and his son, who would recite what he had studied in the *Ḥeder* in the course of the preceding week.

All this made the Sabbath infinitely more than a weekly day of rest—it made it a great day of holiness, of nearness to God (whose resting on the seventh day of Creation the Sabbath both commemorated and imitatively reenacted), of elevation high above the worries and profaneness of the week, of festive mood in which one was conscious of being endowed with an "additional soul" (*n'shama y'tera*). When, at the end of the Sabbath, the *Havdala* ("Separation") ceremony was performed, with the smallest child holding high the big, braided, multicolored candle whose flame was extinguished in the overflow of the wine cup, and the tall turret-like silver box with the aromatic spices made the rounds of the whole family, the sadness over the departure of the Queen Sabbath was mitigated by the lingering memory of the spiritual nourishment which one had absorbed and which gradually, in the course of the week, became replaced by the anticipation of the next Sabbath.

Festive meals in the home were part of every Jewish holyday, taken, most importantly, in the evenings after returning from the synagogue. Outstanding among these was the Seder (lit. "order"), a ceremonial family meal on the eve of the first and second days of Passover, preceded and followed by much chanting and singing, and comprising several dishes of special commemorative and symbolic significance. Again, as at the *Havdala*, the youngest child in the family had a special role in the Seder: as soon as he was old enough to read or to memorize, it was his privilege to ask the "Four Questions," in answer to which the head of the family would recite the miraculous story of God's deliverance of the Israelites from Egyptian slavery. And, as if calculated to keep the interest of all the children alive to the very end of the songful ritual, they were traditionally expected and enabled to "steal" the *Afikoman*, one-half of a *Matza*, which they then returned to the father only after he promised to give them whatever present they stipulated—since without distributing and eating the *Afikoman*, the Seder could not be concluded.

Sukkot or Tabernacles was another holiday which ever since Biblical times has been celebrated in the home and in which children took an active part. In commemoration of the wanderings of the Israelites in the desert, during which they lived in tents, every Jewish family was commanded to build a *Sukka* (booth) in the courtyard (or, failing this, on an uncovered balcony or roof) of its home, and to take all its meals in it for the eight (originally seven) days of the holiday. The roof of the *Sukka* must consist only of twigs, but there is no limitation as to its decoration with flowers, garlands, tinsel, colored paper cut into stars and chains, and so on. The building and decorating of the *Sukka* used to occupy the whole family for four full days, from the end of *Yom Kippur* (Day of Atonement) until the onset of the Sukkot holiday.

Purim, commemorating the story of Queen Esther, was primarily a children's holiday. In the synagogue, during the reading of the Biblical Book of Esther, the children were allowed to make as much noise as they could with the wooden rattles provided for them by their parents for the occasion. At home, they would don fanciful costumes and, representing Queen Esther, her uncle Mordecai, King Ahasuerus, the evil Haman, and others, would perform Purim-plays. Presents would be given to them by parents and relatives in appreciation of their efforts. On this joyous holiday it was also the custom of families to send presents to one another, with the children acting as messengers.

Hanukka, the only traditional holiday of post-Biblical origin, commemorates the cleansing of the Temple of Jerusalem and the restoration of the sacred services after the victory of the Maccabees over their oppressors, the Syrian Greeks, in 164 B.C.E. It lasts eight days, during which every evening one more candle is lit in the family's Hanukka-lamp. At the light of the candles, after singing the traditional *Ma'oz Tzur*, the children play with the *dreydel* or *trenderl*—the small, four-sided wooden top marked with four Hebrew letters, the initials of the four Hebrew words meaning, "A great miracle was there." Depending on how the top fell, he who spun it won or lost; however, the stake usually consisted of nothing more than a few walnuts.

In addition to these annual holidays, the home was the scene of important family celebrations and observations marking the birth of a child, the circumcision of a boy on his eighth day, the redemption of the firstborn son, the day on which a boy started to go to the *Ḥeder*, his *Bar Mitzva* at the age of thirteen, the marriage of a son or a daughter, and, of course, death and burial. In all these, not only the immediate family but all the close and even the distant relatives were involved. In participating in such events, the growing children got firsthand demonstration of the importance of the family and the home.

These, then, were the rules and tales of conduct between parents and children and between man and wife contained in the Bible and the Talmud, the two prime sourcebooks of Jewish religion, education, and conduct for some fifteen centuries. The Talmudic laws and rulings were successively codified from the eighth to the sixteenth centuries by great Jewish scholars known as *Posqim* or "decisors." Their codes were intended to make the *Halakha* more easily accessible to the average learned Jew; and as a result of their works, the Talmudic law remained a practical guide for Jewish life until the Enlightenment.

What the laws prescribed and the stories described carried divine sanction: no sane person would deny that it was his religious duty to obey the first and to try to emulate the second. Together they reflected, and determined once and for all, the specific Jewish variant of family life, which in turn shaped the Jewish mind and became a basic factor in Jewish survival.

I have purposely used the past tense in describing the role the home played in the religious life of the Jews, because, as far as the majority of the Jews of today are concerned, almost every observance touched upon is now a thing of the past. Except for a minority of Jews who are Orthodox, none, or almost none, of the rites and ceremonies which made the Jewish home as important a center of religious life as the synagogue had survived. This desacralization of Jewish home life (and Jewish life in general) was a result of the Enlightenment.

The Family Today

With the onset of the Enlightenment, more and more Jews were deprived of the knowledge of the Jewish sources and with it of the possibility of molding their lives after old exemplars and prototypes. Yet even when the access of the children and youngsters to the Bible and Talmud had become limited, the atmosphere of the home, permeated for centuries by the lofty ideals of parental responsibility for the children and filial devotion to the parents, and by the mutual love which was the ground for everything else in the parent-child and husband-wife relationship, persisted and continued to influence the budding personality of the young generation. The figure of the Jewish mother, with her total devotion to her husband and children, has long been a central theme in Jewish folklore and folk consciousness and has remained a source of strength and confidence to her whole family, quite in contrast to its caricature, which has been popularized recently by several modern American Jewish novelists. Parental concern for the well-being, development, studies, marriages, and careers of their children is, unquestionably, more general and more intense among the Jews than among any other ethnic group. Hence, in any country in the world, relatively more Jewish than Gentile children grow up in a family atmosphere which provides them with emotional security and, as a non-Jewish American sociologist put it, "enables them to surmount the pressures of a competitive and sometimes prejudiced world." [70]

Another residual consequence of the close family relations which have characterized Jewish life throughout history is the greater cohesion among adult members of the family who do not live in the same home. A 1952 survey carried out in the Detroit area found that no less than 75 percent of the Jews reported weekly visits with relatives, as against only 56 percent of white Catholics, 49 percent of white Protestants, and 46 percent of black Protestants.[71] This is not a sufficient basis to draw conclusions, but it is an indication of greater family interaction among Jews than among other Americans.

But it is much more than emotional security and cohesion that the Jewish family gives to its children. The Jewish home, to a greater extent or more frequently than the non-Jewish, imbues them with the values which, in traditional circumstances, secured Jewish survival, and which, in a modern industrialized and urbanized environment, are necessary for advancement. It encourages, and channels them toward, studiousness. It influences the aspirations of the growing children toward professional, technical, managerial, and administrative careers, which in the early 1970's were the occupations of 70 percent of all employed American Jewish males.[72] It can thus be taken for granted—at least in America and Israel, which between them account for some two-thirds of all the Jews in the post-Hitler era—that the present-day Jewish occupational structure is largely the result of the influences, conditionings, and expectations prevailing in the Jewish home environment and thus ultimately the outcome of age-old traditional Jewish values.

To recapitulate, these traditional values were passed on within the family from generation to generation. As Rabbi Louis Isaac Rabinowicz put it, the

> constant insistence upon the value of the family as a social unit for the propagation of domestic and religious virtues and the significant fact that the accepted Hebrew word for marriage is *kiddushin*, "sanctification," had the result of making the Jewish home the most vital factor in the survival of Judaism and the preservation of the Jewish way of life, much more than the synagogue or school.[73]

To which we may add that the specific way in which the Jewish home was constituted and functioned, coupled with the central importance it had in molding the Jewish child's personality, ensured the continued adherence to those values of intellectual endeavor which have survived among the Jews down to the present, long after the decline of religious observances and other Jewish traditions.

2. An Excursus on Sex

A tradition which assigned such a high value to the family inevitably had to have a most positive view of sex—as long as it was exercised legitimately between man and wife. And this, indeed, is what we find in the Bible and the Talmud, whose influence was decisive in molding the Jewish psyche throughout history.

THE VALUE OF SEX

The importance of married life is underlined in the great Biblical myth-cycle of Creation. After creating man, God said: "It is not good that the man should be alone. I will make him a helpmeet for him." As soon as Adam saw Eve, he recognized that she was "bone of his bones and flesh of his flesh." Thus, woman proved irresistible to man; for her sake he, for all times, would "leave his father and mother and cleave to his wife and they shall be one flesh." [1] In Talmudic times, the rabbis were convinced that a man cannot and must not live without a woman, nor a woman without a man, that without a wife there was neither gladness nor bliss in life, and that "a man who had no wife is not a man," that is to say, that he was an incomplete being. Therefore, it was held that it was forbidden for a man to live without a wife. [2]

The view that a man achieved full human stature only if he had a wife was applied by the Spanish medieval Kabbalist Moses de Leon to the godhead (in whose image man was created!), and he taught that without the Matronit, God's divine consort, God was not King, nor great, nor potent. This was the ultimate extension into the divine realm of the Kabbalistic principle that "blessings are found only where male and female are together." Moreover, in the Kabbalistic view, the sexual act itself was elevated to cosmic significance: when the learned men have union with their wives, they do so in imitation of the union between the Supernal Couple. But even more than that. When a pious couple performs the act, by doing so it sets in motion all the generative forces of the mystical universe and causes God the King and his consort the Matronit to unite and to give birth to human souls and angels. [3] No greater accolade of the married state and of the sex act than this could be invented by the human mind.

From the Biblical, Talmudic, and rabbinic references to sexual customs one can piece together a general picture of the sex life of the ancient Hebrews, and of their views as to the value of sex, what sexual acts were forbidden and what allowed. As for the appreciation of sexual pleasure, the following pithy saying by one of the Talmudic sages sums it up: "Three things are a semblance of heaven: the Sabbath, sunshine and intercourse." [4]

However, in a churchless and non-hierarchical religion such as Judaism, in which every rabbinic scholar exercised authority to the extent to which his decisions were accepted by others, we cannot expect to find a uniform view on the value of sex. In fact the views of the rabbinical authorities on sex varied greatly. Maimonides taught that all the prohibitions against illicit unions "are directed to making sexual intercourse rarer and to instilling disgust for it so that it should be sought only very seldom." Elsewhere, he repeatedly recommends moderation and modesty in copulation and in "all the habits consequent upon desire and anger," in eating and drinking, and in "all matters." [5] Evidently Maimonides, who was not only a strict halakhist and a great rationalistic philosopher, but also an outstanding physician and medical author (he wrote an entire book on sexual intercourse), regarded sex only from the doctor's viewpoint and saw it as a purely physiological process, akin to eating and drinking.

As against him, Nahmanides (1194–1270), who was an equally great rabbinical authority, asserted that "the act of sexual union is holy and pure" and that, since man was created by God with sexuality, "whatever He created cannot possibly be shameful or ugly. . . . When a man is in union with his wife in a spirit of holiness and purity, the Divine Presence is with them." [6] This view of Nahmanides, who was a Kabbalist, was undoubtedly influenced by those prevalent in the early Spanish Kabbala of his time which have been touched upon above. [7] Subsequently, the Kabbalistic concept of the sanctity of sex spread in all parts of the Jewish world, and the old Talmudic rule of sexual union between man and wife on Friday night became a generally accepted ideal and practice which gave a special glow to the observance and enjoyment of the Sabbath. [8]

LICIT AND ILLICIT SEX

Biblical legislation made a sharp distinction between illicit and legitimate sexual practices. The former were sharply condemned and prohibited; the latter, within the bonds of marriage and concubinage, approved and recommended. [9] Certain forms of illicit sex, subsumed under the category of "uncovering of nakedness," were considered to be among the gravest sins a man could commit and were punishable by death. [10] On the other hand, the legitimate performance of the sex act was considered a duty, which it was sinful to neglect. [11]

In both Biblical and Talmudic times the sexual needs of women were fully recognized; women were often represented as taking the initiative sexually, and husbands were instructed to satisfy the wives' sexual demands. In fact, for a woman to invite her husband to cohabit with her was considered a most meritorious act. A woman who did this was promised "to have children the like of whom did not exist even in the days of Moses." [12]

The sexuality of women was considered so strong that some Talmudic rabbis opined that a woman would rather live in poverty and have sexual license than have ample means and live in chastity. Others held that a man

who teaches his daughter Tora opens for her thereby the door to licentiousness, because she is apt to utilize her knowledge of the Law for shrewdly cir-
cumventing the rules of chastity. [13]

The Talmudic sources also contain practical advice as to what to do in
order to ensure having male children, which has remained the great desire of
Middle Eastern parents to this day—the marital bed should be placed in
north-south direction; or the man should make sure that his wife has her
orgasm first; or he should have union with her twice in succession. [14]

Judging from the many Talmudic interdictions, the libido of the ancient
Jews was readily aroused. The sight of any exposed part of a woman's body
was considered a well-nigh irresistible temptation for a man. Various passages contain warnings against looking at the arms of a woman while she
launders, her legs while she crosses a stream, her hair, or even her little
finger. Nor was one supposed to touch a woman's hand or listen to her singing. [15] Women, when out of doors, had to wear garments which modestly hid
the contours of their bodies, but even so men were forbidden to walk behind
a woman in the street lest they be aroused to licentious thoughts or acts. [16] At
the mere sight of a woman a man could be overpowered by violent desire for
her, which condition, according to the contemporary doctors, could only be
remedied by enabling him to cohabit with her, or, at least, by letting him
see her naked. The rabbis, however, flatly forbade such a man even to talk to
her across the fence; others went so far as to warn against chatting with any
woman. [17]

These Talmudic opinions were given legal force by Maimonides, who held
that winking at a woman, or gesturing to her playfully, or even admiring her
beauty or smelling her perfume were sinful acts which were punishable by
flogging. [18] Of course, one must not overlook the fact that Maimonides lived
in a Muslim Arab environment in which there was a considerable amount of
segregation between the sexes. His extremely strict view on any contact between a man and a woman not married to each other seems therefore to be
colored to some extent by Muslim influences.

The libido of outstanding men was believed to be more powerful than that
of the common folk, which was expressed in the saying, "The greater the
man the greater his evil inclination." [19] While the expression "evil inclination," which is the common Talmudic term for libido, seems to indicate a
generally condemnatory attitude to the sex urge, this, in fact, was not at all
the case. The sexual urge was evil only when it induced man to commit a
sinful sex act. It also did, however, prompt man to approved sexual activity
and even to several other constructive acts. That is, the rabbis used the term
"evil inclination" in precisely the same sense in which psychoanalysts use
libido: the driving force behind human action in general. Thus one rabbi,
Naḥman bar Sh'muel, is reported as having said, "Were it not for the evil in-

clination, no man would build a home, get married, beget children, and engage in commerce." Because of this constructive, culture-producing function of the "evil inclination," only with its emergence was the creation of the world completed, and when God saw it He pronounced it "very good." [20] Thus the Talmudists arrived at the paradoxical conclusion that the "evil inclination" made the world "very good."

However, the "evil inclination" had to be kept within legitimate bounds, and especially so in times of festive joy, such as the Sukkot celebration in the Temple of Jerusalem. At such occasions special precautions had to be taken lest the sexual urge overpower the men and women who thronged the great courtyard of the Temple. [21]

Despite all the limitations on contact between men and women, many sages had an eye for female pulchritude and enjoyed its sight. Once, while he was standing on the steps leading to the Temple Mount, the patriarch Shim'on ben Gamliel (second century C.E.) saw an exceedingly beautiful Gentile woman, whereupon he exclaimed, "How great are Thy works, O Lord!" And when his contemporary Rabbi Akiba saw the beautiful wife of the Roman governor Tinnius Rufus, he cried because he thought of her end, which was to rot away in the earth. [22] Others, however, taught that it was altogether forbidden to look at a beautiful woman, and even to glance at her many-colored dresses. [23]

At the age of eighteen a youth was supposed to marry; and if he passed the age of twenty without being married, he was living in a sinful state, unless he devoted himself to the study of the Law. [24] If a man remained a bachelor, he was in general considered to be living a life of unchastity; in the rare case that a bachelor led a chaste life, God Himself proclaimed his chastity daily. [25]

While love was to be more than mere passion, [26] cohabitation was a duty which a man owed his wife just as he owed it to her to provide her with food and clothing. [27] The frequency of cohabitation depended on the husband's occupation: men of leisure ("idlers") had to cohabit with their wives daily; workers, twice weekly; donkey drivers, once a week; camel caravaneers, once in thirty days; seafarers, once in six months. As for scholars who devoted themselves to the study of the Law, they must cohabit with their wives every Sabbath night. [28] From its Talmudic source these instructions were taken over by medieval Jewish law codes, down to the last one, the *Shulḥan 'Arukh*, compiled in the sixteenth century, which, however, makes the fulfillment of these marital duties contingent upon the husband's strength. [29]

A wife, on her part, must not refuse cohabitation; if she does, this is a ground for divorce, as is the husband's failure to fulfill his marital sexual duty. But a man must not coerce his wife to cohabit with him. [30] The Talmudic rabbis considered every smallest detail in connection with the sex act important enough to pay attention to it and to advise on the right way of doing it. Thus the times, positions, places, lighting, behavior, etc., proper for cohabitation are all discussed and decided on in the sources.[31]

In fact, proper conduct before and during sexual intercourse was considered such an important issue that the Talmud reports of a scholar, Rav Kahana, that he hid under the bed of his master Rav to be able to observe him in the act: "He heard him chatting and joking with his wife and doing as he required." At this point Rav Kahana could not keep quiet and exclaimed, "One would think that you had never tasted of this dish before!" Taken aback, Rav reproached him: "Kahana, is that you there? Get out! It is rude!" But Kahana, not at all embarrassed, said, "It is a matter of Tora, and I need to learn." [32] Some warnings against irregular practices notwithstanding, the prevalent view was that "a man may do whatever he pleases with his wife." [33] In the *Shulḥan 'Arukh*, its Sephardi author Joseph Caro recommends great restraint during intercourse (although he permits conversation on sexual matters in order to increase the man's desire). However, his contemporary Moses Isserles, who adapted the *Shulḥan 'Arukh* to Ashkenazi use, comments: "It is permissible for a man to do with his wife whatever he wishes. He may have intercourse at any time he wishes, and he may kiss any part of her body he wishes, and he may mount her in the usual manner or in an unusual manner." But then he adds, "Although all these things are permissible, he who sanctifies himself by avoiding that which is permitted to him is considered holy." [34]

The importance attached to sex was inevitably accompanied by a concern about the waning of male potency. This, in turn, led to the use of various remedies which were believed to increase both a man's desire and his performance, among them the mandrakes, saffron mixed in wine, myrrh, and balsamum. The contemplation of lewd pictures was also known to increase the libido.[35] Voluptuous thoughts during the day, or sleeping on one's back, were believed to result in nocturnal emissions.[36]

The Biblical dichotomy between licit and illicit sex was greatly elaborated in the Talmudic period. The Talmudic specifications, in turn, became incorporated into the medieval halakhic codes, the last one of which, the *Shulḥan 'Arukh*, formed the basis of the nineteenth-century handbook of Jewish Law, the *Qitzur Shulḥan 'Arukh*, referred to at the beginning of this chapter. Thus, until the Enlightenment, the sexual conduct of all the Jews, and after it of those who remained faithful to Orthodox tradition, was governed by rules which were laid down in Biblical and Talmudic times.

DEFERRED GRATIFICATION

What the careful dichotomy between licit and illicit sex amounted to was a pattern of deferred gratification. On the one hand, there was the insistence on the pernicious nature of all extramarital sex, which had to be avoided at all costs. Incest and its related offenses were regarded in particular as constituting a category of mortal sin, as great as idolatry and bloodshed, from which one had to abstain even if it meant giving up one's life, and which caused the national catastrophe of the destruction of the Temple. On the other, there was the equally strong emphasis on the duty to engage in the sex act within the bonds of marriage, at least at stated intervals, and the entirely positive view of the pleasure one derived from it. These rules demanded that one desist from gratifying the lust which could be aroused by the sight of exposed parts of a woman's body, by erotic thoughts, or by the enticements of harlots. They demanded that unmarried young men forego sexual gratification altogether until marriage. And even in married life, it was required that a man refrain from having intercourse with his wife for twelve days during each of her menstrual cycles.[37] Thus the Jew's sexual life, which he was commanded to enjoy, was in effect a lifelong training in deferring gratification. The psychological effect of observing these rules for many generations was that the requirement to defer sexual gratification became internalized.

The same process took place in many other areas of life, so that deferred gratification became the typical Jewish attitude and guiding principle of existence. To do something here and now, not because one enjoyed the act itself but because it would bring about future rewards—and, conversely, to desist from things which would produce immediate pleasure for the sake of a later and greater good—these were among the fundamental demands of moral life put by the great Hebrew prophets to their recalcitrant contemporaries. From Talmudic times on, deferred gratification has, in effect, become the basis of demeanor and conduct. The relationship of man to man, within and outside the family; the relationship of man to God; the devotion to studying the Law; the performance of "works of charity"; and many other values incumbent upon the Jew—all this presupposed, and was made possible by, the internalization of deferred gratification, by subordinating the present for the sake of a greater, better future. To the Jewish mind, the proverb about a bird in the hand would have appeared childish. The Jew was convinced that it was better, infinitely better, to work at the chance of getting the many birds which, he knew, nested in the bush of the future.

Deferred gratification is the psychological mechanism which made it possible, inevitable, for the Jew to hold on to the hope of the coming of the Messiah through two millennia of painful Diaspora life. Jewish Messianism was but the enlargement to national dimensions of the individually internalized conviction that one must bear hardships in the present so as to reap rewards in the future. For the individual, the time of future rewards was either later in life, or in afterlife, or vicariously in the achievements of one's children. For the people as a whole, it was the Days of the Messiah, the great futurity, which, although it never arrived, was always just around the corner. In this eschatological view of deferred gratification, the suffering of the present, of the Exile, was a necessary precondition to the triumph of the future. And just as the certainty that the individual reward would come kept the individual Jew working at his unavoidable and self-imposed tasks, so the conviction that redemption was a fact of the future made Jewish survival in every doleful present a matter of preordained destiny.

In modern life, deferred gratification is a hallmark of middle-class, as against lower-class, outlook. This was brought out clearly in a study carried out among Israeli children aged six to ten years, who were partly of Oriental Jewish and partly of European Jewish parentage, and of either middle-class or lower-class background. No ethnic differences were manifested, but it was found that lower-class children preferred immediate gratification (they opted for taking a small chocolate bar immediately rather than wait for a week and get a much larger one), while middle-class children preferred delayed gratification and made the opposite choice.[38] It so happens, of course, that the great majority of the Oriental Jewish families belong to the lower class, while the great majority of the European Jewish families even in Israel belong to the middle class. In the Diaspora, and especially in the West, almost all Jews belong to the middle class, which makes the traditional Jewish tendency to deferring gratification a practically general Jewish phenomenon.

MODERN JEWISH SEX PATTERNS

The extent to which these rules still influence the sex life of the Jews in the modern American and Israeli societies of the mid-twentieth century has become evident from a number of recent studies.

The Kinsey Reports touch upon Jewish sexual behavior only incidentally, but their findings are nevertheless instructive. Kinsey and his associates point out that the American systems of sex mores "certainly go back to the Old Testament philosophy on which the Talmud is based and which was the philosophy of those Jews who first followed the Christian faith." As a result of this chain of origins, "in many details, the proscriptions of the Talmud are nearly identical with those of our present-day legal codes governing sexual behavior." [39] Nevertheless, certain differences were found to exist between the Jewish and the non-Jewish Americans who were interviewed by Kinsey and his associates.

Thus it was found that as far as the weekly frequency of total sexual outlet was concerned in the thirteen-to-twenty age group of single males, the lowest was that of Orthodox Jews: they had a mean frequency of less than twice per week, as against close to two and one-half times a week for religious ("active") Protestants and "devout" Catholics. On the other hand, it was found that, in the same age group, among non-observant Jews, Protestants, and Catholics, the mean frequency was somewhat less than three times a week. That is to say, from adolescence to the age of twenty, non-observant Jewish and non-Jewish single males showed no difference in the frequency of total sexual outlet, but observant Jews were inhibited to a much greater extent than observant non-Jews.

From the age of twenty-one to thirty, the mean frequency of the total sexual outlet of single and married male non-observant Jews was higher than that of non-observant non-Jews; while from the age of thirty-one to forty, the frequencies of the two groups was about equal, with those of the Jews being somewhat lower.

The same kind of difference was found with regard to nocturnal emission: the unmarried Orthodox Jews had a lower frequency than the observant non-Jews, but the non-observant Jews had a higher one than the non-observant non-Jews.

The picture with regard to premarital and extramarital intercourse is rather complex. For one thing, the Kinsey data show that in the sixteen-to-twenty age group, surprisingly, Orthodox Jews had a slightly higher frequency of non-marital intercourse than non-observant Jews, and that in the twenty-six-to-thirty age group, the non-observant Jews had a frequency more than four times higher than the non-observant Protestants. As for marital intercourse, the non-observant Jews showed a slightly higher mean frequency than the non-observant Protestants. Homosexual outlet was, on the whole, of lower frequency among the Jews than the non-Jews and was extremely rare among Orthodox Jews.

Explaining the low frequency of sexual activity among Orthodox Jews (who are the least active of all groups studied both in regard to the frequencies of their total sexual outlet, and in regard to the incidences and frequencies of masturbation, nocturnal emissions, and homosexuality), Kinsey, et al., refer to the "pervading asceticism of Hebrew philosophy." It would be more correct to say that the low frequency of all forms of non-marital sexual outlet among Orthodox Jews is due to the cumulative effect of three thousand years of prohibitions of all forms of illegitimate sex, which to this day inhibits all such activities among Orthodox Jews while it channels their sex into the only legitimate and approved outlet—that of marital intercourse. It is regrettable that the Kinsey Report contains no data on the frequency of marital sex among Orthodox Jews. All it shows is that marital sex among non-observant Jews is more frequent in all age groups than among either observant or non-observant Protestants.

Kinsey and his associates are somewhat puzzled at the freedom with which a high proportion of the Jewish subjects recorded the details and discussed their own sexual histories, which, they find, "has surprisingly little relation to the extent of the overt activity in their individual sexual histories." [40] The analysis presented in this section should have made it clear that this freedom is the result of the age-old attitude to sex which has characterized the Jews ever since Biblical times, and which considered sex in an entirely matter-of-fact manner which can be discussed with the same openness as any other aspect of life, and which, like all those others, is a subject of religious and educational concern.

As for women, no significant differences were found between religious and non-observant, Jewish and non-Jewish, women in the weekly frequencies of masturbation to orgasm, dreams to orgasm, petting to orgasm, and premarital coitus, except that the last one was engaged in by non-observant Jewish as well as non-Jewish women with greater frequency than by their devout sisters. As far as marital and extramarital coitus is concerned, again no significant differences were found among the various groups. Homosexual contacts to orgasm by single females were less frequent among religious Jewish women than among non-religious Jewish, and both religious and non-religious Protestant and Catholic women.

As for total sexual outlet to orgasm of single women, devout Jewish women had lower frequencies than devout Protestant and Catholic women, but among the non-religious the Jewish women tended to have higher frequencies, especially in the twenty-six-to-thirty-five age group. Among married women there were no significant differences.[41]

Thus it appears that the sexual behavior of the American Jewish woman is more similar to that of the American Gentile woman of the same socioeconomic background than is the sex pattern of the American Jewish man to that of the American Gentile man. One can assume that the factors responsible for this greater similarity among the women lie in the historical position of the Jewish woman—she has never been exposed to religious indoctrination to any degree approaching that of the Jewish male. Hence she could not acquire the inner resources which have kept the Orthodox Jewish man from conforming with the sex mores of the Gentile environment. This differential factor must be invoked also with reference to the sexual behavior of Israeli and Iraqi Jews to which we now turn.

A study carried out in 1954 by Samuel Klausner and based on interviews with about fifty native-born Israelis (in their twenties or thirties) of Eastern European parentage from the middle and upper economic strata showed a number of differences when compared with the Kinsey Reports' findings on American males and females. The total sexual outlet from age eleven to twenty-five among the Israeli males was about the same as that of the American males. However, among the Israelis spontaneous orgasm and masturbation as the main form of sexual outlet was replaced by petting and intercourse as they approached their twenties, while among the Americans this changeover occurred only in the late twenties.

The total outlet of the Israeli females (same ages) was about the same as that of the Israeli and American males, but five times that of the American females. Klausner attributes these differences to the Israeli society and culture. The Israeli youth studied were, in their adolescence, members of youth movements in which boys and girls mixed freely and most activities could be carried on by either. Israeli youth culture was more independent of adult culture than was the American at the time of the Kinsey study, in the 1940's, and thus attempts by the adult community to restrict the sexuality of the youth were less effective than in America.[42]

While these findings indicate that the middle- and upper-class Israeli women of East European extraction have achieved sexual liberation and parity with the men of the same background, developments in the kibbutz took a different direction. While in the kibbutz there is no separation between the sexes in the dormitories or even in the shower room until the young people graduate from the *Mosad* (as the high school is termed) at the age of eighteen, in effect the boys and girls develop techniques of preventing exposure which amount to sexual segregation. Taboos and prohibitions in regard to sex play and sexual contacts are strictly observed, in a manner resembling the relationship between brothers and sisters in the conventional family. It is well known that marriages between men and women who grew up in the same kibbutz are rare.

The attitude toward premarital sex or sex play is negative. This is both the official position and that of the young people themselves. Sex without love is considered degrading. The expectation is that "true love," of which sexuality is a part, will be experienced upon reaching maturity, when it will lead to marriage. The picture is one typical of traditional Jewish deferred gratification in the sexual area.

A battery of tests administered by A. I. Rubin to kibbutz children, adolescents, and adults bore out these general observations. As for sexual differentiation—that is, awareness of and concern with the differences between the sexes—non-kibbutz Israeli and American children (age ten) showed no significant differences whatever, with girls superior in both groups to boys; but kibbutz children achieved a lower level of sexual differentiation than non-kibbutz Israeli and American children. Adolescents (age seventeen) in the kibbutz were found to be more repressed than their non-kibbutz peers and were "consciously opposed to immature expression in this area." However, once having reached maturity (age eighteen and one-half to twenty-one), the kibbutz-bred young men showed "relatively reduced impulse control and increased concern with heterosexuality and promiscuity" and "readily dropped their defenses" against sexuality.[43]

A comparison of Middle Eastern Jewish sex patterns with those of native Israelis of East European parentage, as well as with American sex patterns, has been made possible by a study of Klausner whose work was mentioned above. He interviewed sixty Iraqi Jews in Israel (all in their twenties and thirties) who belonged to the upper economic brackets, had completed secondary school in Baghdad (i.e., were an élite group, and hence far from typical of all Iraqi Jews, let alone other Middle Eastern Jews), and subsequently immigrated to Israel. The total sexual outlet of the Iraqi Jewish males was about the same as that of the Israeli-East European males and the Americans. However, the Iraqi males' total outlet peaked between the ages of sixteen and twenty, while that of the American males showed a gradually decreasing trend from the age of sixteen on. Intercourse with companions accounted for more, and with prostitutes far less, among the Americans than among the Iraqis. Masturbation rapidly declined after the age of eighteen among the Iraqis (in accordance with the prevalent Arab view which considers masturbation a shameful, "passive" form of sexual gratification),[44] while among the Americans it continued to be an important outlet into the later twenties.

Among the Iraqi Jewish females, spontaneous orgasm accounted for a remarkably higher percentage of the outlets than among the American. Intercourse was altogether absent, and petting began only about the age of eighteen and remained relatively negligible. Masturbation was engaged in at all ages (twelve to twenty-three). The total outlet was somewhat more among the Iraqi Jewish females than among their American sisters, but considerably less than among the Israeli-East European females.[45]

The sex pattern of these upper-class Iraqi Jews reflected that of the upper- and middle-class Muslims in Iraq and in the more conservative countries of the Middle East in general. Segregation of the sexes was still practiced, and great emphasis was put on female chastity. This, in practice, ruled out all premarital social sex for females with solitary sex remaining the sole source of satisfaction for them. At the same time, women were supposed to be highly sexed (this is a general assumption in Middle Eastern culture and the traditional justification of female circumcision in those Arab countries in which it is practiced),[46] and this cultural expectation had undoubtedly something to do with the higher share of spontaneous orgasms and masturbation among Iraqi Jewish females than among American females.

As for the Iraqi Jewish men, their sex life, too, was a reflection of the general Middle Eastern pattern, in which masturbation was considered shameful but visits to prostitutes were viewed as manifestations of virility,[47] in which petting or intercourse with lower-class females (such as serving women, etc.) was condoned, and in which any woman who could be seduced was fair game.

Summary

In sum, we find that Jewish sexual behavior is influenced, in the first place, by the Biblical and Talmudic sex mores which have been transmitted throughout the ages via two channels: the incessant study of the original an-

cient sources detailing rules and presenting the example of great men to be
followed; and the sequential halakhic codes based upon them. The last one of
these, the *Shulhan 'Arukh* (1565), is—as has been pointed out repeatedly—still being followed by Orthodox Jews for whom familiarity with it, or
(among the Ashkenazim) at least with its abridgment, the *Qitzur Shulhan
'Arukh*, is a religious prerequisite. Until the Enlightenment, this tradition
imposed upon all Jews rigorous restraint from all non-marital sexual outlet,
while it encouraged a ritually regulated practice of sex within the framework
of marriage as both a pleasure and a duty. Among Orthodox Jews these traditions are still effective.

The second source of Jewish sexual conduct in both historical and modern
times is the influence of the Gentile environment. This is clearly indicated
by the evident similarities between American Jews and American Christians,
and between Iraqi Jews and Iraqi Muslims. On the basis of these two examples, one can perhaps extrapolate and hypothesize that the sexual behavior of a Jewish group will be found to approximate that of its Gentile environment to the extent that it is influenced in general by the latter's culture. The
greater this influence, the greater the similarity in the sex pattern, while the
smaller this influence, the smaller the similarity and the more the Jewish
sexual behavior will conform to the one upheld as the ideal in the traditional
Jewish sources.

The two modern Israeli studies show that the specific cultural atmosphere
developed either among middle- and upper-class Jews of East European extraction or in the kibbutz has its clear-cut sexual concomitant: among the former, a sexual freedom of women equaling that of the men; and, among the
latter, a strong restraint on both sexes with a postponement of sexual gratification until about the age of twenty.

3. Education

In discussing the Jewish family it was necessary to refer repeatedly to education for the simple reason that throughout Jewish history it was always considered a religious duty for the father to provide proper education for his
children, first of all for his sons, but secondarily also for his daughters. Here
we shall proceed systematically, albeit rapidly, to show that education was a
prime concern and a central value in Jewish life from the very beginning.

BIBLICAL TIMES

In the earliest times, education meant using paternal authority to impress
children with the duty of obeying the commandments of God. Thus we read
in the Biblical story of Abraham that the Lord said to Himself, "I have

known him [i.e., I have singled out Abraham], to the end that he may command his children and his household after him, that they may keep the way of the Lord, to do righteousness and justice. . . ." [1] Subsequently, this instruction of the children came to include the explanation of the religious rites. When the Israelites in Egypt are commanded to offer up the Passover sacrifice, the description of the ritual concludes with the precept: "And it shall come to pass, when your children shall say unto you : What mean ye by this service? That ye shall say: It is the sacrifice of the Lord's passover, for that He passed over the houses of Israel in Egypt, when He smote the Egyptians, and delivered our houses." The same instruction accompanies the commandment of eating unleavened bread during the seven days of the Passover: "And thou shalt tell thy son in that day, saying: It is because of that which the Lord did for me when I came forth out of Egypt." Similarly, other festivals, rites, and laws are the subject of instruction to the children. [2]

The most important and most frequently recited Jewish prayer consists of six verses contained in Deuteronomy 6:4–9, known from its initial words as the *"Sh'ma' Yisra'el"* ("Hear, O Israel"), or the Jewish confession of faith. This is its full text as recited during the morning and evening prayers and in the reading of the bedtime Sh' ma':

> Hear, O Israel: the Lord our God, the Lord is One. And thou shalt love the Lord thy God with all thy heart, and with all thy soul, and with all thy might. And these words, which I command thee this day, shall be upon thy heart. And thou shalt teach them diligently unto thy children, and shall talk of them when thou sittest in thy house, and when thou walkest by the way, and when thou liest down, and when thou risest up. And thou shalt bind them for a sign upon thy hand, and they shall be for frontlets between thine eyes. And thou shalt write them upon the door-posts of thy house, and upon thy gates. [3]

When precisely this Biblical passage became the basic prayer in Judaism, we do not know; but by Mishnaic times (first century B.C.E. to second century C.E.) it was taken for granted that it was the religious duty of every Jew to recite it morning and evening. [4] Therewith, the teaching of "these words" (i.e., God's Law) assumed an importance equal to that of declaring the oneness of God and loving God.

Several Biblical passages make it clear that the father and the mother had equal shares in fulfilling the duty of instructing and teaching the children. [5] The legendary King Lemuel is represented as having received strict instruction in wisdom from his mother. [6]

Other Biblical commandments make it mandatory for the king and the leader of the people to study God's Law "in all the days of his life" so as to enable him "to keep all the words of this law and these statutes, to do them." [7] The words of God addressed to Joshua to this effect have subsequently become the classic and oft-repeated formulation of the duty to study the Law: "This book of the law ('Tora') shall not depart out of thy mouth, but thou shalt meditate therein day and night, that thou mayest observe to do according to all that is written therein; for then thou shalt make thy ways prosperous, and then thou shalt have good success." [8] For three thousand years thereafter this verse remained the finest and most succinct description of the Jewish attitude to study, observance, and worldly achievement.

Nor was the knowledge of God's Law, from the very earliest, confined to priests and leaders. A passage in Deuteronomy provides that, once the Children of Israel crossed the Jordan, they were to write on large steles "all the words of this law very plainly" for everybody to see, read, and study. [9] To make sure that the knowledge of the Law was kept alive in the mind of the people, the priests were commanded to "read this law before all Israel in their hearing," on the Feast of Tabernacles in every Sabbatical (seventh) year to "the people, the men and women and the little ones, and thy stranger that is within thy gates, that they may hear, and that they may learn and fear the Lord your God, and observe to do all the words of this law; and that their children who have not known, may hear, and learn to fear the Lord your God. . . ." [10]

A brief historical reference from the Book of Chronicles tells us that Yehoshaphat (870–846 B.C.E.), one of the early kings of Judah, actually carried out this commandment: he sent out princes of the royal family and priests and Levites, to teach "in Judah, having the Book of the Law of the Lord with them; and they went about throughout all the cities of Judah, and taught among the people." [11]

Before the end of the Biblical era the instruction of children passed from the hands of the parents to those of professional teachers whose importance is indicated, among other things, by the fact that they are referred to by no less than five terms. [12] The paternal relationship of the teacher to his pupils is shown in his addressing them as "sons": "Come, ye sons, hearken unto me, I will teach you the fear of the Lord." [13]

By the early second century B.C.E., the "House of Study" was an established institution, as we can gather from a passage in the apocryphal Hebrew Book of Wisdom of Ben Sira, known as Ecclesiasticus, whose author flourished about 170 B.C.E. In it the teacher of wisdom says, "Turn unto me, O you fools, and sojourn in my House of Study." [14]

The central purpose of all study was to achieve a right attitude to God and man. Without learning about God one would not be able to know and fulfill His will, nor relate properly to one's fellow men. Hence, "the fear of the Lord is the beginning of wisdom" and "the fear of the Lord is the beginning of knowledge." [15] The method of instruction consisted, to a great extent, of the recitation of historical occurrences—incidentally, an educational device which has remained in use in Jewish education down to the present time.

The method was celebrated in Biblical times in a type of psalm called *Maskil* or "instructional song," which praised the importance of teaching through history. Thus Psalm 44 begins:

> *For the Leader; a* Maskil *of the sons of Korah.*
> *O God, we have heard with our ears,*
> *Our fathers have told us:*
> *A work Thou didst in their days,*
> *In the days of old.*
> *Thou with Thy hand didst drive out nations*
> *And didst plant them in . . .*

A second example is contained in Psalm 78:

> *A* Maskil *of Asaph.*
> *Listen, my people, to my teaching,*
> *Bend your ears to the words of my mouth.*
> *I shall open my mouth with a parable*
> *Utter dark sayings of old.*
> *What we have heard and known,*
> *And our fathers have told us,*
> *We shall not hide from our children,*
> *But tell to the last generation*
> *The praises of the Lord and His strength,*
> *And the wondrous works He hath done.*
> *For He established a witness in Jacob*
> *And appointed a Law in Israel*
> *Which he commanded our fathers*
> *That they make them known to their children,*
> *That the last generation might know,*
> *The children that will be born should rise*
> *And tell their children.*
> *That they put their confidence in God*
> *And forget not the works of God*
> *But keep His commandments.* [16]

Here one has, in poetic form, the method and aim of education in the Biblical world: the deeds of the Lord are taught by father to son so that each generation may "keep His commandments." The method has worked throughout Jewish history and has been retained down to the present time as a major educational device for inculcating children with obedience to God's will. Among traditional Jews, knowledge of the past is still imparted as a means of identification on the part of the children with the ancestral Jewish people and as the framework for recognizing the obligatory nature of the commandments issued and elaborated fifteen to twenty-five centuries ago.

Thus studying itself remains a prime religious duty. Reciting the prayers is, in this view, a constituent element of study. The intrinsic identity between studying and praying was indicated as early as the first century C.E. when the synagogues were called "places for instruction" [17] and is attested to this day by the Judeo-Italian and Yiddish terms for synagogue, *scuola* and *shul*, which are derived from the Latin *schola* and the German *Schule*, meaning school. Another Yiddish term for synagogue is *besmedresh*, which comes from the Hebrew *Bet haMidrash*, meaning "House of Study."

TALMUDIC TIMES

The development of the Jewish school system from the first century on is a large and important subject which cannot be treated in the present context.[18] However, it should not be left without mentioning that the first two Jewish authors who wrote in Greek with the intention of presenting a picture of Jewish history and thought to the Hellenistic world, the historian Josephus Flavius and the philosopher Philo of Alexandria (both in the first century C.E.) point with pride to the education Jewish children received from the earliest age in the Law and traditions of their fathers.[19]

Nor should we omit the Talmudic objection to instructing girls in the Law, which has remained a characteristic feature of Jewish education down to the nineteenth century. A passage in the Mishna quotes Ben ʿAzay to the effect that "a man is obliged to teach his daughter Tora," but this is followed by the contrary opinion of Rabbi Eleʿazar, who said, "He who teaches his daughter Tora teaches her obscenity." [20] While the acceptance of this view excluded girls in general from all formal instruction,[21] there were always exceptions, and in every place and age there were educated, even learned, Jewish women. In fact, some sages went so far as to recommend the instruction of daughters in Greek because they regarded the knowledge of Greek language (and, probably, of Greek culture as well) an "adornment" for girls—in other words, a refinement or social accomplishment.[22]

In Talmudic times education meant primarily studying "the Law," Tora. To begin with, a child would study the Bible, with its Aramaic translation, the Targum; in many cases this did not render the Biblical text literally but paraphrased it, giving it a specific interpretation of its own. After this elementary phase of education, a select few went on to higher studies in a Talmudic academy. In them, the central subject of a study was still the Bible but the emphasis was on the interpretation given to the text by the teachers at whose feet the students sat, or by their predecessors, the venerated masters of earlier generations. As often as not, the point of departure was not the Biblical verse or phrase or word itself, which could be interpreted in different ways, but an idea a teacher had, such as a legal precept, or a moral law; this then was underpinned by finding a Biblical text which, with considerable virtuosity, was interpreted as proving the master's point. After a student had acquired a thorough familiarity with the teachings of his elders, he was ready, if he had the ability, to proceed to putting forward new interpretations of his own. If he did so successfully, he was ordained by his teachers and became a "Rabbi," or master, ready to pass on his Tora to younger men who would become his students.

This system had a built-in guarantee for the expansion of the Law. With every passing generation the body of knowledge increased, and finally the original principle of passing down the interpretation of the Bible only by word of mouth had to be abandoned. The "Oral Law" became so voluminous that even a student with the keenest mind could not memorize all of it. After one or two preliminary attempts by outstanding sages, finally Rabbi Y'huda the Prince codified the Oral Law about 200 C.E. in Palestine—and what he produced is the so-called Mishna.

The discussions in the Talmudic academies of Palestine and Babylonia continued; the Mishna was supplemented, augmented, and refined; Aggadic material was added; and so the G'mara came into being, codified in two independent versions, one in Palestine in circa 425, the other in Babylonia circa 500. The Mishna together with the Palestinian G'mara is known as the Palestinian or Jerusalem Talmud; the Mishna together with the Babylonian G'mara is the Babylonian Talmud. The latter is, after the Bible, the most authoritative and most venerated religious sourcebook of traditional Judaism. Until the Enlightenment it was the main, and almost the only, text studied in yeshivot, and throughout a pious Jew's lifetime.

Numerous Talmudic passages refer to the duty of the father to teach his son. We have already heard that he had to teach him Tora and a trade. The teaching of the Tora (the traditional Jewish Law in the widest sense) consisted, as early as Talmudic times, of the three subjects of Scripture, Mishna, and Talmud. The study of the Talmud had to comprise both *Halakha*, i.e., the strictly legal material, and *Aggada*, homilies, legends, stories, and other non-legal material which constitute a major part of the Talmudic text. Bible, Mishna, and Talmud had to be pursued each for one-third of the total time devoted to study.[23]

The nature of the *Aggada* can be illustrated by adducing samples relevant to our subject. The Talmudic sages not only considered studying a supreme value in itself, but also believed that it was a remedy for physical ills, as well as the means to overcome temptation. An oft-quoted Talmudic saying advises, "He who suffers from headache, let him study the Law." [24] As for temptation, this was objectified in the Talmud as "the Evil Inclination" (*yetzer hara'*), which was believed to assume, occasionally at least, a visible form. The antidote against it is Tora study: "The masters taught . . . The Holy One, blessed be He, spoke to Israel: My children, I created the Evil Inclination, and I created for it the Tora as a remedy. If you occupy yourselves with the Tora, you will not be delivered into its hands. . . . But if you do not occupy yourselves with the Tora, you will be delivered into its hands." In the school of Rabbi Yishma'el, it was taught: "My son, if that ugly one [i.e., the Evil Inclination] meets you, drag him to the House of Study: if it is like a rock, it will be ground to dust, and if it is like iron, it will break into bits." [25]

Aggadic also are the Talmudic passages which show that the sages considered the merit of a man who taught his son Tora so great that he counted in their eyes (or in the eyes of the Bible, as they put it) as if he had personally received the Tora on Mount Sinai, and as if he had taught it to his son's son, his son, and so forth until the end of all generations. Stories are told about the importance Talmudic sages attributed to taking a boy, not necessarily one's own son, to the House of Study: some would rush out from their houses, without even having put on the proper head covering, in order to lead a boy to school; others would not touch breakfast unless and until they came back from this important duty. Still other sages started their day with teaching a boy some new material and took breakfast only thereafter. [26]

MIDDLE AGES

The Talmudic principles of education, while emphasizing concentration on the Jewish Law or halakhic studies, did not exclude secular studies, which, as we saw in Chapter 5 on Jews and Hellenes, meant, in the first place, "Greek Wisdom." This tradition received a strong boost after the spread of Islam and with it Arab culture. The Jewish religious and intellectual leadership in the Arab countries recognized the value of the arts and sciences developed by the Arabs and actively and effectively participated in their cultivation. Some of the greatest physicians, philosophers, mathematicians, astronomers, etc., who wrote in Arabic were Jews, and Arabic poetry and grammatical studies profoundly influenced the Jews in writing Hebrew poetry and engaging in a grammatical study of the Hebrew language. [27]

These developments went hand in hand with the incorporation of secular subjects into the curriculum of Jewish schools in Arab lands. Two twelfth-century Jewish authors, Judah ibn Tibbon of Granada and Joseph ibn Aknin of Barcelona, detailed in their writings the subjects that should be studied in the schools. They consisted of the three R's, reading, writing, and arithmetic; the traditional Jewish religious subjects of Tora, Mishna, and Talmud; the relatively new Jewish subjects of Hebrew grammar, poetry, and philosophy of religion; and the secular subjects of logic, geometry, optics, astronomy, music, mechanics, medicine, and, lastly, metaphysics. The same writings also contain detailed rules as to the required qualifications of the teachers, rules of conduct for both teachers and pupils (among them, the teacher must look upon his pupils as if they were his own sons, and the pupils must show their teachers even greater honor than their parents), and advice as to the value of study—pupils should make the acquisition of knowledge an end in itself, and should pass no moment of the day or night in idleness.[28] Here we have, in a fully developed form, the extension of the Biblical-Talmudic principle of studying the Law as a religious duty, to the acquisition of general education as a supreme human value in itself.

Among Sephardi Jews and the Jews of Italy and Provence who were influenced by them, this attitude continued in the thirteenth and fourteenth centuries, as attested by the numerous writers who variously enumerated the "seven sciences" which must be comprised in the curriculum, insisted on having education placed on a scientific basis, and argued that faith must be founded on knowledge. Take, for instance, the argument of Joseph ibn Caspi (1297–1340), the Provençal Bible commentator, grammarian, and philosopher, who wrote no less than twenty-nine books, all of them in Hebrew, and all (except one dealing with logic and one with grammar) devoted to traditional Jewish studies. In one of his books, Caspi lays down the principles which should guide a believing Jew in undertaking secular studies:

> How can I know God and that He is one, unless I know what knowing means and what constitutes unity? . . . No one really knows the true meaning of loving God and fearing Him, unless he is acquainted with natural science and metaphysics, for we love not God as a man loves his wife and children, nor fear we Him as we would a mighty man. I do not say that all men can reach this intellectual height, but I maintain that it is the degree of highest excellence, though those who stand below it may still be good. Strive, thou, my son, to attain this degree; yet be not hasty in commencing metaphysical studies, and constantly read moral books.[29]

The basic principle followed by these authors, and, in general, by Sephardi Jewry whose views they both molded and expressed, was that knowledge must be sought wherever it could be found and that the Gentile provenance of a science, or even of moral teachings, should be no hindrance to their incorporation into the Jewish curriculum.

While this was the dominant viewpoint in the Mediterranean area, farther to the north, especially in northern France and Germany, among the Ashkenazi Jews, a diametrically opposed position developed. Here it was felt that any foreign influence was a menace to the traditional Jewish religion and way of life, and that its penetration must therefore be prevented. To be sure, there were aspects of the Gentile culture whose adoption by the Jews was not opposed or was opposed unsuccessfully. The most significant of these foreign influences was in the sphere of language. With the exception of a relatively short period, roughly from the sixteenth to the nineteenth century, the Jews everywhere spoke either the colloquial of their Gentile neighbors or a specific Jewish dialect of it. One of the first languages adopted by

Ashkenazi Jews was French, which they spoke in northeastern France and in the Rhineland. In fact, French received a sort of canonization by Rashi, one of the greatest Jewish scholars of all times, who lived in the eleventh century in Troyes (some eighty miles southeast of Paris); his Biblical and Talmudic commentaries contain thousands of French words in explanation of difficult Hebrew and Aramaic words.[30] Some French Jews even went so far as to write religious poems in Judeo-French.[31]

German came later, but its attraction proved more permanent. From the eleventh century on it replaced French as the Jewish colloquial in the Rhineland, and by the twelfth century Yiddish had emerged as "a distinct fusion language with Germanic as its main component."[32] With the migration of Jews from German lands to East Europe, Yiddish became the language of all Ashkenazi Jews who, it is true, constituted in 1300 no more than 15 percent (or 300,000) of world Jewry.[33] Only in about 1700 did Ashkenazi Jewry reach the 50 percent mark; but thereafter it multiplied rapidly while the number of the Sephardi and Oriental Jews first decreased, then remained stagnant until about 1900. About 1900, Yiddish was the language of almost 90 percent of all Jews.[34]

The ready adoption of a Germanic tongue by the Ashkenazi Jews contrasted sharply with their rejection of Germanic (or other Central and East European) cultural influences. True, at the time of the adoption of Yiddish by the Ashkenazi Jews, the culture of the countries in which they lived was much less advanced than the Arab culture to which their southern brethren were exposed, and, being less advanced, its attraction for them was weaker. True, too, their Gentile environment was hostile in many cases which was not conducive to the adoption of cultural influences. Still, it comes as a surprise to see how narrowly self-contained and self-enclosed Ashkenazi education was in the Middle Ages (which for Central and East European Jews lasted until the eighteenth or even nineteenth century). As Israel Abrahams succinctly put it, among the Jews of Europe outside Spain and Italy, "nothing but the literature of religion was considered worthy of study."[35] Despite this self-imposed limitation of the curriculum, the Ashkenazi Jews, for whom religious study was a foremost commandment, were much better educated than their Christian contemporaries who, with the exception of the clergy, were largely illiterate. On the other hand, the Jews shared with the Gentiles large areas of ignorance: they knew almost nothing about the physical world and natural phenomena, and the varied subjects which formed part of the school curriculum among the Sephardim remained utterly unknown to them. What did penetrate the world of the Ashkenazi Jews from their Gentile environment was a steady stream of superstitions, beliefs in demons and monsters, in dreams as omens, and in the efficacy of magic and folk cures comprising many items subsumed in German under the term *Dreckapotheke*.[36] The belief in the efficacy of these quack remedies was so great that rabbis rarely opposed them, even when they involved the ingestion of Biblically forbidden foods such as parts of a hare, a fox, a wolf, or other unclean animals. Even in Holland, where from 1500 on Sephardi influence was strong, the school curriculum in the seventeenth century consisted of nothing more than reading, Bible, Hebrew grammar, Talmud, responsa, and the halakhic code of Maimonides. And yet this limited course of study, to which six hours daily were devoted, was held up as an example to be emulated by the Jewish communities of Germany, Austria, and Poland.[37] In these latter countries Jewish education concentrated on the Talmud, compared to which even instruction in the Bible was secondary.[38] Although many rabbis spoke up against this system, it remained in force generally until the early nineteenth century and thereafter was changed only sporadically and gradually.

Yet whether the school curriculum was well rounded or confined to Jewish religious literature, education had one thing in common among Sephardim and Ashkenazim. In both divisions of the Jewish people it was predicated upon the conviction that to study was a primary duty of the Jew—whether the subject matter studied was limited to the old confines of "the four cubits of the *Halakha*" or was broadened so as to tap all the available resources of Jewish and Gentile learning. By the Middle Ages the old Jewish value of studying had become second nature to the Jews to such an extent that every Jewish father considered it his foremost obligation to see to it that his son studied, both at school and at home. Happy the Jew who had the means to enable his son or son-in-law to devote himself exclusively to studying the Law. Happy, too, the Jew who was able to help another Jew's son to study, even to the modest extent of sharing with him a meal once a week.[39] But woe to the Jew who was so poor that he had to let his son start working at an early age, depriving him thereby of the greatest value, duty, and joy of the Jew. In eighteenth-century Poland (as well as in other countries of East Europe) the economic conditions of the Jews were so bad that many of them were forced to stop studying after the first few years, during which they barely managed to learn enough to be able to read the Bible and the prayer book. In the prevailing value system of Judaism, these poor and ignorant Jews felt themselves utterly *déclassé*, worthless people who were unable to fulfill the central commandment of their religion. They tried, but in vain, to make up for what they lacked in learning by being very pious; but even that was practically impossible, for meticulous observance was feasible only for those who knew the Law, and without studying one could not know it. Little wonder that in this situation many took refuge in myriad superstitious customs, put their trust in amulets (*qame'ot*), and resorted to the help of the half-learned magic healers known as *ba'ale shem* (lit. "Masters of the Name"), who were believed to be capable of exorcising demons, invoking spirits, performing miraculous cures, and other marvelous acts with the "name" of God. When one of these healers, Rabbi Israel Ba'al Shem Tov, in response to the misery of the Jewish poor and ignorant masses, began to preach his revolutionary doctrine of Hasidism, the Polish Jews flocked to him and hailed him as a saint and a savior. The teachings of Rabbi Israel, or the BeShT, can be summed up again briefly: What God wants of the Jew is not that he devote himself to the study of the Law, but that he serve God with joy, with love, and with enthusiasm.[40]

The reaction of those who were not impressed by the teachings of the BeShT and his successors was typical. They took no exception to the tenet of loving God with joy and enthusiasm—these teachings, after all, had good Scriptural bases. But they were utterly alienated by the Hasidic claim that the study of the Law was not the central and most important Jewish duty. In their eyes, this denial shook the foundations of Judaism. Does not the Bible command the study of the Law "day and night," and does not the Talmud declare that the study of the Law equals all the other commandments? Soon, as shown in Chapter 8, the Jews of East Europe were split into two camps facing each other with a bitterness formerly unknown among Jews.

WOMEN'S EDUCATION

It was part of the Ancient Near Eastern heritage of the Jewish people that, until the Enlightenment, and with a few earlier exceptions (e.g., in Renaissance Italy), institutionalized Jewish education was reserved for men only. As I had occasion to point out, it was a Talmudic tenet that all positive religious commandments, the "do's," which were tied to time were obligatory only for men. This meant, among other things, that women were exempt from the duty of reciting prayers (which have to be said at definite times of the day, the week, etc.), and of studying the Law which was a Biblical commandment: "Thou shalt meditate therein day and night that thou mayest observe to do according to all that is written therein." (Josh. 1:8; cf. Deut. 6:7). That is to say, studying the Law, too, was tied to definite periods ("day and night") and hence its observance was not mandatory for women. Therefore, the reasons for learning to read did not apply to women. (The knowledge of writing was of secondary importance even for men, and in some very traditional Middle Eastern Jewish communities, such as that of the Yemenite Jews, while all men could read Hebrew, by no means could all of them write.)

While thus, in general, no schools or other educational facilities were provided for girls, this did not at all mean that women grew up ignorant. First of all, there were several commandments which applied to women in particular and which they were taught to observe (usually by their mothers) with great meticulousness. These revolved mostly around the women's menses, sexual intercourse, childbirth, the lighting of the Sabbath candles, the separation of the *halla* offering from the dough when kneading bread—to which were added many customs of an almost equally obligatory nature. In addition, women in many places went beyond what was required of them by the *Halakha*, learned to read Hebrew in order to be able to pray, and, once having mastered the art of reading, used it to read, for enjoyment as well as ethical uplift, works available in the language they understood, Yiddish in East Europe, Ladino in the Mediterranean lands. The most popular women's book, which served as the main intellectual fare of many generations of Yiddish-speaking women, was the *Tzene-rene* referred to earlier (cf. page 247). All in all, one can say that the average Jewish woman, while she had little education as compared to her much more learned husband or brother, was much better educated than her Gentile women neighbors.

What was psychologically more important than her own educational attainment was the immense pride the Jewish woman took in the scholarliness of her menfolk. It was through them that she fully participated in the study-centered religious life of the Jewish community, and that she identified with the world and values of learning. The women basked in the reflected glory of whatever scholarly eminence their fathers, brothers, husbands, and sons attained. While the women scrupulously observed whatever religious duties tradition imposed upon them, their prestige and standing in the community depended upon the scholarly reputation of their male next-of-kin. In the Middle Eastern Jewish communities, the situation was largely the same except that the lower degree of scholarliness which was generally the case among the men was paralleled by a lower frequency of literacy among the women. However, as far as the European Jewish woman was concerned, when the Enlightenment opened to her the doors to general secular education, she was both intellectually and emotionally ready to take the plunge and, in fact, not infrequently to beat her menfolk in the race toward the irresistible culture of the Western world.

MODERN TIMES

The emergence of the *Haskala*, the Jewish Enlightenment, in the late eighteenth century and its spread from Central into East Europe in the nineteenth, was one of the main factors that prevented a religious schism between Hasidim and Mitnagdim. Both felt threatened by the new wave of this secularistic movement. Faced with a common enemy, their own antagonism was, if not forgotten, at least put aside. Another development that reduced the differences between the two was that the old Jewish value of studying gradually reasserted itself in the Hasidic camp. The Tzaddiq (the Hasidic rabbi) was venerated because of his saintly piety which was the basis—following an ancient Talmudic prototype—for his ability to make God perform miracles for him. But the Tzaddiq had to be also learned: he had to know *Halakha*, because only by knowing the *Halakha* can one observe the

Law without which a man cannot be truly pious. He also had to know the *Aggada*, and primarily the great body of *musar* (ethics) literature, in which were laid down the guidelines to the Tzaddiq's moral saintliness, and to which each Tzaddiq, in turn, contributed. Thus it came about that the Hasidim, while still not concentrating on the study of the Law, devoted themselves more and more to studying the books containing the sayings or sermons (*d'rashot*) of the Tzaddiqs, or else descriptions of their lives and acts, such as the *Shivḥe haBeShT* or "Praises of the BeShT."

While the Hasidim developed a type of learning of their own which differed from that of the Mitnagdim, they both shared the concentration on Jewish religious studies to the exclusion of all secular education. Rare, indeed, was a secularly educated person among the Ashkenazi Jews prior to the Enlightenment. In the seventeenth and eighteenth centuries there were a very few Ashkenazi Jewish physicians and scientists, and none of them attained the stature of their Sephardi predecessors. Among the Ashkenazi rabbis, Elijah ben Solomon, the Gaon of Vilna (1720–97), is an exception in that he wrote, in addition to his numerous Biblical, Talmudic, and Kabbalistic studies, a few minor treatises on astronomy, trigonometry, geometry, and algebra, and a Hebrew grammar. For almost all the Ashkenazi Jews, education meant halakhic study, which commenced at the tender age of four in the *Ḥeder* (lit. "room"), as the elementary Tora school was called. The insistence of the average Ashkenazi father on sending his four-year-old son to the *Ḥeder* often bordered on fanaticism; it can only be understood in the light of the paramount importance attributed to education as the supreme parental religious duty. While the Enlightenment put an end to this type of *Ḥeder* education in large segments of the Ashkenazi world, in East Europe it survived in most places down to the present century.

In this connection I am reminded of a childhood experience of my father and my uncle Philip ("Feivel"), told to me by each of them separately. At five o'clock every morning, Grandfather, who by that time had been up studying the Talmud for an hour or so, would call out: "Yosel! Feivel! Get up!" Before he even finished his call, the five-year-old Yosel and the four-year-old Feivel had to be out of the bed, or else. On winter mornings it would be still dark when the boys set out for school, and Grandfather would give them a lamp to take along. The path to the house of the *Melamed* ("teacher") led across a brook spanned by a plank. One day, as the children set out for school, they found everything covered with a heavy blanket of snow, under which the plank disappeared. Trying to make their way across by the dim light of their lamp, the boys missed their foothold and fell into the water. Wet to their knees, with the lamp extinguished, they returned home. Their mother helped them out of their shoes and pants, dried them, and gave them new clothes, while their father relit the lamp, and so they were sent back into the night. Unfortunately, the same thing happened again: the boys fell into the brook a second time and returned home. After another change of clothes, their father put on his own heavy coat and boots, took the lamp in one hand and a shovel in the other, and motioned the children to follow him. When they reached the brook, he shoveled the snow off the length of the plank, handed the lamp to Yosel, and said to the boys, "Now go to the *Ḥeder!*"

Grandfather took most seriously also the duty of personally teaching his children. He himself was a learned Talmudist, who eked out a living as the owner of a small "general store" in the Hungarian village of Pata, but spent many hours every day and night studying the Talmud, although he was an adherent of and believer in the Rabbi of Belz and, being a Hasid, could have dispensed with study as the supreme Jewish religious duty. His wife bore him eight children, five sons and three daughters. (My father, born in 1882, was the second child and first son.) When his children reached the age of three, Grandfather began to teach them the Hebrew alphabet. In the store they learned from him the Hebrew names of many articles which lined the shelves. Before my father was four, and his older sister five, they could read the Hebrew prayers fluently and had to recite them daily, aloud, to the satisfaction of their father, who listened to every word they uttered whether he was in the same room with them or in the adjoining store and sternly corrected them whenever they made a mistake. At four, my father began to attend the village *Heder*, where within two years he finished the study of the Bible with Rashi's commentary. At six, he began to study the Talmudic tractate of *Baba Metzi'a*, again with Rashi. A few months later, he had to start going also to the Roman Catholic elementary school of the village. [41]

Some thirty years later I, in turn, became the object of the millennial Jewish duty of "teach them diligently unto thy children." Every Sabbath afternoon, my father would call me to his book-lined study, draw up a stool next to his swivel-chair behind the large mahogany desk, take down a volume of the Talmud, and teach me. I still remember that I went to each of these sessions unwillingly, because they meant that I had to interrupt something in which I was engrossed, such as the reading of a book of adventures by Jules Verne or Karl May. But as the lesson progressed, the Talmud reached out for me, and I enjoyed delving in its depths, so that when, hours later, my mother would come in and say, "Yoshka, stop torturing the boy!" I would demur in heartfelt unison with my father, and we would go on until it grew dark and the time came to perform the *Havdala* ceremony. It was during these Sabbath afternoon sessions, which went on for some six or seven years, that I acquired the basis of my knowledge and understanding of Judaism. It is strange to think that ultimately I must thank my grandfather, whom I barely knew, for all this. Many years later, after my father's death, my brother in Jerusalem got his desk and chair; I got his set of the Talmud, which he himself had inherited from his father. It is the set I am using in locating and verifying all the Talmudic quotations contained in this book.

It is not for vain musing that I have indulged for a few minutes in these childhood reminiscences of two generations. My father's early education, first at the hand of his own father, then in the village Ḥeder, and finally in several yeshivot, was an experience he shared with millions of Jewish boys who preceded him along the same path for many centuries or were his contemporaries, members of the last generation before Enlightenment and assimilation reduced their numbers to mere few thousands.[42] Although he went on to acquire a secular education, earned a Ph.D. at the University of Budapest, and became a high school teacher of Hungarian and German language and literature, and an editor, publisher, poet, writer, translator, and Zionist leader, he could never tear himself away from the world of the Talmud in which he was first grounded, and at last I became the beneficiary of this unsevered attachment. For all those who preceded him in Jewish homes, Ḥeders, and yeshivot, education in Bible and Talmud was the key to the world of the mind. As soon as they could read (in Hebrew, of course, and not in the language of their Gentile environment), the lifelong process of becoming imbued with, and upholding, the values of traditional Judaism began—at the early age of three in the case of my father. The first textbooks they read were the prayer book and the Pentateuch. The Biblical stories were for them what folk stories, fairy tales, fables, animal stories, were for the Gentile children, most of whom, however, until the nineteenth century, never learned to read, so that they acquired a knowledge of the folklore of their elders by word of mouth, listening to mother or grandmother.

There was, in addition, another important difference between what the folk stories meant to the Gentile children and what the Bible stories meant to the Jewish child. For the Gentile children, the stories they were told were entertainment, delight, and fascination, with a moral which they may or may not have understood. For the Jewish child, the Bible stories, which he read and studied as the one supreme duty imposed upon him, certainly meant all this and much more. The patriarchs and matriarchs and other heroes figuring in the Biblical tales were, he knew, his ancestors. Every one of their acts was either approved or disapproved by God. Hence whatever deed or event was recorded in the holy pages had a direct bearing on him, contained a lesson he had to take to heart, an injunction he had to follow. In this manner, from the age of three or four, the Jewish child was exposed to formative influences, impressed with ideas of morality, permeated with a religious attitude, and convinced that he was accountable to God for his thoughts, words, and acts. Next to, and simultaneously with, the parental example, the study of the Bible and the Talmud instilled into the Jewish child those values which were to remain with him throughout his life.

The heritage of education, of studying, as a supreme value has remained with the Jews to this day. This fact is too well known and too well documented to need elaboration. And we know that it is primarily the parental home which inculcates in Jewish children the attitude of studiousness that is a prerequisite of educational achievement. I shall refer only to a few studies which indicate the serious and productive orientation of the Jewish parents. A study carried out in the Detroit area in 1953 showed that a considerably higher percentage of middle-class Jewish than non-Jewish mothers showed a preference for the use of leisure time for productive and constructive activities—such as social service work, sewing, gardening, decorating, art work, reading, taking a job, working around the house, etc.—rather than for spending their free time in shopping, visiting friends, relaxing, loafing, attending or participating in athletic events, attending movies or the theater, going out on picnics, vacationing, watching TV or listening to the radio, attending meetings of social clubs, and going out to eat. No less than 80 percent of the Jewish women, as against 54 percent of Protestant women and 51 percent of Catholic women, preferred the productive or constructive activities listed.[43] These findings paralleled those of another survey which indicated that among men the Jews had the most positive attitudes toward work and were active much more frequently than Protestants and Catholics in organizations of a "serious" nature.[44] Moreover, Jewish mothers were much more future-oriented in relation to their children than either Protestant or Catholic mothers.[45] In a New Haven study it was found that 90 percent of the Jewish respondents had a positive attitude toward planning for the future as against only 62 percent of the Italians.[46] All this together with several other such studies shows that the Jewish home is "achievement-oriented" to a greater degree than the homes in which non-Jews grow up, which, of course, cannot fail to make an impression on the children and to influence them in their school performance and in their career choices and efforts.

4. Charity

Charity, like the other dominant Jewish values discussed in the foregoing pages, goes back to Biblical times, was institutionalized in the Talmudic era and was at the same time incorporated into the Jewish psyche as a central feature and a virtue of the first magnitude.

The duty of charity is fulfilled by the act of giving and helping. Its observance is a *mitzva*, a meritorious deed, for which one reaps rewards in the World to Come. Psychologically, the syndrome of charity produces the emotion of compassion. Individuals growing up in a society where charity is a basic value will tend to develop a modal personality in which compassion is not only an important feature but one of which they, and the society as a whole, are proud, something which they uphold as a noble, desirable, distinguishing mark, as a characteristic of the positive self-stereotype. In fact, the assertion that "Israel are compassionate, sons of compassionates" has for long been the most favored self-characterization of Jews.

BIBLICAL AND TALMUDIC TIMES

The Biblical books have so many things to say about the proper relationship between man and man, and especially about the attitude and behavior toward the poor (under the varied headings of charity [*hesed*], righteousness [*tzedeq*], loving-kindness [*tz'daqa*], and several other related concepts) that a brief summary of this important area of ancient Hebrew ethics could not do justice to it. In Biblical and Jewish encyclopedias, the articles dealing with charity run into many thousands of words. But here, a few highlights will have to suffice.

The basic concept was that the poor were *entitled* to help; that is to say, to give charity was not a virtue but a duty. This is epitomized in the commandment, "For the poor shall never cease out of the land; therefore I command thee, saying: 'Thou shalt surely open thy hand unto thy brother, thy poor, and thy needy in thy land.' " [1] The way in which the poor must be helped is regulated by detailed laws: they are allocated tithes,[2] theirs are the corners of the field which must not be harvested, and the sheaves of grain, the olives, and the grapes which were overlooked at harvest time.[3] The tithe given to the poor was called by the same name (*ma'aser*) as that given to the Levites, which made the two of equal importance and made the status of the poor practically equal to that of the Sons of Levi who had no land because they were dedicated to the service of God.

The Hebrew prophets' insistence that God wants charity rather than the observance of rituals is too well known to require more than passing mention. Some of them speak of charity (*hesed*) in general terms; others are specific and untiringly hammer their demand into the consciousness of the people:

> Is not this the fast that I have chosen:
> To loose the fetters of wickedness
> To undo the bands of the yoke,
> And to let the oppressed go free,
> And that ye break every yoke?
> Is it not to deal thy bread to the hungry,
> And that thou bring home the poor that are cast out,
> When thou seest the naked, that thou cover him,
> And that thou hide not from thine own flesh?
>
> . . .
>
> And if thou draw out thy soul to the hungry
> And satisfy the soul of the afflicted,

Then shall thy light rise in darkness
And thy gloom be as the noonday . . .[4]

In the words of many other prophets and of the authors of Biblical books of wisdom, charity is upheld in similar terms as the supreme duty of man to man and the truest way of serving God.[5] Since the lifetimes of the authors of these writings span many centuries, one must conclude that this concept of charity was a persistent tradition shared by all the Biblical teachers of religious morality.

After the Biblical era, charity was accorded even greater importance. At some time close to the end of the Biblical period or shortly thereafter, the frequently occurring Biblical term *tz'daqa*, which meant "righteousness," acquired the meaning of "almsgiving." Thus the statement which is found twice in the Book of Proverbs, "Righteousness *(tz'daqa)* delivers from death,"[6] was reinterpreted to mean "Almsgiving delivers from death" and became in this sense a very frequently voiced exhortation to giving charity. At traditional Jewish funerals this verse is still repeated unceasingly by beggars and collectors of donations for charitable institutions. By the second century B.C.E. charity *(tz'daqa)* was considered to possess an atoning or redemptive effect.[7] At the same time increasing attention was paid to the sensibilities of the receiver of alms who, it was taught, must not be humiliated or hurt in any way. "My son," says Ben Sira, "defraud not the poor of his sustenance, and grieve not the eyes of him that is bitter in [his] soul. Despise not the needy soul, and vex not the heart of the oppressed. Hurt not the feelings of the afflicted, and withhold not a gift from the poor. . . . He that created him heareth his plaint."[8]

A century later, the great Jewish sage Hillel was said to have carried the consideration for the needs of the poor to an extreme. A Talmudic passage refers to his behavior to illustrate the extent to which a person who had been well off and subsequently became impoverished must be provided with the comforts to which he had been used. The rabbis taught that such a man must even be given a horse to ride and a slave to run in front of him. It is in this connection that they mention the example of Hillel and quote a tradition according to which he not only supplied a horse to a poor man of noble descent and a slave to run in front of him, but, on one occasion, when he found no slave, he himself ran in front of him for three miles.[9]

The principle of maintaining the poor in the style in which they had lived prior to their impoverishment was generally accepted by the Talmudic masters, who taught that one must not force a poor man who applies for alms to sell his house or his dishes, but must allow him to retain such personal property while giving him support.[10]

In Talmudic times the notion developed that to give charity was not only a duty and a moral obligation, but that, by practicing it, the donor merely re-

turned to God part of what he had received from God. It is in this sense that
Rabbi Eliezer of Bartota said, "Give unto God of what is His, since you and
what you have are His." [11] Therewith the station of the poor was elevated to
that of representatives of God on earth; if a man of means wished to fulfill his
duty of returning to God part of what he had received from God, he was *in
need* of the poor, for only by giving to the poor could his donation reach
God. The poor were fully aware of this important function of theirs in the
circulation of goods between God and man. A story is told of a poor man who
was so well supplied with food by the community that Rava, a leading
teacher in the early fourth century in Babylonia, felt constrained to ask him,
"Are you not concerned that you are a burden on the community?" But the
poor man answered: "Do I eat what is theirs? I eat what is God's," and being
not only poor but also learned, he quoted Psalm 145:15 which says, "The
eyes of all wait for Thee, and Thou givest them their food in due season." [12]

Many more such stories are contained in the Talmud. They all have one
and the same didactic purpose: to teach that the poor only receive what is
their due, and that the donor merely transmits to them what God wants
them to receive.

Two stories told about Mar Uqba, the head of the Babylonian Jewish community in the third century C.E., illustrate the utmost considerateness which
was the ideal behavior toward the poor. Close to the house of Mar Uqba
there lived a poor man to whom he used to give every day 4 *zuzim* (silver
coins). Since it was considered wrong to give alms publicly or even to let the
recipient know the identity of the donor, Mar Uqba always placed the
money into the door-pivot of the poor man's house. One day the man said, "I
want to go and see who does me this good deed." That day Mar Uqba tarried
late in the House of Study and his wife went to fetch him. When the poor
man saw the door move, he followed them, but they ran and hid in an oven
so that he should not learn their identity. Mar Uqba's feet became scorched
by the hot ashes, and his wife said to him, "Place your feet on mine." He became distraught at the greater immunity his wife had against the fire, but she
said to him, "I am always at home, the poor can always find me, and what I
give them they can eat right away; while you give them money with which
they must go and buy what they need." Thus her merits were greater than
Mar Uqba's and afforded her greater protection against the embers. [13]

The other story, too, tells about a poor man to whom Mar Uqba used to
send 400 *zuzim* on the eve of every Day of Atonement. On one occasion he
sent the money with his son who, upon returning, told him, "He does not
need it." "What did you see?" Mar Uqba asked. "I saw," answered his son,
"that they sprinkled old wine for him." "So he is used to such luxury!"
exclaimed Mar Uqba and thereupon doubled the amount and sent it to him.
When Mar Uqba was about to die he said, "Bring me the accounts of my
charity!" When it was found that he had given away 7,000 dinars, he said:

"The provision is small, and the voyage long," and right away distributed half of his fortune. [14]

The view of the Talmudic sages about charity is best summed up in the words of Rav Asi, who said, "Charity [tz'daqa] is as important as all the other commandments put together," and of Rabbi Ele'azar who taught that charity was greater than all the sacrifices. [15]

The examples presented by these sages and upheld in popular stories as the highest ideals of moral conduct, together with the incessant admonitions of prophets, other Biblical authors, and leading sages, could not fail to make a deep impression on the Jewish mind from Talmudic times on. In fact, they produced an almost automatic Jewish readiness to help those in distress and to alleviate suffering and made social justice one of the most fundamental and enduring Jewish values.

COMPASSION AS IMITATION OF GOD

From Biblical times down to the latest trends in Hasidism, it has been a basic tenet of Jewish religion that one must imitate God. Since, however, God's attributes comprise many which are totally beyond the ken, and even the comprehension, of man, such as His eternity, incorporeality, omniscience, omnipotence, and omnipresence, the *imitatio dei* which the Jew was supposed to endeavor had evidently to be confined to a small area of God's actions. The very old Biblical idea that God created man in His own image [16] still contains some residual mythical overtones since it reflects the belief that God in some way looked like man. The Biblical concept and commandments that man should imitate God are of a completely different character. They impose upon man the duty to be like God in those features which were morally an ideal for man and which God represented to a degree of perfection. God is perfectly holy, therefore man must endeavor to be holy. [17] The imitation of God is implied also in the repeated admonitions which enjoin the Children of Israel "to walk in the ways of God" [18] and stated explicitly in the commandments of the Sabbath rest and of loving the stranger. [19]

But there is one attribute of God whose imitation as a human duty overshadows all the rest: His compassion. In the Bible, as well as in rabbinic literature, God's compassion is referred to many times; in fact, so often that this appears to have been the chief attribute of the deity. [20] The classical passage is that of the great theophany on Mount Sinai, where God proclaimed: "I am Yahweh, Yahweh, merciful and compassionate God, long suffering and abundant in goodness and truth; keeping mercy unto the thousandth generation, forgiving iniquity and transgression and sin; and that will by no means clear the guilty. . . ." [21] This Biblical passage came to form the basis of the traditional Talmudic "thirteen attributes of God": "Rabbi Yohanan said: Thirteen divine attributes of mercy are listed in Scripture: 1) Lord, 2) Lord, 3)

God, 4) merciful, 5) compassionate, 6) long suffering, 7) abundant in goodness, 8) truthful, 9) keeping mercy unto the thousandth generation, 10) forgiving iniquity, 11) and transgression, 12) and sin, 13) and cleansing." [22] Characteristically, God's compassion was made tangible for the people by comparing it to that of a father and pronouncing it even greater than that of a mother. [23]

In Talmudic times, one of the most frequently used designations for God was "The Compassionate" (haRahman in Hebrew or Rahmana in Aramaic), and the duty of being like God in this respect was repeatedly emphasized. God said to the Children of Israel, "My people, just as I am compassionate in heaven, so you be compassionate on earth." [24] The Tanna Abba Shaul said: "Be like God. Just as He is gracious and merciful, so be thou also gracious and merciful." [25] Commenting on the verse, "You shall be holy as I the Lord your God am holy," Abba Shaul said, "The household of the king, what is their duty? To imitate the king." [26]

The Biblical verse, "After the Lord your God shall ye walk," was explained by Hama bar Hanina as follows: "Man ought to follow the acts of the Holy One, blessed be He. Just as He clothes the naked, so you too shall clothe the naked. Just as He visits the sick, so you too shall visit the sick. Just as He comforts the mourners, so you too shall comfort the mourners. Just as He buries the dead, so you too shall bury the dead." [27]

The frequent admonitions to imitate God in being compassionate did, in effect, turn the Jews into a compassionate people. According to a Talmudic passage: "This nation [the Israelites] are distinguished by three traits: they are compassionate, they are bashful [i.e., chaste], they practice charity. . . . Only he who has these three traits is worthy of being joined to his nation." [28] Accordingly, the practice of compassion was used as a criterion to distinguish between Jew and non-Jew. Thus Shabbatai ben Marinos said, "He who is merciful to his fellow men is certainly of the children of our father Abraham, and he who is not merciful to his fellow men is certainly not of the children of our father Abraham." [29] At the same time it was also recognized that to be compassionate constituted a considerable psychological burden: "There are three types of people whose life is no life: the compassionate, the irascible, and the fastidious." [30]

From the Talmudic sources, the commandment of imitating God in His merciful ways was taken over by medieval Jewish authorities. Maimonides lists the duty of "emulating God in His beneficent and righteous ways to the best of one's ability" and considers the imitation of the ways of God by seeking loving-kindness, justice, and righteousness, the ultimate end of the acquisition of knowledge. [31] Among the Kabbalists, Moses Cordovero (1522–70) held that man, whose body resembled God, must, because of this very fact, endeavor to imitate his Creator in deeds; otherwise he debases the divine image: "Consequently, it is proper for man to imitate the acts of the Supernal Crown [i.e., God] which are the thirteen attributes of mercy." [32] The Hasidic heirs of the Kabbalists upheld compassion as the greatest human moral distinction. One of their leaders, Rabbi Moshe Leib of Sasov (1745–1807), said, "To know the needs of men and to bear the burden of their sorrow—that is the true love of men." He himself was known for his abounding love of all Jews and for his charity, on account of which he was called "father of widows and orphans." [33]

While God and Israel were one in compassion, the other nations were lacking in this important divine and human attribute. [34] After the Roman Exile, Israel had ample occasion to experience Gentile cruelty. In Jewish eyes, the Gentiles appeared harsh and heartless to one another as well, and grossly neglectful of the duty of charity. However, their greatest cruelties were manifested in their relationship to Israel. Had it not been for God's compassion, the Gentiles would have long ago exterminated the Jews.

The world was thus divided into two enemy camps: that of the weak, small, and dispersed Jewish people, whose hearts were full of compassion and who were protected only by their compassionate Heavenly Father; and that of the Gentiles, who were strong and many, all of whom hated the Jews, and who did not know, or did not want to know, God, but served others instead. Only when the Holy One, blessed be He, will in his infinite mercy cause the Messiah to come will this sad state of the world come to an end, when all nations will unite in the service of God and be filled with the spirit of mercy and compassion.

THE PRACTICE OF CHARITY

As far as the actual practice of charity was concerned, with their penchant for systematization, the rabbinical authorities distinguished seven branches in it: (1) giving food and drink to the needy, (2) clothing the naked, (3) visiting the sick, (4) burying the dead and comforting the mourners, (5) redeeming the captive, (6) educating the fatherless and sheltering the homeless, and (7) providing poor maidens with dowries. [35]

On the basis of the Biblical laws prescribing the manner in which the poor must be aided, in the days of the Second Jewish Commonwealth the distribution of charity was organized and institutionalized. From among the foremost citizens, "charity overseers" or wardens were chosen to take charge of relief work. By Mishnaic times (c. 100 B.C.E. to 200 C.E.), every community had a charity box, in charge of three trustees. Two other men of utter respectability and trustworthiness went from door to door every week to collect the assessed charity tax from each family, amounting to one-tenth of its income. Those who did not give charity according to the court's assessment could be flogged and their property, in the amount of the charity owed, attached. [36] In addition to cash, three other officers collected and distributed food. Clothing, too, had to be donated by citizens who had resided in the place for at least six months. Many communities built and maintained hospices to shelter the poor travelers and the homeless and to feed them. These institutions remained functioning throughout the Middle Ages and were supplemented by a *heqdesh* (lit. "consecrated place"), which served as a poorhouse and asylum for the old, the sick, and the stranger.[37]

From the thirteenth century, Jewish charitable societies were organized all over Europe for the practice of these seven charities. The members paid weekly dues and, in addition, were subject to various fees. In some places, these societies proliferated (in Rome, their number reached thirty; in the small Verona community, fifteen) and became highly specialized, and subsequently a tendency for centralization developed. Common to all Jewish communities, even the smallest and poorest ones, was the maintenance of organized charity institutions which made it entirely impossible for any individual Jew to shirk his moral obligations toward his poorer fellow men.

The practice of charity became an almost instinctive Jewish response to such an extent that there was no difference among the Jewish communities, however far removed from one another and however different the surrounding Gentile environment. Nor did it make much difference whether a community was big or small; those who had, even if their means were most limited, gave to those in need, whether local people or transients. The latter, even in the smallest and poorest community, would be invited for a meal and given a place to spend the night.

A typical picture of how charity functioned in a tradition-bound Oriental Jewish community was described to me some thirty-five years ago by Mr. Farajullah Nasrullayoff, at the time head of the community of Meshhedi Jews in Jerusalem. Recalling the way things were another thirty or forty years back in Meshhed, the capital of Khurasan—the northeastern province of Persia, and the most sacred city of Shī'ite Islam—Mr. Nasrullayoff first told me of the life of the Meshhedi Jews as *Jadid al-Islam*, "new Muslims" (i.e., crypto-Jews), ever since their forced conversion to Islam in 1839. It was the duty of the richest Jews in Meshhed, who were the recognized heads of the Jewish community, to see to it that no Jew should suffer want. The poor Jews were ashamed of their poverty and would not ask for charity. It was therefore up to the "heads" to make discreet inquiries so as to find out who was in need. The main seasons for the distribution of food and clothes for the poor were the days prior to *Rosh haShana* and Passover. The "heads" would get up before dawn and, under the cover of darkness, deposit bundles containing food and clothing at the doorsteps of the poor. In this manner nobody knew who received donations, and those who received gifts did not know who were the donors.

In the traditional East European Jewish *shtetl*, people of means were expected to contribute to up to twelve charitable purposes which were served either by institutions or associations. They were: (1) the *G'milut Ḥesed*, ("Act of Charity") society, which advanced loans without interest; (2) the *'Ozer Dalim* ("Helpers of the Poor") society, which distributed alms to the poor too proud to go begging; (3) the *Malbish 'Arumim* ("Clother of the Naked"), which provided clothes for the needy; (4) *Hakhnasat Kalla* ("Sheltering of the Bride"), which gave dowries to poor brides and defrayed their wedding expenses; (5) *Bet Y'tomim* ("House of Orphans"), which maintained an orphanage; (6) *Talmud Tora* ("Studying the Law"), which supported free schools for the poor; (7) *Biqqur Ḥolim* ("Visiting the Sick"), whose members actually visited the sick and provided medical expenses for the needy; (8) *Heqdesh* (lit. "consecrated place"), a hospice for the poor and the sick; (9) *Hakhnasat Orḥim* ("Sheltering of Guests"), which provided food and shelter for indigent visitors; (10) *Moshav Z'qenim* ("Seat for the Old"), for old people whose families could not or would not take care of them; (11) *Ma'ot Ḥittin* ("Coins for Wheat"), which provided the poor with *matzot* for Passover; and (12) the *Ḥevra Qadisha* ("Holy Society"), the general burial society, which served everybody and took care of the burial of the poor free of charge. In addition, larger communities also supported a yeshiva, which attracted students from afar, many of whom would have to be given food one day a week by different households.[38]

From the nineteenth century in the Western world, the traditional Jewish charity institutions were gradually replaced by modern social welfare agencies. The very term "charity" fell into opprobrium (except for the continued use of its Hebrew equivalent at traditional burials, where the mourners and their friends are endlessly admonished to give donations because "charity delivereth from death").[39] However, while the support of the poor, the sick, and the stranger, the orphan and the widow has thus been transformed into modern and largely depersonalized aid and service institutions, the age-old Jewish commitment to the principle that those who have must give to those who have not has in no way diminished. In the Western world, where after the Emancipation a large Jewish middle and wealthy class developed, the dimensions and variety of Jewish welfare, social service, and other philanthropic institutions rapidly surpassed their Gentile equivalents. The Jewish interest in the welfare of all Jews embraced not only those near home but also those in remote lands; from the middle of the nineteenth century Jewish organizations were set up in the United States, France, England, and Germany, whose purpose was to aid the needy Jews in the less fortunate communities of Eastern Europe and the Muslim world. In America, the establishment and maintenance of hospitals has become since the 1850's a hallmark of all the sizable Jewish communities, and it has been observed that in virtually all cities with a Jewish population of over 30,000 there are hospitals under Jewish auspices, which in general are among the best such facilities. In addition, there are highly specialized institutions serving the blind, the deaf, the dumb, the tubercular, the insane, the delinquent, the defective, as well as boarding and foster home placement and homemaker services, orphanages, sheltered workshops, recreation programs, etc. Much care was devoted to the new immigrants whose integration in the new country was facilitated by educational, training, and aid institutions, and to the education of the Jewish poor in general. All this resulted in the Jewish community being by far the best-served group as far as institutional support is concerned.

The first half of the twentieth century saw the unification and centralization of the formerly independent and very numerous Jewish fund-raising agencies. Central Jewish welfare agencies on a countrywide scale came into being in several West European countries and achieved an unparalleled size in America. When political Zionism was organized, and especially when it became a major global Jewish concern after World War I, its fund-raising work became part of Jewish philanthropy in many lands. Since the establishment of Israel, the funding of immigrant absorption in the new state and of its other needs has been part of the general centralized fund-raising effort in the United States and several other countries of the Western world.

Another aspect of the survival of the ancient Jewish value of charity in the modern world is the adoption by the Jews of the principles embodied in the welfare state. As Lenski correctly recognized, the strong commitment of the Jews to these principles (as well as other features characterizing what he calls "the Jewish subculture" in America) "can only be fully understood when the social heritage of the Jewish group is taken into account." [40] He also calls attention to the extensive literature of Judaism, "by means of which men of the past have effectively influenced subsequent generations." [41]

The road from the first Biblical commandments enjoining charity to the large-scale bureaucracies handling centralized Jewish social work in America, other Western countries, and Israel has been a long one. Needs, dimensions, and methods of collection and allocation have profoundly changed in the course of the intervening three thousand years. Yet the commitment to charity as a supreme Jewish value has remained the same throughout. The great majority of the Jews still feel, as they did in Biblical and Talmudic times, that charity is a sacred duty. As long as Jews subscribe to this tenet, they have not ceased to be a compassionate people, sons of compassionate fathers.

19

Conclusion

Our exploration of the Jewish mind has taken us on a long journey from the early Hebrews' encounter with the austere desert and the fertility-centered culture of Canaan to the influence of the Joneses on the new suburban "frontier" of America. We looked into the way in which the Jews reacted to their encounters with six significantly different cultural environments, and in which they interacted with them, emerging each time with a changed intellectual physiognomy. We followed the manifestations of their unique determination to remain true to the ancient heritage handed down to them from Biblical and Talmudic times, which became more precious with the passage of each generation. We recognized the Jewish mind for what it was in every age: the product of two major types of influences—one which ever and again impinged upon it from the outside, from the Gentile world into which fate had placed the Jews since their Exile from their ancestral homeland; and the other which was exerted by the unceasing process of internal ferment and distillation, resulting in constant modifications—but never in a total transformation—of the age-old essence and substance of Jewishness. The interaction between these two types of influence, each of which consisted of many factorial components, was the psycho-cultural process which brought forth the many differential varieties of the Jewish mind in the spatial and temporal expanses of the global Diaspora.

Our inquiry led us to recognize that the mental configuration of those who are considered Jews by both themselves and others is as varied as is their physical form; that just as genetically the Jews do not constitute a single race, so mentally, too, they are far from conforming to a single pattern. Hence one cannot paint a portrait of the Jewish mind which would be valid for all the Jews everywhere, or even for the modal variant in every place. All one can attempt is to ascertain the mode in one Jewish community after another, and to be prepared to find that the mode in one is significantly different from that in another.

At this point I cannot refrain from voicing the often heard complaint of the social scientist about the insufficiency of data on which to base his conclusions. While the Jews are possibly the most studied people in the world, still when it comes to specifics that one would like to see presented from two or more Jewish communities so as to be able to compare them, one is quite likely to find that they have not been researched. As far as the Oriental Jews are concerned, what we know about their mentality, intelligence, talents, values, and so on, prior to their immigration to Israel is pitifully meager. The energetic psychological investigations carried out among them after their settlement in Israel and in comparison with Ashkenazi Jews, while most valuable and welcome, fill the gap only partly because they show both population elements in the flux of transition, after several years of exposure to the Israeli environment, and not in the original state of their more quiescent traditional cultures. What is most regrettable is the lack of psychological studies on the differences between Jews and Muslims in countries like Morocco, Algeria, Yemen, Iraq, and Iran in which members of the two faiths had lived in close proximity, although in partial isolation, for many centuries. In the Western world, and especially in America, such comparative studies have been carried out by psychological investigators for several decades. The similarities and differences ascertained by them would gain immensely in significance if they could be matched by parallel studies in the Muslim world.

Because of the absence of such studies, the reader will inevitably be struck by the marked disparity between the available information pertaining to the Jews in the United States (and Canada) on the one hand, and in the other parts of the world (and especially the Middle East) on the other. The abundance of information on the United States has been a temptation for many a social psychologist to base himself on American data and then present his conclusions or observations as relating to "the Jews." True, American Jewry is the largest Jewish community at present, and, together with that of Israel, the most important. But even so, there is no justification for speaking of "the Jews" on the basis of American findings. Such a procedure disregards what is precisely one of the most remarkable traits of "the Jews": their great and unique cultural, social, and above all psychological diversity, overlaying, and occasionally even masking, the common Biblical and Talmudic foundations of their heritage.

The lack of data on Jews living in the Muslim orbit makes it impossible to answer the question of whether the Jews are more intelligent than other peoples; or, to formulate it in the only way in which even under optimum conditions such a question could possibly be answered, whether the Jews are superior in intelligence in every place to the non-Jews among whom they live. In the Western world, and especially in America, where comparative studies on the subject are available, the findings show that Jews tend to achieve higher scores than non-Jews on I.Q. tests, and especially on those which test verbal ability. Even if these test results are taken to indicate a certain Jewish superiority in I.Q., they only speak of America and say nothing about Jews in other cultural environments—let alone in such very different ones as are represented by the Middle Eastern countries. In the absence of Middle Eastern data, and faced with the paucity of data from most European countries, all one can say is that in those places where tests have been administered to compare scores achieved by Jews and non-Jews, the former have performed better than the latter. However, if I might be allowed to speculate, I would say that there is a set of factors which makes it likely that if the tests were or had been administered to Jews and Muslims in an Arab or other Muslim country, the results would show differences similar to those found in America. My reason for making this assumption is that the socio-cultural differences between Jews and Muslims are largely of the same kind as those between Jews and Christians in the West. In the Middle East as well, the Jews were (or are) more literate, more educated in general, and more urbanized than the Muslims. Furthermore, more Jews than Muslims are bilingual (or even polyglot), more of them are engaged in non-manual labor, and, as a talented minority, they are more exposed than the Muslims to societal pressure. All these are factors which, in the long run, have probably resulted in the same kind of differences in intelligence there as they did in the West.

As for differences in intelligence between Ashkenazi and Oriental Jews, data gathered in Israel give us an indication as to how they are reflected in tests after some exposure to a common environment. For one thing, it was found that Ashkenazi children exceed the Oriental Jewish children in command of language, a feature in which Jewish children in the West are, as a rule, found superior to their Gentile peers. Regrettably, no studies are available to indicate what is the level of the command of language shown by Oriental Jewish children in relation to that of their Muslim peers. Likewise, one would very much like to know how the superior command of numbers shown by the Oriental Jewish children relates to the command of numbers of the Middle Eastern Muslim children. Another important result of the Israeli comparative studies is that they show clearly the high correlation between social class and test scores achieved. In fact, the significant differences in class structure between the Ashkenazim and the Oriental Jews (with the middle class preponderant in the former and the lower class in the latter) tend to obscure the etiology of differences in the test scores achieved by the two groups. That is, it is difficult to determine whether such differences as are found in the tests are due to class differences or to ethnic differences, or to a combination of both.

As for the incidence of genius among Jews other than those assimilated to modern Western culture, the question is purely academic for the simple reason that a "genius" in the modern world is understood to be an individual who chalks up quite extraordinary achievements in one of those realms of intellectual activity whose sum total makes up Western culture. All the yardsticks currently used to measure genius in the modern world come up with persons who either live in the West or are culturally part of it. Since the very concept of genius is thus confined to the sphere and spell of the West, the question whether Jews evince a higher incidence of genius than non-Jews could not be raised in relation to the Muslim orbit in modern times. In the past, the situation was different. As we have seen (pages 316–18), in the Middle Ages the Jews had a disproportionately large share of genius, whether they lived in a Christian or in a Muslim environment. Those data, so ably gathered by George Sarton, allow us to speculate that, given the requisite change in the cultural environment, the incidence of genius among the Oriental Jews will catch up with that among the Ashkenazim. Such a change has been taking place for those 1.5 million Oriental Jews who today live in Israel. It can therefore be expected that within a generation, or two at the utmost, there will be no difference in this respect between the two major divisions of the Israeli Jewish population.

As far as talents below the rank of genius are concerned, we do not have to wait even that long. As we have seen (in Chapter 13), wherever social and cultural contact was established between the Jews and their Gentile environment, they manifested talent in those fields whose cultivation received special attention from the non-Jews. In modern times, the great watershed in this respect was the Enlightenment. Prior to it, the artistic, musical, and literary activity of Ashkenazi Jewry was of a tradition-bound Jewish-Middle Eastern type. After it, with amazing speed, the Jews became important contributors to the most essentially Western cultural expressions in all these fields, and in several others which up to that time had not existed outside the West. It was with their penetration of these areas—made possible by many factors, but first of all by genuine Jewish talent—that the rapid process of their transition from their basically Middle Eastern to Western culture culminated.

The lesson contained in this large-scale and rapid nineteenth-century emergence of Jewish talent in many new fields is that the same process can be expected to take place among the Oriental Jews in Israel, France, and wherever they live in a modern Western cultural environment. In fact, the process of transculturation, entirely analogous to that which took place among the Ashkenazi Jews in the nineteenth century, is already well under way among the Oriental Jews. Because of the numerical relations, the process is most crucial in Israel, where the new Oriental Jewish majority is by now quite advanced on the road to adopting the Western culture transplanted into the country by the earlier Ashkenazi immigrants. In the Israeli atmosphere, emphatically favorable for activity in all artistic, literary, and scientific fields, whatever latent or overt talents the Oriental Jews had brought along with them have been stimulated to develop and come to fruition. The favorite example to which many have pointed is that of Yemenite Jewish music and art-crafts (silver filigree work, embroidery, basketry), which not only have blossomed in Israel but have influenced the general Israeli musical and artistic scene. Equally significant is the increasing number of Oriental Jewish and Sephardi authors, poets, painters, and composers whose work is today an integral part of the Israeli cultural production. On a smaller scale, the absorption of French culture has had a similar effect on those North African Jews who settled in France.

Our survey of what is known about the Jewish personality and character (Chapter 14) disclosed that it is futile to attempt a portrayal of "the Jewish personality," for the simple reason that the two millennia of dispersion in the far corners of the world created as many different Jewish modal personalities as there are major Jewish ethnic groups. What we did find was that there are more or less significant differences between the Jewish and the Gentile modal personality in those few places from which data for both population elements are available. These differences must be attributed to the special cultural traditions of the Jews, and to their special position within the Gentile environment, factors which counteract to varying extents the assimilatory forces emanating from the Gentile culture and its product, the Gentile personality. We also found that, because of the latter influences, marked differences exist between the Ashkenazi and the Oriental Jews, with smaller differences evinced by the ethnic groups which make up each of these two major divisions of the Jewish people. We paid special attention to the modal personality of the Sephardim, the Italian Jews, the American Jews, the Israeli *sabras*, and the "Kibbutzniks." We found that, as far as Ashkenazi Jews are concerned, they are characterized by a greater intensity, sensitivity, and impatience than the Gentiles among whom they live. These differences are marked in non-Mediterranean Europe and in the English-speaking world, but not in the Latin lands, nor did they seem to have existed in the Muslim orbit. It stands to reason that these three personality traits have been retained by the Jews from their remote Mediterranean past, and that they appear as specifically Jewish features only where the Jews live among non-Mediterranean peoples. In concluding the discussion of the Jewish personality it was found that, in the modern Jewish Diaspora, Jewish self-identification has remained a more potent factor than religiosity.

Important features of the Western Jewish mentality are the concern over physical health and the sensitivity to pain. A typical manifestation of this concern is the readiness to seek and obtain medical help for either physical or mental disorders. As far as mental illness itself is concerned, it was found that, in the Western world, the incidence among the Jews of psychoses is lower and of neuroses higher than among the Gentiles; that there are significant differences in types of mental disorder between Ashkenazi and Oriental Jews; and that there is an analogy in the symptomatology of mental illness between the Ashkenazi Jews and their Christian neighbors, as well as between the Oriental Jews and their Muslim neighbors. These two major divisions of the Jewish people differ from each other in both their normal and their abnormal personalities, with the latter mirroring the former in each case.

In connection with mental disorder we looked into the personality of the Jewish version of the marginal man, the individual who is straddled between two cultures and consequently beset by a specific syndrome of emotional problems. Then we glanced (in Chapter 16) at three types of addiction. To the first, alcoholism, the Jews have been immune throughout their history; only in recent times, and only in the Western world, have some of those who are thoroughly assimilated to their Gentile compeers begun to succumb to it. The second, overeating, with its resultant obesity, has been shown by recent studies to be more frequent among Jews than non-Jews in the Western world. The third, drug addiction, has long been endemic with low rates of incidence among the Oriental Jews, although for lack of studies nothing definite can be said about it. Among Ashkenazi Jews, and especially in America and England, it is a new development, and from them it has spread to the young generation in Israel. The spread of alcoholism and drug addiction among the Jews shows that, once the religious and traditional barriers crumble, the addictions to which members of the Gentile environment are subject not only take their toll among Jews, but do so occasionally to an even higher degree than among the non-Jews.

Ethnic self-hate is a phenomenon known from various minorities, but its "classical" form is found among the Jews, or at least it is among them that its symptomatology has been most intensively studied (Chapter 17). In any case, no other people has been so consistently accused of "parasitism" and has so emphatically incorporated this contemptible feature into its self-stereotype. Incessant allegations of Jewish inferiority and damaging traits have produced in many Jews a feeling of collective guilt which has become the counterfoil to the Jewish conviction of collective excellence. Moreover, the differences among Jews themselves, such as those between the Sephardim and other Jewish ethnic groups, between the Enlighteners and the non-enlightened, the Ashkenazim and the Oriental Jews, and so on, have often assumed the character of contempt directed by those who felt superior toward those whom they considered inferior. That these centrifugal forces did not succeed in disrupting Jewish unity is an eloquent testimony to the power of the common Jewish tradition to hold together actually disparate and emotionally antagonistic subdivisions of the Jewish people.

A recurring theme throughout our inquiry was that of the values which have informed the Jewish mind in the past and still influence it even beyond the extent of the individual's conscious knowledge of Jewish traditions. In discussing the various aspects of the working of the Jewish mind, such as intelligence, genius, special talents, personality, character, and so on, the issue of values was kept in the background and their presence tacitly assumed rather than made explicit. In the last chapter (Chapter 18), we singled out for intensive treatment those Jewish values which appear to us the most basic and most influential at all times and in every subdivision of the Jewish people. They are: familial attitudes, the position on sex, the imperative of education, and the duty of charity. Each of these values represents an old Hebrew–Jewish–Middle Eastern heirloom handed down from Biblical times, developed in the Talmudic period, and preserved through the Middle Ages up to and beyond the Enlightenment. Each was first implanted into the psyche of every Jewish child in the parental home and subsequently, under the influence of the Jewish socio-cultural environment, made into guidelines of feeling and thinking, of speech and behavior. If nothing else identifies an individual as a Jew, if he does not consider himself a Jew and is not so considered by others, in many cases the residual presence in his psyche of these values remains as the last vestige of his Jewish background. To get rid of the feeling of compassion—to mention only one feature—is evidently more difficult than to decide against all conscious Jewish identification.

Having reached the end of our road, with what final thought can we leave the reader who has patiently followed thus far? Perhaps this: Our examination of the Jewish mind disclosed the *homo Judaeus* to be a human specimen with great and many internal variations and with significant differences everywhere between him and his Gentile environment. Some of these differences show him to be superior to the Gentiles; in others he is inferior to them. On balance, it would seem a pity, and a loss to humanity as a whole, if Jewish assimilation should lead to a stage where the Jewish mind would in no way differ from the Gentile mind. Conversely, it appears that mankind would be better off if it could acquire more of the characteristics of the Jewish mind than it has done heretofore.

NOTES
INDEX

NOTES

ABBREVIATIONS

B.   Babylonian Talmud
B.C.E.   Before the Common Era
C.E.   Common Era
M.   Mishna
T.   Tosefta
Y.   Yerushalmi, or the Palestinian Talmud

CHAPTER I

1. Cf. Raphael Patai, *The Arab Mind*, New York: Scribners, 1973; Raphael Patai and Jennifer Patai Wing, *The Myth of the Jewish Race*, New York: Scribners, 1975.
2. Num. 23:9.
3. Raphael Patai, *Tents of Jacob: The Diaspora Yesterday and Today*, Englewood Cliffs, N.J.: Prentice-Hall, 1971, p. 284; and below, Chapter 6.
4. Cf. Chapter 16.
5. Cf. Chapter 10.
6. B. Yeb. 79a.
7. M. Avot 1:2 and 18.
8. B. Shab. 31a.
9. Lev. 19:18.
10. Deut. 6:5.
11. Bernard Lazare, *L'Antisémitisme: Son histoire et ses causes*, Paris, 1894; reprinted Paris: Jean Crés, 1934, 2:137; English translation: *Antisemitism: Its History and Causes*, New York: International Library Publ. Co., 1903.
12. David Hadler (pseudonym for Ferdynand Zweig), *The Jew: His Tragedy and Greatness*, London: Victor Gollancz, 1947, p. 19. On pp. 103ff. Hadler discusses five basic features of the Jewish mind, namely: (1) belief in Oneness (of God); (2) belief in Israel, the One People; (3) the values of justice and love; (4) faith and reason; and (5) Messianic hope. Elsewhere (p. 79) he discerns yet another feature which is "unique in the Jewish mind, character, and experience": "the coincidence of opposites, a deep-seated dichotomy and polarity."
13. Erich Kahler, *Israel unter den Völkern*, Zurich: Humanitas Verlag, 1936, pp. 31, 89–90, 119.
14. Jacques Maritain, *Antisemitism*, London: Geoffrey Bles, The Centenary Press, 1939, p. 18.
15. 2 Chron. 20:20.
16. Exod. 20:2; Deut. 5:6.
17. Deut. 7:6ff.
18. Lev. 25:55; cf. also Lev. 25:45; Deut. 14:1ff.

19. Isa. 41:8–9.
20. Josh. 24:22.
21. Louis Ginzberg, *The Legends of the Jews*, Philadelphia: Jewish Publ. Soc. of America, 1911, 3:92.
22. Raphael Patai, *Man and Temple in Ancient Jewish Myth and Ritual*, 2nd ed., New York: Ktav, 1967, pp. 123, 126–28, 132.
23. Cf. references in Chapter 12, n. 8.
24. The concept of the noosphere is developed by Pierre Teilhard de Chardin (1881–1955) in several of his books; it is discussed in detail in Raphael Patai, *Myth and Modern Man*, Englewood Cliffs, N.J.: Prentice-Hall, 1972, pp. 61–65.
25. Ernest van den Haag, *The Jewish Mystique*, New York: Stein and Day, 1969, pp. 27, 45.

CHAPTER 2

1. Cf. the three criteria of Jewishness arrived at by Salo W. Baron, "Who Is a Jew?" in *History and Jewish Historians: Essays and Addresses*, by Salo W. Baron, Philadelphia: Jewish Publ. Soc. of America, 1964, pp. 21–22.
2. Cf. Raphael Patai and Jennifer Patai Wing, *The Myth of the Jewish Race*, New York: Scribners, 1975. The quotation is from L. C. Dunn and Theodosius Dobzhansky, *Heredity, Race and Society*, New York: New American Library; as quoted in Patai and Wing, *op. cit.*, p. 15.
3. Maimonides, *Yad haHazaqa*, Issure Bi'a, 15:3; *Shulḥan 'Arukh, Even ha'Ezer*, 4:19.
4. Gen. 17:1ff.
5. Deut. 26:5.
6. Isa. 51:1–2. My translation from the Hebrew.
7. Gen. 22:17.
8. Cf. Jer. 31:15.
9. Cf. R. Patai, *The Hebrew Goddess*, New York: Ktav, 1967, pp. 28, 178, 267.
10. Cf. Patai and Wing, *op. cit.*, p. 57.
11. Exod. 24:7.
12. M. Sh'vu'ot 3:6.
13. Cf. Louis Finkelstein, *The Beliefs and Practices of Judaism*, New York: Devin-Adair, 1941, pp. 4, 6, 14.
14. For Germany and other countries, cf. *Encyclopedia Judaica*, Berlin: Verlag Eschkol, 1931, 7:210ff., s.v. Gemeinde. For Hungary, cf. *Magyar Zsidó Lexikon*, Budapest: A Zsidó Lexikon kiadása, 1929, pp. 69, 369–70.
15. Cf. B. Akzin, "Return, Law of," in R. Patai (ed.), *Encyclopedia of Zionism and Israel*, New York: Herzl Press and McGraw-Hill, 1971, 2:951.
16. Simon N. Herman, *Israelis and Jews*, New York: Random House, 1970, p. 94.
17. Cf. Aimé Pallière. *Le Sanctuaire Inconnu*, Paris, 1926; also in English translation, *The Unknown Sanctuary*, New York: Bloch Publ. Co., 1928.
18. Brief biographies of some two dozen of them can be located in the *Enc. Jud.*, with the help of the index, s.v. Proselytes, Famous.
19. Although Swann was Catholic (his family's conversion from Judaism having taken place two generations earlier), he remained a Jew in the eyes of the high society

into which he was accepted, as well as in his own eyes and in his feelings, as evidenced, among other things, by his reaction to the Dreyfus affair. See Seth L. Wolitz, *The Proustian Community*, New York: New York University Press, 1971, pp. 155–56, 169, 173.

20. *American Jewish Year Book*, 1974–75, New York: American Jewish Committee, and Philadelphia: Jewish Publ. Soc. of America, 1974, 75:295, 561.

CHAPTER 3

* This chapter was first published in the July 1976 issue of *The Jewish Quarterly Review*, 67(1):1–15.

1. The centrality of the Exodus in Jewish religion is discussed in R. Patai, *Tents of Jacob*, Englewood Cliffs, N.J.: Prentice-Hall, 1971, pp. 10–11; and in greater detail, *idem, Myth and Modern Man*, same publisher, 1972, pp. 145–50.
2. Cf. Maimonides, Commentary to the Mishna, *ad* Sanhedrin 10, Mishna 1.
3. Nahum N. Glatzer, "The Beginnings of Modern Jewish Studies," in Alexander Altmann (ed.), *Studies in Nineteenth-Century Jewish Intellectual History*, Cambridge, Mass.: Harvard University Press, 1964, pp. 33, 36.

CHAPTER 4

1. Gen. 25:20; 28:5; 31:20, 24.
2. Deut. 26:5. That Aramaic was "the language of the fathers" is referred to in the Middle Ages by Saʿadya Gaon in his Commentary to the *Sepher Yʾtzira*, text, p. 45.
3. Gen. 24:15; 25:20.
4. Gen. 25:20; 29–30.
5. Gen. 46:8–26. Sixty-six males, including the two sons of Judah, Er and Onan, who had died in Canaan, are enumerated in this passage; to them are added Joseph and his two sons Ephraim and Manasseh who were in Egypt, plus Jacob himself, resulting in the traditional figure of "seventy souls." The only two women mentioned, Dinah the daughter of Jacob, and Serah the daughter of Asher, are not counted in the total.
6. Isa. 19:18.
7. 2 Kings 18:26, 28; Isa. 36:11, 13; Neh. 13:24; 2 Chron. 32:18.
8. Cf. Sources in Louis Ginzberg, *Legends of the Jews*, 1:181; 3:94, 113, 205.
9. Gen. 24:3.
10. Gen. 26:34–35; 27:46.
11. Gen. 28:6–9.
12. Cf. especially Gen. 32:23; 33:1–2, 5–6, where they are consistently referred to as "children."
13. Gen. 46:10; 38:2, 6.
14. Gen. 41:45.
15. Gen. 34:29.
16. Gen. 31:19, 30–35.

17. Exod. 2:21; Lev. 24:10; Exod. 12:38.
18. For an earlier appraisal of modern Middle Eastern sedentarization, cf. R. Patai, *Golden River to Golden Road: Society, Culture and Change in the Middle East*, 3rd. ed., Philadelphia: University of Pennsylvania Press, 1969, pp. 268–71.
19. William F. Albright, *Yahweh and the Gods of Canaan*, New York: Doubleday, 1968, Chapter II.
20. *Ibid.*, p. 183.
21. 2 Chron. 2:4.
22. Cf. G. E. Mendenhall, *Law and Covenant in Israel and the Ancient Orient*, The Biblical Colloquium, Pittsburgh, 1955, reprinted from *Biblical Archaeologist*, 17, 1954, 24–26, 49–76. As quoted by Albright, *op. cit.*, p. 167.
23. Gen. 31:19, 34; 1 Sam. 19:13.
24. Ezek. 1:26, 28.
25. Ezek. 8:14.
26. Cf. R. Patai, *Man and Temple in Ancient Jewish Myth and Ritual*, 2nd ed., New York: Ktav, 1967, pp. 24ff.
27. Cf. Ezek. 8; Jer. 44; and *passim* in the prophets.
28. Cf. R. Patai, *The Hebrew Goddess*, New York: Ktav, 1967, pp. 97–98. In the peripheral Jewish colony on the Upper Egyptian island of Elephantine, these paganizing worships held out for almost another two centuries; cf. *ibid.*, pp. 99–100.
29. Cf. Maimonides, *Guide of the Perplexed*, trans. by M. Friedländer, New York: Hebrew Publ. Co., n.d., Part 3, Chapter 32, p. 151.
30. Exod. 15:11.
31. Albright, *op. cit.*, p. 12.
32. Ps. 92:10.
33. Albright, *op. cit.*, p. 6.
34. Theodor Gaster, "Canaanite Mythology," in Samuel N. Kramer (ed.), *Mythologies of the Ancient World*, Garden City, N.Y.: Doubleday-Anchor Books, 1961, pp. 193, 199, 202, 210.
35. Pss. 68:5; 74:14; Isa. 27:1.
36. Albright, *op. cit.*, p. 201; Gaster, *op. cit.*, p. 200.
37. Rev. 12:3ff.
38. Cf. Patai, *The Hebrew Goddess; idem*, "The Goddess Cult in Hebrew-Jewish Religion," in A. Bharati (ed.), *The Realm of the Extra-Human: Agents and Audiences* (a volume in the series *World Anthropology*), the Hague-Paris: Mouton Publ., 1976, pp. 197–210.
39. Cf. Patai, *The Hebrew Goddess*, plates 24, 26–28, and 31.
40. Cf. *Entziqlopedia Miqra'it*, Jerusalem, 1955–, Vol. 4, pp. 238–44, s.v. *k'ruv*.
41. Gen. 3:24; Ezek. 28:14; 1 Kings 6:23–28; 8:7.
42. 1 Sam. 4:4; 2 Sam. 6:2; 2 Kings 19:15; Isa. 37:16; Pss. 80:2; 99:1; 1 Chron. 13:6.
43. Ezek. 10:1.
44. 1 Enoch 20:7.
45. 1 Kings 12:26–33; 2 Chron. 11:14f.; cf. Exod. 32:5.
46. 1 Kings 6:29–39; 7:29, 36; Exod. 26:1, 31; 36:8, 35; 2 Chron. 3:7, 14; Ezek. 41:18–20, 23, 25.
47. 1 Kings 6:23–28; 8:6–7; 2 Chron. 3:11–13; 5:7–8.

48. This whole question is discussed in detail in Patai, *The Hebrew Goddess*, pp. 121–36. We shall return to it briefly below, in Chapter 5.
49. Albright, *op. cit.*, p. 197.
50. Cf. the evidence in Patai, *The Hebrew Goddess*, pp. 45–52.

CHAPTER 5

1. Cf. sources in Raphael Patai and Jennifer Patai Wing, *The Myth of the Jewish Race*, New York: Scribners, 1975, p. 52.
2. 2 Kings 18:26; Ezra 4:8–6:18; 7:12–26; Dan. 2:4–7:28.
3. Ezra 7:11–21, etc.; Neh. 8:2–8.
4. B. Meg. 3a. Cf. also B. Ber. 8a.
5. 1 Macc. 1:15; Josephus Flavius, *Ant.* 12:241.
6. Victor Tcherikover, *Hellenistic Civilization and the Jews*, Philadelphia: Jewish Publ. Soc. of America, 1959, pp. 160–64.
7. 2 Macc. 4:13–15. Cf. 1 Macc. 1:13–14.
8. Patai and Wing, *op. cit.*, pp. 52, 58–61.
9. Cf. Jacob Neusner, "Jewish Use of Pagan Symbols After 70 C.E.," *Journal of Religion*, 43:4, 1963, p. 294 n. 23.
10. B. Rosh Hash. 24b.
11. As quoted by Tcherikover, *op. cit.*, p. 368.
12. Cf. sources in W. Bacher, *Aggadat haTannaim*, Tel Aviv: D'vir, 1922, Vol. 2, Part 1, pp. 1–2.
13. Saul Lieberman, *Hellenism in Jewish Palestine*, New York: The Jewish Theological Seminary of America, 1950, p. 112.
14. This is the conclusion reached by Lieberman, *op. cit.*, pp. 109–14, after a thorough examination of all the relevant Talmudic passages.
15. *Ibid.*, pp. 104–14.
16. Cf. Samuel Krauss, *Griechische und lateinische Lehnwörter im Talmud, Midrasch und Targum*, 2 vols., Berlin: S. Calvary, 1898–99.
17. Erwin Goodenough, *Jewish Symbols in the Greco-Roman Period*, Princeton, N.J.: Princeton University Press, Bollingen Series, 1953–68, Vols. 9–11.
18. *Ibid.*, 8:3–21; 12:65, 145–57.
19. *Ibid.*, 12:58–63.
20. R. Patai, *The Hebrew Goddess*, New York: Ktav, 1967, pp. 282–87.
21. Goodenough, *op. cit.*, 12:62.
22. *Ibid.*, 12:51.
23. B. Bab. Qam. 82b–83a.
24. Louis Finkelstein, *The Pharisees: The Sociological Background of Their Faith*, Philadelphia: Jewish Publ. Soc. of America, 1938, 2:573.
25. *Ibid.*, 2:570–74.
26. Goodenough, *op. cit.*, 12:187, 197.
27. *Ibid.*, 12:168. Goodenough's interpretation of the Hellenistic Jewish use of Greco-Roman symbols gave rise to numerous critical appraisals which are aptly summarized by Gerhard Delling, "Perspektiven der Erforschung des Hellenis-

tischen Judentums," in *Hebrew Union College Annual*, 45, Cincinnati, 1974, pp. 170–74.

28. In one scene at Dura, Ares is shown, but as a decoration over the gate of Egypt (i.e., an idol of pagans), just as the idols of the Philistines are shown in another panel.

29. 2 Sam. 22:11; Ps. 18:11; Ezek. 1; Zech. 6:1–8.

30. Goodenough, *op. cit.*, 12:155.

31. Louis Ginzberg, *The Legends of the Jews*, Philadelphia: Jewish Publ. Soc. of America, 1909–46, 1:97; 2:173, 237, 316–17. Cf. the numerous entries in the index (Vol. 7), s.v. Chariots.

32. Ezek. 1:26, 28.

33. Cf. Goodenough, *op. cit.*, 10:9; 11: figs. 227, 229, 230, 232.

34. E.g., Exod. 15:6, 12, 16, etc.

35. Cf. Patai, *The Hebrew Goddess*, pp. 113–15, 121–23.

36. Goodenough, *op. cit.*, 4:28; 12:69.

37. Cf. R. Patai, *Man and Temple in Ancient Jewish Myth and Ritual*, 2nd ed., New York: Ktav, 1967, pp. 108, 112, 115, 117, 127, and 134 n. 42.

38. Goodenough, *op. cit.*, 4:71–98; 12:79–83.

39. Amos 2:6–8; 3:9–15; 5:10–13; Zech. 1:2–17; 2:1–17; Ezek. 30:2f.

40. Gen. 5:24.

41. 2 Chron. 33:12–13.

42. Cf. especially his *Ant.* 16:6:8.

43. Cf. Emil Schürer, *Geschichte des jüdischen Volkes im Zeitalter Jesu Christi*, Vol. 3, 4th ed., Leipzig: J. C. Hinrich, 1909, pp. 12, 503.

44. *Ibid.*, 3:504. My translation from the German.

45. *Ibid.*, 3:507–8.

46. 4 Macc. 17:20f.

47. Cf. Patai, *The Hebrew Goddess*, pp. 114–15.

48. Schürer, *op. cit.*, 3:700–701.

49. Gen. 2:7.

50. Schürer, *op. cit.*, 3:698–716.

51. *Ibid.*, 3:703.

52. Cf. literature in Schürer, *op. cit.*, 3:715–16.

53. Cf. *ibid.*, 3:553, and also 704 n. 23. However, Schürer misplaces the emphasis in his interpretation of Philo's orthodoxy.

54. Cf. Tcherikover, *op. cit.*, p. 351, and sources on p. 527 n. 39.

55. George Sarton, *A History of Science*, Cambridge, Mass.: Harvard University Press, 1952–59, 1:x.

56. F. E. Peters, *The Harvest of Hellenism*, New York: Simon and Schuster, 1970, p. 194.

57. Cf. the fine portraiture of the Alexandrian mathematical sciences in Peters, *op. cit.*, pp. 208ff.

58. Cf. Schürer, *op. cit.*, 2:404; 3:271, 283, 477, 482.

59. *Ibid.*, 3:15f., 134.

60. Tcherikover, *op. cit.*, p. 375.

61. Cf. Sarton, *op. cit.*, 2:245–47; *idem*, *Introduction to the History of Science*, Washington, D.C.: Carnegie Institution of Washington, 1927–48, 3:363.

62. Schürer, *op. cit.*, 3:422; emphasis in the original. My translation from the German.

CHAPTER 6

1. Thus according to the *Sepher haQabbala* of Abraham ibn Daud (see below, Section 4).
2. Cf. M. Steinschneider, *Arabische Literatur der Juden*, Frankfurt a. M.: J. Kauffmann, 1902, p. 13, where the date 883 must be corrected to read 783. Cf. also *Enc. Jud.* 11:1187.
3. Cf. Abraham A. Neuman, *The Jews in Spain*, Philadelphia: Jewish Publ. Soc. of America, 1944, 2:100–101.
4. M. Steinschneider, *Jewish Literature from the Eighth to the Eighteenth Century*, London: Longman, Brown, 1857, pp. 183–84; *idem, Allgemeine Einleitung in die jüdische Literatur des Mittelalters*, reprint, Jerusalem: Bamberger and Wahrman, 1938, p. 72; Neuman, *op. cit.*, 1:50; 2:93–94, 100–102, 300 n. 163, 305 n. 32; *Enc. Jud.* 15:247ff.
5. Steinschneider, *Allgemeine Einleitung*, pp. 68, 71, and pp. 73–74, where he mentions a translation into Spanish of the Hebrew prayer book, a Spanish polemical tract by Moses Cohen de Tordesilla, and a few writings on medicine.
6. *Enc. Jud.* 10:1343, 1348; 11:360.
7. Neuman, *op. cit.*, 2:65, 98–100.
8. Cf., e.g., Abraham S. Halkin, "Judeo-Arabic Literature," in Louis Finkelstein (ed.), *The Jews: Their Religion and Culture*, 4th ed., New York: Schocken Books, 1971, p. 128; Aharon Mirsky, " 'Erke haShira ha'Ivrit biS'farad (The Principles of Hebrew Poetry in Spain)," in Hebrew with an English summary, in R. D. Barnett (ed.), *The Sephardi Heritage*, London: Vallentine, Mitchell, 1971, 1:187.
9. Raphael Patai, *The Arab Mind*, New York: Scribners, 1973, pp. 41ff.
10. Cf. the analysis of the various categories of the musive style by Franz Delitzsch, *Zur Geschichte der jüdischen Poesie*, Leipzig: Tauchnitz, 1836, pp. 164–72. In David Ginzburg's annotated edition of Moses ibn Ezra's long poem, *Sepher ha'Anaq Hu haTarshish* (Berlin: Itzkowski for Meqitze Nirdamim, 1886), expressions in every second line are identified as Biblical quotations, allusions, or references, often with the original meaning twisted or changed.
11. Steinschneider, *Arabische Literatur*, pp. 15–34; George Sarton, *Introduction to the History of Science*, Washington, D.C.: Carnegie Institution of Washington, 1927–48, 1:531, 565, 569, 574–75.
12. Eliyahu Ashtor, *Qorot haY'hudim biS'farad haMuslimit (History of the Jews in Muslim Spain)*, Jerusalem: Qiryat Sepher, 1960, 1:160.
13. Maimonides, *Commentary on the Mishna*, Sanh. 10, Mishna 1, in *Talmud Bavli Sanhedrin*, Vienna: Schlossberg, 1867, p. 128d.
14. Carl Brockelmann, *Geschichte der arabischen Litteratur*, 2nd ed., Leiden: Brill, 1943, 1:104ff., 382ff.; Franz Rosenthal, *A History of Muslim Historiography*, Leiden: Brill, 1952; rev. ed., 1968.
15. Patai, *op. cit.*, pp. 41ff.
16. Cf. M. Sota 7:1; Saul Lieberman, *Greek in Jewish Palestine*, New York: Jewish

Theological Seminary of America, 1942, p. 30; Moshe Attais, "The Bedtime Shema in Ladino," *Edoth* (Jerusalem), 1947, 2:211ff.

17. *Jewish Enc.* 9:25, s.v. Samuel Ha-Nagid.

18. Cf. Israel Davidson, *Thesaurus of Medieval Hebrew Poetry*, 4 vols., New York: Jewish Theological Seminary of America, 1924–33; *idem*, "Supplement," *Hebrew Union College Annual* 12–13 (1937–38): 715ff. Shalom Spiegel, "On Medieval Hebrew Poetry," in Louis Finkelstein (ed.), *The Jews*, *op. cit.*, p. 106, cf. 82–120. Israel Zinberg, *A History of Jewish Literature: The Arabic Spanish Period*, trans. and ed. by Bernard Martin, Cleveland & London: Case Western Reserve University Press, 1972.

19. Y'huda haLevi (Judah Halevi), *Kuzari* 2:70–78, ed. by Hartwig Hirschfeld, New York: Pardes, 1946, pp. 110–12.

20. This and all other translations from Hebrew, Aramaic, Arabic, etc., are mine unless otherwise noted.

21. Cf. Eliyahu Ashtor, *The Jews in Moslem Spain*, Philadelphia: Jewish Publ. Soc. of America, 1973, 1:396.

22. Num. 12:3, where the Hebrew *'anav* is usually translated as "meek." B. Bab. Metz. 58b, in ref. to Lev. 25:17.

23. Patai, *op. cit.*, pp. 213–15, 352. n. 21.

24. Cf. Samuel haNagid, *Shire Milḥama* ("War Songs"), ed. by A. M. Haberman, Tel Aviv: Maḥbarot l'Sifrut, 1948, pp. 64, 73; *idem*, *Shire Tza'ar w'Sha'ashu'im* ("Songs of Pain and Play"), ed. by Haberman, Tel Aviv, same publ., 1946, p. 15. On p. 162 of *Shire Milḥama*, Haberman makes the comment that "the self-praise and self-aggrandizement which are usual in Arabic poetry and in Spanish-Hebrew poetry, and are most pronounced in the poetry of Ibn Gabirol, are few in the poems of haNagid."

25. Israel Tzinberg, *Toldot Sifrut Yisrael* (*History of Jewish Literature*), Tel Aviv: Shreberk, 1955, 1:58.

26. *Ibid.*, 1:37.

27. Zinberg, *op. cit.* (English), 1:44, 55.

28. Leopold Dukes, *Shire Sh'lomo*, Hannover: Telgener, 1858, p. 22.

29. Moses ibn Ezra, *Sepher ha'Anaq Hu haTarshish*, pp. 88 and 4.

30. *Otzar Neḥmad*, Vienna, 1857, 2:184, as translated and quoted in Zinberg, *op. cit.*, (English), 1:79.

31. H. Brody and K. Albrecht, *Sha'ar haShir* ("The Gate of Song"), Leipzig: Hinrichs, 1905, pp. 70–71. Leopold Dukes, *Moses ben Ezra aus Granada*, Altona: Gebr. Bonn, 1839, p. 95. The lowly grass that grows on roofs is contraposited with the proud "cedars of cypress" (*sic!*) also in Ibn Ezra's *Sepher ha'Anaq Hu haTarshish*, p. 7.

32. Tzinberg, *op. cit.* (Hebrew), 1:81.

33. *Ibid.*, p. 82.

34. Moses ibn Ezra, *Kitāb al-Muḥāḍara wal-Mudhākara* (*Book of Discussion and Remembrance*), Chapter 6, as quoted in *Jewish Enc.* 6:525.

35. H. Brody, *Diwan des Abul-Hasan Jehuda Ha-Levi*, Berlin: Itzkowski, 1894–1930, 1:49; reprinted by Gregg Intern. Publ., England, 1971.

36. Tzinberg, *op. cit.* (Hebrew), 1:95.

37. Zinberg, *op. cit.* (English), 1:155.

38. Y'huda haLevi, *Kuzari* 5:16, *op. cit.*, p. 242.

39. Tzinberg, *op. cit.* (Hebrew), 1:96.

40. Moses ibn Ezra, *Sepher ha'Anaq Hu haTarshish*, p. 42.

41. Zinberg, *op. cit.* (English), 1:154. My translation from the Hebrew.

42. Aharon Mirsky (ed.), *Shire R. Yitzḥaq ibn Khalfun*, Jerusalem: Mosad Bialik, 1961, p. 92.

43. Spiegel, *op. cit.*, p. 105.

44. Cf. A. R. Nykl, *Hispano-Arabic Poetry*, Baltimore: no publisher, 1946, p. 246; Brody, *Diwan*, *op. cit.*, 1:136. The transliteration of the Arabic has been changed to conform with the customary one. The translations which follow from the Arabic and Hebrew are mine.

45. On astronomy in the Talmud, cf., e.g., B. Shab. 75a; B. Suk. 28a. M. Steinschneider, *Die jüdischen Mathematiker*, Frankfurt a. M.: J. Kauffmann, 1901.

46. Cf. the masterly thousand-page compilation of Steinschneider, *Die hebraeischen Übersetzungen des Mittelalters*, reprinted, Graz: Akademische Druck- und Verlagsanstalt, 1956.

47. Cf. Steinschneider, "Die Mathematik bei den Juden," in *Bibliotheca Mathematica* (Stockholm), 1896, n.s. 10, no. 2, p. 34.

48. The interested reader can find good summaries of this subject in the articles of Charles Singer, "Science and Judaism," in Finkelstein (ed.), *The Jews*, *op. cit.*, pp. 216ff; and of J. M. Millás Valicrosa, "La Ciencia entre los Sefardies hasta su expulsion de España," in Barnett (ed.), *The Sephardi Heritage*, 1:112ff. (in Spanish with an English summary).

49. Sarton, *Introduction to the History of Science*, Vol. 2, Part 1, pp. 323–29; Part 2, pp. 533–41, 808–18. The figures for 1250–1300 include scientists in Spain as well as in Morocco.

50. The subject is discussed in Raphael Patai and Jennifer Patai Wing, *The Myth of the Jewish Race*, New York: Scribners, 1975, pp. 43, 48.

51. Cf. below, Chapter 12, where an analysis of the Jewish share in the Nobel Prizes is given.

52. Alexander Altmann, "Judaism and World Philosophy," in Finkelstein (ed.), *The Jews: Their Role in Civilization*, p. 75.

53. Abraham Halkin, "Judeo-Arabic Literature," in Finkelstein, *The Jews: Their Religion and Culture*, pp. 142f. Cf. Altmann, *op. cit.*, pp. 78–79.

54. Altmann, *op. cit.*, pp. 80–82.

55. *Ibid.*, pp. 85, 87–88.

56. Sarton, *op. cit.*, Vol. 2, Part 1, p. 279.

57. Maimonides, *Guide of the Perplexed*, trans. by Shlomo Pines, Chicago: University of Chicago Press, 1963, p. 9.

58. *Loc. cit.*

59. *Guide* 2:29, Pines, p. 347; 2:47, Pines, p. 409.

60. *Guide* 2:13 and 25, Pines, pp. 282, 284, 327–28.

61. Cf. Leo Strauss, "The Literary Character of the *Guide* . . ." in Salo W. Baron (ed.), *Essays on Maimonides*, New York: Columbia University Press, 1941; *idem*. "Introduction to Maimonides' *Guide* . . ." in Pines, *op. cit.*

62. A. Halkin, "Judeo-Arabic Literature," in Finkelstein (ed.), *The Jews: Their Religion and Culture*, p. 139; *idem*, "The Judeo-Islamic Age," in Leo W. Schwarz

(ed.), *Great Ages and Ideas of the Jewish People*, New York: Random House, 1956, pp. 250–51.

63. *Guide* 3:26, Pines, p. 507.

64. Halkin, "The Judeo-Islamic Age," p. 251; *Jewish Enc.* 9:79–80.

65. *Guide* 3:32, Pines, pp. 526–27. Maimonides quotes 1 Sam. 15:22; Isa. 1:11; Jer. 7:22–23. Cf. Pines, p. 530.

66. Cf. Max Meyerhof, "The Medical Work of Maimonides," in Baron, *op. cit.*, pp. 270–71. However, in his letter to Samuel ibn Tibbon, Maimonides states that "people, prominent and common, gentlemen, theologians and judges" fill the waiting room in his house; *ibid.*, p. 271. Since the intention of this letter was to dissuade Ibn Tibbon from visiting him, Maimonides may have added the word "common" for the sake of effect.

67. Pines, *op. cit.*, pp. 4, 5, 10, 16, etc. Cf. also Strauss, *op. cit.*, p. 71.

68. Meyerhof, *op. cit.*, p. 282. H. Z. Hirschberg, *Toldot haY'hudim b'Afrika haTz'fonit* (*History of the Jews in North Africa*), Jerusalem: Mosad Bialik, 1965, 1:123. Cf. also Maimonides' well-known letter to the Jews of Lunel, and below, Chapter 17, where the letter of Maimonides to his son is quoted.

69. *Guide* 3:18, Pines, pp. 475–76. The idea is repeatedly elaborated in *Guide* 3:17, 18, and in 51, where Maimonides says even more explicitly, "The intellect which overflowed from [God] to us is the bond between us and Him," Pines, p. 621. The reference to the *Mutakallimūn* is in *Guide* 1:71, Pines, p. 176.

70. Maimonides, *Mishne Tora* or *Yad haHazaqa*, book 1: Book of Knowledge, Hilkhot 'Avodat Kokhavim, Chapter 11, Part 16.

71. *Guide* 3:51; 1:introd.; 1:1, 2, 4, 5, 8; 2:22, Pines, pp. 624, 20, 24, 28, 31, 34, 319. The quote is from Zinberg, *op. cit.* (English), 1:148.

72. Tzinberg, *op. cit.* (Hebrew), Vol. 2, Merhavya: Sifriyat Po'alim, and Tel Aviv: Shreberk, 1966, pp. 92–94.

73. Thomas Aquinas, *Summa Theologiae*, as quoted by Gershom G. Scholem, *Major Trends of Jewish Mysticism*, New York: Schocken Books, 1961, p. 4.

74. G. Scholem in *Enc. Jud.* 10:526.

75. G. E. von Grunebaum, *Islam: Essays in the Nature and Growth of a Cultural Tradition*, Amer. Anthropological Ass., Memoir no. 81, April 1955, p. 29.

76. Scholem, *Major Trends*, p. 379 n. 30.

77. *Ibid.*, pp. 194–95, 189. Cf. G. Vajda in *Enc. Jud.* 16:1206–7.

78. The difficulty is well illustrated by the fact that the long article by Scholem in the *Enc. Jud.* 16:1193–1215, s.v. Zohar, does not contain a summary of the contents or teachings of the Zohar, and that in his book-length article on the Kabbala in the same *Enc.* (10:489–653) the subject is again avoided and instead a very long discussion included (pp. 556–638) on "The Basic Ideas of the Kabbalah" as a whole.

79. The main teachings of the Zohar have been systematized and presented in a Hebrew translation by Y. Tishby and F. Lachover, *Mishnat haZohar* (*The Wisdom of the Zohar*), 2 vols., Jerusalem: Mosad Bialik, 1957–61. But even Tishby refrains from attempting to give a summary of the contents of the Zohar, and confines himself instead to individual introductions to each of the subjects into which he groups the material, e.g., The Infinite, The Sephirot, the Shekhina, etc.

80. J. Gonda, *Viṣṇuism and Śivaism*, London: Atherton Press, 1970, p. 142.

81. Scholem, *Major Trends*, p. 139.
82. *Ibid.*, pp. 25, 217; *idem*, *On the Kabbalah and Its Symbolism*, New York: Schocken Books, 1965, p. 102.
83. Śatapatha Brāhmana 6.1.1.109, as quoted by Heinrich Zimmer, *Philosophies of India*, New York: Bollingen Series xxvi, Pantheon Books, 1951, pp. 242–43; *idem*, *Myths and Symbols in Indian Art and Civilization*, New York: Bollingen Series vi, Pantheon Books, 1946, pp. 206–7; cf. p. 214.
84. Zimmer, *Myths*, p. 197.
85. Scholem, *Major Trends*, p. 209; *idem*, *On the Kabbalah*, pp. 100, 101; Menaḥem Recanati, *Ta 'ame haMitzvot* (*Meaning of the Commandments*), Basel, 1581, 3a, as quoted by Scholem, *On the Kabbalah*, p. 124.
86. Cf. above, p. 130. Cf. Moses de Leon's symbolism of the point as the center of the circle, in his *Sepher haRimmon* (*Book of the Pomegranate*), Ms. British Museum 579f. 125–230, as quoted by Scholem, *Major Trends*, p. 218; and most of the figures illustrating Scholem's article "Kabbalah" in *Enc. Jud.* 10:491ff., figs. 1, 2, 4, 5, 6, 7, 8, 14.
87. Zimmer, *Philosophies of India*, p. 412.
88. For a list of all ten *Tattvas* and their explanation, cf. J. C. Chatterji, *Kashmir Shaivaism*, The Kashmir Series of Texts and Studies, Vol. 2, Fasc. 1, Srinagar: The Research Dept. Kashmir State, 1914, pp. 141–47. In the abundant Hindu literature on the *Tattvas* they are often subdivided into twenty-five or even thirty-six units, cf., e.g., the mid-thirteenth-century book *Unamivilakham* (*Explanation of the Truth*) by Manavācakam Kaṭantār, as quoted by Mariasusai Dhavamony, *Love of God According to Saiva Siddhanta*, Oxford: Clarendon Press, 1971, pp. 252–57, 322; see also Gonda, *op. cit.*, p. 44. Similarly in the Kabbala, by adding the twenty-two letters of the Hebrew alphabet to the ten *Sephirot*, the "thirty-two secret paths of wisdom" were arrived at, through which God created all that exists; cf. Scholem, *Major Trends*, p. 76.
89. Raphael Patai, *The Hebrew Goddess*, New York: Ktav, 1967, pp. 164–70, 173–74.
90. Zohar 1:162a–b, explaining the secret meaning of Ps. 37:25. Cf. Patai, *op. cit.*, p. 172.
91. Zohar 3:290b; Patai, *op. cit.*, p. 171.
92. Patai, *op. cit.*, p. 191.
93. Zohar 3:77b; 1:30b–31a: cf. Patai, *op. cit.*, pp. 163, 174–75. The Kabbalist Joseph Gikatila (1248–1305) explains the "mystery of the androgyne" in detail in his *Sha- 'are Ora* (*Gates of Light*), Offenbach, 1715, pp. 61b–62a; cf. Patai, *op. cit.*, p. 172.
94. Cf. Hastings' *Enc. of Religion and Ethics* 6:701, s.v. Hinduism; Zimmer, *Maya der indische Mythos*, Stuttgart: Deutsche Verlags-Anstalt, 1936, p. 463. Cf. also the Iranian myth of the androgynous god Zurvān, in S. N. Kramer (ed.), *Mythologies of the Ancient World*, New York: Doubleday-Anchor Books, 1961, pp. 355–56.
95. Zohar 1:30b–31a; cf. Patai, *op. cit.*, p. 175.
96. Zimmer, *Myths*, p. 186.
97. Zohar Ḥadash, Midrash haNe'elam to Ekha, Warsaw, n.d., p. 183. My summary of the Hebrew original, cf. Patai, *op. cit.*, pp. 194–95.

98. Zimmer, *Myths*, pp. 137–39, and pl. 34. Cf. also Zimmer's earlier book, *Maya*, p. 463.

99. Zohar 3:5a, 69a. Cf. Patai, *op. cit.*, p. 178.

100. W. Norman Brown, "Mythology of India," in Kramer (ed.), *op. cit.*, p. 312.

101. Zimmer, *Myths*, p. 186.

102. Patai, *op. cit.*, pp. 196–97 and sources there.

103. Zimmer, *Myths*, pp. 176–78.

104. Patai, *op. cit.*, pp. 197–98.

105. Zimmer, *Myths*, pp. 139–40, 170 n.

106. Patai, *op. cit.*, p. 115.

107. *Ibid.*, p. 200.

108. Zimmer, *Myths*, pp. 190–92.

109. Patai, *op. cit.*, pp. 201–2 and sources there.

110. Cf. Scholem, *On the Kabbalah*, p. 107.

111. Zimmer, *Myths*, p. 213.

112. *Ibid.*, pp. 183–84, 213.

113. Scholem, *Major Trends*, pp. 177–78, 237.

114. *Ibid.*, pp. 239, 267, 280, 311.

115. Cf. Dhavamony, *op. cit.*, p. 171.

116. Cf. Raphael Patai, *Man and Temple in Ancient Jewish Myth and Ritual*, 2nd ed., New York: Ktav, 1967, pp. 66, 70, 72, 88ff.

117. Scholem, *On the Kabbalah*, p. 108.

118. Patai, *The Hebrew Goddess*, pp. 195–96.

119. Zohar 1:164a and often; quoted by Scholem, *Major Trends*, p. 233.

120. Subramaniar Katiresu, *A Handbook of Saiva Religion*, Madras: G. A. Natesan, rev. ed., 1950, p. 45.

121. Scholem, *Major Trends*, pp. 74, 242; *idem*, in *Enc. Jud.* 7:574.

122. Zohar 2:99b. In the fourteenth century many detailed and explicit Kabbalistic writings appeared on the doctrine of transmigration.

123. *Enc. of Islam*, new ed., s.v. Hind, 3:436; s.v. Ḥallādj, 3:99ff.; s.v. Hindū, 3:459.

124. Cf. Elkan Nathan Adler, *Jewish Travellers*, London: Routledge, 1930, pp. 2–3; Louis Isaac Rabinowitz, *Jewish Merchant Adventurers*, London: E. Goldstone, 1948.

125. Scholem, *On the Kabbalah*, p. 184.

126. Isaac Albalag, as quoted in the Hebrew original by Tzinberg, *op. cit.*, 2:94. Cf. Georges Vajda, *Isaac Albalag*, Paris: J. Vrin, 1960, p. 148.

127. As Vajda remarked, *op. cit.*, p. 148 n. 2.

128. Cf. *Enc. of Religion and Ethics* 1:201, 4:160; Zimmer, *Myths*, pp. 5, 16 n., 17, 18.

129. Cf. Maimonides, "Thirteen Principles of Faith," contained in the Jewish *Siddur* (prayer book), e.g., *Seder 'Avodat Yisrael*, Redelheim, 1868, reprinted by Schocken Books, New York, 1937, p. 160.

130. However, the interested reader can find a discussion of it in Scholem's article "Kabbalah" in *Enc. Jud.* 10:638ff.

131. Scholem, *Enc. Jud.* 10:638.

CHAPTER 7

1. The historical material on which most of this chapter is built is admirably presented in three books: two by Cecil Roth, *The History of the Jews of Italy* (Philadelphia: The Jewish Publ. Soc. of America, 1946) and *The Jews of the Renaissance* (same publisher, 1959); and one by Moses A. Shulvass, *The Jews in the World of the Renaissance* (Leiden: Brill, and Chicago: Spertus College, 1973). Sources other than these are listed in the footnotes below.
2. Salo W. Baron, *A Social and Religious History of the Jews*, New York: Columbia University Press, and Philadelphia: The Jewish Publ. Soc. of America, 1952–69, Vol. X, pp. 278, 280; Vol. XII, p. 25.
3. Roberto Bachi, "The Demographic Development of Italian Jewry from the Seventeenth Century," *The Jewish Journal of Sociology* IV:2, December 1962, p. 173.
4. Raphael Patai and Jennifer Patai Wing, *The Myth of the Jewish Race*, New York: Scribners, 1975, p. 45.
5. Cf. Roth, *The Jews of the Renaissance*, p. ix.
6. *Jewish Enc.* 8:5, s.v. Leon (Judah Aryeh) of Modena.
7. However, in Padua in the sixteenth century the Committee of the Jewish Community forbade "ball games" on the Sabbath in all places, and on weekdays in the courtyard of the synagogue, cf. *ibid.*
8. Patai and Wing, *op. cit.*, pp. 108–10.
9. Baron, *op. cit.*, Vol. XIV, p. 123.
10. H. J. Zimmels, *Die Marranen in der rabbinischen Literatur*, Berlin: Rubin Mass, 1932, pp. 67–68.
11. Baron, *op. cit.*, Vol. XIV, p. 123.
12. Cf. Daniel Carpi (ed.), *Pinqas Wa'ad Q. Q. Padova 5338–5363 (Protocols of the Committee of the Jewish Community of Padua, 1577–1603)*, Jerusalem: The Israel Academy of Sciences and the Central Archives for Jewish History, 5734 (1974).
13. *Jewish Enc.* 7:266–67, s.v. Joseph ben Joshua ben Meir Hakohen.
14. Patai and Wing, *op. cit.*, pp. 377–79.
15. Shulvass, *op. cit.*, p. 267.
16. Roth, *The History of the Jews of Italy*, pp. 191–92.

CHAPTER 8

1. Simon Dubnow, *Geschichte des Chassidismus*, Berlin: Jüdischer Verlag, 1931, I:67–68. Hereinafter quoted as Dubnow.
2. Ruth Benedict, *Patterns of Culture*, London: Routledge, 1935, pp. 56–57.
3. *Ibid.*, pp. 56, 126.
4. A detailed analysis of the way in which Jewish historians present Hasidism is contained in Torsten Ysander, *Studien zum B'eštschen Hasidismus in seiner religionsgeschichtlichen Sonderart*, Uppsala Universitets Årsskrift 1933, Teologi 2. However, in addition to the studies discussed there, a large number of works

have been published both prior to the appearance of Ysander's book and in the
four decades that have elapsed since.

5. Cf. S. A. Horodezky, *HaHasidut w'haHasidim*, Tel Aviv: Dvir, 1928; Dubnow, *op. cit.*; Gershom G. Scholem, *Major Trends in Jewish Mysticism*, New
   York: Schocken Books, 1961. Cf. also Jacob Katz, *Massoret uMashber (Tradition
   and Crisis)*, Jerusalem: Mossad Bialik, 1958, p. 265.

6. S. J. Hurwitz, *HaHasidut w'haHaskala (Hasidism and Enlightenment)*, Berlin:
   H. Itzkowski, 1911.

7. Ysander, *op. cit.*, pp. 372–92; Scholem, *op. cit.*, p. 340.

8. Yaffa Eliach, "The Russian Dissenting Sects and Their Influence on the Baal
   Shem Tov, Founder of Hassidism," *Proceedings of the American Academy for
   Jewish Research*, 36 (1968):57–83.

9. James H. Billington, *The Icon and the Axe: An Interpretive History of Russian
   Culture*, New York: Knopf, 1966, pp. 72ff.

10. *Ibid.*, pp. 73–74, 154, 174, 178–79, 688–89.

11. Cf. Scholem, *op. cit.*, pp. 237–38.

12. Billington, *op. cit.*, p. 310.

13. Of the rich literature on the subject, mention can be made of the following: Karl
    Konrad Grass, *Die russischen Sekten*, Leipzig, 1905–14; Frederick C. Cony-
    beare, *Russian Dissenters*, Harvard Theol. Studies X, 1921; Paul Miliukov, *Out-
    lines of Russian Culture, Part I. Religion and the Church*, Philadelphia: Univer-
    sity of Pennsylvania Press, 1943, p. 59; and Serge Bolshakoff, *Russian
    Nonconformists*, Philadelphia: Westminster Press, 1950, pp. 46–57. See also
    Nicholas V. Riasanovsky, *A History of Russia*, New York: Oxford University
    Press, 1969, p. 221.

14. Miliukov, *op. cit.*, pp. 63, 67, 71ff., 74, 78f., 86f., 92, 94, 100ff., 105; Bolshakoff,
    op. cit., p. 80, cf. pp. 58ff.; Billington, *op. cit.*, pp. 174, 176–78, 239, and p. 695
    n. 32 for Judaizing influences on the Dukhobors and the Molokans.

15. Miliukov, *op. cit.*, pp. 87–91.

16. Billington, *op. cit.*, pp. 238ff.; Miliukov, *op. cit.*, pp. 95–96.

17. Miliukov, *op. cit.*, p. 98.

18. *Ibid.*, pp. 103–4; Bolshakoff, *op. cit.*, pp. 95–96.

19. Miliukov, *op. cit.*, pp. 114–17, 147–50; cf. also Billington, *op. cit.*, p. 700 n. 71.

20. Ysander, *op. cit.*, pp. 362–67, quoting studies on the mysticism of the Russian
    Orthodox Church.

21. Cf. Igor Smolitsch, *Leben und Lehre der Starzen*, 2nd ed., Köln: J. Hegner,
    1952.

22. Ysander, *op. cit.*, p. 371, quoting E. Belenson, "Der verborgene Christus (Mes-
    sias) bei Jiden," *Der Weg*, Warsaw, 1930, No. 4; and F. Haase, *Die religiöse
    Psyche des russischen Volkes*, Leipzig: Teubner, 1921, pp. 55ff.

23. William I. Thomas and Florian Znaniecki, *The Polish Peasant in Europe and
    America*, New York: Dover Publ., 1958, I:206–7; cf. also *The Cambridge History
    of Poland*, Cambridge: The University Press, 1950, I:560.

24. Bolshakoff, *op. cit.*, p. 59.

25. Raphael Mahler, *A History of Modern Jewry*, New York: Schocken Books, 1971,
    p. xv.

26. *Ibid.*, pp. 279, 281, 283–85, 301.

27. *Ibid.*, pp. 289–91, 299.

28. *Ibid.*, pp. 292–301, 315–16; *Cambridge History of Poland*, I:566.

29. Cf. *Shivhe haBeShT*, first printed in Khpust (Kapust) and Berdichev, 1815. English translation: Dan Ben-Amos and Jerome R. Mintz (translators and editors), *In Praise of the Baal Shem Tov*, Bloomington, Ind.: Indiana University Press, 1970. Hereinafter quoted as Ben-Amos.

30. Cf. the bibliography about the BeShT in *Enc. Jud.* 9:1058, s.v. Israel ben Eliezer Ba'al Shem Tov.

31. Ben-Amos, pp. 12, 22, 24, 27.

32. As quoted by Dubnow, II:63.

33. Ben-Amos, pp. 77, 106, 112, 145, 164, 218.

34. Horodezky, *op. cit.*, I:60; Ben-Amos, pp. 124, 250; Mahler, *op. cit.*, p. 458.

35. Dubnow, I:95, quoting *Sepher Tzawa'at haRiBaSh*, pp. 23–25; Mahler, *op. cit.*, p. 461.

36. Ben-Amos, pp. 110, 127, 135, 164, 245.

37. *Ibid.*, pp. 50, 55, 60, 79, 83, 107, 136.

38. *Ibid.*, pp. 161–62, 187–88.

39. *Ibid.*, pp. 36, 37, 60.

40. For a convenient summary, cf. *Enc. Brit.* (1973), s.vv. Epilepsy, Hysteria; and *The Merck Manual of Diagnosis and Therapy*, 11th ed., Rahway, N.J., and West Point, N.Y.: Merck & Co., 1966, pp. 1009ff.

41. Eliach, *op. cit.*, p. 81.

42. Dubnow, I:78.

43. Ben-Amos, p. 237.

44. *Ibid.*, pp. 220–21.

45. Cf. *Enc. Brit.* (1973), s.vv. Epilepsy, Drug Addiction.

46. Ben-Amos, pp. 77, 106, 132, 139, 146, 148, 160, 172, 221–22.

47. *Ibid.*, p. 30.

48. *Ibid.*, pp. 22–23, 35–37, 107–8, 177, 192, 196–97, 200–201, 238, 240, 252.

49. *Ibid.*, pp. 71–72, 210, 248, 255.

50. *Ibid.*, pp. 107–8, 140, 163–64, 186, 190, 223, 232.

51. *Ibid.*, pp. 78, 258.

52. Conybeare, *op. cit.*, p. 352.

53. Horodezky, *op. cit.*, I:60 and sources *ibid.*

54. Eliach, *op. cit.*, pp. 79–80.

55. Ben-Amos, pp. 22–23.

56. Dubnow, II:44.

57. Dubnow, I:185–86, 191, 203, 215; Scholem, *op. cit.*, pp. 334–35.

58. Dubnow, I:191, 248–49.

59. Grass, *op. cit.*, I:269f., as quoted by Ysander, *op. cit.*, pp. 386–87.

60. Conybeare, *op. cit.*, p. 303; Bolshakoff, *op. cit.*, pp. 90–91.

61. Ysander, *op. cit.*, p. 387.

62. Dubnow, I:186; Mahler, *op. cit.*, pp. 475–76, 507, 508.

63. Ben-Amos, p. 134.

64. Aylmer Maude, *A Peculiar People: The Dukhobors*, New York: Funk and Wagnalls, 1904, pp. 101, 219, 240–41.

65. Dubnow, I:143. Although neither the "victim" nor Maimon seem to have under-

stood it, the reasons for the flogging are clear enough: firstly, only a boy child was considered a valuable offspring, while the birth of a daughter, in Aggadic interpretation of Gen. 6:1ff., was regarded as being related to a sinful state in the begetter. Secondly, it was believed, in accordance with a Talmudic statement, that if a man reaches orgasm first, the child conceived would be a daughter, but if the woman reaches orgasm first, it would be a son. A man was therefore supposed to practice self-control so as to ensure he would have a son.

66. Dubnow, II:306.
67. Mark Zborowski and Elizabeth Herzog, *Life Is with People*, New York: International Universities Press, 1952, p. 176.
68. *Ibid.*, p. 176.
69. Dubnow, I:202, II:223; Mahler, *op. cit.*, pp. 476–80, 489–90, 492, 514.
70. Zborowski and Herzog, *op. cit.*, pp. 180–81.
71. Dubnow, II:221–22, 225, 234; cf. Benedict, *op. cit.*, pp. 137–39.
72. E.g., Tob. 6:7, 16, 17; Matt. 8:16, 31; 9:34, 38; Mark 1:34, 38; 9:38; Luke 13:32; T. Hul. 2:22; B. M'ila 17b; B. 'Av. Zar. 55b; Josephus, *Ant.*, 8:2:5; etc.
73. Zborowski and Herzog, *op. cit.*, pp. 91, 172; cf. *Jewish Enc.* 4:574–75, s.v. Dibbukim; 5:305–6, s.v. Exorcism; *Enc. Jud.* 6:19, s.v. Dibbuk, and lit. *ibid.*
74. Ben-Amos, pp. 33, 35, 37, 107–8.
75. Cf. the well-known and oft-performed play of S. An-Ski, *The Dybbuk* (1916), first produced in Vilna in 1920; Joseph Patai, *Lelkek és Titkok*, Budapest: Mult és Jövő, 1937, pp. 48–55; *Enc. Jud.* 6:19–21, s.v. Dibbuk.
76. B. Ta'an. 23a. Cf. R. Patai, *Man and Temple in Ancient Jewish Myth and Ritual*, 2nd ed., New York: Ktav, 1967, pp. 184ff., where some relevant material is gathered.
77. Lev. Rab. 27:6.
78. Dubnow, I:172, II:48.
79. Mahler, *op. cit.*, p. 528.
80. Joseph Patai, *op. cit.*, pp. 99–100.
81. B. Ta'an. 25a; B. Ber. 31b–32a.
82. Dubnow, I:194 n. 1, II:71, 252, 285.
83. Conybeare, *op. cit.*, p. 352; Ysander, *op. cit.*, p. 387.
84. Dubnow, II:96–97.
85. *Ibid.*, II:252.
86. *Ibid.*, II:96–97, 300.
87. Menahem Nahum of Chernobyl, *M'or 'Enayim*, Slavuta, 1798, B'reshit, Noaḥ, and *passim*; *idem*, *Y'sammaḥ Lev*, Slavuta, 1798, Noaḥ; reprinted in Zolkiev, 1800; as quoted by Dubnow, II:54.
88. Dubnow, II:66–67.
89. *Ibid.*, II:299 and sources *ibid.*
90. Scholem, *op. cit.*, p. 405 n. 113 (in Hebrew). On sin in the Kabbalistic doctrine, cf. *ibid.*, pp. 231ff., 236, 239, 241.
91. Cf. *Sepher Tzawa'at haRiBaSh*, Warsaw, 1913, p. 13.
92. Scholem, *op. cit.*, pp. 268, 280.
93. Dubnow, I:228, II:24.
94. *Ibid.*, I:95–96.

95. Bolshakoff, *op. cit.*, pp. 85–86.
96. Cf. Joseph L. Hromádka, "Eastern Orthodoxy," in Edward J. Jurji (ed.), *The Great Religions of the Modern World*, Princeton, N.J.: Princeton University Press, 1947, pp. 303–4.
97. Mahler, *op. cit.*, p. 449.
98. Dubnow, II:71–72.
99. *Ibid.*, II:229–30.
100. *Ibid.*, II:229–30; Mahler, *op. cit.*, p. 496.
101. Mahler, *op. cit.*, p. 502.
102. *Ibid.*, pp. 464, 471.
103. *Ibid.*, p. 499.
104. Elimelekh of Lezhaysk, *No'am Elimelekh* (*Elimelekh's Graciousness*), 1786, as summarized by Dubnow, II:22–28 and by Mahler, *op. cit.*, pp. 497–98; cf. p. 500.
105. Patai, *Man and Temple*, pp. 184ff. and cf. what was said above, p. 200, about the Talmudic "Pious Men" who were believed to have exercised considerable control over the acts of God.
106. Mahler, *op. cit.*, p. 515.
107. Joseph Patai, *op. cit.*, p. 144.
108. Cf. Ḥayim Vital, *Sepher haGilgulim* (*Book of Transmigrations*), Przemysl, 1875. Cf. Scholem, *op. cit.*, pp. 281ff.
109. Dubnow, II:38, 67, 227, 251.
110. *Ibid.*, I:59–60.
111. Conybeare, *op. cit.*, pp. 340, 355–56.
112. Miliukov, *op. cit.*, pp. 99–100; Bolshakoff, *op. cit.*, pp. 100–105.
113. Cf. *Encyclopedia of Religion and Ethics* 11:337.
114. Cf. *Enc. Brit.* (1973), s.v. Seraphim, Saint.
115. Dubnow, II:44; Mahler, *op. cit.*, pp. 508, 515.
116. Bolshakoff, *op. cit.*, p. 90; Ysander, *op. cit.*, pp. 322–23; Eliach, *op. cit.*, p. 73; Dubnow, II:62–63.
117. Dubnow, II:72; Mahler, *op. cit.*, pp. 529, 531, 533.
118. Mahler, *op. cit.*, pp. 516, 518.
119. *Ibid.*, pp. 516, 517.
120. *Enc. Jud.* 7:1422ff.
121. *Ibid.*, 7:1422.
122. Joseph Patai, *op. cit.*, p. 68. My translation from the Hungarian original.
123. Cf. Eliyahu Ba'al Shem, *Toldot Adam* (*History of Adam*), Wilmersdorf, 1808; Benjamin Binesh Ba'al Shem, *Sepher Amtahat Binyamin*, Wilmersdorf, 1729; cf. R. Patai, "Jewish Folk-Cures for Barrenness," *Folk-Lore*, London, Vol. 55, September 1944, pp. 117–24; Vol. 56, December 1944–March 1955, pp. 208–18. Cf. also Dubnow, I:59–60, 84–85.
124. Cf. e.g. Oskar V. Hovorka and Adolf Kronfeld, *Vergleichende Volksmedizin*, Stuttgart: Strecker und Schröder, 1908–9, II:513ff; Patai, "Jewish Folk-Cures for Barrenness," pp. 208ff.
125. Ben-Amos, p. 83; Dubnow, I:86–87.
126. Mahler, *op. cit.*, pp. 450, 527.

127. Dubnow, I:186.

128. *Ibid.*, I:68, 98, 133, 135, 159.

129. *Ibid.*, I:185, II:69, and sources *ibid.*

130. I heard this song in the 1930's in Jerusalem. *Bakhurim* are young men, and especially yeshiva students.

131. Dubnow, I:140; cf. also pp. 183, 197, 201, 213, 217, 251.

132. Ephraim of Sudilkov, *Degel Maḥane Ephrayim (The Banner of the Camp of Ephraim)*, Koretz, 1811, sections WaYiqra, Ḥayye Sara, MiQetz, as quoted by Dubnow, II:64; cf. also pp. 32, 61.

133. Dubnow, II:73, 90, 109.

134. M. Pe'a I:1.

135. Dubnow, II:108.

136. Edward William Lane, *The Manners and Customs of the Modern Egyptians*, London: J. M. Dent (Everyman Library), n.d., p. 241. The book was first published in 1836. Lane lived in Egypt from 1825 to 1828, and again from 1833 to 1835.

CHAPTER 9

1. Azariah dei Rossi, *M'or 'Enayim (Light of the Eyes)*, Mantua, 1575; reprinted in Berlin, 1794, and Vienna, 1829.

2. Salo W. Baron, "The Modern Age," in Leo W. Schwarz (ed.), *Great Ages and Ideas of the Jewish People*, New York: Random House, 1956, p. 379.

3. The latter view is argued by Ellis Rivkin, *Leon da Modena and the Kol Sakhal*, Cincinnati: Hebrew Union College Press, 1952.

4. Leon da Modena, *Historia de gli Riti Hebraici*, Venice, 1638, Part II, Chapter 5, Par. 3, as quoted by Rivkin, *op. cit.*, p. 36.

5. Simone Luzzatto, *Discorso circa il stato degli Hebrei*, Venice, 1638.

6. As quoted by Heinrich Graetz, *History of the Jews*, Philadelphia: Jewish Publ. Soc. of America, 1967 (reprint), 5:83–84.

7. Isaac (Fernando) Cardozo, *Las Excelencias y Calumnias de los Hebreos*, Amsterdam, 1679.

8. Graetz, *op. cit.*, 5:341–43.

9. Isaac de Pinto, *Apologie pour la Nation Juive*, Amsterdam, 1762. The Paris edition of the book (n.d.) had the title *Reflexions critique sur le premier chapitre du VIIe tome des oeuvres de monsieur Voltaire au sujet des Juifs.*

10. Cf. Raphael Patai, *Tents of Jacob: The Diaspora Yesterday and Today*, Englewood Cliffs, N.J.: Prentice-Hall, 1971, pp. 280–81, and sources there.

11. Graetz, *op. cit.*, 5:346; Simon Dubnow, *Weltgeschichte des jüdischen Volkes*, Berlin: Jüdischer Verlag, 1925–29, 7:405–6.

12. Arthur Hertzberg, *The French Enlightenment and the Jews*, New York: Columbia University Press, 1968, pp. 153, 182.

13. Graetz, *op. cit.*, 5:166.

14. Reuel Jesurun, *Dialogo dos Montes*, Amsterdam, 1767.

15. On the characteristics of the love of God according to Spinoza, and on his concept of *amor dei intellectualis* and its Biblical and other sources, cf. Harry A. Wolfson, *The Philosophy of Spinoza*, New York: Schocken Books, 1969, 2:274, 276–83,

302ff. All the statements of Spinoza on *amor dei* are gathered in the Spinoza concordance of Emilia Giancotti Boscherini, *Lexicon Spinozarum*, The Hague: Martinus Nijhoff, 1970, 1:66–68. The quotation above is from the *Ethics* V, Prop. XVI (II:290, 26).

16. Graetz, *op. cit.*, 5:167.

17. *Enc. Jud.* s.v. Brazil.

18. Jacob Katz, "The Term 'Jewish Emancipation': Its Origin and Historical Impact," in Alexander Altmann (ed.), *Studies in Nineteenth-Century Jewish Intellectual History*, Cambridge, Mass.: Harvard University Press, 1964, pp. 4–5.

19. On Toland's indebtedness to Simone Luzzatto, cf. S. Ettinger, "The Beginnings of Change in the Attitude of European Society Towards the Jews," in *Scripta Hierosolymitana*, 1961, 7:216.

20. Hertzberg, *op. cit.*, p. 276.

21. *Ibid.*, pp. 276–80. The quotation is from Jean Baptiste de Boyer d'Argens, *Lettres Juives, ou correspondence philosophique, historique et critique entre un Juif voyageur à Paris et ses correspondants en divers endroit*, The Hague, 1736–37; unpaged introduction of Vol. 3 of the 1738 edition.

22. *Jewish Enc.* 8:481, s.v. Mendelssohn; also quoted in Milton Himmelfarb, *The Jews of Modernity*, New York: Basic Books, 1973, p. 23.

23. Abbé Antoine Guénée, *Lettres de quelques Juifs portugais et allemands à M. de Voltaire*, Paris, 1769; Jean Baptiste de Mirabaud, *Opinions des anciens sur les Juifs*, London, 1769; Jean Baptiste Nicolas de Lisle de Sales, *De la philosophie de la nature*, Amsterdam, 1770.

24. As quoted in the *Enc. Jud.* 14:352–53, s.v. Rousseau.

25. Rousseau, *Émile*, trans. by Barbara Foxley, 1911 (reprinted 1957), New York: Dutton, 4:268.

26. Abbé Henri Grégoire, *Sur la régeneration physique, morale, et politique des Juifs*, Metz, 1789.

27. *Jewish Enc.* 6:90, s.v. Grégoire, Henri.

28. Mirabeau, *Sur Moses Mendelssohn, sur la réforme politique des Juifs*, London, 1787.

29. *Enc. Jud.* 12:73, s.v. Mirabeau.

30. *Ibid.*, 6:702–3, s.v. Emancipation.

31. Raphael Mahler, *A History of Modern Jewry*, London: Vallentine, Mitchell, 1971, p. 33.

32. Christian Wilhelm von Dohm, *Ueber die bürgerliche Verbesserung der Juden*, 1781. Cf. Katz, *op. cit.*, p. 13.

33. Bernard D. Weinryb, "East European Jewry (Since the Partitions of Poland, 1772–1795)," in Louis Finkelstein (ed.), *The Jews: Their History*, 4th ed., New York: Schocken Books, 1970, pp. 347–48, 358.

34. Levi Israel, *Schreiben eines Juden an einem (!) Philosophen nebst der Antwort: Mit Anmerkungen*, Hamburg, 1753; as cited by Katz, *op. cit.*, p. 11.

35. *Moses Mendelssohns gesammelte Schriften*, Leipzig: Brockhaus, 1843, 3:355. My translation from the German.

36. *Ibid.*, 3:182. My translation from the German.

37. Graetz, *op. cit.*, 5:336, 369, 371. Mahler, *op. cit.*, p. 163.

38. Cf. *HaM'assef*, Königsberg, September 1784, *Naḥal haB'sor*, p. 3. My translation

from the Hebrew. Cf. Isaac Eisenstein-Barzilay, "The Background of the Berlin Haskala," in *Essays on Jewish Life and Thought Presented in Honor of Salo Wittmayer Baron*, New York: Columbia University Press, 1959, p. 196.

39. Zalkind Hourwitz, *Apologie pour les Juifs*, Paris: Gattey et Royser, 1789.

40. *Jewish Enc.* 2:332, s.v. Austria.

41. Mahler, *op. cit.*, pp. 308–9, 311–13.

42. Graetz, *op. cit.*, 5:68–70; Rivkin, *op. cit.*, p. 27, and sources in n. 32.

43. Michael R. Marrus, *The Politics of Assimilation: A Study of the French Jewish Community at the Time of the Dreyfus Affair*, Oxford: Clarendon Press, 1971, pp. 39–40.

44. François J. A. Hell, *Observations d'un alsacien sur l'affaire présente des Juifs d'Alsace*, Frankfurt a. M., 1779, p. 69, as quoted by Hertzberg, *op. cit.*, p. 288. Foissac, *Le cri du citoyen contre les Juifs de Metz par un capitaine d'infanterie*, Lausanne (Metz), 1786, esp. p. 19.

45. As shown by Hannah Emmrich, *Das Judentum bei Voltaire*, Breslau: Priebatsch, 1930.

46. Voltaire, *Lettres de Memmius à Ciceron*, in *Oeuvres Complètes*, 52 vols., Paris: Louis Moland, 1877–85, 28:439–40, as quoted by Hertzberg, *op. cit.*, p. 300.

47. All this material is systematically presented in Emmrich, *op. cit.*, pp. 127–46, whose book is a complete and thorough examination of Voltaire's views on Jews and Judaism. I first read Miss Emmrich's book in the year it was published when I was a student at the Jüdisch-Theologisches Seminar in Breslau where she worked as a librarian. Its publication created quite a stir.

48. Mirabeau, *op. cit.*, p. 57, as quoted by Hertzberg, *op. cit.*, p. 294.

49. Cf. above, Chapter 5 on "Jews and Hellenes."

50. Emmrich, *op. cit.*, pp. 10–20.

51. Montesquieu, *Oeuvres complètes*, ed. Roger Caillois, Paris, 1949, 1:218–19; as quoted by Hertzberg, *op. cit.*, 275.

52. J. Weill, "Un texte de Montesquieu sur le Judaïsme," *Revue des Études Juives*, 1904, 49:151–52. My translation from the French.

53. Graetz, *op. cit.*, 5:532.

54. As quoted in Salo W. Baron, *A Social and Religious History of the Jews*, New York: Columbia University Press, 1937, 2:243.

55. E.g., Mordecai Benet (1753–1829), chief rabbi of Moravia; Eleazar Fleckeles (1754–1826) and Samuel Landau (? –1834), rabbi and chief *dayyan*, respectively, in Prague.

56. Moses Sofer, *D'rashot*, 1:101, as quoted by Tz'vi Zahavi, *MehaḤatam Sofer 'Ad Herzl (From Moses Sofer to Herzl)*, Jerusalem: Sifriya Tziyonit, 1966, p. 75. My translation from the Hebrew.

57. *Ibid.*, 2:312b, as quoted by Zahavi, *ibid.*, p. 58; and 2:379a, Zahavi, p. 72. My translation from the Hebrew.

58. Jacob S. Raisin, *The Haskalah Movement in Russia*, Philadelphia: Jewish Publ. Soc. of America, 1913, p. 241.

59. Raphael Patai, *The Arab Mind*, New York: Scribners, 1973, pp. 279ff., 305.

60. Salo W. Baron, "The Modern Age," in Schwarz (ed.), *op. cit.*, p. 317.

61. Cf. the texts of the relevant documents collected by Raphael Mahler, *Jewish*

Emancipation: A Selection of Documents, New York: American Jewish Committee, 1941.

62. Martin Phillipson, *Neueste Geschichte des jüdischen Volkes*, Leipzig: Gustav Fock, 1907, 1:13.

63. Published in Königsberg, 1804, as cited in Phillipson, *op. cit.*, 1:53.

64. Cf. Bezalel Sherman, "Galut Nationalism," in R. Patai (ed.), *Encyclopaedia of Zionism and Israel*, New York: Herzl Press and McGraw-Hill, 1971, 1:369; and *ibid.*, s.v. Bund.

65. Raisin, *op. cit.*, pp. 131, 167, 239–40, 425.

66. Raphael Patai, *Israel Between East and West: A Study in Human Relations*, Philadelphia: Jewish Pub. Soc. of America, 1953.

67. Patai, *The Arab Mind*, pp. 247ff.

68. Arthur Ruppin, *Soziologie der Juden*, Berlin: Jüdischer Verlag, 1930, 1:246ff.

CHAPTER 10

1. Melvin M. Tumin, "The Cult of Gratitude," in Peter I. Rose (ed.), *The Ghetto and Beyond: Essays on Jewish Life in America*, New York: Random House, 1969, p. 76.

2. Cf. *Enc. Jud.* 8:272, s.v. Heine, Heinrich.

3. Milton Himmelfarb, *The Jews of Modernity*, New York: Basic Books, 1973, pp. 28, 29.

4. Graetz, *op. cit.*, 5:587.

5. *Jewish Enc.* 4:252–53, s.v. Conversion; *Enc. Jud.* 3:207, s.v. Apostasy.

6. *Jewish Enc.* 4:253, s.v. Converts.

7. Thorstein Veblen, "Intellectual Preeminence of Jews in Modern Europe," *Political Science Quarterly*, 1919, pp. 33–42.

CHAPTER 11

1. Charles Spearman, " 'General Intelligence,' Objectively Determined and Measured," *American Journal of Psychology*, 1904, 15:201–93; *idem*, *The Abilities of Man*, New York: Macmillan, 1927.

2. L. L. Thurstone, "Multiple-Factor Analysis," *Psychological Review*, 1931, 38:406–27; *idem*, "Primary Mental Abilities," *Psychometric Monographs*, 1938, No. 1, pp. 1–121; *idem*, *Multiple-Factor Analysis*, Chicago: University of Chicago Press, 1947.

3. Joy Paul Guilford, *The Nature of Human Intelligence*, New York: McGraw-Hill, 1967; J. P. Guilford and R. Hoepfner, *The Analysis of Intelligence*, New York: McGraw-Hill, 1971.

4. Cohen also believes that all three processes can be improved chemically, leading to the improvement of thinking abilities. Cf. Edward A. Sullivan, "Medical, Biological, and Chemical Methods of Shaping the Mind," *Phi Delta Kappan*, April 1972, 53(8), p. 485.

5. David Wechsler, *The Measurement and Appraisal of Adult Intelligence*, 5th ed., Baltimore, Md.: Williams & Wilkins, 1972, p. 79.

6. As quoted by Richard J. Herrnstein, *I.Q. in the Meritocracy*, Boston-Toronto: Little, Brown, 1973, p. 107. Cf. also Ronald J. Samuda, *Psychological Testing of American Minorities*, New York: Dodd, Mead, 1975, p. 26.

7. P. E. Vernon, "Development of Current Ideas About Intelligence Tests," in J. E. Meade and A. S. Parks (eds.), *Genetic and Environmental Factors in Human Ability*, Edinburgh and London: Oliver & Boyd, 1966, p. 11.

8. William W. Trumbull, "Foreword," in Samuda, *op. cit.*, p. viii.

9. Those statistically sophisticated will, of course, recognize that the examples selected above correspond to one standard deviation: 68 percent of a normal distribution falls within -1 and $+1$ standard deviation; about 95 percent within -2 and $+2$; and about 99.7 percent within -3 and $+3$.

10. In all normal distributions (whatever they are the distributions of) this is the case.

11. Raphael Patai and Jennifer Patai Wing, *The Myth of the Jewish Race*, New York: Scribners, 1975, p. 149; cf. pp. 146ff.

12. In 1970, Morris B. Gross reported the results of a test of reasoning ability administered to Jewish and Gentile seventh- and tenth-grade groups. Of both paired groups the Jewish were significantly superior. Cf. Morris B. Gross, "Reasoning Ability of Hebrew Parochial School Students," *Perceptual and Motor Skills*, December 1970, 31(3):837–38.

13. Gerald S. Lesser, Gordon Fifer, and Donald H. Clark, *Mental Abilities of Children from Different Social-Class and Cultural Groups*, Monographs of the Society for Research in Child Development, Chicago: University of Chicago Press, No. 102, 1965, 30(4):54–58.

14. Margaret E. Backman, *Relationship of Ethnicity, Socio-Economic Status, and Sex to Patterns of Mental Abilities*, Columbia University Ph.D. Thesis. Results presented by author in "Patterns of Mental Abilities of Adolescent Males and Females from Different Ethnic and Socioeconomic Backgrounds," in *Proceedings, 79th Annual Convention, APA*, 1971, pp. 511–12.

15. Christopher Jencks, "What Color Is I.Q.? Intelligence and Race," in Carl Senna (ed.), *The Fallacy of I.Q.*, New York: The Third Press, Joseph Okpaku Publ. Co., 1973, p. 39.

16. Carl Senna, "Speed and Direction," in *ibid.*, p. 42.

17. E.g., James O. Whittaker, *Introduction to Psychology*, 2nd ed., Philadelphia-Toronto-London: W. B. Saunders, 1970, p. 444; John Radford and Andrew Burton, "Changing Intelligence," in Ken Richardson, *et al.* (eds.), *Race and Intelligence*, Baltimore, Md.: Penguin Books, 1972, p. 29; Joanna Ryan, "The Illusion of Objectivity," in *ibid.*, p. 42; Samuda, *op. cit.*, p. 36.

18. A few typical statements of representatives of the two schools can serve as illustrations of their positions. "By evaluating the total evidence . . . and by a procedure too technical to explain here [Arthur R.] Jensen concluded (as have most experts in the field) that the genetic factor is worth about 80 percent and that only 20 percent is left to everything else—the social, cultural, and physical environment, plus illness, prenatal factors, and what have you" (Herrnstein, *op. cit.*, p. 170). Similarly in England, J. L. Jinks and D. W. Fulker concluded that "the rel-

ative contribution of the genes to measured intelligence falls between about 70 and 85 percent. . . . They show . . . convergence of the overwhelming body of data on measured intelligence to a figure in the vicinity of 80 percent or higher for the genetic contribution to scores on standard I.Q. tests" (*ibid.*, p. 171). Herrnstein himself concludes that "the hereditarian's most impressive argument is simply to note the convergence of dozens, if not hundreds, of studies over the past sixty years. With only occasional, and usually explainable, exceptions . . . all investigations of the relative contributions of nature and nurture have found the first to be predominant" (*ibid.*, p. 167; cf. also p. 165). But he cautions that these results are "based almost entirely on data from whites" (p. 185).

Whatever the estimated or calculated share of the environment in the measurable aspects of intelligence, developmental biologists consider as "environment" everything external to the genotype, which itself is fixed at conception and remains unchanged throughout the individual's lifetime. It is upon this genetic base that the environment exerts its influence. This influence can go so deep as to affect the very functioning of the genes. "For example it is known that hormones, which can be produced in response to external stimuli may be involved in switching genes on and off. . . . [While] there is no evidence that environment can cause directed adaptive change in the genetic material itself, the mediation is by changes in the rates and numbers of genes acting over time" (John Hambley, "Diversity: A Developmental Perspective," in Richardson, *et al.*, *op. cit.*, p. 116). It is because of observations such as this that geneticists are unhappy with the simplistic approach which considers heredity and environment two discrete units, of which one, heredity, is the passive recipient of influences impinging upon it from the environment, and view instead the two as a "*process* whereby an individual's unique genetic endowment is influenced by and contributes to his environment" (*ibid.*, p. 119).

Applying these insights to the question of the interrelationship between intelligence and environment, modern educators have argued that "the environment of the individual is in his head" (Donald Swift, "What Is the Environment?" in *op. cit.*, p. 156). This is the conclusion reached from the understanding that "Man . . . does not react passively to physical and social stimuli. . . . He selects a particular niche, modifies it, develops ways to avoid what he does not want to perceive, and emphasizes that which he wants to experience" (R. Dubos, *So Human an Animal*, London: Hart-Davis, 1970, as quoted by Swift, *ibid.*, p. 156). Cf. also the environmentalist argument as presented by Samuda, *op. cit.*, pp. 42–50.

19. Theodosius Dobzhansky, "Race, Intelligence and Genetics: Differences Are Not Deficit," *Psychology Today*, December 1973, pp. 97, 98. Emphases in the original.

20. Cf., e.g., Benjamin Fine, *The Stranglehold of the I.Q.*, New York: Doubleday, 1975; Carl G. Liungman, *What Is IQ? Intelligence, Heredity and Environment*, New York: Gordon Cremonesi/Atheneum, 1975.

21. Cf. Hans J. Eysenck, *The I.Q. Argument: Race, Intelligence and Education*, New York: The Library Press, 1971, pp. 22–23. Cf. also Senna, *op. cit.*, pp. 26–27.

22. Kenneth Eells, "What Is the Problem?" in Kenneth Eells, Allison Davis, Robert J. Havighurst, Virgil E. Herrick, and Ralph W. Tyler, *Intelligence and Cultural Differences*, Chicago: University of Chicago Press, 1951, p. 4.

23. Robert J. Havighurst, "What Are the Cultural Differences Which May Affect Performance on Intelligence Tests?" in *ibid.*, pp. 16–21. "The impressive case for the link between I.Q. and class level" has been discussed by Herrnstein, *op. cit.*, pp. 115ff., and we shall return to it in the last section of this chapter.

24. Dobzhansky, *op. cit.*, pp. 99–101.

25. Steven Rose, "Environmental Effects on Brain and Behavior," in Richardson, *et al.*, *op. cit.*, pp. 136–39.

26. Ashley Montagu, *Current Anthropology*, March 1975, 16(1):142. Cf. literature quoted in Charles A. Valentine and Bettylou Valentine, "Brain Damage and the Intellectual Defense of Inequality," *op. cit.*, p. 119.

27. Cf. Harold M. Schmeck, Jr., "Brain Harm in U.S. Laid to Food Lack," *The New York Times*, Sunday, November 2, 1975, main section, p. 32.

28. Robert B. Livingston, *et al.*, "U.S. Poverty Impact on Brain Development," in Mary A. B. Brazier (ed.), *Growth and Development of the Brain*, International Brain Research Organization Monograph Series, Vol. 1, New York: Raven Press, 1975, p. 388.

29. Rose, *op. cit.*, p. 143.

30. Matt. 6:11; Luke 11:3.

31. Prov. 30:8. Cf. Israel Abrahams, *Studies*, 2nd ser., p. xii.

32. Isa. 58:7.

33. Prov. 10:2; 11:4.

34. Cf. on this whole issue Ashley Montagu, "Sociogenic Brain Damage," *American Anthropologist*, 1972, 74:1045–61; Valentine, *op. cit.*, pp. 117–50.

35. Montagu, *op. cit.*, p. 1054; Patai and Wing, *op. cit.*, pp. 143–45.

36. Mark Zborowski and Elizabeth Herzog, *Life Is with People*, New York: International Universities Press, 1952, p. 327.

37. Benjamin S. Bloom, *Stability and Change in Human Characteristics*, New York: Wiley, 1964, pp. 76ff.

38. Hans F. K. Günther, *Rassenkunde des jüdischen Volkes*, Munich: J. F. Lehmann, 1930, pp. 202–3. My translation from the German.

39. Julius B. Maller, "Studies in the Intelligence of Young Jews," *Jewish Education*, January–March 1931, 3(1):10–11 (offprint).

40. Cf. sources in Patai and Wing, *op. cit.*, pp. 151 and 323 n. 26.

41. Ernest van den Haag, *The Jewish Mystique*, New York: Stein and Day, 1969, pp. 14–18.

42. Cf. Norbert Wiener, *Ex-Prodigy: My Childhood and Youth*, New York: Simon and Schuster, 1953, pp. 11–13; Lewis S. Feuer, *Scientific Intellectual: The Psychological and Sociological Origins of Modern Science*, New York: Basic Books, 1963, p. 308. Haldane is referred to by Feuer, *ibid.*, without, however, giving the source.

43. Cf. Patai and Wing, *op. cit.*, where this subject is discussed in detail.

44. Cf. R. Patai, *Golden River to Golden Road: Society, Culture and Change in the Middle East*, 3rd ed., Philadelphia: University of Pennsylvania Press, 1969, pp.

19, 22, 31, 37, 350ff., 412ff.; *idem, The Arab Mind,* New York: Scribners, 1973, pp. 82, 90ff., 150, 158, 308.

45. Gina Ortar, "Comparative Analysis of the Jewish Communities as to Structure of Intelligence" (in Hebrew), *Megamot,* 1953, 4(2):107–22.

46. Gina Ortar, "Educational Achievement as Related to Socio-Cultural Background of Primary School Graduates in Israel" (in Hebrew), *Megamot,* 1967, 15:220–30.

47. Avram H. Shapiro, "Effects of Family Density and Mothers' Education on Pre-schoolers' Motor Skills," *Perceptual and Motors Skills,* February 1974, 38(1):79–86.

48. Helen F. Antonovsky and Dina Feitelson, "An Observational Study of Intellec-tual Stimulation of Young Children," *Early Child Development and Care,* 1973, 2(3):329–44.

49. Shlomo Sharan (Singer) and Leonard Weller, "Classification Patterns of Under-privileged Children in Israel," *Child Development,* June 1971, 42(2):581–94.

50. *Ibid.,* p. 591.

51. Blanka Burg, *Mental Abilities of Israeli Children from Different Socio-Cultural Groups,* Yeshiva University Ph.D. Thesis, 1972.

52. Dina Feitelson, "Teaching Reading to Culturally Disadvantaged Children," *The Reading Teacher,* October 1968, 22(1):55–61.

53. Cf. sources in Ilana Preale, Yehuda Amir, and Shlomo Sharan (Singer), "Percep-tual Articulation and Task Effectiveness in Several Israeli Subcultures," *Journal of Personality and Social Psychology,* 1970, 15(3):190.

54. *Ibid.,* pp. 190–91.

55. *Ibid.,* p. 190, referring to works by J. W. Berry, J. Z. M. Dawson, and H. A. Witkin.

56. Cf. the generalized psychological portraiture of the Middle Eastern family in R. Patai, *Israel Between East and West: A Study in Human Relations,* Philadelphia: Jewish Publ. Soc. of America, 1953, p. 108; *idem, Golden River,* pp. 350ff. For the Kurdish Jews, cf. Dina Feitelson, "Some Changes in the Educational Pat-terns of the Kurdish Community in Israel" (in Hebrew), *Megamot,* 1954, 6:275–97. For the Moroccans, cf. M. Kohls, "Culture Patterns and Adjustment Processes of Moroccan Immigrants from Rural Areas" (in Hebrew), *Megamot,* 1956, 7:345–76. Cf. also Preale, *et al., op. cit.,* p. 191.

57. Preale, *et al., op. cit.,* p. 194.

58. Yehuda Amir, "Adjustment and Promotion of Soldiers from Kibbutzim (Commu-nal Settlements" (in Hebrew), *Megamot,* 1967, 15(2–3):250–58.

59. Joseph Marcus, Alexander Thomas, and Stella Chess, "Behavioral Individuality in Kibbutz Children," *Israel Annals of Psychiatry and Related Disciplines,* April 1969, 7(1):43–54.

CHAPTER 12

1. The term "genius" is being used much too loosely even by scholars. For instance, Lewis M. Terman's important forty-year study of some 1,500 individuals who at the ages of six to fourteen had a mean I.Q. of 151 is entitled *Genetic Studies of Genius,* although the subtitle of Volume I reduces "genius" to "gifted children."

Cf. Lewis M. Terman, *et al.*, *Genetic Studies of Genius*, Vol. I. *Mental and Physical Traits of a Thousand Gifted Children*, Stanford, Calif.: Stanford University Press, 2nd ed., 1926. Wishing to avoid this pitfall, I clearly spelled out in the title of this chapter that it deals with both giftedness and genius as manifested among Jews.

2. Terman, *op. cit.*, Vols. 1–5.

3. Otto Klineberg, "Race and Psychology," in *Race and Science* (a UNESCO publication), New York: Columbia University Press, 1971, p. 442. An assortment of definitions of genius and some insightful comments on the phenomenon are contained in Alfred Hock, *Reason and Genius: Studies in Their Origin*, New York: Philosophical Library, 1960, reprinted Westport, Conn.: Greenwood Press, 1971, esp. pp. 63ff. Cf. also Sir Walter Russell Brain, *Some Reflections on Genius*, Philadelphia: Lippincott, 1960, pp. 9ff.

4. George Sarton, *Introduction to the History of Science*, 5 vols., Washington, D.C.: Carnegie Institution of Washington, 1927–48.

5. Sarton, *op. cit.*, Vol. II, Part I, pp. 323–29; Part II, pp. 533–41, 808–18. I included above among the Jews Samuel ibn Abbas, who late in life converted to Islam, and whom Sarton lists among the Muslims.

6. *Loc. cit.* I included two Catalan Jews among the Jewish scientists of Spain; Sarton lists them among the Provençaux. The thirty-five Jewish scientists listed in Spain also include a few who lived in Morocco.

7. The estimates of the total and the Jewish populations are those of Salo W. Baron, *A Social and Religious History of the Jews*, New York: Columbia University Press, and Philadelphia: Jewish Publ. Soc. of America, 1967, Vol. XII, p. 25.

8. Joseph Jacobs, *Jewish Contributions to Civilization*, Philadelphia: Jewish Publ. Soc. of America, 1920; Abraham A. Roback, *Jewish Influence on Modern Thought*, Cambridge, Mass.: Sci-Art Publishers, and New York: The Jewish Forum Publ. Co., 1929; Cecil Roth, *The Jewish Contribution to Civilization*, London: Macmillan, 1938, new ed., Oxford: East and West Library, 1943; Dagobert D. Runes (ed.), *The Hebrew Impact on Western Civilization*, New York: Philosophical Library, 1951.

9. Edouard Drumont, *La France Juive*, Paris: Marpon et Flammarion, 1886, p. 9, as translated and quoted by Seth L. Wolitz, *The Proustian Community*, New York: New York University Press, 1971, p. 150.

10. The anti-Semitic belief that Jews wield enormous and disproportionate influence over the body politic is still alive in America today. Cf. Arnold Foster and Benjamin R. Epstein, *The New Anti-Semitism*, New York: McGraw-Hill, 1974, pp. 121ff.

11. Terman, *op. cit.*, I:56.

12. Lewis M. Terman and Melita H. Oden, *The Gifted Child Grows Up*, Stanford, Calif.: Stanford University Press, 1947, p. 14. (Vol. IV of *Genetic Studies of Genius*.)

13. *Ibid.*, p. 296.

14. *Ibid.*, pp. 296–97.

15. *Ibid.*, p. 345.

16. *Ibid.*, pp. 297, 349–50.

17. *Ibid.*, pp. 349–50.

18. *Ibid.*, p. 350.
19. *Ibid.*, pp. 350–52.
20. *Ibid.*, p. 379.
21. Lewis M. Terman and Melita H. Oden, *The Gifted Group at Mid-Life*, Stanford, Calif.: Stanford University Press, 1959, p. 15. (Vol. V of *Genetic Studies of Genius.*)
22. Roth, *op. cit.*, p. xiii.
23. Menahem Nahum of Chernobyl, *M'or 'Enayim*, Slavuta, 1798, sections *Lekh L'kha, Toldot, Yithro, Emor*, as quoted by Simon Dubnow, *Geschichte des Chassidismus*, Berlin: Jüdischer Verlag, 1931, 2:57.
24. Heber Marini, *Le Fin Mot sur la question juive*, Paris, 1886, pp. 21–24, as quoted by Michael R. Marrus, *The Politics of Assimilation: A Study of the French Jewish Community at the Time of the Dreyfus Affair*, Oxford: Clarendon Press, 1971, p. 113.
25. Adolphe Franck, "Le rôle du judaïsme dans le mouvement politique contemporain," *Les Archives Israélites*, August 19, 1886, p. 258, as quoted by Marrus, *op. cit.*, p. 113.
26. Theodore Reinach, writing in 1893, as quoted by Marrus, *op. cit.*, p. 16 n. 3.
27. Marrus, *op. cit.*, pp. 16–17, quoting Alfred Legoyt, *De certaines immunités biostatiques de la race juive*, Paris, 1868, and Caravallo's comments in it, pp. 9–10, 15–16.
28. Joseph Jacobs, "The Comparative Distribution of Jewish Ability," *Journal of the Anthropological Institute of Great Britain and Ireland*, 1886, 15:365.
29. Cesare Lombroso, *The Man of Genius*, London: Walter Scott, and New York: Scribners, 1891, pp. 133–37.
30. Cf., e.g., Max Weinreich, *Hitler's Professors: The Part of Scholarship in Germany's Crimes Against the Jewish People*, New York: Yiddish Scientific Institute (YIVO), 1946; Karl Saller, *Die Rassenlehre des Nationalsozialismus in Wissenschaft und Propaganda*, Darmstadt: Progress Verlag, 1961.
31. Patai and Wing, *op. cit.*, p. 11.
32. Fritz Lenz, "The Inheritance of Intellectual Gifts," in Erwin Baur, Eugen Fischer, and Fritz Lenz, *Human Heredity*, New York: Macmillan, 1931, p. 666. This English translation is based on the third German edition of *Menschliche Erblichkeitslehre* by the three authors, Munich: Lehman, 1931.
33. *Ibid.*, p. 677, quoting, in part, Theodor Fritsch, *Handbuch der Judenfrage*, which in 1944 reached its forty-ninth edition. Lenz mentions Fritsch (p. 677) among anti-Semitic authors, together with Houston Stewart Chamberlain and Henry Ford (!).
34. *Ibid.*, pp. 667–68, quoting Felix von Luschan, *Völker, Rassen, Sprachen*, Berlin: Weltverlag, 1922, pp. 168–69.
35. *Ibid.*, p. 671.
36. *Ibid.*, p. 674.
37. *Ibid.*, p. 676–77.
38. *Ibid.*, p. 677.
39. *Ibid.*
40. Jacques-Henri Dreyfuss, *Sermons et allocutions*, 2 vols., Paris: L. Kahn, 1908–13, 1:277–83; *idem*, "Le génie français et l'esprit du judaïsme," *La Vraie*

Parole, April 19, 1893; Zadoc Kahn, *Sermons*, 3:20–23; as quoted by Marrus, *op. cit.*, p. 111.

41. *Political Science Quarterly*, 1919, pp. 33–42.

42. Chaim Weizmann, *Trial and Error*, Philadelphia: Jewish Publ. Soc. of America, 1949, 2:356.

43. Lewis S. Feuer, *Scientific Intellectual: The Psychological and Sociological Origins of Modern Science*, New York: Basic Books, 1963, pp. 297, 304, 315.

44. Cf. above, p. 326.

45. R. Patai, *Tents of Jacob: The Diaspora Yesterday and Today*, Englewood Cliffs, N.J.: Prentice-Hall, 1971, pp. 91–105.

46. Patai and Wing, *op. cit.*, pp. 151–53.

47. Patai, *Tents of Jacob*, p. 165.

48. An attempt to explain the absence of Jews among England's Nobel Prize winners up to 1969 was made in Patai, *Tents of Jacob*, pp. 165–66. The Russian and Austrian high percentages of Jews among the Nobel Prize winners could also be attributed to the error of the small figure.

CHAPTER 13

1. On the issue of Arab cultural stagnation, cf. R. Patai, *The Arab Mind*, New York: Scribners, 1973, pp. 247ff.

2. William Charles White, *Chinese Jews: A Compilation of Matters Relating to the Jews of K'ai-feng Fu*, 2nd ed., 3 vols., New York: Paragon Book Gallery, 1966. Cf. also Donald Daniel Leslie, "The Kaifeng Jewish Community," *Jewish Journal of Sociology*, 1969, 11(2):175–85.

3. Juan Huarte de San Juan, *Examen de ingenios para las ciencias*, Pamplona, 1575, pp. 409ff., as quoted by Werner Sombart, *Die Juden und das Wirtschaftsleben*, Leipzig: Dunker und Humblot, 1911, p. 419.

4. Ernest Renan, "Les religions de l'antiquité" (originally published in 1853), in *Études d'histoire religieuse*, 1857, in *Oeuvres complètes d'Ernest Renan*, edition définitive établie par Henriette Psychari, Paris: Calmann-Lévy, n.d., Vol. VII, p. 44. My translation from the French.

5. *Ibid.*, pp. 75–76. My translation.

6. Ernest Renan, "L'histoire du peuple d'Israel," in *ibid.*, pp. 88–89. My translation.

7. Cf., e.g., Maurice Muret, *L'Esprit juif*, Paris: Perrin, 1901, pp. 42–43, 50–51.

8. In saying "unique" I do not overlook Ikhnaton's attempt at introducing a quasi-monotheistic worship in Egypt in the fourteenth century B.C.E.

9. Stonequist speaks of "the genius for religion which the Jews have revealed," cf. Everett V. Stonequist, "The Marginal Character of the Jews," in Isacque Graeber and Steuart H. Britt (eds.), *Jews in a Gentile World*, New York: Macmillan, 1942, p. 305.

10. Joseph Jacobs, "The Comparative Distribution of Jewish Ability," *Journal of the Anthropological Institute of Great Britain and Ireland*, 1886, 15:365–66.

11. Lenz, *op. cit.*, pp. 670ff.

12. Exod. 20:3–6; cf. Deut. 5:7–10.

13. Deut. 4:15–18.

14. Cf. *Enc. of Islam*, old ed., s.v. Sūra, and literature *ibid.*

15. Karl Schwarz, *Die Juden in der Kunst*, 2nd ed., Vienna and Jerusalem: R. Löwit, 1936, pp. 199–200. My translation from the German.

16. A 100-page summary of the historical role of Jews in Western art can be found in Karl Schwarz, "The Hebrew Impact of Western Art," in Dagobert D. Runes (ed.), *The Hebrew Impact on Western Civilization*, New York: Philosophical Library, 1951, pp. 405–504. Cf. also the more complete presentation of the subject in the book mentioned in note 15; and Robert Gordis and Moshe Dawidowitz (eds.), *Art in Judaism*, New York: National Council on Art in Jewish Life, and *Judaism*, 1975 (a collection of essays originally published in *Judaism*).

17. Abraham A. Neuman, *The Jews in Spain*, 2:146–48, and plate opposite p. 148.

18. Cf. Rachel Wischnitzer, *The Architecture of the European Synagogue*, Philadelphia: Jewish Publ. Soc. of America, 1964, pp. xxvii–xxix.

19. Cf. Erwin Goodenough's thirteen-volume magnum opus on Jewish symbols in the Greco-Roman period, discussed in Chapter 5.

20. Cf. Wischnitzer, *op. cit.*, p. 33, fig. 28.

21. Cf. Maimonides, *Yad haḤazaqa*, Ahava, Hilkhot T'filla, xi:5.

22. Cf. Wischnitzer, *op. cit.*, *passim*.

23. *Enc. Jud.*, 3:359.

24. On the Cherubim, cf. R. Patai, *The Hebrew Goddess*, New York: Ktav, 1967, pp. 101ff.

25. Cf., e.g., Lev. 23:24; 25:29; Num. 10:10; 29:1; 2 Sam. 5:15; Ps. 98:6; etc.

26. B. Rosh Hashana 26a.

27. Zborowski-Herzog, *op. cit.*, p. 283.

28. B. Ber. 24a.

29. The Jewish role in music is discussed by Paul Nettle, "Judaism and Music," in Runes, *op. cit.*, pp. 363–404.

30. Cf., e.g., Joseph J. Rivlin, "Moses and Batyah the Daughter of Pharaoh," *Edoth: A Quarterly for Folklore and Ethnology*, Jerusalem, 1945, 1(1):44–54.

CHAPTER 14

1. For a review of definitions of personality, cf. Victor Barnouw, *Culture and Personality*, rev. ed., Homewood, Ill.: The Dorsey Press, 1973, pp. 7–10.

2. Cf. Milton Singer, "Survey of Culture and Personality Theory and Practice," in Bert Kaplan (ed.), *Studying Personality Cross Culturally*, New York: Harper & Row, 1961, pp. 9ff.

3. Bert Kaplan, "Editor's Introduction," in Kaplan, *op. cit.*, p. 3.

4. E.g. Bert Kaplan, "Personality and Social Structure," in J. Gittler (ed.), *Review of Sociology: Analysis of a Decade*, New York: Wiley, 1957, p. 121.

5. Raphael Patai and Jennifer Patai Wing, *The Myth of the Jewish Race*, New York: Scribners, 1975, pp. 259–62.

6. Cf. Exod. 17:2–7; Num. 20:10,13, etc.; Ps. 78:8, etc.

7. Num. 23:21, 24.

8. Isa. 1:2; 30:1; Ps. 78:8.

9. Jer. 5:23; Isa. 45:9.

10. Deut. 32:5. Cf. Ps. 18:27, etc.; Prov. 17:20.

11. Num. 23:9; Esth. 3:8.

12. B. Ket. 112a; B. Shab. 88a, 55b.

13. Gen. 49:4.

14. B. Yeb. 79a; B. Shab. 133b.

15. Joseph Jacobs, *The Jewish Race: A Study in National Character.* Plan of a projected work. London: privately printed, 1889, pp. 12–21.

16. Maurice Fishberg, *The Jews: A Study of Race and Environment,* London: Walter Scott, and New York: Scribners, 1911, p. 462.

17. *Ibid.*, pp. 461, 531–32.

18. Arthur Ruppin, *Soziologie der Juden,* Berlin: Jüdischer Verlag, 1930, 1:54–59.

19. Sigmund Freud, *Moses and Monotheism,* in Vol. 23 of *The Complete Psychological Works of Sigmund Freud,* standard edition, ed. by James Strachey, London: Hogarth Press, 1964. First German edition published in 1939.

20. *Ibid.*, p. 106.

21. *Ibid.*, pp. 105–6.

22. *Ibid.*, p. 134.

23. Sigmund Freud, "An Autobiographical Study," in Vol. 20 of *The Complete Psychological Works of Sigmund Freud* (1959), p. 9.

24. Sigmund Freud, "Address to the Society of B'nai B'rith," in Vol. 20 of the *Complete Works,* pp. 273–74.

25. Sigmund Freud, "A Comment on Anti-Semitism," in Vol. 23 of the *Complete Works,* p. 292. After quoting the passage from which the above sentences are taken, Freud adds that he can no longer recall where he read the statement or who was its author. Ernest Jones in his *Sigmund Freud: Life and Works,* London-New York: Basic Books, 1957, p. 256, suggests that the quotation is in fact from Freud himself, and the editors of the Standard Edition of Freud's works concur, cf. pp. 289–90.

26. R. Patai, *The Arab Mind,* New York: Scribners, 1973, pp. 90–96, 98–106, 120, and cf. Index, s.vv. Face, Honor.

27. I am, of course, fully aware of the controversy concerning the meaning of these two letters, and their various interpretations, such as *sefa ṭava* or *sofo ṭov* ("good end"), or *siman ṭov* ("good sign"). However, the fact remains that only Sephardi Jews used it, and that in general they interpreted it as *S'faradi ṭahor*—"pure Sephardi." Cf. H. J. Zimmels, *Ashkenazim and Sephardim,* London: Oxford University Press, 1958, pp. 286–87.

28. Raphael Patai, *Tents of Jacob: The Diaspora Yesterday and Today,* Englewood Cliffs, N.J.: Prentice-Hall, 1971, p. 284, quoting Zimmels, *op. cit.,* pp. 279, 281.

29. Zimmels, *op. cit.,* p. 281.

30. Meyer Kayserling, "Sephardim," *Jewish Enc.* 11:197.

31. Joseph Nehama, *Histoire des Israélites des Salonique,* Paris: Durlacher, and Salonica: Molho, 1935, 2:39–42. My translation from the French.

32. Additional examples of Gentile influence on the personality of the Spanish Jews were adduced in Chapter 6 above, especially in the sections on "Poetry and Swagger" and "Philosophy: Faith and Arrogance."

33. Cf. above, Chapter 7, "The Renaissance Jew."

34. David Efron, *Gesture and Environment*, New York: King's Crown Press, 1941, pp. 41ff., as quoted by Barnouw, *op. cit.*, pp. 252–54.

35. W. D. Breuer, "Patterns of Gesture among the Levantine Arabs," *American Anthropologist*, 1951, 53:237.

36. H. E. Garrett, "Some Group Differences in Personality and College Achievement," *Personnel Journal*, 1929, 7:341.

37. J. Rumyaneck, "The Comparative Psychology of Jews and Non-Jews," *British Journal of Psychology*, 1930–31, 21:404–26.

38. Keith Sward and Meyer Friedman, "Jewish Temperament," *Journal of Applied Psychology*, February 1935, 19:70–84.

39. Keith Sward, "Patterns of Jewish Temperament," *Journal of Applied Psychology*, 1935, 19:410–25.

40. M. Sukov and E. Williamson, "Personality Traits and Attitudes of Jewish and Non-Jewish Students," *Journal of Applied Psychology*, 1938, 22:487–92.

41. Abraham P. Sperling, "A Comparison between Jews and Non-Jews with Respect to Several Traits of Personality," *Journal of Applied Psychology*, 1942, 828–40.

42. A. M. Shuey, "Personality Traits of Jewish and Non-Jewish Students," *Archives of Psychology*, New York, 1944, No. 290, p. 38.

43. Anton Lourié, "The Jews As a Psychological Type," *American Imago*, 1949, 6:119–55.

44. Edward L. Clark, "Motivation of Jewish Students," *Journal of Social Psychology*, 1949, 29:113–17.

45. J. Veroff, Sheila Feld, and Gerald Gurin, "Achievement Motivation and Religious Background," *American Sociological Review*, 1962, 27(2):205–17.

46. Fred L. Strodtbeck, Margaret R. McDonald, and Bernard C. Rosen, "Evaluation of Occupations: A Reflection of Jewish and Italian Mobility Differences," *American Sociological Review*, 1959, 22:546–53.

47. Boris M. Levinson, "The Problems of Jewish Religious Youth," *Genetic Psychology Monographs*, 1959, 60:309–48; *idem*, "Vocational Interests of Yeshiva College Freshmen," *Journal of Genetic Psychology*, 1961, 99:235–44.

48. Nathan Hurwitz, "Sources of Middle Class Values of American Jews," *Social Forces*, 1958, 37(2), December, 117–23.

49. John M. Cuddihy, *The Ordeal of Civility*, New York: Basic Books, 1974.

50. Several examples of greater intensity in Jewish family relations can be found in Marshall Sklare, *America's Jews*, New York: Random House, 1971, pp. 82–83, 88–89, e.g., Jewish parents give their children "everything."

51. Cf. Mark Zborowski, "Cultural Components in Responses to Pain," *Journal of Social Issues*, 1952, 8:16–30. Cf. below, Chapter 15.

52. Harris N. Kertzer, *Today's American Jews*, New York: McGraw-Hill, 1967, p. 79.

53. *Ibid.*, pp. 74–75.

54. Fishberg, *op. cit.*, p. 522.

55. Kertzer, *op. cit.*, pp. 41, 43, 46.

56. The term *sabra* is derived from the Arabic word meaning cactus, a plant which grows wild in Israel. The native Israeli fondly compares himself to the *sabra* whose fruit is prickly on the outside but sweet inside. Interestingly, the word has

retained its foreign flavor, as indicated most clearly by its plural which is construed by adding the suffix -s ("*sabras*") which exists neither in Arabic nor in Hebrew.

57. G. R. Tamarin and D. Ben-Zwi, "Two Stereotypes of the National Mythology: The Sabra-Superman and the Diaspora Jew," *Israel Annals of Psychiatry and Related Disciplines*, April 1965, 3(1):150–51.

58. As early as 1959 the Israel Ministry of Education and Culture published a booklet entitled *Ha'amaqat haToda'a haY'hudit b'Vet haSefer haMamlakhti: Hanhayot w'Tokhniyot Limudim* (*Deepening Jewish Consciousness in the Government Schools: Directions and Study Plans*), Jerusalem: The Government Printer, 1959. This publication includes outlines of curricula covering the subject. Subsequently the ministry published a large amount of material for use in the schools for the purpose of presenting to Israel's youth the achievements of various Jewish communities in the Diaspora.

59. Ferdynand Zweig, *Israel: The Sword and the Harp*, London: Heinemann Educational Books, 1969, pp. 3–12.

60. Elliott Oring, " 'Hey, You've Got No Character'—Chizbat Humor and the Boundaries of Israeli Identity," *Journal of American Folklore*, October–December 1973, 85:342, p. 365.

61. The *moshav* is a cooperative village in which each family owns its own home and the members cooperate in the agricultural work. The *moshava* is a regular village in which each person (or family) works his own land.

62. Albert I. Rabin, "Personality Study in Israeli Kibbutzim," in Kaplan (ed.), *op. cit.*, pp. 527–28.

63. Albert I. Rabin, *Growing Up in the Kibbutz*, New York: Springer Publ. Co., 1965, pp. 110–11, 144, 179, 194–209.

64. Simon N. Herman, *Israelis and Jews*, New York: Random House, 1970, p. 225.

65. Eva Etzioni-Halevy and Rina Shapira, "Jewish Identification of Israeli Students: What Lies Ahead," *Jewish Social Studies*, 1975, 37(3–4):256.

66. *Ibid.*, pp. 256, 258.

67. *Ibid.*, pp. 255–56, 259–60.

68. Bernard Lazerwitz, "A Comparison of Major United States Religious Groups," *Journal of the American Statistical Association*, 1961, 56(295):573, 575.

69. Jack Elinson, Paul W. Haberman, and Cyrille Gell, *Ethnic and Educational Data on Adults in New York City, 1963–1964*, New York: School of Public Health and Administrative Medicine, Columbia University, 1967, p. 147, as quoted by Sklare, *America's Jews*, p. 121.

70. Sklare, *op. cit.*, p. 114.

71. Sidney Goldstein and Calvin Goldscheider, *Jewish Americans: Three Generations in a Jewish Community*, Englewood Cliffs, N.J.: Prentice-Hall, 1968, p. 201, as quoted by Sklare, *op. cit.*, pp. 113–14.

72. Sklare, *op. cit.*, pp. 114–17; Marshall Sklare and Joseph Greenblum, *Jewish Identity on the Suburban Frontier*, New York: Basic Books, 1967, pp. 57–59.

73. Bernard Lazerwitz, "Some Factors in Jewish Identification," *Jewish Social Studies*, 1953, 15(1):5.

74. Cf. Nathan Rottenstreich, *HaMahshava haY'hudit ba'Et haḤadasha* (*Jewish*

Thought in Modern Times), Tel Aviv: Am Oved, 1966; Etzioni-Halevy and Shapira, *op. cit.*, p. 253.

75. Cf. Herman, *op. cit.*, p. 199.

76. Doris Bensimon-Donath, *L'intégration des Juifs nord-africains en France*, Paris-La Haye: Mouton, 1971, pp. 199, 203. *Pied-noir*, lit. "blackfoot," is the French term for the French settlers in Algeria.

77. Bernard Wasserstein, "Jewish Identification among Students at Oxford," *The Jewish Journal of Sociology*, 1971, 13(2):135–51. Cf. also Ernest Krausz, "The Edgeware Survey: Factors in Jewish Identification," *op. cit.*, 1969, 11(2):151–63.

78. Sklare-Greenblum, *op. cit.*, pp. 51–53, 63, 91, 253, 272, 322–23.

79. Arnold A. Lasker, "Motivations for Attending High Holy Day Services," *Journal for the Scientific Study of Religion*, Fall 1971, 10(3):241–48; reprinted in Patrick McNamara (ed.), *Religion American Style*, New York: Harper & Row, 1974, pp. 225–34.

80. Cf. Lasker in McNamara, *op. cit.*, p. 233.

CHAPTER 15

1. B. ʿAv. Zar. 8a.

2. B. Meg. 13b.

3. M. Sheq. 5:1; B. Yoma 85b; B. Pes. 25a; B. Ned. 10a; B. Taʿan. 11b; B. Sanh. 17b; cf. Maimonides, *Yad haHazaqa* Yʿsode haTora v.7, Deʿot iv.23.

4. B. Pes. 42a, 112a; B. Bab. Metz. 107b; B. Ber. 40a, 44a, 62b; B. Taʿan. 5b.

5. Cf. Julius H. Greenstone, "Health Laws," *Jewish Enc.* 6:294f.

6. Maimonides, *Yad haHazaqa*, Rotzeaḥ, xi; *Shulḥan ʿArukh*, Ḥoshen Mishpat, 427, 9, 10; *ibid.*, Yore Deʿa, 116, 5, gloss of Moses Isserles.

7. B. Git. 61a.

8. B. Sota 14a; Gen. Rab. 8, 13.

9. B. Ned. 39b.

10. Cf. Julius Preuss, *Biblisch-Talmudische Medizin*, Berlin: S. Karger, 1911. An excellent summary of the history of Jewish medicine is found in the *Enc. Jud.* 11:1178–1211.

11. Cf. sources in R. Patai and Jennifer Patai Wing, *The Myth of the Jewish Race*, New York: Scribners, 1975, pp. 64–65, and p. 315 n. 47.

12. Mark Zborowski and Elizabeth Herzog, *Life Is with People*, New York: International Universities Press, 1952, pp. 354–55.

13. Margaret Mead and Martha Wolfenstein (eds.), *Childhood in Contemporary Cultures*, Chicago: University of Chicago Press, 1955, p. 15.

14. Cf. T. Schrire, *Hebrew Amulets: Their Decipherment and Interpretation*, London: Routledge, 1966, pp. 12ff.

15. *Ibid.*, p. 50. Schrire, however, is wrong in stating that because of the Talmudic prohibition of amulets as a direct means of cure, they were used only as a prophylactic measure. I have in my collection several Hebrew amulets inscribed with explicit requests for cure.

16. *Enc. Jud.* 16:179, s.v. Vital Statistics.

17. Odin W. Anderson, "Infant Mortality and Social and Cultural Factors: Historical Trends and Current Problems," in Egbert G. Jaco (ed.), *Patients, Physicians, and Illness*, Glencoe, Ill.: The Free Press, 1958, pp. 21–22. (2nd ed. New York: Free Press, 1972.)

18. *Ibid.*, p. 23.

19. David Mechanic, "Religion, Religiosity, and Illness Behavior: The Special Case of the Jews," *Human Organization*, 1963, 22(3):206.

20. Mark Zborowski, "Cultural Components in Responses to Pain," *Journal of Social Issues*, 1952, 8:16–30; reprinted in Jaco (ed.), *op. cit.*, p. 267.

21. Sydney H. Croog, "Ethnic Origins, Educational Level, and Responses to a Health Questionnaire," *Human Organization*, Summer 1961, 65–69.

22. Victor D. Sanua, "Sociocultural Factors in Responses to Stressful Life Situations: The Behavior of Aged Amputees As an Example," *Journal of Health and Human Behavior*, 1960, 1:17–24.

23. David Mechanic, *op. cit.*, pp. 203, 205–6.

24. Theodor Reik, *Jewish Wit*, New York: Gamut Press, 1962, p. 129.

25. Mechanic, *op. cit.*, p. 207.

26. Patai and Wing, *op. cit.*, pp. 242ff.

27. The data are gathered in Maurice Fishberg, "Insanity," *Jewish Enc.* 6:603ff. and *idem, The Jews: A Study of Race and Environment*, London: Walter Scott, and New York: Scribners, 1911, pp. 337ff. Later data are found in Arthur Ruppin, *Soziologie der Juden*, Berlin: Jüdischer Verlag, 1930, 1:250–54.

28. Israel S. Wechsler, "Nervousness and the Jew: An Inquiry into Racial Psychology," *Menorah Journal*, April 1924, 10(2):119, quoting A. Goldberg, *Social Aspects of the Treatment of the Insane*.

29. Fishberg, *The Jews*, p. 350; cf. pp. 338–39.

30. Fishberg, "Nervous Diseases," *Jewish Enc.* 9:225ff; *idem, The Jews*, pp. 324ff., 330.

31. I. D. Rinder, "Mental Health of American Jewish Urbanites: A Review of Literature and Predictions," in Ailon Shiloh and Ida Cohen Selavan (eds.), *Ethnic Groups in America: Their Morbidity, Mortality and Behavior Disorders*, Vol. I, *The Jews*, Springfield, Ill.: Charles C. Thomas, 1973, pp. 312–13.

32. August B. Hollingshead and F. C. Redlich, *Social Class and Mental Illness: A Community Study*, New York: Wiley, 1958, p. 204.

33. Leo Srole, Thomas S. Langner, Stanley T. Michael, Marvin K. Opler, and Thomas A. C. Rennie, *Mental Health in the Metropolis: Midtown Manhattan Study*, Vol. I, New York: McGraw-Hill, 1962, p. 302.

34. As quoted by Fishberg, in *Jewish Enc.* 6:604.

35. Fishberg in *Jewish Enc.* 9:225; *idem, The Jews*, pp. 349–50.

36. Wechsler, *op. cit.*, pp. 121–23, 130.

37. Bertram H. Roberts and Jerome K. Myers, "Religion, National Origin, Immigration, and Mental Illness," *American Journal of Psychiatry*, 1954, 110(10):762; cf. Jerome K. Myers and Bertram H. Roberts, "Some Relationships Between Religion, Ethnic Origin, and Mental Illness," in Marshall Sklare (ed.), *The Jews: Social Patterns of an American Group*, Glencoe, Ill.: The Free Press, 1958, p. 556.

38. Rinder, *op. cit.*, p. 313.
39. Myers and Roberts, *op. cit.*, p. 556.
40. Srole, *et al.*, *op. cit.*, p. 317.
41. Rinder, *op. cit.*, p. 314.
42. Paul Barrabee and Otto von Mering, "Ethnic Variations in Mental Stress in Families with Psychotic Children," in A. M. Rose (ed.), *Mental Health and Mental Disorder*, New York: Norton, 1955, as quoted by Rinder, *op. cit.*, p. 315.
43. Srole, *et al.*, *op. cit.*, p. 306.
44. *Ibid.*, p. 319.
45. Rinder, *op. cit.*, p. 318.
46. Harold Orlansky, "Jewish Personality Traits: A Review of Studies on an Elusive Problem," *Commentary*, 1946, 2:379–80.
47. Louis A. Berman, *Jews and Intermarriage*, New York: Yoseloff, 1968, pp. 469–76.
48. T. Berman-Yeshurun, "Morbidity in the Old Population and Newcomers Since the Establishment of the State of Israel," *Dapim R'fu'iyim*, 1956, 15:1; A. Sunier, *Mental Illness and Psychiatric Care in Israel: A Report*. Amsterdam University Ph.D. Thesis, 1956.
49. Louis Miller, "Mental Illness," in *Enc. Jud.*, 11:1373–76.
50. H. S. Halevi, "Frequency of Mental Illness Among Jews in Israel," *International Journal of Social Psychiatry*, 1963, 9:268–82; Louis Miller, "Social Change, Acculturation, and Mental Health in Israel," *Israel Annals of Psychiatry and Related Disciplines*, 1966, 4:11.
51. Susan Skea, Juris G. Draguns, and Leslie Phillips, "Ethnic Characteristics of Psychiatric Symptomatology Within and Among Regional Groupings: A Study of an Israeli Child-Guidance Population," *Israel Annals of Psychiatry and Related Disciplines*, 1969, 7(1):31–42.
52. Irle M. Goldman, *Psychopathology of European and "Oriental" Jews*, Rutgers University Ph.D. Thesis, 1971, pp. 67–68.
53. R. Patai, *The Arab Mind*, New York: Scribners, 1973, pp. 79, 108–11, 126–29, 134–35, 159ff., 163–64, 297. While the pages quoted discuss the Arab personality, analogous traits can be found, perhaps in a somewhat modified form, also among the Jews who for many centuries had lived in an Arab or Muslim-dominated environment.
54. Myers and Roberts, *op. cit.*, p. 557.
55. Goldman, *op. cit.*, pp. iii, 47, 64, 103; H. B. M. Murphy, E. D. Wittkower, J. Fried, and H. Ellenberger, "A Cross-Cultural Survey of Schizophrenic Symptomatology," *International Journal of Social Psychiatry*, 1963, 9(4):240.
56. Arnold M. Rose and Holger R. Stub, "Summary Studies on the Incidence of Mental Disorders," in Arnold M. Rose (ed.), *Mental Health and Mental Disorder*, New York: Norton, 1955, p. 111.
57. H. B. M. Murphy, E. D. Wittkower, and N. A. Chance, "Crosscultural Inquiry into the Symptomatology of Depression: A Preliminary Report," *International Journal of Psychiatry*, 1967, 3(1):11.
58. M. Fakhr el-Islam, "Depression and Guilt: A Study at an Arab Psychiatric Clinic," *Social Psychiatry*, 1969, 4:56–58.

59. Murphy, Wittkower, and Chance, *loc. cit.*

60. Kurt Lewin, *Resolving Social Conflicts*, New York: Harper and Brothers, 1948, p. 179.

61. *Ibid.*, p. 179. Emphases in the original.

62. Cf. Patai, *The Arab Mind*, pp. 180ff.

63. The concept was first introduced by Robert Ezra Park (1864–1944) and subsequently made the subject of a full-length study by Everett V. Stonequist, *The Marginal Man: A Study in Personality and Culture Conflict*, New York: Scribners, 1937. A few years later Stonequist discussed Jewish marginality in his paper "The Marginal Character of the Jews," in Isacque Graber and Steuart H. Britt (eds.), *Jews in a Gentile World*, New York: Macmillan, 1942, pp. 296–310.

64. Jessie Bernard, "Biculturality: A Study in Social Schizophrenia," in Isacque Graeber and Steuart H. Britt (eds.), *op. cit.*, pp. 265ff.

65. Milton Steinberg, *A Partisan Guide to the Jewish Problem*, New York: Bobbs-Merrill, 1946, pp. 115–30.

66. Salo W. Baron, "Modern Capitalism and the Jewish Fate," *Menorah Journal*, 1942, 30(2):127.

67. Ernest M. Wolf, "The Varieties of Jewish Self-Hate," *The Reconstructionist*, April 19, 1957, 23(5):9.

68. Orlansky, *op. cit.*, p. 383.

69. S. J. Fernando, "A Cross-Cultural Study of Some Familial and Social Factors in Depressive Illness," *British Journal of Psychiatry*, 1975, 127:45–53.

70. Robert E. Park, "Human Migration and the Marginal Man," *American Journal of Sociology*, 1928, 33(6):891–93.

71. Lewin, *op. cit.*, pp. 181–82.

72. Victor Sanua, *Differences in Personality Adjustment among Different Generations of American Jews and Non-Jews*, Michigan State University Ph.D. Thesis, 1956, pp. 70ff.; *idem*, "Minority Status and Psychological Adjustment," *Jewish Journal of Sociology*, 1962, 4:242–52.

73. Rinder, *op. cit.*, p. 317.

CHAPTER 16

1. Gen. 9:22; Midrash Agada, ed. Buber, 1:22–23; B. Sanh. 70a. Cf. a different version cited in Robert Graves and Raphael Patai, *Hebrew Myths*, New York: Doubleday, 1964, 21.a–f, pp. 121–22.

2. Gen. Rab. 36:4, ed. Theodor, pp. 338–39, quoting Isa. 5:11 and 28:7.

3. B. Sanh. 70a–b.

4. B. Git. 68a and parallel sources.

5. Lev. 10:8–11; cf. Ezek. 44:21; 1 Sam. 1:13–15; Hos. 4:11.

6. Prov. 20:1; 21:17; 23:19–21, 29–35; 31:4–5.

7. Ben Sira 31:25ff.

8. Philo, *De ebrietate*, 39:161, Loeb Class. Libr. ed., 3:403.

9. Deut. 21:18–21.

10. M. Sanh. 8:2; B. Sanh. 70a.

11. Prov. 23:31–32; B. Sanh. 70a.

12. Jud. 9:13; Ps. 104:15.
13. Song 4:10; 5:1.
14. Prov. 9:1–6; 31:6–7.
15. Ben Sira 31:27ff.; 39:26–27. My translation from the Hebrew.
16. B. Ber. 35b, 51a, 57a; B. Pes. 42a, 109a; B. Yoma 76b; B. Sanh. 70a; B. 'Av. Zar. 29a; B. Bab. Bath. 58b.
17. B. Ket. 8b.
18. 1 Sam. 25:36; 2 Sam. 13:28–29; 1 Kings 16:9; 20:16ff.
19. Deut. 14:25–26.
20. Zech. 9:17.
21. 2 Kings 18:32; Hos. 9:2; Num. 15:1–16; etc.
22. Num. 6:3–4; Jud. 13:4, 7; Amos 2:11–12; Jer. 35:5–8.
23. Esth. 5:6.
24. Max M. Glatt, "Alcoholism and Drug Addiction Amongst Jews," *British Journal of Addiction*, 1970, 64:297–304; reprinted in Shiloh and Cohen Selavan (eds.), *op. cit.*, pp. 265ff.
25. *Seder 'Avodat Yisrael*, Redelheim, 1868, p. 198.
26. B. Pes. 107a; Y. Ber. 8:1 (11d bot.).
27. B. 'Av. Zar. 29b, 31a–b, 36a; B. Sanh. 106a.
28. Zborowski and Herzog, *op. cit.*, p. 176.
29. *Enc. Jud.* 7:1408.
30. Ruppin, *Soziologie der Juden*, 1:251; 2:99.
31. *Enc. Jud.* 11:1376.
32. *Ibid.*, s.v. Drunkenness.
33. Charles R. Snyder, *Alcohol and the Jews*, Glencoe, Ill.: The Free Press, and New Haven: Yale Center of Alcohol Studies, 1958, pp. 3–4.
34. Don Cahalan, *Problem Drinkers*, San Francisco: Jossey-Bass Inc., 1970, pp. 53–54, 56, 57, 188.
35. As quoted in Snyder, *op. cit.*, pp. 89–90 n. 10.
36. Benjamin Malzberg, *Mental Health of Jews in New York State: A Study of First Admissions to Hospitals for Mental Disease 1949–51*, Albany, N.Y.: Research Foundation for Mental Hygiene, Inc., 1963 (mimeogr.), p. 65.
37. Snyder, *op. cit.*, pp. 85, 92, 98, 101.
38. *Ibid.*, p. 125.
39. Howard Jones, *Alcoholic Addiction: A Psycho-Social Approach to Abnormal Drinking*, London: Tavistock Publ., 1963, pp. 23–24.
40. Max M. Glatt, "Jewish Alcohol Addicts in the London Area" (in French), *Toxicomanies*, January 1974, 6(1):33–39; as summarized in *Psychological Abstracts*, 1974, No. 1207.
41. "Expert Says Alcohol Use Growing Among Jews of All Ages," J.T.A. (Jewish Telegraphic Agency) *Community News Reporter*, March 26, 1976, 15:12; Y. Safra, "B'Yahadut Artzot haB'rit umiSaviv La: Shatyanim Y'hudim b'ArhaB'r," *HaDoar*, New York, March 12, 1976, pp. 292–93.
42. Immanuel Kant, *Anthropologie*, 1789, Part 1, Book 1, Par. 29, as translated by E. Morton Jellinek, "Immanuel Kant on Drinking," *Quarterly Journal of Studies on Alcohol*, 1941, 1(4):778.
43. Snyder, *op. cit.*, p. 202.

44. Peter B. Field, "A New Cross-Cultural Study of Drunkenness," in David J. Pitt-
    man and Charles R. Snyder (eds.), *Society, Culture and Drinking Patterns*, Car-
    bondale and Edwardsville, Ill.: Southern Illinois University Press, 1962, p. 70.
45. Robert F. Bales, "Attitudes Toward Drinking in the Irish Culture," in Pittman
    and Snyder, *op. cit.*, p. 165, citing various Midrashic and other Jewish sources.
46. M. Keller, "The Great Jewish Drink Mystery," *British Journal of Addiction*,
    1970, 64:287–95.
47. Song 4:4–5; 5:15. Cf. also 7:5, 8.
48. Num. 11:4–6.
49. Num. 11:11–35.
50. Jud. 3:17.
51. B. Bab. Metz. 84a.
52. Zborowski and Herzog, *op. cit.*, pp. 338, 372–73.
53. *Ibid.*, p. 372.
54. H. Bruch and G. Touraine, "Obesity in Childhood. V. The Family Frame of
    Obese Children," *Psychosomatic Medicine*, 1940, 2:141–206, as quoted by Sny-
    der, *op. cit.*, p. 10.
55. D. Hall, "Section Meeting on Culture and Personality," *American Journal of
    Orthopsychiatry*, 1938, 8:619–22, as quoted by Snyder, *op. cit.*
56. R. F. Bales, "The 'Fixation Factor' in Alcohol Addiction: An Hypothesis Derived
    from a Comparative Study of Irish and Jewish Social Norms," unpublished doc-
    toral dissertation, Harvard University, 1944, as quoted by Snyder, *ibid.*
57. Hall, *op. cit.*; O. G. Brim, personal communication to Snyder, *op. cit.*
58. As quoted by Theodor Reik, *Jewish Wit*, New York: Gamut Press, 1962, p. 83.
    English translation of Heine by Herman Salinger, New York, 1944.
59. Reik, *ibid.*
60. *Ibid.*, quoting Alfred Kazin, *A Walker in the City*, New York, 1951, p. 32.
61. Kaufmann Kohler, "Dietary Laws," in *Jewish Enc.* 4:600. Cf. also *Enc. Jud.*
    6:26–45, s.v. Dietary Laws.
62. John D. Rayner, *Liberal Judaism*, London: Liberal Jewish Synagogue, 1968, p. 12.
63. Seymour Leventman, "From Shtetl to Suburb," in Peter I. Rose (ed.), *The
    Ghetto and Beyond*, New York: Random House, 1969, p. 54.
64. Cf., e.g., the probable opium addiction of the Ba'al Shem Tov in Chapter 8.
65. *Enc. Jud.* 5:1097, 1102–3, s.v. Crime; 11:1376–77, s.v. Mental Illness.
66. Glatt, in Shiloh and Cohen Selavan (eds.), *op. cit.*, pp. 268–70.
67. Leo Landman (ed.), *Judaism and Drugs*, New York: Commission on Synagogue
    Relations, Federation of Jewish Philanthropies, 1973.
68. Norman E. Frimer, "Jewish Students and Drugs on the Campus," in Landman
    (ed.), *op. cit.*, pp. 156–57, quoting Samuel Pearlman, *Religious Affiliation and
    Patterns of Drug Usage in an Urban University Population*, 1971, and other
    sources.
69. *Ibid.*, quoting Pearlman, p. 28.
70. Rashbam ad B. Pes. 113a.
71. Jerome Hornblass, Commissioner, City of New York Addiction Services Agency,
    as quoted in J.T.A. *Community News Reporter* of March 26, 1976, 15:12. Cf. also
    xeroxed news release of Commissioner Hornblass' remarks, Addiction Services
    Agency of the City of New York, March 3, 1976, p. 2.

CHAPTER 17

1. Cf. Edmund Silberner, "Proudhon's Judeophobia," *Historia Judaica*, April 1948, 10(1):67.

2. Alphonse Toussenel, *Les juifs, rois de l'époque: histoire de la féodalité financière*, Paris: de Gonet, 1847 (first published in 1844), I:1,7, as quoted by Victor M. Glasberg, "Intent and Consequences: The 'Jewish Question' in the French Socialist Movement of the Late Nineteenth Century," *Jewish Social Studies*, January 1974, 36(1):61, 66.

3. Auguste Chirac, *Le droit de vivre: analyse socialiste*, Paris, 1896, pp. 225–26, as quoted by Glasberg, *op. cit.*, p. 65; cf. also p. 67.

4. As quoted in Jerry Hirsch, "Genetics and Competence," in J. M. McVicker Hunt (ed.), *Human Intelligence*, New Brunswick, N.J.: Transaction Books, 1972, p. 12.

5. Goldwin Smith, in various books and articles quoted in the *Jewish Enc.* 1:648–49, s.v. Anti-Semitism.

6. McVicker Hunt, *loc. cit.*

7. M. Haberlandt, *Die Völker Europas und des Orients*, 1920, as quoted by Hans F. K. Günther, *Rassenkunde des jüdischen Volkes*, Munich: J. F. Lehmann, 1930, pp. 306–7.

8. F. Roderich-Stoltheim (pseudonym of Theodor Fritsch), *Das Rätsel des jüdischen Erfolges*, Leipzig: Hammer Verlag, 6th ed., 1923, p. 100. My translation from the German. The book was also published in an English translation as *The Riddle of the Jew's Success*, Leipzig: Hammer Verlag, 1927.

9. Arno Schickedanz, *Sozialparasitismus im Völkerleben*, Leipzig: Lotus Verlag, 1927, p. 119.

10. Theodor Herzl, *The Jewish State*, New York: Herzl Press, 1970, p. 31. The German original, entitled *Der Judenstaat*, was published in Vienna in 1896.

11. *Ibid.*, p. 89.

12. All the above quotes were assembled by Yehezkel Kaufman, "Anti-Semitic Stereotypes in Zionism," *Commentary*, 1949, 7:241. This article was originally published in a somewhat different form in Hebrew in *Moznayim*, Tel Aviv, Teveth 1934, and *Davar*, 27 Tammuz 1934, and reprinted in Kaufman's *B'Havle haZ'man*, Tel Aviv: D'vir, 1936, pp. 257–74 and 293–307. Schwadron's articles appeared in *Moznayim*, February 9–March 9, Nos. 33–38.

13. As quoted in Ande Manners, *Poor Cousins*, New York: Coward, McCann & Geoghegan, 1972, p. 249.

14. Cf. *Enc. Jud.* 1:644.

15. Yehezkel Kaufman, *B'Havle haZ'man*, pp. 296ff.

16. A faint memory of this attitude still lingers in the term *y'rida*, lit. "descent," which is applied to emigration from Israel. The designation *yored*, lit. "descender," for emigrant has an even more negative connotation. On the *sabra* attitude to Galut-Jews, cf. Chapter 14 on "Personality and Character."

17. Subsequently the Hebrew word *tafil* was adopted for "parasite."

18. Benjamin Akzin, in the Israeli daily *Y'di'ot Aharonot*, as reprinted in *HaDoar* (in Hebrew), New York, January 23, 1976, 55(12):187–88.

19. Moritz Lazarus, *Die Ethik des Judentums*, Frankfurt a. M.: J. Kauffmann, 1898;

English translation: *The Ethics of Judaism*, Philadelphia: Jewish Publ. Soc. of America, 1900–1901, 2 vols., Sections 40 and 41.

20. Cf. Miriam Lewin Papanek, "Psychological Aspects of Minority Group Membership: The Concepts of Kurt Lewin," *Jewish Social Studies*, January 1974, 36(1):72–79, and literature on pp. 75–76.

21. Kurt Lewin, *Resolving Social Conflicts*, New York: Harper and Brothers, 1948, p. 193. Cf. also pp. 169–200; J. Sarnoff, "Identification with the Aggressor: Some Personality Correlates of Anti-Semitism among Jews," *Journal of Personality*, 1951, 2:199–218; C. Greenberg, "Self-Hatred and Jewish Chauvinism," *Commentary*, 1950, 10:426–33.

22. Solomon Liptzin, *Germany's Stepchildren*, Philadelphia: Jewish Publ. Soc. of America, 1944, p. 187; David Abrahamsen, *The Mind and Death of a Genius*, New York: Columbia University Press, 1946, pp. 183ff.

23. Maimonides, *Igrot uSh'elot uT'shuvot (Letters and Responsa)*, Amsterdam: Sh'lomo ben Yoseph Proops, 1712, p. 3a. My translation from the Hebrew.

24. Alḥarizi, Maqama 46:8, 28ff., ed. Lagarde, p. 176, as quoted (in Hebrew) by Erich Breuer, *Y'hude Kurdistan*, completed, ed., and trans. by R. Patai, Jerusalem: The Palestine Institute for Folklore and Ethnology, 1947, p. 44. Cf. also Maqama 24, which satirizes the ignorance of the Mosul community and its cantor.

25. Simon Dubnow, *Geschichte des Chassidismus*, Berlin: Jüdischer Verlag, 1931, 1:45 n. 2.

26. Arthur Hertzberg, *The French Enlightenment and the Jews*, New York: Columbia University Press, 1968, pp. 181–82.

27. Cf. Mahler, *A History of Modern Jewry*, p. 161.

28. *Ibid.*, p. 165.

29. Eisig Silberschlag, "Parapoetic Attitudes and Values in Early Nineteenth Century Hebrew Poetry," in Altmann (ed.), *op. cit.*, p. 137.

30. Raphael Mahler, *HaḤasidut w'haHaskala (Hasidism and Haskala)*, Merḥavya: Sifriyat Po'alim, 1961, pp. 397–508 (documents in German and Polish).

31. Lazarus Bendavid, *Etwas zur Characteristick der Juden*, Leipzig-Vienna, Gustav Fock, 1907, 1:149–50. My translation from the German.

32. Cf. Nahum Glatzer, "The Beginnings of Modern Jewish Studies," in Altmann (ed.), *op. cit.*, p. 40.

33. Graetz, *History of the Jews*, 5:292, 294–96, 298, 300–301, 328, 582.

34. *Ibid.*, 5:294, 295, 335.

35. Theodor Lessing, *Der jüdische Selbsthass*, Berlin: Zionistischer Bücher-Bund, 1930.

36. Both Dubnow and Blumenberg are cited, without identifying the source, by Sir Isaiah Berlin, "Benjamin Disraeli, Karl Marx, and the Search for Identity," in *Jewish Historical Society of England, Transactions, Sessions 1968–1969*, XXII, London: The Jewish Historical Society of England, 1970, p. 16.

37. *Ibid.*, pp. 3, 17.

38. Ernest Renan, *Histoire générale et système comparé des langues sémitiques*, Paris: M. Lévy Frères, 1855, pp. 4–5.

39. Édouard Drumond, *La France Juive: essai d'histoire contemporaine*, 2 vols., Paris: C. Marpon & E. Flammarion, 1886 (reissued in 1938), 1:12–13; Henri

Dagan, *Enquéte dur l'antisémitisme*, Paris: P. V. Stock, 1899, pp. 1–2; cf. Michael R. Marrus, *The Politics of Assimilation: A Study of the French Jewish Community at the Time of the Dreyfus Affair*, Oxford: Clarendon Press, 1971, pp. 14–15.

40. Ben Moshé, "Ce que disent les noms israélites," *Annuaire des Archives Israélites pour l'an du monde 5654 (1893–4)*, p. 58, as quoted by Marrus, *op. cit.*, pp. 18–19.

41. Louis-Germain Lévy, "L'antisémitisme et la question des races," *L'Univers Israélite*, April 1, 1895, p. 462, as quoted by Marrus, *op. cit.*, p. 23.

42. Marrus, *op. cit.*, pp. 23–24, quoting Alfred Naquet in *Journal officiel, Chambre*, 27 Mai, 1895, p. 1493.

43. Camile Dreyfus, "Filles des juifs et fils des preux," *La Nation*, 26 Janvier, 1890, as quoted by Marrus, *op. cit.*, p. 24.

44. Théodore Reinach, *Histoire des israélites depuis de la ruine de leur indépendance nationale jusqu'à nos jours*, 5th ed., Paris: Hachette, 1914, p. 371.

45. *Ibid.*, 1st ed., Paris: Hachette, 1884, p. xiii, as quoted by Marrus, *op. cit.*, p. 93.

46. *Enc. Jud.* 14:56, s.v. Reinach; Solomon Reinach, "L'émancipation intérieure du judaïsme," *L'Univers Israélite*, 26 Octobre, 1900, p. 172, as quoted by Marrus, *op. cit.*, p. 161.

47. Léon Kahn, *Les Juifs de Paris pendant la Révolution*, Paris, 1898, p. 356, as quoted by Marrus, *op. cit.*, p. 96; my translation from "all these miasmas" on.

48. Julien Benda, *Dialogue à Byzance*, Paris, 1909 (first publ. in 1900), pp. 71–73, as quoted in French by Marrus, *op. cit.*, p. 161; my translation.

49. Cf. Marrus, *op. cit.*, pp. 169–72, with all the source references to Lazare's writings in the footnotes.

50. Bernard Lazare, *L'Antisémitisme: Son histoire et ses causes*, Paris, 1894; reprinted Paris: Jean Crés, 1934. English translation: *Antisemitism: Its History and Causes*, New York: International Library Publ. Co., 1903.

51. Marrus, *op. cit.*, p. 173 and n. 2.

52. Lazare, *op. cit.*, pp. 267, 277, 314–16, 326.

53. Marrus, *op. cit.*, p. 178, quoting Hannah Arendt, "From the Dreyfus Affair to France Today," *Jewish Social Studies*, July 1942, 4(3):239.

54. Bernard Lazare, "Nécessité d'être soi-même," *Zion*, April 30, 1897, and *Le Nationalisme juif*, Paris, 1898, pp. 7–9; as quoted by Marrus, *op. cit.*, p. 189.

55. Bernard Lazare, "La conception sociale du judaisme et du peuple juif," *La Grande Revue*, 1 Septembre, 1899, pp. 615, 617, as quoted by Marrus, *op. cit.*, pp. 190–91.

56. Marrus, *op. cit.*, p. 192.

57. Bernard Lazare, *Le Fumier de Job: Fragments inédits précédés du portrait de Bernard Lazare* par Charles Péguy, Paris: Éditions Rieder, 1928, p. 97. My translation from the French. The English edition, *Job's Dungheap*, New York: Schocken Books, 1948, does not contain this passage.

58. *The Complete Diaries of Theodor Herzl*, ed. by R. Patai, trans. by Harry Zohn, New York and London: Herzl Press-Thomas Yoseloff, 1960, 1:424, 431; 2:443, 480, 805, 809–10; 3:942, 1201.

59. R. Patai, *Israel Between East and West: A Study in Human Relations*, Philadelphia: Jewish Publ. Soc. of America, 1953, p. 314.

60. *Ibid.*, 2nd ed., Westport, Conn.: Greenwood, 1970, pp. 371–73.

61. Judith T. Shuval, "Self-Rejection Among North African Immigrants to Israel," *Israel Annals of Psychiatry and Related Disciplines*, Spring 1966, 4(1):101–10.

62. Henri Tajfel, Gustav Jahoda, Charlan Nemeth, Y. Rim, and N. B. Johnson, "The Devaluation by Children of Their Own National and Ethnic Group: Two Case Studies," *British Journal of Social and Clinical Psychology*, 1972, 11:235–43.

63. Yehuda Amir, Aharon Bizman, and Miriam Rivner, "Effects of Interethnic Contact on Friendship Choices in the Military," *Journal of Cross-Cultural Psychology*, September 1973, 4(3):361–73.

64. Y. Rim and R. Aloni, "Stereotypes According to Ethnic Origin, Social Class, and Sex," *Acta Psychologica*, Amsterdam, 1961, 31(4):312–25.

65. Cf. *Enc. Jud.* 12:1031–34, s.v. New Left; M. S. Chertoff (ed.), *The New Left and the Jews*, New York: Pitman, 1971.

66. Bernard Lewis, *Islam in History*, New York: The Library Press, 1973, p. 155.

67. For a detailed analysis of the Radical Left, which comprises elements of both the Old and the New Left, cf. Arnold Foster and Benjamin R. Epstein, *The New Anti-Semitism*, New York: McGraw-Hill, 1974, pp. 7ff., 125–54. Cf. also Nathan Glazer, "The New Left and the Jews," *Jewish Journal of Sociology*, 1969, 11(2):121–32; and the articles by Amos Kenen, Itzhak Epstein, and J. J. Goldberg in Jack Nusan Porter and Peter Dreier (eds.), *Jewish Radicalism: A Selected Anthology*, New York: Grove Press, 1973, pp. 51–81.

68. Cf. Ernest M. Wolf, "The Varieties of Jewish Self-Hate," *The Reconstructionist*, April 19, 1957, 23(5):12.

69. Lewin, *Resolving Social Conflicts*, p. 193.

CHAPTER 18

1. *International Encyclopedia of the Social Sciences* 16:283, s.v. Values, quoting Stephen C. Pepper, *The Sources of Value*, Berkeley, Calif.: University of California Press, 1958, p. 7.

2. M. Pe'a 1:1; cf. B. Qid. 40a.

3. Cf. B. Qid. 40a where references are made to Deut. 5:16, Prov. 21:21, Ps. 34:15, and Deut. 30:20, although the last-mentioned verse speaks not of the reward of Tora study, but of that of the love of God and of obeying Him. It seems as if the sages equated obeying God with studying His Law.

4. B. Qid. 39b.

1. The Family

5. Cf. Patai, *Golden River*, pp. 84–94.

6. Cf. R. Patai, *Sex and Family in the Bible and the Middle East*, New York: Doubleday, 1959, pp. 127ff., where the extent of the patriarch's powers over his family, including life and death, is discussed.

7. Ex. 20:12. In the second version of the Ten Commandments, in Deut. 5:16, this commandment is amplified: "Honor thy father and thy mother, *as the Lord thy God commanded thee*; that thy days may be long, *and that it may go well with thee*, upon the land which the Lord thy God giveth thee." The words in italics

are not found in Exodus. Cf. also Lev. 19:3, where the Children of Israel are commanded to fear their mothers and fathers.

8. Y. Pe'a 15d; Y. Qid. 61b; B. Qid. 32a, quoting Exod. 20:12 and Prov. 3:9.
9. B. Qid. 30b.
10. M. Ket. 12:3; B. Ket. 103a.
11. B. Ket. 103a.
12. Y. Pe'a 15c top; Y. Qid. 61b top: B. Qid. 31a; Gen. Rab. 1:15.
13. B. Qid. 31b.
14. *Ibid.*
15. Y. Pe'a 15c mid.; Y. Qid. 61a.
16. B. Qid. 31b.
17. B. Qid. 31b; Y. Qid. 61b.
18. Y. Qid. 61b; Y. Pe'a 15c mid.
19. B. Qid. 31b.
20. B. Qid. 31b; Y. Qid. 61b.
21. Gen. 27:29.
22. Gen. Rab. 65:27, ed. Theodor, p. 728; Ginzberg, *Legends of the Jews*, 5:278; Graves and Patai, *Hebrew Myths*, 40.c; Deut. Rab. 1:15.
23. Natalie F. Joffe, "The Dynamics of Benefice Among East European Jews," *Social Forces*, 1949, 29:241.
24. B. Ḥul. 84a.
25. Tos. Qid. 1:11; B. Qid. 29a.
26. M. Qid. 4:14; B. Qid. 82b.
27. B. Ket. 49b, etc. Cf. J. D. Eisenstein, *Otzar Yisrael*, Berlin-Vienna: Hebräischer Verlag, 1924, s.v. *Av.*, Vol. I, pp. 3–5.
28. Lev. 19:29; Gen. 38:24ff.
29. B. Qid. 30a; *Shulḥan 'Arukh*, Even ha'Ezer, par. 71.
30. B. Qid. 30b.
31. Yalqut Shim'oni, Mishle 963.
32. Gen. 37:3.
33. Gen. 44:20.
34. 2 Sam. 19:1ff.
35. Ps. 103:13.
36. Gen. 16:1ff.; 21:8ff.
37. Gen. 25:1–6, 28.
38. Gen. 27:1–46.
39. 2 Sam. 21:8–13.
40. Gen. 24:67.
41. Ps. 35:14.
42. Jer. 31:15.
43. Isa. 66:10, 11, 12, 13.
44. B. Shab. 10b; my translation.
45. Y. Pe'a 15c mid.
46. Cf. Graves and Patai, *Hebrew Myths*, Chapter 12.
47. Exod. 20:14; Deut. 5:18.
48. Exod. 21:10–11.
49. B. Yeb. 62b.

50. B. Yeb. 63b.
51. B. Yeb. 63b, quoting Gen. 5:2.
52. B. Yeb. 62b; B. Sanh. 76b, quoting Job 5:24.
53. B. Yeb. 63a–b.
54. B. Bab. Metz. 59b; cf. Midrash Leqaḥ Tov to Num. 16.
55. B. Git. 6b.
56. B. Bab. Metz. 59b.
57. B. Sota 17a.
58. B. Git. 90b; B. Sanh. 22a.
59. B. Sanh. 22a.
60. B. Sanh. 22b.
61. Gen. 8:20; 13:4; 22:13–14; 31:19, 31–32; 35:14; 38:24; 46:27; Exod. 4:25; Num. 35:9–34; Deut. 19:1–13; Jud. 11:30–31; 2 Sam. 3:22–27, 30; 14:4–11.
62. Lev. 25:25, 47–49; Ruth 4:1–9; Jer. 32:7–15.
63. Deut. 25:5–10; cf. Gen. 38:6ff.; Ruth 4:10.
64. Exod. 12:3, 21–27; Deut. 16:10–14; cf. 1 Sam. 20:6, 29; Job 1:15.
65. Ps. 128:3–4.
66. Ps. 133:1.
67. B. Bab. Bat. 109b, 110b.
68. B. Bab. Bat. 109b–110a.
69. Deut. 6:9; 11:20.
70. W. Seward Salisbury, *Religion in American Culture*, Homewood, Ill.: The Dorsey Press, 1964, p. 154.
71. Gerhard Lenski, *The Religious Factor*, Garden City, N.Y.: Doubleday, 1961, p. 196.
72. While "laborers" constituted less than 0.3 percent of the entire Jewish male population. Cf. Will Maslow, *The Structure and Functioning of the American Jewish Community*, New York: American Jewish Congress and American Section of the World Jewish Congress, 1974, p. 8, reporting on the findings of the 1972 National Jewish Population Study of the Council of Jewish Federations and Welfare Funds.
73. *Enc. Jud.* 6:1172, s.v. Family.

2. An Excursus on Sex

1. Gen. 2:18, 23–24.
2. B. Yeb. 61a, 63a.
3. Zohar 3:69a; cf. Patai, *The Hebrew Goddess*, pp. 195–97.
4. B. Shab. 57b. The Hebrew term used for "heaven" is *'olam haba*, lit. "The World to Come." The Hebrew term I translated above as "intercourse" is *tashmish*, which is the usual Talmudic term for it. In the sequel of the passage quoted, the opinion is expressed that *tashmish* here must be taken to mean "elimination." However, this is a forced interpretation, giving the word an entirely unusual sense.
5. Maimonides, *Guide of the Perplexed*, 3:8 and 49, in the translation of Pines, pp. 434, 606, 611.
6. As quoted by Rabbi Samuel Glasner, "Judaism and Sex," in Albert Ellis and Albert Abarbanel (eds.), *The Encyclopedia of Sexual Behavior*, New York: Jason

Aronson, 1973, p. 576; cf. Louis M. Epstein, *Sex Laws in Judaism*, New York: Bloch Publ. Co., 1948, p. 23, quoting Nahmanides, *Igeret haQodesh*, beginning.

7. Cf. above, Chapter 6, "Hebrew Arabesque."

8. On the erotic aspect of the Sabbath observance, cf. Patai, *The Hebrew Goddess*, pp. 246ff.

9. E.g., Gen. 16:2; 30:3, 9.

10. Lev. 18:6–30; 20:10–21.

11. Exod. 21:20; B. Yeb. 62b.

12. Cf., e.g., Gen. 3:16; 19:30–38; 30:14–16; Exod. 21:10; B. Yeb. 62b; M. Ket. 5:6; B. Ket. 62b; B. 'Er. 100b.

13. M. Sota 3:4; B. Sota 21b.

14. B. Nid. 31a–b, 71a; B. 'Er. 100b.

15. B. Ber. 24a, 61a; B. Mak. 24a.

16. B. Ber. 61a; B. 'Er. 100b; B. Bab. Qam. 82a; cf. *Qitzur Shulḥan 'Arukh* 4:20, Chapter 152, Par. 8.

17. M. Avot 1:5; B. Sanh. 75a.

18. Maimonides, *Yad haḤazaqa, Issure Bi'a*, 21:1–2. Cf. Talmudic sources in Epstein, *Sex Laws*, p. 16.

19. B. Suk. 52a.

20. Gen. Rab. 9:7 and parallels.

21. This entire issue is dealt with in Patai, *Man and Temple*, pp. 27–28. Cf. also M. Avot 3:17: "Rabbi Akiba said: Merriment and levity lead a man to licentiousness."

22. B. 'Av. Zar. 20a.

23. *Ibid.*; cf. *Qitzur Shulḥan 'Arukh* 4:20, Chapter 152, Par. 8, for the latest formulation of this prohibition.

24. B. Qid. 29b; *Qitzur*, etc., 4:6, Chapter 145, Par. 1.

25. B. Pes. 113a.

26. M. Avot 5:18.

27. Based on Exod. 21:10.

28. M. Ket. 5:6; B. Ket. 61b, 62b.

29. *Shulḥan 'Arukh*, Even ha'Ezer 76:1, 3; cf. *Qitzur*, etc., 4:15, Chapter 150, Par. 7.

30. B. 'Er. 100; *Qitzur* 4:16, Chapter 150, Par. 13.

31. E.g., Avot diR. Natan 41; B. Shab. 87a; B. Pes. 112b; B. Suk. 52b; B. Git. 70a; B. Ket. 60b, 65a; B. Sanh. 37b–38a; B. Nid. 17a; etc. Cf. also *Qitzur* 4:13ff., Chapter 150.

32. B. Ber. 62a.

33. B. Ned. 20b.

34. *Shulḥan 'Arukh*, Even ha'Ezer 25:2.

35. B. Shab. 62b; B. Sanh. 39b; B. Git. 70a.

36. B. Ket. 46a; B. Ber. 13b.

37. Lev. 20:18; B. Nid. 31b; B. Yoma 9a,b.

38. Leonard Weller, "A Research Note on 'Delayed Gratification' and Ethnicity and Social Class in Israel," *Jewish Journal of Sociology*, 1975, 17(1):29–35.

39. Alfred C. Kinsey, *et al.*, *Sexual Behavior in the Human Male*, Philadelphia and London: W. B. Saunders, 1948, p. 465.

40. *Ibid.*, pp. 467, 474–75, 480, 482, 484, 486.

41. Alfred C. Kinsey, *et al.*, *Sexual Behavior in the Human Female*, Philadelphia and London: W. B. Saunders, 1953, pp. 187–88, 224–25, 279, 345, 398, 498, 557.

42. Samuel Klausner, "Israel, Sex Life in," in Ellis and Abarbanel, *The Enc. of Sexual Behavior*, pp. 558–66.

43. A. I. Rubin, *Growing Up in the Kibbutz*, New York: Springer Publ. Co., 1965, pp. 32–34, 41, 114–17, 119, 195, 209.

44. Patai, *The Arab Mind*, pp. 134–35.

45. Samuel Klausner, "Islam, Sex Life in," in Ellis and Abarbanel, *The Enc. of Sexual Behavior*, pp. 545–57.

46. Patai, *The Arab Mind*, pp. 123–24; *idem*, *Golden River to Golden Road*, pp. 445–59.

47. Patai, *The Arab Mind*, p. 135.

3. Education

1. Gen. 18:19.

2. Exod. 12:26–27; 13:8 (Passover); Exod. 13:14 (redemption of the firstborn); Deut. 4:9; 6:20ff.; 32:1, 46 (the Laws of the Lord in general).

3. Deut. 6:4–9. In the morning and evening prayers, this passage is followed by a recitation of Deut. 11:13–21 and Num. 15:37–41, which passages are also considered parts of the complete Sh'ma' prayer, and which, in Deut. 11:19, repeat the injunction of teaching the children.

4. M. Ber. 1:1, 2.

5. Prov. 1:8; 6:20; 10:1; 15:20; 19:26; 20:20; 23:22, 25; 30:17.

6. Prov. 31:1ff.

7. Deut. 17:19.

8. Josh. 1:8.

9. Deut. 27:1–8.

10. Deut. 31:10–13.

11. 2 Chron. 17:7–9.

12. *Omnim*, 2 Kings 10:1, 5; *morim*, *m'lammdim*, both in Prov. 5:13; cf. Ps. 119:99; *m'vinim*, Neh. 8:7; Ezra 8:16; 1 Chron. 25:8; *maskilim*, Dan. 11:33, 35; 12:3.

13. Ps. 34:12; cf. Ben Sira 2:1; 3:1ff., 12, 17; etc., where the context shows that it is the teacher who addresses his pupils as "sons" (*banim*, also meaning "children").

14. Ben Sira 51:23.

15. Ps. 111:10: Prov. 1:7.

16. Ps. 78:1–7, with some minor emendations.

17. Philo, *De Vita Mos.*, 2:40 (216), Loeb Class. Libr. edition 6:557.

18. The interested reader can easily find the history of Jewish education in any Jewish encyclopedia.

19. Josephus Flavius, *Contra Apionem* 1:12;2:18; *Ant.* 4:8:12: Philo, *Legatio ad Caium* 16, 31.

20. M. Sota 3:4. Cf. above, "Excursus on Sex."

21. Cf. B. Qid. 29b.

22. Y. Pe'a 15c top.

23. B. Qid. 30a.

24. B. 'Er. 54a.

25. B. Qid. 30b.
26. *Ibid.* 30a.
27. Cf. above, Chapter 6, "Hebrew Arabesque."
28. Israel Abrahams, *Jewish Life in the Middle Ages*, New York: Meridian Books (reprint), 1958, pp. 364–67.
29. Joseph ibn Caspi, *Sefer haMusar*, in Eliezer Ashkenazi's *Ta'am Z'qenim*, Frankfurt a. M.: I. Kauffmann, 1854, as quoted by Abrahams, *op. cit.*, p. 370.
30. Cf. sources in Patai, *Tents of Jacob: The Diaspora Yesterday and Today*, p. 437 n. 13.
31. *Ibid.*
32. Cf. Yudel Mark, "The Yiddish Language: Its Cultural Impact," *American Jewish Historical Quarterly*, 1969, 59(2):101–2.
33. Patai, *Tents of Jacob*, p. 79, table.
34. *Ibid.*
35. Abrahams, *op. cit.*, p. 369.
36. Cf. R. Patai, "Jewish Folk-Cures for Barrenness," *Folk-Lore* (London), 1944, 55:117–24, and 1944–45, 56:209–18.
37. By Shabbatai Sheftel Hurwitz (c. 1561–1619), *Wawe ha'Amudim* 9b, as quoted in the *Jewish Enc.* 5:47, s.v. Education; and other sources quoted by Zimmels, *Ashkenazim and Sephardim*, London: Oxford University Press, 1958, p. 66 n. 1.
38. *Jewish Enc. loc. cit.*
39. This system, known in Yiddish as *Teg essen* (i.e., "day eating"), enabled many a yeshiva *bokher* ("student") to survive while devoting himself to the study of the Law. This is how my father maintained himself while studying at the Yeshiva of Neutra (Nyitra) in the 1890's.
40. Cf. above, Chapter 8, "Jewish Dionysians: The Hasidim."
41. These and many other details of my father's early life were described by him in a book he wrote in the 1920's. Cf. József Patai, *A Középső Kapu: Egy Kis Gyermek és Egy Nagy Könyv Élete* (*The Middle Gate: The Life of a Small Child and a Big Book*), Budapest: Mult és Jövö, 1927 (date of the Preface). The book was subsequently published also in German and Hebrew translations.
42. Cf. the detailed description of the teaching method in the East European *Ḥeder* in Zborowski and Herzog, *Life Is with People*, pp. 88ff.
43. Lenski, *op. cit.*, pp. 204–6.
44. *Ibid.*, pp. 205–6.
45. *Ibid.*, p. 208. This was also found in New Haven by Fred L. Strodtbeck, "Family Interaction, Values and Achievements," in Marshall Sklare (ed.), *The Jews: Social Patterns of an American Group*, Glencoe, Ill.: The Free Press, 1958, pp. 151–52.
46. Strodtbeck, *op. cit.*, pp. 159–60.

4. Charity

1. Deut. 15:11.
2. Deut. 14:22–30; 26:12–14.
3. Exod. 23:11; Deut. 24:19–21; Lev. 19:9–10; 23:22.
4. Isa. 58:6–7, 10.

5. Cf., e.g., Ezek. 16:49; Prov. 31:20; Job 22:5–9; 29:12–13; Neh. 8:10. Cf. also Isa. 1:17; Mic. 6:8; Jer. 21:12.

6. Prov. 10:2; 11:4.

7. Cf. Ben Sira 3:30ff.; Tob. 4:7–11.

8. Ben Sira 4:1–8.

9. B. Ket. 67b.

10. B. Ket. 68a.

11. M. Avot 3:7.

12. B. Ket. 67b.

13. B. Ket. 67b; cf. B. Ḥag. 5a.

14. B. Ket. 67b.

15. B. Bab. Bat. 9a; 49b, expounding Prov. 21:3.

16. Gen. 1:27.

17. Lev. 19:2.

18. Deut. 10:12; 11:22; 26:17; 28:9.

19. Exod. 20:10–11; Deut. 10:18–19.

20. Exod. 33:19; Deut. 13:17; 30:3; 2 Kings 13:23; 2 Chron. 30; 36:15; Pss. 78:38; 145:3; B. Pes. 151b, 155a; Lev. Rab. 29; etc.

21. Exod. 34:6–7.

22. Pesiqta diR. Kahana, ed. Buber, 57a, and parallels. The thirteenth attribute is found by Rabbi Yoḥanan in the first word of the phrase w'naqqe lo y'naqqe in Exod. 34:7, which in literal translation would read, "and cleansing He does not cleanse," or, as the standard translations have it, "will by no means clear the guilty." The arbitrary separation of the word w'naqqe from the phrase of which it is an integral part in order to give it an opposite meaning is characteristic of the procedure often adopted by the Talmudic sages. Since all the divine attributes Rabbi Yoḥanan discerned in the passage had to have to do with mercy, such a violation of the actual meaning of the phrase was considered a permissible license.

23. Ps. 103:13; Isa. 49:15.

24. Y. Ber. V, 9c mid.; Y. Meg.·IV, 75c top.

25. Mekhilta Shira 3; B. Shab. 133b. Cf. Sifre Deut. 49, where more divine attributes which man should strive to imitate are enumerated.

26. Sifra 19:2, quoting Lev. 19:2.

27. B. Sota 14a; and parallels, explaining Deut. 13:5.

28. B. Yeb. 79a; Y. Qid. IV, 65c mid., and parallels.

29. B. Yom Tov 32b.

30. B. Pes. 113b.

31. Maimonides, Sefer haMitzvot, positive commandment no. 8; idem, Guide, 3:54.

32. Moses Cordovero, Tomer D'vora, Venice, 1588, beginning.

33. Enc. Jud. 5:856, s.v. Charity, and 12:432, s.v. Moses Leib of Sasov.

34. Amos 1:11; Jer. 6:23; 2 Chron. 36:17.

35. Jewish Enc. 3:669, s.v. Charity.

36. B. Ket. 49b; Maimonides Yad haHazaqa, Matnot 'Aniyim 7:10.

37. Jewish Enc. 3:669–70, s.v. Charity, and Enc. Jud. 8:281–86, s.v. Hekdesh.

38. Cf. Natalie F. Joffe, "The Dynamics of Benefice Among East European Jews,"

Social Forces, 1949, 29:243–45; Zborowski and Herzog, *Life Is with People*, pp. 203–5.

39. B. Shab. 156b, etc.
40. Lenski, *op. cit.*, p. 319.
41. *Ibid.*, p. 320.

INDEX

Aaron, 31, 435
Abahu, Rabbi, 486
Abba Shaul, 529
Abbasids, 97, 105
'Abd al-Raḥmān III, 107
Abigail, 437
Abimi, Rabbi, 485–86
Abraham, 18–20, 23, 31, 42, 44, 45, 93, 350, 404, 409, 484, 490, 493, 509–10, 529
Abraham bar Ḥiyya, 124
Abraham ben David of Posquières, 135
Abraham ibn Daud, 108–9
Abrahamic: descent, 18; family, 21, 46
Abrahams, Israel, 517
Abravanel: Don Isaac, 127; Judah, *see* Leone Ebreo
Absalom, 437, 489
Abstention from alcohol, 442. *See also* Sobriety
Abulafia, Abraham, 135–37, 147
al-Abyad, poet, 122
Academia de los Floridos, de los Sitibundos, 230
Accomplishment, Jewish concern with, 378. *See also* Achievement
Acculturation, Italian Jewish, 158
Achievement: motivation, 390; orientation, 422, 426, 524
Acosta (da Costa), Uriel, 233, 383
Actors, Jewish, 353, 378
Adam, 43, 434, 491, 498; and Eve, 197
Adam, Rabbi, 192
Adam Qadmon (primordial man), 138
Adjustment, 389, 432
Adler, Alfred, 353
Adon, Adonis, 49
Adret, Solomon ben, 135
Adrianople, 109
Aesthetic sense, 358
Affective disorders, 415–16
Afikoman, 494

"Agad'te", 30
Agdistis, 433
Aggada, 59, 80, 88, 149, 210, 514, 521
Aggression, aggressiveness, 390, 420, 422, 425–26, 431, 461
Agriculture, 47, 49, 189, 240–41, 574
Agrippa II, 84–85
Ahab, King, 54
Akiba, Rabbi, 492, 501
Akkadian, 54
Akzin, Benjamin, 460
Alamanno, Yohanan, 171
Albalag, Isaac, 133, 147–48
Albertus Magnus, 127
Albo, Joseph, 101
Albright, William F., 47
Alchemy, 161
Alcohol(ism), 190, 203, 218, 274, 329, 379, 413, 415–16, 436, 438, 440–47, 539
Alertness, 390
Alexander Polyhistor, 83, 95
Alexander VI, Pope, 153
Alexander the Great, 59, 85
Alexandria, 57, 78, 82–83, 92, 96, 106, 123, 279, 344, 464; Jews of, 67; library of, 93
Alfasi, Yitzhaq, 30
Alfonsine Tables, 125
Algebra, 106, 123, 521
Algeria, 151, 263, 479
Alharizi, Judah, 464
'Alī, 100
Alienation, 22, 471
'Aliya, 459
Allah, 448
Allegorical interpretation, 128
Alliance Israélite Universelle, 270, 324–25
al-memor, 362. *See also* Minbar
Almohads, 98, 100, 103
Alphonso X of Castile, 101, 125

Alsace and Lorraine, 236–39

Altmann, Alexander, 126

Amatus Lusitanus, 160

America, 269, 303, 305, 362, 371, 415, 429–30, 444, 480, 497, 533–34, 536, 539; Jews in, 6, 23, 280–81, 374, 388–94, 399, 401–2, 424, 426, 430–32, 444–45, 450, 452–53, 458, 509, 538

Americanization of Jews, 432

American Jewish Congress, 264

American Jewish literature, 370–71

Ami, Rabbi, 488

Ammon, 69, 437

Amoraim, 96

Amor dei, 9

Amor dei intellectualis, 204, 232, 560–61

Amphitheaters, 61, 66

Amsterdam, 102, 228–30, 234, 259–61, 383

Amulets, 67, 160, 187, 194, 217, 383, 411, 518, 575

Anahita, 65–66, 69–70, 72

Anath, 50, 53–54

Anau family, 155

Ancona, 173

Andalusia, 98, 107; Sephardim in, 464

Androgyne, 148, 183, 553

Angels, 53–56, 67, 69–71

Aniconic character: of Judaism, 56, 73, 86, 90, 95; of Yahwism, 48, 55

Animistic concepts, 186–87

Antinomianism, of Hasidim, 206

Antioch, 60

Anti-Semites, 456, 467, 475

Anti-Semitic: authors, 463; caricature of the Jew, 474; doctrine, 459; literature, 457; myth, 476

Anti-Semitism, 23, 250–52, 287, 319–20, 327, 346–47, 422–23, 458, 470–75, 479; black, 479–80; Jewish, 431. *See also* Self-hate

Anxiety, 397, 419, 421, 423, 450

Aphrodite, 65–66, 68–70, 72

Apion, 85, 90

Apocalyptic literature, 78

Apocrypha, 77–79, 83, 200

Apollonian Judaism, 180–81, 196, 207

Apologetics, 89–92, 226, 321

Apostasy, 21, 346. *See also* Conversion

Apulia, 156

Aquila, 83

Arab: anti-Israelism, 269, 479; conquest, 7, 97, 99; countries, 398, 480, 508; culture, 354, 515, 517; environment, 248; gestures, 389; personality, 577; poets, 99; rule, 97; science, 123; world, 100

Arabia, 97, 100, 348, 350

Arabic: language, 7, 41, 43, 101–3, 105, 109–10, 127, 152, 157, 515; poetry, meter, 103–4, 114–15, 157, 168; translation of the Bible, 105

Arabization, 99–100, 102

Arabs, 12, 26, 97, 251, 347, 350, 365, 385–86, 410, 429, 448, 453; in Israel, 370

Aragon, 98, 125

Aram(aean), 18, 42, 437

Aramaic language, 7, 41, 43–44, 46, 57–59, 63, 66, 77–78, 80–82, 84, 100, 105, 110, 112, 136, 367, 369

"Arbol de las vidas," study house, 231

Archaeology, 169, 358

Architecture, 172, 353, 360–62, 369

Ares, 548

d'Argens, marquis, 236–37, 245

Aristeas, *Letter* of, 82, 91

Aristobulus, 87

Aristotle, 85–86, 88, 129–30, 172

Arithmetic, 123

Ark: of the Covenant, 49, 54–55, 74; of Yahweh, 48

Armenians, 476–77

Army, Israeli, 478–79

Arnstein: Fanny von, 249; Nathan Adam von, 249

Arslan Tash, Syria, 53–54

Artaxerxes, 58

Artists' Equity, 394

Arts, Jews in the, 160–62, 177, 272, 282, 318, 349, 369–70, 380, 422, 537

Aryan(s), 320, 326, 347, 462, 473

Ascendancy, 390

Asher, 545
Asherah, 46, 55
Ashkelon, 485
Ashkenazi, Jacob ben Isaac, 247
Ashkenazi: communities, 442; Jews, 222,
    224, 227–28, 242, 245, 268, 282, 310,
    312, 314–15, 333, 345, 354, 359, 368,
    380, 386, 399, 400, 422, 427–29, 453,
    460, 464, 477–78, 516–17, 521, 536,
    538–39; world, 260, 387
Ashkenazim, 80, 154, 169, 227, 233–34,
    267, 309–10, 382, 385, 423–27, 442,
    465, 479, 518, 537, 539
Ashmodai, 434–35
Asi, Rabbi, 486, 488
Asi, Rav, 528
Aspirations, 421; intellectual, 303
Assembly of Jewish Notables. See
    Sanhedrin of Paris
Assimilants, 387, 389
Assimilation, 98, 171, 243, 268, 280, 339,
    360, 399, 404, 430, 444–45, 447, 465,
    474–75, 540
Assyrian(s), 19, 54, 252
Astarte, 46, 72
Astrology, 93, 105–6, 123, 132, 161
Astronomical tables, 101, 123–24
Astronomy, 103, 105, 123, 255, 465, 521
Atheism, 280
Athens, 67, 92
'Atzvut, sadness as sin, 207, 219
Australia, 319
Austria, 240–41, 245, 266–67, 282,
    318–19, 342, 518, 570
Authoritarianism, parental, 314
Auto-da-fé, 150, 230
Autonomy, Jewish, 259, 263
Avant garde, Jews in, 370, 474
Averroës (Ibn Rushd), 127
Avicebron, 126. See also Ibn Gabirol,
    Solomon
Avicenna (Ibn Sina), 126
Avignon, 236; Jews in, 228, 239
Avoidance, 425
Avvakum, Russian raskol prophet, 212
Ayin, nothing, 137
Azazel, 48–49

Baal, 46, 52
Ba'ale Shem, magic healers, 216–17, 518
Ba'al Shem Tov, Israel, 181–82, 191,
    199–203, 205–7, 211, 214, 216–17,
    219–20, 256, 441, 518–19
Ba'al t'qi'a, 365
Babel, Tower of, 43
Babylonia, 50, 58, 61, 67, 78, 96, 97, 99,
    106, 361, 440, 481, 514, 527; exile in,
    216
Bachi, Roberto, 152
Backman, Margaret E., 294–95
Bactria, 62
Badge, Jewish, 171, 174, 240
Badis, king of Granada, 112
Baer, Yitzhaq Fritz, 125
Baghdad, 147, 508
Bahir, book of, 146
Bahya ibn Paquda, 127
Bakhurim, 560
Balaam, 4, 375
Bales, Robert F., 446
Ball games on the Sabbath, 555
Ban (herem), 21
Bandits, 190, 383
Bankers, banking, 171, 173, 247
Baptism, 16, 178, 281. See also Conver-
    sion
Baptized Jews, 319
Baraita, 80
Barbary states, 233, 464
Barcelona, 124
Bari, 155–56
Bar Mitzva, 393, 402, 495
Baron, Salo W., 125, 152, 166, 259, 431
Barrabee, Paul, 420
Barrès, Maurice, 475
Barrios, Daniel Levi (Miguel) de, 234
Baruch, Book of, 79
Barukh of Tulczyn, 202, 204, 208, 211,
    213, 219
Basic personality, 4
Bas Mitzva, 393, 402
Baur, Erwin, 327
Beck, Tobias, 231
Bel and the Dragon, 79
Beliar, 78

Belief in God, 10–11. *See also* God, belief in
Bell Adjustment Inventory, 389–90
Belligerence, 425
Belmonte: Isaac Nuñez (Don Manuel) de, 230; Jacob Israel, 229; Moses, 230
Belonging, consciousness of, 9, 23, 25–27
Belz, Rabbi of, 522
Benaiah, 434–35
Ben-Ammi, 434
Ben ʿAzay, 513
Benda, Julien, 473
Bendavid, Lazarus, 466–67, 470
Bene, Judah del, 172
Benedict, Ruth, 180
Benedictions, 365–66, 398, 408, 439, 452. *See also* Blessing
Ben-Hadad, 437
Benjamin, 19, 43, 489
Benjamin Binesh Baʿal Shem, 216
Benjamin of Tudela, 147, 157
Benreuter Personal Inventory, 389
Ben Sira, Yeshuʿa (Jesus), 78–79, 86, 88, 91, 436–37, 511, 526
Berbers, 385–86; language of, 112
Bergson, Henri, 338
Berlin, Sir Isaiah, 470
Berlin, 242, 245, 247–48, 250, 256–57, 414; Jews in, 239, 281, 469
Berman, Louis A., 423
Bernal: Abraham Nuñez, 230;ʹ Isaac de Almeida, 230
Bernard, Jessie, 430
Berr, Berr Isaac, 237
Beruria, wife of R. Meir, 488–89
BeShT. *See* Baʿal Shem Tov, Israel
Bet Alpha synagogue, 65, 360
Bet din, 64
Bet haMidrash, 366, 513. *See also* House of Study
Bethel, 55
Bethuel, 42
Bet Shearim, 66
Bible, 4, 9, 18, 29, 33, 36, 43, 46, 51, 54, 58, 76–77, 82, 88–89, 96, 101–2, 104, 110–11, 120, 126, 128–29, 157, 176–77, 184, 219–20, 226, 231, 244,

247, 270, 275, 278, 300, 355, 365, 367, 369, 435, 438, 446, 471, 481–82, 486–87, 491–92, 495–96, 498, 514, 518, 523; translations, 110, 169
Biblical: commandments, 10; commentaries, 171; custom, 451; Hebrews, 18, 120, 347–49, 358, 375, 418, 483, 493; historians, 37; historiography, 36; history, 20, 46; Israel, 31; Jews, 6; law, 491; myth, 433; period, 41; poetry, 51; society, 483; stories, 523; times, 36, 145, 216, 438, 481, 483, 488, 493, 495, 509–13, 540
Billington, James H., 183
Bima, 362. *See also* Minbar
Binet, Alfred, 288, 296
Bin-Gorion (Berdyczewsky), Mikha Yosef, 458
Biqqur Ḥolim, 409. *See also* Visiting the sick
Birthrate, 411
al-Bīrūnī, 147
Black children, 296. *See also* Negro children
Blacks in America, 297, 309–10
Blake, William, 181
Blessing, 302. *See also* Benedictions
Blood libel, 263. *See also* Ritual murder libel
Bloodshed, 434, 503
Bloom, Benjamin, 302
Blum, Robert, 475
Blumenberg, Werner, 470
B'nai B'rith, 379
Bohemia, 240, 361
Böhme, Jacob, 183
Bokher, yeshiva-student, 589. *See also* Bakhurim
Bologna, 179
Book trade, 166
Bor Confederacy Rebellion, 190
Bordeaux, 227–28, 236, 239, 267, 465
Boring, Edwin, 289
Börne, Ludwig, 249, 282, 475
Boston, 420
Brāhman community, 147
Brahmin, 138

Brain: damage, 299–302; development, 299; weight, 299

Brandeis, Louis D., 428

Bratslav Hasidim, 214

Brazil, 151, 232–33

Brenner, Yosef Hayim, 458

Breslau, 458, 468

Brody, 203

Bronfn, 411

Brother Daniel (Oswald Rufeisen), 22–23

Brotherly love, 493

Budapest, 267; ghetto, 268

Buddhism, Buddhists, 146–47

Bund, the, 264, 268

Burial, 495, 532. *See also* Funeral

Buschan, Georg, 418

Business, Jews in, 422

Cabinet ministers, Jewish, 319

Caesar, 61

Caesarea, 110

Cahalan, Don, 442

Caillavet, Mme Arman de, 250

Cairo, 427

Calderon, Horacio, 13

Calé, Walter, 470

Canaan, 20, 42–43, 50, 275, 350, 434, 534, 545; deities of, 46, 50; language of, 42–46; religion of, 46–56

Canaanites, 7, 42–56, 77

Canaanization of tribes of Israel, 47

Canada, 411, 442, 453, 535

Canon, Biblical, 79–80

Cantillation, 366

Cantorial singing, 366

Capernaum synagogue, 65

Cappa, worn by Jewish savants, 168

Caravallo, Jules, 325

Cardozo, Isaac (Fernando), 227

Caro, Joseph, 30, 151, 170, 482, 502

Carvajal, Luis de, 99

Cassuto, Umberto, 157

Castile, 98, 118–19, 125, 383; Jews in, 381–83; Spanish, 101–2

Catalan: language, 101; Jews, 568

Catatonic: traits, 425; types, 427

Catherine, Empress of Russia, 245

Cellini, Benvenuto, 172

Census, Jewish, 26

Centaurs, 63, 65

Central Europe, 308, 317–18, 339, 345, 366, 404, 517, 520

Cerf Berr, Herz, 237

Cesare Borgia, 161

Character, 5, 328, 372–407, 466, 538; disorders, 416

Chariot, divine, 71

Charisma, charismatic leadership, 194, 210

Charitable societies, 531

Charity, 8, 174, 209, 300, 379–80, 406, 438, 461, 483, 503, 524–28; as a value, 482; in Biblical and Talmudic times, 525–28; institutions, 531; overseers, 530–31; practice of, 530–33

Charles of Anjou, 156

Chastity, rules of, 500–501

Cheinisse, 443

Chelm, Poland, 216, 246

Cherubim, 54–55, 69, 71–72, 74–75, 88, 143, 172, 363

Chess, Jews in, 353

Child(ren), 421–22, 439, 446, 478, 494, 496, 540; Ashkenazi, 536; honoring of, 488; intelligence of, 291, 293–94, 296–97, 310–11, 328; Israeli, 504; kibbutz, 396; Oriental Jewish, 536; teaching of, 510, 514

Childbed, 411

Childlessness, 301, 493

Children of Israel, Biblical, 20, 29, 42–43, 47, 142, 348, 375, 448, 511, 529

Chile, 151

China, 147; children in, 291–93; Jews in, 346

Chirac, Auguste, 456

Chizbat humor, 395

Choirs in synagogues, 366

Chorazin synagogue, 65

Chosen people, Jews as, 378, 461

"Christ" among Russian dissenters, 206, 212

Christian(s), 25, 30, 97–98, 221, 278, 300, 440, 446; Arabs, 398; Church, 473;

churches, 22, 77, 80, 83; environment, 479, 537; Europe, 123; habits, 469; mysticism, 149; peasants, 441; sectarians, 7; Spain, 100, 102, 118, 120; world, 337, 475

Christianity, 10, 14, 16, 51, 53–54, 91, 252, 278, 280–81, 300, 326, 351, 357

Christmas, 393

Church fathers, 87

Cicero, 171–72, 251

Circumcision, 49, 89, 495; female, 508

Class structure, 174. *See also* Lower class; Middle class

Clement VII, Pope, 179

Clermont-Tonnerre, Count Stanislas de, 238

Climate, influence of, on character, 326

Clothing, 98, 174–75, 223, 447–48, 450, 488, 530. *See also* Dress; Garb

Clothing of the poor, 530–32

Codes of Jewish Law, 30, 102, 104, 276, 495, 509. *See also* Shulḥan 'Arukh

Cohabitation, 501. *See also* Copulation; Sexual intercourse

Cohen, Berlin banker, 248

Cohen, Sidney, 289

Collectors of art, Italian Jewish, 170

Colleges, Jews in, 336, 443–44, 454

Columbus, 125, 150

Comité des Délégations Juives, 264

Commandments, religious, 408, 512, 519

Commensality, Jewish-Gentile, 171, 440, 451

Commerce, Jews in, 352, 376–77. *See also* Merchants

Commitment, Jewish, 454

Communist countries, 273, 480

Community: of fate, 269; Jewish, 21, 398, 403

Compassion, 8, 227, 364, 375, 384, 461, 489, 524–25, 533, 540; as imitation of God, 528–30

Compassionate, the (God), 529. *See also* haRaḥman

Composers, 162, 369

Concept Mastery Test, 323

Concubines, concubinage, 43, 47, 165, 499

Condotta, 156

Confessional among Hasidim, 213

Consciousness, Jewish, 24, 395, 574

Conservative: Jews, Judaism, 282, 406, 444; rabbis, 23

Constans, Jean-Antoine-Ernest, 476

Constantinople, 160

Constellations, 130

Content of Jewishness, 221. *See also* Core of Jewishness; Essence of Jewishness

Conversion, 19, 21, 24–25, 34, 92, 178, 223, 260, 273, 279–82, 404, 467

Cookbooks, 453

Cooperation, 574

Copts, 98, 398

Copulation, 499. *See also* Cohabitation; Sexual intercourse

Cordova, 107, 112, 119

Cordovero, Moses, 529

Core of Jewishness, 176–79, 276–77. *See also* Content of Jewishness; Essence of Jewishness

Corpulence, 448–50. *See also* Obesity; Overeating

Corpus mysticum, Israel as, 10

Cossacks, 98

Country clubs, 393

Courtesans, 164

Court Jews, 265

Courts of law, 246

Covenant, 48, 68

Cracow, 482

Crafts(men), 172, 356–57, 385, 538

Creatio ex nihilo, 128–29

Creation, 128–29, 494, 498

Cremona, 166

Crescas, Ḥasdai, 101

Crime, criminality, 163, 379, 383

Cromwell, Oliver, 231

Crusaders, 36, 98

Cuddihy, John M., 392

Cultural: decline, 344; environment, 314, 343, 482; influences, 4, 5, 517; isolation, 35; life, 394; pluralism, 477; synthesis, 175–79

Culture: Gentile, 239, 314; Jewish, 3, 18, 95, 283
Curriculum, 518
Czartoryski, Prince Adam, 201

Dagon, temple of, 74
Dama ben Nethina, 485
Damascus, 54, 100, 464
Dan, township, 55
Dances, dancing, 157, 161, 172, 214, 215, 276, 344
Daniel, Book of, 79
Dante, 157
Dār ul-Islām, 97. *See also* House of Islam
Darwin, Charles, 330
Datchisher Yid, 267
David, King, 8, 31–32, 34, 71–74, 116, 120, 489–90, 492
Davidson, Israel, 113
Day of Atonement, 49, 213, 401, 527. *See also Yom Kippur*
Days of Awe, 364, 406–7
Death rate, 411
Decadence, 473
Deism, 280
Delirium tremens, 441–42
Delmedigo, Elijah, 127; Joseph Solomon, 244, 464
Delusions: of grandeur, 425; of guilt, 426
Demetrius of Phalerum, 82
Demons, 160, 194, 517
Denmark, 414
Dentistry, 160
Depression, 423–25, 427, 431
Depressive: psychoses, 427; states, 425; syndrome, 425
Derekh eretz, 488
Descartes, 231
Desert: and monotheism, 348; wanderings, 495
Detroit, 497, 524
Deutero-Isaiah, 18
Deuteronomy, 11, 18, 42, 355, 437, 511
Dhimmis, 96–98, 429
Dialoghi d'Amore, 127, 159
Dialogue, 176

Diaspora, 5, 6, 16, 34, 36, 43, 59, 64, 66–67, 81, 179, 222, 253, 260, 307, 337, 343, 346, 357, 360–61, 365–66, 369–70, 394, 399, 403, 418, 421, 423, 429, 451, 458–59, 471, 482, 534, 538, 574. *See also* Dispersion
Diaspora Jew, 395, 458; life of, 503
Dibbuqim, 200
Dietary laws, 89, 402, 406, 409, 451, 493. *See also Kashrut; Kosher food
Dinah, 45, 545
Dinstagishe Kurant, 230
Dionysian element in Hasidism, 180–81, 195–207
Dionysus, 433
Discrimination in Israel, 310
Diseases, 412. *See also* Illness
Dispersion, 308, 538. *See also* Diaspora
Disraeli, Benjamin, 24–25, 282, 319, 475
Divine: Presence, 499, *see also* Shekhina; Providence, 67, 129, 132; Wisdom, 88, 183
Divorce, 301
DNA, 298–300
Dobzhansky, Theodosius, 295–97
Dohm, Wilhelm von, 239, 243
Domination of Gentiles by Jews, 320–21
Donnolo, Shabbatai, 155
Dov Ber ben Samuel of Linits, 191
Dov Ber Maggid of Mezhirich, 198
Dowry, 488
Dragon (*tannin*), 52–53, 74, 76. *See also* Leviathan; Sea-monsters
Dramatists, 162
D'rashot, 521. *See also* Sermon(s)
Dreams as omens, 517
Dreckapotheke, 517
Dress, 488, 501. *See also* Clothing; Garb
Dreyfus, Camille, 472
Dreyfus affair, 9, 263, 473, 475, 545
Dreyfuss, Rabbi J. H., 330–31
Drinking: as ritual, 445–46; moderate, 440; pattern, 442–43
Drive, Jewish, 323
Drug addiction, 415–16, 445, 453–55, 539
Drumont, Édouard, 320–21, 471

Drunkenness, 434–35. *See also* Inebriation, inebriety

Dubayet, Jean Baptiste Annibal Aubert, 251

Dubnow, Simon, 17, 180, 182, 264, 470

Dugma, archetype, 139

Dukhobors, spirit wrestlers, 184, 212

Duns Scotus, 127

Dura Europos synagogue, 65, 68, 70–72, 74, 360, 548

Dutch Jews, 245. *See also* Holland; Netherlands

Dutch West Indies Company, 233

D'vekut, cleaving, 181

Eastern Christianity, 207

Eastern Europe, 150, 218, 221–22, 240, 263, 308, 337, 345, 347, 366, 377, 396, 449, 467–68, 488, 517–18, 520; Jews of, 182, 188–91, 195–96, 246, 264, 266, 276, 368, 411, 440, 443, 465, 473–74, 508, 419

Eating habits, 447, 449

Ecclesiastes, 79

Ecclesiasticus, 78, 511. *See also* Ben Sira, Yeshu'a

Economics, 353

Ecumenism, 175

Eden, Garden of, 54, 486

Edom, 487

Education, 28, 102, 167, 270, 303, 309–11, 313–14, 322, 327, 336, 396, 411, 421, 483, 509–24; as a value, 482; attitude toward, 297; duty of, 514; in Middle Ages, 515–19; in modern times, 520

Educational toys, 304

Efron, David, 388

Eglon, king of Moab, 448

Egypt, 11, 43–45, 50, 57, 72–73, 92, 96–98, 106, 151, 221, 350, 406, 429, 448, 464, 490, 492, 510, 545, 548, 560

Egyptian: influence, 54; Jews, 63; slavery, 448, 494

Egyptians, 221, 510

Einstein, Albert, 14, 329, 338, 377

Eisner, Kurt, 353

Elah, King, 437

Ele'azar, Rabbi, 491–92, 513, 528

Ele'azar ben Shim'on, 448

Election of Israel, 11

Elections, Jews in, 394

Eliach, Yaffa, 182, 193

Eliezer, 42, 44

Eliezer of Bartota, Rabbi, 527

Elijah, 73–74, 202

Elijah Gaon of Vilna, 197, 256, 521

Elimelekh of Lezhaysk, 205, 209–10

Elisha ben Abuya, 63

Elite, 174, 246–47; intellectual, 273, 276

Elitism, 131, 133

Eliyahu Ba'al Shem, 216

Elohim, 88, 143. *See also* God

El Transito synagogue, 362

Emanations. *See Sephira, Sephirot*

Emancipation, 8, 13, 22, 151, 175, 222–24, 233, 238–39, 242–43, 245, 247, 250, 253, 257, 259–62, 266, 272–73, 300, 318–19, 328–29, 339, 386, 419, 428–29, 431, 446, 461, 532

Emigration from Israel, 581

Emmrich, Hannah, 562

Emotional development, 421

Emotionalism, 376, 389–90, 395–96

Emotions, display of, 393

Empathy, 305, 353, 378

Endogamy, 45–46

Engels, Friedrich, 470

England, 151, 154, 183, 235, 242, 281–82, 318–19, 342, 368, 453, 539, 570; Jews in, 354

Enlighteners, 177–78, 223, 225, 252, 260–61, 279, 367, 386–87, 404, 462, 465–66, 474, 539. *See also Maskilim*

Enlightenment, 7–8, 11–12, 15, 17, 19, 21–22, 27, 30–37, 41, 80, 96, 109, 151, 159, 222–24, 234–75, 277–78, 280–83, 301, 303, 306, 314, 318, 321, 333, 337–38, 344, 350, 356, 359–60, 362, 365–69, 371, 380, 384, 386–87, 394, 397, 399, 404, 428, 431, 438, 446–47, 451–52, 461–63, 465, 467, 471, 480, 482, 496, 509, 514, 517, 519–21, 523, 537, 540. *See also Haskala*

Enoch, 78, 93; Book of, 54–55
En Sof, infinite, 137–38
Enthusiasm, 218–19, 390. *See also Hitlahavut*
Environment, 298–99, 307–8, 323–24, 334–35, 472, 480, 564–65; anti-Semitic, 459; cultural, 343, 482; Gentile, 305, 314, 355, 523, 531; home, 302–4, 312, 314; social, 312; socio-cultural, 540; urban, 497
Environmental: factors, 304–5, 336; influence, 294–95, 344, 371, 444
Environmentalists, 294, 296–97, 347–48
Ephebeion, 60
Ephod, breastplate, 485
Ephraim, 18, 545
Ephraim, Berlin banker, 248
Ephraim of Sudilkov, 192, 209, 220
Epikoyres, 267
Epispasm, 60
Er, 44, 545
'*Erev rav*, mixed multitude, 46
Eroticism, 148, 200, 203–4, 276, 503, 587
Esau, 44, 487
Esdras, Book of, 79
Eskeles: Bernhard von, 249; Cecilia von, 249
Essence of Jewishness, 8–12, 217, 221, 274, 406, 534. *See also* Content of Jewishness; Core of Jewishness
Essenes, 67
Estates, 258
Esther, 79, 177; Book or Scroll of, 356, 365
Ethic, humanistic, 280
Ethics, 86, 88; of Judaism, 268
Ethnic groups, Jewish, 307–10
Ethnohistory, 28–37
Ethrog, 65, 71, 74–75; boxes, 356
Euripides, 88
Europe, 21, 41, 125, 224, 259–60, 263, 266, 296, 316, 319, 327, 344, 362, 411, 462, 536, 538. *See also* Central Europe; Eastern Europe; Western Europe
European: culture, 222, 253, 260, 271–72, 279, 359, 368, 386, 462, 466;

Jews, 26, 153, 309, 354, 477–78, 504, *see also* Ashkenazi Jews, Ashkenazim; languages, 271, *see also* Languages of Jews
Eusebius, 84–85
Eve, 43, 491, 498. *See also* Adam and Eve
Evil, 206; eye, 411, 425, 428; Inclination, 205, 500–501, 514–15, *see also* Libido
Excellence, intellectual, 335
Exegesis, 105–6
Exile, 19–20, 34–35, 46, 57, 115, 142, 210, 220, 226, 253, 358–59, 361, 381, 434, 441, 459–60, 462, 467, 504, 530, 534, *see also* Galut; Spanish, 5, 102, 150, 154
Exodus, 29, 45, 375, 406
Exorcism, 200, 212, 518
Expressionism, 353
Extroversion, 390, 424–25
Ezekiel, 48, 54, 71–72, 74, 134, 138
Ezekiel, tragedian, 85
Ezra, 29, 31–32, 57–58

Family, 314, 421; as a value, 482; background, 322; cohesion, 497; importance of, 492–93; names, 240; purity, 226; relations, 483–97, 573; sense, 329; ties, 330
Fano, Jacob, 161
al-Fārābī, 126
Farissol: Abraham, 170; Judah, 170
Fatalism, 161, 383
Father and Mother, divine couple, 140
Federation of Jewish Philanthropies, 445
Feeding the poor, 299, 525
Feitelson, Dina, 311–12
"Felix Libertate" society, 233
Feltscher, feltscherkeh, 410
Ferdinand III of Castile, 119
Ferrara, 167, 173, 179, 244
Fertility, 309; cult, 48, 50–51
Feuer, Lewis S., 306, 334
Fez, 112
Field, Peter B., 446
Fifth Commandment, 484–85
Finance, 352
Finkelstein, Louis, 66

Fischer, Eugen, 327

Fishberg, Maurice, 375–76, 394, 414–15, 418, 423

Flamboyant behavior, 426

Flogging, 183, 198–99, 409, 500, 530

Florence, 162

Foissac. *See* Dubayet, Jean Baptiste Annibal Aubert

Folk: heroes, 31; lore, 28–29, 496, 523; medicine, 216; tunes among Hasidim, 214

Fons vitae, 116, 126

Food, Italian Jewish, 171–72

Forced feeding, 450–51

Ford, Henry, 320

Forli, 173

Fornication, 165, 436. *See also* Sexual license

Fostat, Egypt, 127

Fould, Achille, 319

France, 151, 222, 235, 239, 241, 245, 270, 282, 317–19, 342, 368, 398, 404, 452, 474, 479, 516–17, 537–38

Franchetti, Judith, 161

Francis II, Emperor of Austria, 240, 257

Franck, Adolphe, 324–25

Frankfurt am Main, 268

Frankists, 189

Frederick the Great, 236, 238, 469

Frederick II of Hohenstaufen, 156

Freitagishe Kurant, 230

French: culture, 538; Jews, 124, 324, 387, 471–77, 517; language, 517; people, 330; Revolution, 233, 235, 245, 258; society, 474

Freud, Sigmund, 338, 351, 353, 378–80, 572

Friedmann, Meyer, 389

Frimer, Norman E., 454

Frischmann, David, 458

Fritsch, Theodor, 457

Fromm, Erich, 373

Frustration, 461

Fulker, D. W., 564–65

Funeral, 526. *See also* Burial

Future, planning for, 524

Gabriel, 103

Galicia, 205, 239, 374, 384

Galilee, 66

"Galizianer," 267

Galton, Sir Francis, 325, 456, 471

Gallichi, Abraham Yaghel, 157

Galut, 35–37, 115, 434, 459, 461, *see also* Exile; -Jew, 396, 460; -Jewry, 459; nationalism, 17, 264, 268

Gambling, 161–65, 276, 383

Gamliel, Rabban, 61–63

Ganzfried, Solomon, 482

Gaonim, 108, 132

Garb, 271. *See also* Clothing; Dress

Garrett, H. E., 389

"Gastronomic syndrome," 452

Gazeta de Amsterdam, 230

Geiger, Abraham, 30

Geistesgeschichte (intellectual history), 34, 37

Genesis, 18, 42–45, 87, 375, 433, 435, 491

Genetic: potential for genius, 335; selection for intelligence, 306–7; variation, 16

Genetic factors: in drinking patterns, 446; in intelligence, 306, 335; in personality, 373

Genetics, 294–97, 308, 327–28, 564–65

Genius, 314–15, 337–38, 342, 350, 536–37, 567; and insanity, 327; national, 475

Genocide, 34, 327. *See also* Holocaust

Gentile(s), 3–5, 9, 12, 16–17, 22, 25, 27, 31, 34–36, 78, 81, 83, 89–90, 142, 257–59, 266, 271, 277, 287, 291, 299–301, 303–4, 306–8, 315, 319–20, 325–26, 335–37, 344–45, 350–51, 373, 397, 440, 447, 450–51, 454, 462, 471, 473, 538, 585, *see also Goy(im)*; as Jewish ideal, 464; attitude toward Jews, 478; children, 496; converts, 23; cruelty, 530; culture, 283, 332, 338, 354, 516; custom, 313; environment, 8, 11, 44, 275, 279, 309, 339, 355, 362, 366, 370, 372, 380, 402, 443, 465, 472,

480, 509, 517, 523, 531, 537, 540; features, 466; influence, 206–17, 265, 308, 314, 383, 443, 543, 572; personality, 387–88, 463; sectarians, 216; stereotype of Jews, 223; values, 12, 32; wine, 440; women, 520; working classes, 470; world, 29, 428

Geography, 255

Geometry, 123, 521

Gerim, 16. *See also* Proselyte(s)

German: cultural influences, 517; Jews, 154, 178, 228, 237–38, 243, 272, 281, 354, 386–87, 424, 458, 465, 468, 474; lands, 153, 241; language, 247, 255, 278, 368, 469, 517; literature, 271

Germans, Germany, 22, 183, 223, 233, 239, 257, 266, 282, 317–19, 327–29, 342, 361, 371, 386, 457, 516, 518

Gerona, mystics of, 127

Gershom, Rabbenu, 261

Gestures, Jewish, 388–89

al-Ghazālī, 133, 135, 144

Ghetto, 380, 387, 395, 431, 446, 475; Jew, 395

Ghosts, 160

Gibeonites, 490

Giftedness, 315, 321, 323–24. *See also* Genius; Talent(s)

Gikatila, Joseph, 136, 205, 553

Gilgul, 146. *See also* Metempsychosis; Transmigration of souls

Glasgow, 478

G'mara, 58, 514

God, 18, 32, 35–37, 41, 43–44, 48–49, 52, 55–56, 67–70, 73–76, 78, 86, 88–89, 113, 118, 130, 181–83, 186–88, 200–201, 204, 219, 280, 325, 346, 348, 350, 357–58, 364, 366, 384, 400, 409, 427, 437, 440, 452, 460, 484, 488, 490, 498, 501, 509–10, 523, 528; belief in, 405, 467; hand of, 73; imitation of, 375; the King or "Son," 19, 141–42, 145, 150, 498; knowledge of, 516; law of, 511; nature of, 129–30; unity of, 131–32, 149, 516; will of, 29, 481–82, 512

Go'el, 492

Golden Age in Spain, 100, 104, 106–8, 113–16, 134, 154–55, 169, 380, 383

Gonzaga: Guigliermo, 160; house of, 162

Goodenough, Erwin H., 64–66, 68, 72, 75, 547

Gordon, Aharon David, 458

Goudchaux, Michel, 319

Goy(im), 260, 271, 413. *See also* Gentile(s)

Goyisher kop, "Gentile head," 287

Graetz, Heinrich, 30, 109, 232, 467–70

Grammar, 93, 515. *See also* Hebrew grammar

Grammarians, 465

Granada, 101, 112, 117–18, 120, 125, 150

Grand Duke of Muscovy, 160

Grandezza, 154, 381

Gratification, deferred or instant, 312, 426, 502–4, 509

"Graven image," 355–57, 360, 363

Great Mother, Hindu, 142

Greco-Roman: art, 68; pantheon, 90; period, 361; temples, 361; world, 57

Greece, 151, 154, 196, 381

Greek: cities in Palestine, 59; cults, 53; language, 7, 41, 43, 59, 61, 63, 66, 76–78, 81–83, 85, 97, 102, 110–11, 123, 152, 170, 275, 513; philosophers, 63, 85, 128; philosophy, 7, 119; polytheism, 86; religion, 59, 75–76, 97; science, 92, 123; temples, 69; wisdom, 61–63, 67, 81, 85–86, 515

Greek Orthodox Arabs, 398

Greeks, ancient, 251

Grégoire, Abbé Henri, 238

Gregory XIII, Pope, 160

Group: identity, 17–18, 403; mind, 3–4; survival, 346

Guardian angels, 187

Guénée, Abbé Antoine, 237

Guide of the Perplexed, 127–29, 131–33

Guilford, J. P., 289

Guilt: collective, 461, 539; feelings, 379, 422, 427–28

Günther, Hans F. K., 304

Gymnasion, gymnasia, 59–60, 66, 85
G'zerot, persecutions, 36. *See also* Massacres; Pogroms

Habad Hasidim, 214
Habakkuk, 211–12
Haberlandt, M., 457
Haberman, A. M., 550
Ḥabus, king of Granada, 112–13
Hadler, David, 10, 453
Hagar, 490
Haggada, 356
Hague, The, 234
Haidamak uprising, 189
Haifa, 478
al-Ḥākim, caliph, 98
Halakha, 15, 17, 22, 31, 36, 59, 64, 80,
    88, 104, 132, 134, 149, 151, 154,
    167–68, 176, 210, 224–25, 247,
    254–57, 265, 267–68, 272, 277–78,
    282, 318, 333, 338, 387, 454, 482, 496,
    514, 518, 520
Halakhic: curriculum, 30, 33; law, 23;
    studies, 106; writings, 105
Haldane, J. B. S., 306
haLevi, Y'huda, 99, 114, 118–22, 140
Halévy, Fromenthal, 250; Geneviève,
    250
al-Ḥallāj, 147
Ḥalla offering, 519
Hallucinations, 427;
Hallucinatory activity, 425
Ham, son of Noah, 433
Ḥama bar Ḥanina, Rabbi, 491, 529
Haman, 365
haM'assef, 244–45
Hamat of Tiberias, synagogue, 65–66
haNagid, Samuel, 112–17, 121, 550
Handicrafts, 352
Handmaids, 43
Ḥanilay, Rabbi, 491
Ḥanina, Rabbi, 485, 489
Hanna, 202
Hanukka, 31, 173, 393, 401–2, 406, 495;
    lamps, 356
Hara, 387. *See also* Ghetto

Haran, 42–43, 490
Harden, Maximilian, 470
"Harmfulness" of Jews, 241
Hashish, 453
Hasidic: Jews, 411, 440; movement, 351,
    377; mysticism, 185–86; rabbis, 324
Hasidim, 199, 246, 272, 366, 402, 466,
    520–22, 530; in ancient Palestine, 67;
    of Ashkenaz, 134; pre-Talmudic, 409
Hasidism, 7, 135, 149, 151, 180–83,
    185–86, 188, 191, 195–98, 212–22,
    256, 268, 276–77, 384, 440–41,
    466–67, 519
Haskala, 178, 237, 243–44, 253, 255–56,
    261, 271–72, 283, 467, 520. *See also*
    Enlightenment
Hasmoneans, 84
Haughtiness, Sephardi, 381. *See also*
    Pride
Havdala, 192, 439, 494, 522; cup, 356,
    489
Hayim of Cyprus, physician, 160
Hayim Haykel, Tzaddiq of Amdur, 198
Ḥayyot, angelic beasts, 144
Hayyuj, Y'huda ben David, 112–13
Hazael, king of Damascus, 53
Healers, 216. *See also Ba'ale Shem*
Health: attitudes toward, 413; mental,
    413–28; physical, 408–13, 538
Hebephrenic traits, 425, 427
Hebrew: grammar, 107–8, 112, 154, 232,
    256, 276, 518, 521; language, 7, 41–44,
    51, 57, 63, 66, 77–78, 82–83, 101–4,
    110, 119, 123, 127, 155, 177, 247, 271,
    367, 369, 468–69; linguistics, 105–6,
    109–13, 169; literature, 369; poetry,
    103, 113–22, 154–55; poets, 104;
    printing, 229, 231; reading knowledge
    of, 519–20; script, 102; teaching read-
    ing, 522
Hebrews: ancient, 349–50, 534; Biblical,
    251, 316
Hebrew Union College, 452
Ḥeder, elementary Tora school, 301–2,
    333, 337, 366, 418, 435, 494–95,
    521–23
Heidbrecher questionnaire, 389

Heine, Heinrich, 24–25, 281–82, 368, 450, 475

Helios, 65, 67–68, 70–71

Hell, François J. A., 251

Hellenism, 7, 21, 56–57, 59–95, 102, 149, 253, 275, 357

Hellenistic: age, 109, 123; Jewish literature, 30, 77; Jewish philosophers, 128; Judaism, 149; world, 111

Hellenization, 126

Henry IV, 160

"Hep, hep!" 252

Heqdesh, 531–32

Heracles, 65, 68, 72

Hereditarians, 295–97, 565

Hereditary factors in intelligence, 294–95, 304–7, 336

Heredity, 296, 298, 307, 323–27, 329, 353, 414, 565

Herem, excommunication, 404. See also Ban

Heritage, 21, 431, 534

Herod, 60, 61, 361

Herrnstein, Richard J., 564–65

Herschel, Sir William, 377

Hersey, John, 368

Hersh Ostropoler, 208

Hertz, Heinrich, 377

Herz: Henrietta, 248–49; Markus, 225, 243, 248

Herzl, Theodor, 263, 269, 273, 338, 457–58, 476–77

Hesed, 203, 525

Hesiod, 76, 87, 92, 111

Hess, Moses, 475

Hevra Qadisha, 337, 532

Hidalgo, 381–82

High Holy Days, 401–2, 406–7

High priest, 82, 485

Hijā, poetic diatribe, 115

Hillel, 9, 64, 221, 526

Himalaya, 141–43

Himmelfarb, Milton, 281

Hindu: cosmogony, 148; mysticism, 147; mythology, 148

Hinduism, 136–37, 144–45, 147

al-Hira, 99

Hirsh, Tzaddiq of Zhydaczov, 204

Histadrut, 459

Historiography, 83–84, 94, 108–9, 177, 255

History: external and inner, 34–37; Jewish, 5, 28–37, 404

Hitlahavut, 181. See also Enthusiasm

Hitler, 252, 327

Hitlerjugend, 458

Hittites, 44

Hiyya, Rabbi, 492

Hofstein, Israel, of Kozienice, 201, 217

Holland, 151, 183, 227, 319, 344, 361, 518. See also Netherlands

Holocaust, 23, 283, 308, 460. See also Genocide

Holy Ark, 196, 200, 356

Holy Land, 115, 179, 262, 359. See also Israel, Land of

Holy of Holies, 55–56, 74, 88

Holy Spirit, 195, 212

Holy Tongue, 110. See also Hebrew language

Homberg, Herz, 240

Home, Jewish, 421, 493–96; environment of, 338; life in, 326; parental, 524

Homer, 63, 76, 87–88, 92, 111, 316

Homosexuality, 505–6

Honi the Circle-Drawer, 200

Honoring: of children, 488; of parents, 483–84; of wife, 491–92

Hornblass, Jerome, 445

Horodezky, S. A., 182

Hosea, 435

Hospitality, 226, 483

Hospitals, 22, 352

Hostility, Gentile-Jewish, 380

Hourwitz, Zalkind, 238, 245

House of Islam, 98. See also Dār ul-Islām

House of Study, 489, 511, 513, 515, 527. See also Bet haMidrash

Huarte de San Juan, Juan, 348

Hundt, Hartwig, 252

Hungary, 22, 214–15, 266–67, 282, 318–19, 371; Jews in, 387

Hunger, 300. See also Feeding the poor

Hunting, 174

Hurwitz: Nathan, 390–91; S. J., 182
Husband and wife, 491–92
"Husk," Evil, 148, 184, 205, 220. See also
    Q'lippot
Hutzpa, "cheek," 375
Hygiene, 410
Hygienic conditions, 411
Hypochondriasis, 412, 423
Hypostases, 69–70, 88
Hysteria, 415, 424–25
Hysterical: conversion, 425; mood, 376

Iberian Jews, 106. See also Spanish Jews;
    Portugal, Jews in
Ibn Abbas, Samuel, 568
Ibn Aknin, Joseph, 515
Ibn Caspi, Joseph, 516
Ibn Ezra: Abraham, 114, 124; Moses,
    113–14, 117–20, 122
Ibn Gabirol, Solomon, 113–14, 116–17,
    119, 126, 550
Ibn Jannaḥ, Abu 'l-Walid Merwan
    (Yona), 112–13
Ibn Khaldūn, 47, 108
Ibn Khalfūn, Yitzḥaq, 121
Ibn Khurradādhbih, 147
Ibn Labrat, Dunash, 107, 112–14
Ibn Quraysh, Y'huda, 112
Ibn Saruq, M'naḥem Ya'aqov, 107,
    112–13
Ibn Shaprut, Ḥasdai, 107–8, 112, 248
Ibn Sid, Isaac, 125
Ibn Tibbon: Judah, 515; Samuel, 552
Ibn Verga: Joseph, 30, 109; Solomon, 109
Ibn Waqar, Joseph, 136
Ibtidā', innovation, 258
Iconography: Israelite, 53–56; Jewish,
    67–77
Iconolatrous environment, 360
Iconolatry, Christian, 357
Ideational symptomatology, 425
Idelsohn, A. Z., 214
Identification: group, 223; Jewish, 24, 27,
    176, 400, 454, 540
Identity, Jewish, 9, 159, 222, 345–46,
    388, 397–400, 402–6; of Freud, 378
Idolatry, 31, 86, 434, 460, 503

Illness, 410–11; behavior, 412
Imitatio dei, 409, 528
Imitation of God, 528
Immanuel haRomi, 157, 168
Immigrants, 374, 396, 412, 423, 453, 477;
    in Israel, 310, 423, 537; support of, 533
Impatience, 392–93, 538
Impressionism, Jews in, 369
Incantation, 132
Incense-shovel, 75
Incest, 436, 503
Income, 322
Incunabula, 167
India, 62, 147
Individualism, 419
"Indo-European race," 348
Industry, 318
Inebriation, inebriety, 202, 218, 435,
    438. See also Alcohol(ism)
Infant: care, 412; mortality, 412
Inferiority, 389, 422, 426, 471–73, 539
Influences on the Jewish mind, 6–8
Ingathering of the Exiles, 308–9
Inquisition, 99, 150, 166, 227, 229–30,
    232–33, 383
Insanity, 414
Intellect: divine, 552; primal cause, 130
Intellectual: development, 421; elitism,
    130; life, 422
Intelligence, 130, 287–89; Jewish, 287,
    291–314, 320–21, 328, 331–35, 337,
    535–36, 564–65
Intensity, 392, 394, 538
Intermarriage, 21, 261–62, 310, 381,
    405, 440. See also Mixed marriages
Internalization of cultural values, 333
Introversion, 389
I.Q. (Intelligence Quotient), 287,
    289–91, 294–99, 301, 303–5, 307,
    313–15, 321, 323; tests, 335–37,
    535–36, 565
Iranian immigrants in Israel, 424
Iraq, 99–100, 104–5, 311, see also
    Babylonia, Mesopotamia; Jews in,
    105–6, 424–25, 506–9; Muslims in,
    508–9
Isaac, 31, 42, 44–45, 484, 487, 490

Isaac the Blind, 146
Isaiah, 14, 52, 72, 131, 134, 300, 337–38, 346, 375, 435
Ishmael, 44, 490
Ishtar, 72
Islam, 14, 53–54, 77, 96–97, 110, 132, 147, 252, 278, 351, 357, 515, 531
Islamic thought, 126
Isolation, 384
Israel: Biblical, 4, 19, 434; Land of, 201, 459, 462, 481, 486
Israel, State of, 6, 17, 22, 26, 98, 223, 269–70, 273, 308–9, 311–13, 334, 360, 369, 385, 398–400, 405, 423, 428, 430, 442, 451, 453, 456, 460, 477–78, 480, 497, 533, 535, 537–39; literature of, 370
Israeli, Isaac ben Solomon, 126
Israeli: art, 370; architecture, 370; -born Jews, 309, 394, 397, 424, 573; children, 504, see also Sabra(s); Defense Forces, 313, see also Army, Israeli; Jews, 399–400, 537; music, 370
Israelites: ancient, 438, 448, 493, 510; religion of, 275
Israel Levi of Hamburg, 242
Isserles, Moses, 502, 582
Istituto Rabbinico Lombardo-Veneto, 240
Istrioni Ebrei, 162. See also Theater, Jews in
Italian: Jewish intellectuals, 260–61; Jews, 152–79, 225, 236, 244, 276, 387, 468, 516, 538; language, 7, 153, 160, 172
Italians, gestures of, 388–89
Italy, 5, 7, 21, 28, 127, 227, 318–19, 327, 344, 380, 383
Itzig, Daniel, Berlin banker, 248–49
'Ivrit, Hebrew language, 43

Jacob, 11, 18, 31, 42–45, 484, 487, 489–90, 492, 545
Jacob ben Asher, 30
Jacob Isaac, "the Jew of Przysucha," 202–3, 211

Jacob Isaac Horowitz of Lublin, 213
Jacob Joseph of Polonnoye, 203, 205, 209
Jacobs, Joseph, 325–26, 334, 352, 354, 375
Jadid al-Islam, 531. See also "New Muslims"
"Jargon," 468–69
Jason, high priest, 60
Jason of Cyrene, 84
Jecke, 387
Jehoshaphat, 10
Jencks, Christopher, 294
Jensen, Arthur R., 564
Jerba, Island of, 464
Jeremiah, 19, 131, 375, 490; Letter of, 79
Jeroboam, 55
Jerusalem, 32, 50, 55, 58, 60, 66, 82, 84, 115, 453, 464, 490, 560
Jesurun: David, 230; Reuel (Paulo de Pina), 230
Jesus, 14, 184, 209, 338, 351
Jew, definition of, 19, 24
Jewelry of Yemenite Jews, 385
Jewish Chronicle, 438
Jewish Free School, 466
Jinks, J. L., 564–65
Jizya, head tax, 97
Job, Book of, 176
Jokes, Jewish, 413, 450
Jones: Ernest, 572; Howard, 444
Jordan River, 47, 511
Josefowitz, Rabbi Herschel, 246
Joseph, 43–44, 203, 429, 489–90, 545
Joseph, Rabbi, 486
Joseph ben Joshua haKohen, 169
Joseph ben Y'huda, 131
Joseph II, Emperor of Austria, 239–40, 244
Josephus Flavius, 30, 57, 84–85, 90, 200, 513
Joshua, 510
Joshua Heshel of Opatov, 211
Jost, Isaac Marcus, 30, 109, 467, 470
Journalism, Jews in, 318, 378
Joy in serving God, 218, 440, 519; among Hasidim, 219–20
Judah, 19, 44, 545

Judah: Kingdom of, 53, 57, 511; land of, 58, 78, 438; tribe of, 228, 465
Judah ben David, Rabbi (Bonjudes ben Davin), 163
Judah Maccabi, 79
Judengassen, 382
Judeo-: Arabic, 102, 369; French, 517; Italian, 153, 169, 172, 513; Persian, 102, 369
Judeophobia, 250, 287, 327, 430. *See also* Anti-Semitism
Jüdisch-theologisches Seminar, Breslau, 458, 562
Judith, Book of, 79
Julian the Apostate, 91
Jupiter, 69
Justus of Tiberias, 84-85
Juval, 176

Kabbala, 19, 127, 134-51, 182-83, 205, 226, 232, 256, 351, 467, 499, 552-53
Kabbalism, 142-43, 183, 200
Kabbalistic doctrine, teaching, view, 133, 206, 498
Kabbalists, 19, 158, 205, 212, 529
Kahana, Rav, 502
Kahler, Erich von, 10
Kahn, Léon, 473; Rabbi Zadoc, 476
K'ai-feng Fu, Jews of, 346
Kalām, 126, 129
Kali, 144
Kalila waDimna, 156
Kallir, Eleazar, 104-5
Kalov Hasidim, 214. *See also* Nagykálló
Kammerer, Paul, 330
Kant, Immanuel, 445-46, 467
Kapustin, Savely, 212
Karaism, Karaites, 80, 108, 119, 132, 226, 464
Kardiner, Abram, 373
Karibu, winged genii, 54
Karma, wheel of, 146
Kashrut, 5, 171, 401-2, 405. *See also* Dietary laws; Kosher food
Kaufman, Yehezkel, 459
Kayserling, Meyer, 381
Kazin, Alfred, 451

Kehilla, Kehillot, 190, 199, 246
Kelim, vessels, in the Kabbala, 206
Keter, crown, in the Kabbala, 138-39
Ketubba, marriage contract, 173, 177, 356
Khazaria, 107
Khlysty, flagellants, 184, 195, 197, 202, 206, 212
Kibbutz, kibbutzim, 254, 313-14, 396-97, 509; children, 507; movement, 396; personality, 397
Kibbutzniks, 396, 538
al-Kindī, 126
King, God the, 142, 145. *See also* God
"Kingdom," Sephira of, 139
Kinsey reports, 504-7
Kivrot haTa'ava, "Graves of Lust," 448
K'lal Yisrael, Community of Israel, 255
Klausner, Samuel, 506-8
Kle zemer, "klezmer," musicians, 364-65
Klineberg, Otto, 315
Kloyz, 219
Knesset, Parliament, of Israel, 22-23
Koenigswarter, Frédérique, 250
Kohen, 19
Kohler, Rabbi Kaufmann, 452
Königsberg, 245
Kosciuszko, Tadeusz, 246
Kosher food, 404, 452. *See also* Dietary laws; *Kashrut*
Kovno, 257
Kraeling, Emil G., 73
Kufa, 100
Kultur, German, 469
Kulturgeschichte (cultural history), 37
Kurdish Jews, 370, 398-99
Kurdistan, 398-99, 464
Kurland, 267
Kuzari, 114, 119-20

Laban, 43, 45, 487, 490
Ladino, 43-44, 100, 102, 110, 150, 153, 369, 382-83, 398, 520
Laird Personal Inventory B2, 389
Lakeville study, 405
Lakhmid state, 99

Lamarckism, 330
Landau, Ezekiel, 256
Landauer, Gustav, 353
Landsmannschaften, 6
Lane, Edward William, 221, 560
Language, command of, 312, 314, 536
Languages of Jews, 7–8, 41, 43, 241, 245, 260, 267, 277–78, 352, 367, 369, 398, 468, 516–17
Lasker, Arnold A., Rabbi, 407
Lassalle, Ferdinand, 353, 470, 475
Latin language, 63, 101–3, 112, 123–24, 152, 157, 160, 170, 172
"Latin" Renaissance, 156
Lavater, John Caspar, 242
Law: codes, 482; of God, 58; Jewish, 28, 94, 266; of Moses, 91; study of the, 8–9, 35; traditional, 64
Lawyers, 378
Lazare, Bernard, 9, 403, 474–77
Lazarus, Morris, 461
Leah, 43, 489
Learning: as supreme value, 266, 272–73, 301, 303, 338, 355, 406; zest for, 168. *See also* Study(ing)
Lebanon, 98
Legoyt, Alfred, 325
Leisure time, utilization of, 524
Lemuel, King, 436, 510
Lenski, Gerhard, 533
Lenz, Fritz, 327–31, 353–54, 378
Leone Ebreo (Judah Abravanel), 127, 159
Lesser, Gerald S., 292
Lessing: Gotthold Ephraim, 242; Theodor, 470
Leventman, Seymour, 452
Levi, Rabbi, 202
Leviathan, 48, 52, 74, 76
Levi ben Abraham, 133
Leviné, Eugen, 353
Levites, 19, 511, 525
Levi Yitzhaq of Berdichev, 201, 213
Lewin, Kurt, 428, 461–62
Lewinian law or rule, 462–63
Lewis, Bernard, 479
Lewisohn, Ludwig, 430–31
Liberalism, Jewish, 390

Libido, 202, 204, 500, 502
Lieberman, Saul, 547
Lilith(s), 48, 53–54, 194
Linguistics, 93. *See also* Hebrew linguistics
Lippmann, Auguste, 250
Literacy, 166–67, 174, 309
Literary talent, 367–68
Literature: Jewish, 41, 168–71, 247, 367–71; Jews in, 318, 537
Lithuania, Lithuanians, 182, 186, 233; Jews, 253, 374, 384; language, 367
Liturgical poetry, 104–6. *See also Paytanim; Piyyut(im)*
Llerena, Spain, 179
Löb Melamed, 203
Locke, John, 234
Lodz, 441
Logic, gift for, 353
Logos, 88
Lombroso, Cesare, 326–27, 347
London, 235, 453; Jews in, 444; Liberal Synagogue, 452
Lord's Prayer, 300
Lorelei, Die, 368–69. *See also* Heine, Heinrich
Lorenzo the Magnificent, 171, 175
Lot, 434–35
Lotan, 52. *See also* Leviathan
Louis XV, 228
Louis XIV, 236
Love: aspect of Judaism, 9; between parents and children, 489–90; of God, 11, 37, 129, 188, 204, 232, 262, 384, 462, 510, 516, 519, *see also Amor dei*; marital, 501; of nature, 218; of neighbor, 37; of People of Israel, 262; of strangers, 262, 528; of wife, 491; of Zion, 262
Lower class, 297, 303, 311–12, 420, 504, 536
Lublin, 202, 213, 245
Luftmenschen, 460
Lulabh, 65, 71, 74–75
Lunel, Jews of, 552
Luria, Yitzhaq, 205, 211, 220
Lurianic Kabbala, 181
Luschan, Felix von, 330

Luxemburg, Rosa, 353

Luxury, 173, 177, 384

Luzzatto: Samuel David, 240; Simone, 152, 226, 235

Maacah, 55

Ma'amad, 383

Ma'ase Merkava, "Work of the Chariot," 134

Ma'aser, tithe, 525

Maccabean(s), 32, 58, 60, 79, 87, 409, 411, 459

Maccabees, Books of the, 79, 84, 87

Magic, 147, 150, 160–61, 194, 383, 424–25, 428, *see also* Sorcery, Witchcraft; cures, 517; formulas, 411; healers, 418, *see also Ba'ale Shem;* name(s), 67

Magnes, Judah L., 458

Mahler, Raphael, 208

Maimon, Solomon, 198, 249, 268, 557–58

Maimonides (Moses ben Maimon), 11, 14, 30, 50–51, 108, 127–33, 135, 149, 151, 278, 338, 343, 464, 499, 500, 529, 552

Majlis, 107

Majorca, 123

Mala, "husk," in Hinduism, 144–45

Maladaptive behavior, 425

Maladjustment, 389, 426

Malesherbes, 237

Malfunctioning of the mind, 414

Maller, Julius B., 305

Malnutrition, 299–301

Manasseh, 18, 545

Manasseh ben Israel, 151, 225, 231, 235, 243–44

Mandrakes and other aphrodisiacs, 502

Manic-depressive psychoses, 416

Manic syndrome, 425

Mann, Thomas, 368

Manna, 448

Mannerisms, 432

Manners, 376

Mantua, 161–63, 167, 179, 225

Manuscript collections, 166

Map making, 123

Maramarosh Hasidim, 214

Marginality, 22, 24, 283, 332, 428–32, 539

Marijuana, 453

Marini, Heber, 324

Maritain, Jacques, 10

Marital union, 494. *See also* Cohabitation; Copulation; Sexual intercourse

Maronites, 98

Marranos, 25, 99, 150–51, 153, 229–32; "inverted," 431

Marriage, 495, 497, 499, 503; consanguineous, 418; preference, 335

Martyrs, 230

Marx, Karl, 14, 24, 282, 338, 351, 353, 377, 470, 475

Marxism, 14, 273, 351, 479

Masarjuwayh of Basra, 100

Mashallah, 105

Maskil, instructional song, 512

Maskilim, 177, 255, 260–61, 271–72, 279, 466–67, 480. *See also* Enlighteners

Masora, 111

Masoretic text of the Bible, 83

Massacres, 98, 376

Masturbation, 506, 508

Maternal love, 449

Mathematics, Jews in, 103, 123–24, 344, 352–53, 465

Matronit, 19, 53, 139–43, 145, 498

Matthew, 409

Matza, matzot, 494, 532

Maya, demon-tyrant in Hinduism, 142

Mayer, Berlin banker, 248

Mayerl, Tzaddiq of Przemyslany, 201

Meals, festive, 494

Meals given to students, 518. *See also Teg essen*

Mechanic, David, 413

Medalists, 360

Medical: help, 538; works, 160

Medicine, 63, 103, 157, 159–60, 167, 173–74, 216, 276, 344, 353, 409; study of, 93, 515

Mediterranean heritage, 392–93

Meir, Rabbi, 63, 434, 488–89

Melamed, teacher, 521

Mellah, 387. *See also* Ghetto

Menahem Nahum, Maggid of Chernobyl, 204, 324, 569

Mendelssohn, Moses, 30, 178, 224–25, 228, 231–32, 236, 238–39, 242–45, 248–49, 256, 261, 271, 346, 466, 468–71

Mendelssohn Veit, Dorothea, 248–49

Menora, 65–66, 71, 74–76, 401

Menstrual cycle, 503

Mental: abilities, see I.Q.; age, 290; agility, 377; disorders, 538–39; illness in Israel, 423

Mentality, 308

"Mental race," Jews as, 328, 353–54

Merchants, 147, 156–57, 173, 265. See also Commerce, Jews in

Mering, Otto von, 420

Merkava, divine chariot, 48; mysticism, 134

Meshhedi Jews, 531

Mesopotamia, 42–44, 46, 54, 92, 350. See also Babylonia; Iraq

Messer Leon, Judah, 171, 176

Messiah, 124, 193, 231, 359, 441, 461, 503–4, 530

Messianic: end, 205; fervor, 467; hope, 543; meaning, 215; promise, 89

Messianism, 135, 503

Metatron, 144

Metempsychosis, 146. See also Reincarnation; Transmigration of souls

Metz, 238, 245

Mexico, 151

Mezhirich: Hasidim, 198; Maggid of, 208

Mezuza, 493

Michel, Maggid of Zloczov, 211

Middle Ages, 11, 14, 16, 19, 153, 155, 244, 252, 258, 306, 316–18, 356, 360, 367, 377, 409, 537

Middle class, 246, 291–95, 297, 303, 311–12, 314, 413, 417–18, 444, 479, 504, 524, 536

Middle East, 97, 269, 345–46, 357, 385, 398, 447–49, 453, 535; countries, 312, 536; culture, 399; Jews, 269–70, 308–9, 311, 313, 399–400, 464, 477, 479, 507–8, 519–20, see also Oriental Jews

Midrash(im), 11, 30, 64, 72, 81, 104, 128, 136, 367, 433

Midtown Manhattan study, 418–20

Migrations, 6, 266, 374

Military, Jews in Italian, 171

Milk and meat dishes, 452. See also Dietary laws; Kashrut; Kosher food

Minbar, 362. See also al-memor; Bima

Minhag, custom, 225, 255, 265

Miniature art, 356, 360

Minority, low status, 461

Minyan(im), 199, 337

Minz, Rabbi Judah, 173

Miqve, ritual bath, 204, 337

Mirabaud, Jean Baptiste de, 237

Mirabeau, Count, 238, 245, 251

Mirandola, Pico della, 127, 158, 171

Mishna, 32, 58–59, 63, 67, 78, 80, 96, 110, 127–28, 130, 435, 483–84, 514

Mishnaic: sages, 483; times, 510, 530

Mission civilisatrice, 429

"Mission" of Israel, 331

Mitnaged, Mitnagdim, 181, 198–99, 203, 205, 213, 220–21, 246, 272, 366, 441, 520–21

Mitzva, mitzvot, 219, 279, 299, 446, 487, 524

Mixed marriages, 22, 24. See also Intermarriage

Moab, 434, 448

Mobility, upward, 422

Modal personality, 4, 28, 372–73, 384–85, 388, 391, 423, 426, 538

Modena, Leon da, 162, 164, 225–26, 248

Modesty, 8

Molokans, 183–84

Moneylending, 223

Monolatry, 48

Monotheism, 48, 53–54, 59, 83, 86, 91, 123, 348, 351

"Monotheistic races," 348

Monotheists, 68

Montagu, Ashley, 299

Montesquieu, 242, 252

Monti di Pietà, 174

Moorish: rule, 152; -style synagogues, 77, 361

Morality, 405, 523

Moral life, 406

Mordecai, 74, 211
Mordecai (Motel) of Chernobyl, 208
Morocco, 151, 386, 479, 568; Jews in, 112, 153, 308, 374, 385–86, 449, 478
Mortality, 309, 411
Mosad (school), 507
Mosaic law, 89
Moses, 14, 31–32, 45, 52, 64, 68, 70, 72–73, 87–89, 108, 115, 129, 131–32, 202, 217, 237, 337, 346, 350, 378, 448, 469
Moses ben Abraham, 125
Moses ben Maimon. *See* Maimonides
Moses ben Nahman. *See* Nahmanides
Moses de Leon, 136, 498, 553
Moses ibn Ḥanokh, 107
Moses of Marseilles, 134
Moses of Palermo, 156
Moshav, 107, 396, 574
Moshava, 396, 574
Moshe Leib of Sasov, 530
Mosul, Jews of, 464, 582
Mother: honoring of, 484–86; influence of, 373; Jewish, 450–51
Motivation, 301, 390, 421
Mount Sinai, 11, 20, 28, 64, 406, 482, 515, 528
Muḥammad, 97, 103, 110–11, 350
Munkacs Hasidim, 214
Muntafil, Arab poet, 113
Musar, 521. *See also* Ethics
Music, 123, 161–62, 176–77, 189, 213–15, 256–57, 276, 362–67, 538; Jews in, 318, 344, 353, 537; talent, 352; virtuosos, 378
Musical instruments, 363, 365
Musive style, 104, 120, 549
Muslim: countries, 309, 411, 536; environment, 385, 423, 537; lands, 362; mystics, 147; mysticism, 127, 135, 149; orbit, 537
Muslim Arab: civilization, 168; culture, 21, 156; environment, 500; world, 316
Muslim Arabs, 276, 374, 380
Muslims, 221, 278, 300, 317, 427–28, 449, 453, 508
Muslim Spain, 103, 119, 155; Jews in,

269–70; world, 165, 429, 365, 398, 535
Mussolini, 319
Mutakallimūn, 126, 132, 552
Mu'tazila, Mu'tazilites, 126, 145
Myers, Jerome, 420, 426
"Mystery of copulation," 204
Mystical literature, 256
Mysticism, 19, 183. *See also* Kabbala
Mythology, 51, 63, 111

Nabal, 437
Nagykálló (Kalov), Tzaddiq of, 215
Naḥman bar Sh'muel, 500
Nahmanides, 10, 134–35, 146, 449
Nahman of Bratslav, 211, 213–14
Nahman of Horodenka, 201
Najaf, 99
Nakedness: among Hasidim, 197; among Khlysty and Dukhobors, 197
Names, 165
Naples, University of, 156
Napoleon, 237, 245, 252, 261–62, 451
Naquet, Alfred, 472
Nashn, to nibble, 449
Nasrullayoff, Farajullah, 531
Nasser, Gamal Abdul, 320–21
Nathan ben Yehiel, 155
Nation, Jews as, 259–60
Nation, La, 472
National character, 4, 28, 326, 372. *See also* Modal personality
National consciousness, 475
Nationalism, 10, 258–65, 429, 475, 477; Israeli, 396
National minority, Jews as, 264, 266
National Socialist Party in Germany, 458. *See also* Nazis
Naumann, Max, 458
Navarre, 125
Nazirites, 438
Nazis, 26, 98, 287, 305, 308, 327, 368, 404, 410, 458–60
Necromancy, 132
Negro: children, 291–93; students, 294–95. *See also* Black; Blacks
Nehama, Joseph, 381–83

Nehardea, 33, 61
Nehemia, 29, 31–32, 57–58
Neo-Aramaic, 369
Neofiti, 178
Neo-Orthodoxy, 268, 282
Neo-Platonism, 89, 126–27
Nervousness, 376, 418–19
Nesakh-wine, 446
Nestorian Christians, 399
Netherlands, 154, 229–34, 389. *See also* Holland
Neuroses, 274, 389, 414–16, 418, 420–24, 432, 538
Neurotic: pattern, 423; symptoms, 430
Neutra (Nyitra), 589
"New Christians," 16, 150, 178
New Haven, 415–17, 420, 426, 443
New Left, 479–80
New Moon, 48
"New Muslims," 16. *See also Jadid al-Islam*
New Netherlands, 151
New Testament, 53, 200
New World, 151–52
New Year, 65, 401–2, 406. *See also Rosh haShana*
New York City, 388, 394, 401, 414, 416–17, 442, 454–55
Nietzsche, Friedrich, 180
Niggunim, 214. *See also* Cantorial singing; Music; Singing
Nike, winged victory, 72–73
Nile, 72
Ninth of Av, 406
Nirvana, 146
Nitzotzot, sparks, in the Kabbala, 215
Noah's drunkenness, 433–35, 437
Nobel Prize, 339–43, 570
"Non-Aryans," 282
Nonconformists in Russia, 184. *See also* Russian dissenters, sectarians
Noosphere, 13, 207
Norsa, Solomon Jedidiah, 171
North Africa, 7, 97, 154, 233, 311; immigrants from, 478; Jews in, 132, 386, 404–5, 477, 479, 538
N'shama y'tera, 494

Numbers, command of, 536
Nuremberg laws, 24, 282

Obesity, 447–53. *See also* Overeating
Obsessive syndrome, 425
Occupations, 223, 261, 273, 318, 322, 337–38, 376–77, 411, 418, 470, 488, 497
Oden, Melita H., 321
Okhrana, 320
'Olam haba, 586. *See also* World to Come
Old peoples' homes, 22, 392
'Olim, immigrants to Israel, 269
Olympian family, 70
Olympus, gods of, 63
Onan, 545
Onias, 60
Opium, 193
Oppression, 377–78, 473
Optics, 123
Optimism, 378
Oral: Law, 58, 67, 514; tradition, 33
Organ music in synagogues, 77, 366
Orgies of Dukhobors, 198
Oriental: Jews, 154, 270, 308–10, 312, 314–15, 363, 384, 398–99, 422–28, 442, 453, 460, 477–78, 504, 517, 535–39, *see also* Middle Eastern Jews; peoples, 472; students, 294–95
Oring, Elliott, 395
Orlansky, Harold, 422, 431
Orphanages, 22, 392
Orpheus, 72, 92
Ortar, Gina, 309
Orthodox: Christian Arabs, 98; Jews, 17, 25, 30, 223, 244, 267–68, 387, 402, 406, 408, 440, 444, 451, 455, 482, 496, 504–6, 509; Judaism, 25, 253–58; rabbis, 23, 277; tradition, 502
Osiris, 69
"Ostjuden," 267
Ostraha, Jews of, 195
Otherness, 464–65
"Other (evil) Side," 144. *See also Sitra ahra*
Otranto, 155–56
Ottoman Empire, 154. *See also* Turkey
Overeating, 539. *See also* Obesity

Ovid, 75
Oxford, 478; University, 405

Paddan-aram 42–44, 487
Padua, 160–61, 173, 240, 555
Pain, attention, response, sensitivity to, 392–93, 412, 538
Painting, Jews in, 161, 174, 318, 344, 353, 355–60
Pale of Settlement, Jewish, 188, 239
Palermo, 156
Palestine, 34, 57–59, 61, 63, 66–67, 78, 80, 96–97, 106, 151, 261, 361, 386, 399, 514. See also Israel, State of
Pallière Aimé, 25
Palmistry, 161, 383
Paranoia, 424–25
Paranoid: reactions, 424; syndrome, 425
"Parasitism," Jewish, 305, 456–60, 471, 539, 581
Parental: concern, 421, 496; expectations, 390, 422; home, 540
Parents, 392, 454, 573; honoring of, 484–88
Paresis, 416–17
Paris, 236, 250, 261, 320, 330, 443, 473–74, 479; Commune, 245; Liberal Synagogue, 25; Peace Conference of 1919, 264
Park, Robert Ezra, 431–32, 578
Parliament, British, 235
Parnasim, 233
Parsons, Talcott, 373
Passover, 48, 356, 401–2, 406, 439, 494, 510, 531
Pata, village of, 522
Pathological features, 423
Patriarchal: rule, 309; structure, 313
Patriarchs, Biblical, 41–42
Patriotism, 262–63, 387, 474
Patron saints, 187
Patrons of arts and scholarship, 168
Paytanim, 103. See also Poetry, poets
Peacemaking, 483
Pearson, Karl, 457, 471
Pentateuch, 58, 87, 247, 523
Pentecost, 49. See also Shavu'ot

Peoplehood of Jews, 16–17, 23
"People of Israel," 17, 37
"People of the Book," 31
Perceptual articulation, 312–13
Pereira, Jacob Rodriguez, 228
Peripatetics, 87
Persecution of Jews, 326, 334, 338, 418, 423, 461, 473. See also Massacres; Pogroms
Persia, 16, 97, 106, 365, 398; language of, 41, 399
Personality, 372–407, 422, 481, 496, 538–39; disorders, 424
Peru, 151
Perugia, 161
Peyrefitte, Roger, 13
Pharaoh, 429
Pharisaic: Judaism, 87; order, 67
Pharisees, 58, 67, 87, 253
Philanthropy, 406, 532. See also Charity
Philistine(s), 74, 548
Philo, epic poet, 85
Philology, Jews in, 352
Philo of Alexandria, 57, 68, 71, 74, 82, 87–90, 111, 126, 137, 143, 343, 435, 513
"Philosophers' stone," 161
Philosophes, French, 235, 239
Philosophy, 85–89, 94, 102, 123, 126, 154, 176–77; Jews in, 276, 343–44, 352–53; of religion, 105, 515
Philostratus, 62
Phoenician: influence, 51; pantheon, 50
Phylacteries (tefillin), 356
Physicians, 189, 265, 409–10, 413, 521
Physics, 353
Physiognomy, science of, 161, 383
Picard, Edmund, 471–72
Pidyon, redemption money, 208
Pied-noir, 405
Pilcz, A., 418
Pilgrimages, 187; festivals, 407
Pilpul, 333
Pinhas ben Yair, 75
Pinto, Isaac de, 228, 267, 465
"Pious Men," 200, 210, 218, 559
Pisa, Vitale (Yehiel Nissim) da, 171, 176

Piyyut(im), 103–4. *See also* Liturgical poetry
Plato, 86–88
Plato of Tivoli, 124
Pobirokhin, Hilarion, 212
Podolia, 205
Poetry, poets, 103, 108, 177, 229, 465; Hebrew, 276, 367, 515
Pogroms, 263, 268–69. *See also* Massacres; Persecutions
Poland, 7, 182, 186–87, 205, 208, 233, 241, 245–46, 268, 344, 361, 464, 518; partition of, 188
Polemical works, polemics, 101, 105–6
Polis, Greek city, 60
Polish: folk life, 216; folklore, 213; folk religion, 186–88; Jews, 16, 181, 228, 267, 276, 344, 384, 387, 424, 441, 464, 466, 468–69, 471; language, 367; peasants, 5, 215, 218
Politics, 319, 394
Polygamy, 261
Polyglottism, 352, 367–68, 536
Polytheism, 50, 53, 59, 62, 90, 349
Poor, helping, 476, 484, 519, 525–27, 530–32. *See also* Clothing the poor; Feeding the poor
Portaleone, Abraham, 160, 163, 169–71
Portraits of Italian Jews, 174
Portugal, 25, 109, 151; Jews in, 227–29, 233, 237, 239, 244–45, 465, 468, *see also* Iberian Jews; language, 101
Poshe Yisroel, 267
Posqim, decisors, 496
Potocki, Count Valentine, 25
Poverty, 309. *See also* Poor, helping
Prague, 256
Prayer(s), 110, 197, 220, 365–66, 401, 408, 410–11, 489, 510, 513, 519, 522; women's, 247
Prayer: of Azariah, 79; of Manasseh, 79
Prayer book, 110, 177, 356, 518
Prayerless, Russian sect, 184
Prayer-shawl, 356
Praying aloud among Hasidim, 196–97
Preeminence, 324–27, 331–35, 442
Pregnancy, 300–301

Prejudice, 379, 480
Presence of God, 492. *See also* Shekhina
Pressburg, 257, 359
Pride, 396; Arab, 380; Jewish, 378; Sephardi, 154; Spanish, 5, 380
Priesthood, priests, 306, 409, 511
P'ri 'Etz Hayyim, 231
Printing presses, Hebrew, 166–67
Projective tendencies of Arab culture, 427
Proletarians, 476
Promised Land, 46–47
Prophets, 31–32, 37, 46, 49–51, 62, 128, 131–32, 251, 350–51, 471, 490, 503, 525
Proselyte(s), 16, 18, 23, 25, 61, 83, 92. *See also Gerim*
Prostitutes, 164–65, 508
Protocols of the Elders of Zion, 12, 320–21
Proudhon, Pierre Joseph, 456, 471
Proust, Marcel, 25, 250, 368
Provence, 124, 146; Jews in, 516, 568
Proverbs, Book of, 435–36
Providence, R.I., 401
Prussia, 239, 281, 328–29, 414, 441–42
Psalmist, 436, 493
Psalms, 52, 78, 130, 201, 363; of Solomon, 78
Pseudepigrapha, 79
Psychiatric symptomatology, 425–27
Psychoanalysis, 14, 273, 334, 351, 420
Psychology, Jews in, 353
Psychoneuroses, 415–17, 420. *See also* Neuroses
Psychopathology, 419
Psychoses, 414–15, 417–18, 421, 423, 431, 538
Psychosis-neurosis pattern, 443
Psychotic belligerence, 425
Ptolemy, 82, 84, 106
Publishing, Jews in, 371
Puerto Rican children, 291–93
Pumbeditha, 33, 107
Purim, 162, 173, 177, 198, 365, 406, 439–40, 495; plays, 495
"Purity of blood," 381
"Push," "pushiness," 376, 392

Pythagoras, 87–88
Pythagoreans, 86

Qame'ot, 518. *See also* Amulets
Qetina, Rab, 75
Qiddush, 439, 494; cup, 356
Qitzur Shulḥan 'Arukh, 482, 502, 509
Q'lippot, 144. *See also* Husk
Qohelet Musar, periodical, 231
Quadriga, 71
Queen: Esther, 495; of Heaven, 50, 53;
  Sabbath, 494
Quintilian, 171
Qur'ān, 98, 103–4, 110–11

Rabāb, 365
Rabbinate in Israel, 23
Rabbinical Seminary, Breslau. *See*
  Jüdisch-theologisches Seminar
Rabbinic Judaism, 80
Rabbis, 59, 61–62, 81, 86, 246, 252–53,
  261, 278, 306, 383, 409, 517–18
Rabinowicz, Rabbi Louis Isaac, 497
Rab-shakeh, 438
"Race," Jewish, 15–16, 325, 327, 468, 472
Race differences in intelligence, 297
Rachel, 18–19, 43, 45, 489–90
Rachel Felix, 282
Racine, 370
Radanites, 147
Radziwill, Duke, 464
haRahman, Rahmana, 529
Raimundo, Archbishop, 101
Raisin, Jacob S., 268
Ramah, 490
Rashi, 36, 171, 486, 517, 522
Raskol (dissenting) sect in Russia, 188, 195
Ras Shamra, 51, 53. *See also* Ugarit
Rathenau, Walter, 470
Rationalism, 377
Rav, 490, 502
Rava, 436, 493, 527
Rayner, John K., 452
al-Rāzī, 106
Reason: and Faith, 128; and Revelation,
  126

Rebekah, 42–45, 489–90
Rebelliousness, 375
Recanati, Menahem, 139
Rechabites, 438
Reconquista, 100, 150
Redemption, 504
Rée, Paul, 470
Reform, religious, 225, 272, 466; congre-
  gations, 77; Jews, 277, 406, 444;
  Judaism, 13, 452; movement, 225, 282;
  rabbis, 23; temples, 366
Refugees, 474
Reggio, 165
Rehoboam, 55
Reik, Theodor, 413, 450
Reinach: Joseph, 473; Solomon, 473;
  Theodore, 325, 473
Reincarnation, 145–46. *See also* Metem-
  psychosis; Transmigration of souls
Religio-centrism, 106
Religion: attitude toward, 278–79; Israel-
  ite, 42; Jewish, 3, 16, 23, 29, 81, 94,
  171–73, 260–61, 326, 350–52, 445–46
Religionsgeschichte, history of religion, 37
Religiosity, 390, 397–407, 444, 538
Religious: character of Jewish culture, 275;
  cultures, 62; debates, 175; differences,
  259; laxity, 384; observance, 265, 271,
  280; philosophy, 106; reform, *see* Re-
  form, religious; skepticism, 178; talent,
  345–46; tradition, 447
Remedy books, 216–17
Renaissance, 5, 7, 21, 127, 151–79, 244,
  276, 344, 380, 383–84
Renan, Ernest, 347–49, 471–72
Repentance, 161
Resit Joxma, 234
Responsa, 102, 105, 107, 113
Return, Law of, 22–23
Reuben, 375
Reubeni, David, 179
Revelation, 53, 482
Revolt against the Romans, 33
Revolutionary: movements, 353–54;
  spirit, 475
Rhineland, 517
Rhodes, 153

Ricardo, David, 282
Riesman, David, 373
Rieti, Moses, 157
Rimmonim, 356
Rinder, I. D., 417, 420, 423, 432
Ritual, 22, 48, 50–51, 90, 149, 402, 404, 438; murder libel, 189, *see also* Blood libel; objects, 356; purity, 411
Rivlin, Joseph J., 370
Rizpah, 490
Roberts, Bertram, 420, 426
Robespierre, 239
Roman: authors, 62; empire, 57, 61, 68, 102
Romance languages, 100–101
Romans, 487
Rome, 28, 62, 74, 84, 102, 135, 152–53, 156–57, 162, 531
Romulus and Remus, 28
Rorschach Multiple Choice Test, 432
Rosh haShana, 363, 531. *See also* New Year
Rossi, Azariah de, 170, 225
Roth, Cecil, 157–58, 324
Rothschild, House of, 250
Rousseau, Jean Jacques, 237, 258
Royal Society of Arts and Sciences of Metz, 238, 245
Ruah, spirit, 357
Rub' al-Khali, 350
Rubin, A. I., 507
Rubinstein, Anton, 282
Rufeisen, Oswald. *See* Brother Daniel
Ruge, Arnold, 470
Rūh (spirit), 357
Rumyaneck, J., 389
Rundquist-Sletto Test, 389
Runners, Russian sect, 184
Ruppin, Arthur, 377–78
Rural-urban distribution, 336–37
Russia, 26, 160, 223, 263, 268–69, 308, 319, 339, 342, 392, 570
Russian: anti-Zionism, 479–80; dissenters, 182, 188, 202, 206, 208, 212; Jews, 245, 264, 266, 268, 384, 442, 456, 476, 480; language, 367; Old Believers, 183; Orthodoxy, 182, 185–86, 213; peasants,

5; schismatics, 185; sectarians, 183–85, 191, 193, 213–15, 217, 276

Sa'adya Gaon, 105, 107, 126, 545
Sabbath, 48, 51, 89, 164, 191–92, 196, 225, 254, 399–400, 404–6, 448–50, 486, 489, 492–94, 498–99, 501, 522, 555; candles, 519; meal, 439, 449; rest, 528
Sabbatical year, 64, 511
Saboraim, 96
Sabra(s), 394–96, 459, 538, 573, 581
Sacrifices, 51, 131
Sadducees, 67
Sadness as sin. *See* 'Atzvut
Safed, 211, 318, 482; Kabbalists, 136, 151
Salamanca, 108
Salanter, Rabbi Israel, 257
Salerno, medical school, 156
Sales, Jean Baptiste Nicolas de Lisle de, 237
Salon, Jewish, 246–50
Salonica, 381, 383
Salonnardes, 250
Samael, 142
Samaria, 54
Samaritan alphabet, 169
Samaritans, 80, 317
Samuel, 131
Samuel ben Meir, Rabbi, 454
Sanhedrin, 58, 64, 200, 487; of Paris, 237, 245, 261–62, 264
Sanua, Victor, 432
Saragossa, 108, 112, 117
Sarah, 18, 42, 489–90
Sardinia, 163
Sarton, George, 92, 125, 316–17, 537, 568
Satan, 144, 184, 203, 364, 433
Śatapatha Brāhmana, 137
Satyrs, 48, 160
Saul and Jonathan, 120
Savasorda. *See* Abraham bar Hiyya
Saviorites, Russian sect, 184
Sayings of the Fathers, 78
Scapegoat, 49
Schickedanz, Arno, 457

Schizophrenia, 424, 427
Schizophrenic excitement, 425
Schlegel, Friedrich von, 249
Scholarship, 355, 473, 520
Scholem, Gershom G., 137, 146, 150, 182–83, 552, 554
Schools, 22
Schrire, T., 575
Schürer, Emil, 86, 95
Schwadron, Abraham, 458
Schwarz, Karl, 357–58, 360
Science of Judaism, 268. *See also Wissenschaft des Judenthums*
Sciences, 96, 257; Jews in, 282, 318, 340–41, 343, 353, 380
Scientists, 122–26, 521
Scribes, 58–59, 62, 166. *See also Sofer*
Sculptors, 174
Sculpture, Jews in, 318, 344, 353, 356–60
Scuola (synagogue), 513
Sea-monsters, 65, 74, 76. *See also* Dragon; Leviathan
Second Commandment, 32
Secular: knowledge, 255; studies, 167, 515
Secularism, 278
Secularization, 400–402, 405
Sedentarization, 47, 546
Seder, Passover, 356, 401, 439, 494
Segregation between the sexes, 500
Sejm, 246
Selection, 326–28; sexual, 328
Self-aggrandizement in poetry, 115
Self-alienation, 471
Self-blame, 426
Self-castration, 183
Self-directed symptoms, 425–26
Self-esteem, 378
Self-hate, 27, 263, 274, 430, 461–64, 470–71, 474, 477–80, 539
Self-identification, 538
Self-praise, 550
Self-preservation, 346
Self-rejection, 478
Self-stereotype, 223, 461, 466, 471, 539
Selivanov, Conrad, 185
Semites, 347–51, 472

Semitic: "blood," 472; peoples, 349; "race," 348, 471
Semmelweis, Dr. Ignaz Philipp, 410
Senna, Carl, 294
Sensitivity, 392, 538
Sephardi: dignity, 381; *élan vital*, 227; in England, 281; excellence, 151; in France, 236; heritage, 150–51; in Holland, 224, 227, 234, 518; intellectuals, 260–61; Jews, 5, 100, 102, 110, 151, 153–55, 225, 233, 236, 244, 266–67, 270, 361, 363, 380–82, 398, 464–65, 479, 516–18, 538–39, 572; prejudice, 227; pride, 381; refugees, 265
Sepher Y'tzira, 138
Sephira, *Sephirot*, emanations, 138–39, 141, 144–45, 148, 553
Septuagint, 59, 82, 87–88, 111
Serah, 545
Seraphim, angels, 210, 213
Seraphim, Saint, 213
Sermon(s), 172, 237, 263. *See also D'rashot*
Serpent, the, 43
Sex, 497–509; attitude toward, 192; conversations about, 502; illegitimate, 505; licit and illicit, 499–502; mores of, Biblical and Talmudic, 508; pattern, 446–47, 507–9; play, 507; premarital, 507–8; preoccupation with, 194–95; rules of, 501–2; value of, 498; views on, 436, 497–98, 503
Sex act as duty, 503
Sexual: awareness, 507; behavior, 194, 504, 508–9; conduct, 509; freedom of women, 509; impulses, 202; intercourse, 409, 498–99, 502, 586, *see also* Cohabitation, Copulation; liberation, 507; license, 164–65, 276, 384, 499–500; modesty, 172, 500; needs of women, 499; outlet, 504–9; relations, 196, 501; segregation, 500, 508; temptation, 203; union, 499; urge, 501
Sexuality, 169, 204; in the divinity, 498; divinization of human, 145, 148; of women, 506
S'faradi ṭahor (pure Sephardi), 381

Sha'atnez, 447
Shabbataian heresy, 205–6
Shabbatai ben Marinos, 529
Shabbatai Zevi, 151, 183, 359
Shadkhan (matchmaker), 449
Shakespeare, 370
Shakti, Indian goddess, 138–44
Shapira, Pinhas, of Koretz, 217
Shaul, son of Simeon, 44
Shavu'ot, 406. *See also* Pentecost
Shechem, 45, 85
Sheitel (wig), 268
Shekhina ("Presence"), 53, 66, 69–72, 139–45, 150, 206, 209–10, 219; the mother as the, 486
Shevet Y'huda, 30
Shī'ite Islam, 398, 531
Shim'on ben Gamliel, Rabban, 8–9, 487, 501
Shim'on ben Yohai, 136, 484
Shim'on the Just, 8
Shiva, Hindu god, 137–43, 145
Shivaic teachings, 149
Shivaism, 139, 142–44
Shivhe haBeShT, 191, 521
Shklov, 203
Sh'ma' prayer, 9, 110, 197, 268, 493, 510
Shneur Zalman of Lyadi, 219–20
Shofar, 65, 71, 75, 200, 363–64
Shohat, Alexander, 191
Shohet, ritual slaughterer, 337
Shore-dwellers, Russian sect, 184
Shtetl, 410, 440, 449, 488, 531
Shua, 44
Shuey, A. M., 390
Shul (synagogue), 513
Shulhan 'Arukh, 17, 170, 203, 254, 409, 482, 501–2, 509
Sibylline oracles, 90–91
Sicily, 135, 152–53, 155–56, 159–60, 167, 173
Siena, 162
Simeon, 44
Sin, 187, 202, 205, 409, 427–28, 434, 460; sadness as, *see* '*Atzvut*
Singing, 215, 363, 366, 450, *see also Niggunim*, Vocal music; of women, 162

Sirens, 63
Sitra ahra, 144. *See also* "Other (evil) Side"
Six Day War of 1967, 400–401, 453, 479
Skepticism, 332–33
Sklare, Marshall, 402
Sklare-Greenblum study, 405
Skoptsy ("Castrated"), Russian sect, 184–85, 202
Skovoroda, Gregory, 184, 215
Skverer Hasidim, 199
Slavery, slaves, 47, 98, 165, 493
Smith, Goldwyn, 457
Smyrna, 381
Snyder, Charles R., 443, 445
Sobriety, 5, 329, 420, 446. *See also* Alcoholism; Inebriety
Social contact, Gentile-Jewish, 174–75, 380
Social hygiene, 353
Socialists, French, 456
Social work, 533
Société des Études Juives, 325
Socio-economic Status (SES), 296, 308–11
Socrates, 87
Sodom, 434
Sodomy, 433
Sofer, 58. *See also* Scribes
Sofer, Rabbi Moses (Schreiber), 257, 268, 359
Soldiers in Israel, 313
Solidarity, 326
Solomon, King, 32, 34, 48, 175, 178, 211, 434–35
Somaticization, 425–26
Sombart, Werner, 378
Sommi, Leon, 162
Son and Daughter in the divinity, 140
Song of Songs, 79, 204, 436, 447
Songs, 172, 214, *see also Niggunim*, Singing; of the Hasidim, 192
Soothsayers, 133
Sophia, 183. *See also* Wisdom
Sorcery, 132, 147, 160–61, 383, 427. *See also* Magic; Witchcraft
Sorski, Nil, 186
Southwest Asia, 7

Soviet: Jewry, 445; Russia, 456

Spain, 5, 16, 97–100, 130, 134, 151, 155, 317–18, 344, 380, 383, 568

Spaniards, 380

Spanish: exiles, 153, *see also* Exile; expulsion, 265; Golden Age, 94, *see also* Golden Age in Spain; Hebrew poetry, 99; Jews, 7, 109, 239, 572, *see also* Sephardi Jews; Kabbala, 134; language, 100, 123

"Sparks" in the Kabbala, 144, 205

Spearman, Charles, 288

Sperling, Abraham P., 389–90

Spheres in the Kabbala, 130

Spiegel, Shalom, 122

Spinoza, Baruch, 14, 151, 231–32, 329, 338, 343, 377, 383, 560–61

Spirit, Jewish, 329

Spirit possession, 200

Spirits, 160

Sports, 163, 176, 276

Srole, Leo, 416, 418, 421, 443

Stanford-Binet Test, 291, 297, 315, 321

Starets, Startsy, 186

Stars, influence of the, 161, 383

Stchetinin, Alexis, 206

Steinberg, Milton, 431

Steiner, Max, 470

Steinschneider, Moritz, 102, 123

Stereotypes: derogatory, 266–67; Jewish, 470–73, 477–78. *See also* Self-stereotype

Stiff-necked people, 475

Stimulation, effect on intelligence, 301

Stoics, 86–88

"Stomach Judaism," 451

Stonequist, Everett V., 578

Storm-god, 55

Straus, Émile, 250

"Strong drink," 435–36, 438, 446–47

Struggle for survival, 306

Students, 23, 294–95, 413, 454

Studiousness, 220–21, 497

Study(ing), as a duty, 254–55, 302, 513, 516, 518; the Law (Tora), 483, 501, 503, 519; valuation of, 270, 273, 304; zeal for, 273

Sufi(sm), 135, 147, 149

Suicide, 274, 282, 424, 427

Sukka, booth, 495

Sukkot, Tabernacles, 49, 406, 484, 495, 501, 511

Sukov, M., 389

Sullam, Sarah Copia (Coppio), 248

Sumerian, 54

Sunni Islam, 398

Superiority, 324–26, 379, 390

Supernal: Father, 138–40; Mother, 138–40

Superstitions, 160–61, 383, 517

Supreme Court of Israel, 22–23

Sura, Babylonia, 33, 105, 107

Survival, 221, 496–97, 504

Susa, 62

Susanna, 79

Sward, Keith, 389

Sweatshops, 303

Swimming, instruction in, 488

Symmachus, 83

Synagogue(s), 22, 56, 61–62, 64, 67, 69–70, 75–76, 94, 172, 192, 247, 272, 337, 357, 360–61, 363, 381, 393, 400–401, 404–5, 407, 439, 450, 492, 495; architecture, 358, 361–62

Synanon, 453

Syria, 54, 97

Syro-Arabian desert, 350

Szamuely, 353

Szlachta, Polish nobility, 189–90

al-Ṭabarī: ʾAhī, 106; Sahl Rabbān, 106

Tabernacle, 74

Tabernacles. *See Sukkot*

Talent(s), 316, 335, 343–71, 377–78, 392, 537

Talmud, 20, 30–31, 44, 58–59, 62–63, 67, 80–81, 96, 99, 104, 115, 127, 157, 160, 200, 240, 253, 269–70, 302, 408–9, 435, 438, 446, 454, 467–69, 471, 473, 484–85, 491, 495–96, 498, 500, 504, 518, 522–23, 527; Palestinian and Babylonian, 514; study of, 366

Talmudic: academies, 155–56, 513–14; age, period, time, 9, 13, 21, 43, 145,

201, 210, 338, 363, 365, 375, 409, 438, 440, 481–82, 493, 498, 502–3, 513–15, 540; commentaries, 102, 278; custom, 217; dictionaries, 104; Judaism, 46; law, 33, 496; learning, 306, 318; literature, 78, 485; myths, 433, 435; rabbis, sages, teachers, 8, 55, 58–59, 63, 67–68, 128, 132, 409, 434–35, 437, 448, 484, 486–88, 490–91, 515; scholars, 123, 155; students, 469; study, studies, 25, 220, 266, 271–72, 303, 307, 333, 336, 377, 469; tradition, 227

Talmudism, 181, 190–91, 255, 268, 276
Tamar, 44
Tammuz, death of, 49
Tanḥum, Rabbi, 491
Tannaim, 32, 80–82, 96
Tannaitic literature, 80–81
Tantra texts, 144
Tantric teachings, 149
Tarfon (Tryphon), Rabbi, 486
Targum(s), 58, 64, 513
Tatarinova, Catherine, 185
Tattvas in Hinduism, 139, 553
Taxation, 22
Tcherikover, Victor, 94
Teachers and pupils, 515–16
Teaching children as a duty, 522. See also Education
Technical ability, 353
Technology, Jews in, 162, 380
Teg essen, 589. See also Meals given to students
Teilhard de Chardin, 207
Tel Aviv, 395, 459; University, 400
Temperament, 389
Temple: of Jerusalem, 10, 32–33, 51, 54–55, 60–61, 69, 72–75, 88, 143, 170, 215, 233, 361, 363, 408–9, 437, 485, 495, 501, 503; ritual, service, 8, 438
Temple as Divine Bedroom, 141–42
Ten Commandments, 10, 355, 487, 491. See also Fifth Commandment; Second Commandment
"Tent of Meeting," 48. See also Tabernacle
Teraphim, household gods, 45, 48
Terman, Lewis M., 315, 321–23, 567–68

Tetrad, Kabbalistic, 139
Teutons, 329–30, 353. See also Germans, Germany
Theater, Jews in, 161–62, 173, 177, 276, 344
Thematic apperception measures, 390
Thematic influence in poetry, 114–15
Theodotion, 83
Theodotus, 84–85
Thierry, 238
Third Reich, 252
Third World countries, 480
Thirteen attributes of God, 528–29, 590
Thirteen principles of faith, 11
This World, 487
Thomas and Znaniecki, 186
Thomas Aquinas, 134
Throne of God or of Yahweh, 54, 71
Thurstone, L. L., 288–89, 335
Thurstone Intelligence Test, 390
Thurstone Neurotic Inventory, 432
Tinnius Rufus, 501
Tishby, Y'shayahu, 552
Tiszaeszlár, blood libel, 263
Tithes, 525. See also Ma'aser
Titus, 84; Arch of, 74, 76
Tobit, 79
Toland, John, 226, 235
Toledo, 101, 119, 125, 136, 362
"Toleranzpatent," 239, 244
Toller, Ernst, 353
Tora, 8–9, 68, 88, 133–34, 168, 204, 257, 362, 381, 462, 486, 488–89, 500, 502, 513–15; scrolls, 200, 356; shrine, 75; study, 180, 220, 483
Tortosa, debate of, 101
Tosefta, 63, 81
Toussenel, Alphonse, 456
Tradition(s), 313–14, 407, 445, 476, 539
Traditionalism, 268
Translators, 100–101, 103, 106, 124, 156, 158, 170, 173–74
Transmigration of souls, 145–46, 148, 211–12, 554. See also Metempsychosis; Reincarnation
Trebitsch, Arthur, 470
T'refa food, 257, 262, 447

Treitschke, Heinrich von, 458
Tre nazioni in Italy, 154
Trieste, 244
Trigonometry, 124, 521
Trotsky, Leon, 353
Troyes, France, 36, 517
Tunis, 109, 464
Tunisia, 151
Turkey, 109, 179, 233, 398. *See also* Ottoman Empire
Turkish immigrants, 424
Turks, 179
Twelve tribes of Israel, 18
Tzaddiq(im), 182, 186, 196, 198–205, 207, 211–12, 217–18, 410–11, 441, 520; "Courts" of, 207–8; dynasties, 208
Tzaddiqism, 181, 209–10, 217
Tz'daqa, 525–26, 528. *See also* Charity
Tzedeq, justice, 525
Tzene-rene, 247, 520

'Ūd, lute, 365
Ugarit, 51–53. *See also* Ras Shamra
Ukraine, Ukrainians, 7, 182, 186, 189; folk life, 216; folklore, 213; Jews, 384; language, 367
'Ulamā, Muslim scholars, 258
Umaner Hasidim, 199
Umayyads, 97, 100, 105
Unchastity, 501
Uncontrolled temper, 426
Ungvár, 482
United Nations, 26, 243
United States, 25, 173, 293, 296, 299, 312, 319–20, 342, 388, 442–43, 453, 479, *see also* America; Jews in, 26, 223, 535, *see also* America, Jews in
L'Univers Israélite, 472–73
Universities, Jews in, 167, 328–29. *See also* Colleges
Upanishads, 147
Upper class, 418, 508
Uqba, Mar, 527
Urban concentration, urbanism, 336–38, 411, 418
"Usefulness" of Jews, 241

Usque, Solomon, 248
Usury, 223, 228, 235, 237, 261

Value: charity as, 524–28; education as, 524; learning as, 335; studying as, 514, 518
Values, 12, 34, 41, 115, 182, 223, 301, 481–533; cultural, 420; European, 279, 466; Jewish, 277, 461, 523, 539–40; systems of, 380, 481
Van den Haag, Ernest, 13
Variance in personality, 373–74
Varnhagen, Rachel Levin, 249–50
Varnhagen von Ense, Karl August, 250
Veblen, Thorstein, 283, 331–32, 339
Veit, Simon, 249
Venereal diseases, 411
Venice, 152–53, 162, 164, 226, 244, 248
Venus, 72
Verbal ability, 535
Verband National-deutscher Juden, 458
Vernon, P. E., 289
Verona, 156, 162, 531
Vespasian, 84
Vienna, 247, 249, 267; Jews in, 240
Vigilance Committee, 173
Vilna, 256, 264
Violence among Hasidim, 199
Violinists, 345, 367
Virdimura, woman physician, 160
Vishnitza Hasidim, 214
Visiting the sick, 409. *See also* Biqqur Ḥolim
Visual: ability, 353, 359; arts, 359, *see also* Painting, Sculpture, Jews in
Vital, Hayim, 211
Vocabularies, 105
Vocalization, 105, 111
Vocal music, 363, 365. *See also* Cantorial singing; *Niggunim*; Singing
Völkerpsychologie, 461
Voltaire, 228, 251, 465, 562
Vulgate, 112

Wanderers, Russian sect, 184
Warsaw, 246, 253, 441
Washing of hands, 452

Washington, George, 28
Weber, Max, 373
Wechsler: David, 289; Israel S., 419
Weddings, 173, 199, 365, 393, 400
Weil, Simone, 470
Weininger, Otto, 430, 463, 470
Weismann, August, 330
Weizmann, Chaim, 33–34
Welfare institutions, 532–33
Werfel, Franz, 368
Wessely, Naphtali Herz (Hartwig), 244, 466, 470
Western: art, Jews in, 571; countries, 319; culture, 7–8, 21, 536–37; Jews, 313, 452; society, 471; world, 28, 259, 300, 341, 404, 430, 447, 520, 532, 535
Western Europe, 264, 266, 318, 339, 345, 366–67, 377, 404, 429, 479, 533
West Indies, 151
"Whisperers," 210
White garments among Hasidim, 191, 195, 213
White Russia(ns), 182, 186, 189
Whites, intelligence of, 294–97, 565
Wiener, Norbert, 306
Wife, valuation of, 498
Williamson, E., 389
Wine: as medicine, 437; drinking, 171, 192, 196, 205, 434–36, 438, 440, 447, 449, 494, see also Alcoholism; in Jewish ritual, tradition, 438–40, 454; making, 438
Wisdom, 69, 122, 140, 436, 510, 553; literature, 58, 78, 436; of Solomon, 78, 86. See also Greek wisdom
Wissenschaft des Judentums, 282. See also Science of Judaism
Wit, Jewish, 450. See also Jokes, Jewish
Witchcraft, 132, 383, 425. See also Magic; Sorcery
Wolf, Ernst M., 431, 480
Women, 49, 165–66; alcoholics, 442; American Jewish, 506; authors, 165; education of, 513, 519–20; exemption from commandments, 519; Gentile, 520; Iraqi Jewish, 508; physicians, 160, 166; position of, 309; ritual slaughterers,

166; salons of Jewish, 246–50, see also Salon; sex life of, 506, see also Sexual freedom of women, Sexuality, Sexual needs of women; singing, 365; in synagogues, 365; teachers, 102
Word, The, 69
Working class, 418, 471, 479. See also Lower class
World to Come, 436, 483, 487, 524
World War I, 99, 208, 264, 266, 269, 414, 533
World War II, 26, 199, 308, 371
Writing, knowledge of, 519

Yad haḤazaqa, 127
Yahweh, 48, 50–52, 54–55, 68, 70–71, 88, 143, 528. See also God
Yahwism, 37, 48, 53, 55, 351
Yahwists, 32, 46, 50
Yavne, 33, 79, 82
Yehoshaphat, King, 511
Yemen, 311, 385–86
Yemenite: immigrants, 424; Jews, 16, 308, 374, 385, 424–25, 519, 537–38
Yeshiva, yeshivot, 30, 101, 305, 337, 366, 435, 464, 523, 532, 589; students, 271
Yetzer hara', 514. See also Evil Inclination
Y'huda, Rabbi, 61
Y'huda ben B'thera, Rabbi, 437
Y'huda haLevi. See haLevi, Y'huda
Y'huda the Prince, Rabbi, 66, 80, 484, 514
Y'hudit, language, 43
YHWH as mystical name of God, 139
Yiddish, 7, 43–44, 99, 169, 227, 236, 247, 263, 267–68, 278, 287, 303, 367, 369, 449, 466–68, 513, 517, 520
Yiddisher kop ("Jewish head"), 287
Yiddishisms, 432
Yiddishkayt (Jewishness), 303
Yiddish stage, 476
Yishma'el, Rabbi, 491, 515
Yishma'el ben Yose, 448
Yishuv, 386
Yitzhaq, Rabbi, 436
Y.M. and Y.W.H.A., 394
Yoga, 137, 146, 149
Yogis, 147

Yohanan, Rabbi, 434, 437, 486, 492, 528, 590
Yohanan ben Zakkai, 33, 79–80
Yohanan (John) Hyrcanos, 60
"Yoke" of the commandments, of the Law, of religion, 20, 35, 404
Yom Kippur, 193, 363, 402, 406, 495. *See also* Day of Atonement
Yoni in Hindu mysticism, 142
Yored, emigrant from Israel, 581
Yoshvim, sitters, 208
Yotapata, Galilee, 84
Youth, in Israel, 574; and drug addiction, 455
Y'rida, emigration from Israel, 581
Ysander, Thorsten, 182, 197
Y'sod, Foundation, in the Kabbala, 141
Yuga, world age, in Hindu doctrine, 148

Zacuto, Abraham, 108–9, 125
Zamosc, Israel, 202
Zborowski and Herzog, 410
Zechariah, 78, 438

Zeno, 88
Zerubbabel, 361
Zeus, 69–70, 72, 91
Zhitlovsky, Chaim, 17, 264
Zimmer, Heinrich, 142
Zimmerman, Rabbi S., 445
Zimri, 437
Zinberg, Israel, 133
Zion, 115, 215, 237, 262
Zionism, 273, 277, 334, 480, 533; equated with racism, 26, 243–44
Zionist: Congress, 476; "Imperialism," 479; movement, 17, 269, 405, 459, 475; writings, 459
Zionists, 403, 458
Z'ira, Rabbi, 486
Z'mirot, Sabbath songs, 494
Zodiac, 65, 76
Zohar, 134, 136, 138, 140–41, 143–44, 146, 204, 220, 552
Zoroastrians, 97–98
Zunz, Leopold, 30
Zweig, Ferdynand, 395